Frommer's®

Washington, D.C.

Here's what the critics say about Frommer's:

"Crammed with informed opinions."
—Town & Country Magazine

♦

"Amazingly easy to use. Very portable, very complete."
—Booklist

♦

"The only mainstream guide to list specific prices. The Walter Cronkite of guidebooks—with all that implies."
—Travel & Leisure

♦

"Complete, concise, and filled with useful information."
—New York Daily News

♦

"Hotel information is close to encyclopedic."
—Des Moines Sunday Register

Other Great Guides for Your Trip:

Frommer's Washington, D.C., from $60 a Day

Frommer's Washington, D.C., with Kids

Frommer's Portable Washington, D.C.

The Complete Idiot's Travel Guide to Washington, D.C.

(Available February 1999)

Frommer's Irreverent Guide to Washington, D.C.

Frommer's By Night Guide to Washington, D.C.

Frommer's Memorable Walks in Washington, D.C.

Frommer's USA

Frommer's Virginia

Frommer's Maryland & Delaware

Frommer's® 99

Washington, D.C.

by Elise Hartman Ford

MACMILLAN • USA

ABOUT THE AUTHOR

Elise Hartman Ford has been a freelance writer in the Washington, D.C., area since 1985. She contributes regularly to such newspapers as the *Washington Post,* and to *Washingtonian* and other magazines. In addition to this guide, she is the author of two books about places to rent for special events and meetings: *Unique Meeting, Wedding and Party Places in Greater Washington,* now in its fourth edition, and *Unique Meeting Places* in Greater Baltimore.

MACMILLAN TRAVEL

A Simon & Schuster Macmillan Company
1633 Broadway
New York, NY 10019

Find us online at **www.frommers.com**

Copyright © 1999 by Simon & Schuster, Inc.
Maps copyright © by Simon & Schuster, Inc.

ISBN 0-02-862325-8
ISSN 0899-3246

Editor: Vanessa Rosen
Production Editor: Donna Wright
Photo Editor: Richard Fox
Design by Michele Laseau
Digital Cartography by Ortelius Design and Jim Moore
Cover Photo: Jefferson Memorial
Page Creation by John Bitter, Jena Brandt, Jerry Cole, Sean Monkhouse, Angel Perez, and Heather Pope

SPECIAL SALES

Bulk purchases (10+ copies) of Frommer's and selected Macmillan travel guides are available to corporations, organizations, mail-order catalogs, institutions, and charities at special discounts, and can be customized to suit individual needs. For more information, write to Special Sales, Macmillan General Reference, 1633 Broadway, New York, NY 10019.

Manufactured in the United States of America

Contents

List of Maps

AN INVITATION TO THE READER

In researching this book, we discovered many wonderful places—hotels, restaurants, shops, and more. We're sure you'll find others. Please tell us about them, so we can share the information with your fellow travelers in upcoming editions. If you were disappointed with a recommendation, we'd love to know that, too. Please write to:

Frommer's Washington, D.C. '99
Macmillan Travel
1633 Broadway
New York, NY 10019

AN ADDITIONAL NOTE

Please be advised that travel information is subject to change at any time, and this is especially true of prices. We therefore suggest that you write or call ahead for confirmation when making your travel plans. The authors, editors, and publisher cannot be held responsible for the experiences of readers while traveling. Your safety is important to us, however, so we encourage you to stay alert and be aware of your surroundings. Keep a close eye on cameras, purses, and wallets, all favorite targets of thieves and pickpockets.

WHAT THE SYMBOLS MEAN

✪ Frommer's Favorites

Our favorite places and experiences—outstanding for quality, value, or both.

The following abbreviations are used for credit cards:

AE	American Express	EURO	Eurocard
CB	Carte Blanche	JCB	Japan Credit Bank
DC	Diners Club	MC	MasterCard
DISC	Discover	V	Visa
ER	EnRoute		

FIND FROMMER'S ONLINE

Arthur Frommer's Outspoken Encyclopedia of Travel (www.frommers.com) offers more than 6,000 pages of up-to-the-minute travel information—including the latest bargains and candid, personal articles updated daily by Arthur Frommer himself. No other Web site offers such comprehensive and timely coverage of the world of travel.

Introducing
Washington, D.C.

All the news out of Washington these days aims to shock, or so it seems. With all the talk of scandal and corruption, one might almost expect to see the White House behind bars, the U.S. Capitol shaking its shiny dome in dismay, or the Washington Monument swaying in the wind blown by each hint of wrongdoing. But, as you will observe when you visit, the capital's famous monuments stand strong and unwavering, where they were planted decades and centuries ago. The very presence of the White House; the Capitol; the Washington Monument; the Supreme Court; the Lincoln, Jefferson, Franklin Delano Roosevelt, and Vietnam Veterans' Memorials; the Library of Congress; and the many other significant landmarks in this white marble town remind us of the constancy of our government and the strength that lies within our country's history. Tour these sites and be reassured that democracy is alive and well in the land. Such an experience is reason enough to come to Washington, D.C.

The museums are another. Nowhere else in the world will you find such vast and diverse collections of art and inventions—for free, courtesy of the Smithsonian Institution. Most of the institution's 14 Washington museums are on the National Mall, with a couple—the National Portrait Gallery and National Museum of American Art—off the Mall in Chinatown, another couple—the Anacostia Museum and the National Zoo—set in residential neighborhoods, and the National Postal Museum right next to Union Station. Scattered throughout the city are nearly 30 other museums, from the Corcoran Gallery of Art, near the White House, where you can view Whistlers and Warhols alike, to the National Museum of Women in the Arts, an imposing downtown building filled with the masterpieces of women artists you may never have heard of but wish you had.

So numerous are monuments, memorials, and museums, in fact, that officials worry about edifice gridlock. The reality is that Washington, D.C., remains a lovely town. The Potomac River will always catch the rays of the sun and reflect the light off the monuments as it wends its way along the banks of Georgetown, on past the Kennedy Center for Performing Arts and south alongside the shores of Virginia. The capital's planners stay true to Pierre Charles L'Enfant's vision of a city with abundant green parks, plazas, squares, and gardens, and the federal government maintains these spaces beautifully.

Count on an inviting sameness in Washington each time you visit, then, of historic and cultural sites to see, within a gorgeous landscape. Know that certain adventures are ever yours. You can dine on the cuisine of any country, Indonesian to French; admire the splendidly preserved architecture of old town houses as you stroll residential sections of Capitol Hill, Dupont Circle, and Georgetown; and stay out all night, or pretty late, anyway, at a bar in Adams-Morgan or a nightclub along U Street.

But always expect lots of changes: New museum shows, for example, such as the Edward Hopper watercolors on view at the National Museum of American Art, October 22, 1999, to January 3, 2000; new memorials: the Women in Military Service Memorial, next to Arlington Cemetery, which opened in mid-1997; new trends: the rise of intimate late-night spots around town, like Dupont Circle's XandO, where people converge to actually converse. Undoubtedly the city's most notable new thing is, in fact, a neighborhood. Not long ago you would have found the part of town just northwest of Capitol Hill mostly office worker territory by day and fairly deserted at night; now this area, dubbed the Historic Penn Quarter, is turning into a vibrant crossroads of history, art, culture, dining, shopping, sports, and theater. The MCI Center, the sports arena that opened in December 1997, has served as a catalyst for much of the neighborhood's revitalization.

The combination of the historic and the hip; fine dining and bar grub; brilliant art and jock options; party-hearties and workaholics; home-grown and international is what Washington, D.C., is all about. It's a mix that derives from the diversity of people who reside and work here. Just take a look around.

Washington, D.C., has a youthful American attitude about trying new things, so youthful that it may not offer age-old sophistication, but it is cosmopolitan enough to know what is worth trying. Contained within its compact 67 square miles are many tried, true, and new attractions. This book will help point you to them.

1 Frommer's Favorite Washington Experiences

- **Visit the Lincoln Memorial After Dark.** During the day, hordes of rambunctious schoolchildren may distract you; at night, the experience is infinitely more moving. See chapter 7.
- **Take a Monument and Memorials Walking Tour.** You'll need a good map for this one. Take the Metro to Foggy Bottom, and start out with a hearty breakfast at Aquarelle, in the Watergate Hotel. (For a quicker, cheaper, but still delicious fix, stop at the Watergate Pastry shop on the lower level of the complex.) Explore the Kennedy Center across the street (save in-depth touring for another time, but do go to the upper-level promenade that girds the building and enjoy the magnificent city and river views). Then double back to the Vietnam and Lincoln Memorials; follow the cherry tree–lined Tidal Basin path to the Jefferson Memorial; and finish your tour at the Washington Monument. This is a long but beautiful hike; for more information, see chapter 7. Afterward, head to the charming Old Ebbitt Grill (make reservations in advance) for a strength-restoring lunch, or eat at the food court in the nearby Shops at National Place. See chapter 6.
- **Ramble through Rock Creek Park.** This is a good place to ride a bike, run, or even work out. A paved bike and walking path extends 11 miles from the Lincoln Memorial to the Maryland border. You can hop on the trail at many spots throughout the city—it runs past the National Zoo, behind the Omni Shoreham Hotel in Woodley Park (where you can use the 1½ -mile Perrier parcourse, jogging to each of the 18 calisthenics stations), near Dupont Circle, and across

from the Watergate/Kennedy Center complex. You can rent a bike from Big Wheel Bikes at 1034 33rd St. NW (☎ **202/337-0254**), in Georgetown, and from the Thompson Boat Center (☎ **202/333-4861**), on the path across from the Kennedy Center. For a really long bike ride, trek to the Lincoln Memorial, get yourself across the busy stretch that connects the parkway to the Arlington Memorial Bridge, and cross the bridge to the trail on the other side; this path winds 19 miles to Mount Vernon. See chapters 7 and 11.

- **Spend a Day in Alexandria.** Just a short distance (by Metro, car, or bike) from the district is George Washington's Virginia hometown. Roam the quaint cobblestoned streets; browse charming boutiques and antique stores; visit the Boyhood Home of Robert E. Lee and other historic attractions; and dine in one of Alexandria's fine restaurants. See chapter 11.

- **Sip Afternoon Tea at the Top of Washington National Cathedral.** On Tuesday and Wednesday afternoons at 1:30pm, you can tour the world's sixth largest cathedral, then succumb to tea, scones, and lemon tarts served on the seventh floor of the west tower, whose arched windows overlook the city and beyond to the Sugarloaf Mountains in Maryland. Call ☎ **202/537-8993.** Reserve as far in advance as possible, $15 a person. See chapter 6.

- **You Be the Judge.** If you're in town when the Supreme Court is in session (October through late April; call ☎ **202/479-3000** for details), you can observe a case being argued; it's thrilling to see this august institution at work. See chapter 7.

- **Admire the Library of Congress.** The magnificent Italian Renaissance–style Thomas Jefferson Building of the Library of Congress—filled with murals, mosaics, sculptures, and allegorical paintings—is one of America's most notable architectural achievements. Be sure to take the tour detailed in chapter 7.

- **See the Earth Revolve.** The Foucault Pendulum at the National Museum of American History provides empirical evidence that the Earth is revolving; don't miss it. See chapter 7.

- **Spend a Morning on the Mall.** Arrive at about 8:30am (take the Metro to the Smithsonian), when the Mall is magical and tourist-free. Stroll behind the Smithsonian Information Center (the Castle) through the magnolia-lined parterres of the beautiful Enid A. Haupt Garden. Exit on Jefferson Drive, walk east to the Hirshhorn, and cross the street to its sunken Sculpture Garden, an enchanting outdoor facility. Then cross back on Jefferson Drive, walk past the Hirshhorn, and turn left on the brick path that leads into the lovely Ripley Garden—yet another gorgeous green space on the Mall. See chapter 7 for more information. (If it's Sunday, brunch is served in the Castle Norman-style dining room from 11am to 3pm. For details, call ☎ **202/357-2957** before 10am and after 3pm.)

- **Debark at Union Station.** Noted architect Daniel H. Burnham's turn-of-the-century beaux arts railway station is worth a visit even if you're not trying to catch a train. Dawdle and admire its coffered 96-foot-high ceilings, grand arches, and great halls, modeled after the Baths of Diocletian and the Arch of Constantine in Rome. Then shop and eat: The station's 1988 restoration filled the trilevel hall with shops and eateries, everything from Ann Taylor and Crabtree & Evelyn to a high-quality food court and the refined B. Smith's restaurant. See chapter 7 for more information about Union Station.

- **Cut a Deal at the Georgetown Flea Market.** Spend a pleasant Sunday browsing through castoffs of wealthy Washingtonians, hand-painted furniture of local artists, and a hodgepodge of antiques and collectibles. Everybody shops here at one time or another, so you never know who you'll see or what you'll find. Wisconsin Avenue NW at S Street NW in Georgetown. March to December, Sunday from 9am to 5pm. See chapter 9.

- **Enjoy an Artful Evening at the Phillips Collection.** Thursday evenings from 5 to 8:30pm, you pay $5 to tour the mansion-museum rooms filled with Impressionist, Postimpressionist, and modern art, ending up in the paneled Music Room, where jazz, blues, or other musical combinations are performed by fine local musicians, topped off by an artful lecture. It's a popular mingling spot for singles (there's a cash bar and sandwich fare). Call ☎ **202/387-2151** or see chapter 7 for more information.
- **Stroll Along Embassy Row.** Head northwest on Massachusetts Avenue from Dupont Circle. It's a gorgeous walk along tree-shaded streets lined with beaux arts mansions. Built by fabulously wealthy magnates during the Gilded Age, most of these palatial precincts today are occupied by foreign embassies. See chapter 8.
- **People-Watch at Dupont Circle.** One of the few "living" circles, Dupont's is the all-weather hangout for mondo-bizarre biker-couriers, Washingtonians of all sorts who like to play chess (stone pedestals ring an inside section of the circle), street musicians, and lovers. Sit on a bench and be astounded by the passing scene. See chapter 8.
- **Order Drinks on the Sky Terrace of the Hotel Washington.** Posher bars exist, but none with this view. The experience is almost a cliché in Washington: When spring arrives, make a date to sit on this outdoor, rooftop terrace; sip a gin and tonic; and gaze at the panoramic view of the White House, Treasury Building, and the monuments. Open from the end of April through October, for drinks and light fare (☎ **202/347-4499**). See chapter 5 for more details.
- **Attend the Kennedy Center Open House.** In late September/early October, the weather almost always cooperates for this fun, free, mostly outdoor celebration of the arts. Diplomats and office drones alike can't resist shimmying to the beat of music played by top Washington musicians on the terraces. Call ☎ **800/444-1324** or 202/467-4600. See chapter 10.
- **Shop Saturday Morning at Eastern Market.** Capitol Hill is home to more than government buildings; it's a community of old town houses, antique shops, and Eastern Market, a veritable institution. Here, the locals barter and shop on Saturday mornings for fresh produce and baked goods, and on Sunday for flea market bargains. At 7th Street SE, between North Carolina Avenue and C Street SE. See chapter 9.
- **View Washington from the Water.** Cruise the Potomac River aboard one of several sightseeing vessels (see options in chapter 7) and relax from footweary sightseeing. River cruises not only offer a pleasant interval for catching a second wind, but also treat you to a marvelous perspective of the city. See chapter 7.

2 Washington Today

Washington today is nothing if not a paradox. In 1997, the city was on the brink of financial collapse, with a projected deficit of $74 million; a year later, Washington boasts a budget surplus of $185.9 million. Our population is diminishing, even as residential home sales rise 33% and income tax revenue increases. In an area gaining renown as a center for high-tech research and development, especially in telecommunications, the D.C. government's office and public works infrastructures remain antiquated (today, a full 40% of the government's telephones are still rotary!).

Impressions

The whole aspect of Washington is light, cheerful, and airy; it reminds me of our fashionable watering places.

—Mrs. Frances Trollope

Washington . . . enormous spaces, hundreds of miles of asphalt, a charming climate, and the most entertaining society in America.

—Henry James

These things can be explained. Home sales and tax revenue are rising because those moving in tend to be more affluent than those moving out. The district's financial turnaround was partly due to a strong economy and conservative budgeting but is really nothing short of a miracle worked by chief financial officer Anthony A. Williams. As for the dilapidated and woefully old city service systems, these are the legacy of decades of waste and mismanagement, spearheaded during many of those years by Mayor Marion Barry.

The truth is that Washington, D.C., from its inception, has been a contradiction. It is the capital of our country and a city unto itself, and therein lies a host of complications—control of the city being the main issue. Because it's the seat of our country's government, Washington is under Congress's thumb (by order of the U.S. Constitution), which means, in particular, that Congress controls the city budget. Washingtonians may vote for president but not for Congressional representatives. (Residents do elect a delegate, a kind of lobbyist for the district without power to vote within Congress.) And Washingtonians elect their own mayor and council to govern the city, thanks to Congress's granting of home rule to D.C. in 1974.

At least, that's how it's supposed to work. By 1997, Mayor Barry's disastrous run of home rule had nearly destroyed the city. Congress stepped in to limit Barry's power and clean up his mess, with the appointment of a financial control board and the assignment of a chief financial officer (miracle worker Anthony Williams) to improve fiscal management. By 1998, Washington was being governed by a mayor; a control board; a chief management officer; a city council; and Congress, itself. As we head into 1999, Washington stands at a crossroads, desperate for a more manageable form of government and a strong leader. A mayoral election is scheduled for late 1998 and, thankfully, Marion Barry is not running (Anthony Williams is, though!). Whatever the results of the mayoral election held in late 1998, the new mayor can expect intense scrutiny, not only from D.C. citizens but from Congress, which is contemplating a permanent restructuring of the city's seats of authority.

The awkwardness of Washington's unique relationship with the federal government is compounded by other factors. For instance, the city's economy relies heavily upon the presence of the federal government, the city's single largest employer: About 16.7% of area residents are federal employees. The flow of tourists who come here to visit federal buildings and sightseeing attractions nourishes D.C.'s hotels, restaurants, and other hospitality businesses, and makes tourism the city's second-largest industry.

As paradoxical, as cumbersome, as humbling as the district's relationship is with Congress, the fact is that Washington depends upon this relationship. It is because of the work done by the financial control board appointed by Congress that the district's budget is in fine fettle for the first time in years. Not only that, but President

Clinton included in the 1998 federal budget a D.C. rescue package of $190 million, later adding another $120 million for "extras" like schools and the economy.

All in all, the district's outlook is almost rosy. Crime is down in the city by 22%. Tourism is up by more than 7%. In recent surveys, Washington ranked fourth in the lineup of "best places" in the country to live and work, and eighth in a listing of top cities. Based on criteria that measured the abundance and quality of such items as the arts, jobs, climate, crime, recreation, and transportation system, the two surveys found a lot to praise in the capital. And, during your visit, so will you. The capital is still the capital, and federal funds will always see to the upkeep and appeal of much of Washington. Most of the city's attractions are in relatively safe parts of town, and they're operating normally. And if the city has suffered at the hands of Mayor Barry, it nevertheless continues to thrive from the resources and attention showered upon it from other quarters.

Today, even as some homeowners and renters flee, developers and entrepreneurs are flocking in. The neighborhoods of Georgetown, Foggy Bottom, Dupont Circle, Adams-Morgan, and Capitol Hill are as charming as ever. But the really remarkable news concerns the downtown area, especially the district bounded by Pennsylvania and Massachusetts Avenues, between 7th and 15th streets NW. This part of town is blooming after a 50-year decline. Within a few short blocks are at least five theaters, including the National, the Warner, and the Shakespeare Theater. (The term "revitalization" is apropos, since this area was the city's center of theatrical activity during the 19th and first half of the 20th centuries.) A nonprofit organization of business, not government, leaders has banded together to form the Business Improvement District (BID), which uses funds raised privately from downtown property owners to keep city streets clean and safe, and which hopes to raise more money to finance other attractive projects, like national museums for music and photography and a downtown baseball stadium.

In the meantime, the immense MCI Center continues to make a big splash. This is the arena for Washington's basketball (the Wizards) and hockey (the Capitals) teams, but the 5-acre complex also stages concerts and conferences and includes a four-level Discovery Channel retail store, an interactive National Sports Gallery, and several large restaurants.

Restaurants like Hard Rock Cafe, Planet Hollywood, Cafe Atlantico, and Jaleo are already entrenched in the community, and more restaurants are opening all the time. Local artists continue to take over the empty spaces of old office buildings along the 7th Street corridor, in particular, sometimes forming cooperative arrangements, intent on creating a flourishing new arts scene. Nightclubs, always loyal to the heart of the city, are prospering here and along the U Street strip, farther north. The clincher, though, is that people are now venturing downtown, prompting a push for the development of more apartment buildings and condos along these streets.

The upshot of all this activity is . . . well, activity. Streets once dark are bustling into the wee hours. And while Congress talks of a federal takeover, artists, entrepreneurs, and die-hard Washingtonians are bringing new life to the capital.

3 History 101

Dateline

- 1608 Captain John Smith sails up the Potomac River from Jamestown; during the

continues

All of this city, from marble monuments to Marion Barry, grew out of what started as nothing more than "a howling, malarious wilderness." Two hundred years ago, the world wondered why America had chosen this swampy locale as its capital. Washington's transformation from bumpkin backwater to international hub of power, diplomacy, and beauty took place over the course of 100 years.

A WANDERING CONGRESS   It all began in 1783, when 250 Revolutionary War soldiers, understandably angered because Congress was ignoring their petitions for back pay, stormed the temporary capitol, the State House in Philadelphia, demanding justice. The city of Philadelphia sympathized with the soldiers and ignored congressional pleas for protection; when the soldiers rioted outside, the lawmakers huddled inside behind locked doors. After the soldiers finally returned to their barracks, Congress deemed it politic to move on to Princeton. They also decided that they needed a capital city whose business was government and the protection thereof.

This was not a new idea. Congress had been so nomadic during its first decade that when a statue of George Washington was authorized in 1783, satirist Francis Hopkinson suggested putting it on wheels so it could follow the government around. Before settling in Washington, Congress met in New York, Baltimore, Philadelphia, Lancaster, Princeton, Annapolis, York, and Trenton.

A DEAL MADE OVER DINNER   When Congress proposed that a city be designed and built for the sole purpose of housing the government of the new nation, fresh difficulties arose. There was a general feeling that wherever the capital might be built, a great commercial center would arise; thus, many cities vied for the honor. Then, too, northerners were strongly opposed to a southern capital—and vice versa. Finally, after 7 years of bickering, New Yorker Alexander Hamilton and Virginian Thomas Jefferson worked out a compromise over dinner one night in New York. The North would support a southern site for the capital in return for the South's assumption of debts incurred by the states during the Revolution. As a further sop to the North, it was agreed that the seat of government would remain in Philadelphia through 1800 to allow suitable time for surveying, purchasing land, and constructing government buildings.

ENTER L'ENFANT TERRIBLE   An act passed in 1790 specified a site "not exceeding 10 miles square" to be located on the Potomac. President and experienced surveyor George Washington, charged with selecting the exact site, chose a part of

- next 100 years, Irish-Scotch settlers colonize the area.
- 1783 The Continental Congress proposes new "Federal Town"; both North and South vie for it.
- 1790 A compromise is reached: If the South pays off the North's Revolutionary War debts, the new capital will be situated in its region.
- 1791 French engineer Pierre Charles L'Enfant designs capital city but is fired within a year.
- 1792 Cornerstone is laid for Executive Mansion.
- 1793 Construction begins on the Capitol.
- 1800 First wing of the Capitol completed; Congress moves from Philadelphia; President John Adams moves into Executive Mansion.
- 1801 Library of Congress established.
- 1812 War with England.
- 1814 British burn Washington.
- 1817 Executive Mansion rebuilt and its charred walls painted white; becomes known as White House.
- 1822 Population reaches 33,000.
- 1829 Smithsonian Institution founded for "increase and diffusion of knowledge."
- 1861 Civil War; Washington becomes North's major supply depot.
- 1865 Capitol dome completed; Lee surrenders to Grant April 8; Lincoln assassinated at Ford's Theatre April 14.
- 1871 Alexander "Boss" Shepherd turns Washington into a showplace, using many of L'Enfant's plans.
- 1900 Population reaches about 300,000.

continues

- **1901** McMillan Commission plans development of Mall from Capitol to Lincoln Memorial.
- **1907** Union Station opens, largest train station in country.
- **1912** Cherry trees, a gift from Japan, planted in Tidal Basin.
- **1914** World War I begins.
- **1922** Lincoln Memorial completed.
- **1941** First plane lands at National Airport; United States declares war on Japan.
- **1943** Pantheon-inspired Jefferson Memorial and Pentagon completed.
- **1960** Population declines for first time, from 800,000 to 764,000.
- **1963** More than 200,000 March on Washington and hear Martin Luther King's "I Have a Dream" speech," supporting civil rights.
- **1971** John F. Kennedy Center for Performing Arts opens.
- **1976** Metro, city's first subway system, opens in time for Bicentennial.
- **1982** Vietnam Veterans Memorial erected in Constitution Gardens.
- **1991** Population drops to 600,000.
- **1993** U.S. Holocaust Memorial Museum opens near Mall.
- **1994** Marion Barry is elected to a fourth term as mayor, after serving time in prison.
- **1995** Korean War Veterans Memorial is dedicated. Pennsylvania Avenue closed to vehicular traffic in front of the White House.
- **1996** The city goes through tough times, plagued by municipal and federal budget woes.
- **1997** Federal government offers aid package to save

continues

the Potomac Valley where the river becomes tidal and is joined by the Anacostia. Maryland gladly provided 69¼ square miles and Virginia 30¾ for the new Federal District. (In 1846, Virginia's territorial contribution was returned to the state.) The district today covers about 67 square miles.

President Washington hired French military engineer Pierre Charles L'Enfant to lay out the federal city. It has since been said that "it would have been hard to find a man better qualified artistically and less fitted by temperament" for the job. L'Enfant arrived in 1791 and immediately declared Jenkins Hill (today Capitol Hill) "a pedestal waiting for a monument." He surveyed every inch of the designated Federal District and began his plan by selecting dominant sites for major buildings. He designed 160-foot-wide avenues radiating from squares and circles centered on monumental sculptures and fountains. The Capitol, the "presidential palace," and an equestrian statue (the last to be erected where the Washington Monument stands today) were to be the focal points. Pennsylvania Avenue would be the major thoroughfare, and the Mall was conceived as a bustling ceremonial avenue of embassies and other distinguished buildings.

L'Enfant's plan dismayed landowners who had been promised $66.66 per acre for land donated for buildings, while land for avenues was to be donated free. L'Enfant's 160-foot-wide avenues and 2-mile-long Mall were therefore not appreciated. Of the 6,661 acres to be included in the boundaries of the federal city, about half would be avenues and the Mall.

A more likable man might have won over the landowners and commissioners, inspiring them with his dreams and his passion, but L'Enfant exhibited only a peevish and condescending secretiveness that alienated one and all. A year after he had been hired, L'Enfant was fired. A grateful Congress offered him $2,500 compensation for his year of work, and James Monroe urged him to accept a professorship at West Point. Insulted, he spurned all offers and sued the government for $95,500 instead. He lost and died a pauper in 1825. In 1909, in belated recognition of his services, his remains were brought to Arlington National Cemetery. Some 118 years after he had conceived it, his vision of the federal city became a reality.

HOME NOT-SO-SWEET HOME   In 1800, the government (106 representatives and 32 senators) and its effects arrived, according to schedule. What they found bore little resemblance to a city. "One might take a ride of several hours within the precincts without meeting with a single individual to disturb one's meditation," commented one early resident. Pennsylvania Avenue was a mosquito-infested swamp, and there were fewer than 400 habitable houses. Disgruntled Secretary of the Treasury Oliver Wolcott wrote his wife, "I do not perceive how the members of Congress can possibly secure lodgings, unless they will consent to live like Scholars in a college or Monks in a monastery. . . ." The solution was a boom in boarding houses.

D.C. from bankruptcy. Franklin Delano Roosevelt Memorial is dedicated.
- 1998 White House beset by scandal

Abigail Adams was dismayed at the condition of her new home in the presidential mansion. The damp caused her rheumatism to act up, the main stairs had not yet been constructed, not a single room was finished, and there were not even enough logs for all the fireplaces. And since there was "not the least fence, yard, or other convenience," she hung the presidential laundry in the unfinished East Room. To attend presidential affairs or visit one another, Washington's early citizens had to drive through mud and slush, their vehicles often becoming embedded in bogs and gullies—not a pleasant state of affairs, but one that would continue for many decades. There were many hitches in building the capital. Money, as always, was in short supply, as were materials and labor. The home of the world's most enlightened democracy was built largely by slaves. And always, in the background, there was talk of abandoning the city and starting over somewhere else.

REDCOATS REDUX   Then came the War of 1812. At first the fighting centered on Canada and the West—both too far away to affect daily life in the capital. (In the early 1800s, it was a 33-hour ride from Washington, D.C., to Philadelphia—if you made good time.) In May 1813, the flamboyant British Rear Admiral Cockburn sent word to the Executive Mansion that "he would make his bow" in the Madisons' drawing room shortly. On August 23, 1814, alarming news reached the capital: The British had landed troops in Maryland. On August 24, James Madison was at the front, most of the populace had fled, and Dolley Madison created a legend by refusing to leave the President's House without Gilbert Stuart's famous portrait of George Washington. As the British neared her gates, she was calmly writing a blow-by-blow description to her sister:

> Our kind friend, Mr. Carroll, has come to hasten my departure,
> and is in a very bad humour with me because I insist on waiting until the
> large picture of General Washington is secured, and it requires to be unscrewed
> from the wall. This process was found too tedious for these perilous moments;
> I have ordered the frame to be broken, and the canvas taken out; it is done. . . .
> And now, dear sister, I must leave this house, or the retreating army will
> make me a prisoner in it, by filling up the road I am directed to take.

When the British arrived early that evening, they found dinner set up on the table (Dolley had hoped for the best until the end), and according to some accounts, ate it before torching the mansion. They also burned the Capitol, the Library of Congress, and newly built ships and naval stores. A thunderstorm later that night saved the city from total destruction, and a tornado the next day added to the damage but daunted the British troops.

It seemed that the new capital was doomed. Margaret Bayard Smith, wife of the owner of the influential *National Intelligencer,* lamented, "I do not suppose the Government will ever return to Washington. All those whose property was invested in that place, will be reduced to general poverty. . . . The consternation about us is

Impressions

I know of no other capital in the world which stands on so wide and splendid a river. But the people and the mode of life are enough to take your hair off!
—Henry James

My God! What have I done to be condemned to reside in such a city!
—A French diplomat in the early days

general. The despondency still greater." But *the National Intelligencer* was among the voices speaking out against an even temporary move. Editorials warned that it would be a "treacherous breach of faith" with those who had "laid out fortunes in the purchase of property in and about the city." To move the capital would be "kissing the rod an enemy has wielded." Washingtonian pride rallied, and the city was saved once again. Still, it was a close call; Congress came within nine votes of abandoning the place!

In 1815, leading citizens erected a brick building in which Congress could meet in relative comfort until the Capitol was restored. The Treaty of Ghent, establishing peace with Great Britain, was ratified at Octagon House, where the Madisons were temporarily ensconced. And Thomas Jefferson donated his own books to replace the destroyed contents of the Library of Congress. Confidence was restored, and the city began to prosper. When the Madisons moved into the rebuilt mansion, its exterior had been painted gleaming white to cover the charred walls. From then on, it would be known as the White House.

THE CITY OF MAGNIFICENT INTENTIONS   Between the War of 1812 and the Civil War, few people evinced any great enthusiasm for Washington. European visitors especially looked at the capital and found it wanting. It was still a provincial backwater, and Pennsylvania Avenue and the Mall remained muddy messes inhabited by pigs, goats, cows, and geese. Many people were repelled by the slave auctions openly taking place in the backyard of the White House. The best that could be said—though nobody said it—was that the young capital was picturesque. Meriwether Lewis kept the bears he had brought back from his 4,000-mile expedition up the Missouri in cages on the president's lawn. Native American chiefs in full regalia were often seen negotiating with the white man's government. And matching them in splendor were magnificently attired visitors from European courts. The only foreigner who praised Washington was Lafayette, who visited in 1825 and was feted with lavish balls and dinners throughout his stay.

Charles Dickens gave an expression of discontent in 1842:

> *It is sometimes called the City of Magnificent Distances, but it might with greater propriety be termed the City of Magnificent Intentions. . . . Spacious avenues, that begin in nothing and lead nowhere; streets, miles long, that only want houses, roads, and inhabitants; public buildings that need but a public to be complete; and ornaments of great thoroughfares, which only lack great thoroughfares to ornament—are its leading features.*

Tobacco chewing and sloppy senatorial spitting particularly appalled him:

> *Both houses are handsomely carpeted, but the state to which these carpets are reduced by the universal disregard of the spittoon with which every honorable member is accommodated, and the extraordinary improvements on the pattern which are squirted and dabbled upon it in every direction, do not admit of being*

*described. I will merely observe, that I strongly recommend all strangers not to
look at the floor; and if they happen to drop anything . . . not to pick it up with an
ungloved hand on any account.*

But Dickens's critique was mild when compared with Anthony Trollope's, who declared Washington in 1860 "as melancholy and miserable a town as the mind of man can conceive."

A NATION DIVIDED   During the Civil War, the capital became an armed camp, with thousands of camp followers. It was the principal supply depot for the Union Army and an important medical center. Parks became campgrounds, churches became hospitals, and forts ringed the town. The population doubled from 60,000 to 120,000, including about 40,000 former slaves who streamed into the city seeking federal protection. More than 3,000 soldiers slept in the Capitol, and a bakery was set up in the basement. The streets were filled with the wounded, and Walt Whitman was a familiar figure, making daily rounds to succor the ailing soldiers. In spite of everything, Lincoln insisted that work on the Capitol be continued. "If people see the Capitol going on, it is a sign we intend the Union shall go on," he said. When the giant dome was completed in 1863 and a 35-star flag was flown overhead, Capitol Hill's field battery fired a 35-gun salute, honoring the Union's then 35 states.

There was joy in Washington and an 800-gun salute in April 1865 when news of the fall of the Confederacy reached the capital. The joy was short-lived, however. Five days after Appomattox, President Lincoln was shot at Ford's Theatre while attending a performance of *Our American Cousin.* As the city went into mourning, the festive tricolored draperies disappeared into blackness.

The war enlarged the city's population but did nothing to improve its facilities. Agrarian, uneducated former slaves stayed in the city, and poverty, unemployment, and disease were rampant. A red-light district remained, the parks were trodden bare, and tenement slums mushroomed within a stone's throw of the Capitol. Horace Greeley suggested that the capital go west.

LED BY A SHEPHERD   Whereas L'Enfant had been aloof and introverted, his glorious vision was destined to be implemented 70 years later by Alexander "Boss" Shepherd, a swashbuckling and friendly man. A real-estate speculator who made his money in a plumbing firm, Shepherd shouldered a musket in the Union Army and became one of General Ulysses S. Grant's closest friends. When Grant became president, he wanted to appoint Shepherd governor, but blue-blooded opposition ran too high. Washington high society considered him a parvenu and feared his ambitions for civic leadership. Instead, Grant named the more popular Henry D. Cooke (a secret Shepherd ally) governor and named Shepherd vice-president of the Board of Public Works. No one was fooled. Shepherd made all the governor's decisions, and a joke went around the capital: "Why is the new governor like a sheep? Because he is led by A. Shepherd." He became the actual governor in 1873.

Shepherd vowed that his "comprehensive plan of improvement" would make the city a showplace. But an engineer he wasn't. Occasionally, newly paved streets had to be torn up because he had forgotten to install the sewers first. But he was a first-rate orator and politician. He began by hiring an army of laborers and starting them on projects all over town. Congress would have had to halt work on half-finished sidewalks, streets, and sewers throughout the district to stop him. It would have been a mess. The press liked and supported the colorful Shepherd; people forced out of their homes because they couldn't pay the high assessments for improvements hated him. Between 1871 and 1874, he established parks, paved and lighted the streets, installed sewers, filled in sewage-laden Tiber Creek, and planted more than 50,000 trees. He left the city bankrupt—more than $20 million in debt. But he got the job done.

L'ENFANT REBORN Through the end of the 19th century, Washington continued to make great aesthetic strides. The Washington Monument, long a truncated obelisk and major eyesore, was finally dedicated in 1885. Pennsylvania Avenue was becoming the ceremonial thoroughfare L'Enfant had envisioned, and important buildings were completed one after another. Shepherd had done a great deal, but much was still left undone. In 1887, L'Enfant's "Plan for the City of Washington" was resurrected. In 1900, Michigan Senator James McMillan—a retired railroad mogul with architectural and engineering knowledge—became determined to complete the job L'Enfant had started a century earlier. A tireless lobbyist for government-sponsored municipal improvements, he persuaded his colleagues to appoint an advisory committee to create "the city beautiful."

At his personal expense, McMillan sent this illustrious committee—landscape architect Frederick Law Olmsted (designer of New York's Central Park), sculptor Augustus Saint-Gaudens, and noted architects Daniel Burnham and Charles McKim—to Europe for 7 weeks to study the landscaping and architecture of that continent's great capitals. Assembled at last was a group that combined L'Enfant's artistic genius and Shepherd's political savvy.

> *"Make no little plans,"* counseled Burnham. *"They have no magic to stir men's blood, and probably themselves will not be realized. Make big plans, aim high in hope and work, remembering that a noble and logical diagram once recorded will never die, but long after we are gone will be a living thing, asserting itself with ever growing insistency."*

The committee's big plans—almost all of which were accomplished—included the development of a complete park system, selection of sites for government buildings, and the designing of the Lincoln Memorial, the Arlington Memorial Bridge, and the Reflecting Pool (the last inspired by Versailles). They also got to work on improving the Mall; their first step was to remove the tracks, train sheds, and stone depot constructed there by the Baltimore and Potomac Railroad. In return, Congress authorized money to build the monumental Union Station, the design of which was inspired by Rome's Baths of Diocletian.

Throughout the McMillan Commission years, the House was under the hostile leadership of Speaker "Uncle Joe" Cannon of Illinois, who, among other things, swore he would "never let a memorial to Abraham Lincoln be erected in that goddamned swamp" (West Potomac Park). Cannon caused some problems and delays, but on the whole the committee's prestigious membership added weight to their usually accepted recommendations. McMillan, however, did not live to see most of his dreams accomplished. He died in 1902.

By the 20th century, Washington was no longer an object of ridicule. The capital was coming into its own as a finely designed city of sweeping vistas studded with green parks and grand architecture. Congress's 1899 mandate limiting building height in downtown Washington ensured the prominence of landmarks in their landscape. As the century progressed, the city seamlessly incorporated additional architectural marvels, including the Library of Congress, Union Station, and the Corcoran Gallery, which were all built around the turn of the century; several more Smithsonian museums; and the Lincoln Memorial, completed in 1922. A Commission of Fine Arts was appointed in 1910 by President Taft to create monuments and fountains, once again with Olmsted as a member. Thanks to Mrs. Taft, the famous cherry trees presented to the United States by the Japanese in 1912 were planted in the Tidal Basin.

During the Great Depression in the 1930s, Franklin Delano Roosevelt's Works Progress Administration—WPA, We Do Our Part—put the unemployed to work erecting public buildings and artists to work beautifying them. By the 1930s, too, increasing numbers of automobiles, nearly 200,000, were traversing Washington's wide avenues, joining the electric streetcars that had been in use since about 1890.

Washington's population, meanwhile, also was growing, spurred by the influx of workers remaining after each of the world wars. In 1950, the city's population reached a zenith of more than 800,000 residents, an estimated 60% of which were black. At the same time that Washington was establishing itself as a global power during the world wars, economic hard times, and technological advances, the city was gaining renown among African Americans as a hub of black culture, education, and identity. Washington, from the 1920s to the 1960s, drew the likes of Cab Calloway, Duke Ellington, and Pearl Bailey, who performed at speakeasies and theaters along a stretch of U Street called the Black Broadway. (The reincarnated "New U," as it is dubbed, now attracts buppies and yuppies to its nightclubs and bars.) Howard University, created in 1867, distinguished itself as the nation's most comprehensive center for the higher education of blacks. And when the Civil Rights movement gained momentum throughout the country in the '60s and '70s, Washington's large black presence (nearly 75% of the city's overall population) and activist spirit were instrumental in furthering the cause.

On August 28, 1963, black and white Washingtonians joined the ranks of the more than 200,000 who "marched on Washington" to ensure passage of the Civil Rights Act. It was at this event that Rev. Martin Luther King, Jr., delivered his "I Have a Dream" speech at the Lincoln Memorial, where 41 years earlier, during the memorial's dedication ceremony, black officials were required to stand and watch across the road, segregated from the whites. When King was assassinated on April 4, 1968, rioting erupted here as it did in many cities around the country. From that point to this, black and white Washingtonians have continued to thrash out race relations in a city whose population has declined to a little more than 530,000— about 60% are African Americans.

Nevertheless, Washington, the federal city, proceeds apace, adding more jewels to its crown: 1971 saw the opening of the John F. Kennedy Center for the Performing Arts, on the Potomac's east bank, filling a longtime need for a cultural haven. The 1974 dedication of the Hirshhorn Museum and Sculpture Garden on the Mall met the need for a major museum of modern art. Another storehouse of art treasures is the modernistic I. M. Pei–designed East Building of the National Gallery of Art, which debuted in 1978. It was designed to handle the overflow of the gallery's burgeoning collection and to accommodate traveling exhibits of major importance. In time for the Bicentennial, the National Air and Space Museum opened in splendid new quarters, and the first leg of the capital's much-needed subway system, Metro, was completed. The 45 acres between the Washington Monument and the Lincoln Memorial were transformed into Constitution Gardens, and in 1982 the park became the site of the Vietnam Veterans Memorial.

In 1987, Washington got a new $75 million Smithsonian complex on the Mall; it houses the Arthur M. Sackler Gallery of Art, the relocated National Museum of African Art, the International Center, and the Enid A. Haupt Garden. In 1989, renovation of the city's magnificent Union Station was completed. Its brilliant architect, Daniel Burnham, also designed the palatial City Post Office Building, which in 1993 became part of the Smithsonian complex as the National Postal

Museum. The same year saw the opening of the United States Holocaust Memorial Museum, adjoining the Mall. In 1995, the Korean War Veterans Memorial was dedicated. Washington's fourth presidential monument—and the first in more than half a century—was dedicated in May 1997 to honor Franklin Delano Roosevelt; it is the first memorial in Washington designed to be totally wheelchair accessible. Finally, the Women in Military Service Memorial, next to Arlington Cemetery, was inaugurated in October 1997, followed, in June 1998, by a Civil War memorial recognizing the efforts of African-American soldiers who fought for the Union.

4 Hollywood on the Potomac

On a brisk April Saturday morning in 1998, police cars and orange cones cordon off 15th Street NW, between Pennsylvania Avenue and G Street NW. It's early still, about 9am, but the sidewalks are already bustling with activity. Otherwise nondescript, T-shirt-and-jeans-attired types strut about the sectioned-off area, talking into their headsets or walkie-talkies; roadies remove camera equipment from the backs of huge trucks parked along the curb. A collection of brown canvas director's chairs ("Director Mark Pellington, Producer Peter Samuelson") take up a corner of the sidewalk across from the Treasury Building at F Street. This seems to be center stage, where men and women in black shades and jean jackets are congregating, greeting each other with hugs, talking, and gesticulating. Out of this cluster of VIPs steps actor Jeff Bridges, who hops nimbly into a shiny black car, as bystanders gather and gape. The car pulls away and people wave to Bridges, who responds with a smile and a goofy wagging up-and-down of the wrist out the window.

It's a movie shoot: *Arlington Road,* whose plot centers on domestic terrorism, with Jeff Bridges playing a university professor who teaches history, including a class on terrorism, and Tim Robbins in the role of the mad domestic terrorist. If you've seen the movie, you may remember the chase scene, which takes in a sweeping view of the Hotel Washington, the imposing, block-long Treasury Building, and the Washington Monument. The scene, which lasts no more than a couple of minutes in the finished film, took at least a day to shoot, and this is what is going on, here on 15th Street on an otherwise unremarkable Saturday in April.

Washingtonians, long used to stopped traffic and sectioned-off streets because of political demonstrations, presidential cavalcades, and historic visits by world dignitaries, are growing accustomed to traffic jams caused by movie shoots. *Arlington Road* is just one of scores of Hollywood productions that are using Washington as a location for a movie, TV program, commercial, music video, or documentary. These projects create $42 million in revenue for the city, according to Crystal Palmer, director of the Washington, D.C., Office of Motion Picture and TV Development. Palmer reports that, on the average, 6 films and anywhere from 10 to 35 TV productions are shot here each year. The number of Washington-based films tends to increase in election years: 14 movies were made here in 1996, including *Mars Attacks, The People vs. Larry Flynt, Absolute Power,* and *Independence Day.* Among the films shot here in 1998 were *7 Days, Enemy of the State, Marshall's Law, X-Files* (based on the TV series), and *Adversaries* (which may become a TV series). When you are in Washington, you may stumble upon a filming or taping in progress, because the capital's most famous tourist attractions are also producers' favorite backdrops. Nothing packs a Washington punch like a flash of the White House on the screen.

But if movie- and TV series-making are on the rise in Washington, the practice of using Washington—and politicians—as a subject for films has long been fashionable. Starting in 1915 with *Birth of a Nation,* the lineup includes *Mr. Smith Goes to Washington* (1939), *All the King's Men* (1949), *Advise and Consent* (1962), *Dr. Strangelove* (1963), *All the President's Men* (1976), *Broadcast News* (1987), *Bob Roberts* (1992), *Nixon* (1995), and *Contact* (1997), to name just a few.

Given Washington's popularity among TV and film producers, its sometime nickname, "Hollywood on the Potomac," seems appropriate. The funny thing is, though, that the appellation derives not from the capital's frequent use as a film location or subject, but from its magnetic appeal for Hollywood celebrities. Although an actor was elected president, it isn't Ronald Reagan with whom the concept is associated, but our current president, Bill Clinton. His affinity for movie stars has been matched by his aptitude for employing star power in fund-raising and electioneering efforts.

Barbra Streisand, music meister/billionaire David Geffen, and studio chairman Lew Wasserman are among those who have raised major bucks for Clinton's campaigns. The most honored friends of Bill's ("FOBs") have been invited to spend the night in the Lincoln Bedroom (guests have included such stars as Candice Bergen and Richard Dreyfuss). Clinton's inaugural balls in 1993 and 1997 brought so many Hollywood types to Washington that it was difficult to wander anywhere in the city without spotting a star: Kim Basinger coming out of H.H. Leonards' B&B on O Street, Gregory Hines puffing on a cigar in the Fairfax Bar of the Ritz-Carlton (now the Westin Fairfax), Kevin Costner walking down a hallway of the Willard.

As much as Clinton enjoys hobnobbing with Hollywood types, he could never have wished himself portrayed on screen in quite the ways Hollywood recently has shown him. In 1998, the public witnessed a surreal moment in moviemaking: The film *Wag the Dog,* about the administration's attempts to distract the American people from a scandal involving the president's dalliance with a young "Firefly Girl," was released only weeks before allegations about intern Monica Lewinsky's affair with President Clinton hit the papers. The movie *Primary Colors,* based on the book about a womanizing Clintonlike governor running for president, seemed like old news when it opened shortly after *Wag the Dog,* which may explain why turnout was less than expected.

The phrase "Hollywood on the Potomac" refers to another growing phenomenon, the use of "star" testimony on Capitol Hill. Depending on the type of hearings being held in the Capitol, you might see Andie MacDowell lobbying for more oil pipeline regulations or Alec Baldwin lobbying for federal funding for the arts.

Politicians, on the whole, rarely mind doing a star turn for the cameras. Next time you watch a movie or TV show with a Washington twist, be on the lookout. You may spy George Stephanopolous popping up on the sitcom *Spin City,* Congressman Barney Frank and a whole raft of his colleagues in cameo roles for the series *Lateline,* or senators Christopher Dodd, Alan Simpson, Paul Simon, and Howard Metzenbaum playing themselves in the film *Dave.*

It is easy to see similarities between politics and moviemaking. Both businesses are about creating stars, wooing the public, building power bases, and fanning egos. It's a connection that Hollywood impresarios and politicians themselves perceive. In a Maureen Dowd column that appeared last year in the *New York Times* on the subject of Warren Beatty's then-new film, *Bulworth,* Dowd quotes Beatty as saying: "Washington *is* Hollywood. The techniques and events and the people are the same. As though if the actors left the party, there'd be a more serious discussion? Dream on."

Presidential Scandals

Public and media interest in President Bill Clinton's private affairs, Whitewater to Lewinsky, have been so great, you'd think the country had never before grappled with presidential scandals. But starting with George Washington and his innocent friendship with Sally Fairfax, presidential shenanigans, real or imagined, have often been in the news. The current crisis is remarkable for its sleaze quotient and because the president is combating accusations of sexual misconduct while still in office. To some extent, however, we have been here before.

Sometimes allegations are politically provoked or arise solely from conjecturing troublemakers. Anti-federalist and British journalists were never able to prove anything unseemly about Washington's friendship with Fairfax and, despite what the movies depict of Thomas Jefferson's liaison with Sally Hemmings, most historians believe that Jefferson never fathered a child with the former slave.

Some presidential scandals prove to be the real thing. Warren Gamaliel Harding, our 29th president, is a prime example. Harding was suspected but never implicated in the Teapot Dome Case, in which several of his cabinet members were exposed for accepting bribes in return for arranging the private development of federal oil reserve lands. A more salacious scandal surfaced after Harding's death. (He died in office, after serving less than 3 years.) Harding, a debonair fellow with an eye for the ladies, had carried on several affairs during his unhappy marriage, and one, with the much-younger Nan Britton, overlapped his time in the White House. The couple was so passionate that they once made love in a hidden part of Central Park. That was before he became president. Later, Harding had Secret Service agents smuggle Britton into the White House, where, on one occasion, they cuddled together in a coat closet to evade detection by the prowling Mrs. Harding. It may have been this tryst that produced Elizabeth Ann, Britton's daughter. Though the Harding estate never recognized the child, Harding was indeed her father, Britton revealed in her book, *The President's Daughter.*

Though he never came right out and admitted it, our 22nd president, Grover Cleveland, probably fathered a child out of wedlock, giving his girlfriend's son his last name, paying for his support, and arranging for his adoption. Cleveland was a bachelor at the time, and his affair with the woman, a widow, occurred in 1874, 10 years before Cleveland ran for president. During Cleveland's presidential campaign in 1884, newspapers made the most of the disclosure, portraying him as a drunk and a frequenter of "harlots." Republicans taunted the Democratic candidate with the cry, "Ma, Ma, Where's my pa? Gone to the White House, ha, ha, ha." But the incident only served to play up Cleveland's honesty, for which voters rewarded him by voting him into office. Although Cleveland lost the 1888 reelection, he ran again in 1892 and won, making him the only president to serve two nonconsecutive terms.

Andrew Jackson committed adultery, but not on purpose, he claimed. Jackson married his wife, Rachel, in 1791, when both believed that Rachel's divorce from her first husband was legal, which it was not. The couple legally remarried in

1794, but accusations of adultery surrounded them all their lives. In 1806, Jackson fought a duel and killed his accuser, Charles Dickinson, over the matter, although not before Dickinson had fired a bullet into Jackson that landed so close to his heart that doctors were never able to remove it. The adultery became such an issue when Jackson ran for president in 1828 that he credited Rachel's sudden death just after he won the election to the stress of her having to deal constantly with vituperative comments. This embittering experience touched off a rather unexpected turn of events. When President Jackson was putting his cabinet together, he appointed his good friend and supporter John Eaton as secretary of war, disregarding the rumors that swirled around Eaton's beautiful wife, Peggy, said to be a woman of low morals. Jackson believed that society's vitriolic attacks on Peggy Eaton's character were as baseless as those made on his wife. Jackson's support for the Eatons divided his cabinet and society as he tried to force his administration, and their wives, to treat the Eatons properly. (At parties, the women would scram as soon as Peggy and John arrived.) In 1831, Jackson was compelled to dissolve his cabinet, make new appointments, and dispatch the Eatons to Spain, where John served as minister and Peggy found herself welcome, by the queen, no less.

Scholars disagree about the nature of the relationship Woodrow Wilson shared with Mary Hulbert Peck. Wilson met Peck, a divorcée, in Bermuda, where he was vacationing (without his wife, Ellen) during a break from his job as president of Princeton University. Some believe that Wilson paid her off so she wouldn't talk about their affair. The press never got wind of the friendship, which lasted, in correspondence anyway, until Wilson died. Wilson caused a bit of a scandal while president, when he remarried only 16 months after the death of his first wife. Journalists relentlessly followed Wilson's whirlwind romance with Edith Galt. The *Washington Post* (a Republican bastion at the time) caused a sensation one day by reporting that "The President spent last evening entering Mrs. Galt." A typo, the newspaper apologized; the word "entering" should have read "entertaining."

Much has been made of John F. Kennedy's escapades with women, from Marilyn Monroe to Judith Exner, while occupying the White House and married to the beautiful Jacqueline. But, like Harding's infidelities, Kennedy's affairs did not become public until after his death. Franklin Delano Roosevelt, too, was linked romantically with many women, most notably Lucy Page Mercer Rutherfurd, Eleanor Roosevelt's social secretary. Letters and papers document genuine affection, but not the existence of a sexual relationship.

Until Bill Clinton's presidency, history books would have recorded Richard Nixon's tenure as the most scandalous of the 20th century. Facing impeachment proceedings in 1974 for his knowledge of and participation in the 1972 burglary of Democratic National Committee headquarters in the Watergate apartment-office complex, Nixon chose to resign. Talk of impeachment of President Clinton has surfaced during special prosecutor Kenneth Starr's investigation into Clinton's relationship with White House intern, Monica Lewinsky. Stay tuned.

2 Planning a Trip to Washington, D.C.

Washington, D.C., always a popular destination, is experiencing a boom in tourism. Hotels, the Smithsonian museums, and restaurants are seeing the highest numbers of visitors since the 1980s. The most recent figures show that even in the "slowest" month of January, visitors to the Smithsonian now number about 1 million. During the peak month of July, the institution sees more than 3.5 million people come through its doors.

That's the thing about Washington—there's never a bad time of year to visit. This fact alone allows for some flexibility as you plan your trip. But no matter when you go, you can help maximize the pleasure of your trip and minimize hassles by doing a certain amount of advance planning. The earlier you book your room, the greater your chance of finding the best rate at your preferred hotel. If dining at a hot new or favorite old restaurant is important, play it safe by calling ahead to reserve a table—Washingtonians eat out a lot, themselves, so you'll be vying with them, as well as fellow out-of-towners, for tables. A number of sight-seeing attractions (see below) permit you to obtain tickets as far as 6 months in advance. If you have your heart set on seeing one of these well-liked sites, you can avoid the wait of a long line or the ultimate disappointment of missing a tour altogether by simply reserving advance tickets. But if you're the fly-by-the-seat-of-your-pants type, never fear. There's always something happening in Washington. Just keep this guidebook in hand and follow your whim.

1 Visitor Information

Before you leave, contact the **Washington, D.C., Convention and Visitors Association,** 1212 New York Ave. NW, Washington, D.C. 20005 (☎ **202/789-7000**), www.washington.org, and ask them to send you a free copy of the *Washington, D.C., Visitors Guide,* which details hotels, restaurants, sights, shops, and more. They'll also be happy to answer specific questions. **The D.C. Committee to Promote Washington** (☎ **800/422-8644**) will send you free copies of brochures listing additional information about Washington.

What Things Cost in Washington, D.C.	U.S. $
Taxi from National Airport to downtown	$10–$11
Bus from National Airport to downtown	$8
Metro from National Airport to Farragut West (downtown) (non-rush hour)	$1.10
Local telephone call	35¢
Double room at the Jefferson Hotel (very expensive)	$175–$310
Double room at the J.W. Marriott Hotel (expensive)	$139–$234
Double room at the Radisson Barceló Hotel (moderate)	$110–$199
Double room at the Embassy Inn (inexpensive)	$59–$110
Dinner for one, without wine, at the Willard Room (very expensive)	$45
Dinner for one, without wine, at Jaleo (moderate)	$25–$30
Dinner for one, without wine, at Il Radicchio (inexpensive)	$6–$15
Bottle of beer in a restaurant	$3.50–$4
Coca-Cola in a restaurant	$1.50
Cup of coffee in a restaurant	$1.25
Roll of ASA 100 film, 36 exposures	$6.50
Admission to all Smithsonian museums	Free
Theater ticket at the National	$25–$75

ADVANCE-RESERVATION CONGRESSIONAL TOURS

Based on ticket availability, senators and/or representatives can provide their constituents with advance tickets for tours of the Capitol, the White House, the FBI, the Bureau of Engraving and Printing, the Supreme Court, and the Kennedy Center. This is no secret. Thousands of people know about it and do write, so make your request as far in advance as possible—even 6 months ahead is not too early—specifying the dates you plan to visit and the number of tickets you need. Their allotment of tickets for each site is limited, so there's no guarantee you'll secure them, but it's worth a try. (Advance tickets are not necessary to tour an attraction; but they can be helpful in avoiding long waits.)

Address requests to representatives as follows: name of your congressperson, U.S. House of Representatives, Washington, D.C. 20515; or name of your senator, U.S. Senate, Washington, D.C. 20510. Don't forget to include the exact dates of your Washington trip. When you write, also request tourist information and literature.

Note: Before writing, you might try calling a senator or congressperson's local office; in some states you can obtain passes by phone.

One other tip: If you have acquaintances who work at any of the sites, or within a related organization, by all means, contact them. For example, an employee of the Justice Department may be able to obtain FBI tour tickets for you, hassle-free.

THE CAPITOL   Congressional passes are not for tours but allow you to sit and observe Congress in session. (Regular guided tours, for which you need no ticket, take place Monday through Saturday, from 9am to 3:45pm, and last 45 minutes.) Check the Senate and House calendars first to see what days Congress is in session and in recess. Call ☎ **202/225-3121** to check the House schedule and ☎**202/ 224-3121** to check the Senate schedule. The *Washington Post* also publishes a daily calendar that notes the times Congress will be in session and the issues to be debated.

THE WHITE HOUSE   Tuesday through Saturday between 8 and 8:45am, the doors of the White House are open for special VIP tours to those with tickets. Once again, write far, far in advance, because each senator and congressperson receives no more than 10 tickets a week to distribute. These early tours ensure your entrance during the busy tourist season when thousands line up during the 2 hours daily that the White House is open to the public. The VIP tours are also more extensive than those held later; U.S. Secret Service guides provide explanatory commentary as you proceed through the ground floor and state floor rooms. On the later tours, you see the same rooms but you don't get the commentary; however, attendants and Secret Service agents are on hand to answer questions.

THE FBI   The line for this very popular tour can be extremely long; March through September you can expect to wait for 1 or 2 hours. Guided congressional tours take place on the quarter hour, from 9:45 to 11:45am and from 1:45 to 2:45pm. Contact your senator or representative at least 3 months ahead to schedule an appointment for constituent groups of six or fewer. The regular, unscheduled guided tours take place weekdays from 8:45am to 4:15pm, leaving every 20 to 30 minutes.

BUREAU OF ENGRAVING & PRINTING   Guided VIP tours are offered weekdays at 8am, except on holidays, and last about 45 minutes. Write at least 3 months in advance for tickets. Self-guided tours occur weekdays from 9am to 2pm. From September through April, no tickets are required; from May through August, you must obtain a free, same-day timed ticket to tour the building.

THE KENNEDY CENTER   Congressional tours depart Monday through Saturday at 9:30am and 4:45pm year-round and at 9:45am April through September. These tours are free, but you must have a letter from your senator or congressperson. Call ☎ **202/416-8303** at the Kennedy Center for more information on these tours.

THE SUPREME COURT   Contact your senator or congressperson at least 2 months in advance to arrange for guided tours of the building led by a Supreme Court staff member. Self-guided and guided tours are allowed when the court is not in session. Call the Supreme Court information line to find out days and times that court arguments will take place. You may view these on a first-come, first-served basis, choosing between the 3-minute line, which ushers visitors in and out of the court every 3 minutes, or the "regular" line, which admits visitors who wish to stay for the entire argument.

2 When to Go

CLIMATE

If you have a choice of when you can visit, I'd recommend the fall . The weather is lovely, Washington's scenery is awash in fall foliage colors, and the tourists have thinned out.

   If you hate crowds and want to get the most out of Washington sights, winter is your season: There are no long lines or early morning dashes to avoid them, and hotel prices tend to be lower. People like to say that Washington winters are mild—and yes, if you're from Minnesota, you will find Washington warmer, no doubt. But our winters are unpredictable: bitter cold one day, an ice storm the next, followed by a couple of days of sun and higher temperatures. Pack for all possibilities.

Spring weather is delightful, and, of course, there are those cherry blossoms. Along with autumn, it's the nicest time to enjoy D.C.'s outdoor attractions, to get around to museums in comfort, and to laze away an afternoon or evening at the ubiquitous Washington street cafes. But the city is also crowded with visitors and school groups.

The throngs remain in summer, and anyone who's ever spent a summer in D.C. will tell you how hot and steamy it can be. The advantage: This is the season (especially June and July) to enjoy numerous outdoor events—free concerts, festivals, parades, and more. There's something doing almost every night and day. And, of course, Independence Day (July 4) in the capital is a spectacular celebration.

Average Temperatures (°F) in Washington, D.C.

	Jan	Feb	Mar	Apr	May	June	July	Aug	Sept	Oct	Nov	Dec
Avg. High	44	46	54	66	76	83	87	85	79	68	57	46
Avg. Low	30	29	36	46	56	65	69	68	61	50	39	32

WASHINGTON CALENDAR OF EVENTS

The district is the scene of numerous daily special events, fairs, and celebrations. Listed below are the major annual events. When in town, check the *Washington Post,* especially the Friday "Weekend" section. **The Smithsonian Information Center,** 1000 Jefferson Dr. SW (☎ **202/357-2700**), is another good source. For annual events in Alexandria, see chapter 11.

January

• **Martin Luther King, Jr.'s Birthday.** Events include speeches by prominent civil rights leaders and politicians; readings; dance, theater, and choral performances; prayer vigils; a wreath-laying ceremony at the Lincoln Memorial; and concerts. Many events take place at the Martin Luther King Memorial Library, 901 G St. NW (☎ **202/727-0321**). Call ☎ **202/789-7000** for further details. Third Monday in January.

February

• **Chinese New Year Celebration.** A friendship archway, topped by 300 painted dragons and lighted at night, marks Chinatown's entrance at 7th and H streets NW. The celebration begins the day of the Chinese New Year and continues for 10 or more days, with traditional firecrackers, dragon dancers, and colorful street parades. Some area restaurants offer special menus. For details, call ☎ **202/638-1041.** Mid-February.

• **Black History Month.** During this month, numerous events, museum exhibits, and cultural programs celebrating the contributions of African Americans to American life take place. For details, check the *Washington Post* or call ☎ **202/357-2700.** For additional activities at the Martin Luther King Library, call ☎ **202/727-0321.**

• **Abraham Lincoln's Birthday, Lincoln Memorial.** Marked by the laying of a wreath and a reading of the Gettysburg Address at noon. Call ☎ **202/619-7222.** February 12.

- **George Washington's Birthday, Washington Monument.** Similar celebratory events. Call ☎ **202/619-7222** for details. Both presidents' birthdays also bring annual citywide sales. February 22. Mount Vernon also marks Washington's birthday with free admission and activities that include music and military performances on the bowling green. Call ☎ **703/780-2000.** President's Day, third Monday in February.

March

- **St. Patrick's Day Parade,** on Constitution Avenue NW from 7th to 17th streets. A big parade with all you'd expect—floats, bagpipes, marching bands, and the wearin' o' the green. For parade information, call ☎ **301/879-1717.** The Sunday before March 17.
- **Cherry Blossom Events.** Washington's best-known annual event is the blossoming of the 3,700 famous Japanese cherry trees by the Tidal Basin in Potomac Park. Festivities include a major parade (marking the end of the festival) with princesses, floats, concerts, celebrity guests, and more. There are also special ranger-guided tours departing from the Jefferson Memorial. For parade information—or tickets for grandstand seating ($12 per person)—call the D.C. Downtown Jaycees (☎ **202/728-1137**). For other cherry-blossom events, check the *Washington Post* or call ☎ **202/789-7038** or 202/547-1500. Late March or early April (national news programs monitor the budding).
- **Smithsonian Kite Festival.** A delightful event if the weather cooperates—an occasion for a trip in itself. Throngs of kite enthusiasts fly their unique creations on the Washington Monument grounds and compete for ribbons and prizes. To compete, just show up with your kite and register between 10am and noon. Call ☎ **202/357-2700** or 202/357-3030 for details. Last weekend in March.

April

- **Easter Sunrise Services,** Memorial Amphitheater at Arlington National Cemetery on Easter Sunday. Free shuttle buses travel to the site from the cemetery's visitors' center parking lot. Call ☎ **703/607-8052** or 202/789-7000 for details.
- **White House Easter Egg Roll.** The biggie for little kids. In past years, entertainment on the White House South Lawn and the Ellipse has included clog dancers, clowns, Ukrainian egg-decorating exhibitions, puppet and magic shows, military drill teams, an egg-rolling contest, and a hunt for 1,000 or so wooden eggs, many of them signed by celebrities, astronauts, or the president. *Note:* Attendance is limited to children ages 3 to 6, who must be accompanied by an adult. Hourly timed tickets are issued at the National Parks Service Ellipse Visitors Pavilion just behind the White House at 15th and E streets NW beginning at 7am. Call ☎ **202/456-2200** for details. Easter Monday between 10am and 2pm; enter at the southeast gate on East Executive Avenue, and arrive early.
- **Thomas Jefferson's Birthday, Jefferson Memorial.** Celebrated with a wreath-laying, speeches, and a military ceremony. Call ☎ **202/619-7222** for time and details. April 13.
- **White House Spring Garden Tours.** These beautifully landscaped creations are open to the public for free afternoon tours. Call ☎ **202/456-2200** for details. Two days only, in mid-April.
- **Shakespeare's Birthday Celebration.** Music, theater, children's events, food, and exhibits are all part of the afternoon's hail to the Bard at the Folger Shakespeare Library. Call ☎ **202/544-7077.** Free. Mid-April.
- **Filmfest D.C.** The 13th celebration of this annual international film festival takes place in 1999. The festival lasts about 2 weeks in mid- to late April and presents

as many as 75 works produced by filmmakers from around the world. Screenings are staged throughout the festival at movie theaters, embassies, and other venues. Tickets are usually $7 per movie; some events are free. Call ☎ **202/628-FILM;** www.capaccess.org/fillmfestdc.

- **Taste of the Nation.** An organization called Share Our Strength (SOS) sponsors this fund-raiser, which takes place in more than 100 cities throughout the nation every April. In Washington, anywhere from 70 to 90 major restaurants and many wineries set up tasting booths at Union Station and offer some of their finest fare. For the price of admission, you can do the circuit, sampling everything from barbecue to bouillabaisse; wine flows freely, and there are dozens of great desserts. The evening also includes a silent auction. Tickets are $65 if purchased in advance, $75 at the door, and 100% of the profits go to feed the hungry. To obtain tickets, call ☎ **800/955-8278.** Late April.

- **The Smithsonian Craft Show** features one-of-a-kind, limited-edition crafts by more than 100 noted artists (it's a juried show) from all over the country. It takes place at the National Building Museum, 401 F St. NW, during 4 days in late April. There's an entrance fee of about $10 per adult, $7 per child, each day. For details, call ☎ **202/357-2700** (TDD 202/357-1729) or 202/357-4000.

May

- **Georgetown Garden Tour.** View the remarkable private gardens of one of the city's loveliest neighborhoods. Admission (about $18) includes light refreshments. Some years there are related events such as a flower show at a historic home. Call ☎ **202/333-6896** for details. Second Saturday in May.

- **Washington National Cathedral Annual Flower Mart,** on the cathedral grounds. Includes displays of flowering plants and herbs, decorating demonstrations, ethnic food booths, children's rides and activities (including an antique carousel), costumed characters, puppet shows, and other entertainment. Free. Call ☎ **202/537-6200** for details. First Friday and Saturday in May.

- **Memorial Day.** At 11am, a wreath-laying ceremony takes place at the Tomb of the Unknowns in Arlington National Cemetery, followed by military band music, a service, and an address by a high-ranking government official (sometimes the president); call ☎ **202/685-2851** for details. There's also a ceremony at 1pm at the Vietnam Veterans Memorial, including a wreath-laying, speakers, and the playing of taps (☎ **202/619-7222**), and there are activities at the U.S. Navy Memorial (☎ **202/737-2300**). On the Sunday before Memorial Day, the National Symphony Orchestra performs a free concert at 8pm on the West Lawn of the Capitol to officially welcome summer to Washington. Call ☎ **202/619-7222** for details.

June

- **Dupont-Kalorama Museum Walk Day.** This year marks the 15th annual celebration by six museums and historic houses in this charming neighborhood. Free food, music, tours, and crafts demonstrations. Call ☎ **202/667-0441.** Early June.

- **Shakespeare Theatre Free for All.** This free theater festival presents a different Shakespeare play each year, for a 2-week run at the Carter Barron Amphitheatre in upper northwest Washington. Tickets are required and free. Evenings, mid-June. Call ☎ **202/547-3230.**

- **Smithsonian Festival of American Folklife.** A major event with traditional American music, crafts, foods, games, concerts, and exhibits. Past performances have ranged from Appalachian fiddling to Native American dancing, and demonstrations from quilting to coal mining. All events are free; most events take place outdoors on the Mall. Call ☎ **202/357-2700,** or check the listings in the *Washington Post* for details. For 5 to 10 days, always including July 4.

July

- **Independence Day.** There's no better place to be on the Fourth of July than in Washington, D.C. The festivities include a massive National Independence Day Parade down Constitution Avenue, complete with lavish floats, princesses, marching groups, and military bands. There are also celebrity entertainers and concerts. (Most events take place on the Washington Monument grounds.) A morning program in front of the National Archives includes military demonstrations, period music, and a reading of the Declaration of Independence. In the evening the National Symphony Orchestra plays on the west steps of the Capitol with guest artists (for example, Leontyne Price). Big-name entertainment also precedes the fabulous fireworks display behind the Washington Monument. *Note:* You can also attend an 11am free organ recital at Washington's National Cathedral. Consult the *Washington Post* or call ☎ **202/789-7000** for details. July 4, all day.
- **Bastille Day.** This Washington tradition honors the French Independence Day with live entertainment and a race by tray-balancing waiters and waitresses from Les Halles Restaurant to the U.S. Capitol and back. Free, mais oui. 12th and Pennsylvania Avenue NW. Call ☎ **202/347-6848.** July 14.
- **Latino Festival.** Latin American bands from Miami, New York, and Los Angeles entertain the crowds who come to celebrate the music, food, and culture of Latin America. Free admission; purchase tickets for food. Pennsylvania Avenue, between 9th and 14th streets NW. Call ☎ **703/922-0067.** Late July.

August/September

- **National Frisbee Festival,** on the Washington Monument grounds. See world-class Frisbee champions and their disk-catching dogs at this noncompetitive event. For details, call ☎ **301/645-5043.** Labor Day weekend.
- **Labor Day Concert.** The National Symphony Orchestra closes its summer season with a free performance at 8pm on the West Lawn of the Capitol; call ☎ **202/619-7222** for details. Labor Day. (Rain date: same day and time at Constitution Hall.)
- **International Children's Festival,** Wolf Trap Farm Park in Vienna, Virginia. At this 2-day arts celebration, the entertainment—all of it outdoors—includes clowns, musicians, mimes, puppet shows, and creative workshops from 10am to 4:30pm each day. Admission is charged. For details, call ☎ **703/642-0862.** Late September.
- **Washington National Cathedral's Open House.** Celebrates the anniversary of the laying of the foundation stone in 1907. Events include demonstrations of stone carving and other crafts utilized in building the cathedral; carillon and organ demonstrations; and performances by dancers, choirs, strolling musicians, jugglers, and puppeteers. This is the only time visitors are allowed to ascend to the top of the central tower to see the bells; it's a tremendous climb, but you'll be rewarded with a spectacular view. For details, call ☎ **202/537-6200.** A Saturday in late September or early October.
- **Black Family Reunion.** Performances, food, and fun are part of this celebration of the African-American family and culture on the National Mall. Free. Call ☎ **202/383-9104.** Mid-September.

- **Kennedy Center Open House Arts Festival.** A daylong festival of the per-forming arts in early to mid-September, featuring local and national artists on the front plaza and river terrace (which overlooks the Potomac) and throughout the stage halls of the Kennedy Center. Past festivals have featured the likes of Los Lobos, Mary Chapin Carpenter, and Washington Opera soloists. Kids' activities usually include a National Symphony Orchestra "petting zoo," where children get to bow, blow, drum, or strum a favorite instrument. Admission is free, but you may have to stand in a long line to gain admittance to the inside perfor-mances. Check the *Washington Post* or call ☎ **800/444-1324** or 202/467-4600 for details. A Sunday, in early to mid-September, noon to 6pm.

October

- **Taste of D.C. Festival,** Pennsylvania Avenue between 9th and 14th streets NW. Dozens of Washington's restaurants offer international food-tasting opportuni-ties, along with live entertainment, dancing, storytellers, and games. Admission is free; purchase tickets for tastings. Call ☎ **202/724-5430** for details. Three days, including Columbus Day weekend.
- **White House Fall Garden Tours.** For 2 days, visitors have an opportunity to see the famed Rose Garden and South Lawn. Admission is free. A military band pro-vides music. For details, call ☎ **202/456-2200.** Mid-October.
- **Halloween.** There is no official celebration, but costumed revels are on the increase every year. Giant block parties take place in the Dupont Circle area and Georgetown. Check the *Washington Post* for special parties and activities. October 31.
- **Marine Corps Marathon.** More than 16,000 runners compete in this 26.2-mile race (the fourth-largest marathon in the United States). It begins at the Marine Corps Memorial (the Iwo Jima statue) and passes major monuments. Call ☎ **800/RUN-USMC** or 703/784-2225 for details. Anyone can enter; register up to a week ahead. Fourth Sunday in October.

November

- **Veterans Day.** The nation's war dead are honored with a wreath-laying ceremony at 11am at the Tomb of the Unknowns in Arlington National Cemetery, followed by a memorial service. The President of the United States or a very high-ranking government personage officiates. Music is provided by a military band. Call ☎ **202/685-2851** for information. At the Vietnam Veterans Memo-rial (☎ **202/619-7222**), observances include speakers, a wreath-laying, a color guard, and the playing of taps. November 11.

December

- **Christmas Pageant of Peace/National Tree Lighting,** at the northern end of the Ellipse. The president lights the national Christmas tree to the accompani-ment of orchestral and choral music. The lighting inaugurates the 3-week Pageant of Peace, a tremendous holiday celebration with seasonal music, car-oling, a Nativity scene, 50 state trees, and a burning Yule log. Call ☎ **202/619-7222** for details. A select Wednesday or Thursday in early December, at 5pm.
- **White House Candlelight Tours.** On three evenings after Christmas from 5 to 7pm, visitors can see the president's Christmas holiday decorations by candle-light. String music enhances the tours. Lines are long; arrive early. Call ☎ **202/456-2200** for dates and details.

3 Tips for Travelers with Special Needs

FOR TRAVELERS WITH DISABILITIES

Two helpful travel organizations, **Accessible Journeys** (☎ **800/TINGLES** or 610/ 521-0339; www.disabilitytravel.com) and **Flying Wheels Travel** (☎ **800/ 535-6790** or 507/451-5005; www.flyingwheels.com), offer group tours, cruises, and custom vacations worldwide for people with physical disabilities; Accessible Journeys can also provide nurse-companions for travelers. **The Guided Tour Inc.** (☎ **800/783-5841** or 215/782-1370; www.guidedtour.com) offers tours for people with physical or mental disabilities.

Mobility International USA, P.O. Box 10767, Eugene, OR 97440 (☎ **541/ 343-1284,** TDD is the same number; www.miusa.org), provides accessibility and resource information to its members. Individual membership costs $35 a year; the quarterly newsletter, "Over the Rainbow," is included in the membership.

The Society for the Advancement of Travel for the Handicapped (SATH), 347 Fifth Ave., Suite 610, New York, NY 10016 (☎ **212/447-7284;** fax 212/ 725-8253; www.sath.org/), offers travel information for people with disabilities and charges $5 for individual requests for information, $45 for adult memberships, and $30 for seniors and student memberships. SATH's quarterly magazine, *OPEN WORLD for Accessible and Mature Travel* is free to members and $13 annually to nonmembers.

Visually impaired travelers can obtain large-print and braille atlases of the Washington area (though they're slightly out of date) from Washington Ear, 35 University Blvd., E. Silver Spring, MD 20901 (☎ **301/681-6636**).

RECOMMENDED BOOKS A publisher called **Twin Peaks Press,** Box 129, Vancouver, WA 98666 (☎ **800/637-2256** or 360/694-2462, fax 360/696-3210), specializes in books for people with disabilities. Write for their Disability Bookshop Catalog, enclosing $5. Books include *Travel for the Disabled* for $19.95, a directory of travel agencies for travelers with disabilities at $19.95, and a directory of accessible van rentals at $9.95 (shipping is an extra $4).

SIGHTSEEING ATTRACTIONS Washington, D.C., is one of the most accessible cities in the world for travelers with disabilities. The Washington, D.C., Convention & Visitors Association publishes a fact sheet detailing general accessibility of Washington hotels, restaurants, shopping malls, and attractions. For a free copy, call ☎ **202/789-7064** or write to WCVA, 1212 New York Ave. NW, Suite 600, Washington, D.C. 20005.

Here is some accessibility information for specific attractions.

For tours of the White House, visitors in wheelchairs should come to the East Executive Avenue visitors' entrance; visitors arriving in wheelchairs do not need tickets. For details, call ☎ **202/456-2322.**

All Smithsonian museum buildings are accessible to visitors using wheelchairs. A comprehensive free publication called *Smithsonian Access* lists all services available to visitors with disabilities, including parking, building access, and more. To obtain a copy, contact the VIARC, SI Building, Smithsonian Institution, Washington, D.C. 20560 (☎ **202/357-2700** or TTY 202/357-1729). You can also use the TTY number to obtain information on all Smithsonian museums and events.

The Lincoln, Jefferson, and Vietnam Memorials and the Washington Monument are also equipped to accommodate visitors with disabilities and keep wheelchairs on the premises. There's limited parking for visitors with disabilities on the south side of the Lincoln Memorial. Call ahead to other sightseeing attractions for accessibility information and special services.

Call your senator or representative to arrange wheelchair-accessible tours of the Capitol; they can also arrange special tours for visitors who are blind or deaf. If you need further information on these tours, call ☎ **202/224-4048.**

SHOPPING   For shoppers, places well equipped with wheelchair ramps and other facilities for visitors with disabilities include **Union Station, the Shops at National Place,** the **Pavilion at the Old Post Office,** and **Georgetown Park Mall.**

THEATER   The John F. Kennedy Center for the Performing Arts provides headphones to hearing-impaired patrons at no charge, allowing them to adjust the volume as needed. A wireless, infrared listening enhancement system is available in all theaters. Some performances offer sign-language and audio description. A public TTY is located at the Information Center in the Hall of States. Large-print programs are available at every performance; a limited number of braille programs are available from the house manager. All theaters in the complex (except the Terrace) are wheelchair accessible. The 1997 renovation of the Concert Hall has made it the most accessible venue in the city; improvements include ingenious wheelchair seating, increased to 4% of the seats, and enhanced acoustics. To reserve a wheelchair, call ☎ **202/416-8340.** For other questions regarding patrons with disabilities, including information about half-price tickets (you will need to submit a letter from your doctor stating that your disability is permanent), call ☎ **202/416-8727.** The TTY number is ☎ **202/416-8728.**

The **Arena Stage** (☎ **202/554-9066**) has a wheelchair lift and is otherwise accessible. It offers audio description and sign interpretation at designated performances as well as infrared and audio loop assisted-listening devices for the hearing-impaired. Also available are program books in braille, large-print, and (by advance request) on audiocassette. The TTY box-office line is ☎ **202/484-0247.** You can call ahead to reserve handicapped parking spaces for a performance.

Ford's Theatre is wheelchair-accessible and offers listening devices as well as special signed and audio-described performances. Call ☎ **202/347-4833** for details. The TTY number is ☎ **202/347-5599.**

The National Theatre is wheelchair-accessible and offers special performances of its shows for visually and hearing-impaired theatergoers. To obtain earphones for narration, ask an usher before the performance. The National also offers a limited number of half-price tickets to patrons in wheelchairs; seating is in the orchestra section and you may receive no more than two half-price tickets. For details, call ☎ **202/628-6161.**

GETTING AROUND TOWN   Before you arrive in Washington, you may want to order Metro's free guide on bus and rail system accessibility for the elderly and physically disabled; call ☎ **202/635-6434.**

Each Metro station is equipped with an elevator (complete with braille number plates) to train platforms, and rail cars are fully accessible. By the end of 1999, Metro will have installed 24-inch sections of punctuated terra-cotta tiles leading up to the granite-lined platform edge to warn visually impaired Metro riders that they are nearing the tracks. Train operators make station and on-board announcements of train destinations and stops. Most of the district's Metrobuses have wheelchair lifts and kneel at the curb (this number will increase as time goes on). The TDD number for Metro information is ☎ **202/628-2033.** For other questions about Metro services for travelers with disabilities, call ☎ **202/962-1100.** In fact, it's probably a good idea to call this number to verify that the elevators are operating at the stations you'll be traveling to; otherwise, you may find yourself unable to access or exit a station because of ongoing repair work to the system's elevators and equipment.

Regular Tourmobile trams are accessible to visitors with disabilities. The company also operates special vans for immobile travelers, complete with wheelchair lifts. Tourmobile recommends that you call a day ahead to ensure that the van is available for you when you arrive. For information, call ☎ **202/554-5100.**

TRAVELING BY BUS, TRAIN & PLANE   A companion can accompany a person with a disability at no charge aboard a **Greyhound** bus (you must inform Greyhound in advance); call ☎ **800/231-2222** for details. Call ☎ **800/752-4841** at least 24 hours in advance to discuss other special needs. Greyhound's TDD number is ☎ **800/345-3109.**

Amtrak (☎ **800/USA-RAIL**) provides redcap service for Washington and, at many stations, wheelchair assistance and special seats with 24 hours' notice. Passengers with disabilities are also entitled to a discount of 15% off the lowest available rail fare. Documentation from a doctor or an ID card proving your disability is required. Amtrak also provides wheelchair-accessible sleeping accommodations on long-distance trains, and service animals are permitted and travel free of charge. Write for a free booklet called *Amtrak Travel Planner* from Amtrak Distribution Center, P.O. Box 7717, Itasca, IL 60143, which has a section at the back detailing services for passengers with disabilities. Amtrak's TDD number is ☎ **800/523-6590.**

When making your flight reservations, ask the airline or travel agent where your wheelchair will be stowed on the plane and if seeing or hearing guide dogs can accompany you.

FOR SENIORS

Bring some form of photo ID that includes your birth date, since many city attractions, theaters, transportation facilities, hotels, and restaurants grant special senior discounts.

Contact the D.C. Office on Aging, 441 4th St. NW (☎ **202/724-5626**) to request its free directory, *Golden Washingtonian Club Gold Mine.* It lists numerous establishments offering 10% to 15% discounts to seniors on goods and services.

If you haven't already done so, consider joining the **American Association of Retired Persons (AARP),** 601 E St. NW, Washington, D.C. 20049 (☎ **800/424-3410** or 202/434-2277; www.aarp.org). Annual membership costs $8 per person or per couple. You must be at least 50 to join. Membership entitles you to many discounts. Write to Purchase Privilege Program, AARP Fulfillment, 601 E St. NW, Washington, D.C. 20049, to receive AARP's "Purchase Privilege" brochure—a free list of nationwide hotels, motels, and car-rental firms that offer discounts to AARP members.

Elderhostel, a national nonprofit organization that offers low-cost educational programs for people 55 or older and their adult companions, sponsors frequent weeklong residential programs in Washington. Some of these focus on government and American history, others on art, literature, and other subjects. Cost averages about $460 per person, including meals, room, and classes. For information, call ☎ **410/830-3437** or contact Elderhostel headquarters at 75 Federal St., Boston, MA 02110 (☎ **617/426-7788;** www.elderhostel.org).

Saga International Holidays, 222 Berkeley St., Boston, MA 02116 (☎ **800/343-0273**), offers tours in the United States and abroad designed for travelers over 50. In Washington, D.C., their 5-night, 6-day Smithsonian Odyssey Tours program offers a behind-the-scenes look at several museums and other major D.C. institutions. For this specific program, call ☎ **800/258-5885.** Prices are moderate.

Amtrak (☎ **800/USA-RAIL**) offers a 15% discount off the full, one-way coach fare (with certain travel restrictions) to people 62 or older.

Greyhound also offers discounted fares for senior citizens. Call your local Greyhound office for details.

FOR GAY & LESBIAN TRAVELERS

The complete source for the gay and lesbian community is *The Washington Blade*, a comprehensive weekly newspaper distributed free at about 700 locations in the district. Every issue provides an extensive events calendar and a list of hundreds of resources, such as crisis centers, health facilities, switchboards, political groups, religious organizations, social clubs, and student activities; it puts readers in touch with everything from groups of lesbian bird-watchers to the Asian Gay Men's Network. Gay restaurants and clubs are, of course, also listed and advertised. You can subscribe to the *Blade* for $45 a year or pick up a free copy at **Olsson's Books/Records,** 1307 19th St. NW; **Borders,** 18th and L streets; **Annie's Paramount Steak House,** 1609 17th St. NW; **Kramerbooks,** 1517 Connecticut Ave. NW, at Dupont Circle; and **Chesapeake Bagel Bakery,** 215 Pennsylvania Ave. SE, on Capitol Hill. Call the *Blade* office at ☎ **202/797-7000** for other locations. One final source: Washington's gay bookstore, **Lambda Rising,** 1625 Connecticut Ave. NW (☎ **202/462-6969**), also informally serves as an information center for the gay community, which centers in the Dupont Circle neighborhood.

FOR FAMILIES

Field trips during the school year and family vacations during the summer keep Washington, D.C., crawling with kids all year long. Because it is the nation's capital, Washington is a natural place for families to visit. Still, you may be surprised at just how much there is to do. Perhaps more than any other city, Washington is crammed with historic buildings, arts and science museums, parks, and recreational outlets to interest young and old alike. Some of the museums, like the National Museum of Natural History and the Daughters of the American Revolution (DAR) Museum, have hands-on exhibits for children. Many more sponsor regular, usually free, family-oriented events, such as the Corcoran Gallery of Art's "Family Days" and the Folger Shakespeare Library's seasonal activities. It's worth calling or writing in advance for schedules from the sites you're thinking of visiting (see chapter 7 for addresses and phone numbers). There is something here for everyone, and the fact that so many attractions are free is a boon to the family budget.

Hotels are doing their part to make family trips affordable, too. At many of the hotels, children under a certain age (usually 12) sleep free in the same room with their parents. Hotel weekend packages often offer special family rates. An excellent resource for family travel, including information about deals that chains and other hotels offer to families, is *Family Travel Times*, a bimonthly newsletter published by FTT Marketing. To subscribe or get information, contact Family Travel Times, FTT Marketing, P.O. Box 4326, Washington, D.C., 20044 (☎ **888/822-4388** or 212/477-5524). A subscription rate of $39 per year entitles you to six issues of the newsletter, discounts on other publications and back issues, and weekly call-in service for advice. If you want to get an idea of the kinds of family promotion packages hotels sometimes offer, ask for a back issue of the Winter/Spring 1997 newsletter, which included a "Hotel Happenings" article.

Restaurants throughout the Washington area are growing increasingly family-friendly, as well: Many provide kids' menus or charge less for children's portions.

The best news, though, is that families are welcome at all sorts of restaurants these days and need no longer seek out the hamburger/french fries eateries.

Washington, D.C., is easy to get around with children. The Metro covers the city, taking you nearly anywhere you'd want to go, and it's safe. Children under 4 ride free. Remember, however, that eating or drinking on the subway or in the station is prohibited.

Once you arrive, get your hands on a copy of the most recent *Washington Post* "Weekend" section, published each Friday. The section covers all possible happenings in the city, with a weekly feature, called "Saturday's Child," and a column, called "Carousel," devoted to children's activities.

4 Getting There

BY PLANE

D.C.'s Area Airports

Washington, D.C., has three airports serving the area—two of which, Ronald Reagan Washington National (formerly named Washington National) and Baltimore-Washington International, have recently undergone superb renovations. Dulles International is in the midst of a grand expansion, to be completed in stages in the decades to come; a new midfield terminal opened in February 1998.

Ronald Reagan Washington National Airport (everyone still calls it National) lies across the Potomac River in Virginia, about 20 minutes from downtown in non-rush-hour traffic. Nineteen major airlines and shuttles operate at this airport. If you are arriving from a city that is within 1,250 miles of National, this may be your airport; by law only short- and medium-haul flights use National.

Built in 1941, National was long due for an overhaul, and the recently completed, $1 billion project has vastly improved the airport, without increasing the number of flights or passengers it can handle. Enhancements include a new, three-level, 1,600-foot-long terminal with 35 gates and a large window overlooking the city; ticket counters that provide access for passengers with disabilities; 24 restaurants and 38 shops; more parking space; and climate-controlled pedestrian bridges that connect the terminal directly to the Metro station, whose Blue and Yellow lines stop here. For airport information, call ☎ **703/419-8000;** the airport's Web site is www.metwashairports.com. For Metro information, call ☎ **202/637-7000.**

Washington Dulles International Airport (Dulles) lies 26 miles outside the capital, in Chantilly, VA, a 35- to 45-minute ride to downtown in non-rush-hour traffic. The expansion, to be finished over the course of the next few decades, will eventually add an underground "people mover" system to replace the inconvenient and unwieldy mobile lounges that, for now, transport travelers to and from the main and midfield terminals. As of spring 1998, the airport project had increased its capacity to handle 40,000 passengers daily, up from 35,000. Both domestic and international carriers use Dulles. Call ☎ **703/419-8000** for airport information; the airport's Web site is the same as National's, above.

Last but not least is **Baltimore-Washington International Airport (BWI),** which is about 45 minutes from downtown, a few miles outside of Baltimore. Often overlooked by Washingtonians, BWI's bargain fares make it worth considering. Its renovation has added a two-level observation gallery, a Smithsonian Museum Shop, and a Starbucks. Call ☎ **410/859-7111** for airport information; www.baltwashintlairport.com.

THE MAJOR AIRLINES

Scheduled domestic airlines flying into Washington's three airports include **American** (☎ 800/433-7300), **America West** (☎ 800/235-9292), **Continental** (☎ 800/525-0280), **Delta** (☎ 800/221-1212), **Northwest** (☎ 800/225-2525), **TWA** (☎ 800/221-2000), **United** (☎ 800/241-6522), and **US Airways** (☎ 800/428-4322). Scheduled international flights flying into Baltimore-Washington International and/or Dulles International Airport include **Air Canada** (☎ 800/776-3000), **Air France** (☎ 800/237-2747), **All Nippon Airways** (☎ 800/235-9262), **British Airways** (☎ 800/247-9297), **KLM** (☎ 800/374-7747), **Lufthansa** (☎ 800/645-3880), **Saudi Arabian Airlines** (☎ 800/472-8342), **Swissair** (☎ 800/221-4750), and **Virgin Atlantic** (☎ 800/862-8621). For airline Web addresses, see the Appendix at the end of this book.

For a quarterly guide to flights in and out of National and Dulles, write to Metropolitan Washington Airports Authority, P.O. Box 17045, Washington Dulles International Airport, Washington, D.C. 20041. For a BWI flight guide, write to Maryland Aviation Administration, Marketing and Development, P.O. Box 8766, BWI Airport, MD 21240-0766.

BEST-FOR-THE-BUDGET FARES   Fare wars, the Internet, the rise of low-fare airlines, and the use of a smart travel agent will all help to get you a deal. Travel agents and airlines offer greatly varying rates, so shop around, whether you're using the telephone or the Internet. And closely scan the newspaper and airline informational packets to cash in on flash promotions and airline discounts. Read the Sunday travel sections of the *New York Times* and the *Washington Post;* their weekly columns ("Fly Buys" in the *Post* and "Lowest Air Fares for Popular Routes" in the *Times*) highlight bargain airfares.

Contact all the airlines flying into Washington and inquire about charters and specials. When you call, ask about reduced rates for seniors, children, and students, as well as money-saving packages that include such essentials as hotel accommodations, car rentals, and tours with your airfare. One example: The "Golden Opportunities" booklet sold by US Airways, gives seniors savings options on four one-way tickets, good in the United States, Canada, Mexico, St. Croix, St. Thomas, and Puerto Rico. That booklet was priced at $579 in the spring of 1998 and allows you to travel any day of the week, with few restrictions.

If you can, be flexible: The best rates are usually available on off-peak days (Tuesday, Wednesday, and Saturday), time of day (night flights are sometimes cheaper and less crowded), and seasons (winter and August, for flights into Washington). Think about flying into Baltimore-Washington International Airport (see above). The airport lies closer to Baltimore than Washington, but the inconvenience of adding about 20 more minutes to get into Washington may be well outweighed by the savings you receive in booking seats on the low-cost airlines that fly into BWI: **Southwest Airlines** (☎ 800/435-9792) is the main one.

If you can do without frills, find out whether your city is served by any of the other low-cost airlines that serve Washington: **AirTran** (formerly ValuJet) (☎ **800/247-8726**); **Delta Express** (☎ **800/325-5205**); **Midway Airlines** (☎ **800/446-4392**); and **Western Pacific Airlines** (☎ **800/930-3030**). All but Midway use Washington Dulles International Airport; Midway uses National.

If you are booking your airline through a travel agent, ask about consolidator tickets. Consolidators buy up blocks of unsold seats from airlines and resell them at reduced rates to agents and consumers. You don't have to worry about advance purchasing your ticket when you're dealing with consolidators. Look for their ads in

Netting Savings on the Internet

No doubt about it, the Internet can save you lots of money on airfare, hotels, and car rental. The process of surfing the Net for bargains, though, can be frustrating and time-consuming. I have tried to make it a little easier for you by listing some of the better Web sites out there. Most of these on-line travel booking systems are, essentially, the same reservations services that travel agents use, and each system has its own idiosyncrasies for you to master. The services are free, but each usually requires first that you register, which can take some time.

The best deals you'll find are ones that are available at the very moment you are staring at the screen; airlines post discounts as a way to fill seats that otherwise would remain empty. (Ditto hotels and car-rental companies.) Blink and they're gone, snatched up by some other surfer. If you're ready to fly out the door on a dime, you may be able to benefit. If you're in the daydreaming stages of a trip, the practice of learning how to use each Web site should stand you in good stead when you're ready to book your dates. All the services listed are free, but unless your Internet provider subscription covers unlimited access, you should keep track of your time on-line.

- **www/astanet.com** (American Society of Travel Agents). Use this Web site to describe your proposed trip, and ASTA-member agents bid for thebusiness on-line. The ASTA bidder wins the business, and you win the lowest price.

- **www.priceline.com** (Priceline). When you access this Web site, you enter your destination, the price you want to pay, and the dates you intend to travel; participating airlines (America West, American, Continental, Delta, Northwest, TWA, United, and US Airways are the major ones) that can satisfy your request E-mail you a response. You can then either purchase your ticket on-line with a credit card number, or call the toll-free number (☎ **800/774 2354**) to book your flight. Certain restrictions apply: for instance, tickets are for round-trips only; you can't choose your preferred airline or airport; and if your first bid is rejected, you pay $25 for each additional bid.

- **www.travelocity.com** (Travelocity). Owned by American Airlines, Travelocity will E-mail you the lowest fares for up to five destinations and track the three lowest fares for any routes on any dates in minutes. You can also use this site to find and book bargain hotel and car-rental deals. Click on "Last Minute Deals" for the latest travel bargains, including a link to "H.O.T. Coupons" (www.hotcoupons.com), where you can print out electronic coupons for travel in the United States, including Washington, D.C., and Canada.

- **www.bestfares.com** (Best Fares). The same outfit that's been publishing *Best Fares* magazine for 16 years now brings you this all-in-one Web site, with three free sections: **Newsdesk,** with constantly updated information about national and international fares and other travel news; **Scamwatch,** which alerts you to phony or misleading travel advertising; and **Other Good Stuff,** a potpourri of leads on hotel discounts, currency exchange, and the like. Other sections are available if you sign up for the magazine. Best Fares is for information only and is not a booking site.

- **www.expedia.com** (Expedia). The best part of this Microsoft service is the "Fare Tracker," which E-mails you the best airfare deals for your designated destinations. The site's "Travel Agent" can steer you to hotel and car-rental bargains, and then you can book everything on-line, including flights.

- **www.itn.net** (Internet Travel Network). This service is one of the older and more straightforward on-line reservation systems. The site will alert you automatically to a better deal on a fare than the one you're trying to book, and let you know if seats in each price category are booked on a specific flight.

- **www.reservations.com and www.vacations.com** (Preview Travel). This service claims to be the largest on-line travel agency. The reservations.com site has a "Best Fare Finder" function that searches for the three lowest fares for any route on any days of the year. You can also use the site to book your flight, hotel, and car rental. The vacations.com site previews the latest package deals when you click on "Hot Deals."

- **www.thetrip.com** (Trip.Com). The site is geared toward the business traveler, but vacation planners can use Trip.Com's valuable fare-finding engine, which will E-mail you every week with the best city-to-city airfare deals on your selected route or routes.

- **www.discount-tickets.com** (Discount Tickets). Operated by the ETN (European Travel Network), this site offers discounts on airfares, accommodations, car rentals, and tours. It deals in flights between the United States and other countries, not domestic U.S. flights, so it's most useful for travelers coming to Washington from abroad.

E-Savers Programs. Several major airlines offer a free E-mail service, via which they'll send you their best bargain fares on a weekly basis. First, you visit an airline's Web site (see the listing below or in the Appendix) and fill out the on-line form. Or you can subscribe to Epicurious Travel (travel.epicurious.com), which allows you to sign up for a bunch of airline e-mail lists all at once. Then, once a week (usually Wednesday), subscribers receive a list of discounted flights to and from various destinations, both international and domestic. Most of the time, you are required to leave on the upcoming Saturday and return the following Monday or Tuesday. Quick trip.

At least two airlines serving Washington, D.C., do not participate in these aggregated reservations networks: Southwest Airlines and AirTran (formerly ValuJet). If you're surfing the Net to find out the lowest fares to Washington, D.C., your information will not include flights on these airlines. Since these are two of the lowest-priced carriers to the D.C. area, it's worth going directly to the airlines' Web sites to check on their posted discounts. Southwest's site is www.iflyswa.com; AirTran's site is www.airtran.com.

Finally, try these other sources.

www.tiss.com   This site is a reservation system used by consolidators, that is, travel agents who buy discounted tickets in bulk from the airlines, then turn around and sell them to passengers.

www.air-fare.com   The lowest published airfares from 40 cities are posted on this site.

www.americanexpress.com/travel   Travel agencies like this one sometimes prefer that you go directly to their individual Web sites to learn of savings offers, rather than work through an intermediary reservation service.

the Sunday travel sections of the larger newspapers. And while you're at it, ask your agent about hotel consolidators, as well.

Finally, if you're at home in cyberspace, check out last-minute discounted fares posted by airlines on the Internet. See the box in this chapter on "Netting Savings on the Internet" for Web sites that can help you find cheap rates for airfare, lodging, car rental, and other travel items. For specific airline, hotel, and car-rental Internet addresses, consult the "Useful Toll-Free Numbers & Web Sites" appendix at the back of this book.

SHUTTLES TO & FROM NEW YORK   The Delta Shuttle (☎ 800/ 221-1212), which runs between its own terminal at New York's LaGuardia Airport and Ronald Reagan Washington National Airport, departs New York every hour on the half hour weekdays 6:30am to 8:30pm, plus an extra 9pm flight; Saturday from 7:30am to 8:30pm; and Sunday from 8:30am to 8:30pm, plus an extra 9pm flight. On weekdays, the first flight leaves Washington at 6:45am, with flights every hour on the half hour after that until 9:30pm; on Saturday, hourly on the half hour from 7:30am to 8:30pm; and on Sunday, from 8:30am to 9:30pm. The **US Airways Shuttle** (☎ 800/428-4322) flies from the US Airways terminal at LaGuardia Airport in New York to National Airport. Weekday and Saturday departures from LaGuardia Airport are hourly from 7am to 9pm and Sunday from 9am to 9pm. Washington to New York hourly departures weekdays and Saturday are 7am to 9pm and Sunday 9am to 9pm. Ask about student (12 to 24) and senior (62 and older) discounts. *Note:* The US Airways and Delta Shuttle gates, which used to be side-by-side at National Airport, are now located one-third of a mile away from each other, at either end of National's newly remodeled terminal. If you miss one shuttle departing to New York, you'll have the choice of either hightailing it down the marble concourse to catch the other shuttle's flight departing in 30 minutes, or waiting an hour for the next shuttle from your original gate.

FLIGHTS TO & FROM BOSTON   Both **Delta (Business Express)** and **US Airways** offer frequent service weekdays between Boston and Washington; the least expensive tickets must be purchased in advance and entail certain restrictions.

FLIGHTS TO & FROM CHICAGO   **Southwest Airlines** (☎ 800/435-9792) offers almost hourly service between Chicago's Midway Airport and BWI Airport daily between 6:30am and 4pm, with three evening flights scheduled between 7:15 and 9:20pm.

GETTING DOWNTOWN FROM THE AIRPORT

The cheapest and probably the fastest way to get into town from National Airport is by using the Metro: $1.10 (non-rush-hour) or $1.40 (rush hour) and a 15- to 20-minute ride, and you're there. The pedestrian bridges leading from the airport terminal to the Metro station are a great convenience, although the signage throughout the airport directing you to the Metro can be confusing, especially if your airline uses the old terminal (the Delta and US Airways Shuttles, TWA and TW Express, Continental, Midway, and Northwest). Before you proceed too far, you might want to ask an airport attendant to make sure you're headed in the right direction. If you hop on a shuttle bus, tell the driver to let you know when you've reached the Metro stop. Metro is an option at National only. Airport transportation possibilities at the three airports include:

SuperShuttle (☎ 800/258-3826), which operates seven-passenger blue vans that provide shared-ride, door-to-door service between all three airports and downtown and suburban locations in both Baltimore, Washington, and Virginia. Fares are based on ZIP code, so expect to pay anywhere from $6 to $13 to and from downtown, and about $25 for Maryland and Virginia suburbs.

The Washington Flyer (☎ **703/685-1400**) operates buses between the centrally located Airport Terminal Building at 1517 K St. NW and Dulles Airport, and provides transportation between Dulles and National airports. Fares to and from Dulles, to either downtown or National, are $16 one way; $26 round-trip. Children 6 and under ride free. Service between Dulles and downtown runs in each direction about every 30 minutes weekdays; less frequently weekends. Service between the airports runs hourly weekdays; less frquently weekends. At the K Street Terminal Building, you can board a free looshuttle that goes to nine Washington hotels: the Sheraton Washington, Omni Shoreham, Wasington Hilton, Renaissance Mayflower, Washington Renaissance, Grand Hyatt, J. W. Marriott, Capital Hilton, and Hotel Harrington.

The Montgomery Airport Shuttle (☎ **301/990-6000**) operates from Montgomery County, MD, to all three airports, Union Station, and many other locations, from 5am to 11pm. Fares start at $16. Call a day ahead to reserve.

The Airport Connection II (☎ **800/284-6066** or 301/441-2345) runs a door-to-door van service between BWI and Washington, D.C.; Prince George's County, MD; and Montgomery County, MD. A minimum of 24 hours' notice is required. Fares run between $18 and $30 for one person; $26 and $37 for two people. Children 5 and younger ride free.

Amtrak (☎ **800/USA-RAIL**) offers daily train service ($13 per person, one-way), while **Maryland Rural Commuter System** (MARC) ($5 per person, one-way) (☎ **800/325-RAIL**) provides weekday service at the BWI Rail Station, 5 minutes from the airport. A courtesy shuttle runs between the airport and the train station.

Taxi fares are about $10 to $14 between National Airport and the White House, $42 to $45 between the White House and Dulles or BWI.

BY TRAIN

Amtrak offers daily service to Washington from New York, Boston, Chicago, and Los Angeles (you change trains in Chicago). The upgrading of the Boston to New York stretch is scheduled for completion in 1999 and should speed up the trip to Washington from any point along this Northeast Corridor, making train travel competitive with air travel by Delta and US Airways shuttles.

Amtrak trains arrive at historic Union Station, 50 Massachusetts Ave. NE, a turn-of-the-century beaux arts masterpiece that was magnificently restored in the late 1980s at a cost of more than $180 million. Offering a three-level marketplace of shops and restaurants, this stunning depot is conveniently located and connects with Metro service. There are always taxis available there. For rail reservations, contact Amtrak (☎ **800/USA-RAIL;** www.amtrak.com). (For more on Union Station, see chapters 7 and 9.)

Like the airlines, Amtrak offers several discounted fares; although not all are based on advance purchase, you have more discount options by reserving early. The discount fares can be used only on certain days and hours of the day; be sure to find out exactly what restrictions apply. Tickets for children ages 2 to 12 cost half the price of a regular coach fare. At this writing, the lowest round-trip coach fares between Washington's Union Station and five selected cities are:

Lowest Round-Trip Coach Fares on Amtrak

Route	Discount Fare
N.Y.–D.C.	$122
Chicago–D.C.	$152
Atlanta–D.C.	$172
Los Angeles–D.C.	$318
Boston–D.C.	$124

I also suggest that you inquire about money-saving packages that include hotel accommodations, car rentals, tours, and so on with your train fare. Call ☎ **800/321-8684** for details about these "Amtrak Vacations" packages. For example, Amtrak's Air Rail program is a joint venture of Amtrak and United Airlines, allowing passengers to travel one way of a round-trip by train, the other by plane, with three stops permitted on the rail portion.

Metroliner service—which costs a little more but provides faster transit and roomier, more comfortable seating—is available between New York and Washington, D.C., and points in between. The round-trip *Metroliner* fare between New York and D.C. at this writing is $224. Note: *Metroliner* fares are substantially reduced on weekends.

The most luxurious way to travel is First Class Club Service, available on all Metroliners and some other trains, as well. For an additional $72 each way, passengers enjoy more spacious and refined seating in a private car; complimentary meals and beverage service; and Metropolitan Lounges (in New York, Chicago, Philadelphia, and Washington) where travelers can wait for trains in a comfortable, living room–like setting while enjoying free snacks and coffee.

BY BUS

Greyhound buses connect almost the entire United States with Washington, D.C. They arrive at a terminal at 1005 1st St. NE at L Street (☎ **800/231-2222;** www.greyhound.com). The closest Metro stop is Union Station, 4 blocks away. The bus terminal area is not a showplace neighborhood, so if you arrive at night, take a taxi. If you're staying in the suburbs, you should know that Greyhound also has service to Silver Spring, MD, and Arlington and Springfield, VA.

The fare structure on buses is not necessarily based on distance traveled. The good news is that when you call Greyhound to make a reservation, the company will always offer you the lowest fare options. Call in advance and know your travel dates, since some discount fares require advance purchase. In the spring of 1998, the lowest discounted round-trip fare between New York City and Washington was $53.

BY CAR

Major highways approach Washington, D.C., from all parts of the country. Specifically, these are I-270, I-95, and I-295 from the north; I-95, Route 1, and Route 301 from the south; Route 50/301 and Route 450 from the east; and Route 7, Route 50, I-66, and Route 29/211 from the west. No matter what road you take, you are going to have to navigate the Capital Beltway (I-495 and I-95) to gain entry to D.C. The Beltway girds the city, 66 miles around, with 56 interchanges or exits, and is nearly always congested, but especially weekdays, during the morning and evening rush hours, roughly 7 to 9am and 3 to 7pm. Commuter traffic on the

Beltway now rivals that of major Los Angeles freeways, and drivers can get a little crazy, weaving in and out of traffic.

If you're planning to drive to Washington, get yourself a good map before you do anything else. **The American Automobile Association** (AAA) (☎ **800/222-4357** or 703/222-6000) provides its members with maps and detailed Trip-Tiks that give travelers precise directions to a destination, including up-to-date information about areas of construction along the nation's highways and within city boundaries. If you are driving to a hotel in D.C. or its suburbs, contact the establishment and talk to the concierge or receptionist to find out the best route to the hotel's address and other crucial details concerning parking availability and rates. See chapter 4 for information about driving in D.C.

The district is 240 miles from New York City, 40 miles from Baltimore, 150 miles from Philadelphia, 700 miles from Chicago, nearly 500 miles from Boston, and about 630 miles from Atlanta.

3 For Foreign Visitors

In this most American of cities, you will see evidence of other cultures everywhere: in food, fashion, architecture, entertainment, and diversity of the population. Many Washingtonians, after all, hail from somewhere else and have incorporated their own interests and ways of life into the fabric of Washington society. This inviting, cosmopolitan atmosphere should put you at ease, as will the availability and abundance of services catering to foreign visitors, from embassy assistance, to communication assistance provided by multilingual staff at hotels. This section provides information on getting to the United States and facts that should help you understand Washington once you're here.

1 Preparing for Your Trip

In Washington, D.C., several major attractions (the White House; the Kennedy Center; the Library of Congress; and the Smithsonian Institution) offer free brochures in several languages. The Smithsonian also welcomes international visitors at its Information Center with a multilingual slide show and audio phones. You can obtain Metro maps in French, German, Japanese, and Spanish by calling ☎ **888/METRO-INFO** or 888/638-7646 and requesting a Visitor's Kit that includes a map in the specific language that you need.

The **Meridian International Center** (☎ **202/667-6800**), a nonprofit institution dedicated to the promotion of international understanding, extends its special services to D.C.'s many visitors from abroad. Visitors can call the center weekdays from 9am to 5pm for language assistance with sightseeing and other tourist needs. The center has a bank of volunteers who, together, speak more than 400 languages. The center offers the same multilingual services daily at its information desk at Dulles International Airport; call ☎ **703/572-2536**. (A call to Dulles from the district is long distance.)

ENTRY REQUIREMENTS
DOCUMENT REGULATIONS Citizens of Canada and Bermuda may enter the United States without visas, but they will need to show proof of nationality (commonly a passport).

Citizens of the Australia, Argentina, Japan, New Zealand, the United Kingdom, and most Western European countries traveling on valid passports may not need a visa for fewer than 90 days of holiday or business travel to the United States, provided that they hold a round-trip or return ticket and enter the United States either on an airline or cruise line that participates in the visa-waiver program, or cross the land border from Canada or Mexico. Citizens of these visa-exempt countries who first enter the United States may subsequently visit Bermuda and/or the Caribbean islands and then reenter the United States, by any mode of transportation, without needing a visa. (Additional information is available from the U.S. embassy or consulate in your home country. Your travel agency or airline office may also be able to provide additional information.)

Citizens of countries other than those specified above, or those traveling to the United States for reasons or length of time outside the restrictions of the visa-waiver program, or those who require waivers of inadmissibility, must have two documents:

- a valid passport, with an expiration date at least 6 months later than the scheduled end of the visit to the United States (some countries are exceptions to the 6-month validity rule; contact any U.S. embassy or consulate for complete information.); and
- a tourist visa, available from the nearest U.S. consulate. To obtain a visa, the traveler must submit a completed application form (either in person or by mail) with a 1½-inch-square photo and the required application fee. There may also be an issuance fee, depending on the type of visa and other factors.

You should allow at least a week, and even more time during the summer rush period (June to August) to obtain a visa. If you cannot go in person, contact the nearest U.S. embassy or consulate for directions on applying by mail. Your travel agent or airline office may also be able to provide you with visa applications and instructions.

The U.S. consulate or embassy that issues your visa will determine whether you will be issued a multiple- or single-entry visa. The Immigration and Naturalization Service officers at the port of entry in the United States will make an admission decision and determine your length of stay.

MEDICAL REQUIREMENTS   No inoculations are needed to enter the United States unless you are coming from, or have stopped over in, areas known to be suffering from epidemics, particularly cholera or yellow fever.

If you have a condition requiring treatment with medications containing narcotics or drugs requiring a syringe, carry a valid signed prescription from your physician to allay any suspicions that you might be smuggling drugs.

CUSTOMS REQUIREMENTS   Every adult visitor may bring in free of duty and internal revenue tax, not more than 1 liter of wine, beer, or hard liquor, for personal use. Be aware that you are subject to the alcoholic beverage laws of the state in which you arrive. You may also bring in no more than 200 cigarettes, 50 cigars (but no cigars from Cuba), or 2 kilograms (4.4 pounds) of smoking tobacco.

A gift exemption allows you to bring in up to $100 worth of gifts for other people, including 100 cigars, but not including alcoholic beverages. These exemptions are offered to travelers who spend at least 72 hours in the United States and who have not claimed them within the preceding 6 months.

Certain food products, such as bakery items and all cured cheeses, are admissible. Fruits, vegetables, plants, cuttings, seeds, unprocessed plant products, and certain endangered plant species are either prohibited from entering the country or require an import permit. The only meat you may bring in is canned meat that the inspector can determine has been commercially canned, cooked in the container, hermetically sealed, and can be kept without refrigeration; all other meat, livestock, poultry, and their by-products are either prohibited or restricted from entering the country.

Foreign tourists may bring in or take out up to $10,000 in U.S. or foreign currency with no formalities; larger sums must be declared to Customs on entering or leaving the country.

For more information, contact any U.S. embassy or consulate. Various agencies of the U.S. government provide free leaflets of information about travel tips for nonresidents. These include "Visiting the United States: Customs Regulations for Nonresidents," produced by the U.S. Customs Service, within the Department of the Treasury, and "Traveler's Tips," published by the U.S. Department of Agriculture Animal and Plant Health Inspection Service.

INSURANCE

There is no national health system in the United States. Because the cost of medical care is extremely high, I strongly advise every traveler to secure health insurance coverage before setting out.

You may want to take out a comprehensive travel policy that covers (for a relatively low premium) sickness or injury costs (medical, surgical, and hospital); loss or theft of your baggage; trip-cancellation costs; guarantee of bail in case you are arrested; and costs of accident, repatriation, or death. Such packages (for example, "Europe Assistance" in Europe) are sold by automobile clubs at attractive rates, as well as by insurance companies and travel agencies.

MONEY

CURRENCY & EXCHANGE   The U.S. monetary system has a decimal base: 1 American dollar ($1) = 100 cents (100¢).

Dollar bills commonly come in $1 ("a buck"), $5, $10, $20, $50, and $100 denominations (the last two are not welcome when paying for small purchases and are not accepted in taxis or at subway ticket booths). There are also $2 bills (seldom encountered).

There are six denominations of coins: 1¢ (one cent or "a penny"); 5¢ (five cents or "a nickel"); 10¢ (ten cents or "a dime"); 25¢ (twenty-five cents or "a quarter"); 50¢ (fifty cents or "a half dollar"); and the rare $1 piece ("a Susan B. Anthony").

TRAVELER'S CHECKS   Traveler's checks denominated in U.S. dollars are readily accepted at most hotels, motels, restaurants, and large stores. But the best place to change traveler's checks is at a bank. Do not bring traveler's checks denominated in other currencies. American Express, Barclay's Bank, and Thomas Cook traveler's checks are the most commonly accepted.

CREDIT & CHARGE CARDS   The most widely used method of payment is the credit card: Visa (BarclayCard in Britain), MasterCard (Eurocard in Europe, Access in Britain, Diamond in Japan, Chargex in Canada), American Express, Discover, Diners Club, Carte Blanche, Japan Credit Bank, and enRoute. You can save yourself trouble by using "plastic" rather than cash or traveler's checks in most hotels, motels, restaurants, and retail stores (many food and liquor stores now accept credit/charge cards). You must have a credit or charge card to rent a car. It can also be used as proof of identity or as a "cash card," enabling you to withdraw money from banks and automated teller machines (ATMs) that accept it.

You can telegraph money or have it wired to you very quickly using the **Western Union system** (☎ **800/325-6000**), which is linked to thousands of locations throughout more than 100 countries.

Note: The "foreign-exchange bureaus" so common in Europe are rare even at airports in the United States and nonexistent outside major cities. It is best not to change foreign money (or traveler's checks denominated in a currency other than U.S. dollars) at a small-town bank, or even a branch in a big city; in fact, leave any currency other than U.S. dollars at home—it may prove a greater nuisance to you than it's worth.

SAFETY

GENERAL   In recent years, Washington, D.C., has gained a reputation as a high-crime city. But the latest statistics indicate a 22% drop in crime, attributable in large part to an improved police patrol system and better department leadership provided by the new police chief. At any rate, most crime occurs far from tourist areas. The attractions, hotels, and restaurants listed in this book are in reasonably safe areas of town. As in any big city, keep an eye on your purse, wallet, camera, and other belongings in public places, and, in your hotel, keep your door locked. Many hotels these days offer in-room safes; if yours doesn't, and you are traveling with valuables, put them in a safety-deposit box at the front desk.

Try not to "look" like a tourist, if you can help it. That is, get a sense of where you are headed before you leave your hotel and, if you're walking, pay attention to who is near you as you walk. In general, it's better to avoid direct eye contact with people, especially panhandlers, who can be aggressive. If you are attending a convention or an event where you wear a name tag, remove it before venturing outside.

DRIVING   Safety while driving is particularly important. Question your rental agency about personal safety, or ask for a brochure of traveler safety tips when you pick up your car. Obtain from the agency written directions, or a map with the route marked in red, showing you how to get to your destination. If possible, arrive and depart during daylight hours.

If you see someone on the road indicating a need for help, do not stop. Take note of the location, drive on to a well-lit area, and telephone the police by dialing ☎ **911.**

Park in well-lit, well-traveled areas if possible. Always keep your car doors locked, whether the vehicle is attended or unattended. Look around you before you get out of your car, and never leave any packages or valuables in sight. If someone attempts to rob you or steal your car, do not try to resist—report the incident to the police department immediately.

You may wish to contact the local tourist information bureau in Washington, D.C., before you arrive. They may be able to provide you with a safety brochure.

2 Getting to & Around the United States

BY AIR   A number of U.S. airlines offer service from Europe to the United States. If they don't have direct flights from Europe to Washington, they can book you straight through on a connecting flight. You can make reservations by calling the following numbers in the U.K.: **American** (☎ **0181/572-5555**); **Continental** (☎ **04412/9377-6464**); **Delta** (☎ **0800/414-767**); and **United** (☎ **0181/990-9900**). For a more extensive listing of airlines that fly into the Washington area, see "Getting There" in chapter 2. In particular, read the "Netting Savings on the Internet" box in chapter 2. If you are coming from Europe, you will want to look closely at Discount Tickets, a Web site operated by the European Travel Network.

Travelers from overseas can take advantage of the APEX (advance purchase excursion) fares offered by all the major U.S. and European carriers. Aside from these, attractive values are offered by **Virgin Atlantic Airways** (☎ **800/862-8621**), which flies direct from London to Washington Dulles International Airport, as well as from London to New York/Newark.

Some large American airlines (for example, American Airlines, Delta, Northwest, TWA, and United) offer travelers on their transatlantic or transpacific flights special discount tickets allowing travel between any U.S. destinations at minimum rates. (Two such programs are American's Visit USA and Delta's Discover America.) These tickets are not on sale in the United States and must, therefore, be purchased before you leave your foreign point of departure. This arrangement is the best, easiest, and fastest way to see the United States at low cost. You should obtain information well in advance from your travel agent or the office of the airline concerned, since the conditions attached to these discount tickets can be changed without advance notice.

If you are arriving by air, make very generous allowance for delay in planning connections between international and domestic flights—an average of 2 to 3 hours at least.

Air travelers from Canada, Bermuda, and some places in the Caribbean can sometimes go through Customs and Immigration at the point of departure, which is much quicker and less painful.

BY TRAIN   In contrast to airport customs, travelers arriving by rail from Canada will find border-crossing formalities streamlined to the vanishing point. International visitors, except Canadians, can buy a **USA Railpass,** good for 15 or 30 days of unlimited travel on Amtrak trains throughout the United States and Canada. The pass is available through many foreign travel agents. At press time, prices for a nationwide 15-day adult pass were $260 off-peak, $375 peak; a 30-day pass costs $350 off-peak, $480 peak. (With a foreign passport, you can also buy passes at some Amtrak offices in the United States, including locations in Boston, Chicago, Los Angeles, Miami, New York, San Francisco, and Washington, D.C.) Even cheaper are regional USA Railpasses, which allow unlimited travel through a specific section of the United States. Reservations are generally required and should be made as early as possible for each part of your trip. If your travel plans include visiting both the United States and Canada, you need to purchase a North American Railpass. Also available through Amtrak is an Airail pass, a joint venture of United Airlines and Amtrak that is available as part of **Amtrak Vacations packages** (☎ **800/321-8684**). The pass allows you to arrive in Washington (from a location within the United States) by one mode or transportation, plane or rail, and return via the other. During the train portion of your trip, you can make up to three stops along the way at no extra charge.

With a few notable exceptions (for instance, the Northeast Corridor line between Boston and Washington, D.C.), train service is rarely up to European standards: Delays are common, routes are limited and often infrequently served, and fares are rarely significantly lower than discount airfares. Thus, cross-country train travel should be approached with caution.

BY BUS   Bus travel in the United States can be both slow and uncomfortable; however, it can also be quite inexpensive. Greyhound, the sole nationwide bus line, offers an Ameripass for unlimited travel throughout the United States. At press time, prices were $199 for 7 days, $299 for 15 days, and $409 for 30 days.

FAST FACTS: For the Foreign Traveler

Automobile Organizations   Auto clubs will supply maps, suggested routes, guidebooks, accident and bail-bond insurance, and emergency road service. The major auto club in the United States, with nearly 1,000 offices nationwide, is the **American Automobile Association (AAA).** Members of some foreign auto clubs have reciprocal arrangements with AAA and enjoy its services at no charge. In Washington, AAA offers American Express traveler's checks free to members. The D.C. office, at 701 15th St. NW (☎ **202/331-3000**), employs a multilingual staff who may be able to assist you if you are having language problems. If you belong to an auto club, inquire about AAA reciprocity before you leave home.

AAA can provide you with an International Driving Permit validating your foreign license. You may be able to join AAA even if you are not a member of a reciprocal club. To inquire, call ☎ **800/763-9900** or the number listed above for the D.C. office. In addition, some automobile-rental agencies now provide these services, so you should inquire about their availability when you rent your car.

Business Hours   Banks are open weekdays from 9am to 2 or 3pm, with some open on Friday until 6pm and on Saturday morning. Most banks provide 24-hour access to their automated teller machines (ATMs), usually set in the bank's outside wall; other ATM locations include grocery stores and shopping malls.

Generally, public and private offices are open weekdays 9am to 5pm. Stores are open 6 days a week, with many open on Sunday, too; department stores usually stay open until 9pm at least 1 day a week. Some grocery stores and drugstores are open 24 hours.

Climate   See "When to Go" in chapter 2.

Currency Exchange   You will find currency-exchange services in major airports with international service. Elsewhere, they may be quite difficult to come by. A reliable choice in both Washington and New York (should you arrive in Washington via New York) is Thomas Cook Currency Services, Inc. The agency sells commission-free foreign traveler's checks and U.S. traveler's checks at a 1% commission, as well as drafts (for a $10 fee) and wire transfers (for a $25 fee); Thomas Cook also does check collections (including Eurochecks) and purchases and sells foreign banknotes, gold, and silver. Rates are competitive and the service excellent. Call ☎ **800/287-7362** for all locations and office hours. In Washington, there are Thomas Cook offices at Ronald Reagan Washington National Airport and at Washington-Dulles International Airport, at 1800 K St. NW, and at Union Station opposite Gate G on the train concourse, all of which may be reached at ☎ **800/CURRENCY**.

Drinking Laws   See "Liquor Laws" in "Fast Facts: Washington, D.C." in chapter 4.

Electricity   The United States uses 110–120 volts, 60 cycles, as opposed to 220–240 volts, 50 cycles, as in most of Europe. In addition to a 100-volt converter, small appliances of non-American manufacture, such as hair dryers or shavers, will require a plug adapter, with two flat, parallel pins.

Embassies/Consulates   All embassies are located in Washington, D.C., since it's the nation's capital, and many consulates are located here, as well. Here are several embassy addresses: **Australia,** 1601 Massachusetts Ave. NW (☎ **202/797-3000**); **Canada,** 501 Pennsylvania Ave. NW (☎ **202/682-1740**);

France, 4101 Reservoir Rd. NW (☎ **202/944-6000**); **Germany,** 4645 Reservoir Rd. NW (☎ **202/298-4000**); **Ireland,** 2234 Massachusetts Ave. NW (☎ **202/462-3939**); **Netherlands,** 4200 Linnean Ave. NW (☎ **202/244-5300**); **New Zealand,** 37 Observatory Circle NW (☎ **202/328-4800**); and the **United Kingdom,** 3100 Massachusetts Ave. NW (☎ **202/462-1340**). You can obtain the telephone numbers of other embassies and consulates by calling information in Washington, D.C. (dial **411** within D.C. and its metropolitan area). Or consult the phone book in your hotel room.

Emergencies   In all major cities, you can call the police, an ambulance, or the fire brigade through the single emergency telephone number: ☎ **911.**

If you encounter such travelers' problems as sickness, accident, or lost or stolen baggage, call the **Travelers Aid Society,** 512 C St. NE (☎ **202/546-3120**), an organization that specializes in helping distressed travelers, whether American or foreign. See "Orientation" in chapter 4 for further details.

Hospitals in the United States have emergency rooms, with a special entrance where you will be admitted for quick attention. The closest hospital to the downtown area is the **George Washington University Medical Center,** at 901 23rd St. NW, at Washington Circle (☎ **202/994-3211**); the hospital is a major trauma center with a built-in minor emergency care area and 24-hour medical advice line.

Late-night pharmacies include **CVS Pharmacy,** open 24 hours, at 14th Street NW and Thomas Circle NW (☎ **202/628-0720**), and at 6 Dupont Circle NW (☎ **202/785-1466**).

Gasoline (Petrol)   One U.S. gallon equals 3.75 liters, while 1.2 U.S. gallons equal 1 Imperial gallon. You'll notice there are several grades (and price levels) of gasoline available at most gas stations. And you'll also notice that their names change from company to company. The unleaded ones with the highest octane are the most expensive (most rental cars take the least expensive "regular" unleaded), and leaded gas is the least expensive; but only older cars can take leaded gas now, so check if you're not sure.

Holidays   On the following legal national holidays, banks, government offices, post offices, and many stores, restaurants, and museums are closed: January 1 (New Year's Day); third Monday in January (Martin Luther King, Jr., Day); third Monday in February (Presidents' Day, Washington's Birthday); last Monday in May (Memorial Day); July 4 (Independence Day); first Monday in September (Labor Day); second Monday in October (Columbus Day); November 11 (Veterans' Day/Armistice Day); fourth Thursday in November (Thanksgiving Day); and December 25 (Christmas).

Finally, the Tuesday following the first Monday in November is Election Day and is a legal holiday in presidential-election years.

Legal Aid   If you are stopped for a minor infraction (for example, of the highway code, such as speeding), never attempt to pay the fine directly to a police officer; you may wind up arrested on the much more serious charge of attempted bribery. Pay fines by mail or directly into the hands of the clerk of the court. If you are accused of a more serious offense, it's wise to say and do nothing before consulting a lawyer. Under U.S. law, an arrested person is allowed one telephone call to a party of his or her choice. Call your embassy or consulate.

Mail   If you want your mail to follow you on your vacation and you aren't sure of your address, your mail can be sent to you, in your name, ℅ General Delivery at the main post office of the city or region where you expect to be. The addressee must pick it up in person and produce proof of identity (for example, driver's license, credit or charge card, or passport). In Washington, the main post office is located at 900 Brentwood Rd. NE, Washington, DC 20066-9998, USA (☎ **202/636-1532**). It's open weekdays 8am to 8pm, Saturday 8am to 6pm, and Sunday noon to 6pm. Mailboxes, which are generally found at intersections, are blue with a red-and-white stripe and carry the inscription U.S. MAIL.

Newspapers/Magazines   National newspapers include the *New York Times*, *USA Today*, and the *Wall Street Journal*. There are also a great many national newsweeklies, including *Newsweek*, *Time*, and *U.S. News and World Report*. For information on local Washington, D.C., periodicals, see "Visitor Information" in chapter 4.

Post Office   See "Mail," above.

Safety   See "Safety" in "Preparing for Your Trip," above.

Taxes   In the United States, there is no VAT (value-added tax) or other indirect tax at a national level. Every state, and each city in it, has the right to levy its own local tax on all purchases, including hotel and restaurant checks, airline tickets, and so on.

The sales tax on merchandise is 5.75% in the district, 5% in Maryland, and 4.5% in Virginia. The tax on restaurant meals is 10% in the district, 5% in Maryland, and 7.5% in Virginia.

In the district, in addition to your hotel rate, you pay 13% sales tax and $1.50 per night occupancy tax. In suburban Virginia, you pay a 4.5% state sales tax and a 2% occupancy tax on a hotel room; in Maryland, you can expect to pay 5% state sales tax and a 5% room sales tax.

Telephone/Telegraph/Fax   The telephone system in the United States is run by private corporations, so the rates, especially for long-distance service, can vary widely, even on calls made from public telephones. Local calls from public phones now cost 35¢.

Generally, hotel surcharges on long-distance and local calls are astronomical—even if you charge the call to your credit card. Always ask the hotel operator about these charges before making a call from your room. You are usually better off using a public pay telephone, which you will find clearly marked in most public buildings and private establishments as well as on the street.

Most long-distance and international calls can be dialed directly from any phone. It's most economical to charge the call to a telephone charge card or a credit card, or you can use a lot of change (phone cards are catching on in the United States, but they are not nearly as common as they are in Europe). The pay phone will instruct you how much to deposit into the slot box and when. For calls to Canada and other parts of the United States, dial **1** followed by the area code and the seven-digit number. For international calls, dial **011** followed by the country code, city code, and the telephone number of the person you wish to call. It's helpful to write down these codes before you leave your own country.

For reversed-charge or collect calls, and for person-to-person calls, dial **0** (zero, not the letter "O") followed by the area code and number you want; when an operator comes on the line, you should specify that you are calling collect, or person-to-person, or both. If your operator-assisted call is international, ask for the overseas operator.

For local directory assistance ("information"), dial **411;** for long-distance information, dial **1,** then the appropriate area code and **555-1212.**

Like the telephone system, telegraph services are provided by private corporations, including ITT, MCI, and most commonly, Western Union. You can bring your telegram to the nearest Western Union office (there are hundreds across the country), or dictate it over the phone (☎ **800/325-6000**). You can also telegraph money, or have it telegraphed to you, very quickly over the Western Union system.

Telephone Directory   There are two kinds of telephone directories available to you. The general directory is the so-called white pages, in which businesses and personal residences are listed separately, in alphabetical order. The inside front cover lists the emergency numbers for police, fire, ambulance, the Coast Guard, poison-control center, crime-victims hotline, and so on. The first few pages are devoted to community-service numbers, including a guide to long-distance and international calling, complete with country codes and area codes.

The second directory, printed on yellow paper (hence its name, Yellow Pages), lists all local services, businesses, and industries by type of activity, with an index at the back. The yellow pages also include city plans or detailed area maps, which often show postal zip codes and public transportation routes.

Time   The United States is divided into four time zones (six, if Alaska and Hawaii are included). From east to west, these are: eastern standard time (EST), which includes Washington; central standard time (CST); mountain standard time (MST); Pacific standard time (PST); Alaska standard time (AST); and Hawaii standard time (HST). Always keep the changing time zones in mind if you are traveling (or even telephoning) long distances in the United States. For example, noon in Washington, D.C. (EST) is 11am in Chicago (CST), 10am in Denver (MST), 9am in Los Angeles (PST), 8am in Anchorage (AST), and 7am in Honolulu (HST).

Daylight saving time is in effect from the first Sunday in April through the last Saturday in October, except in Arizona, Hawaii, part of Indiana, and Puerto Rico. Daylight saving time moves the clock 1 hour ahead of standard time.

To find out the time, call ☎ **202/844-2525.**

Tipping   Some rules of thumb: bartenders, 10% to 15%; bellhops, at least 50¢ per piece of luggage ($2 to $3 for a lot of baggage); cab drivers, 15% of the fare; cafeterias and fast-food restaurants, no tip; chambermaids, $1 a day; checkroom attendants (restaurants, theaters), $1 per garment; cinemas, movies, theaters, no tip; doormen (hotels or restaurants), not obligatory; gas-station attendants, not obligatory; hairdressers, 15% to 20%; redcaps (airport and railroad station), at least 50¢ per bag ($2 to $3 for a lot of luggage); restaurants and nightclubs, 15% to 20% of the check; valet parking attendants, $1.

Toilets   Visitors can usually find a rest room in a bar, restaurant, hotel, museum, department store, service station (although for reasons of cleanliness, this should be your last choice), or train station.

Getting to Know Washington, D.C.

Unlike other big, scandalous cities, Washington, with its compact size, excellent subway system, trio of nearby airports, and bounty of free attractions, is a great city for visitors. Before you hit the streets, though, you'll need to know the basics about the city's layout, neighborhoods, transportation, and general ways and means. This chapter will point you in the right direction.

1 Orientation

VISITOR INFORMATION

INFORMATION CENTERS   If you haven't already called ahead for information from the **Washington, D.C., Convention & Visitors Association** (☎ 202/789-7038), stop in at their headquarters, 1212 New York Ave. NW, Suite 600, weekdays 9am to 5pm.

Another walk-in visitors center has opened at the more accessible and convenient Ronald Reagan Building and International Trade Center, the very large and newly built structure at 1300 Pennsylvania Ave. NW, next door to the White House Visitors Center (see below). The center occupies space on the ground floor of the building, off the Wilson Plaza entrance, near the Federal Triangle Metro.

There are two other excellent tourist information centers in town, and although each focuses on a specific attraction, they also provide information about other popular Washington sights.

The **White House Visitors Center**, on the first floor of the Herbert Hoover Building, Department of Commerce, 1450 Pennsylvania Ave. NW (between 14th and 15th streets) (☎ 202/208-1631 or 202/456-7041 for recorded information), is open daily 7:30am to 4pm.

The **Smithsonian Information Center**, in the "Castle," 1000 Jefferson Dr. SW (☎ 202/357-2700 or TTY 202/357-1729), is open every day but Christmas, 9am to 5:30pm. For a free copy of the Smithsonian's "Planning your Smithsonian Visit," which is full of valuable tips, write to Smithsonian Institution, VIARC, SI Building, Room 153, MRC 010, Washington, D.C. 20560, or stop at the Castle for a copy. A calendar of Smithsonian exhibits and activities for the coming month appears the third Friday of each month in the *Washington Post*'s "Weekend" section.

Washington, D.C. at a Glance

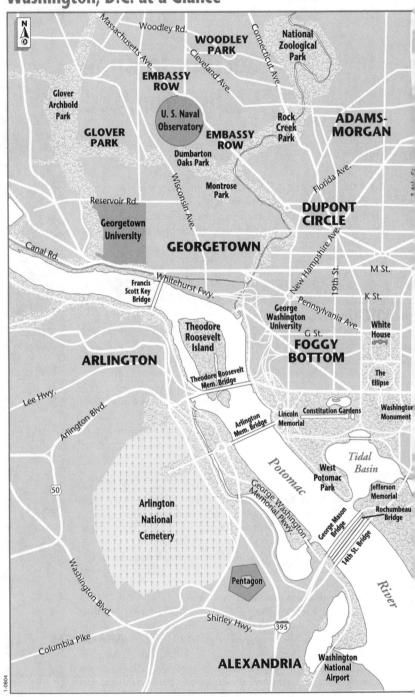

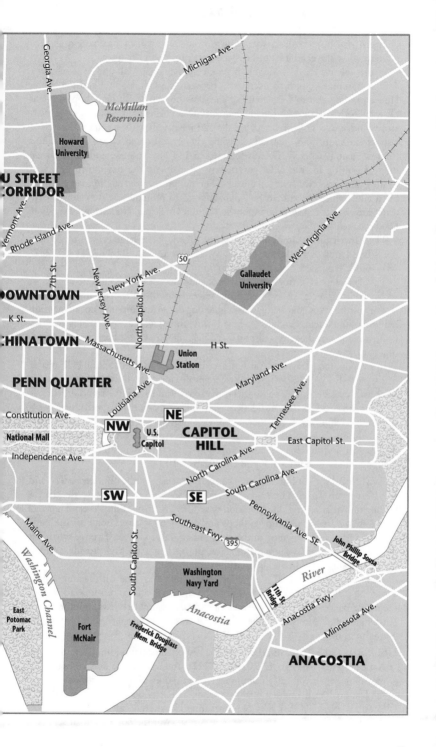

Try to visit both facilities when you're in town to garner information and see interesting on-site exhibits. Further details are provided in chapter 7.

In the downtown area, roughly between the National Mall and Massachusetts Ave. NW running south to north, and between the U.S. Capitol and the White House running east to west, look for the Downtown DC Business Improvement District "SAMs" (safety and maintenance workers). These red-jacket or polo shirt-attired ambassadors of the city patrol the 120-block area with the aim of answering visitors' questions and, generally, keeping the area safe and clean. The Business Improvement District (BID) was founded in 1997 by business leaders who were tired of waiting for the D.C. government to maintain the downtown as a welcoming and attractive spot for tourists. The nonprofit, privately funded BID has hired and trained more than 80 "ambassadors" to promote the downtown. BID teams are expected to form soon for the Dupont Circle and Georgetown neighborhoods, as well.

The **American Automobile Association (AAA)** has a large central office near the White House, at 701 15th St. NW, Washington, D.C. 20005-2111 (☎ **202/ 331-3000**). Hours are weekdays 9am to 6pm.

The **Travelers Aid Society** is a nationwide network of volunteer, nonprofit, social-service agencies providing help to travelers in difficulty. This might include anything from crisis counseling to straightening out ticket mix-ups, not to mention reuniting families accidentally separated while traveling, locating missing relatives (sometimes just at the wrong airport), and helping retrieve lost baggage (also sometimes at the wrong airport).

In Washington, Travelers Aid has a central office in the Capitol Hill area at 512 C St. NE (☎ **202/546-3120**), where professional social workers are available to provide assistance. It's open only on weekdays 9am to 5pm; please call first.

There are also Travelers Aid desks at Washington National Airport (open weekdays 9am to 9pm, weekends 9am to 6pm, ☎ **703/417-3972**); at Dulles International Airport (open weekdays 10am to 9pm, weekends 10am to 6pm, ☎ **703/ 572-8296**); and at Union Station (open Monday through Saturday 9:30am to 5:30pm, Sunday 12:30 to 5:30pm; ☎ **202/371-1937**).

NEWSPAPERS   Washington has two daily newspapers: the *Washington Post* and the *Washington Times.* The Friday "Weekend" section of the *Post* is essential for finding out what's going on, recreation-wise. *City Paper,* published every Thursday and available free at downtown shops and restaurants, covers some of the same material but is a better guide to the club and art-gallery scene. If you're staying in the suburbs, the *Friday Journal Papers* (one for each area county) provide comprehensive coverage of activities beyond the downtown.

Also on newsstands is *Washingtonian,* a monthly magazine with features, often about the "100 Best" this or that (doctors, restaurants, and so on) in Washington; the magazine also publishes a calendar of events, restaurant reviews, and profiles of Washingtonians. Available at the airport for free is *Washington Flyer,* a magazine geared to tourists.

HELPFUL TELEPHONE NUMBERS   Visitor Information lines include:
- **National Park Service** (☎ **202/619-7222**). You reach a real person, not a recording, when you call this number with questions about the monuments, the National Mall, and national park lands, and activities taking place at these locations. National Park Service information kiosks are located near the Jefferson, Lincoln, Vietnam Veterans, and Korean War memorials, and at several other locations in the city.

- **Dial-a-Park** (☎ 202/619-7275). Call this number for information about park service events and attractions.
- **Dial-a-Museum** (☎ 202/357-2020). This recording tells you about the locations of the 14 Washington Smithsonian museums and of their daily activities.
- **Recreation and Parks** (☎ 202/673-7660). To find out about city parks and recreation areas not under federal jurisdiction, dial this number to reach the D.C. Department of Recreation and Parks.

CITY LAYOUT

Pierre Charles L'Enfant designed Washington's great sweeping avenues crossed by numbered and lettered streets. At key intersections he placed spacious circles. Although the circles are enhanced with monuments, statuary, and fountains, L'Enfant also intended them to serve as strategic command posts to ward off invaders or marauding mobs. After the events in Paris during the French Revolution—and remember, that was current history at the time—his design views were quite practical.

The U.S. Capitol marks the center of the city, which is divided into quadrants: **northwest (NW), northeast (NE), southwest (SW),** and **southeast (SE).** If you look at your map, you'll see that some addresses—for instance, the corner of G and 7th streets—appear in four different places. There's one in each quadrant. Hence you must observe the quadrant designation (NW, NE, SW, or SE) when looking for an address.

MAIN ARTERIES & STREETS   From the Capitol, North Capitol Street and South Capitol Street run north and south, respectively. East Capitol Street divides the city north and south. The area west of the Capitol is not a street at all, but the National Mall, which is bounded on the north by Constitution Avenue and on the south by Independence Avenue.

The primary artery of Washington is Pennsylvania Avenue, scene of parades, inaugurations, and other splashy events. Pennsylvania runs northwest in a direct line between the Capitol and the White House—if it weren't for the Treasury Building, the president would have a clear view of the Capitol—before continuing on a northwest angle to Georgetown.

Since May 1995, **Pennsylvania Avenue** between 15th and 17th streets NW has been closed to cars, for security reasons. H Street is now one-way eastbound between 19th and 13th streets N; I Street is one-way westbound between 11th and 21st streets NW.

Constitution Avenue, paralleled to the south most of the way by Independence Avenue, runs east-west flanking the Capitol and the Mall. If you hear Washingtonians talk about the "House" side of the Hill, they're referring to the part of the Capitol that holds Congressional House offices and the House Chamber, on the Independence Avenue side, in other words. The "Senate" side is the part of the Capitol that holds Senate offices and the Senate Chamber, on the Constitution Avenue side.

Impressions

If Washington should ever grow to be a great city, the outlook from the Capitol will be unsurpassed in the world. Now at sunset I seemed to look westward far into the heart of the continent from this commanding position.

—Ralph Waldo Emerson

Washington's longest avenue, **Massachusetts Avenue,** runs north of and parallel to Pennsylvania. Along the way, you'll find Union Station and then Dupont Circle, which is central to the area known as Embassy Row. Farther out are the Naval Observatory (the vice president's residence is on the premises), Washington National Cathedral, American University, and eventually, Maryland.

Connecticut Avenue, which runs more directly north, starts at Lafayette Square, intersects Dupont Circle, and eventually takes you to the National Zoo, on to the charming residential neighborhood known as Cleveland Park, and into Chevy Chase, Maryland, where you can pick up the Beltway to head out of town. (If you are driving to Washington and want a straightforward, albeit traffic-laden, way into town, reverse these instructions, following the Beltway to the Connecticut Avenue exit, and turn south—left off the ramp—toward Chevy Chase.) Downtown Connecticut Avenue, with its posh shops and clusters of restaurants, is a good street to stroll.

Wisconsin Avenue originates in Georgetown and intersects with M Street to form Georgetown's hub. Antique shops, trendy boutiques, discos, restaurants, and pubs all vie for attention. Wisconsin Avenue basically parallels Connecticut Avenue; one of the few irritating things about the city's transportation system is that the Metro does not connect these two major arteries in the heart of the city. (Buses do, and, of course, you can always walk or take a taxi from one avenue to the other.) In fact, Metro's first stop on Wisconsin Avenue is in Tenleytown, a residential part of town. Follow the avenue north, and you land in the affluent Maryland cities, Chevy Chase and Bethesda.

FINDING AN ADDRESS   Once you understand the city's layout, it's easy to find your way around. As you read this, have a map handy.

Each of the four corners of the District of Columbia is exactly the same distance from the Capitol dome. The White House and most government buildings and important monuments are west of the Capitol (in the northwest and southwest quadrants), as are important hotels and tourist facilities.

Numbered streets run north-south, beginning on either side of the Capitol with First Street, northeast (NE) and southeast (SE). Lettered streets run east-west and are named alphabetically, beginning with A Street. (Don't look for a B, a J, an X, Y, or Z Street, however.) After W Street, one-syllable, two-syllable, and three-syllable street names come into play; the more syllables in a name, the farther the street will lie from the Capitol.

Avenues, named for U.S. states, run at angles across the grid pattern and often intersect at traffic circles. For example, New Hampshire, Connecticut, and Massachusetts Avenues intersect at Dupont Circle.

With this in mind, you can easily find an address. On lettered streets, the address tells you exactly where to go. For instance, 1776 K St. NW is between 17th and 18th streets (the first two digits of 1776 tell you that) in the northwest quadrant (NW). Note: I Street is often written Eye Street to prevent confusion with 1st Street.

To find an address on numbered streets, you'll probably have to use your fingers. For instance, 623 8th St. SE is between F and G streets (the sixth and seventh letters of the alphabet; the first digit of 623 tells you that) in the southeast quadrant (SE). One thing to remember: You count B as the second letter of the alphabet even though no B Street exists today (Constitution and Independence Avenues were each at one time the original B streets), but since there's no J Street, K becomes the 10th letter, L the 11th, and so on.

NEIGHBORHOODS IN BRIEF

Adams-Morgan   This increasingly trendy, multiethnic neighborhood is about a minute long, centered around 18th Street and Columbia Road NW. Parking during the day is OK, but forget it at night. But you can easily walk (and be alert; the neighborhood is edgy) or take a taxi here for a taste of Malaysian, Ethiopian, Spanish, or some other international cuisine. On Friday and Saturday nights it's a hot nightlife district, rivaling Georgetown and Dupont Circle.

Capital Hill   Everyone's heard of "the Hill," the area crowned by the Capitol. When people speak of Capitol Hill, they refer to a large section of town, extending from the western side of the Capitol to the D.C. Armory going east, bounded by H Street NE and the Southwest Freeway north and south. It contains not only the chief symbol of the nation's capital, but the Supreme Court building, the Library of Congress, the Folger Shakespeare Library, Union Station, and the U.S. Botanic Garden. Much of it is a quiet residential neighborhood of tree-lined streets and Victorian homes. There are many restaurants in the vicinity.

Downtown   The area roughly between 7th and 22nd streets NW going east to west, and P Street and Pennsylvania Avenue going north to south, is a mix of the Federal Triangle's government office buildings, K Street ("Lawyer's Row"), Connecticut Avenue restaurants and shopping, historic hotels, the city's poshest small hotels, and the White House. Also here is a quadrant known as the Historic Penn Quarter (see profile in box), a part of downtown that is taking on new life with the opening of the MCI Center, trendy new restaurants, and art galleries. The total downtown area takes in so many blocks and attractions that I've divided discussions of accommodations (chapter 5) and dining (chapter 6) into two sections: "Downtown, 16th Street NW and West," and "Downtown, east of 16th Street NW"; 16th Street and the White House form a natural point of separation.

Dupont Circle   My favorite part of town, the Dupont Circle area is a fun place to be any time of day or night. It takes its name from the traffic circle minipark, where Massachusetts, New Hampshire, and Connecticut Avenues collide. The streets extending out from the circle are lively with all-night bookstores, really good restaurants, wonderful art galleries and art museums, nightspots, movie theaters, and Washingtonians at their loosest. It is also the hub of D.C.'s gay community.

Foggy Bottom   The area west of the White House to the edge of Georgetown, Foggy Bottom was Washington's early industrial center. Its name comes from the foul fumes emitted in those days by a coal depot and gasworks, but its original name, Funkstown (for owner Jacob Funk), is perhaps even worse. There's nothing foul about the area today. The Kennedy Center and George Washington University are located here. Constitution and Pennsylvania Avenues are Foggy Bottom's southern and northern boundaries, respectively.

Georgetown   This historic community dates from colonial times. It was a thriving tobacco port long before the District of Columbia was formed, and one of its attractions, the Old Stone House, dates from pre-Revolutionary days. Georgetown action centers on M Street and Wisconsin Avenue NW, where you'll find numerous boutiques (see chapter 9 for details), chic restaurants, and popular pubs (lots of nightlife here). But get off the main drags and see the quiet tree-lined streets of restored colonial row houses, stroll through the beautiful gardens of Dumbarton Oaks, and check out the C&O Canal. One of the reasons so much activity flourishes in Georgetown is because of Georgetown University and its students.

Historic Penn Quarter

Not all neighborhoods are what they seem. Before the days of the MCI Center, the neighborhood that runs north-south from Massachusetts Avenue to Pennsylvania Avenue, and east-west from the White House to the Capitol, attracted visitors who wanted to tour the FBI Building on E Street NW, Ford's Theatre and the Petersen House on 10th Street, and two fantastic Smithsonian museums, the National Portrait Gallery on F Street and the National Museum of American Art on G Street. But a neighborhood within this neighborhood has emerged, where Washington's identity as the nation's capital merges nicely with its identity as its own city. Visitors who want to explore this area should start at the new **MCI Center,** at 601 F St. NW, and proceed to the **Discovery Channel Retail Store** to view the 15-minute film, *Destination DC,* shown every half-hour on the fourth floor. (Tickets are $2.50 per adult, $1.50 per child.) Follow up the film with a **DC Heritage Tour** ($7.50 per adult, $5 per child), which departs from the MCI Center twice daily at 10:30am and 1pm. During this 90-minute walking tour, a costumed guide whisks you in and out of historic spots, offering a view of 19th-century Washington. Among the many stops, the guide will point out the house where John Wilkes Booth plotted Lincoln's assassination and the halls where Walt Whitman cared for the Civil War wounded.

From there, you're on your own. You can tour Chinatown; pop in and out of art galleries, like the **Zenith** on 7th Street. NW; eat at one of the best restaurants in the city, like **Cafe Atlantico** on 8th Street. NW; experience the offbeat **Bead Museum** at 400 7th St. NW; take a ride (maybe) in the oldest working elevator in the world, hand-operated by Mr. Litwin in his Merchants of Antiques and Fancy Furniture store, at 637 Indiana Ave. NW (Mr. Litwin's shop dates from 1951, the elevator from the 1850s); take in a Shakespeare play at the **Lansburgh Theatre** on 7th Street. NW; or shop for gorgeous, glazed Italian pottery at the **Corso De-Fiori Boutique** in Market Square, 8th and D streets NW.

Glover Park   Mostly a residential neighborhood, this section of town, just above Georgetown and just south of the Washington National Cathedral, is worth mentioning because of the increasing number of good restaurants opening along its main stretch, Wisconsin Avenue NW. Glover Park sits between the campuses of Georgetown and American Universities, so there's a large student presence here.

The Mall   This lovely tree-lined stretch of open space between Constitution and Independence Avenues, extending for 2½ miles from the Capitol to the Lincoln Memorial, is the hub of tourist attractions. It includes most of the Smithsonian Institution museums and many other nearby visitor attractions. The 300-foot-wide Mall is used by natives as well as tourists—joggers, food vendors, kite-flyers, and picnickers among them.

U Street Corridor   D.C.'s newest nightlife neighborhood between 12th and 15th streets NW is rising from the ashes of nightclubs and theaters frequented decades ago by African Americans. At the renovated Lincoln Theater, where legends like Duke Ellington, Louis Armstrong, and Cab Calloway once performed, patrons today can enjoy performances by popular though less famous black artists. The corridor offers at least six alternative rock and contemporary music nightclubs and several restaurants (see chapter 10 for details).

Woodley Park   Home to Washington's largest hotel (the Washington Marriott Wardman Park—formerly known as the Sheraton Washington) and another really big one (the Omni Shoreham), Woodley Park also is the site of the National Zoo, many good restaurants, and some antique stores. Washingtonians are used to seeing conventioneers wandering the neighborhood's pretty residential streets with their name tags still on.

2 Getting Around

Washington is one of the easiest U.S. cities in which to get around. Only New York rivals its comprehensive transportation system, but Washington's clean, efficient subways put the Big Apple's underground nightmare to shame. A complex bus system covers all major D.C. arteries, as well, and it's easy to hail a taxi anywhere at any time. But because Washington is of manageable size and marvelous beauty, you may find yourself shunning transportation and getting around on foot.

BY METRO

Metrorail stations are immaculate, cool, and attractive. Cars are air-conditioned and fitted with upholstered seats; tracks are rubber-cushioned so the ride is quiet; service is frequent enough so you usually get a seat, at least during off-peak hours (basically weekdays 10am to 3pm and weeknights after 8pm); and the system is so simply designed that a 10-year-old can understand it. Eating, drinking, and smoking are strictly prohibited on the Metro and in stations.

If you don't want to risk the ire of commuters, be sure to follow these guidelines: Stand to the right on the escalator so people in a hurry can pass you on the left; and when you reach the train level, don't stop at the bottom of the escalator because you'll block the path of those coming behind you. Instead, move down the platform.

Metrorail's 75 stations and 92.3 miles of track (83 stations and 103 miles of track are the eventual goal) include locations at or near almost every sightseeing attraction and extend to suburban Maryland and northern Virginia. If you're in Washington even for a few days, you'll probably have occasion to use the system; but if not, create an excuse. The Metro is a sightseeing attraction in its own right.

There are five lines in operation—red, blue, orange, yellow, and green—with extensions planned for the future. The lines connect at several points, making transfers easy. All but yellow- and green-line trains stop at Metro Center; all except red-line trains stop at L'Enfant Plaza; all but blue- and orange-line trains stop at Gallery Place/Chinatown.

Metro stations are indicated by discreet brown columns bearing the station's name and topped by the letter *M*. Below the *M* is a colored stripe or stripes indicating the line or lines that stop there. When entering a Metro station for the first time, go to the kiosk and ask the station manager for a free "Metro System Pocket Guide" (available in six languages: English, German, Spanish, Korean, Japanese, and French). It contains a map of the system, explains how it works, and lists the closest Metro stops to points of interest. The station manager can also answer questions about routing or purchase of fare cards. Some Metro riders will soon be able to turn to Metro station computers for help. By spring of 1999, Metro will have installed touch-screen computers at nine Metro stations to advise riders on best routes to take to reach a particular destination, provide copies of maps and schedules of bus service, and respond to other transportation-related queries. The nine Metro stations are, in the district, Union Station; in Maryland, New Carrolton and

Metro Stops in Georgetown & Downtown

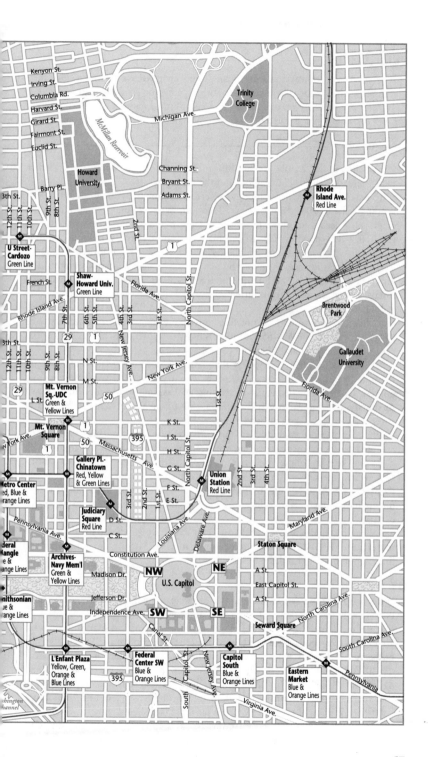

Travel Tip

If you're on the subway and plan to continue your travel via Metrobus, pick up a transfer at the station where you enter the system (not your destination station). Transfer machines are on the mezzanine levels of most stations. Transfers are good for a discount on bus fares in D.C. and Virginia. There are no bus-to-subway transfers.

Greenbelt; and in Virginia, Ronald Reagan National Airport, King Street, Vienna, Franconia/Springfield, Huntington, and the Pentagon.

To enter or exit a Metro station, you need a computerized fare card, available at vending machines near the entrance. Don't throw away your fare card after you enter, you'll need it to get out of the station. The minimum fare to enter the system is $1.10, which pays for rides to and from any point within 7 miles of boarding during off-peak hours; during peak hours (weekdays 5:30 to 9:30am and 3 to 8pm), $1.10 takes you for only 3 miles. The machines take nickels, dimes, quarters, and bills from $1 to $20; they can return up to $4.95 in change (coins only). If you plan to take several Metrorail trips during your stay, put more value on the fare card to avoid having to purchase a new card each time you ride. There's a 10% bonus on all fare cards of $20 or more. Up to two children under 5 can ride free with a paying passenger. Senior citizens (65 and older) and people with disabilities (with valid proof) ride Metrorail and Metrobus for a reduced fare.

Discount passes, called "One-Day Rail passes," cost $5 per person and allow you unlimited passage for the day, after 9:30am weekdays, and all day on weekends and holidays. You can buy them at most stations; at **Washington Metropolitan Transit Authority,** 600 5th St. NW (☎ **202/637-7000**); at Metro Center, 12th and G streets NW; or at a Giant or Safeway grocery store.

When you insert your card in the entrance gate, the time and location are recorded on its magnetic tape, and your card is returned. Don't forget to snatch it up and keep it handy; you have to reinsert it in the exit gate at your destination, where the fare will automatically be deducted. The card will be returned if there's any value left on it. If you arrive at a destination and your fare card doesn't have enough value, add what's necessary at the Exitfare machines near the exit gate.

Metrorail operates weekdays 5:30am to midnight, weekends and holidays 8am to midnight. Call ☎ **202/637-7000** for information on Metro routes. *Warning:* The line is often busy, so just keep trying.

BY BUS

While a 10-year-old can understand the Metrorail system, the Metrobus system is considerably more complex. The 15,800 stops on the 1,489-square-mile route (it operates on all major D.C. arteries as well as in the Virginia and Maryland suburbs) are indicated by red, white, and blue signs. However, the signs tell you only what buses pull into a given stop, not where they go. For routing information, call ☎ **202/637-7000.** Calls are taken weekdays 6am to 10:30pm, weekends and holidays 8am to 10:30pm. This is the same number you call to request a free map and time schedule, information about parking in Metrobus fringe lots, and for locations and hours of those places where you can purchase bus tokens.

Base fare in the district is $1.10; bus transfers cost 10¢. There are additional charges for travel into the Maryland and Virginia suburbs. Bus drivers are not equipped to make change, so be sure to carry exact change or tokens. If you'll be in Washington for a while and plan to use the buses a lot, consider buying a $20 2-week pass, also available at the Metro Center station and other outlets.

Most buses operate daily almost around the clock. Service is quite frequent on weekdays, especially during peak hours. You may not be as lucky late at night or on the weekends.

Up to two children under 5 ride free with a paying passenger on Metrobus, and there are reduced fares for senior citizens (☎ 202/962-7000) and people with disabilities (☎ 202/962-1245 or 202/962-1100). If you should leave something on a bus, train, or in a station, call Lost and Found at ☎ 202/962-1195.

BY CAR

More than half of all visitors to the district arrive by car. If you're one of them, you should know that traffic is always thick during the week, parking spaces are often hard to find, and parking lots are ruinously expensive. You may also discover that street signs, building and parking information, and construction detour and Metro direction signs throughout the district are often missing, confusing, illegible, or contradictory. (On a beautiful spring day, at the height of the tourist season, I noticed that none of the streets stemming off of the Smithsonian Museum-lined Independence Avenue had street signs.) The worst part is that you may well be ticketed if your interpretation of posted parking instructions differs from that of the meter maid's. To keep up with street closing and construction information, grab the day's *Washington Post*, pull out the Metro section and turn to page 3, where the column "Metro, In Brief" tells you about potential traffic and routing problems in the district and suburban Maryland and Virginia.

Even if you don't drive in D.C., you will want a car to get to most attractions in Virginia and Maryland. All major car-rental companies are represented here. Here are the phone numbers for those rental companies with locations at all three airports: **Alamo** (☎ **800/327-9633**); **Avis** (☎ **800/331-1212**); **Budget** (☎ **800/ 527-0700**); **Hertz** (☎ **800/654-3131**); and **Thrifty** (☎ **800/367-2277**). **Kemwel Holiday Auto** (☎ **800/678-0678**) offers discounted rates for major car-rental companies. Be sure to ask about local taxes and surcharges, which can vary from location to location, even within the same car company, and which can add quite a bit to your costs. In fact, even rental rates vary from location to location, with those offered at airport terminals usually among the highest.

If you do drive in the district, you'll have to maneuver through the traffic circles. Traffic law states that the circle traffic has the right of way. No one pays any attention to this rule, however, which can be frightening (cars zoom into the circle without a glance at the cars already there). The other thing you will notice is that while some circles are easy to figure out (Dupont Circle, for example), others are nerve-rackingly confusing (Thomas Circle, where 14th Street NW, Vermont Avenue NW, and Massachusetts Avenue NW come together, is to be avoided at all costs).

Also, sections of certain streets in Washington become one-way during rush hour: Rock Creek Parkway, Canal Road, and 17th Street NW are three examples. Other streets during rush hour change the direction of some of their traffic lanes: Connecticut Avenue NW is the main one. In the morning, traffic in four of its six lanes travels south to the downtown and in late afternoon/early evening, downtown traffic in four of its six lanes heads north; between the hours of 9am and 3:30pm, traffic in either direction keeps to the normally correct side of the yellow line. Lighted traffic signs alert you to what's going on, but pay attention.

Local officials are trying to prevent road-rage accidents, that is, those that occur because an aggressive driver, acting out of impatience and intolerance for others on the road, has tried to force another driver out of the way. A number of these accidents have caused severe injury and even fatalities on local highways and on the George Washington Parkway in the past year. Should you find yourself in such a threatening situation, forget any inclination to stand up to this kind of driver, but change lanes and move out of the way as safely and quickly as you can.

BY TAXI

District cabs operate on a zone system instead of meters. By law, basic rates are posted in each cab. If you take a trip from one point to another within the same zone, you pay just $4, regardless of the distance traveled. So it will cost you $4 to travel a few blocks from the U.S. Capitol to the National Museum of American History, but the same $4 could take you from the Capitol all the way to Dupont Circle. They're both in Zone 1. Also in Zone 1 are most other tourist attractions: the White House, most of the Smithsonian, the Washington Monument, the FBI, the National Archives, the Supreme Court, the Library of Congress, the Bureau of Engraving and Printing, the Old Post Office, and Ford's Theatre. If your trip takes you into a second zone, the price is $5.50, $6.90 for a third zone, $8.25 for a fourth, and so on.

The fares seem modest. But they can add up: There's a $1.50 charge for each additional passenger after the first, so a $4 Zone 1 fare can become $8.50 for a family of four (although one child under 5 rides free). There's also a rush-hour surcharge of $1 per trip weekdays between 7 and 9:30am and 4 and 6:30pm. Surcharges are also added for large pieces of luggage and for arranging a pickup by telephone ($1.50).

The zone system is not used when your destination is an out-of-district address (such as an airport); in that case, the fare is based on mileage covered—$2 for the first half mile or part thereof and 70¢ for each additional half mile or part. You can call ☎ 202/331-1671 to find out the rate between any point in D.C. and an address in Virginia or Maryland. Call ☎ 202/645-6018 to inquire about fares within the district.

It's generally easy to hail a taxi, although the *Washington Post* has reported that taxi cabs, even those driven by black cabbies, often ignore African Americans to pick up white passengers; African-American friends corroborate that this is true. Unique to the city is the practice of allowing drivers to pick up as many passengers as they can comfortably fit, so expect to share (unrelated parties pay the same as they would if they were not sharing). You can also call a taxi, though there's that $1.50 charge. Try **Capitol Cab** (☎ 202/546-2400), **Diamond Cab Company** (☎ 202/387-6200), or **Yellow Cab** (☎ 202/544-1212). To register a complaint, note the cab driver's name and cab number and call (☎ 202/645-6005). You will be asked to file a written complaint either by fax (☎ 202/889-3604) or mail (Commendations/Complaints, District of Columbia Taxicab Commission, 2041 Martin Luther King, Jr., Ave. SE, Room 204, Washington, D.C. 20020).

BY ORGANIZED TOUR

The best way to get acquainted with any city, I'm convinced, is by hopping on a tour bus that circles the major parts of town while a guide narrates. It's a relaxing way to pick up some facts about a place, and usually a tour allows you to jump off the vehicle to visit one site, and then jump back on to continue the circuit. In Washington, you have many choices, including **DC Ducks** (☎ 202/966-3825),

Taxicab Zones

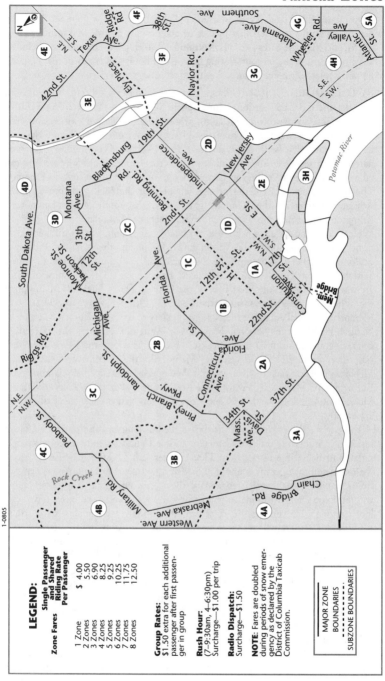

LEGEND:

Single Passenger and Shared Riding Rate Per Passenger

Zone Fares	
1 Zone	$ 4.00
2 Zones	5.50
3 Zones	6.90
4 Zones	8.25
5 Zones	9.25
6 Zones	10.25
7 Zones	11.75
8 Zones	12.50

Group Rates:
$1.50 extra for each additional passenger after first passenger in group

Rush Hour:
(7–9:30am, 4–6:30pm)
Surcharge—$1.00 per trip

Radio Dispatch:
Surcharge—$1.50

NOTE: Fares are doubled during periods of snow emergency as declared by the District of Columbia Taxicab Commission.

—— MAJOR ZONE BOUNDARIES
---- SUBZONE BOUNDARIES

1-0805

a 90-minute land and water tour offered April through September (or later, depending on the weather) that focuses on the capital's historic and military landmarks, and **Bike the Sites** (☎ 202/966-8662), which provides you bikes, helmets, and equipment to use on tours lasting from 1 to 4 hours and led by licensed guides. For a complete listing of organized tours of all sorts, see chapter 7.

BY TOURMOBILE   If you're looking for an easy-on/easy-off tour of major sites, consider the more conventional **Tourmobile Sightseeing** (☎ 202/554-5100 or 888/868-7707; www.tourmobile.com), whose comfortable red, white, and blue sightseeing trams travel to as many as 25 sites, as far out as Arlington National Cemetery and even (with coach service) Mount Vernon. (Tourmobile is the only narrated sightseeing shuttle tour authorized by the National Park Service.) You can take the **Washington/Arlington Cemetery** tour or tour only **Arlington Cemetery.** The former stops at 21 different sites on or near the Mall and four sights at Arlington Cemetery: the Kennedy grave sites, the Tomb of the Unknowns, Arlington House, and the Women in Military Service Memorial.

Here's how the system works: You can board a Tourmobile at 24 different locations—the White House; the Washington Monument; the Arts and Industries Building/Hirshhorn Museum; the National Air and Space Museum; Union Station/National Postal Museum; the East Face of the Capitol/Library of Congress/Supreme Court; the West Face of the Capitol; Ford's Theater/FBI Building; the White House Visitor Center; the Old Post Office Pavilion; the U.S. Navy Memorial/National Archives; the National Gallery of Art; the National Museum of Natural History; the National Museum of American History; the Bureau of Engraving and Printing/U.S. Holocaust Memorial Museum; the Jefferson Memorial; the Franklin D. Roosevelt Memorial; the Kennedy Center; the Lincoln/Vietnam Veterans/Korean War Veterans Memorials; the National Law Enforcement Memorial Visitor's Center/National Portrait Gallery/National Museum of American Art/MCI Center; or Arlington National Cemetery (three separate stops).

You pay the driver when you first board the bus (you can also purchase a ticket inside the Arlington National Cemetery Visitor Center or, for a small surcharge, order your ticket in advance from **Ticketmaster,** call ☎ 800/551-SEAT). Along the route, you may get off at any stop to visit monuments or buildings. When you finish exploring each area, step aboard the next Tourmobile that comes along without extra charge (as long as you can show your ticket). The buses travel in a loop, serving each stop about every 15 to 30 minutes. One fare allows you to use the buses for a full day. The charge for the Washington/Arlington Cemetery tour is $14 for anyone 12 and older, $7 for children 3 to 11. For Arlington Cemetery only, those 12 and older pay $4.75, children $2.25. Children under 3 ride free. Buses follow figure-eight circuits from the Capitol to Arlington Cemetery and back. You can also buy an advance ticket after 3pm June 15–Labor Day or after 1pm the rest of the year, that is valid for the rest of the afternoon plus the following day; these tickets cost $16 per adult, $8 for children 3 to 11. Well-trained narrators give commentaries about sights along the route and answer questions.

Tourmobiles operate daily year-round, except Christmas. From June 15 to Labor Day, they ply the Mall between 9am and 6:30pm. After Labor Day, the hours are 9:30am to 4:30pm. In Arlington Cemetery, between November and March, they start at 8:30am and end at 4:30pm; from April through October, the hours are 8:30am to 6:30pm.

From April through October, Tourmobiles also run round-trip to **Mount Vernon**. Coaches depart from the Arlington National Cemetery Visitor Center at

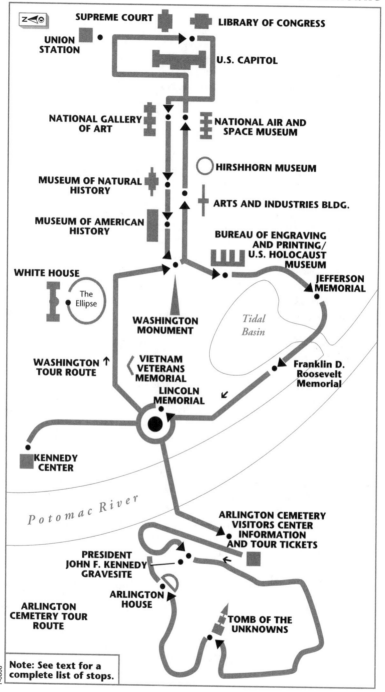

SUPREME COURT

LIBRARY OF CONGRESS

UNION STATION

U.S. CAPITOL

NATIONAL GALLERY OF ART

NATIONAL AIR AND SPACE MUSEUM

HIRSHHORN MUSEUM

MUSEUM OF NATURAL HISTORY

ARTS AND INDUSTRIES BLDG.

MUSEUM OF AMERICAN HISTORY

BUREAU OF ENGRAVING AND PRINTING/ U.S. HOLOCAUST MUSEUM

WHITE HOUSE

The Ellipse

JEFFERSON MEMORIAL

WASHINGTON MONUMENT

Tidal Basin

WASHINGTON TOUR ROUTE ↑

VIETNAM VETERANS MEMORIAL

LINCOLN MEMORIAL

Franklin D. Roosevelt Memorial

KENNEDY CENTER

Potomac River

ARLINGTON CEMETERY VISITORS CENTER INFORMATION AND TOUR TICKETS

PRESIDENT JOHN F. KENNEDY GRAVESITE

ARLINGTON HOUSE

ARLINGTON CEMETERY TOUR ROUTE

TOMB OF THE UNKNOWNS

1-0806

Note: See text for a complete list of stops.

63

10am, noon, and 2pm, with a pickup at the Washington Monument shortly there-after. The price is $22 for those 12 and older, $11 for children ages 3 to 11, including admission to Mount Vernon. A combination tour of Washington, Arlington Cemetery, and Mount Vernon (good for 2 days) is $37 for anyone 12 and older, $18.50 for children ages 3 to 11. Another offering (June 15 to Labor Day) is the **Frederick Douglass National Historic Site Tour,** which includes a guided tour of Douglass's home, Cedar Hill, in southeast Washington. Departures are from Arlington National Cemetery at noon, with a pickup at the Washington Monument shortly thereafter. Those 12 and older pay $7, and children ages 3 to 11 pay $3.50. A 2-day combination Frederick Douglass Tour and Washington/Arlington National Cemetery Tour is also available for $28 for those 12 and older, $14 for children ages 3 to 11. For both the Mount Vernon and Frederick Douglass tours, you must reserve in person at either Arlington Cemetery or the Washington Monument at least an hour in advance.

Tourmobile's newest offering is a **Twilight Tour** that departs each evening at 6:30pm March through December from Union Station, stopping at the Jefferson, FDR, and Lincoln Memorials, the White House, and the Capitol, before returning to Union Station. The tour lasts nearly 4 hours, includes narrated touring on the bus and at each site, and costs $14 per adult, $7 per child ages 3 to 11.

BY OLD TOWN TROLLEY   Another standard is **Old Town Trolley Tours** (☎ 202/832-9800), which offers 2½-hour narrated tours aboard green-and-orange trolleys that stop at more than 19 sites. Both the Tourmobiles and the trolleys are open-air in summer—meaning not air-conditioned. For a fixed price, you can get on and off these green-and-orange vehicles as often as you like for an entire loop around the city. Following a loop, the trolleys stop at 19 locations in the district, including Georgetown; they also go out to Arlington National Cemetery. They operate Memorial Day to Labor Day daily from 9am to 5pm; the rest of the year 9am to 4pm. The cost is $20 for adults, $11 for children 4 to 12, free for children under 4. The full tour, which is narrated, takes 2½ hours, and trolleys come by every 30 minutes or so. Stops are made at Union Station; the Hyatt Regency Hotel (near the National Gallery); the Pavilion at the Old Post Office; Metro Center (near the National Museum of Women in the Arts); the Grand Hyatt (Chinatown, MCI Center); the FBI Building/Ford's Theatre; the J.W. Marriott; the Hotel Washington (near the White House); the Capital Hilton; the Renaissance Mayflower Hotel (near the National Geographic Society); the Washington Hilton (near the Phillips Collection and Adams-Morgan restaurants); the Washington Park Gourmet (near the National Zoo); Washington National Cathedral; the Georgetown Park Mall; Arlington Cemetery; Lincoln Memorial; the Washington Monument/ U.S. Holocaust Memorial Museum/Smithsonian Castle; the Air and Space Museum; and the U.S. Capitol/Library of Congress. You can board without a ticket and purchase it en route.

Old Town Trolley also offers a 2½-hour "Washington After Hours" tour of illu-minated federal buildings and memorials from mid-March to the end of December. Call the number listed above for details.

FAST FACTS: Washington, D.C.

Airports   See "Getting There" in chapter 2.

American Express   There's an American Express Travel Service office at 1150 Connecticut Ave. NW (☎ 202/457-1300), another at Metro Center, 1001

G St. NW (☎ **202/393-2368**), and a third in upper northwest Washington at 5300 Wisconsin Ave. NW, in the Mazza Gallerie (☎ **202/362-4000**). Each office functions as a full travel agency and currency exchange; of course, you can also buy traveler's checks here.

Area Code   Within the District of Columbia, it's 202. In suburban Virginia, it's 703. In suburban Maryland, it's 301.

Baby-sitters   Most hotels can arrange for sitters. If your hotel does not offer a baby-sitting service, you can contact **White House Nannies** (☎ **301/ 652-8088**). In business since 1985, this company checks their caregivers' qualifications, child-care references, and personal histories, including driving and social security records. Each caregiver has been trained in CPR and first aid. Rates are $8 to $12 per hour (4-hour minimum), depending upon the caregiver's experience and how many children you have, plus a one-time referral fee of $20 when you've called at least 24 hours in advance or $25 when you've called less than 24 hours ahead. If the hotel does not pay for parking, you may have to pay that fee, as well.

Business Hours   See "Fast Facts: For the Foreign Traveler" in chapter 3.

Car Rentals   See "Getting Around," earlier in this chapter.

Climate   See "When to Go" in chapter 2.

Congresspersons   To locate a senator or congressional representative, call the Capitol switchboard (☎ **202/224-3121**).

Convention Center   The Washington, D.C., Convention Center, 900 9th St. NW, between H Street and New York Ave. (☎ **202/789-1600**), is a vast multipurpose facility with 381,000 square feet of exhibition space and 40 meeting rooms.

Crime   See "Safety," below.

Doctors/Dentists   Prologue (☎ **800/DOCTORS**) can refer you to any type of doctor or dentist you need. Its roster includes just about every specialty. Hours are weekdays 8:30am to 8pm, Saturday 9:30am to 4pm. **The Washington Hospital Center** (☎ **202/877-DOCS**) referral service operates weekdays 8am to 4pm and will point you to a doctor located as close as possible to where you are staying. **Physicians Home Services**, Suite 401, 2311 M St. NW (☎ **202/331-3888**), will come to your hotel if you are staying in the district (for a hefty $250 to $300 fee, which insurance companies do not reimburse), or will treat you in its downtown office during regular hours. PHS accepts credit cards; traveler's checks; local personal checks with adequate identification; and cash.

Driving Rules   See "Getting Around," earlier in this chapter.

Drugstores   **CVS,** Washington's major drugstore chain (with more than 40 stores), has two convenient 24-hour locations: 14th Street and Thomas Circle NW, at Vermont Ave. (☎ **202/628-0720**), and at Dupont Circle (☎ **202/ 785-1466**), both with round-the-clock pharmacies. These drugstores also carry miscellaneous goods ranging from frozen food and basic groceries to small appliances. Check your phone book for other convenient locations.

Embassies   See "Fast Facts: For the Foreign Traveler" in chapter 3.

Emergencies/Hotlines   Dial ☎ **911** to contact the police or fire department or to call an ambulance. See also "Hospitals," below. To reach a 24-hour **poison**

control hotline, call ☎ **202/625-3333;** to reach a **24-hour crisis line,** call ☎ **202/561-7000;** and to reach the **drug and alcohol abuse hotline,** which operates daily 10am to 2am, call ☎ **888/294-3572.**

Hospitals   In case of a life-threatening emergency, call ☎ **911.** If you don't require immediate ambulance transportation but still need emergency-room treatment, call one of the following hospitals (and be sure to get directions): **Children's Hospital National Medical Center,** 111 Michigan Ave. NW (☎ **202/884-5000** for emergency room and general information); **George Washington University Hospital,** 901 23rd St. NW (entrance on Washington Circle; ☎ **202/994-3211** for emergency room or 202/994-1000 for general information); **Georgetown University Hospital,** 3800 Reservoir Rd. NW (☎ **202/784-2119** for emergency room or 202/687-2000 for general information); **Howard University Hospital,** 2041 Georgia Ave. NW (☎ **202/865-1131** for emergency room or 202/865-6100 for general information).

Laundry/Dry Cleaning   Most hotels provide laundry and dry-cleaning services and/or have coin-operated facilities. Otherwise, try **Washtub Laundromat,** 1511 17th St. NW (☎ **202/332-9455**), for self-service coin-operated laundering. For complete laundry and dry-cleaning services with free pickup and delivery, contact **Bergmann's** (☎ **703/247-7600**). For same-day dry-cleaning service, try **MacDee Quality Cleaners,** at 1639 L St. NW (☎ **202/296-6100**), open Monday through Saturday.

Liquor Laws   The minimum drinking age is 21. Establishments can serve alcoholic beverages weekdays from 8am to 2am, Saturday until 3am, and Sunday 10am to 3am. Liquor stores are closed on Sunday. District gourmet grocery stores, mom-and-pop grocery stores, and 7-Eleven convenience stores often sell beer and wine, even on Sundays.

Luggage Storage/Lockers   Washington National, Dulles, and Baltimore-Washington International Airports each have luggage storage facilities, as do most hotels.

Maps   Free city maps are often available at hotels and throughout town at tourist attractions. You can also contact the Washington, D.C., Convention and Visitors Association, 1212 New York Ave. NW, Washington, D.C. 20005 (☎ **202/789-7000**).

Newspapers/Magazines   See "Visitor Information," earlier in this chapter.

Police   In an emergency, dial ☎ **911.** For a nonemergency, call ☎ **202/727-1010.**

Post Office   If you want your mail to follow you on your vacation and you aren't sure of your address, your mail can be sent to you, in your name, ℅ General Delivery at the main post office of the city or region where you expect to be. The addressee must pick it up in person and produce proof of identity (for example, driver's license, credit or charge card, or passport). In Washington, the main post office is located at 900 Brentwood Rd. NE, Washington, D.C. 20066-9998, USA (☎ **202/636-1532**). It's open weekdays 8am to 8pm, Saturday 8am to 6pm, and Sunday noon to 6pm. Other post offices are located throughout the city, including the one in the National Postal Museum building, opposite Union Station at 2 Massachusetts Ave. NE, at G and North Capitol streets (☎ **202/523-2628**). It's open weekdays 7am to midnight, and weekends until 8pm.

Religious Services   Every hotel keeps a list of places of worship for all faiths. Inquire at the front desk. Among Washington's notable places of worship are: the Washington National Cathedral (the Episcopal church is the sixth largest cathedral in the world), Wisconsin and Massachusetts aves. NW (☎ **202/537-6200**); Saint John's Church (also Episcopal, known as the "church of the Presidents"), on Lafayette Square across from the White House (☎ **202/347-8766**); the Basilica of the National Shrine of the Immaculate Conception (the nation's largest Catholic church), Michigan Ave. and 4th Street NE (☎ **202/526-8300**); Adas Israel (Jewish), Connecticut Ave. and Porter Street NW ☎ **202/362-4433**); and the Islamic Mosque and Cultural Center (Muslim), 2551 Massachusetts Ave. NW (☎ **202/332-8343**).

Rest Rooms   Visitors can usually find a rest room in a bar, restaurant, hotel, museum, department store, train station, or service station (although for reasons of cleanliness, this should be your last choice). You might have to buy a snack or drink in a restaurant/bar to gain bathroom privileges.

Safety   In Washington, you're quite safe throughout the day in all the major tourist areas described in this book, and you can also safely visit the Lincoln Memorial after dark. At nighttime, be alert anywhere you go in Washington. Riding the Metro is quite safe.

Taxes   Sales tax on merchandise is 5.75% in the district, 5% in Maryland, and 4.5% in Virginia. The tax on restaurant meals is 10% in the district, 5% in Maryland, and 4.5% in Virginia.

In the district, in addition to your hotel rate, you pay 13% sales tax and $1.50 per night occupancy tax. The state sales tax on a hotel room is 9.75% in suburban Virginia and 10% in Maryland (where you can expect an additional 5% to 7% in city or local taxes).

Taxis   See "Getting Around," earlier in this chapter.

Tickets   A service called **TICKETplace** (☎ **202/TICKETS**) sells half-price tickets, on the day of performance only, to most major Washington-area theaters and concert halls. It also functions as a Ticketmaster outlet. A same-day half-price ticket booth operates at the Old Post Office Pavilion. For advance sale tickets, call Ticketmaster (☎ **202/432-SEAT**) or Protix (☎ **703/218-6500**). See chapter 10 for details.

Time   To find out the exact time, call ☎ **202/844-2525**.

Transit Information   See "Getting There" in chapter 2 and "Getting Around," earlier in this chapter.

Weather   Call ☎ **202/936-1212**.

5 Where to Stay in Washington, D.C.

Not so long ago, up until 1997, in fact, Washington's peak seasons coincided generally with two activities: the sessions of Congress and springtime, starting with the appearance of the cherry blossoms along the Potomac. Specifically, when Congress was "in," from about the second week in September until Thanksgiving and again from about mid-January through June, hotels were reasonably full with guests whose business took them to Capitol Hill or to conferences scheduled here. The period April through June traditionally has been the peak-peak season, when families and school groups descend upon the city to see the cherry blossoms and enjoy Washington's sensational spring. Weekdays, too, have always been considered prime time, with hotels emptying out on weekends.

No longer. Increased tourism (up by about 7%) and business travel have created a bustling hotel market, blurring the distinctions between peak and off-peak. The only true down time now is the period between Thanksgiving and mid-January. The start of peak-peak season has inched earlier, to the beginning of March. And hotel bookings on weekends have shot up, because business travelers are staying over more and more on weekends either to capture the cheaper "stay over Saturday-night" rate offered by airfares, or to have their families join them for minivacations.

Although the hotel occupancy rate for the year has risen past the 70% mark, the number of accommodations has remained pretty much the same: More than 100 hotels and motels, or about 25,000 guest rooms exist in Washington, and the number increases to 65,000 hotel rooms if you add suburban Maryland and Virginia lodging. With so many accommodations available, you'll probably always be able to snag a room, even in high season, and even at the last minute. But you're either going to pay more or end up way outside of Washington. Room rates, by the way, have risen nearly 6%, with the average hovering around $137.55 for city hotels and $99.50 for less expensive suburban properties.

A NOTE ABOUT PRICE CATEGORIES The hotels listed in this chapter are grouped first by location, then alphabetically by price. I've used the following guide for per-night prices: **Very Expensive,** more than $215; **Expensive,** $150 to $215; **Moderate,** $100 to $149; and **Inexpensive,** less than $100.

Prices are based on published rates for a standard double room on weekdays during high season. As you'll soon find out, you can often do better. Two rates are given, weekday and weekend, since the difference can be enormous. Reduced rates and weekend rates are, generally, subject to availability. Don't forget tax: In the district, in addition to your hotel rate, you'll have to pay 13% in taxes plus $1.50 a night room tax. And keep in mind that parking can cost a bundle, so inquire about parking rates when you make your reservation; some hotels charge more than $20 a night!

HOW TO GET THE BEST RATE

As you peruse this chapter, you should keep certain things in mind. First, consider all the hotels, no matter the rate category. The accepted wisdom is that no one pays the advertised "rack" rate. Even the best and most expensive hotels may be ready to negotiate and often offer bargain rates at certain times or to guests who are members of certain groups, and you may be eligible. If you can be flexible about the time you are traveling, all the better. Second, as a rule, when you call a hotel, you should ask whether there are special promotions or discounts available. Most hotels offer discounts of at least 10% to members of the American Automobile Association (AAA) and the American Association of Retired Persons (AARP). The magnificent Willard Hotel, for instance, offers 50% off its regular rates for guests older than 65—on a space available basis. Many hotels in Washington, like the State Plaza Hotel, discount rates for government, military, or embassy-related guests. Long-term rates, corporate rates, and holiday rates are also possibilities.

Families often receive special rates, as much as 50% off on a room adjoining the parents' room (Hyatt is one chain that offers this, based on availability), or perhaps free fare in the hotel's restaurant (many Holiday Inns let kids 12 and under eat free from children's menus year-round). Every hotel (but not necessarily inns or bed-and-breakfasts) included in this chapter allows children under a certain age, usually 12 or 18, to stay free in the parents' room.

Finally, it pays to know what you want and to do some research. For example, by calling hotels and simply asking if there were special weekend rates, I was quoted the following low prices: $100 to $110 at the Holiday Inn Downtown; about $155 at the posh Watergate Hotel; $125 (as much as $34 off the regular rate) for a "Weekend Superbe" package available through the Hotel Sofitel, entitling couples to a one-night stay with a continental breakfast of croissants and pastries served in the room; and $99, including continental breakfast served in the restaurant, at the Morrison-Clark Inn.

CYBER DEALS   If you are cyber savvy or game to give it a go, you can shop for hotel room bargains on the Internet, just as many do for airfare bargains. Even if you don't discover real deals, you may be able to download pictures of particular hotels and their individual rooms, as well as maps of the neighborhood and area transportation. Refer back to the box in chapter 2, "Netting Savings on the Internet," to find those all-in-one Web sites, like Best Fares, that cover travel needs from airfare, to hotel rooms, to car rentals. In addition to those Web sites, you can book rooms by calling up the home pages of various chain hotels, such as Holiday Inn's **www.holiday-inn.com.** A few of these chains post special rates on the Internet that you wouldn't otherwise know about. Radisson (**www.radisson.com**), for instance, publishes its "Hot Deals" only on the Web. For a complete listing of hotel chain Internet addresses, see the Appendix.

Another possibility is a service like **Travelweb,** at **www.preferredhotels.com/ TravelWeb/clickit.html.** This Web site gives you access to the hotel industry's reservations system, where you may stumble upon last-minute offerings posted by Hilton, Hyatt, Sheraton, and other chains. Another site, Aaron's Hotel and Motel

Directory, at **www.hotel-intl.com,** gives you access to a comprehensive listing of properties for a particular town or zip code and other helpful travel information. If you are more in the mood to stay at an inn, try **www.innsandouts.com.**

RESERVATION SERVICES If you don't have the time or energy to find yourself the right accommodation, these Washington reservations services will do it for you, for free. Because each of these businesses is Washington-based, you can specify your needs and ask for details about neighborhoods that only local people would know.

Capitol Reservations, 1730 Rhode Island Ave. NW, Suite 1114, Washington, D.C. 20036 (☎ **800/VISIT-DC** or 202/452-1270; fax 202/452-0537; www.hotelsdc.com), will find you a hotel that meets your specific requirements and is within your price range, and they'll do the bargaining for you. "Because of the high volume of room nights we book," explains owner Thom Hall, "many properties offer discounts available only through this service and below public rates." Capitol Reservations listings begin at about $55 a night for a double. The 15-year-old service works with about 75 area hotels, all of which have been screened for cleanliness, safe locations, and other desirability factors. **Washington D.C. Accommodations,** 2201 Wisconsin Ave. NW, Suite C110, Washington, D.C. 20007 (☎ **800/554-2220** or 202/289-2220; fax 202/338-4517; www.dcaccommodations. com), has been in business for 14 years and provides the same service. In addition to finding hotel accommodations for you, this service can advise you about transportation and general tourist information and even work out itineraries.

GROUPS If you're planning a meeting, convention, or other group function requiring 10 rooms or more, contact **U.S.A. Groups** (☎ **800/872-4777** or 202/861-1900; fax 703/440-9705). This free service represents hotel rooms at almost every hostelry in the Washington, D.C., and suburban Virginia–Maryland region in all price categories.

BED & BREAKFASTS If a stay in a private home, apartment, or small inn appeals to you, you may want to consider the specific inns I've listed in this chapter, or try calling these two services: **The Bed and Breakfast League/Sweet Dreams and Toast,** P.O. Box 9490, Washington, D.C. 20016 (☎ **202/363-7767;** fax 202/363-8396; e-mail: bedandbreakfast-washingtondc@erols.com), represents more than 65 B&Bs in the district. Through them, you might find a room in a mid-1800s Federal-style Capitol Hill mansion, a Georgetown home with a lovely garden, or a turn-of-the-century Dupont Circle townhouse with Victorian furnishings. The accommodations are screened, and guest reports are given serious consideration. Hosts are encouraged, though not required, to offer such niceties as fresh-baked muffins at breakfast. All listings are convenient to public transportation. Rates for most range from $53 to $120 for a single and $73 to $135 for a double, plus tax, and $10 to $25 per additional person. There's a 2-night minimum-stay requirement and a booking fee of $10 (per reservation, not per night). American Express, Diner's Club, MasterCard, and Visa are accepted.

A similar service, **Bed & Breakfast Accommodations Ltd.,** P.O. Box 12011, Washington, D.C. 20005 (☎ **202/328-3510;** fax 202/332-3885; www.bnbaccom. com), has more than 80 homes, inns, guest houses, and unhosted furnished apartments in its files. Most are in historic districts. Its current roster offers, among many others, a Georgian-style colonial brick home on a tree-lined avenue in Tenley Circle and a restored Capitol Hill Victorian, built in 1859, with working fireplaces and a garden. Rates are $45 to $150 single, $55 to $160 double, $15 for an extra person, and from $65 for a full apartment. At guest houses and inns, rates run the gamut from $89 to $180 single, $89 to $250 double. American Express, Diner's Club, MasterCard, Visa, and Discover are accepted.

1 Best Bets

- **Best Historic Hotel:** The grande dame of Washington hotels is the magnificent **Renaissance Mayflower,** 1127 Connecticut Ave. NW (☎ **800/HOTELS-1** or 202/347-3000), which, when it was built in 1925, was considered not only the last word in luxury and beauty, but also "the second-best address" in town. Harry S Truman preferred it over the White House.
- **Best Location:** The **Willard Inter-Continental,** 1401 Pennsylvania Ave. NW (☎ **800/327-0200** or 202/628-9100), is within walking distance of the White House, museums, theaters, downtown offices, good restaurants, and the Metro. It's also a quick taxi ride to Capitol Hill.
- **Best Place to Stay During an Inauguration:** For the best views of the inaugural parade, book rooms at the **J.W. Marriott,** 1331 Pennsylvania Ave. NW (☎ **800/228-9290** or 202/393-2000), or the **Hotel Washington,** 15th and Pennsylvania aves. NW (☎ **800/424-9540** or 202/638-5900). Be sure to specify a room with a view of Pennsylvania Avenue. Also, know that the best inaugural parties are inevitably held at the Willard Inter-Continental (see "Best Location," above).
- **Best Place for a Romantic Getaway:** The posh **Jefferson,** 16th and M streets. NW (☎ **800/368-5966** or 202/347-2200), is just enough off the beaten track, but still conveniently downtown, to feel like you've really escaped. Because the service, bar, and restaurant (see chapter 6 for a review of the Restaurant at the Jefferson) are outstanding, you have no need to leave the premises. The restaurant itself has one of the most romantic nooks in the city.
- **Best Moderately Priced Hotel:** The newly renovated **Hotel Lombardy,** 2019 Pennsylvania Ave. NW (☎ **800/424-5486** or 202/828-2600), is now slightly more than moderately priced but still conveniently located, with spacious and charmingly decorated accommodations, and concierge-like service from the front desk.
- **Best Inexpensive Hotel:** The **Days Inn Premier,** 1201 K St. NW (☎ **800/562-3350** or 202/842-1020), near the Convention Center and the MCI Center, even has a small rooftop pool. If you reserve far in advance, you may be able to get the special $59 per night "Super Saver" rate.
- **Best Inn:** The stunning **Morrison-Clark Inn,** Massachusetts Avenue and 11th Street NW (☎ **800/332-7898** or 202/898-1200), housed in two beautifully restored Victorian town houses, has exquisite rooms and an acclaimed restaurant.
- **Best B&B: Swann House,** 1808 New Hampshire Ave. NW (☎ **202/265-7677**) is remarkably pretty and comfortable, in a great neighborhood (Dupont Circle), and not outrageously priced.
- **Best Service:** The staff at **The Four Seasons,** 2800 Pennsylvania Ave. NW (☎ **800/332-3442** or 202/342-0444), pampers you relentlessly and greets you by name. The hotels also offers an "I Need It Now" program that delivers any of 100 or more left-at-home essentials (tweezers; batteries; cufflinks; electric hair curlers; and so on) to you in 3 minutes, at no cost.
- **Best Place to Hide If You're Embroiled in a Scandal:** Lovely as it is, the **Normandy Inn,** 2118 Wyoming Ave. NW (☎ **800/424-3729** or 202/483-1350), remains unknown to many Washingtonians—a plus if you need to lay low. Best of all, the neighborhood teems with embassies, in case your trouble is of the I-need-a-foreign-government-to-bail-me-out variety.

- **Best for Business Travelers: The Grand Hyatt Washington,** 1000 H St. NW (☎ **800/233-1234** or 202/582-1234), wins for its convenient central location (in the business district between the White House and the Capitol, directly across from the Convention Center, and 3 blocks from the MCI Center, with direct underground access to the subway) and for its ample on-site meeting facilities. The hotel also offers an inviting, $15-extra "Business Plan," which accommodates travelers in 8th- and 9th-floor rooms equipped with a large desk, fax machine, and computer hookup, with access to printers and other office supplies. Continental breakfast is included in the plan.

- **Best Hotel Restaurant:** The inventive French fare at sumptuous **Lespinasse,** in the Carlton hotel, 923 16th St. NW (☎ **800/325-3535** or 202/638-2626), is the hands-down star. Among the other standouts in this category are: **Citronelle,** in the Latham Hotel, 3000 M St. NW (☎ **800/528-4261** or 202/726-5000); the **Restaurant at the Jefferson,** in the Jefferson Hotel (see "Best for a Romantic Getaway," above); and **Brighton,** in the Canterbury Hotel, 1733 N St. NW (☎ **800/424-2950** or 202/393-3000).

- **Best Health Club:** The **West End Executive Fitness Center,** at the ANA Hotel, 2401 M St. NW (☎ **800/ANA-HOTELS** or 202/429-2400), is the model against which all other hotels measure their own. The 17,500-square-foot center offers classes in yoga and aerobics; seminars in stress management and weight loss; and equipment that includes virtual-reality bike machines, stair climbers with telephones and TV/VCR units, NordicTraks, rowing machines, exercise bikes with telephones, and assorted other torturous machines. The health club also has squash and racquetball courts; a swimming pool; a steam room; a whirlpool; saunas; and a minispa. Personal trainers, fitness evaluation, and workout clothes are available.

- **Best Views: The Hay-Adams,** 16th and H streets NW (☎ **800/424-5054** or 202/638-6600), has such a great, unobstructed view of the White House that the Secret Service comes over regularly to do security sweeps of the place.

2 Capitol Hill/The Mall

EXPENSIVE

Capitol Hill Suites. 200 C St. SE, Washington, D.C. 20003. ☎ **800/424-9165** or 202/543-6000. Fax 202/547-2608. 152 units. A/C TV TEL. Weekdays and weekends $89–$199 double. Extra person $20. Rates include continental breakfast. Children under 18 stay free. AE, CB, DC, DISC, MC, V. Valet parking $15. Metro: Capitol South.

This well-run all-suite property (on the House of Representatives side of the Capitol) comprises two contiguous converted apartment houses on a residential street near the Library of Congress, the Capitol, and Mall attractions—hence its popularity with numerous congresspeople, whose photographs are displayed in the pleasant lobby. Spacious accommodations, ideal for families, offer full kitchens or kitchenettes and dining areas, and you'll find complete living and dining rooms in the one-bedroom units. Decor is residential, with 18th-century mahogany reproduction furnishings and museum art prints adorning the walls. The hotel provides a helpful guide to local shops and services.

A food market and about 20 nearby restaurants (many of which deliver to the hotel) compensate for the lack of on-premises dining facilities. You get complimentary continental breakfast daily in the first floor "salon." The *Washington Post* is available in the lobby daily. There are coin-operated washers and dryers, and guests enjoy free use of extensive facilities at the nearby Washington Sports Club.

⊕ Family-Friendly Hotels

The Premier Hotel (*see p. 102*)   Near the Kennedy Center, this property has a rooftop pool and Ping-Pong area, coin-operated washers and dryers, and a family-friendly diner. Rooms have small refrigerators and TVs equipped with Nintendo games.

Omni Shoreham (*see p. 104*)   Adjacent to Rock Creek Park, the Omni is also within walking distance of the zoo and is equipped with a large outdoor pool and kiddie pool.

One Washington Circle Hotel (*see p. 101*)   A great location in a safe neighborhood; bright and airy suites with full kitchens and sofa beds; an outdoor pool; a coin-operated washer and dryer; a good restaurant on the premises; and a great price that includes continental breakfast. —and a hospital across the street for emergencies—all for a great price, which, if more than $135, includes continental breakfast.

Washington Hilton & Towers (*see p. 89*)   A large, heated outdoor pool; a wading pool; three tennis courts; shuffleboard; and bike rental—what more do you need?

✪ **The Hotel George.** 15 E St. NW, Washington, D.C. 20001. ☎ **800/576-8331** or 202/ 347-4200. Fax 202/347-4213. www.hotelgeorge.com. 147 units. A/C MINIBAR TV TEL. Weekdays $185–$220, weekends $129; suites $375–$500. Ask about seasonal rates. Extra person $20. Children under 14 stay free. AE, CB, DC, DISC, MC, V. Parking $18. Metro: Union Station.

Out with the old, in with the funk. Posters throughout this new hotel, housed in a 1928 building, depict a modern-day George Washington, sans wig—and that's the theme of this hotel. Rather than stick to old-style traditions, this place with a hip attitude brings you Washington à la 2000. The lobby isn't fancy, but it's comfortable, and the decor is "cool retro." The large rooms offer modern amenities: hair dryers; coffeemakers; interactive cable TV with on-demand movies; irons and ironing board; two-line telephones with data port and voice mail; and 5-foot, granite-topped executive desks. I especially loved the spacious, mirrored, marble bathrooms, with a speaker that broadcast TV sound from the other room. So far, the hotel attracts groups and Hill-ites waiting to make their mark on Capitol Hill.

Dining/Diversions: The hotel's restaurant, bis, opened in May 1998 and serves French bistro food, the creation of chef Jeff Buben, who co-owns bis and the acclaimed Vidalia (see chapter 6) with his wife, Sallie.

Amenities: 24-hour concierge, overnight shoe shine, weekday delivery of *Washington Post*, laundry and valet, nightly turndown, room service during restaurant hours, express checkout, VCR and CD player rentals, cigar-friendly billiard room, business/secretarial services, 1,600 square feet of meeting/banquet space, fitness center with men's and women's steam rooms.

Phoenix Park Hotel. 520 N. Capitol St. NW, Washington, D.C. 20001. ☎ **800/824-5419** or 202/638-6900. Fax 202/393-3236. 150 units. A/C MINIBAR TV TEL. Weekdays $189–$219 double, weekends starting from $89 double; suites $199–$799. Extra person $19. Children under 16 stay free. AE, DC, DISC, MC, V. Parking $15. Metro: Union Station.

The Phoenix Park is one of a cluster of hotels across from Union Station and 2 blocks from the Capitol. What distinguishes the this hotel is its popular and authentic Irish pub, the Dubliner, which attempts to set the tone for the entire

Georgetown & Downtown Accommodations

ANA Hotel **8**
The Capital Hilton **23**
Capitol Hill Suites **37**
The Carlton **24**
Channel Inn **39**
Days Inn Premier **29**
Embassy Inn **20**
Four Seasons **7**
George Washington
  University Inn **13**
The Georgetown Dutch Inn **5**
Georgetown Suites **6**
Grand Hyatt Washington **33**
Hay-Adams **25**
Henley Park **31**
Holiday Inn Downtown **22**
Hotel George **36**
Hotel Lombardy **16**
Hotel Washington **26**
J.W. Marriott **27**
The Jefferson **19**
Kalorama Guest House **1**
Latham Hotel **4**
Lincoln Suites Downtown **17**
Loews L'Enfant Plaza **38**
Marriott Wardman Park **2**
Morrison-Clark Inn **30**
Omni Shoreham **3**
One Washington Circle Hotel **10**
Park Hyatt **9**
Phoenix Park Hotel **35**
The Premier Hotel **11**
Red Roof Inn **34**
Renaissance Mayflower **18**
Renaissance Washington, D.C. **32**
St. James Suites **14**
State Plaza Hotel **15**
The Watergate Hotel **12**
Willard Inter-Continental **28**
Windsor Inn **21**

property. Because of this well-worn, wood-paneled pub, which offers Irish fare, ale, and entertainment, the hotel attracts a number of Irish and Irish-American guests, stages a number of Ireland-related events in its ballroom, and attempts an Irish air of hospitality—which, frankly, fails outside the doors of the pub. The attractive rooms have computer connections but are rather cramped with furnishings. Irish linens and toiletries are in the bathroom, along with coffeemakers and hair dryers.

Dining/Diversions: The hotel's pub, the Dubliner, attracts drinkers and guests from all over—see description above.

Amenities: Room service until 11pm, voice mail, some secretarial services (faxing, copying), a small fitness center.

3 Downtown, East of 16th Street NW

VERY EXPENSIVE

Grand Hyatt Washington. 1000 H St. NW, Washington, D.C. 20001. ☎ **800/233-1234** or 202/582-1234. Fax 202/637-4781. www.hyatt.com. 900 units. A/C MINIBAR TV TEL. Weekdays $290 double, weekends $119–$139 double. Extra person $25. Children under 18 stay free. AE, CB, DC, DISC, MC, V. Parking $12. Metro: Metro Center.

Hotel as circus, that's the Grand Hyatt. There's always something going on in the vast lobby—whose atrium is 12 stories high and enclosed by a glass, mansard-style roof. The hotel's waterfalls, baby grand piano floating on its own island in the 7,000-square-foot "lagoon," catwalks, 22-foot-high trees, and an array of bars and restaurants on the periphery will keep you permanently entertained. Should you get bored, head to the nearby nightspots and restaurants, or hop on the Metro, to which the Hyatt has direct access. The hotel is across from the Convention Center, between Capitol Hill and the White House, and 2 blocks from the MCI Center, which has bestowed "official hotel for the MCI Center" status upon the Grand Hyatt (teams and performers at the center stay here).

By contrast to its public areas, guest rooms seem rather tame, which might be a good thing. Each room has a 25-inch cable TV with free HBO service, hair dryers, irons, and ironing boards. One of the best things about the Grand Hyatt is the potpourri of special plans and packages the hotel offers, especially for business travelers. For example, an extra $15 qualifies you for the business plan, which includes an 8th- or 9th-floor room equipped with a large desk, fax machine, computer hookup, and coffeemaker; access to printers and other office supplies on the floor; and complimentary continental breakfast. Tourists should ask about seasonal deals, like the annual winter holiday package.

Dining/Diversions: The Hyatt offers three restaurants: The Zephyr Deli, the informal Grand Cafe, and the smaller Via Pacifica, which features American, Italian, and Asian cuisine; and three bars, the lobby Via's Bar, the large Grand Slam sports bar, and Butler's–The Cigar Bar.

Amenities: Concierge, room service (Monday through Thursday 6am to 1am, Friday through Saturday 6am to 2am), dry cleaning and laundry service, twice daily maid service, express checkout, courtesy car available on a first come, first served basis that takes guests within a 2-mile or 10-minute radius of the hotel; two-story health club with Jacuzzi, lap pool, exercise room, steam and sauna room, and aerobics program; business services that include two large ballrooms, a 102-seat theater, and 40,000 square feet of meeting space; an American Express Travel Center for traveler's checks and ticketing; and direct underground access to the Metro.

✪ **Willard Inter-Continental.** 1401 Pennsylvania Ave. NW, Washington, D.C. 20004.
☎ **800/327-0200** or 202/628-9100. Fax 202/637-7326. 341 units. A/C MINIBAR TV TEL.
Weekdays $410–$440 double, weekends $199 double. Extra person $30. Children under 18
stay free. AE, DC, DISC, JCB, MC, V. Parking $20. Metro: Metro Center. Small pets ok.

Billed as the "crown jewel of Pennsylvania Avenue," the Willard is the crown jewel
of all Washington hotels. Its designation as a National Historic Landmark in 1974
and magnificent restoration in the 1980s helped revitalize Pennsylvania Avenue and
this part of town.

The historic 1901 beaux arts–style hotel occupies the site of the City Hotel, built
in 1815 (renamed the Willard when that family bought it), and plays the same role
it did in the 1860s, when Nathaniel Hawthorne said about it, "You exchange nods
with governors of sovereign States; you elbow illustrious men, and tread on the toes
of generals. . . ." Lincoln spent the eve of his inauguration here, and it was at the
Willard that Julia Ward Howe penned the words to the "Battle Hymn of the
Republic."

The main lobby today is again an awesome entranceway, with massive marble
columns ascending to a lofty ceiling decorated with 48 state seals and hung with
huge globe chandeliers. Alaska and Hawaii seals are located in Peacock Alley, a
plush promenade with potted palms. Artisans were able to incorporate some of the
Willard's original plasterwork and scagliola marble into the updated hotel, along
with marble mosaic tile floors, carpeting, and chandeliers.

Rooms are sumptuous, spacious, and furnished in Edwardian and Federal-period
reproductions. Because of the large number of foreign visitors, many of whom still
smoke, six of the Willard's 12 floors are no-smoking. And, because of the many
heads of state (more than 100 in the last decade) who bunk here, the hotel offers
the 6th floor as "Secret Service–cleared." Eight rooms are outfitted to accommodate
guests with disabilities. The "02" suites allow a partial look at the White House. But
perhaps the best rooms are the ones perched in the curve of the 12th floor's southeast corner—the ones with the round "bull's eye" windows that capture glimpses of
the Capitol. Phones have dual lines with voice mail and cable TVs (with pay-movie
channels and video message, data-port plugs, retrieval/checkout). Each room has an
in-room safe, an iron, and an ironing board. In the marble bathrooms are a hair
dryer, scale, phone, and TV speaker.

Dining/Diversions: The Willard Room (the term power lunch originated here)
is simply stunning (see chapter 6 for a review). The circular Round Robin Bar is
where Henry Clay mixed the first mint julep in Washington (see "Behind Hotel
Bars" in this chapter, for more about the Round Robin and bartender Jim Hewes).
The Café Espresso offers croissant sandwiches, pastas, pastries, and vintage wines by
the glass. The Nest Lounge offers live jazz on weekends.

Amenities: Twice-daily maid service, nightly bed turndown, 24-hour room service, concierge, currency exchange, airline/train ticketing, express checkout, choice
of newspaper delivery, fax and cellular phone rental, full business center, complete
fitness center, VCRs in suites, upscale boutiques.

EXPENSIVE

Henley Park. 926 Massachusetts Ave. NW (at 10th St.), Washington, D.C. 20001. ☎ **800/222-8474** or 202/638-5200. Fax 202/638-6740. 95 units. A/C MINIBAR TV TEL. Weekdays
$145–$225 double, summer and weekends $98 double (including parking and continental
breakfast); junior suite $315, one-bedroom suite $395–$475, Ambassador Suite $725. Senior
discounts. Extra person $20. Children under 14 stay free. AE, CB, DC, DISC, MC, V. Parking
$16. Metro: Metro Center, Gallery Place, or Mt. Vernon Square.

D.C. with Dogs

If you take your dog along when you travel, you're always grateful to find a hotel that accepts pets, let alone one that actually welcomes them with open arms. Well, Fido has a home in Washington at the **Loews L'Enfant Plaza Hotel,** 480 L'Enfant Plaza SW, Washington, D.C. 20024 (☎ **800/235-6397** or 202/484-1000, advance notice of pet required). It's conveniently located for a game of fetch on the Mall (and for you to do some sightseeing at the Smithsonian). Actually, it's a wonderful choice for anyone: Its rooms are comfortable and have nice views; there are terrific amenities for kids (children under 5 eat free from a children's menu and all kids 12 and under receive a welcome gift) and for business travelers; the hotel restaurant is first-rate; and there's a year-round rooftop pool. During my stay here, the doorman took a shine to my dog and remembered us each time we came and went, offering tips on where she was welcome and grabbing up extra towels to protect my car seat when she headed off for a swim.

—Lisa Renaud

The Henley Park caters to a high-end corporate clientele who are not put off by its location: It's off by itself in an iffy part of town, although within walking distance of the Convention Center, restaurants, and nightlife. This is an intimate, English-style hotel housed in a converted 1918 Tudor-style apartment house with 119 gargoyles on its facade. The lobby, with its exquisite Tudor ceiling, archways, and leaded windows, is particularly evocative of the period. Luxurious rooms make this a good choice for upscale romantic weekends. They are decorated in the English country house mode, with Hepplewhite-, Chippendale-, and Queen Anne–style furnishings, including lovely period beds. Bathrooms offer phones, cosmetic mirrors, and luxury toiletries, and in-room amenities include terry-cloth robes, cable TVs with pay-movie options, and, in some rooms, fax machines.

Dining/Diversions: The hotel's posh restaurant, Coeur de Lion, serves classic continental cuisine; the menu highlights seafood; and the wine list is excellent. Adjoining the Coeur de Lion, Marley's, a delightful cocktail lounge, is the setting for piano bar entertainment (and complimentary hors d'oeuvres) weeknights, live jazz nightly, and dancing Friday and Saturday. Afternoon tea is served daily in the octagonal Wilkes Room, a charming parlor with a working fireplace.

Amenities: 24-hour concierge and room service, *Washington Post* delivery each weekday morning, complimentary shoe shine, nightly bed turndown with gourmet chocolate, complimentary weekday 7:30 to 9:30am limo service to downtown and Capitol Hill locations, access to a fitness room in the Morrison-Clark Inn (see listing below) across the street.

Hotel Washington. 515 15th St. NW (at Pennsylvania Ave. NW), Washington, D.C. 20004. ☎ **800/424-9540** or 202/638-5900. Fax 202/638-1594. www.hotelwashington.com. 350 units. A/C MINIBAR TV TEL. Weekdays $174–$240 double; $438–$680 suite. Subject to availability, certain bargain rates apply: weekends $135 single or double; $169 corporate rate, weekdays, double; family plan of $99 for family of 4, with children under 14, including breakfast. Extra person $18. Children under 14 stay free. AE, DC, MC, V. Parking $20. Metro: Metro Center. Pets ok.

Built in 1918, this hotel is the oldest continuously operating hotel in Washington. A major renovation in 1980 restored the hotel to play up the historic angle. The wooden moldings, crystal chandeliers, and marble floors in the two-story lobby are reconstructed originals. Decor in the guest rooms is traditional, with lots of mahogany furnishings and historically suggestive print fabrics and wall coverings.

People choose to stay at the Hotel Washington because of its location and views. From its corner perch at Pennsylvania Avenue and 15th Street, the 12-story hotel surveys the avenue, monuments, Capitol, and the White House. No other hotel in town can top the panoramic spectacle from the hotel's rooftop Sky Terrace where, from late April through October, you can have drinks and light fare. Guest rooms on the Pennsylvania Avenue side have great views, as do the first-floor meeting rooms. Clientele are mostly corporate, often international.

Dining/Diversions: The hotel's main restaurant, the Two Continents, is on the lobby level and serves American cuisine. In the lobby Corner Bar, complimentary coffee is provided daily and free hors d'oeuvres, nuts, and fruit are put out weekdays after 3:30pm during the winter. At the Sky Terrace, you can soak in the views while enjoying light fare.

Amenities: Room service (7am to 11pm), dry cleaning and laundry, express checkout, valet parking, business center and meeting rooms, fitness center, sauna, tour desk (for Old Town Trolley), gift shop.

J. W. Marriott. 1331 Pennsylvania Ave. NW (at E St.), Washington, D.C. 20004. ☎ **800/ 228-9290** or 202/393-2000. Fax 202/626-6991. www. marriott.com. 772 units. A/C TV TEL. Weekdays $234 double, $249 rm with city view, $259 for concierge-level rm. Weekends $109–$234 (concierge level) double with full breakfast. Extra person free. AE, DC, DISC, JCB, MC, V. Parking $20. Metro: Metro Center.

This flagship Marriott property, which opened in 1984, is adjacent to the National Theater, 1 block from the Warner Theater and 2 blocks from the White House. The best rooms on the 7th, 12th, 14th, and 15th floors overlook Pennsylvania Avenue and the monuments (floors 14 and 15 are concierge levels). Conventioneers make up much of the clientele; tourists (including families) and businesspeople traveling on their own will enjoy the extensive facilities and location.

Public areas bustle with groups checking in and locals cutting through to the shops that adjoin the hotel. Decor of the lobby area combines futuristic architecture with lush plantings. Residential-style rooms are furnished with desks and armoires, many of them cherry-wood pieces in traditional styles. You'll find an iron and full-size ironing board in your room, as well as a cable TV that offers HBO and On-Command videos. The hotel's best value is $89 for a double, part of its "home for the holidays" promotion, effective during the 2 weeks prior to Christmas and into early January. Also available from November 21 through December is a "two for breakfast" package, where you pay $109 for a double, including full breakfast (add $10 for city-view room, $40 for concierge level).

Dining/Diversions: The hotel's main dining room is Celadon, a chinoiserie setting for American/continental cuisine. Allie's American Grille overlooks Pennsylvania Avenue and serves American fare; "early-bird" dinners here are priced under $15. The skylit Garden Terrace offers piano music and nightly jazz.

Amenities: Concierge and 24-hour room service, laundry and dry cleaning, delivery of USA Today, nightly turndown, twice daily maid service, baby-sitting, express checkout, a connecting mall with 80 shops and restaurants, complete health club (with indoor swimming pool and hydrotherapy pool), video games, full business center, gift shop.

Renaissance Washington, D.C., Hotel. 999 9th St. NW (at K St.), Washington, D.C. 20001. ☎ **800/228-9898** or 202/898-9000. Fax 202/289-0947. www. renaissancehotel.com. 800 units. A/C MINIBAR TV TEL. Weekdays $199–$229 double, club

Behind Hotel Bars: The Willard's Round Robin Bartender Tells All

A good hotel bar is a haven. Whether you are a woman alone, a couple in love, old friends catching up with each other, colleagues talking business, or a journalist interviewing a subject, a hotel bar can offer a comfortable, relaxing place for quiet conversation and a well-mixed drink or glass of wine. And at the best hotel bars, you will find yourself agreeably looked after but unbothered. In Washington, exceptional bars include those at the **Jefferson, Carlton, Westin Fairfax, Hay-Adams, Mayflower, Canterbury,** and the **Tabard.**

In a class of its own, largely because of bartender Jim Hewes, is the **Willard Hotel's Round Robin Bar.** Hewes, who, with colleagues Carol Randall and Shawn Carey, has bartended at the Round Robin since the renovated Willard reopened in 1986, is steeped in nearly 2 centuries' worth of knowledge of presidential drink preferences and Washington political and social life. A cast of characters from Hewes's stories are depicted in the black-and-white portraits that line the green felt–lined walls of the bar: Charles Dickens, Samuel Clemens, Warren Harding, and Abraham Lincoln are just some of the many famous people who have stopped in or stayed at the Willard. If you care for an easy, amiably given history lesson along with that classically mixed gin and tonic, grab a stool at the round mahogany bar here and listen as the ponytailed Hewes fills you in.

"In the old days, everything took place within 10 blocks of the White House. The center of activity was supposed to be the Capitol, but it was really around here, and the Willard, starting in the 1840s and 1850s, gained a reputation as a meeting place. Presidents Zachary Taylor, Millard Fillmore, James Buchanan, Calvin Coolidge, Warren Harding, and Abraham Lincoln each lived or stayed for a time at the Willard. Washington Irving brought Charles Dickens

---

level $229–$249 double; $295–$2,000 suite. Weekends $109–$129 double. Extra person $25. Children under 18 stay free. AE, CB, DC, DISC, MC, V. Parking $15. Metro: Gallery Place.

Directly across the street from the D.C. Convention Center and 1 block away from the MCI Center, this hotel caters primarily to conventioneers and business travelers, but it also luxury and convenience to tourists.

A renovation completed in 1997 transformed guest rooms from contemporary to traditional decor, with oak furnishings and earth tones. Rooms offer remote-control TVs (with cable stations, pay-movie options, and video message retrieval/checkout) and phones with voice mail and computer jacks. The hotel has 16 rooms for guests with disabilities, including two with roll-in showers. Thirteen rooms are equipped with computer terminals offering unlimited access to the Internet; you pay an extra $20 above the regular room rate. An entire 15-story tower with 153 rooms constitutes the Renaissance Club, which has concierge-level amenities.

Dining/Diversions: Mahogany-paneled and crystal-chandeliered, The Tavern features American regional cuisine; a bar adjoins. Less formal is the cheerful Café Florentine, off the lobby, offering reasonably priced buffets and à la carte meals with a Mediterranean flair. The Caracalla prepares classic Italian cuisine. And the Plaza Gourmet offers take-out sandwiches, salads, and fresh-baked pastries.

Amenities: 24-hour room service and concierge; dry cleaning and laundry service; delivery of *USA Today;* express checkout; valet parking; gift shop; full business (a port, brandy, and wine drinker) here for a drink. Samuel Clemens (better known as Mark Twain) palled around with Senator Stewart from Nevada, imbibing bourbon at the bar. Walt Whitman wrote a poem about the Willard bar. Nathaniel Hawthorne, in the capital to cover the Civil War for *The Atlantic* magazine, wrote "You adopt the universal habit of the place, and call for a mint-julep, a whiskey-skin, a gin cocktail, a brandy smash, or a glass of pure old Rye, for the conviviality of Washington sets in at an early hour and, so far as I have had the opportunity to observe, never terminates at any hour."

"Throughout the 19th century, and up until World War I, people drank constantly throughout the day," says Hewes. "Popular in the 1840s was the Mamie Taylor, a potent mix of Scotch whiskey, lime juice, and ginger soda that was invented in Washington to honor Old Rough and Ready's sweetie, a hard-drinking, corn-cob-smoking first lady," notes Hewes. The mint julep, introduced at the Round Robin by statesman Henry Clay in 1850, quickly caught on and has been associated with the Round Robin ever since. (For the past few Kentucky Derby Days, Hewes has discussed the history of the mint julep for National Public Radio's *All Things Considered*.) Ulysses S. Grant was among the presidents to enjoy the julep.

"President Clinton is a Tanqueray and tonic man, and he likes his beer, though usually he'll have what the others in his party are having. Bush liked martinis. Reagan, and Nixon, too, introduced the city to California wines and Schramsburg sparkling wine," says Hewes.

And Hewes's favorite drink? "A good Irish whiskey, or a beer," he says. If you're intent on hitting the Round Robin when Hewes is tending bar, better call ahead (☎ 202/637-7348) since he's not there everyday.

center including 72,000 square feet of meeting space; 10,000-square-foot health club ($8 a day to use), including pool, whirlpool, sauna, extensive exercise equipment, and aerobics floor.

MODERATE

Holiday Inn Downtown. 1155 14th St. NW (at Massachusetts Ave.), Washington, D.C. 20005. ☎ **800/HOLIDAY** or 202/737-1200. Fax 202/783-5733. 208 units. A/C TV TEL. Weekdays $130–$179 double, weekends $100–$110. Extra person $15. Children under 18 stay free. AE, CB, DC, DISC, JCB, MC, V. Valet parking $10. Metro: McPherson Square. Small pets $25.

Just 5 blocks from the White House, this 14-story Holiday Inn is a good family choice in the moderately priced category. There's a fairly large rooftop swimming pool and sundeck offering nice city views. A renovation in 1997 has spruced up guest rooms, the four meeting rooms, and the lobby. Rooms are equipped with cable TVs offering HBO plus On-Command Video, an electronic key system, and phones with call waiting and modem jacks. The best room is the "junior suite"— not really a suite, but the corner room on each of the top 10 floors. They're much larger and airier than other rooms and include two double beds and sofa beds; they're worth the extra $20.

The hotel's restaurant/lounge serves buffet breakfasts and dinners. Other amenities include coin-operated washers and dryers and a special parking lot for oversize vehicles. Guests have free access to a fitness center next door.

At this writing, all Holiday Inns are featuring a "Great Rates" promotion, offering discounts of 10%–50%, depending on the season and space availability. Be sure to inquire when you call the toll-free number to reserve.

✪ **Morrison-Clark Historic Inn.** 1015 L St. NW (at 11th St. and Massachusetts Ave. NW), Washington, D.C. 20001. ☎ **800/332-7898** or 202/898-1200. Fax 202/289-8576. 66 units. A/C MINIBAR TV TEL. Weekdays $155–$185 double; weekends $99–$129 double; suites $175–$205 weekdays and weekends. Rates include continental breakfast. Extra person $20. Children under 16 stay free. AE, CB, DC, DISC, MC, V. Parking $15. Metro: Metro Center or Mt. Vernon Square.

This magnificent inn, occupying twin 1865 Victorian brick town houses—with a newer wing in converted stables across an interior courtyard—is listed in the National Register of Historic Places. Guests enter via a turn-of-the-century parlor, with velvet- and lace-upholstered Victorian furnishings and lace-curtained bay windows. A delicious continental breakfast is served in the adjoining Club, which is furnished with an original white marble fireplace and 13-foot windows flanking gilded mirrors. In warm weather, you can breakfast in the lovely, two-level, brick-paved courtyard, enclosed by the inn and neighboring buildings.

High-ceilinged guest rooms are individually decorated with original artworks, sumptuous fabrics, and antique or reproduction 19th-century furnishings. Most popular—and the grandest—are the Victorian-style rooms, which have acquired new chandeliers and bedspreads in the past year. Four Victorian rooms have private porches; many other rooms have plant-filled balconies. All have cable TVs, two phones (bed and bathroom) equipped with computer jacks, and hair dryers.

Room service is available from the inn's highly acclaimed restaurant (see chapter 6 for a review). Other amenities include twice-daily maid service with Belgian chocolates at bed turndown, complimentary *Washington Post*, business services, and fresh flowers in every room. A fitness center is on the premises. Look for ads in the *New York Times* to obtain the best rate of $79.

INEXPENSIVE

Days Inn Premier. 1201 K St. NW, Washington, D.C. 20005. ☎ **800/562-3350**, 800/325-2525, or 202/842-1020. Fax 202/289-0336. www.daysinn.com. 219 units. A/C TV TEL. Weekdays $99–$125 double, weekends $69–$99 double. Extra person $15. Children under 18 stay free. AE, CB, DC, DISC, MC, V. Parking $14. Metro: McPherson Square, Metro Center.

Proximity to the Convention Center makes this eight-floor Days Inn a perfect choice for visitors attending events there. A small rooftop pool will appeal to families with young children. Newly renovated rooms are cheerfully decorated and equipped with remote-control satellite TVs (with free and pay-movie channels) in armoires, hair dryers, and coffeemakers. On the top two "executive floors," guests get king-size beds; minirefrigerators; microwaves; views of the Capitol (corner room 919 is probably best); and access to the Executive Club, with its computer, TV, continental breakfast, and kitchen. Rooms are split between smoking and no-smoking. Four rooms are equipped for wheelchair accessibility.

The lobby is always crowded with conventioneers checking in, along with families during the summer. The facility has 12,000 square feet of meeting space, a full-service restaurant, and adjoining lounge. Additional amenities include room service, a small fitness center, and a coin-operated laundry; a car-rental agency is just across the street. City tours depart from the lobby. Inquire about special packages when you reserve. Lower "Super Saver" rates (about $59) are sometimes available if you reserve in advance (the earlier the better) via the central toll-free number, ☎ **800/325-2525**—it's worth a try (you may find better rates by calling this number instead of the one listed above).

Red Roof Inn. 500 H St. NW, Washington, D.C. 20001. ☎ **800/THE-ROOF** or 202/289-5959. Fax 202/682-9152. www.redroof.com. 197 units. A/C TV TEL. Weekdays $97.99–$102 double, weekends $70–$102 double. Children under 18 stay free AE, CB, DC, DISC, MC, V. Parking $8.50. Metro: Gallery Place.

Reserve early. This popular hotel, with endearingly considerate staff, sits in the heart of Chinatown, within walking distance of many attractions, including two (off the Mall) Smithsonian museums; it's also just 1 block from the MCI Center and 3 blocks from the Convention Center. Red Roof Inns purchased the 10-story property (which used to be a Comfort Inn) in 1996 and renovated the rooms, which are attractively decorated and equipped with cable TVs offering free Showtime and pay-movie options plus Nintendo. There's a reasonably priced cafe open 6:30am to 2pm and 5:30 to 10pm. On-premises facilities include coin-operated washers and dryers and a sunny 10th-floor exercise room with sauna. *USA Today* newspapers are free at the front desk.

4 Downtown, 16th Street NW & West

VERY EXPENSIVE

✪ **The Carlton.** 923 16th St. NW, Washington, D.C. 20006. ☎ **800/562-5661** or 202/638-2626. Fax 202/638-4231. 192 units. A/C MINIBAR TV TEL. Weekdays $285–$325 double, weekends $265–$285 double; $450–$2,500 suite. Extra person $15. Children under 10 stay free. AE, CB, DC, DISC, JCB, MC, V. Parking $22. Metro: Farragut West or McPherson Square. Pets under 25lbs ok, with advance notice.

Ah, luxury! Palladian windows dressed in rich damask draperies, elaborately gilded ceilings, Louis XVI chandeliers, plush green oversized sofas, and cozy arrangements of comfortable chairs: This is the lobby of the Carlton, designed to resemble a Milan palazzo. Guest rooms are quietly opulent and decorated in tastefully coordinated colors (for instance, grays and royal blues), with desks set in alcoves, a mirror-covered armoire, and creamy silk moiré wall coverings. Amenities in each room include dual telephone lines; voice mail and modem capabilities; personal safes; terry robes; and hair dryers. Guests have included everyone from Queen Elizabeth to the Rolling Stones.

Dining/Diversions: The Carlton's Lespinasse is quite the elegant restaurant (see chapter 6 for a review). The Library Lounge, which might be the best hotel bar in Washington, has a working fireplace and paneled walls lined with bookcases. High tea is offered daily in the posh lobby.

Amenities: 24-hour concierge and room service, pressing service, complimentary coffee or tea with wake-up call, complimentary newspaper and shoe shine, complimentary bottled water with turndown service, no charge for credit-card calls and local faxes, state-of-the-art fitness room and access to a complete health club (at the University Club), 10,000 square feet of meeting space, ballroom.

Hay-Adams. 16th and H sts. NW, Washington, D.C. 20006. ☎ **800/424-5054** or 202/638-6600. Fax 202/638-3803. 136 units. A/C MINIBAR TV TEL. Weekdays $265–$485 double, weekends $199–$329. Extra person $30. Children under 12 stay free. AE, CB, DC, JCB, MC, V. Parking (valet only) $22. Metro: Farragut West or McPherson Square. Pets ok, with advance notice.

Reserve a room on the 5th through 8th floor, H Street side of the hotel, pull back the curtains from the windows, and enjoy a full frontal view of the White House—with the Washington Monument behind it. One block from the president's abode, the Hay-Adams offers the best vantage point in town. Between the hotel and the White House is Lafayette Square, another landmark.

The Hay-Adams is one in the triumvirate of exclusive hotels built by Harry Wardman in the 1920s (the Jefferson and the Carlton are the other two). Its architecture evokes an Italian Renaissance style, and the building's interior has walnut wainscoting, arched alcoves, and intricate Tudor and Elizabethan ceiling motifs. Among the early guests were Amelia Earhart, Sinclair Lewis, Ethel Barrymore, and Charles Lindbergh. Today's guests tend to be socialites, foreign dignitaries, and powerful business leaders (but the staff won't divulge names).

Rooms are individually furnished with antiques and superior appointments. A typical accommodation might include 18th–century-style furnishings; silk-covered walls hung with botanical prints and fine art; a gorgeous molded plaster ceiling; and French silk floral-print bedspreads, upholstery, and curtains. Many rooms have ornamental fireplaces.

Dining/Diversions: The sunny Lafayette Restaurant (overlooking the White House) is an exquisite dining room that serves contemporary American/continental fare at all meals, plus afternoon tea. The adjoining lounge features nightly piano-bar entertainment. Off the Record is the hotel's newly opened wine and champagne bar.

Amenities: 24-hour room and concierge service, nightly bed turndown, complimentary shoe shine, guest access to a local health club, secretarial and business services, in-room fax on request, meeting rooms.

✪ **The Jefferson.** 1200 16th St. NW (at M St.), Washington, D.C. 20036. ☎ **800/ 368-5966** or 202/347-2200. Fax 202/223-9039. www.slh.com. 100 units. A/C MINIBAR TV TEL. Weekdays $300–$310 double; $350–$1,200 suite; weekends $175 double; $350 and up for suite. Extra person $25. Children under 12 stay free. AE, CB, DC, JCB, MC, V. Parking $20. Metro: Farragut North. Pets under 25lbs ok.

Opened in 1923 just 4 blocks from the White House, the Jefferson is one of the city's three most exclusive venues (along with the Hay-Adams and the Carlton), proffering discreet hospitality to political personages, royalty, literati, and other notables. With a very high staff-to-guest ratio, the Jefferson puts utmost emphasis on service; if you like, a butler will unpack your luggage and press clothes wrinkled in transit (the charge for pressing clothes ranges from $5 for a shirt to $18 for an evening gown).

Set foot in the lobby and you won't want to leave. An inviting sitting room with a fireplace at the rear of an extended vestibule draws you past green-velvet loveseats placed back-to-back down the middle and enclosed terraces opening off each side. A fine art collection, including original documents signed by Thomas Jefferson, graces the public area as well as the guest rooms. You'll hear a Thomas Jefferson–style grandfather clock chime the hour.

Each antique-filled guest room evokes a European feel. Yours might have a four-poster bed with plump eyelet-trimmed comforter and pillow shams (many are topped with canopies), or a cherry-wood bookstand from the Napoleonic period filled with rare books. In-room amenities include two-line speaker phones with hold buttons; fax machines (you get your own fax number when you check in); cable TVs with VCRs; CD players; and, in the bathrooms, terry robes, hair dryers, and phones.

Dining/Diversions: Off the lobby is The Restaurant at the Jefferson, one of the city's premier dining rooms (see chapter 6 for a review) and a cozy bar/lounge. In the paneled lounge, whose walls are hung with framed letters and documents written by Thomas Jefferson, you can sink into a red leather chair and enjoy a marvelous high tea daily from 3 to 5pm, or cocktails anytime—the bar stocks a robust selection of single-malt scotches and a fine choice of Davidoff cigars.

Amenities: 24-hour butler service, overnight shoe shine, nightly bed turndown with Godiva chocolate, morning delivery of *Washington Post* or any other major newspaper, 24-hour room and multilingual concierge service, video and CD rentals, express checkout. Business/secretarial services and meeting rooms, for a fee of $20, guests have access to full health club facilities (including Olympic-size pool) at the University Club across the street.

Renaissance Mayflower. 1127 Connecticut Ave. NW (between L and M sts.), Washington, D.C. 20036. ☎ **800/228-7697** or 202/347-3000. Fax 202/466-9082. www.marriott.com. 738 units. A/C MINIBAR TV TEL. Weekdays $275–$335 double; weekends $139–$199 double. Extra person $25. Children under 18 stay free. AE, CB, DC, DISC, JCB, MC, V. Parking $12. Metro: Farragut North.

Superbly located in the heart of downtown, the Mayflower is the hotel of choice for guests as varied as Israeli Prime Minister Benjamin Netanyahu and jazz genius Wynton Marsalis. The lobby, which extends an entire block from Connecticut Avenue back to 17th Street, is always active, since Washingtonians tend to use it as a shortcut in their travels.

The hotel is quite historic. Among other things, the Mayflower was the site of Calvin Coolidge's inaugural ball in 1925, the year it opened. (Coolidge didn't attend—he was mourning the death of his son from blood poisoning.) President-elect FDR and family lived in rooms 776 and 781 while waiting to move into the White House, and this is where FDR penned the words, "The only thing we have to fear is fear itself." A major restoration in the 1980s uncovered large skylights and renewed the lobby's pink marble bas-relief frieze and spectacular promenade.

Graciously appointed guest rooms have high ceilings, cream moiré wall coverings, and mahogany reproduction furnishings (Queen Anne, Sheraton, Chippendale, Hepplewhite). Handsome armoires hold 25-inch remote-control TVs. Amenities include ironing board and iron; three phones; a terry robe; hair dryer; and a small color TV in the bathroom. Inquire about "summer value rates."

Dining/Diversions: Washington lawyers and lobbyists gather for power breakfasts in the Café Promenade. Under a beautiful domed skylight, the restaurant is adorned with Edward Laning's murals, crystal chandeliers, marble columns, and lovely flower arrangements. A full English tea is served here afternoons Mon–Sat. The clubby, mahogany-paneled Town and Country is the setting for light buffet lunches and complimentary hors d'oeuvres during cocktail hour. Bartender Sambonn Lek has quite a following and is famous for his magic tricks and personality. The Lobby Court, a Starbucks espresso bar just opposite the front desk, serves coffee and fresh-baked pastries each morning, and becomes a piano bar serving cocktails later in the day.

Amenites: Coffee, tea, or hot chocolate and *USA Today* with wake-up call, 24-hour room service, twice-daily maid service, complimentary overnight shoe shine, concierge, courtesy car takes you within 3-mile radius, express checkout, valet parking, business center, full on-premises fitness center, florist, gift shop.

EXPENSIVE

The Capital Hilton. 1001 16th St. NW (between K and L sts.), Washington, D.C. 20036. ☎ **800/HILTONS** or 202/393-1000. Fax 202/639-5784. www.hilton.com. 591 units. A/C MINIBAR TV TEL. Weekdays $126–$275 double, add $30 more for Tower units; weekends (including continental breakfast) $133, Tower $155. Extra person $25; children under 12 stay free. AE, CB, DC, DISC, JCB, MC, V. Parking $22. Metro: Farragut West, Farragut North, or McPherson Square. Pets ok.

This longtime Washington residence has hosted every American president since FDR, and the annual Gridiron Club Dinner and political roast takes place in its ballroom. The Hilton's central location (2 blocks from the White House) makes it convenient for tourists, and business travelers appreciate the Tower's concierge floors (10 to 14) and extensive facilities.

During a 5-year, $55-million renovation in the late 1980s, the public areas were upgraded (note the gorgeous cherry paneling in the lobby). And in 1993, the rooms were redecorated in Federal-period motif with Queen Anne– and Chippendale-style furnishings. Each room has three phones equipped with call waiting and a cable TV featuring pay-movie stations. In the bathroom, you'll find a small TV and hair dryer. Ask about special rates for AAA members, senior citizens, military, and families.

Dining/Diversions: Steak and seafood highlight the menu at Fran O'Brien's Steakhouse, an upscale sports-themed restaurant named for its owner, a former Redskin. American regional fare is served at the sunny, gardenlike Twigs and the more elegant Twigs Grill, which adjoins. The Bar is the hotel's lobby lounge.

Amenities: 24-hour room service, concierge (7am to 11pm), full business center including 25,000 square feet of conference rooms, morning delivery of *USA Today*, tour and ticket desk, unisex hairdresser, gift shop, facial salon, shoe-shine stand, air-line desks (American, Continental, Northwest), fitness center, ATM with foreign-currency capabilities.

MODERATE

Lincoln Suites Downtown. 1823 L St. NW, Washington, D.C. 20036. ☎ **800/424-2970** or 202/223-4320. Fax 202/223-8546. 99 suites. A/C TV TEL. Weekdays $129–$159, weekends $99–$129. Children under 16 stay free. AE, CB, DC, DISC, MC, V. Parking $9 (in adjoining garage). Metro: Farragut North or Farragut West.

Lots of long-term guests stay at this all-suite, 10-story hotel in the heart of downtown, just 5 blocks from the White House. A multimillion dollar renovation was completed in May 1997, refurbishing the large, comfortable suites and sprucing up hallways. About 36 suites offer full kitchens; others have refrigerators, wet bars, coffeemakers, and microwaves. Rooms are fairly spacious, well-kept, attractive, and equipped with cable TVs with free HBO, shower massagers, hair dryers, and irons and ironing boards. The property also has a coin-operated washer and dryer and a small meeting room.

Samantha's, next door (and leased from the hotel), offers reasonably priced American fare. The hotel's own Beatrice is a grotto-like Italian restaurant open for all meals and providing room service Monday through Saturday 7am to 2pm and 5 to 11pm, Sunday 7 to 11am for breakfast only. In the lobby are complimentary copies of the *Washington Post* Monday through Saturday (and for sale on Sunday), complimentary milk and homemade cookies each evening, and complimentary continental breakfast weekend mornings; guests enjoy free use of the well-equipped Bally's Holiday Spa nearby.

INEXPENSIVE

Embassy Inn. 1627 16th St. NW (between Q and R sts.), Washington, D.C. 20009. ☎ **800/ 423-9111** or 202/234-7800. Fax 202/234-3309. 38 units (all with bathroom). A/C TV TEL. Weekdays $79–$110 double, weekends $59 double based on availability. Rates include continental breakfast, evening sherry, and snacks. Smoking rms on lower level. Extra person $10. Children under 14 stay free. AE, CB, DC, MC, V. Metro: Dupont Circle.

This four-story 1910 brick building, a former inn, was rescued from demolition some years back, spruced up, and restored to become a quaint, homey, small hotel. Its Federal-style architecture harmonizes with other turn-of-the-century town houses along this block, falling within a district designated "historic" in 1964.

Accommodations are comfortable, clean, and a little quirky in design: the sink is in the bedroom, not the bathroom; bathrooms have only shower stalls, no tubs; and middle rooms have no windows. Cable TV with free HBO and hair dryers, are unexpected perks. The recently redone lobby doubles as a parlor where breakfast (including fresh-baked muffins and croissants) is served daily and fresh coffee brews all day; tea, cocoa, and evening sherry are also complimentary. You can pick up maps and brochures, read a complimentary *Washington Post*, or request sundries you may have forgotten (toothbrush, razor, and the like). *Note:* There is no elevator, and there's street parking only.

Windsor Inn. 1842 16th St. NW (at T St.), Washington, D.C. 20009. ☎ **800/423-9111** or 202/667-0300. Fax 202/667-4503. 47 units. A/C TV TEL. Weekdays $79–$125 double; $125–$150 suite; weekends $59 based on availability. Rates include continental breakfast, evening sherry, and snacks. Smoking rms on lower level Extra person $10. Children under 14 stay free. AE, CB, DC, MC, V. Metro: Dupont Circle.

Under the same ownership and just a couple of blocks north of the above-mentioned Embassy Inn, the Windsor Inn occupies two brick buildings, side by side but with separate entrances. The Windsor annex has slightly larger rooms and more charming features, such as the occasional bay window or arched ceiling; the annex and the main building maintain the old-fashioned feel of the Embassy. Some of the public areas are done in art deco motif, and hallways are lighted by sconces and hung with gilt-framed lithographs. All rooms are neat and comfortable, and a few have sofas and/or decorative fireplaces. As at the Embassy, the Windsor offers cable TV with free HBO and hair dryers in each room. Six of the 39 rooms have tub and shower in bathrooms, the rest have only showers. Suites offer the greatest value, are very roomy and attractively furnished, and cost much less than you'd usually pay in Washington. Lower-level rooms (the smoking floor) face a skylit terrace with lawn furnishings and colorful murals. Continental breakfast, which includes croissants and muffins, is served in the lobby, as are complimentary coffee, tea, hot chocolate, and sherry. Ice machines, a refrigerator, and a handsome conference room are available to guests. The very friendly multilingual staff is a big plus. *Note:* There is no elevator, and parking is on the street.

5 Georgetown
VERY EXPENSIVE

✪ **The Four Seasons.** 2800 Pennsylvania Ave. NW, Washington, D.C. 20007. ☎ **800/332-3442** or 202/342-0444. Fax 202/944-2076. www.rshr.com. 260 units. A/C MINIBAR TV TEL. Weekdays $370–$465 double; $775–$3,500 suite; weekends $275 double, starting at $550 for suites. Extra person $40. Children under 16 stay free. AE, DC, JCB, MC, V. Parking $22. Metro: Foggy Bottom. Pets ok if on leash at all times.

Since it opened in 1979, this most glamorous of Washington's haute hotels has hosted everyone from Tom Hanks to Aretha Franklin, Puff Daddy to King Hussein. Open the front door and you enter a plush setting where thousands of plants and palm trees grow and large floral arrangements enhance the garden-like ambience.

Service is what sets this hotel apart. Staff are trained to know the names, preferences, even allergies of guests, and repeat clientele rely on this attention. Accommodations, many of them overlooking Rock Creek Park or the C&O Canal, have walls hung with gilt-framed antique prints, beds outfitted with down-filled bedding, dust ruffles, and scalloped spreads, and large desks and plump cushioned armchairs with hassocks to drive home the residential atmosphere. In-room amenities include cable TVs with free HBO and Spectravision movie options; VCRs (movies and video games are available); CD players (the concierge stocks CDs); bathrobes; and, in the bathrooms, hair dryers, lighted cosmetic mirrors, and upscale toiletries. Under construction now, in an adjoining building, are 40 luxury suites for clients who want state-of-the-art business amenities (each suite will be sound-proofed and have an office equipped with fax machine, at least 3 telephones with 2-line speakers, portable telephones, and headsets for private TV listening).

Dining/Diversions: The elegant and highly acclaimed Seasons is reviewed in chapter 6. The delightful Garden Terrace is bordered by tropical plants, ficus trees, and flower beds and has a wall of windows overlooking the canal. It's open for lunch, a lavish Sunday jazz brunch, and classic English-style afternoon teas.

Amenities: Twice-daily maid service, 24-hour room service and concierge, com-plimentary sedan service weekdays within the district, gratis newspaper of your choice, car windows washed when you park overnight, complimentary shoe shine, beauty salon, gift shop, jogging trail, business facilities, children's programs, exten-sive state-of-the-art fitness club that includes personal trainers; and a spa that offers a Vichy shower, hydrotherapy, and synchronized massage (two people work on you at the same time).

EXPENSIVE

The Latham. 3000 M St. NW, Washington, D.C. 20007. ☎ **800/528-4261** or 202/726-5000. Fax 202/337-4250. 143 units. A/C TV TEL. Weekdays $160–$180 double, week-ends $119–$139; suites $175–$290. Extra person $20. Children under 18 stay free. AE, DC, DISC, MC, V. Valet parking $14.

The Latham is at the hub of Georgetown's trendy nightlife/restaurant/shopping scene, but since its accommodations are set back from the street, none of the noise of nighttime revelers will reach your room. It's also the only Georgetown hotel with a swimming pool. Charming earth-tone rooms are decorated in French-country motif, with pine furnishings and multipaned windows; cable TVs (offering cable and pay-per-view movie selections) are housed in forest-green armoires. All rooms are equipped with large desks; hair dryers; terry robes; irons; and ironing boards. Tenth-floor rooms offer gorgeous river views; third-floor accommodations, all two-room suites, have windows facing a hallway designed to replicate a quaint George-town street. Most luxurious are two-story carriage suites with cathedral ceilings, full living rooms, and stocked minibars. Fax printers are in all suites and in one-third of the guest rooms; CD players with headphones are in third-floor and carriage suites.

Dining/Diversions: The highly acclaimed Citronelle, one of D.C.'s hottest restaurants, is on the premises (see chapter 6 for a review). And fronting the hotel is the country-French La Madeleine, another branch of which is fully described among Alexandria restaurants in chapter 11.

Amenities: Room service during restaurant hours, concierge, valet parking, nightly turndown, free delivery of morning newspaper, business services, express checkout, small outdoor nearby pool and bilevel sundeck, fitness room, jogging and bike path along the C&O Canal, meeting rooms, and audiovisual services.

MODERATE

The Georgetown Dutch Inn. 1075 Thomas Jefferson St. NW (just below M St.), Wash-ington, D.C. 20007. ☎ **800/388-2410** or 202/337-0900. Fax 202/333-6526. 47 units. A/C TV TEL. Weekdays $125–$195 one-bedroom suite for 2; $250–$320 two-bedroom duplex penthouse (sleeps 6); weekends $105–$115 one-bedroom suite for 2; $195–$250 penthouse suite. Rates include continental breakfast. Extra person $20. Children under 14 stay free. AE, CB, DC, DISC, MC, V. Limited free parking for small to midsize cars. Metro: Foggy Bottom, with a 10-minute walk. Bus: Bus no. 32, 34, and 36 go to all major Washington tourist attractions.

Many European and South American guests, usually embassy folks, stay at this inn. It's also a favorite for families here to celebrate weddings or graduations; they book several suites, or maybe a whole floor. Personalized service is a hallmark of the hotel, whose staff greet you by name and protect your privacy, should you be a celebrity of some sort—which many guests are.

Accommodations are spacious one- and two-bedroom, apartment-like suites, nine of them duplex penthouses with 1½ bathrooms; all have full kitchens but no microwaves. Amenities include cable TVs with HBO; irons and ironing boards; coffeemakers with free coffee; and three phones (bedside, living room, and bathroom). You'll also find a cosmetic mirror in the bathroom; a hair dryer is provided on request.

Although there's no restaurant on the premises, an extensive room-service menu is available. Complimentary continental breakfast is served in the lobby each morning. Guests also enjoy free use of nearby state-of-the-art health clubs. The C&O Canal towpath, just down the block, is ideal for jogging and cycling, though be wary of going at night.

Georgetown Suites. 1000 29th St. NW (between K and M sts.), Washington, D.C. 20007. ☎ **800/348-7203** or 202/298-1600. Fax 202/333-2019. www.georgetownsuites.com. 78 suites. A/C TV TEL. $139 studio suite (for 2); $149 one-bedroom suite (for up to 4); weekends $99 studio suite; $109 one-bedroom suite. Rates include extended continental breakfast. Roll-aways or sleeper sofa $10 extra. AE, DC, MC, V. Limited parking $15. Metro: Foggy Bottom. Pets ok.

This property, in the heart of Georgetown, was designed to meet the needs of business travelers making extended visits, but it works well for families, too. You enter the hotel via a brick courtyard with flowering plants in terra-cotta pots and Victorian white wooden benches. You'll find yourself in a large lobby area that seems much like a student lounge. The TV's going; games, books, magazines, and daily newspapers lie scattered across table tops in front of loveseats and chairs; and a cappuccino machine rests on the counter. Tea and coffee are available throughout the day, and a substantial continental breakfast is served daily.

Accommodations have fully equipped kitchens, living rooms, and dining areas and are furnished with large desks, cable TVs with HBO, hair dryers, and irons and ironing boards. The biggest, if not the best, suite is probably the two-level, two-bedroom town house, which has its own entrance on 29th Street; this goes for $250 a night. Among the on-premises facilities are an outdoor barbecue grill for guest use, coin-operated washers and dryers, and a small exercise room. Hotel services include complimentary grocery shopping and food delivery from nearby restaurants. M Street buses (a block away) will take you to most major D.C. attractions.

Georgetown Suites maintains another 136 suites (same phone number, rates, and amenities) close by, at 1111 30th St. NW, between K and M streets.

6 Adams-Morgan/North Dupont Circle

VERY EXPENSIVE

Washington Hilton & Towers. 1919 Connecticut Ave. NW (at T St.), Washington, D.C. 20009. ☎ **800/HILTONS** or 202/483-3000. Fax 202/797-5755. www.hilton.com. 2,206 units. A/C MINIBAR TV TEL. Weekdays $230–$270 double, Towers rms $265–$305 double; weekends (and selected weekdays and holidays) $119–$129 double, Towers rms $149–159. Extra person $20. Children of any age stay free. AE, CB, DC, DISC, JCB, MC, V. Parking $12. Metro: Dupont Circle. Pets ok with advance notice.

This superhotel/resort occupies 7 acres and offers every imaginable amenity. The Hilton caters to group business travelers and is accustomed to coordinating meetings for thousands. Its vast conference facilities include the largest ballroom on the East Coast between New York and Orlando (it accommodates nearly 4,000, theater-style). Besides conventions, the Hilton also hosts inaugural balls, debutante cotillions, and state banquets. Numerous smaller meeting rooms are available, and a business center is open during regular business hours.

Guest rooms are cheerful and attractively furnished; the artwork on the walls was commissioned by local artists. From the fifth floor up, city-side, you'll have panoramic views of Washington (as well as a view of the Olympic-size pool). The 10th floor comprises a concierge level called the Towers. The 9th and 10th floors are the executive levels, where rooms have two telephones with data ports and a fax machine.

Dining/Diversions: The handsome mahogany-paneled 1919 Grill specializes in steaks, seafood, and pasta dinners. The Capital Café, for buffet meals and full restaurant fare, has a wall of windows overlooking the pool. A poolside eatery serves light fare under a striped tent top in season. The clubby McClellan's is a handsome brass-railed mahogany bar lounge. Capital Court, an elegant lobby lounge, features a nightly piano bar.

Amenities: Concierge, room service during restaurant hours, transportation/ sightseeing desk, paper delivery of your choice upon request (*USA Today, Washington Post,* or *Wall Street Journal*), express checkout, extensive health club facilities, Olympic-size, lighted, and heated outdoor pool, children's pool, three lighted tennis courts, shuffleboard, lobby shops, comprehensive business center, shoe-shine stand.

EXPENSIVE

⭕ **Hotel Sofitel.** 1914 Connecticut Ave. NW, Washington, D.C. 20009. ☎ **800/424-2464** or 202/797-2000. Fax 202/462-0944. 144 units. A/C MINIBAR TV TEL. Weekdays from $199–$259; weekends $139–$159 for double or suite. Extra person $20. Children under 12 stay free. AE, CB, DC, MC, V. Valet parking $15. Metro: Dupont Circle. Small pets ok.

The front desk greets you with "Bonjour"; your room amenities include a bottle of Evian and Nina Ricci toiletries; the hotel's Trocadero restaurant serves French bistro food; and you get a fresh baguette at checkout. It's not hard to guess that the Sofitel is part of a French hotel chain. The 1906 building is a registered historic property on a hill a short walk from lively Dupont Circle; its elevated position allows for great city views from rooms on the upper level, Connecticut Avenue–side of this eight-floor hotel. You're also a short walk away from trendy Adams-Morgan: cross Connecticut and walk up Columbia Road. Rooms are spacious, each with a breakfast/study alcove and many with sitting areas, and are decorated in muted shades of champagnes and peach. A multilingual staff sees to the needs of an international clientele of diplomats, foreign delegations, and corporate travelers. If you're looking for a romantic getaway at a reasonable rate, ask about the hotel's "Romantic Rendezvous" and "Weekend Superbe" packages.

Dining/Diversions: The Trocadero is open for breakfast, lunch, and dinner; the adjoining Pullman Lounge features a pianist weeknights starting at 5:30pm.

Amenities: Full-service concierge, 24-hour room service (5:30am to 11pm), dry cleaning and laundry, major national and European newspapers available in lobby or delivered to your door upon request, nightly turndown, twice daily maid service, baby-sitting, secretarial services including faxing and copying, express checkout, courtesy limo available weekdays 7 to 9am and 5 to 7pm for city jaunts, but not to the airport. Fitness center with Nautilus and other equipment, newly renovated conference rooms.

Adams-Morgan & Dupont Circle Accommodations

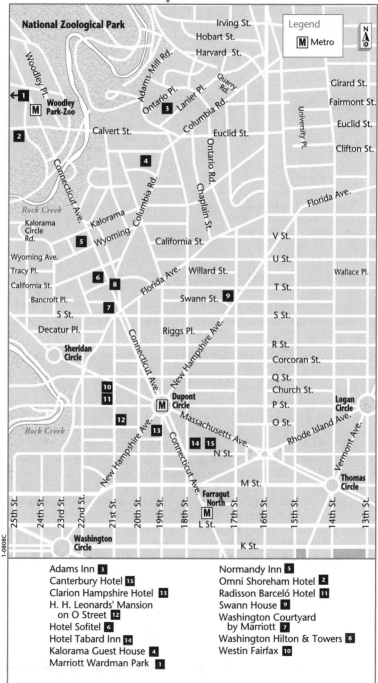

Adams Inn **3**
Canterbury Hotel **15**
Clarion Hampshire Hotel **13**
H. H. Leonards' Mansion
  on O Street **12**
Hotel Sofitel **6**
Hotel Tabard Inn **14**
Kalorama Guest House **4**
Marriott Wardman Park **1**

Normandy Inn **5**
Omni Shoreham Hotel **2**
Radisson Barceló Hotel **11**
Swann House **9**
Washington Courtyard
  by Marriott **7**
Washington Hilton & Towers **8**
Westin Fairfax **10**

MODERATE

⊙ **Normandy Inn.** 2118 Wyoming Ave. NW (at Connecticut Ave.), Washington, D.C. 20008. ☎ **800/424-3729** or 202/483-1350. Fax 202/387-8241. www. washingtonpost.com/yp/normandyinn. 75 units. A/C TV TEL. Weekdays and weekends $79–$155 double. Extra person $10. Children under 18 stay free. AE, DC, DISC, MC, V. Parking $10 plus tax. Metro: Dupont Circle.

This gracious small hotel is a gem. Situated in a neighborhood of architecturally impressive embassies, the hotel receives many embassy-bound guests (the French Embassy is the Normandy's largest customer). You may discover this for yourself on a Tuesday evening, when guests gather in the charming Tea Room to enjoy complimentary wine and cheese served from the antique oak sideboard. This is also where continental breakfast is available daily, complimentary coffee and tea throughout the day, and cookies after 3pm. In nice weather, you can move outside to umbrella tables on a garden patio. A glass and brick conservatory was added in 1998 to offer guests a casual lounge for sitting and conversing or watching TV.

The six-floor Normandy has pretty twin and queen guest rooms, all remodeled in 1998, with tapestry-upholstered mahogany and cherry-wood furnishings in 18th-century styles, pretty floral-print bedspreads, and gilt-framed botanical prints gracing the walls. Amenities include minirefrigerators; coffeemakers; remote-control cable TVs; access to the neighboring Washington Courtyard's pool and exercise room; and complimentary *Washington Post* (in lobby). The Normandy is an easy walk from both Adams-Morgan and Dupont Circle. The Irish company that owns the Normandy also owns the Washington Courtyard by Marriott (see below).

Washington Courtyard by Marriott. 1900 Connecticut Ave. NW (at Leroy Place), Washington, D.C. 20009. ☎ **800/842-4211** or 202/332-9300. Fax 202/328-7039. www. courtyard.com. 147 units. A/C TV TEL. Weekdays and weekends $89–$190 double. Extra person $15. Children under 18 stay free. AE, DC, DISC, MC, V. Parking $10. Metro: Dupont Circle.

A major renovation in 1994 has given the Courtyard a European feel and a well-heeled look. Waterford crystal chandeliers hang in the lobby and in the restaurant, and you may hear an Irish lilt from time to time (an Irish management company owns the hotel). Guests tend to linger in the comfortable lounge off the lobby, where coffee is available all day and cookies each afternoon.

Guest rooms, located off charming hallways, are equipped with cable TVs (offering HBO and Spectravision); coffeemakers; hair dryers; and phones with modem jacks. Accommodations on the 7th to 9th floors, facing the street, provide panoramic views. Especially nice are the corner "executive king" rooms, which are a little larger and are equipped with marble bathrooms, a refrigerator, terry robes, pants press, and fax machine.

In addition to an outdoor pool and sundeck, facilities include Claret's, serving American fare at breakfast and dinner. (Room service is available during restaurant hours.) Bailey's, a clubby bar, adjoins. *USA Today* is available gratis at the front desk. A small exercise room and a meeting room are on site. For a fee, guests can use the well-equipped Washington Sports Club just across the street.

INEXPENSIVE

Adams Inn. 1744 Lanier Place NW (between Calvert St. and Ontario Rd.), Washington, D.C. 20009. ☎ **800/578-6807** or 202/745-3600. Fax 202/319-7958. www.adamsinn.com. E-mail adamsinn@adamsinn.com. 25 units (14 with bathroom). A/C. $55 double without bathroom, $70–$95 double with bathroom. Rates include continental breakfast. Extra person $10. Weekly rates available. AE, CB, DC, DISC, MC, V. Limited parking $7. Metro: Woodley Park–Zoo (7 blocks away).

Close to Adams-Morgan eateries, shops, and a Safeway supermarket, the homey Adams Inn occupies three turn-of-the-century brick town houses on a residential tree-lined street. Each has a cozy Victorian parlor with decorative fireplace, lace-curtained windows, and books, games, and magazines for guests.

The well-kept accommodations are furnished with flea market and auction finds; many are covered in flowery wallpaper, and some have bay windows or handsome oak paneling. There are no phones or TVs, but you do get a clock radio. Rooms that share bathrooms have in-room sinks. The best deal for families or friends traveling together are the two rooms that connect through a bathroom on the first floor of 1746 Lanier (the two rooms easily sleep four, for as little as $115). The continental breakfast, served daily between 8 and 9:30am, includes a fruit cup, breads, doughnuts, tea, and coffee.

A coin-operated washer and dryer are in the basement, a pay phone is in the lobby, and the desk takes incoming messages. Other pluses: a TV lounge and a refrigerator and microwave oven for communal guest use. Anne Owens is your genial host.

Kalorama Guest House. 1854 Mintwood Place NW (between 19th St. and Columbia Rd.), Washington, D.C. 20009. ☎ **202/667-6369.** Fax 202/319-1262. 29 units (15 with bathroom). 5 suites. A/C. $45–$75 double with shared bathroom, $65–$105 double with bathroom; $95–$135 suite ($5 each additional occupant). Rates include continental breakfast. AE, CB, DC, DISC, MC, V. Limited parking $7. Metro: Woodley Park–Zoo or Dupont Circle.

This San Francisco–style B&B was so successful, it expanded in a short time from a six-bedroom Victorian town house (at 1854 Mintwood) to include four houses on Mintwood Place and two on Cathedral Avenue NW in Woodley Park (☎ **202/ 328-0860;** fax 202/328-8730). The Mintwood Place location is near Metro stations, dozens of restaurants, nightspots, and shops. And the Cathedral Avenue houses, even closer to the Woodley Park–Zoo Metro, offer proximity to Rock Creek Park and the National Zoo. It is the Adams-Morgan location, also, that includes a small, two-room apartment with a kitchen, cable TV, telephone, and fax machine.

Common areas and homey guest rooms are furnished with finds from antique stores, flea markets, and auctions. Students, Europeans, and conferees are usually your fellow guests.

Over at 1854 is the cheerful breakfast room with plant-filled windows. The morning meal includes bagels, croissants, and English muffins. There's a garden behind the house with umbrella tables. At each location, you have access to laundry and ironing facilities, a refrigerator, a seldom-used TV, and a phone (local calls are free) for long-distance credit- or charge-card calls (incoming calls are answered around the clock, so people can leave messages for you). It's customary for the innkeepers to put out sherry, crackers, and cheese on Friday and Saturday afternoons. Magazines, games, and current newspapers are available. Some of the houses are no-smoking.

7 Dupont Circle

VERY EXPENSIVE

Westin Fairfax. 2100 Massachusetts Ave. NW, Washington, D.C. 20008. ☎ **800/325-3589** or 202/293-2100. Fax 202/293-0641. www.luxurycollection.com. 206 units. A/C MINIBAR TV TEL. Weekdays $215–$235 double, suites $350–$2,100 for Presidential Suite; weekends $195 double, including breakfast. Children under 18 stay free. AE, CB, DC, MC, V. Valet parking $23. Metro: Dupont Circle. Small pets ok.

Inside Washington: Hotel Stories

Washington hotels have seen a lot of history (not to mention gossip-column fodder), from pre–Civil War days when the Willard maintained separate entrances for pro-Union and secessionist factions, to pre-Trump wedding (and divorce) days when Marla Maples flung a shoe (and a 7½-carat engagement ring) at Donald in the lobby of the Four Seasons.

Washington "Mayor-for-Life" Marion Barry experienced a brief power outage—in the form of a 6-month jail sentence—when he was lured to the **Vista Hotel** (now known as The Westin City Center) by former girlfriend Rasheeda Moore, arrested for smoking crack cocaine, and led off in handcuffs muttering curses.

Franklin Delano Roosevelt lived at the **Mayflower,** the grande dame of Washington hotels, between his election and inauguration, and both Lyndon Johnson and John F. Kennedy called the Mayflower home while they were young congressmen. For 20 years before his death, J. Edgar Hoover ate the same lunch at the same table in the hotel's **Grille Room** every day—chicken soup, grapefruit, and cottage cheese (one wonders what he ate for dinner to maintain his portly frame). One day he spotted Public Enemy No. 3 at an adjoining table and nabbed him!

Back at the **Willard:** Brought to the capital by her lover and manager, P. T. Barnum, the "Swedish Nightingale," Jenny Lind, received a steady stream of visitors during her stay, among them Daniel Webster and President Millard Fillmore. Ulysses S. Grant, who often partook of cigars and brandy at the Willard, coined the term lobbyists to describe the people who pestered him there seeking to influence government business. Thomas Marshall, vice president under Woodrow Wilson, also liked to smoke cigars at the Willard, but found the

---

A dispute between the proprietor and the hotel's management company in 1997 resulted in the sale of this property and a few name changes (Ritz-Carlton to Luxury Collection to the St. Regis), but the essential upscale quality you'd hope to find is still here. The hotel was built in 1927 and has served ever since as a D.C. haunt of the rich and famous. (Al Gore lived here as a kid.) In 1998, the Westin Fairfax was the host hotel for the Kennedy Center Honors Celebration, counting among its guests Gregory Peck, Katherine Hepburn, and Kathleen Turner.

A 1994 renovation gussied up its top-drawer appearance, from canopied entrance angled on Embassy Row, to the rich, walnut-paneled lobby, to pristine Oriental-carpeted hallways and lovely rooms. The latter are handsomely appointed with traditional dark-wood pieces; rich, brocade draperies; and French architectural watercolor renderings. Front-of-the-house rooms overlook Embassy Row. Some 6th- to 8th-floor rooms at the back of the house give you a glimpse of the Washington Monument and Georgetown. In-room amenities include cable TVs (with HBO) concealed in armoires; safes; three phones; and terry robes. Gorgeous marble bathrooms are equipped with hair dryers and upscale toiletries (some also have small black-and-white TVs). The seventh floor of the eight-story hotel is the Club level, with its own lounge, and is where a concierge attends you.

Dining/Diversions: The Jockey Club is one of Washington's most prominent restaurants (see chapter 6 for a review). The elegant Fairfax Club, with a working fireplace, is an intimate setting for cocktails, light fare, and piano music. The back room of the bar is an exclusive club and disco for certain wealthy Washingtonians.

prices scandalous, commenting, "What this country needs is a good 5-cent cigar."

During JFK's inaugural festivities, Frank Sinatra and his Rat Pack cronies took over a dozen rooms on the 10th floor of the **Capital Hilton** so they could visit each other without being bothered by autograph-seekers in the halls.

Speaking of JFK, he courted Jackie over drinks in the **Blue Room** at the **Shoreham,** a famous nightclub where Rudy Vallee, Lena Horne, Bob Hope, Maurice Chevalier, Judy Garland, and Frank Sinatra performed; today the room is a meeting facility. In its heyday, the Shoreham entertained the rich and the royal. Prominent socialites such as Perle Mesta and Alice Roosevelt Longworth threw private parties here, and Truman held poker games in Room D-106 while his limousine waited outside. But the hotel's most ostentatious guest was Saudi Arabian King Ibn-Saud who, traveling with a full complement of armed guards and 32 limos, dispensed solid gold watches as tips.

Suite 205 at the **Jefferson** served as backdrop for the year-long dalliance between President Bill Clinton's chief political strategist, Dick Morris, and call girl Sherry Rowlands. The scandal broke in August 1996, when Rowlands reported to the *Star* that Morris sometimes allowed her to listen to telephone conversations he was having with the president as well as read speeches that were to be delivered at the 1996 Democratic National Convention.

More recently, the **Ritz-Carlton, Pentagon City** (across the Potomac), took a turn in the spotlight when newspapers revealed the hotel to be the place where special prosecutor Ken Starr confronted Monica Lewinsky about her alleged affair with President Clinton. If you're interested in visting this hotel, it's located at 1250 S. Hayes St., Arlington, ☎ **703/415-5000.** Metro: Pentagon City.

The Terrace Court Salon is the setting for daily continental breakfast and afternoon tea ($16 for traditional, $23 with champagne).

Amenities: Complimentary morning newspaper delivery and shoe shine, nightly turndown with imported chocolates, 24-hour concierge and room service, in-room massage; twice daily maid service, express checkout, dry cleaning and laundry service. Fitness room with Stairmasters, Life cycles, treadmills, sauna, massage, and separate locker areas, meeting rooms and services.

EXPENSIVE

Canterbury Hotel. 1733 N St. NW, Washington, D.C. 20036. ☎ **800/424-2950** or 202/393-3000. Fax 202/785-9581. 99 units. A/C MINIBAR TV TEL. Weekdays $160–$400 suite for 2 (most are under $200), weekends and off-season weekdays $119–$140. Rates include continental breakfast served in restaurant. Extra person $35. Children under 12 stay free. AE, CB, DC, DISC, MC, V. Parking $15. Metro: Dupont Circle.

Located on a lovely residential street, this small, European-style hostelry is close to many tourist attractions. Enter the hotel via a graciously appointed lobby hung with British prints that conjure up shades of Jane Austen. Classical music is played in public areas.

Each room is actually a junior suite and differently appointed, although all have a sofa/sitting area, dressing room, and kitchenette or full kitchen. Attractively decorated, these spacious accommodations sport 18th-century mahogany English-reproduction furnishings (a few have four-poster beds). Among the amenities: cable

TVs with CNN and pay-movie stations; iron and ironing board; coffeemakers; electronic locks; and multifeature phones with voice mail. Bathrooms are supplied with cosmetic mirrors; hair dryers; phones; and baskets of fine toiletries.

Dining/Diversions: The hotel's wonderful new restaurant, Brighton (see chapter 6 for details), serves American-regional fare at all meals. And the Tudor-beamed Union Jack Pub, complete with dartboard and a menu featuring fish-and-chips, is the perfect place to relax after a busy day on the town. English beers on tap are served in pint mugs.

Amenities: Nightly turndown with fine chocolate, room service during restaurant hours, morning delivery of the *Washington Post,* complimentary *Wall Street Journal* available in lobby and restaurant, express checkout, secretarial services, meeting space for up to 75 people. Guests enjoy free use of the nearby YMCA/National Capital Health Center's extensive workout facilities, including an indoor lap pool.

Radisson Barceló Hotel. 2121 P St. NW, Washington, D.C. 20037. ☎ **800/333-3333** or 202/293-3100. Fax 202/857-0134. www.radisson.com. 301 units. A/C TV TEL. Weekdays $155–$180 double, weekends $99–$139 double; suites $250–$500 weekdays in season, $150–300 weekends and off-season. Extra person $20. Children under 18 stay free. AE, CB, DC, DISC, MC, V. Parking $14. Metro: Dupont Circle.

The first American venture for a Mallorca-based firm, the 10-story Barceló offers friendly European-style service, an unbeatable location midway between Dupont Circle and Georgetown, and a superb restaurant. The Barceló's art deco–style, marble-floored lobby is inviting, and its accommodations (formerly apartments) are enormous (the hotel claims these are the largest sleeping rooms in Washington). All offer workspaces with desks and living room areas containing sofas and armchairs. In-room amenities include cable TVs with HBO and more than 200 pay-movie options; three phones with voice-mail and modem jacks; marble bathrooms with hair dryers and shaving mirrors; irons and ironing boards; coffee and coffeemakers. *Note:* Weekend "bed-and-breakfast" packages on Friday and Saturday nights in summer can go as low as $89 for a double.

Dining/Diversions: Gabriel features first-rate Latin American/Mediterranean cuisine (see chapter 6 for a review); its simpatico bar/lounge (featuring tapas and sherry) is popular with sophisticated Washingtonians.

Amenities: Concierge, room service (6:30am to 11pm), complimentary *Washington Post* in the morning at the front desk, nightly turndown, faxing and other secretarial services, express checkout, rooftop sundeck, swimming pool in the courtyard, sauna, small fitness room, bike rentals, gift shop.

MODERATE

Clarion Hampshire Hotel. 1310 New Hampshire Ave. NW (at N St.), Washington, D.C. 20036. ☎ **800/368-5691** or 202/296-7600. Fax 202/293-2476. 82 units. A/C MINIBAR TV TEL. Weekdays $109–$159 suite for 2, weekends and off-season weekdays $79–$109 per suite. Extra person $20. Children under 12 stay free. AE, CB, DC, DISC, JCB, MC, V. Parking $12. Metro: Dupont Circle.

The Hampshire is within easy walking distance of Georgetown and 2 blocks from Dupont Circle, convenient to numerous restaurants, nightspots, and offices. The hotel serves mostly an association, corporate, and government clientele, so you should inquire about low summer rates.

Spacious, junior-suite accommodations are furnished with 18th-century reproductions and offer lots of closet space; big dressing rooms; couches; coffee tables; and desks. Fifty of the 82 rooms have kitchenettes, which come with microwaves and coffeemakers; some have cooking ranges. Balconies at the front of the hotel offer city views. Amenities include a hair dryer; chocolates on arrival; multifeature, data port–equipped phones; cable TVs; and morning delivery of the *Washington Post.* Guests also receive free passes to a large health club with indoor pool, 10 minutes away.

The hotel's Peacock Bistro, with an outdoor cafe, a fresh juice bar, and a coffee bar, serves fresh salads, pastas, grilled meats, and sandwiches. Room service is available during restaurant hours.

✪ **H. H. Leonards' Mansion on O Street.** 2020 O St. NW, Washington, D.C. 20036. ☎ **202/496-2000.** Fax 202/659-0547. E-mail: mansion@erols.com. 6 suites and a 5-bedroom guest house. A/C TV TEL. $150–$1,000. Government and nonprofit rates available. Except for the guest house, rates include breakfast, whatever you want. MC, V. Parking $15 and $6 (for garage a block away). Metro: Dupont Circle. Small pets ok.

A legend in her own time, H. H. Leonards operates this Victorian property, made up of three five-story town houses, as an event space, an art gallery, an antiques emporium, and—oh, yeah—a B&B. If you stay here, you may find yourself buying a sweater, a painting, or (who knows?) an antique bed. Everything's for sale. Guest rooms are so creative they'll blow you away; most breathtaking is a log cabin loft suite, with a bed whose headboard encases an aquarium. The art deco–style penthouse takes up an entire floor and has its own elevator, 10 phones, and seven televisions. The International Room has a nonworking fireplace and three TVs (one in the bathroom). All rooms have king-size beds, computer-activated telephones that can hook you up to the Internet, at least one television, and out-of-this-world decor; most have a whirlpool, and some have kitchens. Elsewhere on the property are an outdoor pool; eight office/conference spaces; 21 far-out bathrooms; art and antiques everywhere; an exercise room; and thousands and thousands of books. Full business services are available, including multiline phones; fax machines; IBM and Mac computers; and satellite feeds. The Light House (guest house) has a separate entrance and five bedrooms, all white walls with light streaming in from windows and skylights; rates include maid service.

Hotel Tabard Inn. 1739 N St. NW, Washington, D.C. 20036. ☎ **202/785-1277.** Fax 202/785-6173. 40 units (13 with shared bathroom). A/C TEL. Weekdays and weekends $90–$110 with shared bathroom, $114–$165 with private bathroom. Extra person $15. $10 for crib. Inquire about reduced summer rates. All rates include continental breakfast. AE, DC, MC, V. Street parking, $14 valet parking, $10 self-parking. Metro: Dupont Circle.

In 1914, three Victorian town houses were joined to form the Tabard Inn, named for the famous hostelry in Chaucer's Canterbury Tales. The inn's owners live on the West Coast, but their son manages the Tabard, with the help of a chummy, peace-love-and-understanding sort of staff who clearly love the inn.

At the heart of the ground floor is the dark, paneled lounge, with a wood-burning fireplace and original beamed ceiling and bookcases. This is a favorite place for Washingtonians to come for a drink, especially in winter, or to linger before or after dining in the charming Tabard Inn restaurant (see chapter 6 for a review).

From the lounge, the inn leads you through nooks and crannies to guest rooms: Can you dig chartreuse? How about aubergine? Rooms are painted in these unconventional colors and decorated in similar style. Each is different, though N Street–facing rooms are largest and brightest, and some have bay windows. Furnishings are a mix of antiques and flea-market finds. Perhaps the most eccentric room is the top floor "penthouse," which has skylights; exposed brick walls; its own kitchen; and a deck accessed by climbing out a window.

✪ **Swann House.** 1808 New Hampshire Ave. NW, Washington, D.C. 20009. ☎ **202/265-7677.** Fax 202/265-6755. www.bestinns.com. E-mail: swannhousse@aol.com. 11 units. A/C TV TEL. $110–$235 depending on unit and season. Extended stay and government rates available. Extra person $20. Rates include expanded continental breakfast. Limited off-street parking. No pets. MC, V. Metro: Dupont Circle.

This stunning 1883 mansion angled prominently on a corner 4 blocks north of Dupont Circle has nine exquisite guest rooms, two with private entrances. The coolest is the Blue Sky Suite, which has the original rose-tiled (working) fireplace, a queen-size bed and sofa bed, a gabled ceiling, and its own roof deck. The most romantic room is probably the Il Duomo, with Gothic windows; cathedral ceiling; working fireplace; and a turreted bathroom with angel murals. The Jennifer Green Room has a queen-size bed; another working fireplace; an oversized marble steam shower; and a private deck overlooking the pool area and garden. The Regent Room has a king-size bed in front of a carved working fireplace, a whirlpool, double shower, outdoor hot tub, TV, VCR, and stereo. The beautiful window treatments and bed coverings are the handiwork of innkeeper Mary Ross. You'll want to spend some time on the main floor of the mansion, which has 12-foot ceilings; fluted woodwork; inlaid wood floors; a turreted living room; columned sitting room; and a sunroom (where breakfast is served) leading through three sets of French doors to the garden and pool. Laundry facilities, meeting space, and business services are available.

8 Foggy Bottom/West End

VERY EXPENSIVE

ANA Hotel. 2401 M St. NW, Washington, D.C. 20037. ☎ **800/ANA-HOTELS** or 202/429-2400. Fax 202/457-5010. 415 units. A/C MINIBAR TV TEL. Weekdays $280 double, weekends $139 double; suite $700–$1,700. Extra person $30. Children under 18 stay free. AE, CB, DC, DISC, JCB, MC, V. Valet parking $19. Metro: Foggy Bottom.

The ANA is famous for its newly remodeled 17,500-square-foot West End Executive Fitness Center, which includes a pool and spa facilities, squash and racquetball courts, and every kind of exercise equipment. When in town, this is where Arnold Schwarzenegger stays, and where other visiting celebrities come to work out, even if they don't stay here. Guests pay $10 a day to use exercise equipment or to take aerobics classes but may use the pool, sauna, steam room, and whirlpool for free.

The ANA's lobby and public areas are especially pretty, thanks to the central interior garden courtyard. The 146 guest rooms that overlook this courtyard are probably the best. An $8 million renovation in late 1998 spruced up all the guest rooms and the lobby. Amenities in guest rooms include large writing desks, terry robes, iron and ironing board, three phones (one in the bathroom) with voice mail, safes, remote-controlled TVs, and Caswell Massey toiletries. The ninth floor is a secured executive club level, popular with many of the business travelers who stay here.

Dining/Diversions: *Washingtonian* magazine's readers' poll named ANA's Sunday brunch the best in Washington; it's served in the lovely Colonnade, which is also a popular site for wedding receptions. The Bistro serves American cuisine with a Mediterranean flair; for Japanese guests (the Japanese-owned hotel is named for its owners, All Nippon Airways, and draws a fair number of travelers from Japan), the Bistro offers an authentic Japanese breakfast daily. Cocktails, coffee, and pastries are available in the Lobby Lounge.

Amenities: 24-hour room service, concierge, dry cleaning and laundry service, nightly turndown, twice daily maid service, express checkout, valet parking, complimentary shoe shine, fitness center, business center, 5,500-square-foot ballroom, 186 fixed-seat auditorium, more than 29,000 square feet of meeting space.

✪ **Park Hyatt.** 1201 24th St. NW, Washington, D.C. 20037. ☎ **800/922-PARK** or 202/789-1234. Fax 202/457-8823. www.hyatt.com. 223 units. A/C MINIBAR TV TEL. Weekdays $255–$320 double, $295–$360 suite; weekends $179–$199 double, $202–$224 suite. Extra person $25. Children under 17 free. Family plan offered, based on availability: 2nd rm for children under 17 is half price. AE, CB, DC, DISC, JCB, MC, V. Valet parking $20 weekdays, $8 weekends. Metro: Foggy Bottom or Dupont Circle. Pets ok.

At this luxury hotel, museum-quality modern art hangs on the walls of the handsome public areas (including a David Hockney lithograph) and the framed reproductions in guest rooms are of works hanging in the National Gallery and other museums in town. Each room has an iron and ironing board, and each bathroom has a TV and radio, telephone, hair dryer, and makeup mirror. You won't see maid carts in the hallways because housekeeping staff use handheld baskets. The 11-year-old, 10-story hotel prides itself on going the extra mile to please a customer, even if it means taking out a wall to enlarge a suite, as the Park Hyatt did for Lily Tomlin, right after the hotel opened. Guests include big names, royal families (who use the Presidential Suite, with its fireplace and grand piano), lobbyists, and tour bus travelers. Executive suites have separate living and dining areas, fax machines, and a second TV. Rooms are handsome and service is superb.

Dining/Diversions: Melrose's bright and lovely dining room offers four-star cuisine with an emphasis on seafood (see chapter 6 for a review); look for the amiable chef, Brian McBride, who's been known to pop into the dining room from time to time to make sure all is well. From Thursday through Sunday in the lounge, afternoon tea is served (traditional $15.95, with champagne cocktail $19), including finger sandwiches, scones, Devon cream, and pastries, plus the services of a palmist ($10 extra). Adjoining Melrose is a bar; outdoors is a smashingly beautiful cafe.

Amenities: 24-hour concierge, room service, business center, valet/laundry service, foreign currency exchange, shoe shine, twice-daily maid service, delivery of *Washington Post* weekdays, nightly turndown, express checkout, gift shop. Hair and skin salon, health club including indoor pool, heated whirlpool, sauna and steam rooms, and extensive exercise room.

✪ **The Watergate Hotel.** 2650 Virginia Ave. NW, Washington, D.C. 20037. ☎ **800/424-2736** or 202/965-2300. Fax 202/337-7915. 231 units. A/C MINIBAR TV TEL. Weekdays $230–$320 double, weekends $155 double; suites from $420 double, with greatly reduced weekend rates. Extra person $25. Children under 17 stay free. AE, CB, DC, DISC, JCB, MC, V. Parking $20 (valet only). Metro: Foggy Bottom. Pets ok.

Don't confuse the immense Watergate condo and office complex—site of the notorious 1972 break-in that brought down the Nixon administration—with the elegantly intimate hotel housed within the complex. This was the hotel of choice for many stars attending 1997 inaugural bashes, including Jimmy Smits, Gloria Estefan, and Stevie Wonder, who gave an impromptu performance in the hotel's sumptuous lobby after one of the balls. Year-round, the Watergate's clientele includes high-level diplomats, business travelers, and Kennedy Center performers (the Kennedy Center is adjacent). Its spa facilities, indoor lap pool and sundeck, state-of-the-art health club, entertainment options, and dozens of adjacent shops are popular with sophisticated travelers, including couples in search of a romantic weekend.

Rooms and suites are spacious—suites are said to be the largest in the city. River-facing rooms give splendid views of the Potomac, and of these, all but the 8th- and 14th-floor rooms have balconies. All rooms have writing desks and fax machines, and most have wet bars; most executive suites have kitchenettes. TVs offer Show-time movies and more than 50 cable stations. In your bathroom you'll find Gilchrist & Soames toiletries; a cosmetic mirror; hair dryer; phone; and terry robes.

Dining/Diversions: Chef Robert Wiedemaier (who ran the Four Seasons's premier restaurant for 7 years) presides over Aquarelle, winning accolades for his Euro-American cuisine. The elegant Potomac Lounge serves British-style afternoon teas Tues–Sun and features special early evening events, such as caviar tastings, sushi/Japanese beer nights, and salmon nights, while a pianist plays on.

Amenities: 24-hour room service and concierge, full business services, nightly turndown, complimentary shoe shine, daily newspaper of your choice, complimentary weekday morning limo to downtown, complimentary coffee in Potomac Lounge. Jacuzzi, steam, sauna, massage and spa treatments; barber/beauty salon (Zahira's, the stylist to three presidents), 10 meeting rooms, gift shop, ballroom overlooking the Potomac, and, in the adjacent complex, dozens of shops including jewelers, designer boutiques, a supermarket, drugstore, and post office.

EXPENSIVE

St. James Suites. 950 24th St. NW (off of Washington Circle), Washington, D.C. 20037. ☎ **800/852-8512** or 202/457-0500. Fax 202/466-6484. www.stjamesuiteswdc.com. 195 units. A/C MINIBAR TV TEL. Weekdays $165–$185, weekends $89–$129. Rates include breakfast. Extra person $20. Children under 17 stay free. AE, DC, DISC, MC, V. Parking $17. Metro: Foggy Bottom.

The St. James is a home away from home for many of its guests, about one-third of whom book these luxury suites for more than 30 days at a time. The suites are all one-bedrooms, with separate living and sleeping areas, marble bathrooms, two-line telephones with modem capability, and kitchens equipped with everything from china and flatware to cooking utensils. Each living room includes a queen-size pullout sofa. Unlike other hotels in this residential neighborhood of old town houses, the St. James is fairly new (only 11 years old), which means accessibility was a factor in its design: A ramp in the lobby leads to the reception area, and 10 suites are available for travelers with disabilities. The St. James is near Georgetown, George Washington University, and the Kennedy Center. Corporate club members receive extra perks, such as evening cocktails and hors d'oeuvres served in the club's pleasant second-floor quarters.

Amenities: Room service (11am to 11pm), dry cleaning, laundry service, *Washington Post, New York Times, Wall Street Journal, USA Today* available in breakfast room or delivered to room on request, nightly turndown on request, baby-sitting, business services including faxing and courier service, daily shoe shine, full kitchens, outdoor pool, 24-hour, state-of-the-art fitness center, nearby tennis courts and jogging/biking paths, conference rooms.

MODERATE

The George Washington University Inn. 824 New Hampshire Ave. NW, Washington, D.C. 20037. ☎ **800/426-4455** or 202/337-6620. Fax 202/298-7499. 94 units. A/C TV TEL. Weekdays $120–$155 double, $130–$175 efficiency, $145–$195 one-bedroom suite; weekends $99–$135 double, $110–$155 efficiency, $125–$170 one-bedroom suite. Children under 18 stay free. AE, DC, MC, V. Limited parking $14. Metro: Foggy Bottom.

This eight-story, whitewashed brick inn, another former apartment building, became a hotel in 1968 and, rumor has it, was a favorite spot for clandestine trysts for high-society types. These days you're more likely to see Kennedy Center performers and visiting professors. The university purchased the hotel (formerly known as "The Inn at Foggy Bottom") in 1994 and renovated it.

Rooms are a little larger and corridors a tad narrower than those in a typical hotel, and each room includes a dressing chamber. One-bedroom suites are especially spacious, with living rooms that hold a sleeper sofa and a TV hidden in an armoire (there's another in the bedroom). Guest rooms are equipped with a minirefrigerator, a microwave oven, and a coffeemaker; efficiencies and suites have kitchens. The roominess and the kitchen facilities make this a popular choice for families and for long-term guests, and if it's not full, the inn may be willing to offer reduced rates. Mention prices quoted in the inn's *New York Times* ad, if you've seen it, or your affiliation with George Washington University, if you can. This is a fairly safe and lovely neighborhood, within easy walking distance to Georgetown, the Kennedy Center, and downtown. But keep an eye peeled—you must pass through wrought-iron gates into a kind of cul-de-sac to find the inn. Off the lobby is the well-received restaurant Zuki Moon, a Japanese "noodle house" designed to reflect a tea garden. The menu offers low-fat, healthy, and inexpensive dishes, mostly Japanese, but some American. Amenities include complimentary newspaper delivered daily, 24-hour message service, and same-day laundry/valet service. There's a coin-operated laundry on the premises, five rooms designed for guests with disabilities, and meeting room for 50.

✪ **Hotel Lombardy.** 2019 Pennsylvania Ave. NW, Washington, D.C. 20006. ☎ **800/424-5486** or 202/828-2600. Fax 202/872-0503. 125 units. A/C MINIBAR TV TEL. Weekdays $140–$180 double, $160–$180 suite for 2; weekends (and sometimes off-season weekdays) $69–$99 double, $119–$140 suite for 2. Extra person $20. Children under 16 stay free in parents' room. AE, CB, DC, DISC, MC, V. Self-parking $17. Metro: Farragut West or Foggy Bottom.

From its handsome walnut-paneled lobby with carved Tudor-style ceilings to its old-fashioned nonautomatic elevator (the hotel is not well suited for travelers with disabilities), the 11-story Lombardy offers a lot of character and comfort for the price and the location (about 5 blocks west of the White House). George Washington University's campus is just across Pennsylvania Avenue, which means this part of town remains vibrant at night, when other downtown neighborhoods have shut down. Peace Corps, World Bank, and corporate guests make up a large part of the clientele, but other visitors will also appreciate the Lombardy's warmly welcoming ambience and the attentive service of the multilingual staff.

Spacious rooms, entered via pedimented louver doors, have undergone a recent redecoration , and each one is slightly different, although all share a 1930s northern Italian motif. Large desks, precious dressing rooms, and roomy walk-in closets are other assets.

Moderately priced and open for all meals, the Café Lombardy, a sunny, glass-enclosed restaurant, serves authentic northern Italian fare. You can also dine in the newly opened Venetian Room, an exquisitely decorated haven with velvet upholstery, antique lanterns, mother-of-pearl-inlaid Moorish cocktail tables, and a custom-made cherry-wood bar. The Venetian Room shares a menu with the cafe, or you may choose from a special menu of appetizers. Amenities include a free overnight shoe shine; fully equipped kitchens and dining nooks in all but 20 rooms; Spectravision pay-per-view movie channel; access to health club 1 block away ($5 per visit); and two small meeting rooms.

One Washington Circle Hotel. 1 Washington Circle NW, Washington, D.C. 20037. ☎ **800/424-9671** or 202/872-1680. Fax 202/887-4989. www.onewashcirclehotel.com. 151 suites. A/C TV TEL. Weekdays $135–$165 for smallest suite, $170–$285 for largest suite; weekends $59–$99 for smallest suite, $109–$149 for largest. Extra person $15. Guests paying rates of $135 or higher receive free continental breakfast weekdays and cocktails/

hors d'oeuvres Mon–Thurs. Children under 18 stay free. AE, CB, DC, MC, V. Underground valet parking $8–$15. Metro: Foggy Bottom.

Built in 1960, this building was converted into a hotel in 1976, making it the city's first all-suite hotel property. Five types of suites are available, ranging in size from 390 to 710 square feet. Every suite has a comfortable decor that includes a sofa bed and dining area, kitchens, and walk-out balconies, some overlooking the circle with George Washington's statue. But keep in mind that across the circle is George Washington University Hospital's emergency room entrance, which is busy with ambulance traffic; although the hotel is well insulated, you may want to ask for a suite on the L Street side. President Nixon liked to stay here on his visits to Washington after Watergate; he preferred Suite 615. Clientele is mostly corporate, but families like the outdoor pool; in-house restaurant; prime location near George-town and the Metro; free shuttle to the Kennedy center; and the kitchens. Ask about bargain room rates available to groups, AAA members, and senior citizens, or through a special value ad for the hotel in the *New York Times*. The well-reviewed West End Cafe serves contemporary American cuisine in a garden room/greenhouse setting. Locals frequently dine here, but guests sometimes benefit from special rates. A pianist plays jazz Tuesday through Saturday nights.

State Plaza Hotel. 2117 E St. NW, Washington, D.C. 20037. ☎ **800/424-2859** or 202/861-8200. Fax 202/659-8601. 221 units. A/C MINIBAR TV TEL. Weekdays $125–$150 efficiency suite for 1 or 2 people, $175–$225 for a large one-bedroom suite (with dining rm) for up to 2 people; weekend (and off-season weeknights, subject to availability) $69–$109. Extra person $20. Children under 16 stay free. AE, DC, DISC, MC, V. Parking $12. Metro: Foggy Bottom.

This eight-floor, all-suite hotel is actually two buildings, known as the North Tower and the South Tower, connected through the garage. They are identical. South Tower suites overlook the Mall, the Washington Monument, and other sights, the higher up you go; the North Tower overlooks downtown Washington and holds the dining room, where three meals are served daily and free hors d'oeuvres are available each evening during happy hour.

Many guests are affiliated with the nearby State Department, World Bank, or George Washington University; if you are, too, inquire about special rates. Suites are pleasant, clean, and fairly spacious; ask for a plaza suite if you want the largest. Each suite has cable TV; iron and ironing board; hair dryer; and full kitchen, including a microwave. On-premises facilities offer nine suites for guests with disabilities; a small fitness center; three conference rooms; the Garden Cafe; self-service laundry; and a sundeck. Among the amenities are room service during restaurant hours; complimentary shoe shine; free local phone calls and no-fee long-distance access; and weekday delivery of the *Washington Post*.

INEXPENSIVE

The Premier Hotel. 2601 Virginia Ave. NW (at New Hampshire Ave.), Washington, D.C. 20037. ☎ **800/965-6869** or 202/965-2700. Fax 202/337-5417. www.premierdc.com. E-mail dcpremier@aol.com. 192 units. A/C TV TEL. Weekdays and weekends $89–$139 double, concierge floor $30 additional. Extra person $10. Children under 18 stay free. AE, DC, DISC, JCB, MC, V. Parking $9 (maximum height 6'2"). Metro: Foggy Bottom.

A short walk from the Kennedy Center, with an entrance through a nicely land-scaped porte cochere, this former Howard Johnson's property has an upscale look following a $3.5 million renovation . It now offers many assets unusual in its price range, including a concierge and a business center. Pluses include a large L-shaped rooftop pool with a sundeck and adjoining Ping-Pong area; a 24-hour workout room; secured underground parking; coin-operated washers and dryers; sightseeing bus tours; and a gift shop. Rooms, attractively decorated in rich earth tones (half with balconies overlooking the Potomac), offer refrigerators, coffeemakers, safes, and cable TVs with HBO, pay-movie options, and Nintendo. Rooms on the executive floor (the seventh) are larger and have either a sofa bed or chair with ottoman. Room 723 on this floor is dubbed the "Watergate Room," commemorating its use by a lookout for the Watergate burglars, who on June 17, 1972, were across the street breaking in to the Democratic National Committee Headquarters, in the Watergate Hotel. You may stay in this room ($250 per night), which is decorated with memorabilia from the Watergate time.

Local calls are free. America's Best, a contemporary diner with an exhibition kitchen, serves all meals and provides room service during breakfast hours only, 6 to 9:30am.

9 Woodley Park

EXPENSIVE

Marriott Wardman Park. 2660 Woodley Rd. NW (at Connecticut Ave. NW), Washington, D.C. 20008. ☎ **800/325-3535** or 202/328-2000. Fax 202/234-0015. www.marriott.com. 1,338 units. A/C TV TEL. Weekdays $189–$235 double; weekends $89–$149 double; suites $350–$1,200. Extra person $30. Children under 17 stay free. AE, CB, DC, DISC, MC, V. Valet parking $17, self-parking $14. Metro: Woodley Park–Zoo. Pets ok.

This is Washington's biggest hotel, resting on 16 acres just down the street from the National Zoo and several excellent restaurants. Its size and location (the Woodley Park–Zoo Metro station is literally at its doorstep) makes it a good choice for large and small conventions, tour groups, and individual travelers. Built in 1918, the property is also one of Washington's oldest hotels. If its name doesn't sound familiar, it's because in 1998 Marriott took over management of the hotel, which was formerly known as the Sheraton Washington. The owners are embarking on a $40 million renovation of the ballroom, meeting rooms, and other areas, split over the course of the summers of 1998 and 1999. With the loss of the usual convention/ business clientele because of the construction, the hotel is offering cheap rates for leisure travelers; inquire about these if you're planning a trip to Washington in the summer of '99.

The hotel feels like a college campus: There's an old part, whose entrance is overhung with stately trees, and a new part, whose entrance is preceded by a great green lawn. The hotel has its own post office; barbershop; florist; jewelry store; two outdoor pools (one of which may be closed for restructuring in 1999); two restaurants; a lobby bar; and a deli.

The oldest part of the Wardman Park is the nicest. The 80-year-old, redbrick Wardman Tower houses 201 guest rooms, each featuring high ceilings, ornate crown moldings, and an assortment of antique French and English furnishings. This was once an apartment building whose residents ranged from presidents Hoover, Eisenhower, and Johnson, to actor Douglas Fairbanks, Jr., and author Gore Vidal. Wardman Tower rooms, which include 54 suites, offer a few more amenities, such as minibars and terry robes, than the hotel's other, more conventional guest rooms. All rooms have room service (6am to 1am); voice mail and data ports; hair dryers; complimentary Starbucks coffee and tea service; and irons and ironing boards. The 10th floor of the Wardman Tower is the club level.

Dining/Diversions: Americus serves dinner (American cuisine); the Courtyard Cafe serves breakfast and lunch; L'Expresso is a gourmet deli and pastry shop; and the Lobby Bar is open for drinks daily.

Amenities: Multilingual concierge, laundry and valet, morning delivery of *USA Today*, express check in and check out, gift shop, 95,000 square feet of exhibit space and 78,000 square feet of meeting space, full business center, outdoor heated pool with sundeck, fitness room, nearby jogging and bike paths, 61 rooms equipped for guests with disabilities.

Omni Shoreham. 2500 Calvert St. NW (at Connecticut Ave.), Washington, D.C. 20008. ☎ **800/843-6664** or 202/234-0700. Fax 202/265-7972. www.omnihotels.com. 860 units. A/C TV TEL. Weekdays and weekends $109–$299 double, depending on availability. Extra person $22. Children under 18 stay free. AE, CB, DC, DISC, JCB, MC, V. Parking $14. Metro: Woodley Park–Zoo.

A massive, $74-million renovation of all guest rooms and the lobby is underway at the Omni and is scheduled for completion by May 1999. The spacious guest rooms will remain twice the size of normal hotel rooms, but their new decor will restore a traditional, elegant look through the use of chintz fabrics, mahogany furnishings, and porcelain fixtures. A new air-conditioning system is being installed throughout the hotel, the pools are being torn out and restructured, and the already excellent health club is being refitted to include extras like a steam room and whirlpool.

In the meantime, the hotel continues to operate as, primarily, a meeting and convention venue, whose business travelers will appreciate the new two-line telephones with voice mail and the ability to program one's own wake-up-call. Leisure travelers should consider the Shoreham for its recreational facilities, such as the large swimming pool with children's pool, and its proximity to the National Zoo and excellent restaurants. Its 11-acre location on Rock Creek Park is a special asset, because of the spectacular views it affords and its immediate access to bike and jogging paths. Built in 1930, the Shoreham has been the scene of inaugural balls for every president since FDR. Do you believe in ghosts? Ask about Room 800G, the haunted suite (available for $2,500 a night).

Dining/Diversions: The elegant Monique Café et Brasserie, reminiscent of the famed La Coupole in Paris, specializes in continental/American fare with an emphasis on steak and seafood. Rock Creek Park provides a fitting backdrop for the lushly planted cocktail lounge, which is housed under a 35-foot vaulted ceiling.

Amenities: Room service (6am to 2am), concierge, dry cleaning and laundry service, express checkout, shops, travel/sightseeing desk, business center and conference rooms; 10 miles of jogging, hiking, and bicycle trails, health and fitness center; 1½-mile Perrier parcourse with 18 exercise stations.

INEXPENSIVE

Kalorama Guest House. 2700 Cathedral Ave. NW (entrance on 27th St.), Washington, D.C. 20008. ☎ **202/667-6369.** Fax 202/319-1262. 19 units, 12 with bathrooms. A/C. $45–$75 double with shared bathroom, $65–$105 double with private bathroom. Rates include continental breakfast. AE, CB, DC, DISC, MC, V. Limited parking $7. Metro: Woodley Park–Zoo.

This is the Woodley Park location of the bed-and-breakfast based in Adams-Morgan—see listing under "Adams-Morgan/North Dupont Circle," above, for more information.

Where to Dine in Washington, D.C.

6

To say that the Washington dining scene is diverse is to state the obvious. Take a look at the list of restaurants by cuisine in the second section of this chapter and you'll see what I mean: from first entry "America" to last entry "Miss Saigon," the capital's restaurants represent a world of tastes. Not quite so obvious, perhaps, is the degree of sophistication you'll find here. For example, not only does Washington have many wonderful Italian restaurants, but the city is also home to many that specialize in the cuisine of a particular region or city, like **Galileo** (Piedmontese), **Villa Franco** (the Amalfi Coast), or **I Ricchi** (Tuscan). Washington has not only superb French restaurants, but also superb inexpensive (**La Fourchette**) and expensive (**Lespinasse**); bistro (**Bistrot Lepic**) and haute cuisine (**Citronelle**); Alsatian (**L'Auberge Provençale**); Provençal (**Provence**); and Parisian (**Vintage**) restaurants. Both red meat and fresh fish emporiums proliferate. If you want a kosher meal, head to **Felix's** on Friday evenings for kosher brisket. If you're into organic, consider **Nora** or the **Tabard Inn.**

Washingtonians are appreciative of the high quality and range of cuisines available in the area, and they eat out often. Surveys show that Washington restaurants take in billions of dollars yearly, rating fourth in a lineup behind Chicago, Los Angeles, and New York. Impressed by this ranking and Washington appetites, restaurateurs and chefs worldwide more and more are drawn to Washington. One result can be seen in the number of chain restaurants that have recently opened here, many of them excellent seafood eateries, like McCormick & Schmick's, originally of Portland, Oregon, and Grillfish, of Miami. Another indication of the thriving dining scene is the spawning of new restaurants by local chefs/proprietors whose first restaurants have succeeded here. Thus, we have Roberto Donna, with his dynasty of 12 Italian dining options, from the affordably delicious Il Radicchio to the sublime Galileo; Yannick Cam, whose French Provence now has a Spanish cousin, El Catalan; and Jeff Buben, chef and owner of the regional Southern Vidalia, who opened the French bis in the Hotel George in May 1998 (to name just a few).

Read over the reviews that follow to see what appeals. A few tips: It's always wise to book a reservation; few places are so formal as to require men to wear jacket and tie, but those that do are so noted; if you're driving, check whether the listing indicates valet parking, complimentary or otherwise—on Washington's crowded streets, this service can prove a true bonus; if your desired restaurant is booked, consider eating at the bar, sometimes a fun alternative, and often the same menu is available.

ABOUT THE PRICES

I've tried to present you with a range of menus and prices, in most every Washington neighborhood. The restaurants listed are grouped first by location, then listed alphabetically by price category. I've used the following price categories: **Very Expensive,** the average main course at dinner is more than $20; **Expensive,** $16 to $20; **Moderate,** $10 to $15; and **Inexpensive,** $10 and under.

Keep in mind that the above categories refer to dinner prices, but some very expensive restaurants offer affordable lunches, early-bird dinners, tapas, or bar meals. Starred entries indicate personal favorites.

Note: A Metro station is indicated when it's within walking distance of a restaurant. If you need bus-routing information, call ☎ **202/637-7000.**

1 Best Bets

- **Best Spot for a Romantic Dinner:** Just ask for the "snug" (tables 39 and 40) at **The Restaurant at the Jefferson,** 1200 16th St. NW, at M Street (☎ **202/ 347-2200**). Two cozy seating areas in alcoves are secluded from the main dining room, complete with banquettes for cuddling. Follow your sumptuous dinner with drinks in front of the fireplace in the adjoining lounge.
- **Best Spot for a Business Lunch:** The upstairs dining room of the **Occidental Grill,** 1475 Pennsylvania Ave. NW (☎ **202/783-1475**), is quiet, with nice-sized booths that guarantee privacy in a restaurant that's centrally located near Capitol Hill and downtown offices. (The food's great, too.)
- **Best Spot for a Celebration: Goldoni,** 1113 23rd St. NW (☎ **202/293-1511**), has a festive air, thanks to the bits of opera bursting through the bubble of conversation in the skylit room. A fun place, and the food is excellent.
- **Best Decor: The Willard Room** (☎ **202/637-7440**), in the Willard Hotel, is simply grand, decorated with paneling, velvet, and silk. (Consider this another contender for most romantic.)
- **Best View:** Washington Harbour is the setting for **Sequoia,** 3000 K St. NW (☎ **202/944-4200**), where a multilevel garden terrace offers a panoramic vista of the Potomac and verdant Theodore Roosevelt Island beyond. If you're dining inside, ask for the bar-level alcove overlooking the Potomac—the best seat in the house.
- **Best Wine List:** At **Seasons,** in the Four Seasons Hotel, 2800 Pennsylvania Ave. NW (☎ **202/944-2000**). For the 11th consecutive year, its wine cellar has been chosen as one of the 100 best worldwide by *Wine Spectator* magazine.
- **Best for Kids:** The **Austin Grill,** 2404 Wisconsin Ave. NW (☎ **202/ 337-8080**), is a friendly, chattering place with a children's menu, spill-proof cups, and an atmosphere to please everyone. Go before 9pm.
- **Best American Cuisine: Kinkead's,** 2000 Pennsylvania Ave. NW (☎ **202/ 296-7700**), concentrates on seafood, but also offers a meat and poultry item on each menu; at any rate, you could eat here every day and not go wrong.
- **Best Chinese Cuisine: Full Kee,** 509 H St. NW (☎ **202/371-2233**), in the heart of Chinatown, is consistently good and a great value.
- **Best French Cuisine:** For fancy French food, **Lespinasse,** in the Carlton Hotel, 923 16th St. NW (**202/879-6900**), is the place to go. The luxuriously decorated

dining room is a fitting backdrop for the divinely prepared (and enormously expensive) creations of chef Troy Dupuy. For French staples served with great enthusiasm and charm in a more relaxed setting, head for **Bistrot Lepic,** at 1736 Wisconsin Ave. NW (☎ **202/333-0111**).

- **Best Italian Cuisine:** Roberto Donna's **Galileo,** 1110 21st St. NW (☎ **202/ 293-7191**), serves the best fine Italian cuisine, preparing exquisite pastas, fish, and meat dishes with savory ingredients like truffles and porcini mushrooms. For more traditional (and affordable) classic Italian fare, Donna's **Il Radicchio,** 1211 Wisconsin Ave. NW (☎ **202/337-2627**) and 1509 17th St. NW ☎ **202/ 986-2627**), does the trick.
- **Best Seafood: Pesce,** 2016 P St. NW (☎ **202/466-3474**) offers reasonably priced, perfectly grilled or sautéed seafood in a convivial atmosphere.
- **Best Southern Cuisine: Vidalia,** 1990 M St. NW (☎ **202/659-1990**). Chef Jeff Buben calls his cuisine "provincial American," a euphemism for fancy fare that includes cheese grits and biscuits in cream gravy.
- **Best Southwestern Cuisine:** It doesn't get more exciting than **Red Sage,** 605 14th St. NW (☎ **202/638-4444**), where superstar chef Mark Miller brings contemporary culinary panache to traditional southwestern cookery. Keep his **Café** and **Chili Bar** in mind for Red Sage cuisine and ambience at lower prices.
- **Best Steak house:** Twenty-three years old and still going strong, the **Prime Rib,** 2020 K St. NW (☎ **202/466-8811**) is the best steak and prime rib place in town, despite some awesome competition.
- **Best Tapas:** The upbeat **Gabriel,** 2121 P St. NW (☎ **202/293-3100**), where you can graze on chef Greggory Hill's ambrosial little dishes, which range from black figs stuffed with Spanish *chorizo* to crunchy fried calamari with fiery *harissa* sauce and lemony thyme aioli.
- **Best Pizza:** At **Pizzeria Paradiso's,** 2029 P St. NW (☎ **202/223-1245**), peerless chewy-crusted pies are baked in an oak-burning oven and crowned with delicious toppings. You'll find great salads and sandwiches on fresh-baked focaccia here, too.
- **Best Desserts:** No frou-frou desserts served at **Café Berlin,** 322 Massachusetts Ave. NE (☎ **202/543-7656**). These cakes, tortes, pies, and strudels are the real thing.
- **Best Diet Meal:** At **Legal Sea Foods,** 2020 K St. NW (☎ **202/496-1111**), follow up a cup of light clam chowder (made without butter, cream, or flour) with an entree of grilled fresh fish and vegetables and a superb sorbet for dessert.
- **Best Late-Night Dining:** To satisfy a yen for Chinese food, go to **Full Kee,** 509 H St. NW in Chinatown (☎ **202/371-2233**), open until 3am on weekends; for more comfortable surroundings and good old American cuisine, try the **Old Ebbitt Grill,** 675 15th St. NW (☎ **202/347-4801**), whose kitchen stays open until 1am on weekends.
- **Best Outdoor Dining: Les Halles,** 1201 Pennsylvania Ave. NW (☎ **202/ 347-6848**), so much fun inside, carries the party outside in warm weather to its partly covered sidewalk cafe, excellently located on the avenue for people-watching and sightseeing (the Capitol lies down the street; the Old Post Office Pavilion is directly across the avenue).
- **Best Brunch:** Combine a Kennedy Center tour or Sunday matinee with a lavish brunch at its on-premises **Roof Terrace Restaurant** (☎ **202/416-8555**). This ornate establishment invites guests into the kitchen Sundays, from 11:30am to 2pm, where a stunning array of food is laid out. Your meal includes a glass of champagne or a mimosa and live entertainment while you dine. Price is $25.95.

- **Best Teas:** This category differs from the above, which is about British-style afternoon repasts. At the charming **Teaism,** 2009 R St. NW (☎ **202/667-3827**), the Asian "tea list," comprising several dozen varieties, is as lovingly composed as the wine list of the most distinguished French restaurant.
- **Best for Pretheater Dinner:** How could you do better than **701's** $22 three-course bargain and its prime location, right around the corner from the Shakespeare Theater and a few blocks from the National and Warner theaters?
- **Best Spot for a Night on the Town:** For an exuberant evening, you can dine to the rhythm of a Brazilian beat at **Coco Loco,** 810 7th St. NW (☎ **202/289-2626**), and stay on to dance the night away.

2 Restaurants by Cuisine

AMERICAN
America (Capitol Hill, *M*)
Aquarelle (Foggy Bottom, *VE*)
Brighton (Dupont Circle, *E*)
Cafe Bethesda (Bethesda, *E*)
Capitol City Brewing Company
   (Downtown East, *M*)
Cashion's Eat Place
   (Adams-Morgan, *M–E*)
Clyde's of Georgetown
   (Georgetown, *M*)
Daily Grill (Downtown West, *E*)
Felix (Adams-Morgan, *M–E*)
The Inn at Little Washington
   (Outside D.C., *VE*)
Martin's Tavern (Georgetown, *M*)
Melrose (Foggy Bottom, *E*)
Mendocino Grille and Wine Bar
   (Georgetown, *E*)
Morrison-Clark Inn (Downtown
   East, *E*)
Mrs. Simpson's (Woodley Park, *E*)
Nora (Dupont Circle, *VE*)
Occidental Grill (Downtown
   East, *VE*)
Old Ebbitt Grill (Downtown
   East, *M*)
Reeve's Restaurant & Bakery
   (Downtown East, *I*)
The Restaurant at the Jefferson
   (Downtown West, *VE*)
Roof Terrace Restaurant/
   Hors d'Oeuvrerie (Foggy
   Bottom, *VE*)
Rupperts (Downtown East, *VE*)
Seasons (Georgetown, *VE*)

Sequoia (Georgetown, *M*)
1789 (Georgetown, *VE*)
Tabard Inn (Dupont Circle, *E*)
Tahoga (Georgetown, *E*)
Trio (Dupont Circle, *I*)
The Willard Room (Downtown
   East, *VE*)

ASIAN FUSION
Asia Nora (Foggy Bottom, *E*)
Oodles Noodles (Downtown
   West, *I*)
Perry's (Adams-Morgan, *M*)
Raku (Dupont Circle, *I*)
Teaism (Dupont Circle, *I*)

BARBECUE
Old Glory Barbecue (Georgetown, *I*)

CAJUN
Louisiana Express (Bethesda, *I*)

CHINESE
City Lights of China (Dupont
   Circle, *I*)
Full Kee (Downtown East, *I*)
Hunan Chinatown (Downtown
   East, *I*)

ETHIOPIAN
Meskerem (Adams-Morgan, *I*)
Zed's (Georgetown, *I*)

FRENCH
Au Pied de Cochon
   (Georgetown, *M*)
Bistrot Lepic (Georgetown, *M*)
Citronelle (Georgetown, *VE*)

Key to Abbreviations: *E*=Expensive; *I*=Inexpensive; *M*=Moderate; *VE*=Very Expensive

The Jockey Club (Dupont Circle, *VE*)
La Colline (Capitol Hill, *E*)
La Fourchette (Adams-Morgan, *M–E*)
Lespinasse (Downtown West, *VE*)
Provence (Foggy Bottom, *E*)
Vintage (Georgetown, *E*)

GERMAN

Café Berlin (Capitol Hill, *M*)

INDIAN

Aditi (Georgetown, *M*)
Bombay Club (Downtown West, *E*)

INTERNATIONAL

Cities (Adams-Morgan, *E*)
New Heights (Woodley Park, *E*)
701 (Downtown East, *E*)

ITALIAN

Barolo (Capitol Hill, *E–VE*)
Cafe Parma (Dupont Circle, *M*)
Cesco Trattoria (Bethesda, *E*)
Coppi's (U Street Corridor, *I–M*)
Galileo (Downtown West, *VE*)
Goldoni (Foggy Bottom, *E*)
Il Radicchio (Dupont Circle, *I*)
I Ricchi (Downtown West, *VE*)
Luigino (Downtown East, *E*)
Obelisk (Dupont Circle, *E*)
Petitto's (Woodley Park, *M*)
Pizzeria Paradiso (Dupont Circle, *I*)
Ristorante Terrazza (Bethesda/Chevy Chase, *V*)
Sostanza (Dupont Circle, *E*)
Villa Franco (Downtown East, *E*)

JAPANESE

Sushi-Ko (Glover Park, *M*)

LATIN

Café Atlantico (Downtown East, *M*)
Gabriel (Dupont Circle, *E*)

MEDITERRANEAN

BeDuCi (Dupont Circle, *M*)
Isabella (Downtown East, *E*)

MEXICAN

Coco Loco (Downtown East, *M*)
Mixtec (Adams-Morgan, *I*)

MIDDLE EASTERN

Iron Gate Inn (Dupont Circle, *M*)
Lebanese Taverna (Woodley Park, *M*)

SEAFOOD

Bethesda Crab House (Bethesda, *M*)
Georgetown Seafood Grill on 19th Street (Downtown West, *E*)
Kinkead's (Foggy Bottom, *E*)
Legal Sea Foods (Downtown West, *E*)
McCormick & Schmick's (Downtown West, *E*)
Pesce (Dupont Circle, *M*)
The Sea Catch (Georgetown, *E*)

SOUTHERN/SOUTHWESTERN/AMERICAN

Austin Grill (Glover Park, Bethesda, *I*)
B. Smith's (Capitol Hill, *E*)
Georgia Brown's (Downtown East, *E*)
Music City Roadhouse (Georgetown, *I*)
Red Sage (Downtown East, *VE*)
Roxanne (Adams-Morgan, *M*)
Vidalia (Downtown West, *E*)

SPANISH

El Catalan (Downtown East, *VE*)
Jaleo (Downtown East, *M*)
Taberna del Alabardero (Downtown West, *VE*)

STEAK HOUSES

Les Halles (Downtown East, *E*)
Morton's of Chicago (Georgetown, *VE*)
The Palm (Downtown West, *E*)
Prime Rib (Downtown West, *VE*)

THAI

Bua (Dupont Circle, *I*)
Busara (Glover Park, *M*)
Haad Thai (Downtown East, *I*)

VIETNAMESE

Miss Saigon (Georgetown, *M*)

3 Capitol Hill

For information on eating at the Capitol and other government buildings, see "Dining at Sightseeing Attractions," later in this chapter.

EXPENSIVE

B. Smith's. Union Station, 50 Massachusetts Ave. NE. ☎ **202/289-6188.** Reservations recommended. Lunch and brunch $8.95–$18.95, $10.95–$21.95. AE, CB, DC, DISC, MC, V. Mon–Thurs 11:30am–4pm and 5–11pm, Fri–Sat 11:30am–4pm and 5pm–midnight, Sun 11:30am–8:30pm. Free validated parking for 2 hours. Metro: Union Station. TRADITIONAL SOUTHERN.

Union Station's most upscale restaurant, the creation of former model Barbara Smith, occupies the room where presidents once greeted visiting monarchs and dignitaries. The dining room has 29-foot ceilings, imposing mahogany doors, white marble floors, gold-leafed moldings, and towering Ionic columns. Background music is mellow (Nat King Cole, Ray Charles, Sarah Vaughan). The restaurant has live jazz on Friday and Saturday evenings and at Sunday brunch. Chef James Oakley's menu offers appetizers such as jambalaya or red beans and rice studded with andouille sausage and tasso (spicy smoked pork). Among the main dishes are sautéed Virginia trout piled high with crabmeat/vegetable "stuffing" and served atop mesclun with rice and a medley of roasted vegetables. A basket of minibiscuits, corn and citrus-poppyseed muffins, and sourdough rolls accompanies all dishes. Desserts include pecan sweet potato pie. An almost all-American wine list features many by-the-glass selections.

Barolo. 223 Pennsylvania Ave. NW. ☎ **202/547-5011.** Reservations recommended. Lunch $11–$14.50, dinner $13.95–$24. AE, DC, MC, V. Mon–Thurs 11:30am–2:30pm and 5:30–10pm, Fri 11:30am–2:30pm and 5:30–10:30pm, Sat 5:30–10:30pm. Free valet parking at dinner. Metro: Capitol South. ITALIAN.

Much needed on Capitol Hill is this excellent upscale Italian restaurant, another pearl in Roberto Donna's string of fine eateries in the area. Situated above another Donna creation, the inexpensive Il Radicchio (see write-up for Dupont Circle location), Barolo has three dining rooms, including a back room for private parties. The intimate main room is paneled and has wooden floors, a working fireplace, and tables placed discreetly apart; encircling the upper reaches of the room is a charming, narrow balcony set with tables for two. Although the menu changes daily, you can expect Piedmontese-style cuisine, such as white asparagus salad with fresh fava beans and slices of Parma prosciutto; saffron pappardelle pasta with fresh sautéed lobster, asparagus, roasted garlic, and fresh basil; or roasted filet of red snapper over sweet potato, rosemary, black olives, and fresh basil. You can also expect to see Washington notables dining here; among recent guests wereMary Bono and Jerry Lewis, both representatives of California, and the owner himself, Roberto Donna. The wine list is entirely Italian and focuses on wines of the Piedmont, with emphasis on those produced from the Barolo grape.

✪ La Colline. 400 N. Capitol St. NW. ☎ **202/737-0400.** Reservations recommended. Breakfast $5–$8.75, lunch $8.75–$16.25, dinner $18.75–$21. AE, CB, DC, MC, V. Mon–Fri 7–10am, 11:30am–3pm, and 6–10pm, Sat 6–10pm. Free garage parking after 5pm. Metro: Union Station. FRENCH.

Mornings are great here if you want to see breakfast fund-raisers in progress. Hill people like La Colline for its convenience to the Senate side of the Capitol: the great bar, the four private rooms, the high-backed leather booths that allow for discrete conversations, and, last but not least, the food. You'll always get a good meal here. The regular menu offers an extensive list of French standards, like the salad niçoise, the terrine of foie gras (a deal for under $9), and the fish—poached, grilled, or sautéed. Almost as long is the list of daily specials, which are worth considering— the soft-shell crab is superb here in season. The wine list concentrates on French and California wines; wine-by-the-glass choices change with the season to complement the menu. Don't let the dessert cart roll past you; the apple pie is a winner.

MODERATE

America. Union Station, 50 Massachusetts Ave. NE. ☎ **202/682-9555.** Reservations recommended. Main courses $6.95–$17.95; sandwiches, burgers, and salads $3.50–$13.95; brunch $7.25–$13.50. AE, DC, DISC, MC, V. Sun–Thurs 11:30am–midnight, Fri–Sat 11:30am– 1am. Free validated parking for 2 hours. Metro: Union Station. AMERICAN REGIONAL.

Our helpful waiter gave us the lowdown: Candice Bergen, Justice Clarence Thomas, Newt Gingrich, and Alec Baldwin are among those who have eaten here at one time or another. People-watching is one reason to come to this vast, four-level restaurant, but sightseeing is another. Ask for a seat in the uppermost Capital Wine Room, where if you look out the window, you see the Capitol dome; look the other direction (between the Roman legionnaire statues), and you've got a grand view of Union Station. (This area seats parties of up to four, not large groups.) Walls are decorated with WPA-style murals, a large painting of the American West, and a whimsical frieze depicting surfers, athletes, astronauts, and superheroes in outer space.

A vast American-classic menu comprises about 150 items, each with the name of the city, state, or region in which the dish supposedly originated: spaghetti and meatballs (Cleveland?), chili dogs (Fort Lee, NJ?). The BLT (Newport) is a safe bet, the nachos (Eagle Pass, TX) are too greasy, and you'll definitely find better crab cakes (Ocean City, MD) elsewhere in the city.

Café Berlin. 322 Massachusetts Ave. NE. ☎ **202/543-7656.** Reservations recommended. Main courses $11.95–$16.95 at lunch and dinner; soups, sandwiches, and salads $4.75–$6.95 at lunch. AE, DC, MC, V. Mon–Thurs 11am–10pm, Fri–Sat 11am–11pm, Sun 4–10pm. Metro: Union Station. GERMAN.

You have to walk past the dessert display on your way to your table at Café Berlin, so forget your diet. These delicious, homemade confections are the best reason to come here. The vast spread might include a dense pear cheesecake, raspberry Linzer torte, sour-cherry crumb cake, or vanilla custard cake. Entrees feature things like the Rahm Schnitzel, which is a center cut of veal topped with a light cream and mushroom sauce, or a wurstplatte of mixed sausages. Seasonal items highlight asparagus in spring, game in the fall, and so on. Lunch is a great deal: a simple chicken salad sandwich (laced with tasty bits of mandarin orange), the soup of the day, and German potato salad, all for $5.75. The owners and chef are German; co-owner Peggy Reed emphasizes that their dishes are "on the light side—except for the beer and desserts." The 12-year-old restaurant occupies two prettily decorated dining rooms on the bottom level of a Capitol Hill town house, whose front terrace serves as an outdoor cafe in warm weather.

4 Downtown, East of 16th Street NW

VERY EXPENSIVE

El Catalan. 1319 F St. NW. ☎ **202/628-2299.** Reservations recommended. Lunch $12.50–$21, dinner $13.50–$28. AE, DC, MC, V. Mon–Thurs 11:45am–2:30pm and 5:30– 10:15pm, Fri 11:45am–2:30pm and 5:30–11:15pm, Sat 5:30–11:15pm. Metro: Metro Center. SPANISH.

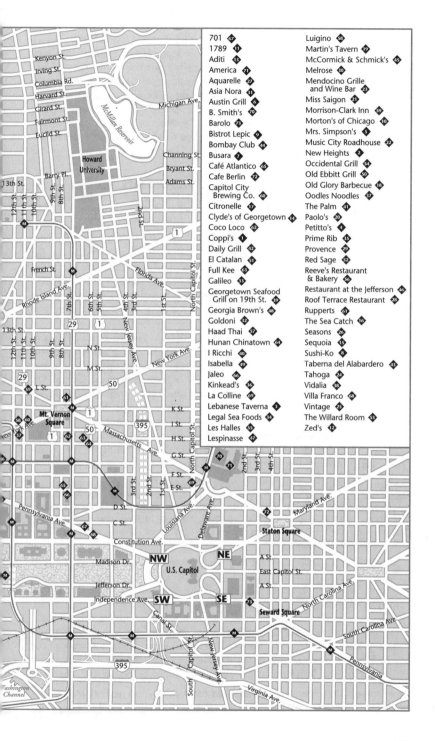

701 **67**
1789 **11**
Aditi **13**
America **71**
Aquarelle **22**
Asia Nora **31**
Austin Grill **6**
B. Smith's **70**
Barolo **73**
Bistrot Lepic **9**
Bombay Club **44**
Busara **7**
Café Atlantico **65**
Cafe Berlin **72**
Capitol City
  Brewing Co. **60**
Citronelle **17**
Clyde's of Georgetown **14**
Coco Loco **62**
Coppi's **1**
Daily Grill **42**
El Catalan **61**
Full Kee **63**
Galileo **33**
Georgetown Seafood
  Grill on 19th St. **39**
Georgia Brown's **48**
Goldoni **32**
Haad Thai **57**
Hunan Chinatown **64**
I Ricchi **40**
Isabella **42**
Jaleo **66**
Kinkead's **36**
La Colline **69**
Lebanese Taverna **3**
Legal Sea Foods **34**
Les Halles **55**
Lespinasse **47**

Luigino **58**
Martin's Tavern **19**
McCormick & Schmick's **45**
Melrose **30**
Mendocino Grille
  and Wine Bar **23**
Miss Saigon **21**
Morrison-Clark Inn **59**
Morton's of Chicago **10**
Mrs. Simpson's **5**
Music City Roadhouse **22**
New Heights **2**
Occidental Grill **54**
Old Ebbitt Grill **50**
Old Glory Barbecue **18**
Oodles Noodles **37**
The Palm **41**
Paolo's **20**
Petitto's **4**
Prime Rib **15**
Provence **29**
Red Sage **52**
Reeve's Restaurant
  & Bakery **56**
Restaurant at the Jefferson **46**
Roof Terrace Restaurant **28**
Rupperts **51**
The Sea Catch **16**
Seasons **26**
Sequoia **15**
Sushi-Ko **8**
Taberna del Alabardero **43**
Tahoga **24**
Vidalia **27**
Villa Franco **68**
Vintage **25**
The Willard Room **53**
Zed's **12**

113

This restaurant would be top-notch if it weren't for the service, which is so slow, it's agonizing. And throughout my meal, the waiter kept addressing me as "lady," not as in "Lady," but as in "hey lady." Restaurant reviews have pointed out the poor service ever since El Catalan opened in 1997, but management apparently doesn't care. The front dining area is the more casual room, the rear dining area elegantly beautiful with, somehow, a Casablanca feel about it. Emerging from the open kitchen are excellent tapas, such as octopus stew with potatoes or the squid sautéed with chorizo, and even more excellent entrees, the best of which is probably the beef rib stew with an orange-and olive-flavored sauce. The desserts are heavenly, try the Catalan cream or the pear gratin.

Occidental Grill. 1475 Pennsylvania Ave. NW. ☎ **202/783-1475.** Reservations recommended. Main courses $12.95–$19.95 at lunch, $12.95–$27.95 at dinner; sandwiches, soups, and salads $4.95–$16.95; pretheater $28. AE, CB, DC, DISC, MC, V. Mon–Sat 11:30am–11pm, Sun noon–9:30pm. Metro: Metro Center, Federal Triangle. AMERICAN.

In the same complex as the Willard Hotel, the Occidental Grill was opened by the Willard family in 1906. Subsequent owner Gus Bucholz started, in the 1920s, the tradition of displaying autographed photographs of his customers, many of whom were famous. The restaurant closed in 1972, but when it reopened with the Willard in 1986, the walls in the lower dining room were covered with those photographs of past patrons—military, political, sports, even royalty figures. They're the first thing you notice when you enter.

The upstairs dining room is more formal, with larger booths, a smaller bar, and no photos. Downstairs feels like a club, with dark wood paneling; a classic bar, walls lined with booths, and leather seats. In 1998, the restaurant opened an outdoor patio on Pennsylvania Avenue, where you have a grand view of the Capitol. On both levels you choose from the same menu, which offers traditional meat-and-potatoes fare along with grilled fish and nouvelle cuisine. Certain things are famous: onion crisps and the swordfish club sandwich. And certain things that aren't famous should be: the black-bean soup with grilled shrimp and lime cream and the grilled Atlantic salmon with crab and potato hash and saffron-fennel broth. The potato dishes are always good.

Red Sage. 605 14th St. NW (at F St.). ☎ **202/638-4444.** Reservations recommended for main dining room, not accepted for chili bar and cafe. Lunch $13–$16, dinner $19–$30; Cafe/Chili Bar $5–$13. AE, CB, DC, DISC, MC, V. Restaurant Mon–Thurs 11:30am–2pm and 5:30–10pm, Fri 11:30am–2pm and 5:30–10:30pm; Sat 5:30–10:30pm, Sun 5–10pm. Cafe/Chili Bar Mon–Sat 11:30am–11:30pm, Sun 4:30–11pm. Metro: Metro Center. WESTERN/CONTEMPORARY AMERICAN.

Nationally renowned chef Mark Miller has created an elegantly whimsical Wild West fantasy. Downstairs, the main dining room comprises a warren of cozy, candlelit alcoves under a curved ceiling with ponderosa-log beams. Upstairs are the more casually gorgeous Cafe and high-ceilinged Chili Bar.

When you look at the menu, think spicy. Red Sage is famous for its house-made sausages, its sautéed Virginia trout with grilled Maryland crab cakes, and for desserts such as the dark chocolate praline tombstone with hazelnut crunch. The wine list is extensive and well researched. The Chili Bar and Cafe offer inexpensive light fare ranging from barbecued brisket quesadillas to catfish tacos.

✪ **Rupperts.** 1017 7th St. NW. ☎ **202/783-0699.** Reservations required. Main courses $25 at lunch and dinner. AE, DC, MC, V. Tues–Wed 6–10pm, Thurs 11:30am–2:30pm and 6–10pm, Fri–Sat 6–11pm. Metro: Mount Vernon Square–UDC, Gallery Place–Chinatown. AMERICAN.

Within spitting distance of the D.C. Convention Center, this one-room, understated restaurant with a casual atmosphere is in a marginal neighborhood; thankfully, a boom in downtown development is rapidly bringing other restaurants and nightlife a little closer.

The restaurant's success is a tribute to the chef's simple but excellent ways with seasonal produce. The chef changes the menu daily, sometimes three times a day, to work with the freshest ingredients. You may see a foie gras and figs dish on the menu in late fall or soft-shell crabs and grilled rhubarb in spring. The food is not heavy, nor laden with sauces. Three different freshly baked breads come with dinner. The wine list is eclectic, everything from a $210 bottle of Borgogno Riserva Barolo to a $15 Domaine Manoir Beaujolais Noveau. Desserts, however, are too hip; black rice with persimmon left me unimpressed. Most people are in business dress at lunch, less formal attire in the evening.

The Willard Room. In the Willard Inter-Continental Hotel, 1401 Pennsylvania Ave. NW. ☎ **202/637-7440.** Reservations recommended. Lunch $8–$22, dinner $10–$32. AE, DC, DISC, JCB, MC, V. Mon–Fri 7:30–10am and 11:30am–2pm; Mon–Sat 6–10pm. Metro: Metro Center. AMERICAN REGIONAL/CLASSIC EUROPEAN.

Like the rest of the hotel (see chapter 5), the Willard dining room has been restored to its original turn-of-the-century splendor, with gorgeous carved oak paneling, towering scagliola columns, brass and bronze torchères and chandeliers, and a faux-bois beamed ceiling. Scattered among the statesmen and diplomats dining here are local couples who have come for romance; the Willard has been the setting for more than one betrothal.

Chef de cuisine Gerard Madani, who changes the lunch menu daily and the dinner menu every 2 or 3 weeks, emphasizes lightness in cooking. Some examples: steamed Dover sole with a sorrel-flavored vermouth cream sauce, veal kidney with celery root mustard-seed sauce, beef tenderloin with bordelaise sauce, and grilled whole Maine lobster. Two of the most popular desserts are the double-vanilla crème brûlée and the chocolate tears, which combines dark chocolate and white chocolate in a tear-shaped, mousse-like confection. The wine list offers more than 250 fine selections.

EXPENSIVE

Georgia Brown's. 950 15th St. NW. ☎ **202/393-4499.** Reservations recommended. Lunch and dinner $9–$19, brunch $22. AE, DC, DISC, MC, V. Mon–Thurs 11:30am–10:30pm, Fri 11:30am–11:30pm, Sat 5:30–11:30pm, Sun 11:30am–4:30pm (brunch 11:30am–2:30pm) and 5:30–10:30pm. Metro: McPherson Square. AMERICAN/SOUTHERN.

In Washington restaurants, seldom do you find such a racially diverse crowd. The harmony may stem from the staff, whose obvious rapport results in gracious service to diners, and certainly extends from the open kitchen, where chef Neal Langerman directs his multicultural staff. But in this large handsome room, whose arched windows overlook McPherson Square, the food may capture all your attention. A plate of corn bread and biscuits arrives, to be slathered with a butter that's been whipped with diced peaches and honey. The menu is heavily southern, with the emphasis on the "low country" cooking of South Carolina and Savannah: collards, grits, and lots of seafood, especially shrimp dishes. The Carolina Perlau is a stewlike mix of duck, spicy sausage, jumbo shrimp, and rice, topped with toasted crumbs and scallions—it has bite without being terribly spicy.

Isabella. 809 15th St. NW (between H and I sts.). ☎ **202/408-9500.** Reservations recommended. Lunch $7.95–$18.95, dinner $8.95–$18.95. AE, DC, DISC, MC, V. Mon–Thurs

Tea at the Washington National Cathedral

✪ **Washington National Cathedral,** Massachusetts and Wisconsin avenues NW (☎ 202/537-8993). Tea at the Washington National Cathedral begins with a tour of the world's 6th largest cathedral (see chapter 7), or, in May and September, a choice of either a garden or cathedral tour, and winds up on the 7th floor of the West tower, whose arched windows take in a stunning view of the city, its monuments, and the Sugarloaf Mountains in Maryland. Tea consists of scones and jam; sandwich triangles of egg salad or smoked salmon, or maybe pastry cups of tarragon chicken salad; tiny pastries such as cream puffs, heart-shaped shortbread, iced chocolate squares, and lemon tarts; and brewed tea. During the school year, you can descend from the tower in time to enjoy even-song services performed at 4pm by the Youth Choir. Tea is served every Tues and Wed at 1:30pm; $15 per person; reserve as far in advance as possible, the cathedral accepts reservations up to 6 months ahead.

11:30am–5:30pm and 5:30–10:30pm, Fri 11:30am–5:30pm and 5:30–11pm, Sat 5:30–11pm. Metro: McPherson Square. MEDITERRANEAN.

Since it opened in early 1997, Isabella has been getting much attention, which continues even though there's a new chef in the kitchen. Chef Caroline Bruder prepares her own twist on classic Mediterranean dishes. Steamed mussels in white wine with garlic and shallots, oyster and brie stew, and lamb shank cooked in a wood-burning oven and presented in a marsh of gorgonzola polenta are some of the dishes people are talking about. The wine list is an interesting mix of Italian, Spanish, French, and California wines. A sidewalk patio fronts Isabella; inside, the restaurant is decorated in shades of purple and gold, has giant palm trees, and two levels of semicircular banquettes. But watch out; tables are packed too closely together. On a recent visit, I saw a woman maneuvering between tables to sit down, knock a glass of wine off of one table, then a glass of water off another.

✪ **Les Halles.** 1201 Pennsylvania Ave. NW. ☎ **202/347-6848.** Reservations recommended. Lunch $11.75–$20, dinner $13.25–$22.50. AE, CB, DC, DISC, MC, V. Daily 11:30am–midnight. Metro: Metro Center, Federal Triangle. FRENCH/STEAK HOUSE.

Anyone who believes that red meat is passé should stop reading here. At lunch and dinner, people are eating the *onglet* (a boneless, French-cut steak hard to find outside France); steak au poivre; steak tartare; New York sirloin; and other cuts of cow—always accompanied by *frites*, of course. The menu isn't all beef, but it is classic French: cassoulet, confit de canard, escargots, onion soup, and such. I can never resist the *frisee aux lardons*, a savory salad of chicory studded with hunks of bacon and toast smeared thickly with Roquefort.

Les Halles is big and charmingly French, with French-speaking staff providing breezy, flirtatious service. The banquettes, pressed tin ceiling, mirrors, wooden floor, and the side bar capture the feel of a brasserie. A vast window overlooks Pennsylvania Avenue and the awning-covered sidewalk cafe, which is a superb spot to dine in warm weather. Every July 14, this is the place to be for the annual Bastille Day race, which Les Halles hosts (See Calendar of Events in chapter 2 for details). Les Halles is a favorite hangout for cigar smokers, but the smoking area is well ventilated.

Luigino. 1100 New York Ave. NW. ☎ **202/371-0595.** Reservations recommended. Lunch $8.25–$14.50, dinner $12.50–$22.50, pretheater $18.50. AE, DC, MC, V. Mon–Thurs 11:30am–2:30pm and 5:30–10:30pm, Fri 11:30am–2:30pm and 5:30–11:30pm, Sat

5:30–11:30pm, Sun 5–10pm. Pretheater daily 5:30–7pm. Free validated parking for garage on 12th St. Metro: Metro Center. ITALIAN.

This classy Italian restaurant occupies the same building (an ex-bus station) as the Capitol City Brewing Company (see below). Here elegance mixes amusingly with informality. Starched white cloths lie upon traditional red-checkered tablecloths; waiters wear colorful vests atop their classic black pants and white shirts, a line of cushioned chairs (not stools) stretch the length of a bar overlooking the open kitchen, and rock and roll plays softly in the background.

The pizza is a bit greasy, but has a good, chewy, thin crust. Grilled fish and meat specials are popular, but we find the fresh pasta dishes satisfying, including the ravioli filled with crabmeat and braised vegetables and the twists of pasta with diced green beans and potatoes topped with a standard (but fine) basil pesto sauce. Among the wine list offerings are some affordable Italian wines.

Morrison-Clark Inn. Massachusetts Ave. NW (at 11th St.). ☎ **202/898-1200.** Reservations recommended. Lunch $12.50–$14.50, dinner $17.50–$23, 3-course Sun brunch (including unlimited champagne) $25. AE, CB, DC, DISC, MC, V. Mon–Fri 11:30am–2:30pm and 5:30–9:30pm, Sat 5:30–9:30pm, Sun 11:30am–2:30pm and 5:30–9pm. Metro: Metro Center. AMERICAN REGIONAL.

The *Washington Post* and *Gourmet* magazine often cite the Morrison-Clark restaurant as one of the best in the city. The dining room is a Victorian drawing room with ornately carved white-marble fireplaces. At night, soft lighting emanates from Victorian brass candelabras, crystal chandeliers, and candles. During the day, sunlight streams through floor-to-ceiling, mahogany- and gilt-trimmed windows. And, weather permitting, you can dine outdoors at courtyard umbrella tables.

Chef Susan McCreight Lindeborg's seasonally changing menus are elegant and inspired. An early spring menu may feature potato and leek soup with country ham toasts as a first course and sautéed salmon with risotto cakes and crimini mushroom butter sauce as a main course. The inn is known for its desserts, like the chocolate caramel tart topped with praline-studded whipped cream. Similar fare is available at lunch and brunch. A reasonably priced wine list offers a variety of premium wines by the glass, plus a nice choice of champagnes, dessert wines, and ports.

701. 701 Pennsylvania Ave. NW. ☎ **202/393-0701.** Reservations recommended. Lunch $12.50–$18.50, dinner $14.50–$22.50, pretheater $22. AE, CB, DC, MC, V. Mon–Tues 11:30am–3pm and 5:30–10:30pm, Wed–Thurs 11:30am–3pm and 5:30–11pm, Fri 11:30am–3pm and 5:30–11:30pm, Sat 5:30–11:30pm, Sun 5–9:30pm. Free valet parking 5:30–11pm nightly. Metro: Archives–Navy Memorial. AMERICAN/INTERNATIONAL.

This restaurant is steps away from the Archives–Navy Memorial Metro stop and a short walk from several theaters. Its plate-glass windows allow you to watch commuters, theatergoers, and tourists scurrying along Pennsylvania Avenue. Walls, glass partitions, and columns in the dining room create pockets of privacy throughout.

701 has gained renown for its extensive caviar and vodka selections. But don't disregard the main menu, which features sophisticated American fare and always includes a few vegetarian items. A signature soup with great texture and flavor is Iowa corn and shrimp chowder, with dry sack sherry and chives. Other dishes to recommend are the barbecue duck strudel and the fingerling potato custard with wild mushrooms. Artful presentation makes the food all the more enticing. Portions are generous, and service is marvelous.

Villa Franco. 601 Pennsylvania Ave. NW. ☎ **202/638-2423.** Reservations recommended. Lunch $12–$16, dinner $13–$28. AE, MC, V. Mon–Thurs 11:30am–3pm and 5:30–11pm, Fri 11:30am–3pm and 5:30–11:30pm, Sat 5:30–11:30pm. Metro: Archives–Navy Memorial. ITALIAN.

Although it has a Pennsylvania Avenue address, Villa Franco's entrance is on Indiana Avenue, just a block up from Pennsylvania. The decor is colorful, with faux stucco wall treatments in bright pastels, trompe l'oeil statuary and fountains, and vividly decorated rotundas in the tiled bar and back dining room. The food represents cuisine from the Amalfi Coast of Italy, near Naples, Palermo, and Capri—think fresh mozzarella, tomatoes, basil, eggplant, and olives. Standouts include a fresh tuna tartare with a sun-dried tomato and black olive purée, a baby spinach salad with frisée and shavings of ricotta cheese, and pan-roasted yellow snapper in a tangy caponata sauce.

MODERATE

Café Atlantico. 405 8th St. NW. ☎ **202/393-0812.** Reservations required. Lunch $9.50–$14.50, dinner $13.95–$16.50, light fare $4.50–$7.50. AE, DC, MC, V. Mon–Tues 11:30am–2:30pm and 5:30–10pm, Wed–Sat 11:30am–2:30pm and 5:30–11pm (Fri 2:30–5:30pm for light fare), Sun 5:30–10pm. The bar stays open until 1am on weekends. Metro: Archives–Navy Memorial. LATIN AMERICAN/CARIBBEAN.

This place, a favorite hot spot in Washington's burgeoning downtown, rocks on weekend nights. The colorful, three-tier restaurant throbs with Latin, calypso, and reggae music, and everyone is having a good time—including, it seems, the staff. If the place is packed, see if you can snag a seat at the second-level bar, where you can watch the genial bartender mix the potent drinks for which Café Atlantico is famous: the caipirinha, made of limes, sugar, and *cachacha* (sugarcane liqueur), or the mojito, a rum and crushed mint cocktail.

After you are seated at the bar or table, your waiter makes fresh guacamole right in front of you. As for the main dishes, you can't get a more elaborate meal for the price. The ceviche, Ecuadorean seared scallops, and Argentine rib eye are standouts, and tropical side dishes and pungent sauces produce a burst of color on the plate. *Beware:* Since the menu changes every week, these items may not be available.

Capitol City Brewing Company. 1100 New York Ave. NW. ☎ **202/628-2222.** Also 2 Massachusetts Ave. NW. ☎ **202/842-2337.** Reservations accepted for groups of 15 or more at this location, for 6 or more at the Mass. Ave. location. Main courses $8.95–$16.95. Sun–Thurs 11am–11pm, Fri–Sat 11am–midnight. Bar stays open until 1am. AE, DC, DISC, MC, V. Metro: Metro Center. AMERICAN.

Both locations of these brewpubs are popular with singles, who enjoy swilling good beer in nicer-than-normal bar surroundings. The huge pubs are each situated within historic buildings: one across from the convention center and near the MCI Center, the other in the old City Post Office Building across from Union Station (upstairs from the National Postal Museum). Daily beer specials are posted on a chalkboard. The menu offers typical bar food, although here and there you find the odd item worth trying (like the grilled portobello mushroom). Custom-cooked burgers and the pan-seared, blackened catfish club sandwich are commendable. The service, however, is not. If you want to be waited on in this decade, sit at the bar. A basket of soft pretzels accompanied by a horseradish-mustard dip is complimentary.

✪ Coco Loco. 810 7th St. NW (between H and I sts.). ☎ **202/289-2626.** Reservations recommended. Tapas mostly $4.95–$12; *churrascaria* with antipasti bar $30 (dinner only); antipasti bar $14 (dinner only). AE, MC, V. Mon–Thurs 11:30am–2:30pm and 5:30–10pm, Fri 11:30am–2:30pm and 5:30–11pm, Sat 5:30–11pm. Metro: Gallery Place. BRAZILIAN/MEXICAN.

At 8pm on a Wednesday night, the dance floor is filled with young, well-dressed couples dancing to salsa. Weekends, you can't even get in the joint. Besides the music and dancing, much of the action emanates from the open kitchen and the

In case you want to see the world.

At American Express, we're here to make your journey a smooth one. So we have over 1,700 travel service locations in over 120 countries ready to help. What else would you expect from the world's largest travel agency?

do more

Travel

In case you want to be welcomed there.

We're here to see that you're always welcomed at establishments everywhere. That's why millions of people carry the American Express® Card – for peace of mind, confidence, and security, around the world or just around the corner.

do more®

Cards

In case you're running low.

We're here to help with more than 118,000 Express Cash

locations around the world. In order to enroll, just call

American Express before you start your vacation.

do more

Express
Cash

And just in case.

We're here with American Express® Travelers Cheques and Cheques *for Two*® . They're the safest way to carry money on your vacation and the surest way to get a refund, practically anywhere, anytime.

Another way we help you…

do more

Travelers Cheques

U-shaped bar. If you want a quieter setting, head for the window-walled front room or the garden patio. The exuberantly tropical interior space centers on a daily changing buffet table. Cheeses, fresh fruits, salads (ranging from roasted tomatoes with mozzarella to garbanzos with figs), cold cuts, and other antipasti are temptingly arrayed on palm fronds and banana leaves.

An extensive selection of Mexican tapas includes interesting quesadillas and pan-roasted shrimp on chewy black (squid-infused) Chinese jasmine rice. Coco Loco's most popular dish is churrascaria, the Brazilian mixed grill. Waiters serve you chunks of the sausage, chicken, beef, and pork from skewers. It comes with salsa, fried potatoes, and coconut-flavored rice and includes antipasti bar offerings. All this and Mexican chocolate rice pudding for dessert, too. The wine list is small but well chosen.

Jaleo. 480 7th St. NW (at E St.). ☎ **202/628-7949.** Reservations accepted until 6:30pm. Lunch $7.50–$10.75, dinner $10.50–$28, tapas $2.95–$7.50. AE, DC, DISC, MC, V. Mon 11:30am–2:30pm and 5:30–10pm, Tues–Thurs 11:30am–2:30pm and 5:30–11:30pm, Fri–Sat 11:30am–2:30pm and 5:30pm–midnight, Sun 11:30am–3pm and 5:30–10pm. A limited tapas menu is served Mon–Sat 2:30–5:30pm. Metro: Archives or Gallery Place. SPANISH REGIONAL/TAPAS.

In theater season, Jaleo's dining room fills and empties each evening according to the performance schedule of the Shakespeare Theater, which is right next door. Lunchtime always draws a crowd from nearby office buildings and the Hill. The restaurant, which opened in April 1993, may be credited for initiating the tapas craze in Washington. Among the menu items are mild but savory warm goat cheese served with toast points, a skewer of grilled chorizo sausage atop garlic mashed potatoes, and a delicious mushroom tart served with roasted-red-pepper sauce. Paella is among the few heartier entrees listed (it feeds four). Spanish wines, sangrias, and sherries are available by the glass, and fresh-baked chewy bread comes in handy for soaking up tangy sauces. Finish with a rum- and butter-soaked apple charlotte in bread pastry or a plate of Spanish cheeses. The casual-chic interior focuses on a large mural of a flamenco dancer based on John Singer Sargent's painting *Jaleo,* which inspired the restaurant's name; on Wednesday evenings at 8 and 9pm, flamenco (Sevillanas) dancers perform in 15- to 20-minute rounds.

Old Ebbitt Grill. 675 15th St. NW (between F and G sts.). ☎ **202/347-4801.** Reservations recommended. Breakfast $4.50–$6.95; brunch $5.95–$12.95; lunch $7.95–$12.95; dinner $9.95–$15.95; burgers and sandwiches $6.25–$10.95; raw bar $8.95–$18.50. AE, DC, DISC, MC, V. Mon–Fri 7:30am–1am, Sat 8am–1am, Sun 9:30am–1am. Bar Sun–Thurs to 2am, Fri–Sat to 3am. Raw bar open daily to midnight. Metro: McPherson Square or Metro Center. Complimentary valet parking from 6pm Mon–Sat, from noon Sun. AMERICAN.

Located 2 blocks from the White House, this is the city's oldest saloon, founded in 1856. Among its artifacts are animal trophies bagged by Teddy Roosevelt and Alexander Hamilton's wooden bears—one with a secret compartment in which it's said he hid whiskey bottles from his wife. The Old Ebbitt is an attractive place, with Persian rugs strewn on beautiful oak and marble floors; beveled mirrors; flickering gas lights; etched-glass panels; and paintings of Washington scenes. The long, dark mahogany Old Bar area gives it the feeling of a men's saloon.

You may see preferential treatment given to movers and shakers, and you'll always have a wait for a table if you don't reserve ahead. The staff is friendly and professional in a programmed sort of way; service could be faster. Menus change daily but always include certain favorites: burgers; trout Parmesan (Virginia trout dipped in egg batter and Parmesan cheese, deep-fried); crab cakes; and oysters (there's an oyster bar). The tastiest dishes are usually the seasonal ones, whose fresh ingredients make the difference.

INEXPENSIVE

Full Kee. 509 H St. NW. ☎ **202/371-2233.** Reservations accepted. Lunch $4.25–$9, dinner $6.95–$14.95. No credit cards. Sun–Thurs 11am–1am, Fri 11am–3am, Sat 11am–3am. Metro: Gallery Place/Chinatown. CHINESE.

This is probably Chinatown's best restaurant, in terms of the actual food. Forget decor: Full Kee's two rooms are brightly lighted and crammed with Chinese-speaking customers sitting upon metal-legged chairs at plain rectangular tables. The restaurant does not have a no-smoking section. A cook works at the small open kitchen at the front of the room, hanging roasted pig parts on hooks and wrapping dumplings.

Chefs from some of Washington's best restaurants often congregate here after hours, and here's their advice: Order from the typed back page of the menu. Two selections are especially noteworthy: the jumbo breaded oyster casserole with ginger and scallions (I can second that) and the whole steamed fish. Check out the laminated tent card on the table and find the soups; if you love dumplings, order the Hong Kong-style shrimp dumpling broth (you get eight shrimp dumplings if you order the broth without noodles, only four if you order the broth with noodles). Bring your own wine or beer (and your own glasses in which to pour it) if you'd like to have a drink, since Full Kee does not serve any alcohol and accepts no responsibility for helping you imbibe.

Haad Thai. 1100 New York Ave. NW (entrance on 11th St. NW). ☎ **202/682-1111.** Reservations recommended. Lunch $6–$8, dinner $7–$11. AE, DC, MC, V. Mon–Fri 11:30am–2:30pm and 5–10:30pm, Sat noon–10:30pm, Sun 5–10:30pm. Metro: Metro Center. THAI.

The Washington area has lots of Thai restaurants, but not many are downtown. Fewer still offer food this good in such pretty quarters. Haad Thai is a short walk from the Convention Center, the MCI Center, and surrounding hotels. Plants and a pink and black mural of the Thai beach decorate the dining room. The dishes to order are the standards: pad thai, *panang gai* (chicken sautéed with fresh basil leaves in curry, with peanut sauce), and satays, although all dishes are flavorful and only mildly spicy. If you happen to like your food really hot, ask for it that way.

Hunan Chinatown. 624 H St. NW. ☎ **202/783-5858.** Reservations recommended for 6 or more. Lunch $7.50–$15, dinner $9–$25. AE, CB, DC, DISC, MC, V. Sun–Thurs 11am–10pm, Fri–Sat 11am–11pm. Metro: Gallery Place-Chinatown. CHINESE.

Classical Muzak playing in the background, comfortably cushioned chairs, and fresh-cut carnations on tabletops covered with pink and white tablecloths are several of the features that set this Chinatown restaurant apart from its neighbors. We liked the tea-smoked duck, the hot and sour soup (thick with shredded mushrooms), the fried wonton, fried dumplings, and shredded chicken in garlic sauce. Go here if you want good Chinese food in a calming atmosphere.

Reeve's Restaurant & Bakery. 1306 G St. NW. ☎ **202/628-6350.** Main courses $5.50–$8; sandwiches $3.50–$6; buffet breakfast $5.25 Mon–Fri, $6.25 Sat and holidays. MC, V. Mon–Sat 7am–6pm. Metro: Metro Center. AMERICAN.

There's no place like Reeve's, a Washington institution since 1886, although in a new building since 1992. J. Edgar Hoover used to send a G-man to pick up chicken sandwiches, and Lady Bird Johnson and daughter Lynda Bird worked out the latter's wedding plans over lunch here. It's fronted by a long bakery counter filled with scrumptious pies and cakes. Brass-railed counter seating on both floors uses the original 19th-century wooden stools. The ambience is cheerful, and much of the seating is in cozy booths and banquettes.

Everything is homemade with top-quality ingredients: the turkeys, chickens, salads, breads, desserts, even the mayonnaise. At breakfast, you can't beat the all-you-can-eat buffet: scrambled eggs, home fries, French toast, pancakes, doughnuts, corned-beef hash, grits, bacon, sausage, stewed and fresh fruit, biscuits with sausage gravy, and more. Hot entrees run the gamut from golden-brown Maryland crab cakes to country-fried chicken with mashed potatoes and gravy. Reeve's pies are famous: strawberry, peach, chocolate cream; you name it. No alcoholic beverages.

5 Downtown, 16th Street NW & West

VERY EXPENSIVE

✪ **Galileo.** 1110 21st St. NW. ☎ **202/293-7191.** www.robertodonna.com. Reservations recommended. Breakfast $2.95–$9.95, lunch $11–$19, dinner $17–$30 at dinner. AE, CB, DC, DISC, MC, V. Mon–Fri 7:30–9:30am, 11:30am–2pm and 5:30–10pm, Sat 5:30–10:30pm, Sun 5–10pm. Complimentary valet parking in evening. Metro: Foggy Bottom. ITALIAN.

Food critics mention Galileo as one of the best Italian restaurants in the country and Roberto Donna as one of our best chefs. The likable Donna opened the white-walled, grotto-like Galileo in 1984; since then, he has opened several other restaurants in the area, including Il Radicchio and Pesce (see Dupont Circle listings), has written a cookbook, and has established himself as an integral part of Washington culture.

Galileo features the cuisine of Donna's native Piedmont region, an area in northern Italy influenced by neighboring France and Switzerland—think truffles, hazelnuts, porcini mushrooms, and veal. A SWAT team of male waiters attend. The atmosphere is relaxed; diners are dressed in jeans and suits alike. For starters, munch on the Piedmont-style *crostini*—paper-thin toast dipped in pureed cannellini beans with garlic. The menu includes more than 900 vintages of Italian wine (40% Piedmontese). Typical entrees include sautéed Chesapeake Bay oysters, served on a bed of leeks and porcini mushrooms; *pansotti* (a pasta) of potatoes with truffles and crispy pancetta in a porcini mushroom sauce; and grilled rack of venison with a wild berry sauce. Finish with a traditional tiramisu or, better yet, the warm pear tart with honey vanilla ice cream and caramel sauce—spectacular.

I Ricchi. 1220 19th St. NW. ☎ **202/835-0459.** Reservations recommended. Lunch $10–$28, dinner $11.95–$32. AE, DC, MC, V. Mon–Fri 11:30am–1:30pm and 5:30–9:45pm, Sat 5:30–10pm. Free valet parking at dinner. Metro: Dupont Circle. ITALIAN.

This restaurant celebrates its 10th year in 1999, and it remains a popular and convivial place to enjoy Italian food à la Tuscany. An open kitchen with a blazing wood-burning grill creates a warming bustle in the large room. What's good here? If you're into fish, check out the daily specials; the minestrone; and the pastas, particularly the one stuffed with spinach and ground veal, the fat noodles wrapped in rabbit sauce, or the spaghettini covered with a thick tomato sauce, with mushrooms and crisp shrimp.

Lespinasse. 923 16th St. NW (in the Carlton Hotel). ☎ **202/879-6900.** Reservations recommended. Jacket required for men. Breakfast $8–$19; lunch prix fixe $36, à la carte $24–$27; tea $19; dinner prix fixe $75, à la carte $28–$39. AE, CB, DC, DISC, MC, V. Mon–Fri 7–10:30am noon–2pm and 6pm–10pm, Sat 7–11am and 6pm–10pm, Sun 7–11am; daily tea (in lobby) 3–5:30pm. Complimentary valet parking for lunch and dinner. Metro: Farragut North. FRENCH.

A $6-million renovation of Lespinasse's opulent dining room endowed it with a castlelike stenciled ceiling with wooden beams; creamy gold-hued walls; royal blue stamped banquettes and floral carpeting; and comfortable yellow leather chairs. The china is Limoges, the crystal Riedel. You pay for the embellishments: This Washington branch of New York's Lespinasse is now the most expensive restaurant in town. Westin Fairfax chef Gray Kunz sent his sous-chef, Troy Dupuy, to command this kitchen. Sommelier Vincent Feraud is the best, having presided at Jean-Louis (now closed). One unexpected thing about the wine list is that it offers a nice selection of reasonably priced good wines by the glass.

Dupuy contrasts textures as he melds exotic fruit and vegetable flavors with meat and seafood dishes. A winning appetizer is the trio of foie gras. The risotto with truffles and coriander, which comes with a silver saucepot of mushroom fricassee, is an established signature dish (a carryover from New York). The perfectly roasted squab entree tastes amazingly rich and is served with mashed and wedged potatoes, leeks, and truffles. If desserts, like stewed quince and green apple in pastry, don't appeal, the after-dinner plate of petits fours might. A dinner at Lespinasse takes time—not because of the service, which is smooth and attentive, but because the kitchen is slow. But maybe that's for the good: lingering over the meal becomes an event unto itself.

Prime Rib. 2020 K St. NW. ☎ **202/466-8811.** Reservations recommended. Jacket and tie required for men. Lunch $10–$18, dinner $18–$29.95. AE, CB, DC, MC, V. Mon–Thurs 11:30am–3pm and 5–11pm, Fri 11:30am–3pm and 5–11:30pm, Sat 5–11:30pm. Free valet parking after 5pm. Metro: Farragut West. STEAKS/CHOPS/SEAFOOD.

The Prime Rib has plenty of competition now, but it makes no difference. Beef lovers still consider this The Place. It has a definite men's club feel about it: brass-trimmed black walls, leopard-print carpeting, comfortable black leather chairs and banquettes. Waiters are in black tie, and a pianist at the baby grand plays show tunes and Irving Berlin classics.

The meat is from the best grain-fed steers and has been aged for 4 to 5 weeks. Steaks and cuts of roast beef are thick, tender, and juicy. For less carnivorous diners, there are about a dozen seafood entrees, including an excellent crab imperial. Mashed potatoes are done right, as are the fried potato skins. Bar drinks here, by the way, are made with fresh-squeezed juices and Evian water.

The Restaurant at the Jefferson. 1200 16th St. NW (at M St.). ☎ **202/833-6206.** Reservations recommended. Lunch $13–$22, dinner $22–$28, Sun brunch $19.50–$28. AE, CB, DC, JCB, MC, V. Daily 6:30–10:30am, 11am–3pm, and 6–10:30pm. Free valet parking. Metro: Farragut North. NATURAL AMERICAN.

Cozy, rather than intimidatingly plush, the Jefferson Hotel's restaurant is very romantic (ask to be seated in "the snug," tables 39 or 40). The emphasis on privacy and the solicitous, but not imposing service also make it a good place to do business.

Chef James Hudock changes his menus seasonally. Appetizers we enjoyed from a late winter menu included a baby spinach salad sprinkled with goat cheese and dressed with tangerine-ginger dressing, and a warm artichoke heart salad with designer lettuce and scallops, resting upon a thin potato galette. Among the entrees were a caramelized black grouper with Kalamata olives, roasted peppers, English peas, and roasted potatoes, and perfectly done lamb chops. Our meal ended with a divine coffee crème brûlée.

✪ **Taberna del Alabardero.** 1776 I St. NW (entrance on 18th St. NW). ☎ **202/429-2200.** Reservations recommended. Jacket and tie required for men. Lunch $10–$18, dinner $18–$28, pretheater $30. AE, DC, DISC, MC, V. Mon–Thurs 11:30am–2:30pm and 6–10pm, Fri 11:30am–2:30pm and 6–11pm, Sat 6–11pm. Metro: Farragut West. SPANISH.

Dress up to visit this elegant restaurant, where you receive royal treatment from the Spanish staff who are quite used to attending to the real thing: Spain's King

Juan Carlos and Queen Sofia and their children regularly dine here when in Washington.

The dining room is old-world ornate, with lace antimacassars placed upon velvety banquettes and heavy brocade-like drapes framing the large front windows. Order a plate of tapas to start: lightly fried calamari; shrimp in garlic and olive oil; thin smoked ham; and marinated mushrooms. Although the à la carte menu changes with the seasons, the four paellas (each requires a minimum of two people to order) are always available. The lobster and seafood paella served on saffron rice is rich and flavorful. (Ask to have the lobster shelled; otherwise, you do the cracking.) Chef Josu Zubikarai's Basque background figures prominently, especially in signature dishes such as Txangurro Gratinado (Basque-style crabmeat).

There are three Taberna del Alabardero in Spain, but this is the only outside the mother country. All are owned and operated by Father Luis de Lezama, who opened his first tavern outside the palace gates in Madrid in 1974, as a place to train delinquent boys for employment.

EXPENSIVE

Bombay Club. 815 Connecticut Ave. NW. ☎ **202/659-3727.** Reservations recommended. Lunch and dinner $7.50–$18.50, Sun brunch $16.50, pretheater $24. AE, CB, DC, MC, V. Mon–Thurs 11:30am–2:30pm and 6–10:30pm, Fri 11:30am–2:30pm and 6–11pm, Sat 6–11pm, Sun 11:30am–2:30pm and 5:30–9pm. Free valet parking after 6pm. Metro: Farragut West. INDIAN.

The Clintons have eaten here many times, and diners know it; when the Secret Service swept the restaurant recently at lunch, the place was abuzz with anticipation, only to see Prince Bandar bin Sultan, the Saudi ambassador, enter the room.

The Indian menu here ranges from fiery green chili chicken ("not for the fainthearted," the menu warns) to the delicately prepared lobster malabar, a personal favorite. Tandoori dishes, like the chicken marinated in a yogurt, ginger, and garlic dressing, are specialties, as is the vegetarian fare—try the black lentils cooked overnight on a slow fire. The staff seems straight out of *Jewel in the Crown,* attending to your every whim. This is one place where you can linger over a meal as long as you like. Slow-moving ceiling fans and wicker furniture accentuate the colonial British ambience.

Daily Grill. 1200 18th St. NW. ☎ **202/822-5282.** Reservations recommended. Lunch $7.95–$15, dinner $8.95–$22. AE, DC, MC, V. Mon–Thurs 11:30am–11pm, Fri–Sat 11:30am–midnight, Sun 10am–3pm (brunch), 3–5pm (limited menu), and 5–10pm. Free valet parking from 5pm Mon–Sat and all day Sun. Metro: Farragut North or Dupont Circle. AMERICAN.

Step right in and get your Cobb salad, your chicken pot pie, your fresh fruit cobbler, your meat and potatoes. Talk about retro; in the case of the Daily Grill, retro means revisiting the food favorites of decades past. The California-based restaurant itself is not that old—about 2 years. It's a big space (seating up to 240), with a nice bar at the front and windows on three sides. Stop at the winding bar first and choose from an extensive selection: good wines, lots of single malts, tequilas, and small-batch bourbons.

Like its chain siblings, the D.C. grill is gaining a reputation for American-friendly service and large portions of grilled meats and fish. Favorite orders are the short ribs and the "Grill Combo" of tiny onion rings over skinny fries.

✪ Georgetown Seafood Grill on 19th Street. 1200 19th St. NW. ☎ **202/530-4430.** Reservations recommended. Lunch $9.95–$17.95, dinner $10.95–$21.95, salads and sandwiches $8.95–$12.95. AE, DC, DISC, MC, V. Mon–Thurs 11:30am–10pm, Fri 11:30am–11pm, Sat 5:30–11pm, Sun 5:30–10pm. Metro: Dupont Circle. SEAFOOD.

In the heart of downtown is this hint of the seashore. Two big tanks of lobsters greet you as you enter, and the decor throughout follows a nautical theme: aquariums set in walls, canoes fastened to the ceiling, models of tall ships placed here and there. Meanwhile, music from another era is heard—"Young at Heart," and the like. It's enough to make you forget what city you're in.

A bar and sets of tables sit at the front of the restaurant, an open kitchen is in the middle, and tall wooden booths on platforms lie at the rear. The lobster thermidor special is a mix of Pernod, scallions, mushrooms, and cream mixed with bits of lobster. But if you want really healthier chunks of lobster, order the lobster club, served on brioche with apple-wood bacon and mayonnaise, or better yet, the fresh lobster delivered daily from Maine. Besides the lobster, you can choose from a list of at least eight "simply grilled" fish entrees. Raw-bar selections list oysters from Canada, Virginia, and Oregon, and these may be the freshest in town. Service is excellent.

Legal Sea Foods. 2020 K St. NW. ☎ **202/496-1111.** Reservations recommended, especially at lunch. Lunch $7.95–$15.95 (sandwiches $6.95–$8.95), dinner $10–$25. AE, DC, DISC, MC, V. Mon–Thurs 11am–10pm, Fri 11am–10:30pm, Sat 4–10:30pm, Sun 4–9pm. Metro: Farragut North or Farragut West. SEAFOOD.

This famous family-run, Boston-based seafood empire, whose motto is "If it's not fresh, it's not Legal," made its Washington debut in August 1995. The softly lighted dining room is plush, with terrazzo marble floors and rich cherry-wood paneling. Sporting events, especially Boston games, are aired on a TV over the handsome marble bar/raw bar, and you can get a copy of the *Boston Globe* near the entrance. In 1998, the restaurant enclosed the bar area to allow for cigar smoking. As for the food, not only is everything fresh, but it's all from certified-safe waters.

Legal's buttery rich clam chowder is a classic. Other worthy appetizers include garlicky, golden-brown, farm-raised mussels au gratin and fluffy pan-fried Maryland lump crab cakes served with zesty corn relish and mayonnaise-mustard sauce. Legal's signature dessert is a marionberry and blueberry cobbler with a brown-sugar oatmeal-crisp crust; it's topped with a scoop of homemade vanilla ice cream. An award-winning wine list is a plus. At lunch, oyster po'boys are a treat.

McCormick & Schmick's. 1652 K St. NW (at corner of 17th St. NW). ☎ **202/861-2233.** Reservations recommended. Lunch and dinner $6.60–$19. AE, DC, DISC, MC, V. Mon–Thurs 11am–11pm, Fri 11am–midnight, Sat 5pm–midnight, Sun 5–10pm. Bar opens at 4pm Sat and Sun. Metro: Farragut North and Farragut West. SEAFOOD.

In this branch of a Pacific Northwest–based restaurant, stained glass in the chandeliers and ceiling evince a patriotic theme. The restaurant boasts its own shoe-shiner, Victor, who has rapidly developed a following. This huge place seats its patrons in booths, at a 65-foot bar, and at linen-laid tables. The vast menu offers selections of fresh fish from both nearby and Pacific waters—the more simply prepared, the better. Oyster lovers will have a tough time choosing from the half-dozen kinds stocked daily. For good value, look at the list of light entrees ranging from oyster stew to chicken picatta and costing $6.60 to $9.95. For best value, head to the bar to enjoy a giant burger, fried calamari, quesadillas, fish tacos, and more—for only $1.95, Monday through Thursday 3:30 to 6:30pm and 10:30pm to midnight, Friday 3:30 to 6:30pm, and Saturday 10pm to midnight. Friendly bartenders make you feel at home as they concoct "handmade from scratch" mixed drinks. A surf-and-turf version of McCormick & Schmick's, the M&S Grill, opened in June 1998 near the MCI Center, at 13th and F Streets NW.

✪ **The Palm.** 1225 19th St. NW. ☎ **202/293-9091.** Reservations recommended. Lunch $8.50–$17, dinner $15–$58. AE, DC, MC, V. Mon–Fri 11:45am–10:30pm, Sat 6–10:30pm, Sun 5:30–9:30pm. Complimentary valet parking at dinner. Metro: Dupont Circle. STEAK HOUSE.

The Palm is one in a chain that started 76 years ago in New York—but here in D.C., it feels like an original. The Washington Palm is 27 years old; its walls, like all Palms, are covered with the caricatures of regulars, famous and not-so. (Look for my friend, Bob Harris.) You can't go wrong with steak, whether it's offered as a 36-ounce, dry-aged New York strip, or sliced in a steak salad. Oversize lobsters are a specialty, and certain side dishes are a must: creamed spinach, onion rings, Palm fries (something akin to deep-fried potato chips), and hash browns. Several of the longtime waiters like to joke around; service is always fast.

✪ **Vidalia.** 1990 M St. NW. ☎ **202/659-1990.** Reservations recommended. Lunch $13–$16.75, dinner $17–$27. AE, DC, DISC, MC, V. Mon–Thurs 11:30am–2:30pm and 5:30–10pm, Fri 11:30am–2:30pm and 5:30–10:30pm, Sat 5:30–10:30pm, Sun 5–9:30pm (closed Sun July 4–Labor Day). Complimentary valet parking at dinner. Metro: Dupont Circle. PROVINCIAL AMERICAN.

Down a flight of steps from the street, the charming Vidalia is a tiered dining room, with cream stucco walls hung with gorgeous dried-flower wreaths and works by local artists.

Chef Jeff Buben's "provincial American" menu (focusing on southern-accented regional specialties) changes frequently, but recommended constants include crisp East Coast lump crab cakes, a fried grits cake with portobello mushrooms, and something that fans refer to simply as "the onion": a roasted whole Vidalia onion that's cut and opened, like the leaves of a flower. Venture from the regular items, and you may delight in a timbale of roasted onion and foie gras.

A signature entree is the scrumptious sautéed shrimp on a mound of creamed grits and caramelized onions in a thyme and shrimp-cream sauce. Corn bread and biscuits with apple butter are served at every meal. Vidalia is known for its lemon chess pie, which tastes like pure sugar; I prefer the pecan pie. A carefully chosen wine list highlights American vintages. Note: In early summer 1998, the Bubens opened bis, a French restaurant, in The Hotel George on Capitol Hill (see chapter 5).

INEXPENSIVE

Oodles Noodles. 1120 19th St. NW. ☎ **202/293-3138.** Reservations recommended for 5 or more at dinner. Main courses $7–$9. AE, DC, MC, V. Mon–Thurs 11:30am–3pm and 5–10pm, Fri 11:30am–3pm and 5–10:30pm, Sat 5–10:30pm. Metro: Dupont Circle, Farragut North. ASIAN.

Asian waiters, Asian background music, and calligraphy figures drawn on the walls put you in the right frame of mind for Pan-Asian noodle dishes. You can order Japanese dumplings; Szechuan dan dan noodles (egg noodles); Vietnamese vermicelli; Thai drunken noodles; and so on. Many of the items come within soup, such as Shanghai roast-pork noodles soup and the Siam noodles soup, which is a spicy sweet and sour broth with shrimp, minced chicken, and squid.

But not everything is a noodle. Appetizers include satays, spring onions cakes, and vegetable spring rolls. Entrees include curry, teriyaki, and similar spicy non-noodle fare.

Although Washington food critics give Oodles Noodles high marks, I find it a hit or miss place. On a recent visit, my Noodles on the Boat (grilled marinated lemon chicken with rice vermicelli, bean sprouts, vegetables, peanuts, and fried onions) was bland, and my husband's Spices Chicken "wasn't spicy at all." You can't beat the prices, though, and my children, at least, were content with their Chicken Wonton Soup and Ravioli (pork dumplings).

6 Georgetown

VERY EXPENSIVE

✪ **Citronelle.** In the Latham Hotel, 3000 M St. NW. ☎ **202/625-2150.** Reservations recommended. Breakfast $7–12, lunch $16–$25, dinner $22–$32. AE, DC, MC, V. Mon–Thurs 6:30–10:30am, noon–2pm, and 5:30–10pm; Fri–Sat 6:30–10:30am, noon–2pm, and 5:30–10:30pm; Sun 6:30–10:30am. Complimentary valet parking at dinner. CONTEMPORARY FRENCH.

In March 1998, Citronelle reopened after a $2-million renovation, with much fanfare provided by enthusiastic Washington foodies and Citronelle's ebullient chef/owner Michel Richard. Richard opened Citronelle in 1992, but left it in the hands of other good chefs while he returned to his flagship restaurant, the famed Citrus, in Los Angeles. Now the Frenchman has moved to Washington, happy to please the palates of Washingtonians, whose tastes he believes to be more sophisticated than Los Angelenos.

In terms of decor, the Citronelle transformation includes a wall that changes colors, a state-of-the-art wine cellar (a glass-enclosed room that encircles the dining room, displaying its 8,000 bottles and a collection of 18th- and 19th-century corkscrews), and a Provençal color scheme of mellow yellow and raspberry red.

Emerging from the bustling exhibition kitchen now are appetizers like the fricassee of escargots, sweetbreads, porcinis, and crunchy pistachios, and entrees like the crispy lentil-coated salmon. The dessert of choice: Michel Richard's rich, layered chocolate "bar" with sauce noisette. Citronelle's extensive wine list offers many premium by-the-glass selections, but with all those bottles staring out at you from the wine cellar, you may want to spring for a full bottle.

Morton's of Chicago. 3251 Prospect St. NW. ☎ **202/342-6258.** Reservations recommended. Main courses $19.95–$29.95. AE, CB, DC, MC, V. Mon–Sat 5:30–11pm, Sun 5–10pm. Free valet parking. STEAKS/CHOPS/SEAFOOD.

Arnie Morton, a flamboyant former Playboy Enterprises executive, created the empire of Morton's steakhouses, of which Washington now has three (the newest is at the corner of Connecticut Avenue and L Street NW; ☎ **202/955-5997**). Politicos, media types, and regular folks come here to sit upon comfortable cream-colored leather booths at white-linen-laid tables lighted by pewter oil lamps in the shape of donkeys or elephants. (Morton's was one of the many restaurants frequented by Monica Lewinsky and her erstwhile attorney William Ginsburg in 1998 throughout special prosecutor Ken Starr's investigation.)

Morton's is known for its huge—some say grotesquely large—portions of succulent USDA prime midwestern beef and scrumptious side dishes. Start off with an appetizer such as smoked Pacific salmon or a lump-crabmeat cocktail served with mustard-mayonnaise sauce. Steaks (rib-eye, double filet mignon, porterhouse, or New York sirloin) are perfectly prepared to your specifications. Other entree choices include veal or lamb chops, fresh swordfish steak in béarnaise sauce, and baked Maine lobster. Side orders of flavorfully fresh al dente asparagus served with hollandaise or hash browns are highly recommended. Consider taking home a doggie bag if you want to leave room for dessert—perhaps a soufflé Grand Marnier or fresh raspberries in sabayon sauce.

Seasons. In the Four Seasons Hotel, 2800 Pennsylvania Ave. NW. ☎ **202/944-2000.** Reservations recommended. Breakfast $10–$17.25, lunch $12.75–$21, dinner $21–$34. AE, DC, DISC, JCB, MC, V. Mon–Fri 7–11am, noon–2:30pm, and 6–10:30pm; Sat–Sun 8am–noon and 6–10:30pm. Metro: Foggy Bottom. Free valet parking. AMERICAN.

Although Seasons is the signature restaurant of one of Washington's most upscale hotels, and a major celebrity haunt, it takes a casual approach to formal dining: relaxed atmosphere, no dress code, and friendly service. Seasons is candlelit at night and sunlit during the day and has windows overlooking the C&O Canal.

Scottish chef William Douglas McNeill's cuisine focuses on fresh market fare. Stellar entrees range from seared tuna with shiitake mushroom-mashed potatoes and peppercorn sauce, to mustard seed-encrusted roast rack of lamb served with Provençal veggies. A basket of scrumptious fresh-baked breads might include rosemary flat bread or sun-dried tomato bread drizzled with Parmesan. For dessert, consider a caramelized ginger crème brûlée. For the 11th consecutive year, *Wine Spectator* magazine has named Seasons' vast and carefully researched wine cellar one of the 100 best worldwide.

1789. 1226 36th St. NW (at Prospect St.). ☎ **202/965-1789.** Reservations recommended. Jacket required for men. Main courses $18–$32, prix-fixe pretheater menu $25. AE, CB, DC, DISC, MC, V. Sun–Thurs 6–10pm, Fri 6–11pm, Sat 5–11pm. Complimentary valet parking. AMERICAN REGIONAL.

The restaurant 1789 is cozy but formal. Housed in a Federal town house, its intimate dining areas are typified by the John Carroll Room, where the walls are hung with Currier and Ives prints and old city maps, a log fire blazes in the hearth, and a gorgeous flower arrangement is displayed atop a hunting-theme oak sideboard. Throughout, silk-shaded brass oil lamps provide romantic lighting. You might spot anyone from cabinet members and senators to Sharon Stone at the next table.

Noted chef Ris Lacoste varies her menus seasonally. Appetizer options might include macadamia-crusted grilled shrimp. Typical entrees range from osso buco with risotto Milanese to roast rack of lamb with creamy feta potatoes au gratin in a red pepper purée-infused merlot sauce. A memorable dessert is the delicate *tuile* (crisp, rounded cookie) filled with chocolate, orange, and pistachio mascarpone on a bitter orange sauce. The wine list is long and distinguished. A great bargain here: The pretheater menu offered nightly through 6:45pm includes appetizer, entree, dessert, and coffee for just $25!

EXPENSIVE

✪ **Mendocino Grille and Wine Bar.** 2917 M St. NW. ☎ **202/333-2912.** Reservations recommended. Lunch $6.75–$18.75, dinner $15.75–$24.75. AE, DC, DISC, MC, V. Mon–Thurs 11:30am–3pm and 5:30–10pm, Fri–Sat 11:30am–3pm and 5:30–11pm, Sun 5:30–10pm. Metro: Foggy Bottom. AMERICAN VIA CALIFORNIA.

Rough-textured slate walls alternate with painted patches of Big Sur sky to suggest a West Coast winery and California's wine-growing region. The wall sconces resemble rectangles of sea glass and the dangling light fixtures look like turned over wineglasses. The California-casual works, and so does the food.

Grilled seafood is the highlight: yellowfin tuna presented on wilted spinach and roasted pepper purée, or Chilean sea bass on a warm salad of french beans. Non-seafood choices include free-range chicken served on roasted red bliss potatoes and sugar snap peas, and grilled tenderloin of beef. Ever in search of the perfect crab cake, I found a close call here in the form of the jumbo lump crabmeat and smoked salmon cake appetizer.

All 85 wines on the list are West Coast selections and have received high ratings from connoisseurs. California casual doesn't mean cheap: Prices hover around $50 a bottle, although you can order a Beringer White Zinfandel for $13 or a Groth Vineyards Reserve 92 Cabernet Sauvignon Napa Valley for $135.

The Sea Catch. 1054 31st St. NW (just below M St.). ☎ **202/337-8855.** Reservations recommended. Lunch $10–$16, dinner $15–$25. AE, CB, DC, DISC, JCB, MC, V. Mon–Sat noon–3pm and 5:30–10:30pm. Complimentary valet parking. SEAFOOD.

The Sea Catch has been catching the eyes of seafood lovers in Washington since 1989—way before the recent onslaught of seafood restaurants. It sits on the bank of the C&O Canal and has an awning-covered wooden deck from which you can watch ducks, punters, and mule-drawn barges glide by while you dine. Inside, the inn-like main dining room has a working fireplace and rough-hewn walls made of fieldstone dug from Georgetown quarries. There's also a handsome white Carrara-marble raw bar and a deluxe brasserie. Classic jazz tapes play in the background.

For openers, plump farm-raised oysters, clams, house-smoked fish, and other raw-bar offerings merit consideration. Entrees focus on daily changing fresh fish and seafood specials, such as big, fluffy jumbo lump crab cakes served with crunchy Oriental-style napa cabbage slaw or grilled marinated squid with fennel and basil aioli. The kitchen willingly prepares fresh fish and seafood dishes to your specifica-tions, including live lobster from the tanks. An extensive wine list highlights French, Italian, and American selections. Fresh-baked desserts usually include an excellent key lime pie.

Tahoga. 2815 M St. NW. ☎ **202/338-5380.** Reservations recommended. Lunch $7.50–$11, dinner $16–$21.50. AE, DC, MC, V. Mon–Thurs 11:30am–2pm and 5:30–10pm, Fri 11:30am–2pm and 5:30–11pm, Sat 5:30–11pm, Sun 5:30–10pm. Metro: Foggy Bottom, with 15-minute walk. AMERICAN.

Even if the food and the sparkling look of the place don't entice you, two other unique features might: its hidden, brick-walled garden patio through French doors at the back, and its lunchtime offering of every wine, by the bottle or glass, at half price. Among the modern American dishes you might try are pan-seared crayfish cakes, barbecued rabbit nachos, roasted pheasant chowder, meatloaf (fancier than the usual version), lamb shank, and sautéed breast of duck. The curving bar lies beyond the main dining room and presents a comfortable spot for even a woman alone to have a drink without being bothered.

Vintage. 2809 M St. NW. ☎ **202/625-0077.** Reservations recommended. Lunch $9.95–$18, dinner $13.95–$18.95. AE, MC, V. Mon–Thurs 11:30am–3pm and 5:30–10:30pm, Fri 11:30am–3pm and 5:30–11pm, Sat 5:30–11pm. Metro: Foggy Bottom, with 15-minute walk. FRENCH.

The restaurant is a little too cool, too spare in design to feel like a French bistro, but the food it serves is authentic French bistro cooking: cassoulet of lamb, salt pork, duck confit, and sausages, or choucroute garni, house-smoked salmon presented on a salad of green lentils lightly dressed in vinaigrette. Each dish is perfectly prepared, transporting you back to Paris. Owner Gérard Pangaud, known for his other upscale French restaurant, Gérard's Place, in downtown Washington (I can't rec-ommend Gérard's in this edition, because I found the staff there to be unrespon-sive), has taken care to offer a pleasing selection of wines in an affordable range, $15–$25. If you arrive early, you can enjoy a drink at the bustling bar, in the front room with a big picture window overlooking Wisconsin Avenue. But make your presence known; it's easy to get lost in the shuffle here.

MODERATE

Aditi. 3299 M St. NW. ☎ **202/625-6825.** Reservations recommended. Lunch $4.25–$9.95, dinner $5.95–$13.95. AE, DC, DISC, MC, V. Mon–Thurs 11:30am–2:30pm and 5:30–10pm, Fri–Sat 11:30am–2:30pm and 5:30–10:30pm, Sun noon–2:30pm and 5:30–10pm. INDIAN.

This charming, two-level restaurant provides a serene setting in which to enjoy first-rate Indian cookery accompanied by Indian music. A must here is the platter of assorted appetizers—*bhajia* (a deep-fried vegetable fritter), deep-fried cheese-and-shrimp *pakoras*, and crispy vegetable *samosas* stuffed with spiced potatoes and peas. Favorite entrees include lamb biryani, which is a basmati rice pilaf tossed with savory pieces of lamb, cilantro, raisins, and almonds; and the skewered jumbo tandoori prawns, chicken, lamb, or beef—all fresh and fork tender—barbecued in the tandoor (clay oven). Sauces are on the mild side, so if you like your food fiery, inform your waiter. A kachumber salad (lettuce, cucumbers, green peppers, and tomatoes topped with yogurt and spices) is a refreshing accompaniment to entrees. For dessert, try *kheer,* a cooling rice pudding garnished with chopped nuts.

✪ **Bistrot Lepic.** 1736 Wisconsin Ave. NW. ☎ **202/333-0111.** Reservations recommended. Lunch $9–$12.25, dinner $14–$18. AE, DISC, MC, V. Tues–Thurs 11:30am–2:30pm and 5:30–10pm, Fri–Sat 11:30am–2:30pm and 5:30–10:30pm, Sun 11:30am–2:30pm and 5:30–9:30pm. FRENCH.

So tiny it has no waiting area for new arrivals, Bistrot Lepic is the real thing, a charming French restaurant like one you might find on a Parisian side street. The atmosphere is bustling and cheery, and you hear a lot of French spoken—not just by the staff and the young proprietress, Cecile Fortin (her husband Bruno is chef), but by customers as well.

This is traditional French cooking, updated. The seasonal menu offers such seafood and meat entrees as grilled rockfish served with green lentils du Puy and aged balsamic sauce, and roasted rack of lamb with Yukon gold mashed potatoes and garlic juice. We opted for specials: tuna prepared quite rare, as it's supposed to be, and served on fennel with a citrusy vinaigrette, and grouper with a lightly spicy lobster sauce upon a bed of spinach.

The modest French wine list offers a fairly good range, but the house wine, Le Pic Saint Loup, is a nice complement to most menu choices and priced at less than $20 a bottle.

Clyde's of Georgetown. 3236 M St. NW. ☎ **202/333-9180.** Reservations recommended. Lunch/brunch $6.95–$10.95, dinner $9.95–$16.95 (most under $12), burgers and sandwiches under $7 all day. AE, DC, DISC, MC, V. Mon–Thurs 11:30am–2am, Fri 11:30am–3am, Sat 10am–3am (brunch is 9am–4pm), Sun 9am–2am (brunch is 9am–4pm). AMERICAN.

Clyde's has been a favorite watering hole for an eclectic mix of Washingtonians since 1963. You'll see university students, Capitol Hill types, affluent professionals, Washington Redskins, romantic duos, and well-heeled "ladies who lunch" bogged down with shopping bags from Georgetown's posh boutiques. A 1996 renovation transformed Clyde's from a saloon to a theme park, whose dining areas include a cherry-paneled front room with oil paintings of sport scenes, and an atrium with vintage model planes dangling from the glass ceiling and a 16th-century French limestone chimneypiece in the large fireplace.

Clyde's is known for its burgers, chili, and crab-cake sandwich. Appetizers are a safe bet, and the Clyde's take on the classic niçoise is also recommended: chilled grilled salmon with greens, oven-roasted Roma tomatoes, green beans, and grilled new potatoes in a tasty vinaigrette. Sunday brunch is a tradition (brunch is also served on Saturday). The menu is reassuringly familiar—steak and eggs, omelets, waffles—with variations thrown in for good measure, like an eggs Benedict that uses a grilled portobello mushroom in place of ham and roasted red pepper hollandaise. Among bar selections are at least ten draft beers and seven microbrews. If you drive, park in the underground Georgetown Park garage; after your meal, stop at the concierge desk in the mall and show your meal receipt to receive parking ticket validation allowing you to pay $1 for 2 hours, a deal in Georgetown.

✪ **Martin's Tavern.** 1264 Wisconsin Ave. NW. ☎ **202/333-7370.** Reservations accepted. Breakfast $5.50–$11.95, brunch $5.50–$11.95, lunch $6.50–$10.95 (sandwiches and salads average $5.95), dinner $5.75–$19.95 (most items under $15). AE, CB, DC, DISC, MC, V. Sun–Thurs 8am–11pm, Fri–Sat 8am–1am. One hour free parking for lunch, 1½ hours for dinner, at Georgetown Inn. AMERICAN.

A good old-fashioned neighborhood pub—that's Martin's. Out-of-towners (especially French and Japanese) come here often, but Martin's has a loyal following of locals as well. I once heard a couple at the bar joking that they chose their new house on the basis of its proximity to Martin's. It has operated continuously since 1933, when it was opened by former New York Giants player William G. Martin, and his father, William S. These days, Billy Martin, great grandson of William S., is behind the bar and, as general manager, pretty much runs the show and supervises the staff, some of whom have been here for more than a decade. Sit at the bar, and you'll hear the lore about famous regulars over the years—from the Kennedys to Art Buchwald. If you crave intimacy, just ask for the "dugout." The menu mainstays are the crab cakes, steak sandwich, the shad and shad roe, and linguine with clam sauce. The place has lots of paneling, old photos, and draft beers on tap.

Miss Saigon. 3057 M St. NW. ☎ **202/333-5545.** Reservations recommended, especially weekend nights. Lunch $5.50–$7.95, dinner $6.95–$22.95. AE, DC, MC, V. Mon–Fri 11:30am–3pm and 3–11pm, Sat–Sun noon–11pm (dinner menu served all day). VIETNAMESE.

This is a charming restaurant, with tables scattered amid a "forest" of tropical foliage, with twinkly lights strewn upon the fronds of the potted palms and ferns.

The food here is delicious and authentic, although the service can be a trifle slow when the restaurant is busy. To begin, there is the crispy calamari, a favorite of Madeline Albright. House specialties include steamed flounder, caramel salmon, and "shaking beef" (Vietnamese steak): crusty cubes of tender beef marinated in wine, garlic, butter, and soy sauce, then sautéed with onions and potatoes, and served with rice and salad. There's a full bar. Desserts range from bananas flambé au rhum to ice cream with Godiva liqueur. Not to be missed is drip pot coffee, brewed tableside and served iced with sweetened condensed milk.

Sequoia. 3000 K St. NW (at Washington Harbour). ☎ **202/944-4200.** Reservations recommended (not accepted for outdoor seating). Main courses $6.95–$28.95; salads and sandwiches $6.95–$12.95. AE, DISC, MC, V. Sun–Thurs 11:30am–midnight, Fri–Sat 11:30am–1am. Paid parking at the harbor discounted after 5pm weekdays and on weekends. AMERICAN REGIONAL.

In the Washington-restaurant-with-a-view category, no setting is more spectacular than Sequoia's terrace, where umbrella-shaded tables overlook the boat-filled Potomac between two bridges. If outside tables are taken, you can enjoy the same river vista from the window-walled interior.

The view is the main reason people frequent Sequoia, and it's especially popular as a place to come for drinks after work. The restaurant is huge and often the setting for large parties, so don't look for intimacy.

The varied and extensive menu runs the gamut from burgers, sandwiches, pastas, and pizzas to mint-marinated lamb chops with garlic smashed potatoes. Save room for one of Sequoia's excellent desserts, perhaps toasted pecan/whiskey pie. Many wines are offered by the glass, and regional beers and ales are featured.

INEXPENSIVE

Music City Roadhouse. 1050 30th St. NW. ☎ **202/337-4444.** Reservations recommended. Family-style meal $12.95, $5.95 for children 6–12, children under 6 can share with adults; late-night courses $3–$7.50; brunch $12.95. AE, CB, DC, DISC, MC, V. Tues–Sat 4:30pm–1am, Sun 11am–9pm (brunch 11am–2pm). SOUTHERN/AMERICAN.

The downstairs of Music City Roadhouse is a large and raucous two-room bar with pool tables. Upstairs is the restaurant where live, mostly blues bands play while you savor fried and barbecued chicken, barbecued spare ribs, fried catfish, pot roast, and country fried steak. The deal is, for $12.95 each, you may choose up to three entrees and three side dishes for your table. The sides, such as mashed regular and sweet potatoes, coleslaw, greens, and green beans with bacon, are replenishable.

The music is great, but so loud it overwhelms conversation, and the small tables are packed tightly next to each other (most seating is family style, at long tables). In good weather, try to sit out on the terrace, which overlooks the C&O Canal. The food is plentiful and tastes of the true South (that is, the greens are soggy). And the roadhouse validates your parking ticket from the underground garage, a rarity for Georgetown. *Note:* If you've got kids, make sure they go to the bathroom before you get here. The only rest room is downstairs in the bar, which, at 6:30 on a Saturday night is already noisy and jammed with beer-guzzling behemoths.

✪ **Old Glory Barbecue.** 3139 M St. NW. ☎ **202/337-3406.** Reservations recommended for 6 or more Sun–Thurs, reservations not accepted Fri–Sat. Main courses $6.50–$17; late-night entrees $5.25–$6.75; brunch buffet $11.95, $5.95 for kids 11 and under. AE, DC, DISC, MC, V. Sun 11:30am–1am (brunch 11am–3pm), Mon–Thurs 11:30am–1am, Fri–Sat 11:30am–3am. Metro: Foggy Bottom. AMERICAN/BARBECUE.

Raised wooden booths flank one side of the restaurant; an imposing, old-fashioned dark wood bar with saddle-seat stools extends down the other. Blues, rock, and country songs play in the background. Old Glory boasts the city's "largest selection of single-barrel and boutique bourbons," a claim that two buddies at the bar were confirming firsthand. In a few hours, when the two-story restaurant is packed with the young and the restless, these two may be swinging from the ceiling's tin-colander lampshade lighting fixtures.

In early evening, though, Old Glory is prime for anyone—singles, families, or an older crowd. Come for the messy, tangy, delicious spare ribs; hickory smoked chicken; tender, smoked beef brisket; or marinated, wood-fried shrimp. Six sauces are on the table, the spiciest being the vinegar-based East Carolina and Lexington, the least spicy but most popular the sweet Memphis sauce. My southern-raised husband favored the Savannah version, which reminded him of that city's famous Johnny Harris barbecue sauce. The complimentary corn muffins and biscuits, side dishes of collard greens, succotash, potato salad, and desserts like apple crisp and coconut cherry cobbler all hit the spot.

Zed's. 3318 M St. NW. ☎ **202/333-4710.** Reservations accepted for parties of more than 5 people. Lunch $5.95–$10.75, dinner mostly $6.95–$12.95. AE, CB, DC, DISC, MC, V. Daily 11am–11pm. ETHIOPIAN.

Although Ethiopian cuisine has long been popular in Washington, few restaurants can match Zed's, which offers authentic, high-quality fare. Zed's is a trilevel, charming little place in Georgetown with indigenous paintings, posters, and artifacts adorning pine-paneled walls.

Diners use a sourdough crepe-like pancake called *injera* to scoop up food. Highly recommended are the *doro watt* (chicken stewed in a tangy, hot, red-chili-pepper sauce), the *infillay* (strips of tender chicken breast flavored with seasoned butter and honey wine and served with a delicious chopped spinach and rice side dish), flavorful lamb dishes, and the deep-fried whole fish. Vegetables have never been tastier. Consider ordering more of the garlicky chopped collard greens, red lentil purée in spicy red-pepper sauce, or a purée (served chilled) of roasted yellow split peas mixed with onions, peppers, and garlic. There's a full bar, and, should you have the inclination, there are Italian pastries for dessert.

7 Adams-Morgan

Although the action in Adams-Morgan centers on just 2 or 3 blocks, the neighborhood is one of D.C.'s liveliest, filled with ethnic and trendy restaurants and happening nightclubs. At nighttime, it's best to come here via taxi, since parking is difficult and the closest Metro stop is a bit of a hike. (During the day, parking isn't a problem.) If you take the Metro, you can get off at Dupont Circle (the Q Street exit) and walk uphill on Connecticut Avenue until you reach the Columbia Road fork, which you follow to Adams-Morgan. Or take Metro to the Woodley Park–Zoo stop, walk south on Connecticut Avenue to Calvert Street, turn left, and cross the Calvert Street bridge to Adams-Morgan. Don't wander too far from the areas described here and in chapter 10; some side streets can be dangerous.

EXPENSIVE

Cities. 2424 18th St. NW (near Columbia Rd.). ☎ **202/328-7194.** Reservations recommended. Main courses $16.50–$24.95. AE, CB, DC, DISC, MC, V. Sun–Thurs 6–11pm, Fri–Sat 6–11:30pm. Bar open Sun–Thurs 5pm–2am, Fri–Sat 5pm–3am. INTERNATIONAL.

Housed in a century-old former five-and-dime store, Cities is a restaurant-cum-travelogue. A year-long, $1.2-million renovation has dressed up the place, with additions like suede drapes, touches of mahogany and Italian leather, and soft lighting provided by hundreds of hanging filament bulbs. Once a year, the restaurant is revamped to reflect the cuisine, character, and culture of a different city. Even the music reflects the city under consideration, and waiters are in native dress or some facsimile thereof. Until spring of 1999 or so, Cities will be embracing Paris, with photos of French street and cafe scenes on the walls and bouillabaisse and fillet of turbot with truffles on the menu. The wine and champagne list is small but expertly conceived, and premium wines are offered by the glass. The bar, at the front of the restaurant, is upscale and loungy, furnished with banquettes and the magnificent bar, and features light-fare specialties of the highlighted city, starting around $7.50.

Upstairs is Privé at Cities, "a private club dedicated to the new age of self-indulgence, available to the restaurant's elite clientele and visiting celebrities." If you think you qualify, talk to your hotel concierge to arrange a visit.

MODERATE TO EXPENSIVE

✪ **Cashion's Eat Place.** 1819 Columbia Rd. NW (between 18th St. and Mintwood Place). ☎ **202/797-1819.** Reservations recommended. Brunch $6–$9, dinner $11–$17. MC, V. Tues 5:30–10pm, Wed–Sat 5:30–11pm, Sun 11:30am–2:30pm and 5:30–10pm. AMERICAN WITH EUROPEAN INFLUENCES.

Adams-Morgan & Dupont Circle Dining

National Zoological Park

Legend
M Metro

N

1 Mrs. Simpson's

Woodley Pl.

Irving St.
Hobart St.
Harvard St.

2 M Woodley Park-Zoo
3   4

Girard St.
Fairmont St.
Euclid St.
Clifton St.

Calvert St.

Adams-Mill Rd.
Ontario Pl.
Lanier Pl.
Quarry Rd.
Columbia Rd.

Euclid St.

University Pl.

Connecticut Ave.

Rock Creek

5

Kalorama Circle Rd.

Kalorama

Wyoming

6 8
7 10 9
   11
12

Ontario Rd.

Chaplain St.

Florida Ave.

California St.

V St.
U St.

Wyoming Ave.
Tracy Pl.
California St.
Bancroft Pl.
S St.
Decatur Pl.

Florida Ave.

Willard St.
Swann St.

T St.
S St.

Wallace Pl.

13

Riggs Pl.

R St.
Corcoran St.

14
15
16
17

Connecticut Ave.

New Hampshire Ave.

Sheridan Circle

18

Q St.
Church St.
P St.
O St.

29
28
27

19
20   24
23 22
21

M Dupont Circle

Massachusetts Ave.

Logan Circle

Rock Creek

New Hampshire Ave.

Connecticut Ave.

25 26

N St.

Rhode Island Ave.

Vermont Ave.

Thomas Circle

M St.

25th St.
24th St.
23rd St.
22nd St.
21st St.
20th St.
19th St.
18th St.
17th St.
16th St.
15th St.
14th St.
13th St.

Farragut North M

L St.
K St.

Washington Circle

BeDuCi 21	Jockey Club 19	Pesce 22
Brighton-on-N 26	La Fourchette 9	Petitto's 2
Bua 27	Lebanese Taverna 4	Pizzeria Paradiso 24
Cafe Parma 15	Meskerem 8	Raku 18
Cashion's Eat Place 7	Mixtec 5	Roxanne 12
Cities 10	Mrs. Simpson's 1	Sostanza 17
City Lights of China 13	New Heights 3	Tabard Inn 25
Felix 11	Nora 14	Teaism 16
Gabriel 20	Obelisk 23	Trio 29
Il Radicchio 28	Perry's 6	

1-0810C

133

⓭ Family-Friendly Restaurants

Baby-boomer parents (and I am one) are so insistent upon taking their children with them everywhere that sometimes it seems all restaurants are, of necessity, family-friendly (although you may wish certain ones were not). Hotel restaurants, no matter how refined, usually welcome children, since they may be guests of the hotel. The cafeterias at tourist attractions (see box "Dining at Sightseeing Attractions," later in this chapter) are always a safe bet, since they cater to the multitudes. Inexpensive ethnic restaurants tend to be pretty welcoming to kids, too. Aside from those suggestions, I offer these:

Old Glory Barbecue *(see p. 131)* A loud, laid-back place where the staff is friendly without being patronizing. Go early, because the restaurant becomes more of a bar as the evening progresses. There is a children's menu, but you may not need it; the barbecue, burgers, muffins, fries, and desserts are so good, everyone can order from the main menu.

Austin Grill *(see p. 148)* Another easygoing, good-service joint, with great background music. Kids will probably want to order from their own menu here, and their drinks arrive in unspillable plastic cups with tops and straws, for taking with you if need be.

Il Radicchio *(see p. 142)* A spaghetti palace to please the most finicky, at a price that should satisfy the family budget.

America *(see p. 111)* The cavernous restaurant with its voluminous menu offers many distractions for a restless brood. No children's menu, but why would you need one, when macaroni and cheese, peanut butter and jelly, pizza, and chicken tenders are among the selections offered to everyone?

A curving bar lies at the center of the agreeable Cashion's Eat Place, up a couple of steps from the main room. People sitting at tables inside the curve tend to prop their arms comfortably upon the half-wall and converse from time to time with the patrons seated in the dining area below.

Owner/chef Ann Cashion has gained renown for her stints at Nora, Austin Grill, and Jaleo. Her menu includes about eight entrees, split between seafood and meat. The side dishes that accompany each entree, such as spiced red cabbage and chestnuts and sautéed foie gras, are worth as much attention. Desserts, like the chocolate cinnamon mousse and the lime tartalette, are worth saving room for.

The glass-fronted Cashion's opens invitingly on to the sidewalk in warm weather. But we were there on a frigid January day when each opening of the door blew a blast of cold over those of us seated at the front of the restaurant. Go to Cashion's, but if it's a wintry day, ask for a table at the back.

Felix. 2406 18th St. NW. ☎ **202/483-3549.** Reservations recommended. Brunch $7–$10, dinner $15–$24. AE, DC, MC, V. Mon–Thurs 5:30–10:30pm, Fri–Sat 5:30–11pm, Sun 11am–3:30pm and 5:30–10:30pm. Live music nightly Sun–Thurs until 1:30am, Fri–Sat until 2:30am. AMERICAN.

Felix and its patrons try hard to be hip. Customers down martinis at the bar and sometimes crush up against dining tables (the areas adjoin on the first floor). Despite an attractive decor that includes a three-dimensional mural of international landmark buildings and a ceiling painted with a celestial scene, the ambience at Felix feels like a party in a group house, an impression reinforced by the dimly

---

Queens for a Day

A drag brunch in conservative, staid D.C.? Only in Adams-Morgan at the whimsically urban-hip **Perry's,** 1811 Columbia Rd. NW (☎ **202/234-6218**). Its cozy-elegant, loungy interior has lots of wood, a fireplace, a 1920s feel, French windows (open in warm weather) framed by imposing floor-to-ceiling red curtains, and a chandelier that looks like an alien octopus suspended from a fire-engine-red plastic cushion. Seating includes dark blue sofas at mahogany coffee tables. During Sunday brunch, drag queens in over-the-top outfits (one slinks around the room in a black vinyl cat costume) appear every 15 minutes or so; they dance, flirt with male customers, camp it up, and lip synch to the music. The crowd is about half straight folks, half gay men and women, and everyone has a great time. Brunch ($15.95, including coffee or tea) consists of an extensive buffet, including paella, French toast, sushi, smoked salmon, eggs and breakfast meats, sesame noodles, grilled vegetables, cold cuts, cheeses, desserts, and more. It's served from 11am to 3pm, and you can't make reservations; arrive early to avoid a wait. Also consider Perry's for moderately priced alfresco Asian-fusion dinners; its lovely rooftop deck, festively strung with yellow lights, opens nightly at 5:30pm.

---

lighted living room setups in the back room and upstairs in the Loft Lounge. You're afraid to peer too closely at what that couple in the corner is doing. (The Loft Lounge, by the way, is open Friday and Saturday nights only, as a bar and music club, not for dining.)

But that's just the atmosphere at this bar-cum-bistro. The food is quite good: Cream of mushroom soup is seasoned just right and delicately creamy; the pork chop, by contrast, is huge and hearty, not at all fatty, and served with potato gallettes and sautéed spinach. A signature dish is the fresh yellowfin tuna, pan-seared rare and presented with sticky rice, snow peas, and wasabi cream sauce. Chocolate lovers will go for the decadent Sundae-upon-a-brownie, but anyone would like the espresso crème brûlée. On Friday evenings, Felix also offers a kosher brisket.

La Fourchette. 2429 18th St. NW. ☎ **202/332-3077.** Reservations recommended on weekends. Main courses $8.95–$21.95. AE, DC, MC, V. Mon–Thurs 11:30am–10:30pm, Fri 11:30am–11pm, Sat 4–11pm, Sun 4–10pm. FRENCH.

Upstairs is no-smoking, but downstairs is where you want to be, among the French-speaking clientele and Adams-Morgan regulars. The waiters are suitably crusty and the ambience is as Parisian as you'll get this side of the Atlantic. So is the food. The menu lists escargots, onion soup, bouillabaisse, and mussels Provençal, along with specials like the grilled salmon on spinach mousse, and the shrimp niçoise, ever-so-slightly crusted and sautéed in a tomato sauce touched lightly with anchovy. A colorful mural covers the high walls, and wooden tables and benches push up against bare brick walls. La Fourchette is Washington's Paris cafe.

MODERATE

Roxanne. 2319 18th St. NW (between Belmont and Kalorama roads). ☎ **202/462-8330.** Reservations recommended. Brunch $4.95–$9.95; dinner $7.95–$14.95; sandwiches, salads, and burgers $3.95–$8.95. AE, MC, V. Mon–Fri 5–11pm, Sat 5pm to midnight, Sun 11am–4pm and 5pm–midnight. Bar Sun–Thurs to 2am, Fri–Sat to 3am. SOUTHWESTERN.

If you want simple tacos and burritos in a smoky bar setting, go downstairs to Peyote Cafe. Roxanne, under the same ownership, offers "cuisine" rather than "eats," says the waitress—which means the atmosphere's still laid-back, but the menu describes things like pepita salmon (baked in a pumpkinseed crust, served over spiced black beans, with chili-grilled shrimp and corn-tomato salsa). You can order from Roxanne's menu if you're in the Peyote Cafe, but not vice versa. (The rooftop On the Rox serves the same menu as Roxanne and is open spring through fall.) If you want a margarita, specify the tequila you want from Roxanne's list of 34 (LARGEST TEQUILA SELECTION IN ADAMS-MORGAN, the sign says); otherwise, you'll end up with the wimp version served in a short highball glass.

INEXPENSIVE

Meskerem. 2434 18th St. NW (between Columbia Rd. and Belmont Rd.). ☎ **202/462-4100.** Lunch $5–$10.50, dinner $8.50–$11.50. AE, DC, MC, V. Mon–Fri noon–midnight, Sat–Sun noon–2am. ETHIOPIAN.

Washington has a number of Ethiopian restaurants, but this is probably the best. It's certainly the most attractive; the three-level, high-ceilinged dining room (sunny by day, candlelit at night) has an oval skylight girded by a painted sunburst and walls hung with African art and musical instruments. On the mezzanine level, you sit at *messobs* (basket tables) on low carved Ethiopian chairs or upholstered leather poufs. Ethiopian music (including live bands after midnight on weekends) enhances the ambience.

Diners share large platters of food, which are scooped up with a sourdough crepe-like pancake called *injera*. Items listed as *watt* are hot and spicy; *alitchas* are milder and more delicately flavored. You might also share an entree—perhaps *yegeb kay watt* (succulent lamb in thick, hot berbere sauce)—along with a combination platter of five vegetarian dishes served with tomato and potato salads. There are also combination platters comprising an array of beef, chicken, lamb, and vegetables. The restaurant has a full bar, and the wine list includes Ethiopian wine and beer.

Mixtec. 1792 Columbia Rd. (just off 18th St.). ☎ **202/332-1011.** Main courses $2.95–$9.95. MC, V. Sun–Thurs 11am–10:30pm, Fri–Sat 11am–11pm. MEXICAN REGIONAL.

This cheerful Adams-Morgan eatery attracts a clientele of Hispanics, neighborhood folks, and D.C. chefs, all of whom appreciate the delicious authenticity of its regional Mexican cuisines. The kitchen is open, the dining room colorfully decorated, and the music is lively mariachi and other kinds of Mexican music.

Delicious made-from-scratch corn and flour tortillas enhance whatever they're stuffed with. Small dishes called *antojitos* ("little whims") are in the $2.50 to $4.95 range, including *queso fundido* (a bubbling hot dish of broiled Chihuahua cheese topped with shredded spicy chorizo sausage and flavored with jalapeños and cilantro). Also popular are the *enrollados Mexicanos,* which are large flour tortillas wrapped around a variety of fillings: grilled chicken, beef, vegetables, salmon. The freshly prepared, from Mexican avocados, guacamole is excellent. A house specialty, a full entree served with rice and beans, is *mole Mexicano*—broiled chicken in a rich sauce of five peppers (the kitchen uses some 200 different spices!), sunflower and sesame seeds, onions, garlic, almonds, cinnamon, and chocolate. Choose from 30 kinds of tequila, tequila-mixed drinks, Mexican beers, and fresh fruit juices.

8 Dupont Circle

VERY EXPENSIVE

The Jockey Club. In the Westin Fairfax, Washington, D.C., 2100 Massachusetts Ave. NW. ☎ **202/659-8000.** Reservations required. Jacket/tie required for men at dinner. Breakfast $10–$20, lunch $12–$30, dinner $24–$30. AE, DC, DISC, MC, V. Daily 6:30–11am, noon–2:30pm, and 6–10:30pm. Metro: Dupont Circle. FRENCH/CONTINENTAL.

The Jockey Club, Washington's longest-running power-dining enclave, opened in 1961 and immediately became a Kennedy-clan favorite (it still is). John F. Kennedy once quipped that when he wanted to reach a staff member, he first called their office, then their home, then the Jockey Club. These days, it's a moneyed bunch who come here, and you're likely to see more than one white-haired gentleman squiring about a much younger woman.

The dining room is cheerful and pubby, with red-leather banquettes; a random-plank oak floor; lanterns suspended from a low beamed ceiling (the subdued amber lighting is as cozy as the glow of a fireplace); and walls of stucco or aged oak paneling hung with English equestrian prints.

Executive chef Hidemasa Yamamoto brings Eastern nuance to classic continental cookery. For instance, an appetizer of sautéed quail with California artichokes and green lentils is garnished with *oba* (Japanese basil). Big fluffy crab cakes meunière comprise the restaurant's signature dish—more than 45,000 are ordered yearly. The pommes soufflés side dish has been on the menu since the restaurant opened. Ask for the chef's menu when you reserve a table; Yamamoto will create a four-course sampling dinner for you from the whole menu.

Nora. 2132 Florida Ave. NW (at R St.). ☎ **202/462-5143.** Reservations recommended. Main courses $18–$29. DISC, MC, V. Mon–Thurs 6–10pm, Fri–Sat 6–10:30pm. Metro: Dupont Circle. ORGANIC AMERICAN.

Owner-chef Nora Pouillon brings haute panache to politically correct organic cookery in this charming restaurant. The main dining room is a converted stable, part of which is skylit, with a weathered-looking beamed pine ceiling, tables lighted by shaded paraffin lamps, and a display of Amish and Mennonite patchwork crib quilts on the walls. The atmosphere is relaxed and cozy, and the dress code is anything goes, with some diners wearing jeans, others fancier duds. Journalists like to eat here, and so does Bill Clinton.

Don't expect brown rice and beans. Instead you'll find listings of chemical-free, organically grown, free-range items, some of which you won't ever have heard of (for example, "mizuna," which is a bitter green), although you can bet they'll be extremely healthful. Nightly menus vary with the seasons. Recent popular dishes included sautéed Maine scallops in a soy-bacon vinaigrette and slow-roasted sesame salmon. A vegetarian entree, like green olive risotto, is always an option. Many desserts use fruits and nuts—for instance, orange-scented shortcake with fresh strawberries. An extensive wine list includes, but is not limited to, selections made with organically grown grapes. The food's so good that I promise you that while you experience the vivid and earthy flavors of natural foods, you won't miss any of the bad-for-you ingredients.

EXPENSIVE

✪ **Brighton.** In the Canterbury Hotel, 1733 N St. NW. ☎ **202/296-0665.** Reservations recommended. Lunch $8–$12.50, dinner $16.50–$22.50. AE, CB, DC, DISC, MC, V. Mon–Fri 11:30am–2pm and 6–10pm, Sat 6–10pm. Metro: Dupont Circle, Farragut North. AMERICAN.

Brighton lies below street level, in the Canterbury Hotel, and yet it is one of the brightest dining rooms you'll find. (If you want cozy, go upstairs to the Union Jack Pub and eat your Brighton dinner there.) Fabric colors are deep salmon and celery, the carpeting a grassy green, the walls lemon yellow. Little vases of fresh-cut yellow roses decorate each table. Diners tend to be locals more than hotel guests.

The food is sublime. First comes a basket of biscuits, sweet bread, and crusty peasant bread. The appetizers and entrees that follow live up to their dramatically artistic presentation. For an appetizer, try the iron-skillet-roasted mussels, with

Dining at Sightseeing Attractions

With so many great places to eat in Washington, I have a hard time recommending those at sightseeing attractions. Most of these are overpriced and too crowded, even if they are convenient. A few, however, are worth mentioning—for their admirable cuisine, noteworthy setting, or both.

CAPITOL HILL AREA   Head to the Capitol's numerous restaurants for a chance to rub elbows with your senators and representatives. But keep in mind these spots are usually open only for lunch and can get very crowded; to lessen the chances of a long wait, try going about 30 minutes before the posted closing time. You'll find the **House of Representatives Restaurant** (also called the "Members' Dining Room") in Room H118, at the south end of the Capitol (☎ 202/225-6300). This fancy, eatery, with chandeliers and gilt-framed pictures on the walls, is open to the public but doesn't take reservations (it's also open for breakfast). Senators frequent the **Senate Dining Room,** but you'll need a letter from your senator to eat here (jacket and tie required for men, no jeans for men or women). More accommodating is the **Refectory,** first floor, Room S112, Senate side of the Capitol (☎ 202/224-4870), which serves sandwiches and other light luncheon fare.

Most Hill staffers eat at places like the **Longworth Building Cafeteria,** Independence Avenue and South Capitol Street SE (☎ 202/225-4410), where they can just grab a bite and go, choosing from a fairly nice selection of food court booths. But by far the best deal for visitors is the **Dirksen Senate Office Building South Buffet Room,** 1st and C streets NE (☎ 202/224-4249). For just $9.50 per adult, $6.50 per child (including a nonalcoholic drink and dessert), you can choose from a buffet that includes a carving station and eight other hot entrees. It's often crowded, but they will take reservations for parties of more than 10.

In the same neighborhood, two institutions offering great deals and views (of famous sites or people) are the **Library of Congress's Cafeteria** (☎ 202/707-8300), and its more formal **Montpelier Room** (☎ 202/707-8300), where the buffet lunch is only $8.50; and the **Supreme Court's Cafeteria** (☎ 202/479-3246), where you'll likely spy a justice or two enjoying the midday meal.

MUSEUM RESTAURANTS   Among museum restaurants, the ones that shine are the Corcoran Gallery of Art's **Café des Artistes** (☎ 202/639-1786); the National Air & Space Museum's two spots, **Flight Line** (☎ 202/371-8750) and the **Wright Place** (☎ 202/371-8778); the National Gallery of Art's **Terrace Café** (☎ 202/216-2492) and **Garden Café** (☎ 202/216-5966); the National Portrait Gallery's and the National Museum of American Art's restaurant, **Patent Pending** (☎ 202/357-2700), situated in a corridor connecting the two museums; and the Phillips Collection's snug **Café** (☎ 202/387-2151).

shaved garlic and diced tomato in a Riesling Dijon broth. Next up, sample the macadamia nut–encrusted Chilean sea bass in a ginger, lime, and coconut sauce. And for dessert, how about the banana, macadamia nut spring roll with ginger ice cream and chocolate sauce.

✪ **Gabriel.** In the Radisson Barceló Hotel, 2121 P St. NW. ☎ **202/956-6690.** Reservations recommended. Breakfast $8; breakfast buffet $10.18; lunch $8–$14; Mon–Fri lunch buffet $9.50; dinner $15–$22; tapas $3.75–$6.50; Sun brunch buffet $17.75, Wed–Fri happy-hour buffet $7.50. AE, DC, DISC, MC, V. Mon–Thurs 6:30am–10pm, Fri 6:30am–10:30pm, Sat 7am–10:30pm, Sun 7am–9pm (brunch 11am–3pm). Free valet parking. Metro: Dupont Circle. LATIN AMERICAN/MEDITERRANEAN.

Like Coco Loco (see above), Gabriel features Latin-accented fare, including tapas; while the former is funky/hip, however, this is a more traditional setting. A large, rectangular, mahogany bar is the centerpiece of a convivial lounge area; outdoors is a small patio cafe with umbrella tables. Noted Washington chef Greggory Hill spent months studying with major chefs in various parts of Spain and Mexico before creating Gabriel's dazzlingly innovative and ever-changing menu.

Sample a variety of tapas at the bar or begin a meal with them—plump chorizo-stuffed black figs or *gambas al ajillo* (shrimp in garlic oil). Entrees might include lamb with mole and sweet potato-plantain mash or pork tenderloin with black bean sauce on basmati rice. Crusty-chewy fresh-baked sourdough bread is great dipped in rosemary/garlic-infused olive oil. There's a well-chosen wine list, with several by-the-glass selections including dry and sweet sherries—the ideal complement to tapas. Incredible desserts here include a warm phyllo purse stuffed with papaya, pineapple, berries, and pistachio nuts, poised on cinnamon custard.

Obelisk. 2029 P St. NW. ☎ **202/872-1180.** Reservations recommended. Prix-fixe 5-course dinners only: $42–$45. DC, MC, V. Tues–Sat 6–10pm. Metro: Dupont Circle. ITALIAN.

In this pleasantly spare room decorated with 19th-century French botanical prints and Italian lithographs, owner/chef Peter Pastan presents his small prix-fixe menus of sophisticated Italian cuisine that uses the freshest possible ingredients. Pastan says his culinary philosophy is to "get the best stuff we can and try not to screw it up." Each night's menu offers diners two or three choices for each course. A recent dinner began with an antipasti of peppers with olivada and anchovies, followed by a Provençal sea bass soup seasoned with saffron, and an artfully arranged dish of pan-cooked snapper with artichokes, thyme, and pancetta. Rather than cheese, I enjoyed a dessert of pear spice cake. Breads and desserts are all baked in-house and are divine. Pastan's carefully crafted wine list represents varied regions of Italy, as well as California vintages. The $40-ish prix-fixe menu seems a deal, but the cost of wine and coffees can easily double the price per person.

✪ Sostanza. 1606 20th St. NW. ☎ **202/667-0047.** Reservations recommended. Lunch $8–$12, dinner $15–$25. AE, CB, DC, MC, V. Daily noon–2pm and 6–10pm. Metro: Dupont Circle. SEAFOOD/ITALIAN.

This is the sort of place you'd hope to stumble upon as a stranger in town. It's pretty, with a sophisticated but relaxed atmosphere, the food is excellent, and the service professional. And although the restaurant has changed its name repeatedly since it opened in 1980, it remains what it has always been, a reliable place to sample classic Italian cuisine. Conceived originally as an Italian steakhouse by owners Vince MacDonald and Roberto Donna, who reigns over a small dynasty of his own restaurants (see Galileo, Barolo, Il Radicchio, Pesce), Sostanza's menu has expanded to offer classic Italian pastas, fish, chicken, and veal dishes. For steak, think alla siciliano: grilled with capers, olives, and sweet pickled peppers. The soft-shell crabs in season, in late spring, are a treat, lightly breaded and fried. Daily specials number about 18, in addition to always-available meat and fish items. The antipasto selection is a holdover from the restaurant's early days, featuring roasted peppers with anchovies, stuffed zucchini, and the like.

At street level is Sostanza's slate terrace, where you can dine at umbrella tables; you go down a short flight of steps to reach Sostanza's exquisite dining room, which resembles a trattoria with its ochre and burnt sienna-toned walls, arched skylight, and tile floor. Across the long, narrow entry hall from the main dining room are the bar and more tables, where, if you're lucky, you can sit and shoot the breeze with owner Vince, who thinks of himself as Italian, though he is, in fact, American, with Italian roots.

Tabard Inn. 1739 N St. NW. ☎ **202/833-2668.** Reservations recommended. Breakfast $2.50–$7.50, lunch $8–$14.50, dinner $16.50–$24.50. AE, DC, MC, V. Mon–Fri 7–10am, 11:30am–2:15pm, and 6–9:45pm; Sat 7–10am (breakfast), 11am–2:15pm (brunch), and 6–9:45pm; Sun 10:30am–2:15pm (brunch) and 6–9:45pm. Metro: Dupont Circle. AMERICAN.

The restaurant here is only a shade more conventional than the inn in which it resides (see listing in chapter 5). From the cozy lounge, where you can enjoy a drink in front of a crackling fire in the fireplace, you enter a narrow room, where hanging plants dangle from skylights and a mural of a ponytailed waiter points the way to the kitchen. A small bar hugs one side of the passage, a series of small tables the other, and both lead to the main space. Or you can head up a set of stairs to another dining room and its adjoining courtyard. Restaurant staff, like inn staff, are disarmingly solicitous.

The food is fresh and seasonal, making use of the inn's own homegrown vegetables and herbs and emphasizing seafood. A curried butternut squash and apple soup was thick and smooth, the floating cilantro leaf providing just the right accent. The inn's version of Caesar salad featured an anchovy dressing and slivers of Parmesan cheese over greens peppered with croutons. Fresh fish, vegetables, and desserts are your best bets.

MODERATE

BeDuCi. 2100 P St. NW. ☎ **202/223-3824.** Reservations recommended. Lunch $9–$18.95, dinner $10–$22.95. AE, DC, DISC, MC, V. Mon–Thurs 11:30am–2:30pm and 5:30–10pm, Fri 11:30am–2:30pm and 5:30–10:30pm, Sat 5:30–10:30pm, Sun 5:30–9:30pm. Complimentary valet parking at dinner. Metro: Foggy Bottom. MEDITERRANEAN.

Mediterranean cuisine is the most recent rage in Washington, but BeDuCi has been serving it since opening 6 years ago. Entrees range from pastas and couscous to paellas and vegetarian stews. Your best bets are the specials, whether you choose an appetizer (maybe cream of cauliflower soup with rock shrimp), or an entree (say, the duck breast filled with lemon zest, wrapped with bacon and figs). Desserts, like the pineapple cobbler, are wonderfully rich and made by Michele Miller, co-owner with Jean-Claude Garrat. The name BeDuCi refers to the restaurant's location: Below Dupont Circle. There's a covered outdoor cafe in warm weather. The white walls in the three inside dining rooms are decorated with paintings and prints. Newly opened is BeDuCi's deli alongside the restaurant.

Cafe Parma. 1724 Connecticut Ave. NW (between R and S sts.). ☎ **202/462-8771.** Reservations recommended. Main courses $8–$14; weekday buffet lunch and daily buffet dinner $9.95, weekend buffet brunch $10.75; pizzas from $6.75; *panini* (sandwiches) and *filoncini* (subs) $5–$6.50. AE, DC, DISC, MC, V. Daily 11:30am–10:30pm. Bar stays open until 1am Sun–Thurs, 2am Fri–Sat. Metro: Dupont Circle. ITALIAN.

Cafe Parma lures diners inside with an exquisite antipasti display in the front window—about 30 items that might include bean salads, marinated eggplant, snow peas with oil-cured olives, creamy egg salad, pasta salads, escarole and pancetta, homemade potato salad, calamari salad, grilled vegetables, and much more. It's always changing and always fabulous, and if you arrive during weekday happy hour, it's free. Pizzas here are baked on flavorful bread dough that's lightly fried in olive oil before toppings are added (more than 30 choices ranging from grilled chicken breast to sun-dried tomatoes). Besides a selection of pastas, the cafe also serves sandwiches and soups (for example, lobster bisque). Italian wines are reasonably priced and available by the glass. Additional breakfast items such as eggs Benedict are offered at brunch, but you can't beat the lavish all-you-can-eat buffet.

The pleasant dining room has pine-wainscoted stucco walls hung with artistic photographs of Washington. A handsome bar and a sunken dining room adjoin.

✪ **Pesce.** 2016 P St. NW. ☎ **202/466-3474.** Reservations accepted for lunch, 6 or more at dinner. Main courses $16.50–$18. AE, DC, DISC, MC, V. Mon–Thurs 11:30am–2:30pm and 5:30–10pm, Fri 11:30am–2:30pm and 5:30–10:30pm, Sat noon–2:30pm and 5:30–10:30pm, Sun 5–9:30pm. Metro: Dupont Circle. SEAFOOD.

Nightly, from about 8:30 until 9:30, a line of people forms inside the cramped waiting area of this restaurant, sometimes trailing out the door, just to enjoy the marvelous grilled or sautéed fresh fish. If you get there earlier than 8:30, you may still have a wait, but not as long. This small restaurant has a convivial atmosphere, brought on, no doubt, by the collective anticipation of a pleasant meal. In this simple setting of exposed brick walls adorned with colorfully painted wooden fish, waiters scurry to bring you a basket of crusty bread, your wine selection, and the huge blackboard menu. Among the many appetizers are blue point oysters on the half shell and several tasty salads. Entrees always list several pastas along with the differently prepared fish. My grilled monkfish entree was firm but tender, and delicious upon its bed of potato purée and wild mushroom ragout. Jointly owned by chefs Roberto Donna and Jean-Louis Palladin, Pesce bears their mark of excellence, even though neither actually works in the kitchen. *Tip:* Try ordering your wine by the glass; depending on the wine you choose, your table may be able to enjoy four glasses of wine and pay less than the cost of a whole bottle.

INEXPENSIVE

Bua. 1635 P St. NW. ☎ **202/265-0828.** Reservations recommended. Lunch $5.95–$7.75, dinner $7.95–$12.95. AE, DC, DISC, MC, V. Mon–Thurs 11:30am–3pm and 5–10:30pm, Fri 11:30am–3pm and 5–11pm, Sat noon–4pm and 5–11pm, Sun noon–4pm and 5–10:30pm. Metro: Dupont Circle, with a 10- to 15-minute walk. THAI.

Walk by on a Friday or Saturday night, and you'll see this two-story restaurant packed (and in summer, tables are full on the second floor outdoor balcony). In spite of its two floors, Bua is not large; it gets mostly a neighborhood crowd, with office people filling the place for weekday lunch. The food is inexpensive and the service gracious and honest; my server steered me away from the "heavenly wings" appetizer, pronouncing them "too crusty." Consider instead the satays, pad thai, and steamed seafood in banana leaves—all house specialties. The peanut sauce accompanying the satays is so good that Bua should sell containers of it for people to stock at home. The spring rolls are very delicate, not greasy.

✪ **City Lights of China.** 1731 Connecticut Ave. NW (between R and S sts.). ☎ **202/265-6688.** Reservations recommended. Main courses $6.95–$11.95 at dinner (a few are pricier). AE, DC, DISC, MC, V. Mon–Thurs 11am–10:30pm, Fri 11:30am–11pm, Sat noon–11pm, Sun noon–10:30pm; Dinner from 3pm daily. Metro: Dupont Circle. CHINESE.

One of Washington's best Chinese restaurants outside of Chinatown, City Lights keeps getting bigger to accommodate its fans, who range from Mick Jagger to Natalie Cole to Jesse Jackson to Attorney General Janet Reno. White House workaholics frequently order deliveries of City Lights carryout. Favorite dishes prepared by Taiwanese chef (and part owner) Kuo-Tai Soug include crisp-fried Cornish hen prepared in a cinnamon-soy marinade and served with a tasty dipping sauce, Chinese eggplant with a garlic sauce, stir-fried spinach, crisp fried shredded beef, and

Dining Rooms that Serve Up Intrigue & Scandal

Have an appetite for espionage? How about gossip? Try out one of these eateries, the locations of which, if not the restaurants themselves, have each provided the backdrop for a rendezvous involving scandal and deception.

Au Pied de Cochon, 1335 Wisconsin Ave. NW. ☎ **202/333-5440.** At this Georgetown bistro, on a November Saturday in 1985, Soviet KGB colonel Vitaly Yurchenko sat with his CIA guard awaiting a late lunch of poached salmon. Three months earlier, the Russian spy had defected to the United States. Since then, Yurchenko had had a change of heart, partly due, some say, to mishandling by the CIA. At any rate, Yurchenko suddenly rose from the table, told his handler that he was going for a walk, headed out the front door and up Wisconsin Avenue to the new Russian embassy compound, about a mile up the hill. A few days later, Yurchenko held a press conference during which he denied that he had ever defected, saying instead that the CIA had kidnapped him. Adopt a Russian accent and order the drink (if you can stomach it) that the restaurant serves to commemorate this little bit of spy lore: the **Original Yurchenko Shooter,** made with equal parts Grand Marnier and Stolichnaya vodka, served chilled. The restaurant also inscribed a plaque with the words, YURCHENKO'S LAST MEAL, which you'll find on the banquette next to the corner table (near the window), at which the spy sat.

Iron Gate Inn, 1734 N St. NW. ☎ **202/737-1370.** Some think this is one of Washington's most romantic restaurants, with its big fire blazing in winter and its private, brick-walled courtyard garden abloom with wisteria in summer. Apparently, Soviet defector Arkady Shevchenko thought so back in October 1978, when he arranged to meet his call girlfriend, Judy Chavez, here for lunch. Shevchenko ordered a double vodka and perused the Middle Eastern restaurant's menu as he waited for Chavez. The former mucky-muck in the Soviet government had once advised Soviet Foreign Minister Andrei Gromyko and had

the Peking duck. The setting is pretty but unpretentious—a three-tier dining room with much of the seating in comfortable pale-green leather booths and banquettes. Neat tables laid with white linen and set with peach napkins, cloth flower arrangements in lighted niches, and green neon track lighting complete the picture.

✪ **Il Radicchio.** 1509 17th St. NW. ☎ **202/986-2627.** Main courses $5.50–$14.50. AE, DC, MC, V. Mon–Thurs 11:30am–10pm, Fri–Sat 11:30am–11pm, Sun 5–10pm. Metro: Dupont Circle, with a 10- to 15-minute walk. ITALIAN.

What a great idea: Order a replenishable bowl of spaghetti for the table at a set price of $6.50, and each of you chooses your own sauce from a long list, at prices that range from $1.50 to $4. Most are standards, like the carbonara of cream, pancetta, black pepper, and egg yolk, and the puttanesca of black olives, capers, garlic, anchovies, and tomato. It's a great deal.

The kitchen prepares daily specials, like Saturday's oven-baked veal stew with polenta, as well as sandwiches and an assortment of 14 wood-baked pizzas, with a choice of 25 toppings. I'd stick with the pizza, pasta, and salad.

Radicchio pops up on one of the thin-crusted pizzas, in salads like the radicchio and pancetta in balsamic vinaigrette, and in a pasta, with sausage, red wine, and tomato, all of which are recommended.

Ingredients are fresh and flavorful, the service quick and solicitous. This branch of the restaurant draws a neighborhood crowd to its long, warm, and cozy room been rewarded by the CIA for his defection with a great deal of money, some of which he had lavished on Chavez, treating her to a car and vacations to the Virgin Islands. Chavez chose to return the favor this particular day by sending an NBC camera crew to the Iron Gate Inn in her place and, later, by writing a book about her experiences with Shevchenko. Stop in for the tagliatelle tossed with grilled shrimp, pancetta, and sugar peas while you mull over this little episode.

The Jefferson, 1200 16th St. NW. ☎ **202/347-2200.** Have a drink in the intimate bar or sup on the delectable dishes served in the fine restaurant. (See write-up this chapter.) And while you're savoring your food, you can be thinking about President Clinton's political strategist, good old Dick Morris, sucking on the toes of his call girlfriend Sherry Rowlands, up there in Suite 205. The scandal broke in August 1996, but Morris had carried on the Jefferson-based affair for a year. Rowlands reported to the *Star* that Morris had allowed her to listen in on telephone conversations he was having with the president.

The Watergate, 2650 Virginia Ave. NW. ☎ **202/965-2300.** In the Watergate Office Building, within the same complex as the hotel, the Democratic National Committee headquarters was the scene of the famous break-in early in the morning of June 17, 1972. Police arrested the five clean-cut, business suit-attired burglars, one of whom proved to be James McCord, a retired CIA official and the security coordinator for the Nixon Re-election Committee. A plaque on the 6th floor commemorates the spot on which the Watergate scandal began. More fun than looking at the plaque is the chance to sit in the Potomac Lounge sipping Scotch (Nixon's favorite drink), or dine in the Watergate's esteemed restaurant, **Aquarelle** (see write-up this chapter), to chew over the events that took place just a few floors up, some 27 years ago.

decorated with wall murals of barnyard animals and radicchio leaves. The Georgetown Il Radicchio (1211 Wisconsin Ave. NW; ☎ **202/337-2627**) attracts college students and families. Il Radicchio on Capitol Hill (223 Pennsylvania Ave. SE; ☎ **202/547-5114**) caters to overworked, underpaid Hill staffers, who appreciate Il Radicchio's food and the price.

✪ **Pizzeria Paradiso.** 2029 P St. NW. ☎ **202/223-1245.** Pizzas $6.75–$15.95, sandwiches and salads $3.25–$6.25. DC, MC, V. Mon–Thurs 11am–11pm, Fri–Sat 11am–midnight, Sun noon–10pm. Metro: Dupont Circle. PIZZA AND PANINI.

Peter Pastan, master chef/owner of Obelisk, right next door, owns this classy, often crowded, 16-table pizzeria. Don't expect Domino's. Instead, an oak-burning oven at one end of the charming room produces exceptionally doughy but light pizza crusts. As you wait, you can munch on the mixed olives placed in a small bowl before you and gaze up at the ceiling painted to suggest blue sky peeking through ancient stone walls. Pizzas range from the plainest Paradiso, which offers chunks of tomatoes covered in melted mozzarella, to the robust Siciliano, a blend of 9 ingredients, including eggplant and red onion. Or you can choose your own toppings from a list of 29. You can also order the daily special and be rewarded with an inspired creation, like potatoes roasted with goat cheese, red onions, and chives atop the chewy crust. Pizzas are available in two sizes, 8-inch and 12-inch, and most toppings cost 75¢ each on the 8-inch, $1.25 each on the 12-inch. As popular as pizza are the panini (sandwiches) of homemade focaccia stuffed with marinated roasted lamb and vegetables and other fillings, and the salads, such as tuna and white bean. Good desserts, but a limited wine list.

Raku. 1900 Q St. NW. ☎ **202/265-7258.** Main courses $3.95–$13.50. AE, MC, V. Mon–Thurs 11:30am–10pm, Fri–Sat 11:30am–11am, Sun 11:30am–10pm. Metro: Dupont Circle. ASIAN.

Raku's glass-fronted location occupies a prominent, excellent people-watching corner near Dupont Circle. Spring through fall, the scene gets even better, when Raku's windowed walls open to its sidewalk cafe. Inside, you find artfully tied bamboo poles and Japanese temple beams, shoji screens, and TV monitors airing campy videos (anything from Godzilla to instructions for using chopsticks), as background music plays Asian pop. A curvilinear bar overlooks the kitchen, where chefs prepare the street food of China, Japan, Korea, and Thailand. Try the skewers, like the soy-sesame, glazed chicken or the "squid sticks" (squid caramelized with a sweet ginger-soy glaze), and dumplings, especially "pork juicy buns" (stuffed with roast pork, cabbage, soy, and ginger, served with black bean sauce). The noodle dishes are unreliable, bland one day and spicy the next, although the *kowloon* (roasted pork, shrimps, ham, and Peking duck dumplings in chicken broth full of bok choy, mustard greens, pea shoots, and thick noodles) may be worth taking a chance on. The Hunan chicken salad is wildly popular. Staff deliver each dish to your table as it is prepared, whether you're ready or not.

Teaism. 2009 R St. NW (between Connecticut and 21st sts.). ☎ **202/667-3827.** All menu items 75¢–$7.75. AE, MC, V. Mon–Thurs 8am–10pm, Fri 8am–11pm, Sat 9am–11pm, Sun 9am–10pm. Metro: Dupont Circle. ASIAN TEAHOUSE.

Occupying a turn-of-the-century neoclassic building on a tree-lined street, Teaism has a lovely rustic interior such as you might find at a teahouse in the countryside of China. A display kitchen and tandoor oven dominate the sunny downstairs room, which offers counter seating along a wall of French windows, open in warm weather. Upstairs seating is on banquettes and small Asian stools at handcrafted mahogany tables.

The tea list, as impressive as the wine list of a top French restaurant, comprises close to 50 aromatic blends, most of them from India, China, and Japan. Many have exotic names such as golden water turtle or jasmine pearl. On the menu is light Asian fare served in lacquer lunch boxes (Japanese "bento boxes") or on stainless-steel plates. Items include salmon cured in lapsang souchong served with chopped bok choy, tandoor-baked lamb kebabs, and stir-fried chicken with coconut. Baked goods, coconut ice cream, and lime shortbread cookies are among desserts. At breakfast you might try cilantro eggs and sausage with fresh tandoor-baked onion *nan* (chewy Indian bread). Everything's available for carryout. Teapots, cups, and other gift items are for sale.

Trio. 1537 17th St. NW (at Q St.). ☎ **202/232-6305.** Lunch and dinner $5.75–$9.50, burgers and sandwiches $1.75–$5.75; full breakfasts $2.75–$5.95. AE, DISC, MC, V. Daily 7:30am–midnight. Metro: Dupont Circle (Q St. exit). AMERICAN.

This art deco coffee shop's roomy red-leather booths (the kind with coat hooks) are filled each morning with local residents checking out the *Washington Post* over big platters of bacon and eggs. In warm weather, the awning-covered outdoor cafe is always packed. The four-decades-old Trio is run by George Mallios, son of the original owners, and is something of a Washington legend.

The food is fresh, and you can't beat the prices. The same menu is offered throughout the day, with low-priced lunch and dinner specials, such as crab cakes with tartar sauce and grilled pork chops with applesauce—all served with two side dishes (perhaps roasted new potatoes and buttered fresh carrots). The wine list has 36 offerings, all but the champagne available by the glass. The à la carte menu is extensive. A full bar offers everything from microbrews to Fuzzy Navels, and a soda fountain turns out hot-fudge sundaes and milkshakes.

Note: If there's no room here, go next door to the Fox and Hounds, under the same ownership and offering the same menu.

9 Foggy Bottom/West End

VERY EXPENSIVE

✪ **Aquarelle.** In the Watergate Hotel, 2650 Virginia Ave. NW. ☎ **202/298-4455.** Reservations recommended. Breakfast $10.75–$18, lunch $15.75–$19.75, dinner $17–$30, pretheater $38. AE, CB, DC, DISC, MC, V. Daily 7–10:30am, 11:30am–2:30pm, and 5–10:30pm for dinner. Free valet parking. Metro: Foggy Bottom. AMERICAN.

The Watergate has a new chef in its new restaurant in the old spot that used to house Jean-Louis's Palladind. In Aquarelle's cheery room overlooking the Potomac, Chef Robert Wiedmaier presents his own version of "Euro-American" cuisine. The menu changes seasonally and focuses on game and fish. Wiedmaier is German-born and Belgian-trained, but he's thoroughly American in his exuberance, which shines in dishes like the flavorful grilled meats and fish, as well as in pastas topped with rich vegetable and garlic sauces. A timbale of salmon mousseline is a treat, as is anything Wiedmaier does with asparagus. Other appetizers might include lobster tail with fennel purée or flan of crabmeat in watercress butter with angel-hair potatoes. Recommended entrees are the rack of lamb and the veal chop with portobello mushroom and Stilton cheese. And for dessert: the crème brûlée. The Aquarelle is popular as a pretheater dinner spot for those going to the Kennedy Center, and wins the drama award for its in-kitchen dinners offered nightly.

Roof Terrace Restaurant/Hors d'Oeuvrerie. In the Kennedy Center, New Hampshire Ave. NW (at Rock Creek Pkwy.). ☎ **202/416-8555.** Reservations recommended for the Roof Terrace Restaurant, but not accepted for the Hors d'Oeuvrerie. Roof Terrace: lunch $12–$19, dinner $25–$29, Sun prix-fixe buffet brunch $25.95 ($12.95 for children under 12); Hors d'Oeuvrerie: light-fare items mostly $9–$16. AE, CB, DC, MC, V. Roof Terrace, matinee days only 11:30am–2pm, Mon–Sat 5:30–8pm, Sun 11:30am–2pm and 5:30–8pm. Hors d'Oeuvrerie, Sun and Tues–Wed 5pm–8pm, Thurs–Sat 5pm until half an hour after the last show ends. *Note:* The Roof Terrace is occasionally closed when there are few shows; call before you go. Metro: Foggy Bottom. AMERICAN REGIONAL.

A meal at the Roof Terrace is convenient for theatergoers, but it's also a gourmet experience in a glamorous dining room, where ornate crystal candelabra chandeliers hang from a lofty ceiling and immense windows provide panoramic views of the Potomac.

Executive chef Dan Storino changes the menu with the seasons, usually keeping the list to 6 or 7 appetizers and 7 to 9 entrees, including one special. You might see listed a grilled salmon on celery root purée with port wine sauce or a grilled filet mignon with roasted garlic mashed potatoes and bordelaise sauce. In season (spring and summer), the Maryland crab cake is a constant among the appetizers. For dessert, look for the chocolate-pecan tart or flourless chocolate cake with vanilla ice cream. Many premium wines are offered by the glass. Every Sunday, the restaurant hosts a kitchen brunch buffet, a lavish spread that includes custom-made omelets, pasta, smoked meats and fish, fancy French toast, and tons of desserts. The $25.95 price entitles you to the buffet and either a glass of champagne, a mimosa, or a glass of fresh-squeezed orange juice.

After-theater munchies and cocktails are served in the adjoining and equally plush Hors d'Oeuvrerie. Stop here before or after a show for a glass of wine or champagne and a light supper—perhaps grilled shrimp or saffron risotto, oven-baked Maryland crab cakes, or the peppered filet mingon sandwich. It's gourmet snack fare. Desserts and coffee are also available.

EXPENSIVE

Asia Nora. 2213 M St. NW. ☎ **202/797-4860.** Reservations recommended. Main courses $18–$24. DISC, MC, V. Mon–Sat starting at 5:45pm, with last reservation at 10pm Thurs, 10:30pm Fri–Sat. Metro: Dupont Circle or Foggy Bottom. ASIAN FUSION.

Everything's set at a slant here: the tables; the bar; the banquette at the back on the first floor; and the triangular cutaway balcony on the second. Museum-quality artifacts from Asian countries—batik carvings, Japanese helmets, and Chinese puppets—decorate the gold-flecked jade-colored walls. It's intimate and exotic, a charged combination. Try sitting at the bar first, on the most comfortable bar stools in town. If you like good bourbons and single-malt Scotches, you're in luck.

Staff dressed in black-satin martial-arts pajamas serve Asian-fusion cuisine, all prepared with organic ingredients. Hence, a salad of smoked trout with field greens and Fuji apples, a "small dish" of crispy spinach and shiitake spring rolls, and a main dish of banana leaf grilled sea bass. It actually sounds more far out than it tastes.

Goldoni. 1113 23rd St. NW. ☎ **202/293-1511.** Reservations recommended. Lunch $11–$19, dinner $17–$24. AE, CB, DC, DISC, MC, V. Mon–Thurs 11:30am–2pm and 5:30–10pm, Fri 11:30am–2pm and 5–11pm, Sat 5–11pm, Sun 5–10pm. Complimentary valet parking for dinner. Metro: Foggy Bottom. ITALIAN.

A lot of restaurants have occupied this space over the years, but with any luck, the year-old Goldoni is here to stay. It's dramatically large, high-ceilinged, and skylit; white walls display modern art evoking the Venetian carnival, and outbursts of operas play now and again during your meal.

The Fred Astaire-ish maitre' d, Julian Russell, escorts you past the bar to your table, where more drama awaits. A risotto with grapefruit, basil, and baby shrimp is cradled in a grapefruit half. Chef/owner Fabrizio Aielli's signature dish, grilled whole fish (we had rockfish, but snapper, sea bass, and others may be available), arrives on a huge platter, served with polenta and shiitake mushrooms. A salad with radicchio, goat cheese, and ground walnuts is excellent. Sorbets are a specialty, as is the beautifully presented tiramisu. Bring a party of people; Goldoni is a good spot for a celebration.

✪ **Kinkead's.** 2000 Pennsylvania Ave. NW. ☎ **202/296-7700.** Reservations recommended. Lunch $10–$18, dinner $18–$26, Sun brunch $7.50–$13. AE, DC, DISC, MC, V. Daily 11:30am–11pm. Metro: Foggy Bottom. AMERICAN/SEAFOOD.

When a restaurant has been as roundly praised as Kinkead's, you start to think no place can be that good—but Kinkead's is. An appetizer like grilled squid with creamy polenta and tomato fondue leaves you with a permanent longing for squid. The signature dish, a pepita-crusted salmon with shrimp, crab, and chilies provides a nice hot crunch before melting in your mouth. Vegetables are simply prepared, usually steamed or sautéed with a touch of lemon or garlic oil.

The award-winning chef/owner Bob Kinkead is the star at this three-tier, 220-seat restaurant. He wears a headset and orchestrates his kitchen staff in full view of the upstairs dining room, where booths and tables neatly fill the nooks and alcoves of the town house. At street level is a scattering of tables overlooking the restaurant's lower level, the more casual bar and cafe, where a jazz group or pianist performs in the evening and at Sunday brunch. *Beware:* If the waiter tries to seat you in the "atrium," you should know that you'll be stuck at a table mall-side, just outside the doors of the restaurant.

Kinkead's menu features primarily seafood, but the menu (which changes daily for lunch and again for dinner) also includes at least one meat and one poultry entree. The wine list comprises more than 300 selections. You can't go wrong with the desserts either, like the chocolate dacquoise with cappuccino sauce.

Melrose. In the Park Hyatt Hotel, 1201 24th St. NW (at M St.). ☎ **202/955-3899.** Reservations recommended. Breakfast $9–$15.50; lunch $14–$22.50; dinner $23.75–$28; pretheater $26.95; Sun brunch $33 ($36 with champagne). AE, CB, DC, DISC, JCB, MC, V. Mon–Sat 6:30–11am, Sun 6:30–10:30am. Daily 11am–2:30pm and 5:30–10:30pm. Complimentary valet parking all day. Metro: Foggy Bottom. AMERICAN.

Situated in an upscale hotel, this pretty restaurant offers fine cuisine presented with friendly flourishes. In nice weather, dine outdoors on the beautifully landscaped, sunken terrace whose greenery and towering fountain protect you from traffic noises. The glass-walled dining room overlooks the terrace and is decorated with more greenery, grand bouquets of fresh flowers, and accents of marble and brass.

Brian McBride is the beguiling executive chef who sometimes emerges from the kitchen to find out how you like the angel-hair pasta with mascarpone and lobster, or his sautéed Dover sole with roasted peppers, forest mushrooms, and mâche. McBride, like Bob Kinkead (see above), is known for his seafood, which makes up most of the entrees and nearly all of the appetizers. Specialties of the house include shrimp ravioli with sweet corn, black pepper, tomato, and lemongrass beurre blanc, and Melrose crab cakes with grilled vegetables in a remoulade sauce. Desserts, like the raspberry crème brûlée or the chocolate bread pudding with chocolate sorbet, are excellent. The wine list offers 30 wines by the glass. Friday nights, the restaurant dispenses with corkage fees; feel free to bring your own bottle. Saturday nights, a quartet plays jazz, swing, and big-band tunes, 7 to 11pm; lots of people get up and dance.

Provence. 2401 Pennsylvania Ave. NW. ☎ **202/296-1166.** Reservations recommended. Lunch $13.50–$23, dinner $20.50–$34. AE, CB, DC, MC, V. Mon–Fri noon–2pm and 6–10pm, Sat 5:30–11pm, Sun 5:30–9:30pm. Complimentary valet parking evenings. Metro: Foggy Bottom. FRENCH.

With an exhibition kitchen arrayed with gleaming copper ware, Provence's interior is country French. Panels of rough-hewn stone are framed by rustic shutters, antique hutches display provincial pottery, and delicate chandeliers and shaded sconces provide a soft amber glow.

Yannick Cam's provincial cuisine "personalisée" refers to his unique interpretations of traditional Mediterranean recipes, which lose nothing in the way of regional integrity. An appetizer of pan-roasted young squid—stuffed with finely ground scallops and shrimp, sautéed shallots and garlic, wild mushrooms, parsley, toasted pine nuts, and lavender blossoms—was complemented by buttery pan juice. And an entree of crisp-skinned organic roast chicken—perfumed with bay leaf, rosemary, sweet garlic, and a soupçon of anchovy—was accompanied by superb roasted potatoes and artichoke hearts in a sauce of red wine, citrus, tomato concassé, garlic, chopped olives, and rosemary-infused olive oil. For dessert, try the terrine of chocolate with walnut-hazelnut sauce. The knowledgeable staff can suggest appropriate wines from the 90%-French list.

10 Glover Park

MODERATE

Busara. 2340 Wisconsin Ave. NW. ☎ **202/337-2340.** Reservations recommended. Lunch $6–$8.25, dinner $7.95–$15.25. AE, DC, DISC, MC, V. Mon–Thurs 11:30am–3pm and 5–11pm, Fri 11:30am–3pm and 5pm–midnight, Sat 11:30am–4pm and 5pm–midnight, Sun 5–11pm. THAI.

Like many Thai restaurants, Busara gives you big portions for a pretty good price. The pad thai is an excellent, not as sweet as the normal version; the satays are well marinated; and an appetizer called "shrimp bikini" serves up not-at-all-greasy deep-fried shrimp in a thin spring-roll covering.

Busara's dining room is large, with a picture window overlooking Wisconsin Avenue, modern art on the neon blue walls, and dimly set track lighting angled this way and that. Service is solicitous, but not pushy. If the dining room is full, you can eat at the bar (at dinner only), which is in a separate, small, and inviting room. In warm weather, Busara also serves diners in its Oriental garden.

Sushi-Ko. 2309 Wisconsin Ave. NW. ☎ **202/333-4187.** Reservations recommended. Lunch $6.50–$17, dinner $7.50–$18. AE, MC, V. Mon 6–10:30pm, Tues–Fri noon–2:30pm and 6–10:30pm, Sat 5–10:30pm, Sun 5–10pm. JAPANESE.

This is the best place in Washington for sushi, and people know it; so even if you've reserved a table, you may have a wait. The sushi choppers are fun to watch at the sushi bar, so try to sit there. At any rate, you can expect superb versions of sushi and sashimi standards, but the best items are those invented by former chef Kaz Okochi (now of Raku)—like a napoleon of diced sea trout layered between rice crackers, or a tuna tartare. If you're not one for sushi, you might enjoy this restaurant's excellent tempuras and teriyakis.

INEXPENSIVE

✪ **Austin Grill.** 2404 Wisconsin Ave. NW. ☎ **202/337-8080.** www.austingrill.com. Main courses $6–$15. AE, DC, DISC, MC, V. Mon 11:30am–10:30pm, Tues–Thurs 11:30am–11pm, Fri 11:30am–midnight, Sat 11am–midnight, Sun 11am–10:30pm. TEX-MEX.

Come with the kids, a date, or your friends for fun and good food. Austin Grill is loud; as the night progresses, conversation eventually drowns out the sound of the taped music (everything from Ry Cooder to Natalie Merchant).

Owner Rob Wilder opened his grill in 1988 to replicate the easygoing lifestyle, Tex-Mex cuisine, and music he'd loved when he lived in Austin. The grill is known for the fresh ingredients used to create outstanding crabmeat quesadillas; "Lake Travis" nachos (tostidas slathered with chopped red onion, refried beans, and cheese); a daily fish special (like rockfish fajitas); key lime pie; and excellent versions of standard fare (chicken enchiladas, guacamole, pico de gallo, and so on).

Austin Grill's upstairs overlooks the small bar area below. An upbeat decor includes walls washed in shades of teal and clay and adorned with whimsical coyotes, cowboys, Indians, and cacti. Arrive by 6pm weekends if you don't want to wait; weekdays are less crowded. This is the original Austin Grill; another District Austin Grill opened in May 1998 at 750 E St. NW. ☎ 202/393-3776; suburban locations are in Old Town Alexandria and West Springfield, Virginia, and in Bethesda, Maryland.

11 U Street Corridor

INEXPENSIVE TO MODERATE

Coppi's. 1414 U St. NW. ☎ **202/319-7773.** Main courses $7–$11.50. AE, DC, DISC, V. Mon–Thurs 5pm–midnight, Fri–Sat 5pm–1am, Sun 5–11pm. Metro: U Street–Cardoza. ITALIAN.

Crowded with neighborhood customers and hungry clubgoers headed for one of the nearby music houses, Coppi's is a narrow room decorated with wooden booths and bicycle memorabilia from Italian bike races. The wood-burning oven turns out a mean pizza, a stiff competitor to that of top-dog Pizzeria Paradiso (see above). The crust is chewy and the toppings of good-quality ham, pancetta, cheeses, and vegetables. You can count on finding an extensive Italian wine list and entrees all under $12. Another Coppi's, the larger Coppi's Vigorelli, is in the Cleveland Park neighborhood, at 3421 Connecticut Ave. NW (☎ **202/244-6437**).

12 Woodley Park

EXPENSIVE

✪ **Mrs. Simpson's.** 2915 Connecticut Ave. NW. ☎ **202/332-8300.** Reservations recommended. Lunch $5.50–$11.95; dinner $6.95–$22.95; Sun brunch $6.95–$13.95, $16.95 for 3-course champagne Sun brunch. AE, CB, DC, DISC, MC, V. Mon–Fri 11:30am–9:30pm, Sat 11:30am–9:30pm, Sun brunch 10:30am–9:30pm. Metro: Woodley Park–Zoo. AMERICAN.

Mrs. Simpson's lies 1 block up and across Connecticut Avenue from the Sheraton Washington Hotel, whose guests often stumble delightedly upon the restaurant. More and more, though, you'll see people from the neighborhood, drawn by the gracious welcome, the popular brunch, and a menu that offers just enough variety to please small and hearty eaters, traditional and inquisitive palates.

Specials are always worth investigating. A smoky mushroom soup of puréed, grilled portobello and shiitake mushrooms tastes creamy, though it is broth-based. The grilled Canadian salmon al pesto is perfectly prepared and worth ordering simply for the vegetable pancake that accompanies it. Crab cakes are the traditional version—mostly crab—and a house specialty.

Your waiter will urge dessert on you, and you should succumb. Chocolate roulade cake, fresh lemon mousse, and raspberry crème brûlée are tops.

✪ **New Heights.** 2317 Calvert St. NW. ☎ **202/234-4110.** Reservations recommended. Brunch $7.75–$11.50, dinner $16–$25. AE, CB, DC, DISC, MC, V. Mon–Thurs 5:30–10pm, Fri–Sat 5:30–11pm, Sun 11am–2:30pm and 5:30–10pm. Free valet parking. Metro: Woodley Park–Zoo. AMERICAN/INTERNATIONAL.

This attractive second-floor dining room has a bank of windows looking out to Rock Creek Park and walls hung with the colorful works of a Florida artist. New Heights attracts a casually upscale clientele, who fill the room every night. Certain features, like the excellent black bean pâté with smoked tomato and green onion sauces, and the choice of appetizer or entree portions, are fixtures. But Matthew Lake, the restaurant's 27-year-old chef, is responsible for innovations such as the heavenly potato-crusted Arctic char, which is prepared with ginger-braised leeks and walnuts in a porcini mushroom beurre blanc. Best to ask about menu items whose descriptions use unfamiliar though intriguing words; for example, "crispy eggplant fritters with rocket pesto and lime tahini." An almond torte dessert proves a perfect antidote.

MODERATE

Lebanese Taverna. 2641 Connecticut Ave. NW. ☎ **202/265-8681.** Reservations accepted for seating before 6:30pm. Lunch $8–$14, dinner $10–$16. AE, CB, DC, DISC, MC, V. Mon–Thurs 11:30am–2:30pm and 5:30–10:30pm, Fri 11:30am–2:30pm and 5:30–11pm, Sat 11:30am–3pm and 5:30–11pm, Sun 5–10pm. Metro: Woodley Park–Zoo. LEBANESE.

This family-owned restaurant gives you a taste of Lebanese culture, not just through the cuisine, but in decor and music as well. It's so popular on weekends that often you'll see people standing in line to get in (reservations are accepted for seating before 6:30pm only). Diners, once seated in the courtyardlike dining room, where music plays and prayer rugs hang on walls, hate to leave. The wood-burning oven in the back bakes the pita breads and several appetizers. Order a demi mezze, with pita for dipping, and you get 12 sampling dishes, including hummus, tabouleh, baba ghannouge, and pastry-wrapped spinach pies (*fatayer b'sbanigh*), enough for dinner for two, or hors d'oeuvres for four. The wealth of meatless dishes will delight vegetarians, while rotisserie items, especially the chicken and the chargrilled kebabs of chicken and shrimp, will please all others. Another plus: complimentary parking at a nearby garage.

Petitto's. 2653 Connecticut Ave. NW. ☎ **202/667-5350.** Reservations recommended. Main courses $11–$17.75. AE, CB, DC, DISC, MC, V. Mon–Sat 5:30–10:30pm, Sun 5:30–9:30pm. Dolce Finale, Mon–Thurs 5pm–midnight, Fri–Sat 5pm–1:30am. Metro: Woodley Park–Zoo. NORTHERN ITALIAN.

This is an old-fashioned neighborhood restaurant whose three dining rooms, each with a working fireplace, occupy the first floor of a turn-of-the-century town house. Operatic arias provide the appropriate background music, with live operas sung every Friday night in the upstairs dining room. In nice weather, you can dine alfresco at tables set out in front of the restaurant, and watch the passersby strolling Connecticut Avenue.

A "symphony of pasta" sampler platter (three varieties) offers the best value. Choices include a *falasche alla Petitto* (homemade spinach and egg noodles tossed with mushrooms, prosciutto, and peas in a cream sauce) and penne tossed with chunks of bacon and hot peppers in red sauce. Aside from the sampler, the linguini with lump crabmeat and black olives and mushrooms is notable for its fresh chunks of crab in a light cream sauce. Two new pasta dishes include the pappardelle with wild mushroom sauce and the agnolotti stuffed with spinach and ricotta. Non-pasta entrees change weekly, but there's always veal and fresh seafood dishes; for example, *cacciucco*, an array of lobster, scallops, mussels, clams, and squid. A moderately priced and well-chosen list of Italian wines is augmented by costlier vintages (including French and California selections).

Dolce Finale, in Petitto's candlelit, brick-walled wine cellar, features a variety of cappuccinos, wines, grappas, liqueurs, fruits, and cheeses, and an array of sumptuous desserts. It can be visited separately from the restaurant.

13 Dining in Bethesda

Dining in Bethesda? Yeah, well, dining is what this Maryland suburb of Washington is all about. Within a few blocks' radius of the Bethesda Metro stop (on the red line) are nearly 200 restaurants. It's not that Bethesda restaurants are any better than the best you'll find in Washington, although many of them are as good. It's not that there are tons of attractions that would attract the tourist here otherwise; Bethesda is a bedroom community, mostly residential, with the grocery stores and shopping malls to match. But a combination of development

A Great Restaurant Outside Washington

Ask a Washingtonian to name his or her favorite local restaurant, and the answer may surprise you: Washingtonians consistently put at the top of their lists, The Inn at Little Washington, which lies 50 miles outside of the city.

The Inn at Little Washington, Middle and Main Streets, Washington, VA (☎ 540/675-3800), with its exquisite American regional food prepared by chef Patrick O'Connell, gains accolades from the world's best chefs. The English-style inn is a Relais et Chateaux property and lies in Washington, Virginia, about 50 miles south of Washington. To get here follow I-66 west to Exit 43A (Gainsville/Warrenton), which takes you to Route 29 south for 12 miles to Warrenton, and then travel through the business section until you reach Route 211 west. Turn right on Route 211 and drive 23 more miles to Washington, Virginia, turning off for the business section, and the middle of town.

and a thriving economy has inspired restaurateurs to open every kind of restaurant you can think of, Afghan to Cajun, within a compact and walkable cross section of this affluent community. Some of the restaurants are very inexpensive, and a few fall into the expensive range, but most of the restaurants are moderately priced.

So if you are visiting friends or relatives in the upper northwest reaches of the district, or in the Bethesda/Chevy Chase vicinity, itself, don't fret that you're in the boondocks. You'll find this part of town lively with pedestrian traffic, people like you, out for a good meal. (Bethesda has a growing number of singles bars and nightspots, too.) And while a number of Washington restaurants are often closed on Sunday or Monday, most Bethesda restaurants are open every day. The downside is that the dining scene can get downright competitive. Forget impromptu, and plan to eat early or late and to make a reservation or expect a wait. Forget parking, too, there's not enough; take the Metro. Here are some of my favorite restaurants in Bethesda, as well as one I think noteworthy in Chevy Chase; all are within walking distance of the Metro. If you want more restaurant and shopping information, call up the Bethesda Web site at **www.bethesda.org.**

Austin Grill. 7728 Woodmont Ave. ☎ **301/656-1366.** Reservations accepted for groups of 8 or more but not on weekends. Lunch and dinner $7–$14. AE, DC, DISC, MC, V. Mon 11:30am–10pm, Tues–Thurs 11:30am–11pm, Fri 11:30am–midnight, Sat 11am–midnight, Sun 11am–10pm. TEX-MEX.

Same food as the Glover Park location (see description above for recommended dishes), this Austin Grill caters more to families in the early evening and to funlovers as the night progresses. This is also a larger restaurant, with a separate bar area, more seating at banquettes, and at sidewalk tables in good weather.

Bethesda Crab House. 4958 Bethesda Ave. ☎ **301/652-3382.** Reservations recommended. Hard-shell crabs: all you can eat for $19.95 per person. Other items available: shrimp, crab cakes, etc.; Main courses $20. AE, MC, V. Daily 9am–midnight. CRABS.

Of all the restaurants recommended, this one is the farthest from the Metro. But it's not a long walk, especially if you're bound and determined to participate in the local Maryland custom of taking mallet to Chesapeake Bay hard-shell crab, cracking it open, and picking it to get the succulent Old Bay seasoned meat inside. This is the only place in the area that offers you the opportunity. Dress down and expect long lines in summer, a shack-like interior, long bare tables where you'll be sitting with strangers, and sore lips.

Cafe Bethesda. 5027 Wilson Lane. ☎ **301/657-3383.** Reservations recommended. Lunch $10–$14, dinner $15–$25. AE, DC, MC, V. Mon–Fri 11:30am–2pm and 5:30–10pm, Sat–Sun 5:30–10pm. MODERN AMERICAN.

This is a comfortable neighborhood place, where the service is thoughtful and the food some of the best in Bethesda. You can choose from straightforward rack of lamb or steak, or go for something a little snazzier, like the tuna served with black olives, pine nuts, and capers, or grilled eggplant rolls, stuffed with goat cheese, roasted peppers, and spinach. Great desserts.

Cesco Trattoria. 4871 Cordell Ave. ☎ **301/654-8333.** Reservations required. Lunch $7.95–$14.95, dinner $10.95–$19.95. AE, MC, V. Mon–Thurs 11:30am–2pm and 5:30–10pm, Fri 11:30am–2pm and 5:30–10:30pm, Sat 5:30–10:30pm. ITALIAN.

Another Roberto Donna endeavor (see Galileo, Il Radicchio, etc.) is this elegant-looking, but informal and bustling restaurant, which the owner opened in collaboration with Francesco Ricchi, who opened I Ricchi (see entry above) in downtown Washington. Wealthy Bethesdans, happy to enjoy fine Italian dining without having to trek in to the city, keep the restaurant packed, which can mean that even if you have a reservation, you may still have a wait. Many think it's worth it, once they've bitten into the prosciutto with fried bread; grilled rockfish with diced tomatoes, olives, and olive oil; and pappardelle pasta with rabbit ragout. The best Italian restaurant in Bethesda, and one of the best in the area.

Louisiana Express. 4921 Bethesda Ave. ☎ **301/652-6945.** Reservations not accepted. Lunch and dinner $2.95–$13.50. Mon–Sat 7:30am–9:30pm, Sun 9am–9pm. CAJUN.

When I want to treat my daughters, ages 6 and 11, I take them here for beignets and hot chocolate, and all of us emerge happy, with confectioner's sugar-rimmed smiles. Unfancy decor, but casual and easygoing as New Orleans itself, Louisiana Express serves authentic versions of po'boys, etouffée, jambalaya, blackened fish, and bread pudding with bourbon sauce. The restaurant is on the same street as the Bethesda Crab House, (see above), and a good walk from the Metro.

Ristorante Terrazza. 12 Wisconsin Circle, Chevy Chase. ☎ **301/951-9292.** Reservations recommended. Lunch $7.95–$13.95, dinner $9.95–$21.95. AE, MC, V. Mon–Fri 11:30am–2:30pm and 5:30–10:30pm, Sat 5:30–10:30pm. Free valet parking at lunch and dinner. Metro: Friendship Heights. ITALIAN.

One Metro stop before the Bethesda station on the red line is Friendship Heights, whose station lies beneath the building that houses Terrazza; because of it prime location and excellent cuisine, it would be remiss of me not to mention it. Even if you're headed to Bethesda, you won't regret this detour, after you've dined on the mushroom risotto, red snapper with white grapes, or the veal scalopini with figs and marsala wine, served with sautéed spinach and saffron potatoes. There's an emphasis here on gracious service, and the restaurant attracts an older crowd.

7

What to See & Do in Washington, D.C.

As you plan your trip to Washington, you may start to wonder: Just how many memorials are there, anyway? The answer is a whopping 155, when you count those throughout the capital area. Many, of course, were constructed long ago and are known world-wide: the Lincoln and Jefferson Memorials and the Washington Monument, for example. Some are so new that you may not even have heard of them. On July 15 through 18, 1998, for example, the African-American Civil War Memorial was dedicated in the Shaw neighborhood; in October 1997, the Women in Military Service for America, adjacent to Arlington Cemetery, opened to the public. On the other hand, the Franklin Delano Roosevelt Memorial, only 2 years old in May, has fast gained popularity, drawing nearly twice the number of visitors as any other presidential memorial.

As for numbers of museums, try more than 50. This figure includes the nine Smithsonian museums, joined by the National Gallery of Art, the United States Holocaust Museum, and the National Archives, all of which are clustered alongside the National Mall, a destination you, no doubt, have placed at the top of your itinerary. Here, too, you can look for something new: the National Gallery's outdoor Sculpture Garden, which encompasses 6.1 acres across from the gallery's west building, between 7th and 9th Streets. The garden, which opened in the fall of 1998, is a welcome addition, especially since renovation work has closed the U.S. Botanic Garden, on the other side of the Mall, until the year 2000.

The Mall rightfully belongs at the top of your list, but the many off-the-mall museums and attractions should not be far behind. These include the Smithsonian's National Portrait Gallery, National Museum of American Art (including the Renwick Gallery, the museum's American crafts annex near the White House), the Anacostia Museum, the National Zoo, and the National Postal Museum; privately funded museums, like the Corcoran Gallery of Art, the National Museum of Women in the Arts, and the Phillips Gallery; and other less famous sites, such as the Woodrow Wilson Historic House Museum, Dumbarton Oaks, and the Newseum (in Arlington).

If it's the Washington-as-the-nation's-capital side you'd most like to see, you should tailor your visit to accommodate tours of the White House, the Capitol, the Supreme Court, and the Library of Congress. And if it's the Washington-as-a-historic city-

Impressions

It has a damp, wheezy, Dickensian sort of winter hardly equalled by London, and a steaming tropical summer not surpassed by the basin of the Nile.

—Alistair Cooke

Take an umbrella, an overcoat, and a fan, and go forth.

—Mark Twain

of-neighborhoods side you'd prefer to get to know, explore on your own or take an organized tour (see "Organized Tours" near the end of this chapter) that sends you in and out of historic homes, gardens, and neighborhoods throughout the city.

Now, are you feeling overwhelmed? At long last, the city has a walk-in visitor center, complete with maps, visitor guides, interactive information kiosks, brochures, and live and talking information specialists, to help you get a grip. In July 1998, the **Washington, D.C., Visitor Information Center** opened in the brand-new Ronald Reagan Building and International Trade Center, at 1300 Pennsylvania Ave. NW (☎ 202/638-3222), just 1 block from the White House Visitor Center. Because the building is so enormous (second largest federal building, the first being the Pentagon), you may have trouble finding the entrance: head for the corner of 13th Street and Pennsylvania Avenue, enter the building, then go down the hall and to the left, and you'll see the center. If you're arriving by Metro, exit the Federal Triangle station and cross Wilson Plaza to the visitor center, whose entrance lies directly across from the station. The center is open Monday to Saturday 8am to 6pm, and Sunday noon to 5pm.

USEFUL WEB SITES

Before you begin: The National Park Service, which maintains many of the attractions reviewed in this chapter, has its own Web site: **www.nps.gov/nacc,** which you may want to access for further information. The Smithsonian Institution, see section 3, further along, also has its own Web site: **www.si.edu,** which will help get you to the home pages for its individual museums.

SUGGESTED ITINERARIES

If You Have 1 Day

Make the Mall your destination, visiting whichever museums appeal to you the most. Then take a breather: If you have young children, let them ride the carousel across from the Smithsonian's Arts and Industries Building. With or without kids, stroll across the Mall to the new National Gallery Sculpture Garden, where you can get a bite to eat in the cafe or sit relaxing next to the reflecting pool. Rest up, dine in the Dupont Circle neighborhood, stroll Connecticut Avenue, then take a taxi to visit the Lincoln Memorial at night.

If You Have 2 Days

On your first day, take a narrated tour of the city (see list of tours at end of this chapter) for an overview of the city's attractions, stopping at the Jefferson, FDR, Lincoln, and Vietnam Veterans Memorials, and at the Washington Monument. Use the tour to determine your choices of mall museums to visit. After taking in the Washington Monument, walk up 15th Street to the Old Ebbitt Grill for lunch (expect a wait unless you made a reservation). Following lunch, visit your top-pick museums on the Mall. Start your second day by visiting the Capitol, followed by a tour of the Supreme Court. Walk to Massachusetts Avenue for lunch at Café Berlin, then spend the afternoon visiting the Library of Congress, the Folger Shakespeare Library, and, if you have time, Union Station and the National Postal Museum.

Have dinner in Georgetown and browse the shops.

If You Have 3 Days

Spend your first 2 days as described above. On the morning of your third day, tour the White House and the National Archives. In the afternoon, ride the bus (an N bus from Dupont Circle, or a 30-series bus from Georgetown) to visit the Washington National Cathedral, or take in some of the non-Mall art museums, for example, the Phillips Collection, the National Portrait Gallery, the Museum of American Art, or the Corcoran. Enjoy a pretheater dinner at one of the many restaurants that offer these good deals (some suggestions: 1789 in Georgetown, the Bombay Club near the White House), then head to the Kennedy Center for a performance.

If You Have 4 Days or More

Spend your first 3 days as suggested above.

On the fourth day, get an early start on the FBI tour, go across the street to Ford's Theatre, then have an early lunch. Head to the Discovery Store in the MCI Center in time to buy tickets and catch the 1pm Heritage Tour, which gives you an inside look at Washington in the 19th century as you walk through Chinatown and other sections of this downtown neighborhood. Use the rest of the afternoon for outdoor activities—go to the zoo or for a hike along the C&O Canal. Alternatively, you might visit the U.S. Holocaust Memorial Museum (not recommended for children under 12); this will require most of a day to see. Have dinner downtown at one of the 7th Street district restaurants, then go on to see Shakespeare performed at the Lansburgh, or head to Coco Loco to practice your samba.

On the fifth day, consider a day trip to Alexandria, Virginia. Or board a boat for Mount Vernon, and spend most of the day touring the estate, with the afternoon set aside for seeing sights you've missed. Have dinner in Adams-Morgan, followed by club-hopping up and down 18th Street. (Or try jazz at one of the clubs; see chapter 10 for suggestions.)

1 The Three Major Houses of Government

Three of the most visited sights in Washington are the buildings housing the executive, legislative, and judicial branches of the U.S. government. All are stunning and offer considerable insight into the workings of America.

✪ **The White House.** 1600 Pennsylvania Ave. NW (visitor entrance gate at E St. and E. Executive Ave.). ☎ **202/456-7041** or 202/208-1631. Free admission. Tues–Sat 10am–noon. Closed some days for official functions; check before leaving your hotel by calling the 24-hour number. Metro: McPherson Square (if you are going straight to the White House), Federal Triangle (if you are getting tour tickets from the White House Visitor Center).

If you think you're going to get the Monica Lewinsky tour, think again. Whether you visit the White House on a VIP guided tour or go through self-guided, you will see just what your escorts (Secret Service agents, by the way) want you to see, and that doesn't include the Oval Office. So forget scandal in the White House, if you can, and soak up the history of this house that has served as a residence, office, reception site, and world embassy for every U.S. president since John Adams.

Before the Tour

Remember, there are no public rest rooms or telephones in the White House, and picture-taking and videotaping are prohibited.

A good idea, before you take any tour, is to pick up a book called *The White House: An Historic Guide,* available at the White House Visitor Center and at many of the top sights. Then you'll know what to look for in each room. You can order it in advance (as well as another book, *The Living White House,* which gives more biographical information about the presidents and their families) from the **White House Historical Association,** 740 Jackson Place NW, Washington, D.C. 20503 (☎ **800/555-2451** or 202/737-8292). Send $8 for a paperback or $9.50 for a hardcover edition of either book (prices include costs for shipping and handling). You can also order a $49.95 CD-ROM, which offers a virtual tour of the White House, including some rooms that aren't on the in-person tour, such as the Lincoln Bedroom and even part of the Oval Office. At the very least, pick up the free brochure given out at the **White House Visitor Center** (see below).

WHITE HOUSE TOURS AND TICKETS   It's not hard to get tickets to visit the White House, but there are a few things that you should know before heading out to the president's home. The White House is open mornings only, Tuesday through Saturday. Tickets are required year-round, although the National Park Service sometimes waives that requirement when things are really slow, usually between January and March.

There are two ways to get tickets: You can write to your congressperson or senator months in advance requesting tickets for the VIP tour (see "Visitor Information" on p.19 in chapter 2 for more information). Or, if you don't have VIP tour tickets, you can pick up your free tickets at the **White House Visitor Center,** 1450 Pennsylvania Ave., in the Department of Commerce Building, between 14th and 15th Streets (see listing below for more information). Tickets are timed for tours between 10am and noon and are issued on the day of the tour on a first-come, first-served basis starting at 7:30am. During the busy season (April through September), people start lining up before 7am, and although a multitude (approximately 4,500 are distributed) of tickets is available, it is essential that you arrive early (even before 7am, to ensure admission). One person may obtain up to four tickets. Each person who gets tickets, also receives an invisible hand stamp detectable only by some high-tech machine. To gain admittance on the tour, someone in your party must have the magic stamp. The ticket counter closes when the supply for that day is gone. Tickets are valid only for the day and time issued.

After obtaining your tickets, you'll probably have quite a bit of time to spare before your tour time; consider enjoying a leisurely breakfast at **Reeve's Restaurant & Bakery** or the **Old Ebbitt Grill,** both close by (see chapter 6 for details).

Both the VIP tour and the not-so-VIP tour go through the same rooms; on the VIP tour, a Secret Service agent guides you; on the self-guided tour, Secret Service Agents are scattered throughout the rooms, and if you approach them, they'll even answer questions. Highlights of the tour include the following rooms:

The Gold-and-White East Room   This room has been the scene of presidential receptions, weddings of presidents' daughters (Lynda Bird Johnson, for one), and other dazzling events. This is where the president entertains visiting heads of state and the place where seven of the eight presidents who died in office (all but Garfield) laid in state. It was also the scene of Nixon's resignation speech. The room is decorated in the early 20th-century style of the Theodore Roosevelt renovation; it has parquet Fontainebleau oak floors and white-painted wood walls with fluted pilasters and classical relief inserts. Note the famous Gilbert Stuart portrait of George Washington that Dolley Madison saved from the British torch during the War of 1812.

The Green Room   Thomas Jefferson's dining room is today used as a sitting room. He designed a revolving door with trays on one side, so servants could leave dishes on the kitchen side. Then he would twirl the door and allow guests to help themselves, thus retaining his privacy. In the room, green watered-silk fabric covers walls hung with notable paintings by Gilbert Stuart and John Singer Sargent, which look down upon a number of early 19th-century furnishings attributed to the famous cabinetmaker Duncan Phyfe.

The Oval Blue Room   This room, decorated in the French Empire style chosen by James Monroe in 1817, is where presidents and first ladies have officially received guests since the Jefferson administration. It was, however, Van Buren's decor that began the "blue room" tradition. The walls, on which hang portraits of five presidents (including Rembrandt Peale's portrait of Thomas Jefferson and G. P. A. Healy's of Tyler), are covered in reproductions of early 19th-century French and American wallpaper. Grover Cleveland, the only president to wed in the White House, was married in the Blue Room; the Reagans, Nancy wearing symbolic yellow, here greeted the 53 Americans liberated after being held hostage in Iran for 444 days; and every year it's the setting for the White House Christmas tree.

The Red Room   Several portraits of past presidents—plus Albert Bierstadt's *View of the Rocky Mountains* and a Gilbert Stuart portrait of Dolley Madison—hang here. It's used as a reception room, usually for afternoon teas. The satin-covered walls and most of the Empire furnishings are red.

The State Dining Room   Modeled after late-18th-century neoclassical English houses, this room is a superb setting for state dinners and luncheons. Theodore Roosevelt, a big-game hunter, hung a large moose head over the fireplace and other trophies on the walls. Below G. P. A. Healy's portrait of Lincoln is an inscription written by John Adams on his second night in the White House (FDR had it carved into the mantel): "I Pray Heaven to Bestow The Best of Blessings on THIS HOUSE and on All that shall here-after Inhabit it. May none but Honest and Wise Men ever rule under This Roof."

A BRIEF HISTORY OF THE WHITE HOUSE   Irishman James Hoban submitted the winning design for the structure, beating out 52 other entries in a contest held by George Washington. Although Washington picked the winner, he was the only president never to live in the White House, or president's palace, as it was called before whitewashing brought the name "White House" into use. The White House took 8 years to build, starting in 1792, when its cornerstone was laid, and its facade is made of the same stone as that used to construct the Capitol. In 1814, during the War of 1812, the British set fire to the White House, gutting the interior; the only reason the exterior endured is because a rainstorm extinguished the fire. What you see today is Hoban's basic creation: a building modeled after an Irish country house; in fact, Hoban had in mind the house of the duke of Leinster in Dublin.

Alterations over the years have incorporated the South Portico in 1824, the North Portico in 1829, and electricity starting with Benjamin Harrison's presidency in 1891. In 1902, repairs and refurnishings of the White House cost nearly $500,000. No other great change took place until Harry Truman added his controversial "balcony" inside the columns of the South Portico. Also in 1948, after the leg of Margaret Truman's piano cut through the dining room ceiling, nearly $6 million was allotted to reconstruct the building. The Trumans lived at Blair House across the street for nearly 4 years while the White House interior was shored up with steel girders and concrete. It's as solid as Gibraltar now.

In 1961, Jacqueline Kennedy formed a Fine Arts Committee to help restore the famous rooms to their original grandeur.

Note: All visitors, even those with VIP congressional tour passes, should call ☎ 202/456-7041 before setting out in the morning; occasionally the White House is closed to tourists on short notice because of unforeseen events.

The White House Visitor Center. 1450 Pennsylvania Ave., NW. (in the Department of Commerce Building, between 14th and 15th sts.) ☎ **202/208-1631** or 202/456-7041 for recorded information. Daily 7:30am–4pm. Closed Thanksgiving, Christmas, and New Year's Day. Metro: Federal Triangle.

The Visitor Center opened in 1995 to provide extensive interpretive data about the White House (as well as other Washington tourist attractions) and serve as a ticket-distribution center. It is run under the auspices of the National Park Service, and the staff is particularly well informed. Also try to catch the 30-minute video about the White House called *Within These Walls*, which provides interior views of the presidential precincts and features footage with both the president and Hillary Clinton (it runs continuously throughout the day). Before you leave the visitor center, pick up a copy of the National Park Service's brochure on the White House, which tells you a little about what you see in the five rooms you tour and a bit about the history of the White House. You should also take a look at the center's on-premises exhibits, which include:

Architectural History of the White House, including the grounds and extensive renovations to its structure and interior that have taken place since its cornerstone was laid in 1792.

Symbol and Image, showing how the White House has been portrayed by photographers, artists, journalists, political cartoonists, and others.

First Families, with displays about the people who have lived here (such as prankster Tad Lincoln, who once stood in a window above his father and waved a Confederate flag at a military review).

The Working White House, focusing on the vast staff of servants, chefs, gardeners, Secret Service people, and others who maintain this institution.

Ceremony and Celebration, depicting notable White House events from a Wright Brothers' aviation demonstration in 1911 to a ballet performance by Baryshnikov during the Carter administration.

White House Interiors, Past and Present, including photographs of the ever-changing Oval Office as decorated by administrations from Taft through Clinton.

✪ **The Capitol.** At the east end of the Mall, entrance on E. Capitol St. and 1st St. NW. ☎ **202/225-6827.** Free admission. Mar–Sept daily 9am–8pm; guided tours Mon–Fri 9:30am–7pm and Sat 9:30am–3:30m, guides posted to assist but not guide you Sun 1–4:30pm. Sept–Feb daily 9am–4:30pm; guided tours Mon–Sat 9am–3:45pm. Closed Jan 1, Thanksgiving Day, and Dec 25. Parking at Union Station or on neighborhood streets. Metro: Union Station or Capitol South.

TOUR INFORMATION For all tours, whether during peak season (March through August) or the slow season (September through February), find the east front side of the Capitol, whose sidewalks extend from the Capitol steps and plaza to 1st Street, across from the Library of Congress and Supreme Court. If you are visiting the Capitol in the off-season, you probably will be able to enter the Capitol without waiting in line: Walk up the long driveway and climb the central grand steps of the Capitol. After you pass through the security-check just inside the doors, you enter the Rotunda, where a Capitol Service Guide (a man or woman in a red jacket) will direct you where to stand if you're interested in a guided tour, or hand you the self-guiding brochure if you want to tour on your own.

During the peak season, you have three options if you'd like a guided tour of the Capitol. If you are part of a group of more than 15 people, you can call ☎ 202/224-4910 to reserve a guided tour time, thus avoiding a wait in line. Reservations are very limited, so call months in advance. When you make your reservation, you will be told to come to the east front side of the Capitol and look for any guide in the official red jacket, who will escort you off to the far right side, away from the other lines, and then take you inside for the tour. If you are touring as individuals or as a family, you can try to arrange ahead to obtain VIP tour tickets from the office of your representative or senator for the morning tours (departing at intervals between 8 and 8:45am); see chapter 2 for details. For these tours, you enter the Capitol through the Law Library door on the east front side of the Capitol, facing the Supreme Court, on the ground level, just to the right of the grand staircase. A Capitol Guide will meet you inside and take you on the tour.

Most people opt for just showing up at the Capitol, and if this is your plan, find the east front side of the Capitol and look for the signs posted at the end of either sidewalk flanking the Capitol. One sign designates the line for guided tours, the other denotes the self-guided tours line. If you want the guided tour, step right up and stand in line; guided tours in peak season take place every 30 minutes and admit 50 people at a time. You may have a long wait, especially if you have arrived in the morning. Your best bet is to arrive midday, late afternoon, or early evening. If you'd rather walk through on your own, you will also have to wait in line in peak season, but this queue moves a little faster, admitting 15 people at a time in faster intervals. All tours are free, the guided tours last 20 to 30 minutes, and the self-guided tours last as long as you like. (See "An Art-Full Tour of the Capitol," below, if you're interested in doing your own tour.) Whether you are self-guided or Capitol Guide Service–guided, you must have a ticket to enter the Capitol during the peak season; the tickets, which do not specify time and date, are handed to you just before you climb the steps and enter the Capitol, which means you're stuck in line and can't go and grab a bite to eat or tour another site in the interim.

The House and Senate galleries are always open to visitors, but passes are required when these galleries are in session. After 6pm, however, you may enter either gallery without a pass and watch the session to its conclusion. Once obtained, the passes are good through the remainder of the Congress. To obtain visitor passes in advance, contact your representative or senator (see chapter 2 for details). If you don't get advance tickets, and if you don't receive visitor passes in the mail (not every senator or representative sends them), they're obtainable at your senator's office on the Constitution Avenue side of the building or your representative's office on the Independence Avenue side. (Visitors who are not citizens can obtain a gallery pass by presenting a passport at the Senate or House appointments desk, located on the first floor of the Capitol). Call the Capitol switchboard at ☎ 202/224-3121 to contact the office of your senator or congressperson. You'll know when the House and/or the Senate is in session when you see flags flying over their respective wings of the Capitol, or you can check the weekday "Today in Congress" column in the *Washington Post* for details on times of the House and Senate sessions and committee hearings. This column also tells you which sessions are open to the public, allowing you to pick one that interests you. To visit the Hall of the House of Representatives Gallery, enter the Capitol through the south door at the end of the building facing Independence Avenue; to visit the Senate Chamber Gallery, enter the building through the Law Library door on the east front side of the Capitol facing the Supreme Court, on the ground level, just to the right of the central grand staircase.

A BRIEF HISTORY OF THE CAPITOL   The Capitol is as awesome up close at it is from afar. As the place where our elected representatives formulate, debate, and pass into law our country's policies and principles, the Capitol is perhaps the most important edifice in the United States. For 135 years it sheltered not only both houses of Congress but the Supreme Court, and for 97 years the Library of Congress as well. When you tour the Capitol, you'll learn about America's history as you admire the place in which it unfolded. Classic architecture, interior embellishments, and hundreds of paintings, sculptures, and other artworks are integral elements of the Capitol.

On the massive bronze doors leading to the **Rotunda** are portrayals of events in the life of Columbus. The Rotunda—a huge, 96-foot-wide, circular hall that is capped by a 180-foot-high dome—is the hub of the Capitol. The dome was completed, at Lincoln's direction, while the Civil War was being fought. Nine presidents have lain in state here; when Kennedy's casket was displayed, the line of mourners stretched 40 blocks. On the circular walls are eight immense oil paintings of events in American history, such as the presentation of the Declaration of Independence and the surrender of Cornwallis at Yorktown. In the dome is an allegorical fresco masterpiece by Constantino Brumidi, *Apotheosis of Washington,* a symbolic portrayal of George Washington surrounded by Roman gods and goddesses watching over the progress of the nation. Brumidi was known as the "Michelangelo of the Capitol" for the many works he created throughout the building. Take another look at the dome and find the woman poised directly below Washington; the triumphant Armed Freedo figure is said to be modeled after Lola Germon, a young and beautiful actress with whom the 60-year-old Brumidi had a child. Beneath the dome is a trompe l'oeil frieze that depicts events in American history from Columbus through the Wright brothers' flight at Kitty Hawk.

Newly added to the Rotunda is the sculpture of suffragists Elizabeth Cady Stanton, Susan B. Anthony, and Lucretia Mott. Until recently, the ponderous monument had been relegated to the Crypt, one level directly below the Rotunda. Women's groups organized to place the statue in its more prominent position in the Rotunda.

National Statuary Hall was originally the chamber of the House of Representatives. In 1864, it became Statuary Hall, and the states were invited to send two statues each of native sons and daughters to the hall. As the room filled up, statues spilled over into the Hall of Columns, corridors, and any space that might accommodate the bronze and marble artifacts. Many of the statues honor individuals who played important roles in American history, such as Henry Clay, Ethan Allen, Daniel Webster, and even a woman or two, like Jeannette Rankin (the first woman to serve in Congress).

The south and north wings are occupied by the House and Senate chambers, respectively. The House of Representatives chamber is the largest legislative chamber in the world. The president delivers his annual State of the Union address here. Before you leave, visit the Capitol's two museum rooms, the **Old Senate Chamber** and the **Old Supreme Court Chamber,** both of which have been restored to their mid-19th-century appearance. The Old Senate Chamber was the

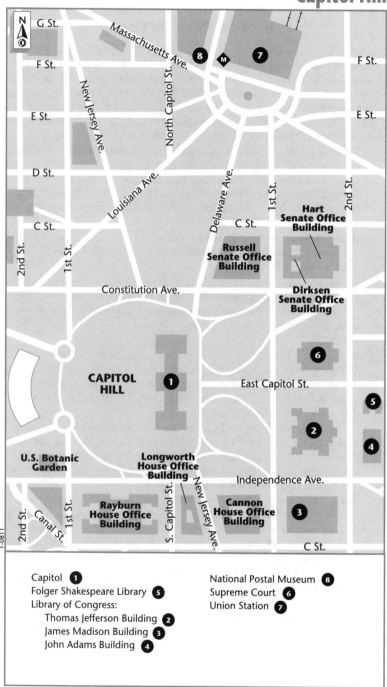

N

G St.

Massachusetts Ave.

F St.   F St.

E St.   E St.

New Jersey Ave.

North Capitol St.

D St.

Louisiana Ave.

Delaware Ave.

C St.   C St.

1st St.

2nd St.

2nd St.

1st St.

Hart Senate Office Building

Russell Senate Office Building

Dirksen Senate Office Building

Constitution Ave.

CAPITOL HILL

East Capitol St.

U.S. Botanic Garden

Longworth House Office Building

Independence Ave.

1st St.

2nd St.

Canal St.

S. Capitol St.

New Jersey Ave.

Rayburn House Office Building

Cannon House Office Building

C St.

1-0811

Capitol ❶	National Postal Museum ❽
Folger Shakespeare Library ❺	Supreme Court ❻
Library of Congress:	Union Station ❼
Thomas Jefferson Building ❷	
James Madison Building ❸	
John Adams Building ❹	

An Art-Full Tour of the Capitol

One glance at the Capitol's grand architecture is enough to tell you that the building is about more than history and politics. The place is also about art. In addition to its superb design, the Capitol also contains more than 800 artworks, from gilded 19th-century frames and the grand paintings they encase, to frescoes, ornamental bronze stair railings, and stained-glass windows. Take a guided tour of the Capitol, if you like, and sit in on a session of Congress, but try to save some time to explore on your own. Here are some special things to look for:

- There's a lot to admire in the Rotunda, but don't miss the life-size marble statue of Lincoln, sculpted by Vinnie Ream—a woman! Ream was only 19 when she received the commission and 23 when she completed it. She sketched Lincoln in half-hour sessions during what proved to be the final 5 months of his life. This is a solemn rendering of a pensive president deep in thought.

- If you like Ream's work, seek out two other statues she sculpted, one of politician Samuel Jordan Kirkwood of Iowa, the other of Cherokee leader Sequoya of Oklahoma, in Statuary Hall.

- For more of Constantino Brumidi's art, find the first floor of the Senate wing. Covering the vaulted ceilings and the crescent-shaped spaces over doorways are Brumidi's decorative paintings of 40 different kinds of birds; plus flowers, fruits, and animals; and portraits of famous Americans and Revolutionary War leaders.

- An immense 20-by-30-foot painting in the east staircase of the Senate wing is William Powell's *1873 Battle of Lake Erie,* depicting the moment during the War of 1812 when Oliver Hazard Perry (known for his victorious pronouncement "We have met the enemy and they are ours.") transfers the colors of his flagship to one in better shape.

- Another huge painting is the 20-by-30-foot fresco by Emanuel Leutze, better known for his *Washington Crossing the Delaware,* than for this *Westward the Course of Empire Takes its Way,* which covers the wall over the west stairway of the House wing. The 1862 painting is a tumultuous display of covered wagons and hopeful immigrants making their way over the Rocky Mountains to the West. It's as colorful as the artist, who was known to drink with his subjects as he worked.

- Albert Bierstadt's works hang in illustrious places, like the White House, the Corcoran Gallery of Art . . . and here, on a private stairway landing in the House wing. It's hard to find it, and when you do, you'll need to peer up from the steps, but it's worth it. Bierstadt was one of the country's best 19th-century landscape painters: *Entrance Into Monterey, 1770* is the name of this superb painting.

site of hotly debated issues, from slavery to territorial expansion; the Old Supreme Court Chamber is where Chief Justice John Marshall established the foundations of American constitutional law. (If you've seen the movie *Amistad,* you'll be interested to know that it was in this chamber that John Quincy Adams argued the Amistad case before the Supreme Court.) Keep your eyes peeled for senators and congressmen and -women as you walk around, because you're likely to see several.

○ **Supreme Court.** East of the Capitol on 1st St. NE (between E. Capitol St. and Maryland Ave.). ☎ **202/479-3000.** Free admission. Mon–Fri 9am–4:30pm. Closed weekends and all federal holidays. Metro: Capitol South or Union Station.

The highest tribunal in the nation, the Supreme Court is charged with deciding whether actions of Congress, the president, the states, and lower courts are in accord with the Constitution, and with applying the Constitution's enduring principles to novel situations and a changing country. It has the power of "judicial review"—authority to invalidate legislation or executive action that conflicts with the Constitution. Out of the 6,500 cases submitted to it each year, the Supreme Court hears only about 100 cases, many of which deal with issues vital to the nation. The Court's rulings are final, reversible only by another Supreme Court decision, or in some cases, an Act of Congress or a constitutional amendment.

Until 1935 the Supreme Court met in the Capitol. Architect Cass Gilbert designed the stately Corinthian marble palace that houses the Court today. The building was considered rather grandiose by early residents: One justice remarked that he and his colleagues ought to enter such pompous precincts on elephants.

If you're in town when the Court is in session, try to see a case being argued (call ☎ **202/479-3211** for details). The Court meets Monday through Wednesday from 10am to noon and, on occasion, from 1 to 2pm, starting the first Monday in October through late April, alternating, in approximately 2-week intervals, between "sittings," to hear cases and deliver opinions, and "recesses," for consideration of business before the Court. Mid-May to late June, you can attend brief sessions (about 15 minutes) at 10am on Monday, when the justices release orders and opinions. You can find out what cases are on the docket by checking the *Washington Post's* "Supreme Court Calendar." Arrive at least an hour early—even earlier for highly publicized cases—to line up for seats, about 150 of which are allotted to the general public.

At 10am the entrance of the justices is announced by the marshal, and all present rise and remain standing while the justices are seated following the chant: "The Honorable, the Chief Justice and Associate Justices of the Supreme Court of the United States. Oyez! Oyez! Oyez! [French for "Hear ye!"] All persons having business before the Honorable, the Supreme Court of the United States, are admonished to draw near and give their attention, for the Court is now sitting. God save the United States and this Honorable Court!" There are many rituals here. Unseen by the gallery is the "conference handshake"; following a 19th-century tradition symbolizing a "harmony of aims if not views," each justice shakes hands with each of the other eight when they assemble to go to the bench. The Court has a record before it of prior proceedings and relevant briefs, so each side is allowed only a 30-minute argument.

The Supreme Court is cloaked in mystery, purposefully. You can't take cameras or recording devices into the courtroom. The justices never give speeches or press conferences. The media reports that Justice Thomas is famously silent, Justice Scalia argumentative, and Justice Ginsburg talkative; all of the justices tend to be intimidating. See for yourself.

If the Court is not in session during your visit, you can attend a free lecture in the courtroom about Court procedure and the building's architecture. Lectures are given every hour on the half hour from 9:30am to 3:30pm.

After the talk, explore the Great Hall and go down a flight of steps to see the 20-minute film on the workings of the Court. On the same floor is an exhibit displaying reproductions of the friezes adorning the tops of the courtroom walls, a gift shop, and a cafeteria that's open to the public and serves good food.

2 The Presidential Memorials

Tributes to American presidents appear in various guises all over the city, and the most recent additions honor Ronald Reagan: the immense new Ronald Reagan Building and International Trade Center at 1300 Pennsylvania Ave. NW and the Ronald Reagan National Airport (known until winter of 1998 as the Washington National Airport). Far fewer in the capital are presidential memorials intended as national shrines to honor the chief executive. In fact, there are four: the Washington Monument, Lincoln Memorial, Jefferson Memorial, and the Franklin Delano Roosevelt Memorial. Unfortunately, none of these lies directly on a Metro line, so you can expect a bit of a walk from the specified station.

Washington Monument. Directly south of the White House (at 15th St. and Constitution Ave. NW). ☎ **202/426-6841.** Free admission. Early Apr–Sept, daily 8am–midnight; Oct–Mar, daily 9am–5pm. Last elevators depart 15 minutes before closing (arrive earlier). Closed Dec 25, open till noon July 4. Metro: Smithsonian, then a 10-minute walk.

TICKET INFORMATION Tickets are required for admission to the Washington Monument in winter (roughly, September through March), from 9am to 5pm, and the rest of the year, from 8am to 8pm. If you come after 8pm in season, go to the Washington Monument and stand in line—always check first with a ranger or at the ticket booth to be sure, though. The ticket booth is located at the bottom of the hill from the monument, on 15th Street NW between Independence and Constitution Avenues. The tickets grant admission at half-hour intervals between the stated hours. You can obtain tickets on the day of the tour; if you want to save yourself the trouble and get them in advance (up to six tickets per person), call Ticketmaster (☎ **800/505-5040**), but you'll pay $1.50 per ticket plus a 50¢ service charge per transaction.

Don't be alarmed when you catch sight of the Washington Monument under wraps. Underneath its radical chic, transparent blue sheath (designed by celebrated architect Michael Graves), the 555-foot marble obelisk is undergoing exterior renovation. The interior was renovated in the spring of 1998, when the monument was closed for tours. Despite its appearance, the monument is open for regular tours; the elevator is refurbished; the climate-control system has been replaced; the 897 steps have been scrubbed; and the 193 carved commemorative stones are polished (see below). The Washington Monument remains the city's most visible landmark, but now, and until at least the year 2000, you will see it through a bluish haze and scaffolding.

VISITING THE WASHINGTON MONUMENT If the building seems to be quivering, it's probably just the wind flapping the blue covering. Even on a still day, the winds are awesome on this summit. The repair work is the monument's first major restoration since it opened in 1888. The restoration has received a lot of attention and brought to light a number of mysterious truths about the obelisk: for example, rangers and workmen have heard it sing as the wind whistles through cracks at the top, and, oddly, the more inferior building materials lie at the base of the monument and the best materials on top. Don't worry, the world's tallest, freestanding masonry work is structurally sound.

The idea of a tribute to George Washington first arose 16 years before his death, at the Continental Congress of 1783. But the new nation had more pressing problems, and funds were not readily available. It wasn't until the early 1830s, with the 100th anniversary of Washington's birth approaching, that any action was taken. Then there were several fiascoes. A mausoleum was provided for Washington's

May the spirit which animated the great founder of this city descend to future generations.

—John Adams

remains under the Capitol Rotunda, but a grand-nephew, citing Washington's will, refused to allow the body to be moved from Mount Vernon. In 1830, Horatio Greenough was commissioned to create a memorial statue for the Rotunda. He came up with a bare-chested Washington, draped in classical Greek garb; a shocked public claimed he looked as if he were "entering or leaving a bath," and so the statue was relegated to the Smithsonian. Finally, in 1833, prominent citizens organized the Washington National Monument Society. Treasury Building architect Robert Mills's design (originally with a circular colonnaded Greek temple base, which was later discarded for lack of funds) was accepted. The cornerstone was laid on July 4, 1848, and for the next 37 years, watching the monument grow, or not grow, was a local pastime. Declining contributions and the Civil War brought construction to a halt at an awkward 150 feet. The unsightly stump remained until 1876 when President Grant approved federal monies to complete the project. Dedicated in 1885, it was opened to the public in 1888.

The transparent blue covering will impede the spectacular view, but you should still be able to pick out the major sites. To the east are the Capitol and Smithsonian Buildings; to the north, the White House; to the west, the Lincoln and Vietnam Memorials, and Arlington National Cemetery beyond; and to the south, the gleaming-white shrine to Thomas Jefferson and the Potomac River. It's a marvelous orientation to the city.

Climbing the 897 steps is verboten, but the large elevator whisks visitors to the top in just 70 seconds. If, however, you're avid to see more of the interior, "Down the Steps" tours are given, subject to staff availability, weekends at 10am and 2pm. For details, call before you go or ask a ranger on duty. On this tour you'll learn more about the building of the monument and get to see the 193 carved stones inserted into the interior walls. The stones, which differ in size, shape, and material, are gifts from foreign countries, states, and individuals.

Light snacks are sold at a snack bar on the grounds, where you'll also find a few picnic tables. There's limited, free, 2-hour parking at the 16th Street Oval.

✪ **Lincoln Memorial.** Directly west of the Mall in Potomac Park (at 23rd St. NW, between Constitution and Independence aves.). ☎ **202/426-6842.** Free admission. Daily 8am–midnight, except Dec 25. Metro: Foggy Bottom, then about a 30-minute walk.

The Lincoln Memorial attracts some 1.5 million visitors annually. It's a beautiful and moving testament to a great American, its marble walls seeming to embody not only the spirit and integrity of Lincoln, but all that has ever been good about America.

Like its fellow presidential memorials, this one was a long time in the making. Although it was planned as early as 1867, 2 years after Lincoln's death, it was not until 1912 that Henry Bacon's design was completed, and the memorial itself was dedicated in 1922.

A beautiful neoclassical templelike structure, similar in architectural design to the Parthenon in Greece, the memorial has 36 fluted Doric columns representing the states of the Union at the time of Lincoln's death, plus two at the entrance. On the attic parapet are 48 festoons symbolic of the number of states in 1922 when the

Washington, D.C. Attractions

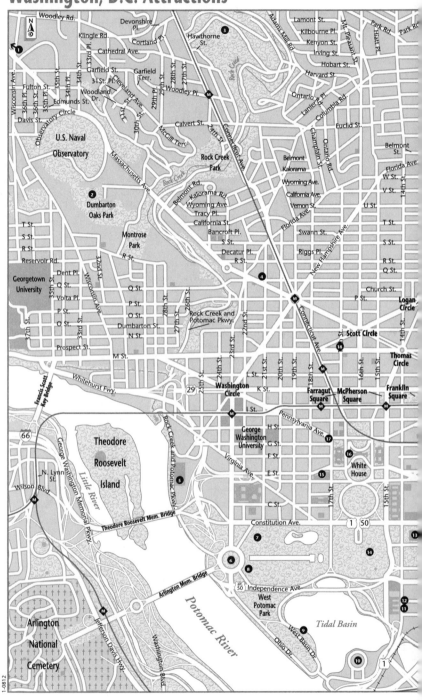

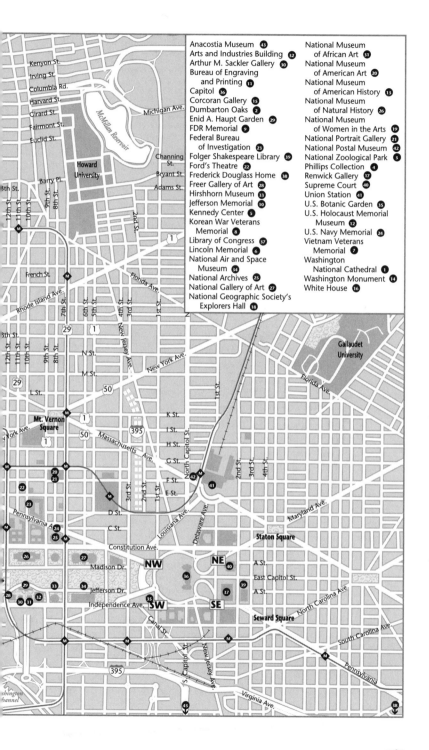

Anacostia Museum **43**
Arts and Industries Building **12**
Arthur M. Sackler Gallery **30**
Bureau of Engraving
  and Printing **11**
Capitol **36**
Corcoran Gallery **15**
Dumbarton Oaks **2**
Enid A. Haupt Garden **29**
FDR Memorial **9**
Federal Bureau
  of Investigation **23**
Folger Shakespeare Library **39**
Ford's Theatre **22**
Frederick Douglass Home **38**
Freer Gallery of Art **28**
Hirshhorn Museum **33**
Jefferson Memorial **10**
Kennedy Center **5**
Korean War Veterans
  Memorial **8**
Library of Congress **37**
Lincoln Memorial **6**
National Air and Space
  Museum **34**
National Archives **25**
National Gallery of Art **27**
National Geographic Society's
  Explorers Hall **18**

National Museum
  of African Art **31**
National Museum
  of American Art **20**
National Museum
  of American History **13**
National Museum
  of Natural History **26**
National Museum
  of Women in the Arts **19**
National Portrait Gallery **21**
National Postal Museum **42**
National Zoological Park **3**
Phillips Collection **4**
Renwick Gallery **17**
Supreme Court **40**
Union Station **41**
U.S. Botanic Garden **35**
U.S. Holocaust Memorial
  Museum **12**
U.S. Navy Memorial **24**
Vietnam Veterans
  Memorial **7**
Washington
  National Cathedral **1**
Washington Monument **14**
White House **16**

monument was erected. Hawaii and Alaska are noted in an inscription on the terrace. To the west, the Arlington Memorial Bridge crossing the Potomac recalls the reunion of North and South. To the east is the beautiful Reflecting Pool, lined with American elms and stretching 2,000 feet toward the Washington Monument and the Capitol beyond.

The memorial chamber, under 60-foot ceilings, has limestone walls inscribed with the Gettysburg Address and Lincoln's Second Inaugural Address. Two 60-foot murals by Jules Guerin on the north and south walls depict, allegorically, Lincoln's principles and achievements. On the south wall, an Angel of Truth freeing a slave is flanked by groups of figures representing Justice and Immortality. The north-wall mural depicts the unity of North and South and is flanked by groups of figures symbolizing Fraternity and Charity. Most powerful, however, is Daniel Chester French's 19-foot-high seated statue of Lincoln in deep contemplation in the central chamber. Its effect is best evoked by these words of Walt Whitman: "He was a mountain in grandeur of soul, he was a sea in deep undervoice of mystic loneliness, he was star in steadfast purity of purpose and service and he abides."

Acting on Lincoln's legacy, on several occasions those who have been oppressed have expressed their plight to America and the world at the steps of his shrine. Most notable was a peaceful demonstration of 200,000 people on August 28, 1963, at which another freedom-loving American, Dr. Martin Luther King, Jr., proclaimed "I have a dream."

An information booth and bookstore are on the premises. Rangers present 20- to 30-minute programs as time permits throughout the day, year-round. Limited free parking is available along Constitution Avenue and south along Ohio Drive.

Jefferson Memorial. South of the Washington Monument on Ohio Dr. (at the south shore of the Tidal Basin). ☎ **202/426-6841.** Free admission. Daily 8am–midnight, except Dec 25. Metro: Smithsonian, with 20- to 30-minute walk, or by Tourmobile.

President John F. Kennedy, at a 1962 dinner honoring 29 Nobel Prize winners, told his guests they were "the most extraordinary collection of talent, of human knowledge, that has ever been gathered together at the White House, with the possible exception of when Thomas Jefferson dined alone." A fascinating and passionate man, Jefferson penned the Declaration of Independence and served in America's government as George Washington's secretary of state, John Adams's vice president, and our third president. He spoke out against slavery, although, like many of his countrymen, he kept slaves himself. In addition, he established the University of Virginia and pursued wide-ranging interests, including architecture, astronomy, anthropology, music, and farming.

The site for the Jefferson Memorial, in relation to the Washington and Lincoln Memorials, was of extraordinary importance. The Capitol, the White House, and the Mall were already located in accordance with L'Enfant's plan, and there was no spot for such a project if the symmetry that guided L'Enfant was to be maintained. So the memorial was built on land reclaimed from the Potomac River, now known as the Tidal Basin. Franklin Delano Roosevelt, who laid the cornerstone in 1939, had all the trees between the Jefferson Memorial and the White House cut down, so he could see the memorial every morning and draw inspiration from it.

It's a beautiful memorial, a columned rotunda in the style of the Pantheon in Rome, whose classic architectural style Jefferson himself introduced to this country (he designed his home, Monticello, and the earliest University of Virginia buildings, in Charlottesville, Virginia). On the Tidal Basin side, the sculptural group above the entrance depicts Jefferson with Benjamin Franklin, John Adams,

---

❷ Did You Know?

- Architect Pierre L'Enfant's bill for designing Washington came to $95,000; scoffed at by Congress, he died a pauper.
- In 1835, Andrew Jackson paid off the national debt; it was the first and last time in U.S. history that the federal books have been balanced.
- When the *Washington Post* sponsored a public music competition, John Philip Sousa was asked to compose a march for the awards ceremony; the result was the "Washington Post March," for which Sousa earned the grand sum of $35.
- The only presidential inauguration ceremony to be held in the White House was that of Franklin D. Roosevelt, in 1941.
- Ambassadors to Washington in the early days were given "hardship pay" for having to endure the inconveniences of living here.
- A famous beverage was concocted for a Missouri lobbyist, Colonel J. K. Rickey. Originally rye whiskey was used, but later some "barbarous New Yorkers" substituted gin—hence, "Gin Rickey."

Roger Sherman, and Robert Livingston, all of whom worked on drafting the Declaration of Independence. The domed interior of the memorial contains the 19-foot bronze statue of Jefferson standing on a 6-foot pedestal of black Minnesota granite. The sculpture is the work of Rudolph Evans, who was chosen from more than 100 artists in a nationwide competition. Jefferson is depicted wearing a fur-collared coat given to him by his close friend, the Polish general Tadeusz Kosciuszko. Inscriptions from Jefferson's writing engraved on the interior walls expand on Jefferson's philosophy, which is best expressed in the circular frieze quotation: "I have sworn upon the altar of God eternal hostility against every form of tyranny over the mind of man."

Rangers present 20- to 30-minute programs throughout the day as time permits, year-round. Spring through fall, a refreshment kiosk at the Tourmobile stop offers snack fare. A new gift shop and bookstore opened in late 1998 on the bottom floor of the memorial. There's free 1-hour parking.

❖ **Franklin Delano Roosevelt Memorial.** In West Potomac Park, about midway between the Lincoln and Jefferson Memorials, on the west shore of the Tidal Basin. ☎ **202/426-6841.** Free admission. Ranger staff on duty 8am–midnight daily, except Dec 25. Free parking along W. Basin and Ohio drs. Metro: Smithsonian, with a 30-minute walk. Transportation: Tourmobile (see "Organized Tours," near the end of this chapter).

One year after it opened on May 2, 1997, the Franklin Delano Roosevelt had attracted twice as many visitors as any other memorial: 3 million. Its popularity has to do as much with the design as the man it honors. This is a 7½-acre, outdoor memorial that lies beneath a wide-open sky. It stretches out, rather than rising up, before you, leading you across the stone-paved floor. Granite walls define the four "galleries," each representing a different term in FDR's presidency, from 1933 to 1945. Architect Lawrence Halprin's design includes waterfalls, sculptures (by Leonard Baskin; John Benson; Neil Estern; Robert Graham; Thomas Hardy; and George Segal), and Roosevelt's own words carved into the stone. These quotes continue to inspire. Try these: from the Depression, "The only thing we have to fear is fear itself.", to the days leading up to World War II, "I have seen war. I have seen war on land and sea. I have seen blood running from the wounded . . . I have seen the dead in the mud. I have seen cities destroyed . . . I have seen children starving. I have seen the agony of mothers and wives. I hate war.", and through World War II, "The structure of world peace cannot be the work of one man, or one party, or one nation . . . it must be a peace which rests on the cooperative effort of the whole world."

I had read much about the memorial before visiting it and nowhere did I read that the memorial is noisy, which it is. Planes on their way to or from nearby Reagan National Airport zoom overhead, and the many displays of cascading water can sound thunderous. All that water tempts both children and adults on warm days (the memorial is unsheltered and unshaded), and, when the memorial first opened, people arrived in bathing suits with towels and splashed around. The park rangers don't allow that anymore, whether out of a sense of propriety or because the structures were not built to withstand so much weight. The rangers do allow you to dip your feet in the various pools, though. A favorite time to visit is at night, when dramatic lighting reveals the waterfalls and statues against the dark parkland.

Conceived in 1946, the FDR Memorial has been in the works for 50 years. Part of the delay in its construction can be attributed to the president himself. FDR had told his friend, Supreme Court Justice Felix Frankfurter, "If they are to put up any memorial to me, I should like it to be placed in the center of that green plot in front of the Archives building. I should like it to consist of a block about the size of this," he said, as he pointed to his desk. In fact, such a plaque sits in front of the National Archives Building. Friends and relatives struggled to honor Roosevelt's request to leave it at that, but Congress and national sentiment overrode them.

On May 2, 1997, President Clinton officiated at the memorial dedication ceremony. The memorial lies directly across the Tidal Basin from the Washington Monument, on a sight line between the Jefferson and Lincoln Memorials, in a spot that the McMillan Commission reserved in 1901 for a presidential memorial, not knowing whose it would be. As with other presidential memorials, this one opened to some controversy. Advocates for people with disabilities were incensed that the memorial sculptures did not show the president in a wheelchair, which he used from the age of 39 after he contracted polio. President Clinton asked Congress to allocate funding for an additional statue portraying a wheelchair-bound FDR; in the works (if not in place by the time you read this) is a bronze relief of FDR in a wheelchair, placed at the front of the memorial. Step inside the gift shop to view a replica of Roosevelt's wheelchair, as well as one of the rare photographs of the president sitting in a wheelchair. The memorial is probably the most accessible tourist attraction in the city; as at most of the National Park Service locations, wheelchairs are available for free use on-site.

If you don't see a posting of tour times, look for a ranger and request a tour; the rangers are happy to oblige.

3 The Smithsonian Museums

The Smithsonian's collection of nearly 141 million objects encompasses the entire world and its history, as well as its peoples and animals (past and present) and our attempts to probe into the future. The sprawling institution comprises 14 museums (9 of them on the Mall) as well as the National Zoological Park in Washington, D.C., plus two additional museums in New York City.

It all began with a $500,000 bequest from James Smithson, an English scientist who had never visited this country. When he died in 1829, he willed his entire fortune to his nephew, stipulating that should the nephew die without heirs (which he did in 1835), the estate should go to the United States to found "at

Parking Near the Mall

Don't drive, use the Metro. If you're hell-bent on driving on a weekday, though, set out early to nab one of the Independence or Constitution Avenues spots that become legal at 9:30am, when rush hour ends. Arrive about 9:15 and just sit in your car until 9:30am (to avoid getting a ticket), then hop out and stoke the meter. So many people do this, that if you arrive at 9:30 or later, you'll find most of the street parking spots gone.

Washington . . . an establishment for the increase and diffusion of knowledge. . . ." In 1846, Congress created a corporate entity to carry out Smithson's will, and the federal government agreed to pay 6% interest on the bequeathed funds in perpetuity. Since then, other munificent private donations have swelled Smithson's original legacy many times over. Major gallery and museum construction through the years stands as testament to thoughtful donors.

In 1987, the Sackler Gallery (Asian and Near Eastern art) and the National Museum of African Art were added to the Smithsonian's Mall attractions. The National Postal Museum opened in 1993. And future plans call for moving the National Museum of the American Indian (currently in New York) here in 2001.

To find out information about any of the Smithsonian museums, you call the same number: ☎ **202/357-2700** or TTY 202/357-1729. The information specialists who answer are very professional and always helpful. As mentioned earlier, you can also access the Smithsonian Institution Web site at **www.si.edu,** which will get you to the individual home pages for each of the museums.

Smithsonian Information Center (the "Castle"). 1000 Jefferson Dr. SW. ☎ **202/ 357-2700** or TTY 202/357-1729. Daily 9am–5:30pm, info desk 9am–4pm. Closed Dec 25. Metro: Smithsonian.

Make your first stop the impressively high-tech and very comprehensive Smithsonian Information Center, located in the institution's original Norman-style red sandstone building, popularly known as the "Castle."

The main information area here is the Great Hall, where a 20-minute video overview of the institution runs throughout the day in two theaters. There are two large schematic models of the Mall (as well as a third in Braille), and two large electronic maps of Washington allow visitors to locate nearly 100 popular attractions and Metro and Tourmobile stops. Interactive videos, some at children's heights, offer extensive information about the Smithsonian and other capital attractions and transportation (the menus seem infinite).

The entire facility is accessible to persons with disabilities, and information is available in a number of foreign languages. Daily Smithsonian events appear on monitors; in addition, the information desk's volunteer staff (some of whom speak foreign languages) can answer questions and help you plan a Smithsonian sightseeing itinerary. Most of the museums are within easy walking distance of the facility. While you're here, notice the charming vestibule, which has been restored to its turn-of-the-century appearance. It was originally designed to display exhibits at a child's eye level. The gold-trimmed ceiling is decorated to represent a grape arbor with brightly plumed birds and blue sky peeking through the trellis. Furnishings are peacock themed, and large Chinese paintings adorn the walls. The Castle Commons Room is the location of a Sunday brunch, 11am to 3pm, open to the public. The price is $18.95 for adults, $8.95 for children (ages 6 to 10) and you must make reservations by calling ☎ **202/357-2957.**

Information, Please

If you want to know what's happening at any of the Smithsonian museums, just get on the phone; **Dial-a-Museum** (☎ **202/357-2020** or 202/633-9126 for Spanish), a recorded information line, lists daily activities and special events. For other information, call ☎ **202/357-2700.**

Anacostia Museum. 1901 Fort Place SE (off Martin Luther King Jr. Ave.). ☎ **202/357-2700.** Free admission. Daily 10am–5pm. Closed Dec 25. Metro: Anacostia, then take a W1 or W2 bus directly to the museum.

This unique Smithsonian establishment was created in 1967 as a neighborhood museum. Expanding its horizons over the years, the museum is today a national resource devoted to the identification, documentation, protection, and interpretation of the African-American experience, focusing on Washington, D.C., and the Upper South. The permanent collection includes about 7,000 items, ranging from videotapes of African-American church services to art, sheet music, historic documents, textiles, glassware, and anthropological objects. In addition, the Anacostia produces a varying number of shows each year and offers a comprehensive schedule of free educational programs and activities in conjunction with exhibit themes. For instance, to complement an exhibition called "The African-American Presence in American Quilts," the museum featured a video about artist/quilt maker Faith Ringgold, quilting workshops for adults and children, talks by local quilting societies, and storytelling involving quilts.

Call for an events calendar (which always includes children's activities) or pick one up when you visit.

Arthur M. Sackler Gallery. 1050 Independence Ave. SW. ☎ **202/357-2700.** Free admission. Daily 10am–5:30pm; summer Fri–Wed 10am–5:30pm, Thurs 10am–8pm. Closed Dec 25. Metro: Smithsonian.

Opened in 1987, the Sackler, a national museum of Asian art, presents traveling exhibitions from major cultural institutions in Asia, Europe, and the United States. In the recent past, these have focused on such wide-ranging areas as 15th-century Persian art and culture; contemporary Japanese woodblock prints and ceramics; photographs of Asia; and art highlighting personal devotion in India. Art from the permanent collection supplements the traveling shows: It includes Khmer ceramics, ancient Chinese jades, bronzes, paintings, and lacquerware; 20th-century Japanese ceramics and works on paper; ancient Near Eastern works in silver, gold, bronze, and clay; and stone and bronze sculptures from South and Southeast Asia. Since the museum's opening, 11th- to 19th-century Persian and Indian paintings, manuscripts, calligraphies, miniatures, and bookbindings from the collection of Henri Vever have enhanced Sackler's original gift.

The Sackler is part of a museum complex that also houses the National Museum of African Art. And it shares its staff and research facilities with the adjacent Freer Gallery, to which it is connected via an underground exhibition space.

The Sackler offers museum programs (including many wonderful experiences for children and families); free highlight tours given daily (highly recommended); films; events; and temporary exhibits.

Arts & Industries Building. 900 Jefferson Dr. SW (on the south side of the Mall). ☎ **202/357-2700.** Free admission. Daily 10am–5:30pm. Closed Dec 25. Metro: Smithsonian.

Am I the only person who confuses this building with the one known as "the Castle"? (See the Smithsonian Information Center, above.) The Arts & Industries

Building lies to the left of said Castle, when you're approaching Mall-side, to the right from the Independence Avenue side. Completed in 1881 as the first U.S. National Museum, this redbrick and sandstone structure was the scene of President Garfield's Inaugural Ball. From 1976 through the mid-1990s, it housed exhibits from the 1876 United States International Exposition in Philadelphia—a celebration of America's centennial that featured the latest advances in technology. Some of these Victorian tools, products, art, and other objects are on permanent display, along with rotating exhibits, including "Speak to My Heart: Communities of Faith and Contemporary African American Life," on view through February 28, 2001.

Singers, dancers, puppeteers, and mimes perform in the **Discovery Theater** (open all year except in August, with performances weekdays and on selected Saturdays—call ☎ **202/357-1500** for show times and ticket information; admission of about $5 is charged). Don't miss the charming Victorian-motif shop on the first floor. Weather permitting, a 19th-century carousel operates across the street.

✪ **Freer Gallery of Art.** On the south side of the Mall (at Jefferson Dr. and 12th St. SW). ☎ **202/357-2700.** Free admission. Daily 10am–5:30pm; summer Fri–Wed 1am–8pm. Closed Dec 25. Metro: Smithsonian (Mall or Independence Ave. exit).

Charles Lang Freer, a collector of Asian art and American art from the 19th and early 20th centuries, gave the nation 9,000 of these works for the Freer Gallery's opening in 1923. Freer's original interest was, in fact, American art, but his good friend James McNeill Whistler encouraged him to collect Asian works as well. Eventually the latter became predominant. Freer's gift included funds to construct a museum and an endowment to add objects of the highest quality to the Asian collection only, which now numbers more than 28,000 objects. It includes Chinese and Japanese sculpture, lacquer, metalwork, and ceramics; early Christian illuminated manuscripts; Iranian manuscripts, metalwork, and miniatures; ancient Near Eastern metalware; and South Asian sculpture and paintings.

Among the American works are more than 1,200 pieces (the world's largest collection) by Whistler, including the famous **Peacock Room.** Originally a dining room designed by an architect named Thomas Jeckyll for the London mansion of F. R. Leyland, the Peacock Room displayed a Whistler painting called *The Princess from the Land of Porcelain.* But after his painting was installed, Whistler was dissatisfied with the room as a setting for his work. When Leyland was away from home, Whistler painted over the very expensive leather interior, and embellished it with paintings of golden peacock feathers. Not surprisingly, a rift ensued between Whistler and Leyland. After Leyland's death, Freer purchased the room, painting and all, and had it shipped to his home in Detroit. It is now permanently installed here. Other American painters represented in the collections are Thomas Wilmer Dewing; Dwight William Tryon; Abbott Henderson Thayer; John Singer Sargent; and Childe Hassam.

Housed in a recently renovated granite-and-marble building that evokes the Italian Renaissance, the pristine Freer has lovely skylit galleries. The main exhibit floor centers on a garden court open to the sky. An underground exhibit space connects the Freer to the neighboring Sackler Gallery, and both museums share the

Freeze Frame

About 90% of the American works in the Freer are in their original frames, many of them designed by architect Stanford White or painter James McNeil Whistler.

Meyer Auditorium, which is used for free chamber music concerts, dance performances, Asian feature films, and other programs. Inquire about these, as well as children's activities and free tours given daily, at the information desk.

Hirshhorn Museum & Sculpture Garden. On the south side of the Mall (at Independence Ave. and 7th St. SW). ☎ **202/357-2700.** Free admission. Daily 10am–5:30pm; summer, Fri–Wed 10am–5:30pm, Thurs 10am–8pm. Sculpture Garden 7:30am–dusk. Closed Dec 25. Metro: L'Enfant Plaza (Smithsonian Museums/Maryland Ave. exit).

This museum of modern and contemporary art is named after Latvian-born Joseph H. Hirshhorn, who, in 1966, donated his vast art collection—more than 4,000 drawings and paintings and some 2,000 pieces of sculpture—to the United States "as a small repayment for what this nation has done for me and others like me who arrived here as immigrants." At his death in 1981, Hirshhorn bequeathed an additional 5,500 artworks to the museum, and numerous other donors have since greatly expanded his legacy.

Constructed 14 feet aboveground on sculptured supports, the museum's contemporary cylindrical concrete-and-granite building shelters a verdant plaza courtyard where sculpture is displayed. The light and airy interior follows a simple circular route that makes it easy to see every exhibit without getting lost in a honeycomb of galleries. Natural light from floor-to-ceiling windows makes the inner galleries the perfect venue for viewing sculpture, second only, perhaps, to the beautiful tree-shaded sunken Sculpture Garden across the street (don't miss it). Paintings and drawings are installed in the outer galleries, along with intermittent sculpture groupings.

A rotating show of about 600 pieces is on view at all times. The collection features just about every well-known 20th-century artist and touches on most of the major trends in Western art since the late 19th century, with particular emphasis on our contemporary period. Among the best-known pieces are Rodin's *The Burghers of Calais* (in the Sculpture Garden); Hopper's *First Row Orchestra;* de Kooning's *Two Women in the Country;* and Warhol's *Marilyn Monroe's Lips.*

Pick up a free calendar when you enter to find out about free films, lectures, concerts, and temporary exhibits. An outdoor cafe is open during the summer. Free tours of the collection are given daily; call about these, and about tours of the Sculpture Garden.

✪ **National Air & Space Museum.** On the south side of the Mall (between 4th and 7th sts. SW), with entrances on Jefferson Dr. or Independence Ave. ☎ **202/357-2700** or 202/357-1686 for IMAX ticket information. Free admission. Daily 10am–5:30pm. Free 1½ -hour highlight tours daily at 10:15am and 1pm. Closed Dec 25. Metro: L'Enfant Plaza (Smithsonian Museums/Maryland Ave. exit).

The National Air & Space Museum is the most visited museum in the world. The museum chronicles the story of our mastery of flight, from Kitty Hawk to outer space, in 23 galleries filled with exciting exhibits. Plan to devote at least 3 or 4 hours to exploring these exhibits and, especially during the tourist season and on holidays, arrive before 10am to make a rush for the film-ticket line when the doors open. The not-to be-missed IMAX films shown in the Samuel P. Langley Theater here, on a screen five stories high and seven stories wide, are immensely popular, and tickets sell out quickly (although the first show seldom sells out). You can purchase tickets up to 2 weeks in advance; tickets are available only at the Langley Theater box office on the first floor. Five or more films play each day, most with aeronautical or space-exploration themes: *To Fly, Cosmic Voyage,* and *Magic of Flight* are the names of three. Tickets cost $5 for adults, $3.75 for ages 2 to 21 and seniors 55 and older; they're free for children under 2. You can also see IMAX films most evenings after closing (call for details and ticket prices, which are higher than daytime prices). At the same time, purchase tickets for a show at the Albert Einstein Planetarium.

In between shows, you can view the exhibits; audio tours are also available for rental. Interactive computers and slide and video shows enhance the exhibits throughout.

Highlights of the first floor include famous airplanes (such as the *Spirit of St. Louis*) and spacecraft (the *Apollo 11* Command Module); the world's only touchable moon rock; numerous exhibits on the history of aviation and air transportation; galleries in which you can design your own jet plane and study astronomy; and rockets, lunar-exploration vehicles, manned spacecraft, and guided missiles. **"How Things Fly,"** a gallery that opened in 1996 to celebrate the museum's 20th anniversary, includes wind and smoke tunnels, a boardable Cessna 150 airplane, and dozens of interactive exhibits that demonstrate principles of flight, aerodynamics, and propulsion. All the aircraft, by the way, are originals.

Kids love the **"walk-through" Skylab orbital workshop** on the second floor. Other galleries here highlight the solar system; U.S. manned space flights; sea-air operations; aviation during both world wars; and artists' perceptions of flight. An important exhibit is **"Beyond the Limits: Flight Enters the Computer Age,"** illustrating the primary applications of computer technology to aerospace.

An attractive cafeteria and a rather nice restaurant, Flight Line and the Wright Place, respectively, are on the premises.

National Museum of African Art. 950 Independence Ave. SW. ☎ **202/357-2700.** Free admission. Daily 10am–5:30pm; summer Wed–Fri 10am–5:30pm, Thurs 10am–8pm. Closed Dec 25. Metro: Smithsonian.

Founded in 1964, and part of the Smithsonian since 1979, the National Museum of African Art moved to the Mall in 1987 to share a subterranean space with the Sackler Gallery (see above) and the Ripley Center. Its aboveground domed pavilions reflect the arch motif of the neighboring Freer.

The museum collects and exhibits ancient and contemporary art from the entire African continent, but its permanent collection of more than 7,000 objects (shown in rotating exhibits) highlights the traditional arts of the vast sub-Saharan region. Most of the collection dates from the 19th and 20th centuries. Also among the museum's holdings are the **Eliot Elisofon Photographic Archives,** comprising 300,000 photographic prints and transparencies and 120,000 feet of film on African arts and culture. Permanent exhibits include **"The Ancient West African City of Benin, A.D. 1300–1897"**; **"The Ancient Nubian City of Kerma, 2500–1500 B.C."** (ceramics, jewelry, and ivory animals); **"The Art of the Personal Object"** (everyday items such as chairs, headrests, snuffboxes, bowls, and baskets); and **"Images of Power and Identity."**

Inquire at the desk about special exhibits, workshops (including excellent children's programs), storytelling, lectures, docent-led tours, films, and demonstrations. A comprehensive events schedule here (together with exhibitions) provides a unique opportunity to learn about the diverse cultures and visual traditions of Africa.

National Museum of American Art. 8th and G sts. NW. ☎ **202/357-2700.** Free admission. Daily 10am–5:30pm. Closed Dec 25. Metro: Gallery Place–Chinatown.

Don't wait to see the National Museum of American Art and the National Portrait Gallery: The two museums will close by the year 2000 for a 2-year overhaul. The National Museum of American Art owns more than 37,500 works representing 2 centuries of the nation's national art history. It is the largest collection of American art in the world. About 1,000 of these works are on display at any given time, along with special exhibits highlighting various aspects of American art. The museum is the country's oldest federal art collection—it was founded in 1829, predating the Smithsonian. The collection, along with the National Portrait Gallery (described below), is housed in the palatial quarters of the 19th-century Greek Revival Old Patent Office Building, partially designed by Washington Monument architect Robert Mills and Capitol dome architect Thomas U. Walter. Fronted by a columned portico evocative of the Parthenon, the building was originally a multi-purpose facility housing a jumble of items ranging from the original Declaration of Independence to a collection of shrunken heads.

Twentieth-century art occupies the most exalted setting, the third-floor Lincoln Gallery, with vaulted ceilings and marble columns. In this room, 4,000 revelers celebrated Lincoln's second inaugural in 1865. On view are works of post–World War II artists (de Kooning, Kline, Noguchi, and others). Other 20th-century works on this floor include paintings commissioned during the New Deal era.

Elsewhere, you'll see the works of mid- to late-19th-century artists such as Winslow Homer, Mary Cassatt, Albert Pinkham Ryder, and John Singer Sargent; a suite of galleries devoted to the Gilded Age; pieces by early American masters Charles Willson Peale, Benjamin West, and Samuel F. B. Morse; an extensive folk art collection; and George Catlin's Native American portraits from the group he showed in Paris in the 1840s (the museum owns 445 of them).

When you enter, pick up a map and calendar of events and ask about current temporary exhibits at the information desk. Free walk-in tours are given at noon weekdays and at 2pm on weekends. The Patent Pending cafe lies in a hall connecting the museum to the National Portrait Gallery; in good weather, you can dine in the lovely courtyard that's enclosed within the walls of the museums.

✪ **National Museum of American History.** On the north side of the Mall (between 12th and 14th sts. NW), with entrances on Constitution Ave. and Madison Dr. ☎ **202/357-2700.** Free admission. Daily 10am–5:30pm. Closed Dec 25. Metro: Smithsonian or Federal Triangle.

The National Museum of American History deals with "everyday life in the American past" and the external forces that have helped to shape our national character. Its massive contents range from General George Washington's Revolutionary War tent to Archie Bunker's chair.

Exhibits on the **first floor** (enter on Constitution Avenue) explore the development of farm machinery, power machinery, transportation, timekeeping, phonographs, and typewriters. The **Palm Court** on this level includes the interior of Georgetown's Stohlman's Confectionery Shop as it appeared around 1900 and part of an actual 1902 Horn and Hardart Automat, where you can stop and have an ice cream. You can have your mail stamped "Smithsonian Station" at a post office that had been located in Headsville, West Virginia, from 1861 to 1971, when it was brought, lock, stock, and barrel, to the museum. An important first-floor exhibit, **"A Material World,"** deals with the changing composition of artifacts—from predominantly natural materials such as wood and stone to the vast range of synthetics we have today. **"Information Age"** considers the ways information technology has changed society during the past 150 years. And **"Science in American Life"** analyzes the impact of science on society from the 1870s to the present.

If you enter from the Mall, you'll find yourself on the second floor. Until late 1998, you would have seen hanging in an alcove here, the huge, original Star-Spangled Banner, 30 by 42 feet, that inspired Francis Scott Key to write the U.S. national anthem in 1814. The flag is undergoing restoration work and will return to its niche by late 2001; in the meantime, you should be able to watch the conservators at work behind a glass wall on this same floor.

A Liberal & Enlightened Donor

Wealthy English scientist James Smithson (1765–1829), the illegitimate son of the duke of Northumberland, never explained why he willed his vast fortune to the United States, a country he had never visited. Speculation is that he felt a new nation, lacking established cultural institutions, stood in greatest need of his bequest. Smithson died in Genoa, Italy, in 1829. Congress accepted his gift in 1836; 2 years later, a shipment of 105 bags of gold sovereigns (about half a million dollars' worth—a considerable sum in the 19th century) arrived at the U.S. Mint in Philadelphia. For the next 8 years, Congress debated the best possible use for these funds. Finally, in 1846, James Polk signed an act into law establishing the Smithsonian Institution and providing "for the faithful execution of said trust, according to the will of the liberal and enlightened donor." It authorized a board to receive "all objects of art and of foreign and curious research, and all objects of natural history, plants, and geological and mineralogical specimens . . . for research and museum purposes."

In addition to the original Smithson bequest—which has been augmented by many subsequent endowments—the Smithsonian is also supported by annual congressional appropriations. Today it comprises a complex of 16 museums in Washington, D.C. and New York, plus the National Zoological Park. Its holdings, in every area of human interest, range from a 3.5-billion-year-old fossil to part of a 1902 Horn and Hardart Automat. Thousands of scientific expeditions sponsored by the Smithsonian have pushed into remote frontiers in the deserts, mountains, polar regions, and jungles.

The museum holds many other major exhibits. **"After the Revolution"** focuses on the everyday activities of ordinary 18th-century Americans. **"Field to Factory"** tells the story of African-American migration, south to north, between 1915 and 1940 . **The Foucault Pendulum** is a copy of the original model that was exhibited in Paris in 1851 with the accompanying teaser, "You are invited to witness the earth revolve." (The pendulum vibrates in a single plane, tracing in sand what seems to be a scattered series of lines, but what is actually the proof of the Earth's rotation.) Don't miss it!

One of the most popular exhibits on the second floor is **"First Ladies: Political Role and Public Image,"** which displays the first ladies' gowns and tells you a bit about each of these women. Infinitely more interesting, I think, is the neighboring exhibit, **"From Parlor to Politics: Women and Reform in America, 1890–1925,"** which chronicles the changing roles of women as they've moved from domestic to political and professional pursuits.

Head for the third floor if you want less of a crowd. Here are a vast collection of ship models, uniforms, weapons, and other military artifacts; major exhibits focus on the experiences of GIs in World War II (and the postwar world) as well as the wartime internment of Japanese Americans. Other areas include Money and Medals, Textiles, Printing and Graphic Arts, and Ceramics. Here, too, is the first American flag to be called Old Glory (1824).

Inquire at the information desk about highlight tours, films, lectures, and concerts, and hands-on activities for children and adults. The gift shop is vast—it's the largest of the Smithsonian shops.

✪ **National Museum of Natural History.** On the north side of the Mall (at 10th St. and Constitution Ave. NW), with entrances on Madison Dr. and Constitution Ave. ☎ 202/357-2700. Free admission. Daily 10am–5:30pm. Closed Dec 25. Free highlight tours Mon–Thur 10:30am and 1:30pm, Fri 10:30am. Metro: Smithsonian or Federal Triangle.

Children refer to this Smithsonian showcase as the dinosaur museum (there's a great dinosaur hall), or sometimes the elephant museum (a huge African bush elephant is the first amazing thing you see if you enter the museum from the Mall). Whatever you call it, the National Museum of Natural History is the largest of its kind in the world, and one of the most visited of all of Washington's museums. It contains more than 120 million artifacts and specimens, everything from Ice Age mammoths to the legendary Hope Diamond.

A **Discovery Room,** filled with creative hands-on exhibits "for children of all ages," is on the first floor. Call ahead or inquire at the information desk about hours.

On the Mall Level, off the Rotunda, is the **fossil collection,** which traces evolution back billions of years with exhibits of a 3.5-billion-year-old stromatolite (blue-green algae clump) fossil—one of the earliest signs of life on Earth—and a 70-million-year-old dinosaur egg. **"Life in the Ancient Seas"** features a 100-foot-long mural depicting primitive whales, a life-size walk-around diorama of a 230-million-year-old coral reef, and more than 2,000 fossils that chronicle the evolution of marine life. The **Dinosaur Hall** displays giant skeletons of creatures that dominated the Earth for 140 million years before their extinction about 65 million years ago. Suspended from the ceiling over Dinosaur Hall are replicas of ancient birds, including a life-size model of the pterosaur, which had a 40-foot wingspan. Also residing above this hall is an ancient shark—or at least the jaw of one—the *Carcharodon megalodon,* which lived in our oceans 5 million years ago. A monstrous 40-foot-long predator, its teeth were 5 to 6 inches long, and it could have consumed a Volkswagen "bug" in one gulp! Here, too, you'll find a spectacular living coral reef in a 3,000-gallon tank, a second 1,800-gallon tank housing a subarctic sea environment typical of the Maine coast, and a giant squid exhibit focusing on the world's largest invertebrates.

Upstairs is the popular **O. Orkin Insect Zoo,** where kids will enjoy looking at tarantulas, centipedes, and the like, and crawling through a model of an African termite mound. The **Ocean Planet** exhibit gives a video tour of what lies beneath the ocean surface, and teaches you about ocean conservation. The **Hope Diamond** is also on display on the second floor, where a renovation of the Gems and Minerals Hall has ended after years of work. The new hall has a new name: the **Janet Annenberg Hooker Hall of Geology, Gems, and Minerals,** and includes all you want to know about earth science, from volcanology to the importance of mining in our daily lives. Interactive computers, animated graphics, and a multimedia presentation of the "big picture" story of the Earth are some of the things that have brought the exhibit and museum up to date. Additional exhibits include **"South America: Continent and Culture,"** with objects from the Inca civilization, among others, and **"Origin of Western Culture,"** from about 10,000 years ago to A.D. 500.

The museum opened a new gift shop in 1997; its cafeteria is closed because of renovations.

National Portrait Gallery. 8th and F sts. NW. ☎ 202/357-2700. Free admission. Daily 10am–5:30pm. Closed Dec 25. Metro: Gallery Place–Chinatown.

If the prospect of a gallery of "heroes and villains, thinkers and doers, conservatives and radicals" fascinates you, don't delay seeing the National Portrait Gallery because, along with the National Museum of American Art, this museum will close for a 2-year overhaul by the year 2000. The gallery enshrines those who have made "significant contributions to the history, development, and culture of the United States" in paintings, sculpture, photography, and other forms of portraiture. Although the museum didn't open until 1968, the concept of a national portrait gallery first arose in the mid-19th century when Congress commissioned G. P. A. Healy to paint a series of presidential portraits for the White House. And American portraiture dates back even further, as evidenced by those predating the Revolution (of Pocahontas, among others), and of those by Rembrandt Peale. In May 1998, Peale's portraits of George and Martha Washington returned to the gallery after a 3-year stint at the Boston Museum of Fine Arts. It's great fun to wander these corridors, putting faces to famous names for the first time. And it's enlightening to discover portraits of accomplished Americans whose names you've never heard.

In addition to the Hall of Presidents (on the second floor), notable exhibits include Stuart's famed "*Lansdowne*" portrait of George Washington; a portrait of Mary Cassatt by Degas; 19th-century silhouettes by French-born artist Auguste Edouart; Jo Davidson's sculpture portraits (including a Buddhalike Gertrude Stein); and photographs by Mathew Brady. On the mezzanine, the Civil War is documented in portraiture, including one of the last photographs ever taken of Abraham Lincoln. Take a look at the magnificent Great Hall on the third floor. Originally designed as a showcase for patent models, it later became a Civil War hospital, where Walt Whitman came frequently to "soothe and relieve wounded troops."

Pick up a calendar of events at the information desk to find out about the museum's comprehensive schedule of temporary exhibits, lunchtime lectures, concerts, films, and dramatic presentations. Walk-in tours are given at varying hours; inquire at the information desk.

✪ **National Postal Museum.** 2 Massachusetts Ave. NE (at 1st St.). ☎ **202/357-2700.** Free admission. Daily 10am–5:30pm. Closed Dec 25. Metro: Union Station.

Bring your address book, and you can send postcards to the folks back home, through an interactive exhibit that issues a cool postcard and stamps it. That's just one feature that makes the museum visitor-friendly. Many of its exhibits involve easy-to-understand activities, like postal-themed video games. Despite our increasing use of E-mail, fax machines, and cellular phones for communicating, the act of writing and receiving letters still holds a special appeal for us—and that appeal is a lot of what this museum is about.

The museum documents America's postal history from 1673 (about 170 years before the advent of stamps, envelopes, and mailboxes) to the present. (**Fun fact:** Did you know that a dog sled was used to carry mail in Alaska until 1963 when it was replaced by an airplane?) In the central gallery, titled **"Moving the Mail,"** three planes that carried mail in the early decades of the 20th century are suspended from a 90-foot atrium ceiling. Here, too, are a railway mail car; an 1851 mail/passenger coach; a Ford Model A mail truck; and a replica of an airmail beacon tower. In **"Binding the Nation,"** historic correspondence illustrates how mail kept families together in the developing nation. Several exhibits deal with the famed Pony Express, a service that lasted less than 2 years but was romanticized to legendary proportions by Buffalo Bill and others. In the Civil War section you'll learn about Henry "Box" Brown, a slave who had himself "mailed" from Richmond to a Pennsylvania abolitionist in 1856. **"The Art of Cards and Letters"** gallery displays rotating exhibits of personal (sometimes wrenching, always interesting) correspondence taken from different periods in history, as well as greeting cards and postcards. And an 800-square-foot gallery called **"Artistic License: The Duck Stamp Story,"** focuses on federal duck stamps (first issued in 1934 to license waterfowl hunters), with displays on the hobby of duck hunting and the ecology of American water birds. In addition, the museum houses a vast research library for philatelic researchers and scholars, a stamp store, and a museum shop. Inquire about free walk-in tours at the information desk.

Opened in 1993, this most recent addition to the Smithsonian complex occupies the lower level of the palatial beaux arts quarters of the City Post Office Building, which was designed by architect Daniel Burnham and is situated next to Union Station. Created to house and display the Smithsonian's national philatelic and postal history collection of more than 16 million objects, it is, somewhat surprisingly, a hit for everyone in the family.

National Zoological Park. Adjacent to Rock Creek Park, main entrance in the 3000 block of Connecticut Ave. NW. ☎ **202/673-4800** (recording) or 202/673-4717. Free admission. Daily May to mid-Sept (weather permitting): grounds 6am–8pm, animal buildings 10am–6pm. Daily mid-Sept to May: grounds 6am–6pm, animal buildings 10am–4:30pm. Closed Dec 25. Metro: Woodley Park–Zoo or Cleveland Park.

It could be argued that one has not truly "done" the zoo until one has spent certain countless hours there pursuant to school field trips and science projects, as well as family excursions. Here are both facts and tips.

The facts: Established in 1889, the National Zoo is home to several thousand animals of some 500 species, many of them rare and/or endangered. A leader in the care, breeding, and exhibition of animals, it occupies 163 beautifully landscaped and wooded acres and is one of the country's most delightful zoos. Among the animals you'll see are cheetahs, zebras, camels, elephants, Hsing-Hsing (the rare giant panda from China), tapirs, antelopes, brown pelicans and other waterfowl, kangaroos, hippos, rhinos, giraffes, apes, orangutans, reptiles, invertebrates, lions, tigers, spectacled bears, beavers, hummingbirds and monkeys (in Amazonia, a rain forest habitat), seals, and sea lions.

Pointers: Consider calling ahead (allow 3 weeks and call during weekday business hours) for a **free 90-minute highlights tour** (☎ **202/673-4954**). Not recommended for kids under 4. The tour guide will tell you how to look at the animals; where, why, and when to look; and fill your visit with lots of surprises. Enter the zoo at the Connecticut Avenue entrance; you will be right by the Education Building, where you can pick up a map and find out about feeding times and special activities taking place during your visit. Note that from this main entrance, you're headed downhill; the return uphill walk can prove trying if you have young children and/or it's a hot day. As noted below, the zoo does rent strollers and offers plenty of refreshment stands. Also remember that zoo animals live in large, open enclosures—simulations of their natural habitats—along two easy-to-follow numbered paths, **Olmsted Walk** and the **Valley Trail.** You can't get lost, and you won't unintentionally miss anything.

You can hang out for an hour in **Amazonia** peering up into the trees and you still won't spy the sloth—do yourself a favor and ask the attendant where it is. However, if your whole purpose is to see the **rare giant panda,** Hsing-Hsing, go at feeding

Smithsonian Touring and Dining Tips

The Information Center opens 1 hour earlier than the museums. The Castle's 19th-century dining room, known as **The Commons,** is the site each Sunday for brunch, 11am to 3pm, featuring everything from omelets to baked ham, for $18.95 per person (less for children and senior citizens). Call ☎ **202/357-2957** before 10am or after 3pm to make a reservation.

time, 11am or 3pm, because otherwise the moody panda seems to hide just to spite you. If Hsing-Hsing isn't cooperating, look next door for the red panda, not as rare but pretty cute.

Throughout the zoo, keep your eyes open, and you'll realize some rather interesting facts: that camels have hair in their ears (to help keep out sand); that birds' feet can look very different, the most dangerous birds being those with sharp claws; and that hippopotamuses stay underwater, usually, for no more than 90 seconds, although everyone thinks they stay under for hours.

Zoo facilities include stroller-rental stations; a number of gift shops; a bookstore; and several paid-parking lots. The lots fill up quickly, especially on weekends, so arrive early or take the Metro. Snack bars and ice-cream kiosks are scattered throughout the park.

Renwick Gallery of the National Museum of American Art. Pennsylvania Ave. and 17th St. NW. ☎ **202/357-2700.** Free admission. Daily 10am–5:30pm. Closed Dec 25. Metro: Farragut West or Farragut North.

A department of the National Museum of American Art (though nowhere near it), the Renwick, a showcase for American creativity in crafts, is housed in a historic mid-1800s landmark building of the French Second Empire style. The original home of the Corcoran Gallery, it was saved from demolition by First Lady Jacqueline Kennedy in 1963, when she recommended that it be renovated as part of the Lafayette Square restoration. In 1965, it became part of the Smithsonian and was renamed for its architect, James W. Renwick, who also designed the Smithsonian Castle. Although the setting—especially the magnificent Victorian Grand Salon with its wainscoted plum walls and 38-foot skylight ceiling—evokes another era, the museum's contents are mostly contemporary. The rich and diverse display of objects here includes both changing crafts exhibits and contemporary works from the museum's permanent collection. Typical exhibits range from **"Uncommon Beauty: The Legacy of African-American Craft Art"** to **"Calico and Chintz: Antique Quilts from the Patricia Smith Collection."** The above-mentioned **Grand Salon** on the second floor, furnished in opulent 19th-century style, displays paintings by 18th- and 19th-century artists. (The great thing about this room, besides its fine art and grand design, is its cushiony, velvety banquettes, perfect resting places for the weary sightseer.)

The Renwick offers a comprehensive schedule of crafts demonstrations, lectures, and films. Inquire at the information desk. And check out the museum shop near the entrance for books on crafts, design, and decorative arts, as well as craft items, many of them for children

4 Elsewhere on the Mall

National Archives. Constitution Ave. NW (between 7th and 9th sts.). ☎ **202/501-5000** for information on exhibits and films or 202/501-5400 for research information. www.nara. gov/nara/events/calendar/calendar.html. Free admission. Exhibition Hall Apr–Aug, daily 10am–9pm; Sept–Mar, daily 10am–5:30pm. Free tours weekdays 10:15am and 1:15pm by appointment only; call ☎ **202/501-5205.** Call for research hours. Closed Dec 25. Metro: Archives.

Keeper of America's documentary heritage, the National Archives display our most cherished treasures in appropriately awe-inspiring surroundings. Housed in the **Rotunda of the Exhibition Hall** are the nation's three charter documents—the Declaration of Independence, the Constitution of the United States, and the Bill of Rights, as well as the 1297 version of the Magna Carta—each on permanent display to the public.

High above and flanking the documents are two larger-than-life murals painted by Barry Faulkner. One, entitled *The Declaration of Independence,* shows Thomas Jefferson presenting a draft of the Declaration to John Hancock, the presiding officer of the Continental Congress; the other, entitled *The Constitution,* shows James Madison submitting the Constitution to George Washington and the Constitutional Convention. In the display cases on either side of the Declaration of Independence are exhibits that rotate over a 3-year period, for instance, **"American Originals,"** which features 26 compelling American historical documents ranging from George Washington's Revolutionary War expense account to the Louisiana Purchase Treaty signed by Napoléon. There are also temporary exhibits in the **Circular Gallery.**

The Archives serve as much more than a museum of cherished documents. Famous as a center for genealogical research—Alex Haley began his work on *Roots* here—it is sometimes called "the nation's memory." This federal institution is charged with sifting through the accumulated papers of a nation's official life—billions of pieces a year—and determining what to save and what to destroy. The Archives' vast accumulation of census figures, military records, naturalization papers, immigrant passenger lists, federal documents, passport applications, ship manifests, maps, charts, photographs, and motion picture film (and that's not the half of it) spans 2 centuries. And it's all available for the perusal of anyone age 16 or over (call for details). If you're casually thinking about tracing your roots, stop by Room 400 where a staff member can advise you about the time and effort that will be involved, and, if you decide to pursue it, exactly how to proceed.

Even if you have no research project in mind, the National Archives merit a visit. The neoclassical building itself, designed by John Russell Pope in the 1930s (also architect of the National Gallery of Art and the Jefferson Memorial), is an impressive example of the beaux arts style. Seventy-two columns create a Corinthian colonnade on each of the four facades. Great bronze doors herald the Constitution Avenue entrance, and allegorical sculpture centered on *The Recorder of the Archives* adorns the pediment. On either side of the steps are male and female figures symbolizing guardianship and heritage, respectively. *Guardians of the Portals* at the Pennsylvania Avenue entrance represent the past and the future, and the theme of the pediment is destiny.

Pick up a schedule of events (lectures, films, genealogy workshops) when you visit.

✪ **National Gallery of Art.** On the north side of the Mall, on Constitution Ave. NW (between 3rd and 7th sts. NW). ☎ **202/737-4215.** www.nga.gov. Free admission. Mon–Sat 10am–5pm, Sun 11am–6pm. Closed Jan 1 and Dec 25. Metro: Archives, Judiciary Square, or Smithsonian.

Most people don't realize it, but the National Gallery of Art is not part of the Smithsonian complex.

Housing one of the world's foremost collections of Western painting, sculpture, and graphic arts from the Middle Ages through the 20th century, the National Gallery has a dual personality. The original West Building, designed by John Russell Pope (architect of the Jefferson Memorial and the National Archives), is a neoclassic marble masterpiece with a domed rotunda over a colonnaded fountain and high-ceilinged corridors leading to delightful garden courts. It was a gift to the nation from Andrew W. Mellon, who also contributed the nucleus of the collection, including 21 masterpieces from the Hermitage, two Raphaels among them. The ultramodern East Building, designed by I. M. Pei and opened in 1978, is composed of two adjoining triangles with glass walls and lofty tetrahedron skylights. The pink

Avoiding the Crowds at the National Gallery of Art

The best time to visit the National Gallery is Monday morning; the worst is Sunday afternoons.

Tennessee marble from which both buildings were constructed was taken from the same quarry; it forms an architectural link between the two structures.

The West Building: On the main floor of the West Building, about 1,000 paintings are always on display. To the left (as you enter off the Mall) is the **Art Information Room,** housing the **Micro Gallery,** where those so inclined can design their own tours of the permanent collection and enhance their knowledge of art via user-friendly computers. Continuing to the left of the rotunda are galleries of 13th-through 18th-century Italian paintings and sculpture, including what is generally considered the finest Renaissance collection outside Italy; here you'll see the only painting by Leonardo da Vinci housed outside Europe, *Ginevra de' Benci.* Paintings by El Greco, Ribera, and Velázquez highlight the Spanish galleries; Grünewald, Dürer, Holbein, and Cranach can be seen in the German; Van Eyck, Bosch, and Rubens in the Flemish; and Vermeer, Steen, and Rembrandt in the Dutch. To the right of the rotunda, galleries display 18th- to 19th-century French paintings (including one of the world's greatest impressionist collections), paintings by Goya, works of late-18th- and 19th-century Americans—such as Cole, Stuart, Copley, Homer, Whistler, and Sargent—and of somewhat earlier British artists, such as Constable, Turner, and Gainsborough. Room decor reflects the period and country of the art shown: Travertine marble heralds the Italian gallery, and somber oak panels define the Dutch galleries. Down a flight of stairs are prints and drawings; 15th-through 20th-century sculpture (with many pieces by Daumier, Degas, and Rodin); American naive 18th- and 19th-century paintings; Chinese porcelains; small Renaissance bronzes; 16th-century Flemish tapestries; and 18th-century decorative arts.

Note: The National Gallery Sculpture Garden, just across 7th Street from the West Wing, should have opened by the time you read this. The completed 6.1-acre park should include open lawns; a central pool with a spouting fountain (the pool is converted into an ice rink in winter); an exquisite, glassed-in pavilion housing a cafe; 20th century sculptures; and informally landscaped shrubs, trees, and plants.

The East Building: The 20th anniversary of the opening of this wing was celebrated in 1998. The wing was conceived as a showcase for the museum's collection of 20th-century art, including Picasso, Miró, Matisse, Pollock, and Rothko; and to house the art history research center. Always on display are the massive aluminum Calder mobile dangling under a seven-story skylight and an exhibit called **"Small French Paintings,"** which I love.

See the box "Exhibits Scheduled at Museums in 1999," later in this chapter, for upcoming special exhibits in both wings (1998 featured works by Mark Rothko and a show entitled "Degas at the Races.")

Pick up a floor plan and calendar of events at an information desk to find out about National Gallery exhibits; films; tours; lectures; and concerts. Highly recommended are the free highlight tours (call for exact times) and audio tours. The gift shop is a favorite. The gallery offers several good dining options, the best being the Terrace Café, which sometimes tailors its menu to complement a particular exhibit.

✪ **United States Holocaust Memorial Museum.** 100 Raoul Wallenberg Place (formerly 15th St. SW; near Independence Ave., just off the Mall). ☎ **202/488-0400.** www.ushmm.org. Free admission. Daily 10am–5:30pm. Closed Yom Kippur and Dec 25. Metro: Smithsonian.

Holocaust Museum Touring Tips

Because so many people want to visit the museum, tickets specifying a visit time (in 15-minute intervals) are required. Reserve them via **Protix** (☎ 800/400-9373). There's a small service charge. You can also get them at the museum beginning at 10am daily (lines form earlier).

When this museum opened in 1993, officials thought perhaps 500,000 people might visit annually. In fact, 2 million come here every year. On a daily basis, the number is 1,650, which is the maximum number of free timed tickets the museum gives out each day to visitors who come to tour the permanent exhibit. The museum opens its doors at 10am and the tickets are usually gone by 10:30am. It's best to get in line early in the morning (around 8am). Most visitors—80 percent—are not Jewish, 14 percent are foreigners, and 18 percent are repeats.

The noise and bustle of so many visitors can be disconcerting and certainly at odds with the experience that follows, when you first enter the lobby of the United States Holocaust Museum, our national institution for the documentation, study, and interpretation of Holocaust history. The museum also serves as a memorial to the 6 million Jews and millions of others (including gypsies, homosexuals, physically challenged, and political prisoners) who were murdered during the Holocaust. But things settle down as you begin your tour.

You will spend most of your time—anywhere from 1 to 5 hours—in the permanent exhibit, which takes up three floors, presenting the information chronologically. When you enter, you will be issued an identity card of an actual victim of the Holocaust. By 1945, 66% of those whose lives are documented on these cards were dead. The tour begins on the fourth floor, where exhibits portray the events of 1933 to 1939, the years of the Nazi uprising. On the third floor (documenting 1940 to 1944), exhibits illustrate the narrowing choices of people caught up in the Nazi machine. You board a Polish freight car of the type used to transport Jews from the Warsaw ghetto to Treblinka and hear recordings of survivors telling what life in the camps was like. This part of the museum documents the details of the Nazis' "Final Solution" for the Jews.

The second floor recounts a more heartening story: It depicts how non-Jews throughout Europe, by exercising individual action and responsibility, saved Jews at great personal risk. Denmark—led by a king who swore that if any of his subjects wore a yellow star, so would he—managed to hide and save 90% of its Jews. Exhibits follow on the liberation of the camps, life in Displaced Persons camps, emigration to Israel and America, and the Nuremberg trials. A highlight at the end of the permanent exhibition is a 30-minute film called *"Testimony,"* in which Holocaust survivors tell their own stories. The tour concludes in the hexagonal Hall of Remembrance, where you can meditate on what you've experienced and light a candle for the victims.

Chartered by a unanimous Act of Congress in 1980 and located adjacent to the Mall, the museum strives to broaden public understanding of Holocaust history. In addition to its permanent and temporary exhibitions, the museum has a Resource Center for educators, which provides materials and services to Holocaust educators and students; an interactive computer learning center; and a registry of Holocaust survivors, a library, and archives, which researchers may use to retrieve historic documents, photographs, oral histories, films, and videos.

The museum recommends not bringing children under 11; for older children, it's advisable to prepare them for what they'll see. There's a cafeteria and museum shop on the premises.

You can see some parts of the museum without tickets. These include two special exhibit areas on the first floor and concourse: **"Daniel's Story: Remember the Children"** and **"Hidden History of the Kovno Ghetto"** (this leaves in 1999); the **Wall of Remembrance** (Children's Tile Wall), which commemorates the 1.5 million children killed in the Holocaust, and the **Wexner Learning Center.**

5 Other Government Agencies

Bureau of Engraving & Printing. 14th and C sts. SW. ☎ **202/874-3188** or 202/874-2330. Free admission. Mon–Fri 9am–2pm (last tour begins at 1:40pm). Closed Dec 25–Jan 1 and federal holidays. Metro: Smithsonian (Independence Ave. exit).

This is where the cash is. A staff of 2,600 works around the clock churning it out at the rate of about 22.5 million notes a day. Everyone's eyes pop as they walk past rooms overflowing with fresh green bills. But although the money draws everyone in, it's not the whole story. The bureau prints many other products, including 25 billion postage stamps per year, presidential portraits, and White House invitations.

As many as 5,000 people line up each day to get a peek at all that moola, so arriving early, especially during the peak tourist season, is essential (unless you have secured VIP tickets from your senator or congressperson; details in chapter 2). April through September, you must obtain a same-day ticket specifying a tour time; the ticket booth on the 14th Street side of the building opens at 8am. The rest of the year no ticket is needed; you just have to line up on 14th Street.

The 40-minute guided tour begins with a short introductory film. Then you'll see, through large windows, the processes that go into the making of paper money: the inking, stacking of bills, cutting, and examination for defects. Most printing here is done from engraved steel plates in a process known as "intaglio," the hardest to counterfeit, because the slightest alteration will cause a noticeable change in the portrait in use. Additional exhibits include bills no longer in use, counterfeit money, and a $100,000 bill designed for official transactions (since 1969, the largest denomination printed for the general public is $100).

After you finish the tour, allow time to explore the **Visitor Center,** open 8:30am to 3:30pm, where exhibits include informative videos, money-related electronic games, and a display of $1 million. Here, too, you can buy gifts ranging from bags of shredded money—no, you can't tape it back together—to copies of documents such as the Gettysburg Address.

Federal Bureau of Investigation. J. Edgar Hoover FBI Building, E St. NW (between 9th and 10th sts.). ☎ **202/324-3447.** Free admission. Mon–Fri 8:45am–4:15pm. Closed Jan 1, Dec 25, and other federal holidays. Metro: Metro Center or Federal Triangle.

At the height of the season, say mid-April, you might be standing in line with 300 people at 8 in the morning to tour the FBI Building, and not get in. If you're coming anytime between April and August, try to arrange for tickets ahead of time; even so, the tour office might tell you that they won't confirm your tickets until a week before your visit.

More than half a million visitors (many of them kids) come here annually to learn why crime doesn't pay. Tours begin with a short videotape presentation about the priorities of the bureau: organized crime; white-collar crime; terrorism; foreign

FBI Touring Tips

To beat the crowds, arrive before 8:45am or write to a senator or congressperson for a scheduled reservation as far in advance as possible (details in chapter 2). Tours last 1 hour and are conducted every 20 to 30 minutes, depending upon staff availability. The building closes at 4:15pm, so you must arrive at least 1 hour before closing if you want to make the last tour (arrive even earlier in high season). Once inside, you'll undergo a security check.

counterintelligence; illegal drugs; and violent crimes. En route, you'll learn about this organization's history (it was established in 1908) and its activities over the years. You'll see some of the weapons used by big-time gangsters such as Al Capone, John Dillinger, Bonnie and Clyde, and "Pretty Boy" Floyd; and an exhibit on counterintelligence operations. There are photographs of the 10 most-wanted fugitives (2 were recognized at this exhibit by people on the tour, and 10 have been located via the FBI-assisted TV show *America's Most Wanted*).

Other exhibits deal with white-collar crime, organized crime, terrorism, drugs, and agent training. On display are more than 5,000 weapons, most confiscated from criminals; they're used for reference purposes.

You'll also visit the **DNA lab;** the **Firearms Unit** (where it's determined whether a bullet was fired from a given weapon); the **Material Analysis Unit** (where the FBI can determine the approximate make and model of a car from a tiny piece of paint); the unit where hairs and fibers are examined; and a **Forfeiture and Seizure Exhibit**—a display of jewelry, furs, and other proceeds from illegal narcotics operations. The tour ends with a bang, lots of them in fact, when an agent gives a sharpshooting demonstration and discusses the FBI's firearm policy and gun safety.

✪ **Library of Congress.** 1st St. SE (between Independence Ave. and E. Capitol St.). **202/707-8000.** www/loc.gov/. Free admission. Madison Building Mon–Fri 8:30am–9:30pm, Sat 8:30am–6pm. Jefferson Building Mon–Sat 10am–5:30pm. Closed Sun and all federal holidays. Stop at the information desk inside the Jefferson Building's west entrance on First Street to obtain same-day, free tickets to tour the Library. Tours of the Great Hall Mon–Sat 11:30am, 1pm, 2:30pm, and 4pm. Metro: Capitol South.

The question most frequently asked by visitors to the Library of Congress is: "Where are the books?" The answer is: On the 532 miles of shelves located throughout the library's 3 buildings. Established in 1800, "for the purchase of such books as may be necessary for the use of Congress," the library today serves the nation, with holdings for the visually impaired (for whom books are recorded on cassette and/or translated into braille), research scholars, and college students. Its first collection of books was destroyed in 1814 when the British burned the Capitol (where the library was then housed) during the War of 1812. Thomas Jefferson then sold the institution his personal library of 6,487 books as a replacement, and this became the foundation of what would grow to become the world's largest library. Today, the collection contains a mind-boggling 113 million items. Its buildings house, among many other things, more than 17 million catalogued books; over 49 million manuscripts; the letters of George Washington; over 13 million prints and photographs; more than 2 million audio holdings (discs, tapes, talking books, and so on); more than 700,000 movies and videotapes; musical instruments from the 1700s; and the papers of everyone from Freud to Groucho Marx. The library offers a year-round program of free concerts, lectures, and poetry readings, and houses the Copyright Office.

As impressive as the scope of the library's effects and activities is its original home, the ornate Italian Renaissance–style Thomas Jefferson Building, which reopened to the public May 1, 1997, after an $81.5 million, 12-year overhaul of the entire library. The Jefferson Building was erected between 1888 and 1897 to hold the burgeoning collection and establish America as a cultured nation with magnificent institutions equal to anything in Europe. Fifty-two painters and sculptors worked for 8 years on its interior. There are floor mosaics of Italian marble; allegorical paintings on the overhead vaults; more than 100 murals; and numerous ornamental cornucopias, ribbons, vines, and garlands within. The building's exterior has 42 granite sculptures and yards of bas-reliefs. Especially impressive are the exquisite marble **Great Hall** and the **Main Reading Room,** the latter under a 160-foot dome. Originally intended to hold the fruits of at least 150 years of collecting, the Jefferson was, in fact, filled up in 13. It is now supplemented by the James Madison Memorial Building and the John Adams Building. On permanent display in the Jefferson Building's Great Hall is an exhibit called **"Treasures of the Library of Congress,"** which rotates a selection of more than 200 of the rarest and most interesting items from the library's collection—like Thomas Jefferson's rough draft of the Declaration of Independence with notations by Benjamin Franklin and John Adams in the margins, and the contents of Lincoln's pockets when he was assassinated.

If you have to wait for a tour, take in the 12-minute orientation film in the Jefferson's new visitors' theater or browse in its new gift shop. Pick up a calendar of events when you visit. Free concerts take place in the Jefferson Building's elegant Coolidge Auditorium; find out more about them on the LOC concert Web site: **lcweb.loc.gov/rr/perform/concert.** **The Madison Building** offers interesting exhibits and features classic, rare, and unusual films in its Mary Pickford Theater. It also houses a cafeteria and the more formal Montpelier Room restaurant, both of which are open for lunch weekdays.

Anyone over high school age may use the library's collections, but first you must obtain a user card with your photo on it. Go to Room G-22 (ground floor level of the Jefferson Building) and present a driver's license or passport, complete a brief, self-registration procedure, and receive your user card. Then head to the Information Desk in either the Jefferson or Madison Buildings to find out about the research resources available to you, and how to use them. Most likely, you will be directed to the Main Reading Room. All books are used on-site; when you know which books you need, and their call numbers, you complete a "call" slip, and submit it to a staff person, who enters your request into a computer. The clerk receiving the request retrieves the books from the stacks and sends them up to the central desk, where you pick them up.

6 War Memorials & Cemeteries

Arlington National Cemetery. Just across the Memorial Bridge from the base of the Lincoln Memorial. ☎ **703/607-8052.** Free admission. Apr–Sept, daily 8am–7pm; Oct–Mar, daily 8am–5pm. Metro: Arlington National Cemetery. If you come by car, parking is $1.25 an hour for the first 3 hours, $2 an hour thereafter. The cemetery is also accessible via Tourmobile.

Upon arrival, head over to the Visitor Center, where you can view exhibits, pick up a detailed map, use the rest rooms (there are no others until you get to Arlington House), and purchase a Tourmobile ticket ($4.75 per adult, $2.25 for children 4–11) allowing you to stop at all major sights in the cemetery and then reboard

Arlington National Cemetery

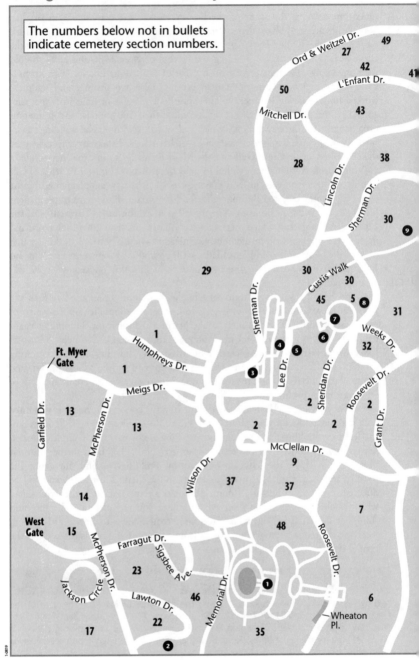

The numbers below not in bullets indicate cemetery section numbers.

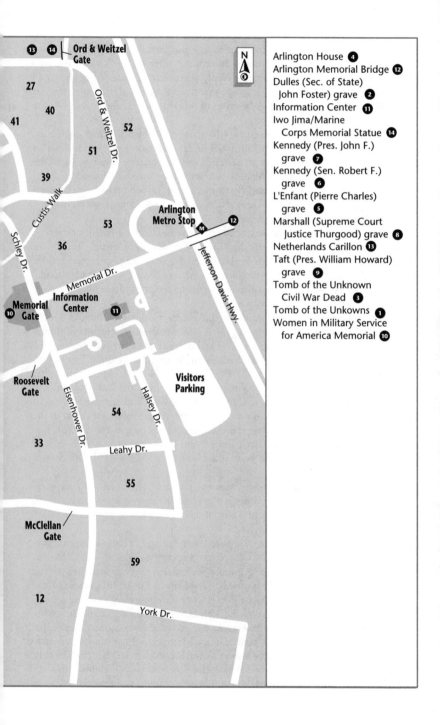

Ord & Weitzel Gate

N

27
40
41
Ord & Weitzel Dr.
52
51
39
Custis Walk
53
Arlington Metro Stop
36
Schley Dr.
Memorial Dr.
Jefferson Davis Hwy.
Memorial Gate
Information Center
Roosevelt Gate
Eisenhower Dr.
Halsey Dr.
Visitors Parking
54
33
Leahy Dr.
55
McClellan Gate
59
12
York Dr.

Arlington House ④
Arlington Memorial Bridge ⑫
Dulles (Sec. of State)
  John Foster) grave ②
Information Center ⑪
Iwo Jima/Marine
  Corps Memorial Statue ⑭
Kennedy (Pres. John F.)
  grave ⑦
Kennedy (Sen. Robert F.)
  grave ⑥
L'Enfant (Pierre Charles)
  grave ⑤
Marshall (Supreme Court
  Justice Thurgood) grave ⑧
Netherlands Carillon ⑬
Taft (Pres. William Howard)
  grave ⑨
Tomb of the Unknown
  Civil War Dead ③
Tomb of the Unkowns ①
Women in Military Service
  for America Memorial ⑩

189

whenever you like. Service is continuous, and the narrated commentary is informative; this is the only guided tour of the cemetery offered. (See "Getting Around" in chapter 4 for details.) If you've got plenty of stamina, consider doing part or all of the tour on foot. Remember as you go that this is a memorial frequented not just by tourists but by those visiting the graves of beloved relatives and friends who are buried here.

This shrine occupies approximately 612 acres on the high hills overlooking the capital from the west side of the Memorial Bridge. It honors many national heroes and more than 240,000 war dead, veterans, and dependents. Many graves of the famous at Arlington bear nothing more than simple markers. Five-star General John J. Pershing's is one of those. Secretary of State John Foster Dulles is buried here. So are President William Howard Taft and Supreme Court Justice Thurgood Marshall. Cemetery highlights include:

The Tomb of the Unknowns, containing the unidentified remains of service members from both world wars, the Korean War, and the Vietnam War. It's an unembellished massive white-marble block, moving in its simplicity. Inscribed are the words: "Here rests in honored glory an American Soldier known but to God." The changing of the guard takes place every half-hour April to September and every hour on the hour October to March.

A 20-minute walk, all uphill, from the Visitor Center is **Arlington House** (☎ **703/557-0613**). For 30 years (1831–61) this was the legal residence of Robert E. Lee, where he and his family lived off and on until the Civil War. Lee married the great-granddaughter of Martha Washington, Mary Anna Randolph Custis, who inherited the estate upon the death of her father. It was at Arlington House that Lee, having received the news of Virginia's secession from the Union, decided to resign his commission in the U.S. Army. During the Civil War, the estate was taken over by Union forces, and troops were buried here. A year before the defeat of the Confederate forces at Gettysburg, the U.S. government bought the estate. A fine melding of the styles of the Greek Revival and the grand plantation houses of the early 1800s, the house has been administered by the National Park Service since 1933.

You tour the house on your own; park rangers are on-site to answer your questions. About 30% of the furnishings are original. Slave quarters and a small museum adjoin. Admission is free. It's open daily 9:30am to 4:30pm but is closed January 1 and December 25.

Pierre Charles L'Enfant's grave was placed near Arlington House at a spot that is believed to offer the best view of Washington, the city he designed.

Below Arlington House, an 8-minute walk from the visitor center, is the **Gravesite of John Fitzgerald Kennedy.** Simplicity is the key to grandeur here, too. John Carl Warnecke designed a low crescent wall embracing a marble terrace, inscribed with memorable words of the 35th U.S. president, including his famous utterance, "And so my fellow Americans, ask not what your country can do for you, ask what you can do for your country." Jacqueline Kennedy Onassis rests next to her husband, and Senator Robert Kennedy is buried close by. The Kennedy graves attract streams of visitors. Arrive close to 8am to contemplate the site quietly; otherwise, it's mobbed. Looking north, there's a spectacular view of Washington.

About 1½ miles from the Kennedy graves, the **Marine Corps Memorial,** the famous statue of the marines raising the flag on Iwo Jima, stands near the north (or Orde & Weitzel Gate) entrance to the cemetery as a tribute to marines who died in all wars. On Tuesday evenings in summer, there are military parades on the grounds at 7pm.

Close to the Iwo Jima statue is the **Netherlands Carillon,** a gift from the people of the Netherlands, with 50 bells. Every spring thousands of tulip bulbs bloom on the surrounding grounds. Carillon concerts take place from 2 to 4pm on Saturday during April, May, and September; and from 6 to 8pm on Saturday from June to August. (Sometimes the hours change; call ☎ **703/285-2598** before you go.) Visitors are permitted to enter the tower to watch the carillonneur perform and enjoy panoramic views of Washington.

✪ In October 1997, the **Women in Military Service for America Memorial** (☎ **800/222-2294** or 703/533-1155) was added to Arlington Cemetery, to honor the more than 1.8 million women who have served in the armed forces from the American Revolution to the present. The impressive new memorial lies just beyond the gated entrance to the cemetery, a 3-minute walk from the Visitor Center. What you see as you approach the memorial is a large, circular reflecting pool, perfectly placed within the curve of the granite wall rising behind it. Arched passages within the 226-foot-long wall lead to an upper terrace and dramatic views of Arlington National Cemetery and the monuments of Washington; an arc of large glass panels (which form the roof of the memorial hall) contains etched quotations from servicewomen (and a couple from men). Currently, only 11 quotations appear, including this one from American Red Cross founder Clara Barton: "From the storm-lashed Mayflower . . . to the present hour, woman has stood like a rock for the welfare and the glory of the history of the country, and one might well add . . . unwritten, unrewarded, and almost unrecognized." Behind the wall and completely underground is the **Education Center,** housing a **Hall of Honor,** a gallery of exhibits tracing the history of women in the military, a theater, and a computer register of servicewomen, which visitors may access for information about individual women, past and present, in the military. Hours are October through March 8am to 5pm and April through September 8am to 7pm. Stop at the reception desk for a brochure that details a self-guided tour through the memorial. The memorial is open every day but Christmas.

The Korean War Veterans Memorial. Just across from the Lincoln Memorial (east of French Dr., between 21st and 23rd sts. NW). ☎ **202/426-6841.** Free admission. Rangers on duty 8am–midnight daily except Dec 25. Ranger-led interpretive programs are given throughout the day. Metro: Foggy Bottom.

This privately funded memorial founded in 1995 honors those who served in Korea, a 3-year conflict (1950–53) that produced almost as many casualties as Vietnam. It consists of a circular "Pool of Remembrance" in a grove of trees and a triangular "Field of Service." The latter is highlighted by lifelike statues of 19 infantrymen, who appear to be trudging across fields, their expressions and stances suggesting that their enemies lurk nearby. The scene is wholly compelling. In addition, a 164-foot-long black granite wall depicts the array of combat and combat support troops that served in Korea (nurses, chaplains, airmen, gunners, mechanics, cooks, and others); a raised granite curb lists the 22 nations that contributed to the UN's effort there; and a commemorative area honors KIAs, MIAs, and POWs. Limited parking is available along Ohio Drive. If you don't mind a walk, try to snag a spot along W. Basin Drive near the FDR Memorial; after you tour that site, you cross Independence Avenue and head in the direction of the Lincoln Memorial.

The Vietnam Veterans Memorial (see below) extends to one side of the Lincoln Memorial, the Korean to the other side, so you'll be able to hit all three while you're here.

United States Navy Memorial and Naval Heritage Center. 701 Pennsylvania Ave. NW. ☎ **800/723-3557** or 202/737-2300. Free admission. Mon–Sat 9:30am–5pm. Closed Thanksgiving, New Year's Day, and Dec 25. Metro: Archives–Navy Memorial.

Authorized by Congress in 1980 to honor the men and women of the U.S. Navy, this memorial comprises a 100-foot-diameter circular plaza bearing a granite world map flanked by fountains and waterfalls salted with waters from the seven seas. A statue *of The Lone Sailor* watching over the map represents all who have served in the navy. And two sculpture walls adorned with bronze bas-reliefs commemorate navy history and related maritime services.

The building adjoining the memorial houses a naval heritage center. The center's museum includes interactive video kiosks proffering a wealth of information about navy ships, aircraft, and history; the **Navy Memorial Log Room,** a computerized record of past and present navy personnel; the **Presidents Room,** honoring the six U.S. presidents who served in the navy and the two who became secretary of the navy; the **Ship's Store,** filled with nautical and maritime merchandise; and a wide-screen 70mm Surroundsound film called *At Sea,* which lets viewers experience the grandeur of the ocean and the adventure of going to sea on a navy ship. The 35-minute film plays every Monday through Saturday at 11am, 1pm, and 3pm; admission is $3.75 for adults, $3 for seniors and students 18 and under.

Guided tours are available from the front desk, subject to staff availability. The plaza is the scene of many free band concerts in spring and summer; call for details.

✪ **The Vietnam Veterans Memorial.** Just across from the Lincoln Memorial (east of Henry Bacon Dr. between 21st and 22nd sts. NW). ☎ **202/426-6841.** Free admission. Rangers on duty 8am–midnight daily except Dec 25. Ranger-led programs are given throughout the day. Metro: Foggy Bottom.

A most poignant sight in Washington is the Vietnam Veterans Memorial: two long, black granite walls inscribed with the names of the men and women who gave their lives, or remain missing, in the longest war in our nation's history. Even if no one close to you died in Vietnam, it's wrenching to watch visitors grimly studying the directories at either end to find out where their husbands, sons, and loved ones are listed. The slow walk along the 492-foot wall of names—it names close to 60,000 people, many of whom died very young—powerfully evokes the tragedy of all wars. It's also affecting to see how much the monument means to Vietnam veterans who visit it. Because of the raging conflict over U.S. involvement in the war, Vietnam veterans had received virtually no previous recognition of their service.

The memorial was conceived by Vietnam veteran Jan Scruggs and built by the Vietnam Veterans Memorial Fund, a nonprofit organization that raised $7 million for the project. The VVMF was granted a 2-acre site in tranquil Constitution Gardens to erect a memorial that would make no political statement about the war and would harmonize with neighboring memorials. By separating the issue of the wartime service of individuals from the issue of U.S. policy in Vietnam, VVMF hoped to begin a process of national reconciliation.

Yale senior Maya Ying Lin's design was chosen in a national competition open to all citizens over 18 years of age. It consists of two walls in a quiet, protected park setting, angled at 125° to point to the Washington Monument and the Lincoln Memorial. The wall's mirrorlike surface reflects surrounding trees, lawns, and monuments. The names are inscribed in chronological order, documenting an epoch in

American history as a series of individual sacrifices from the date of the first casualty in 1959 to the date of the last death in 1975.

The wall was erected in 1982. In 1984, a life-size sculpture of three Vietnam soldiers by Frederick Hart was installed at the entrance plaza. He describes his work this way: "They wear the uniform and carry the equipment of war; they are young. The contrast between the innocence of their youth and the weapons of war underscores the poignancy of their sacrifice. . . . Their strength and their vulnerability are both evident." Near the statue a flag flies from a 60-foot staff. Another sculpture, the *Vietnam Veterans Women's Memorial*, which depicts three servicewomen tending a wounded soldier, was installed on Veterans Day 1993.

The park rangers at the Vietnam Veterans Memorial are very knowledgeable and are usually milling about—be sure to seek them out if you have any questions. Limited parking is available along Constitution Avenue.

7 More Museums

✪ **Corcoran Gallery of Art.** 500 17th St. NW (between E St. and New York Ave.). ☎ **202/ 639-1700.** www.corcoran.com. Free admission. Wed and Fri–Mon 10am–5pm, Thurs 10am–9pm. Suggested contribution $3 adults, $1 students and senior citizens, $5 for families; children 12 and under are free. Free 45-minute tours daily at noon, Thurs 7:30, Sat–Sun 10:30am and 12:30pm. Closed Tues, Jan 1, and Dec 25. Some street parking. Metro: Farragut West or Farragut North.

This elegant art museum is a favorite party site in the city, hosting everything from MTV's ball during the 1996 presidential inauguration (2,800 turned out, twice the number expected, everyone from Sheryl Crow to Lauren Bacall), to wedding receptions for the wealthy. In 1997, the Corcoran made the papers as the site of a standoff between Russian and American sponsors of a Romanov jewels exhibit. The Russians parked a large truck outside the museum, refusing to budge until the American committee returned the jewels to them. The Russians eventually capitulated and the jewels continued on to the next stop on their traveling tour.

The first art museum in Washington (and one of the first in the nation), the Corcoran Gallery was housed from 1869 to 1896 in the redbrick and brownstone building that is now the Renwick. The collection outgrew its quarters and was transferred in 1897 to its present beaux arts building, designed by Ernest Flagg.

The collection, shown in rotating exhibits, focuses chiefly on American art. A prominent Washington banker, William Wilson Corcoran was among the first wealthy American collectors to realize the importance of encouraging and supporting this country's artists. Enhanced by further gifts and bequests, the collection comprehensively spans American art from 18th-century portraiture to 20th-century moderns like Nevelson, Warhol, and Rothko. Nineteenth-century works include Bierstadt's and Remington's imagery of the American West; Hudson River School artists; expatriates like Whistler, Sargent, and Mary Cassatt; and two giants of the late 19th century, Homer and Eakins.

The Corcoran is not exclusively an American art museum. On the first floor is the collection from the estate of Senator William Andrews Clark, an eclectic grouping of Dutch and Flemish masters; European painters; French impressionists; Barbizon landscapes; Delft porcelains; a Louis XVI *salon dore* transported in toto from Paris; and more. Clark's will stated that his diverse collection, which any curator would undoubtedly want to disperse among various museum departments, must be shown as a unit. He left money for a wing to house it, and the new building opened in 1928. Don't miss the small, walnut-paneled room known as

---

Fun Fact ————————————————————————————————

Displayed on the second floor of the Corcoran is the white-marble female nude, *The Greek Slave*, by Hiram Powers, considered so daring in its day that it was shown on alternate days to men and women.

"Clark Landing," which showcases 19th-century French impressionist and American art; a room of exquisite Corot landscapes; another of medieval Renaissance tapestries; and numerous Daumier lithographs donated by Dr. Armand Hammer.

Pick up a schedule of events—temporary exhibits, gallery talks, concerts, art auctions, and more. Families should inquire about the Corcoran's series of Saturday Family Days and Sunday Traditions. (Family Days are especially fun for everyone and always feature great live music.) Both programs are free, but you need to reserve a slot for the Sunday events. The charming Café des Artistes is open for lunch Monday through Saturday 11am to 3pm, for dinner on Thursday, and for Sunday brunch (reservations are not accepted for the brunch, which costs $18.95 per adult, $8.50 per child, and includes live gospel music singers; call ☎ **202/639-1786** for more information). The Corcoran has a nice gift shop.

Dumbarton Oaks. 1703 32nd St. NW (entrance to the collections on 32nd St., between R and S sts.; garden entrance at 31st and R sts.). ☎ **202/339-6401.** Garden Apr–Oct $4 adults, $3 children under 12 and senior citizens, Nov–Mar free admission; collections year-round suggested donation $1. Garden Apr–Oct, daily 2–6pm, Nov–Mar, daily (weather permitting) 2–5pm; collections year-round Tues–Sun 2–5pm. Gardens and collections are closed national holidays and Dec 24. Street parking.

Many people associate Dumbarton Oaks, a 19th-century Georgetown mansion named for a Scottish castle, with the 1944 international conference that led to the formation of the United Nations. Today the 16-acre estate is a research center for studies in Byzantine and pre-Columbian art and history, as well as landscape architecture. Its yards, which wind gently down to Rock Creek Ravine, are magical, modeled after European gardens. The pre-Columbian museum, designed by Philip Johnson, is a small gem, and the Byzantine collection is a rich one.

This unusual collection originated with Robert Woods Bliss and his wife, Mildred. In 1940 they turned over their estate, their extensive Byzantine collection, a library of works on Byzantine civilization, and 16 acres (including 10 acres of exquisite formal gardens) to Mr. Bliss's alma mater, Harvard, and provided endowment funds for continuing research in Byzantine studies. In the early 1960s they also donated their pre-Columbian collection and financed the building of a wing to house it, as well as a second wing for Mrs. Bliss's collection of rare books on landscape gardening. The Byzantine collection includes illuminated manuscripts, a 13th-century icon of St. Peter, mosaics, ivory carvings, a 4th-century sarcophagus, jewelry, and more. The pre-Columbian works, displayed chronologically in eight marble- and oak-floored glass pavilions, feature Olmec jade and serpentine figures, Mayan relief panels, textiles from 900 B.C. to the Spanish Conquest, funerary pottery, gold necklaces made by the lost-wax process, and sculptures of Aztec gods and goddesses.

The historic music room, furnished in European antiques, was the setting for the 1944 Dumbarton Oaks Conversations about the United Nations. It has a beamed, painted 16th-century French-style ceiling and an immense 16th-century stone fireplace. Among its notable artworks is El Greco's *The Visitation*.

Pick up a self-guiding brochure to tour the staggeringly beautiful formal gardens, which include an Orangery; a Rose Garden (final resting place of the Blisses amid

1,000 rose bushes, newly brought back to life after near extinction); wisteria-covered arbors; herbaceous borders; groves of cherry trees; and magnolias. Exit at R Street, turn left, cross an honest-to-goodness Lovers' Lane, and proceed next door to Montrose Park, where you can picnic.

The Folger Shakespeare Library. 201 E. Capitol St. SE. ☎ **202/544-7077** or 202/544-4600. Free admission. Mon–Sat 10am–4pm. Closed federal holidays. Free walk-in tours daily 11am. Metro: Capitol South.

"Shakespeare taught us that the little world of the heart is vaster, deeper, and richer than the spaces of astronomy," wrote Ralph Waldo Emerson in 1864. A decade later, Amherst student Henry Clay Folger was profoundly affected upon hearing a lecture by Emerson similarly extolling the bard. Folger purchased an inexpensive set of Shakespeare's plays and went on to amass a prodigious mass—by far the world's largest—of his printed works, today housed in the Folger Shakespeare Library. By 1930, when Folger and his wife, Emily (whose literary enthusiasms matched his own), laid the cornerstone of a building to house the collection, it comprised 93,000 books, 50,000 prints and engravings, and thousands of manuscripts. The Folgers gave it all as a gift to the American people.

The building itself has a marble facade decorated with nine bas-relief scenes from Shakespeare's plays; it is a striking example of art deco classicism. A statue of Puck stands in the west garden, and quotations from the bard and from contemporaries such as Ben Jonson adorn the exterior walls. An Elizabethan garden on the east side of the building is planted with flowers and herbs of the period, many of them mentioned in the plays. Inquire about docent-led tours identifying these plants, and placing them within the plays, scheduled on certain Saturdays, April to October. The garden is also a quiet place to have a picnic.

The facility, which houses some 250,000 books, 100,000 of which are rare, is an important research center not only for Shakespearean scholars, but for those studying any aspect of the English and continental Renaissance. And the oak-paneled **Great Hall,** reminiscent of a Tudor long gallery, is a popular attraction for the general public. It has an intricate plaster ceiling decorated with Shakespeare's coat of arms, fleurs-de-lis, and other motifs. On display are rotating exhibits from the permanent collection: books, paintings, playbills, Renaissance musical instruments, and more.

At the end of the Great Hall is a theater designed to suggest an Elizabethan inn-yard where plays, concerts, readings, and Shakespeare-related events take place (see chapter 10 for details).

Ford's Theatre & Lincoln Museum. 517 10th St. NW (between E and F sts.). ☎ **202/426-6925.** Free admission. Daily 9am–5pm. Closed Dec 25. Metro: Metro Center.

On April 14, 1865, President Abraham Lincoln was in the audience of Ford's Theatre, one of the most popular playhouses in Washington. Everyone was laughing at a funny line from Tom Taylor's celebrated comedy, *Our American Cousin,* when John Wilkes Booth crept into the president's box, shot the president, and leapt to the stage, shouting "Sic semper tyrannis" (Thus ever to tyrants). With his left leg broken from the vault, Booth mounted his horse in the back alley and galloped off. Doctors carried Lincoln across the street to the house of William Petersen, where the president died the next morning.

After Lincoln's assassination, the theater was closed by order of Secretary of War Edwin M. Stanton. For many years afterward it was used as an office by the

Museums of Special Interest

In addition to the many superb museums described within this chapter, many other lesser-known, but wonderful, ones exist around the city. Often these museums focus on one select subject, architecture, perhaps, or the life of the historic figure who lived within. Peruse the following list to see whether one of these sites covers a topic that happens to be of special interest to you, and then call for further information. Don't try to drop in without calling, because most of these museums are not open daily and some require appointments.

Art Museum of the Americas. 201 18th St. NW (☎ **202/458-3000**). Permanent collection of 20th-century Latin American art. Metro: Farragut West, then walk south about 6 blocks.

B'Nai B'rith Klutznick Museum. 1640 Rhode Island Ave. NW (☎ **202/ 857-6583**). Jewish history and culture. Metro: Farragut North.

Capital Children's Museum. 800 3rd St. NW (☎ **202/675-4120**). Hands-on educational complex. Metro: Union Station.

Daughters of the American Revolution (DAR) Museum. 1776 D St. NW (☎ **202/879-3254**). Permanent collection Early American furnishings and decorative arts. Metro: Farragut West, then walk south about 5 blocks.

Decatur House. 748 Jackson Place (☎ **202/842-0920**). Historic house museum (see chapter 8 for description within Walking Tour 2) with permanent collection of Federalist and Victorian furnishings. Metro: Farragut West or McPherson Square.

Dumbarton House. 2715 Q St. NW (☎ **202/337-2288**). Another historic house museum (also featured in chapter 8 within Walking Tour 3), with permanent collection of 18th- and 19th-century English and American furniture and decorative arts. Metro: Dupont Circle, with a 20-minute walk along Q St.

Frederick Douglass Home. 1411 W St. SE (☎ **202/426-5961**). Last residence of famous African-American, 19th-century abolitionist. Metro: Anacostia, then catch bus no. B2, which stops right in front of the house.

Historical Society of Washington. 1307 New Hampshire Ave. NW (☎ **202/785-2068**). The 1899 Christian Heurich mansion, resplendent in late Victoriana (see chapter 8 for detailed description within Walking Tour 1). Metro: Dupont Circle, 19th Street exit.

Interior Department Museum. 1849 C St. NW (☎ **202/208-4743**). Permanent exhibits relating to American historical events and locales, including murals by prominent Native American artists, newly on view on the 9th floor. Metro: Farragut West, then walk about 6 blocks south.

War Department. In 1893, 22 clerks were killed when three floors of the building collapsed. It remained in disuse until the 1960s, when it was remodeled and restored to its appearance on the night of the tragedy. Except when rehearsals or matinees are in progress (call before you go), visitors can see the theater and trace Booth's movements on that fateful night. Free 15-minute talks on the history of the theater and the story of the assassination are given throughout the day. Be sure to visit the Lincoln Museum in the basement, where exhibits—including the Derringer pistol used by Booth and a diary in which he outlines his rationalization for the deed—focus on events surrounding Lincoln's assassination and the trial of the conspirators. The theater stages productions most of the year (see chapter 10 for information).

Kreeger Museum. 2401 Foxhall Rd. NW (☎ 202/337-3050). Permanent collection of impressionist, Postimpressionist, expressionist, and African paintings and sculpture. No convenient Metro or bus stop; best to drive or take a taxi.

Mary McLeod Bethune House. 1318 Vermont Ave. NW (☎ 202/673-2402). The last official Washington residence of African-American activist/educator Bethune, the house presents and preserves African-American women's history. Metro: McPherson Square.

National Aquarium. 14th St. and Constitution Ave. NW (☎ 202/482-2826). The nation's first public aquarium, tiny but interesting. Metro: Federal Triangle.

National Building Museum. 401 F. St. NW (☎ 202/272-2448). Housed within a historic building of mammoth proportions is this museum devoted to architecture, building, and historic preservation. Metro: Judiciary Square.

Octagon. 1799 New York Ave. NW (☎ 202/638-3105). Another historic house museum (see chapter 8 for detailed description within Walking Tour 2), it also features exhibits on architecture (its neighbor is the American Institute of Architects headquarters). Metro: Farragut West.

Sewall-Belmont House. 144 Constitution Ave. NE (☎ 202/546-3989). A must for those interested in women's history, the historic house displays memorabilia of the women's suffragette movement, which got its start here. Metro: Union Station.

Textile Museum. 2320 S St. NW (☎ 202/667-0441). Historic and contemporary handmade textile arts, housed in historic John Russell Pope mansion (also featured on Walking Tour 1, see chapter 8). Metro: Dupont Circle, Q Street exit, then walk a couple of blocks up Massachusetts Avenue until you see S. Street.

Treasury Department. 15th St. and Pennsylvania Ave. NW (☎ 202/622-0896). An immense building with marvelous architecture and fascinating history. Metro: Metro Center or Federal Triangle.

Tudor Place. 1644 31st St. NW (☎ 202/965-0400). An 1816 mansion with gardens, and home to Martha Washington's descendants until a decade ago. Metro: Dupont Circle, with a 25-minute walk along Q Street.

Woodrow Wilson House. 2340 S St. NW (☎ 202/387-4062). Former home of this president, preserved the way it was when he lived here (see description in Walking Tour 1, chapter 8). Metro: Dupont Circle, then walk a couple of blocks up Massachusetts Avenue until you reach S Street.

The House Where Lincoln Died (the Petersen House). 516 10th St. NW. ☎ **202/426-6830.** Free admission. Daily 9am–5pm. Closed Dec 25. Metro: Metro Center.

After the shooting, the doctors attending Lincoln carried him out into the street, where boarder Henry Safford, standing in the open doorway of his rooming house, gestured for them to bring the president inside. So Lincoln died in the home of William Petersen, a German-born tailor. Now furnished with period pieces, the dark, narrow town house looks much as it did on that fateful April night. It takes about 5 minutes to troop through the building. You'll see the front parlor where an anguished Mary Todd Lincoln spent the night with her son, Robert. Her emotional state was such that she was banned from the bedroom because she was creating havoc. In the back parlor, Secretary of War Edwin M. Stanton held a Cabinet

Exhibits Scheduled at Museums in 1999

The following listing, though not comprehensive, is enough to give you an idea about upcoming or current exhibits at major Washington museums. Because schedules sometimes change, it's always a good idea to call ahead. See individual entries in this chapter for phone numbers and addresses.

Arthur M. Sackler Gallery "The Jesuits and the Mughals" (September 27, 1998 to April 4, 1999) examines the blending of Eastern and Western artistic styles in 22 paintings, books, and objects from Catholic missions in Asia after Vasco de Gama's discovery of the sea route in 1498; "Paintings of Mustang" (January 31 to August 1) displays Australian artist Rober Powell's watercolor paintings of Mustang, a remote area that extends from Nepal into Tibet.

Corcoran Gallery of Art "New Worlds from Old: American and Australian Landscape Painting of the 19th Century" (January 27 to April 20); "Property and Dreams: 1930s Photography in the USA and the USSR" (May 15–Aug 23); "Roy Lichtenstein Sculptures" (June–October, exact dates to be announced).

Freer Gallery of Art "Whistler Prints I: The Leyland Circle, 1867-75" (July 3, 1998 to June 30, 1999) focuses on Whistler's printmaking career, under the patronage of Frederick Richards Leyland, a Liverpool ship owner; "Winged Figures" (opens spring 1999) brings together for the first time Abbott H. Thayer's three monumental winged figure paintings in the Freer collection.

Hirshhorn Museum & Sculpture Garden If you're here at the end of 1998 or early January 1999, you'll want to catch "Chuck Close," a retrospective of the artist's photographs; paintings; drawings; and prints (October 15, 1998 to January 10, 1999).

National Air & Space Museum "Business Wings" (June 12, 1998 to May 31, 1999) examines the role of aircraft in the business community and how aircraft have responded to the time-sensitive and changing needs of business.

National Gallery of Art "Love and War: A Manual for Life in the Late Middle Ages" (November 8, 1998 to January 31, 1999) displays the drawings and pages of a late medieval manuscript known as the "Housebook," as well as 21 prints created by the artist, referred to simply as the "Master of the Housebook," which belong to the Rijksmuseum, in Amsterdam; "John Singer Sargent" (February 21 to May 31) is an exhibit of more than 100 paintings and watercolors, reflecting the main phases of the artist's life.

National Museum of African Art "Heavy Metals or the Alloyed Truth: A Tribute to the African Smith" (March 21 to June 20); "Modern Art from South Africa" (May 23 to September 26); and "Hats Off: A Salute to African Headgear" (July 18 to October 17).

National Museum of American Art "Eyeing America: Robert Cottingham Prints" (September 25, 1998 to January 31, 1999) includes a complete set of the

meeting and began questioning witnesses. From this room, Stanton announced at 7:22am on April 15, 1865, "Now he belongs to the ages." Lincoln died, lying diagonally because he was so tall, on a bed the size of the one you see here, but not this one. (The Chicago Historical Society owns it and other items from the room.)

Twelve years after Lincoln's death, the house was sold to Louis Schade, who published a newspaper called the *Washington Sentinel* in its basement for many years. In 1896, the government bought the house for $30,000, and it is now maintained by the National Park Service.

artist's prints through 1991; "Art of the Gold Rush" (October 27, 1998 to March 7, 1999) displays images of the forty-niners, as seen from both the East and West Coasts, with a companion exhibit of photographs including more than 140 daguerreotypes; "Images of Old New England" (April 2 to August 22) exhibits nearly 180 paintings, sculptures, prints, photographs, and other works, all views of New England made between the Civil War and World War II, as executed by artists such as Norman Rockwell and Winslow Homer; "Watercolors by Edward Hopper" (October 22, 1999 to January 3, 2000) is a show of 50 master watercolors by one of the best-known American artists of the 20th century.

National Museum of Natural History   "Forces of Change" (opening in 1999, dates to be announced) is a new exhibit hall that shows how the Earth changes and how humans participate in (and are affected by) these changes.

National Museum of Women in the Arts   "Painting in A Lonely Arena, Joyce Treiman and the Old Masters" (December 14, 1998 to July 5, 1999) explores the wildly untraditional American artist's figurative paintings, inspired by the works of the Old Masters; "A Narrative Thread, Women's Embroidery in Rural India" (February 4 to May 9) includes 30 communally embroidered quilts.

National Portrait Gallery   "George Washington" (November 20, 1998 to December 19, 1999) commemorates the 200th anniversary of our first president's death, through this display of Washington portraits made during his two terms in office.

National Postal Museum   "More than Magic" (opens in 1999, dates to be determined) has as its theme postal automation, with interactive exhibits showing how letters and parcels race through the U.S. Postal Service's mail system at a rate of more than 600 million pieces per day.

National Zoological Park   A new grasslands exhibit will open in 1999 (dates to be announced).

The Phillips Collection   "An American Century of Photography: From Dry-Plate to Digital" (January 23 to April 11) displays 140 images and surveys the history of photography from the 1880s to the present; "O'Keeffe and Things" (April 24 to July 25) includes 60 works spanning the years 1908 to 1972.

Renwick Gallery   "Shaker: The Art of Craftsmanship" (March 19 to July 25) highlights the furniture, decorative arts, and tools designed, crafted, and used by the Mount Lebanon, New York, Shaker community; "Dominic Di Mare" (March 19 to July 25) offers the first retrospective of the San Francisco Bay area artist's works, which range from the avant-garde, to woven sculptural forms, to shrinelike structures.

National Geographic Society's Explorers Hall. 17th and M sts. NW. ☎ **202/857-7588.** Free admission. Mon–Sat and holidays 9am–5pm, Sun 10am–5pm. Closed Dec 25. Metro: Farragut North (Connecticut Ave. and L St. exit).

I don't know that I'd come here if I didn't have kids. Whatever, as my 11-year-old says. The truth is, anyone over 8 will find something fascinating or enjoyable at Explorers Hall.

The National Geographic Society was founded in 1888 for "the increase and diffusion of geographic knowledge." At Explorers Hall, dozens of fascinating displays, most of them using interactive videos, put that knowledge at your fingertips. In **Geographica,** on the north side of the hall, you can touch a tornado; find out what it's like inside the Earth; and explore the vast Martian landscape. The major exhibit here is **Earth Station One,** an interactive amphitheater (centered on an immense free-floating globe) that simulates an orbital flight. You can also peer into a video microscope that zooms in clearly on slides showing such specimens as a hydra (a simple multicellular animal) or mosquito larva.

Other displays include a scale model of Jacques Cousteau's diving saucer, in which he descended to 25,000 feet; the flag and dog sled, among other equipment, of Admiral Robert E. Peary, the first man to reach the North Pole; an *Aepyornis maximus* egg, from Madagascar's extinct 1,000-pound flightless "elephant bird"; and the world's largest freestanding globe. Also on view are a full-size replica of a giant Olmec stone head dating from 32 B.C. from La Venta, Mexico and a 3.9 billion-year-old moon rock. Video excerpts from the society's TV specials are shown in the National Geographic Television Room. The hall offers an ongoing series of lectures and temporary exhibits.

National Museum of Women in the Arts. 1250 New York Ave. NW (at 13th St.). ☎ **202/783-5000.** Suggested contribution: $3 adults. Mon–Sat 10am–5pm, Sun noon–5pm. Closed Jan 1, Thanksgiving Day, and Dec 25. Metro: Metro Center, 13th St. exit.

Celebrating "the contribution of women to the history of art," this relatively new museum (opened 1987) is Washington's 72nd but a national first. Its 10th anniversary in 1997 saw the opening of the **Elizabeth A. Kasser Wing,** which adds 5,300 square feet and two new galleries to the museum. Founders Wilhelmina and Wallace Holladay, who donated the core of the permanent collection—more than 200 works by women from the 16th through the 20th century—became interested in women's art in the 1960s. After discovering that no women were included in H. W. Janson's *History of Art,* a standard text (this, by the way, did not change until 1986!), the Holladays began collecting art by women, and the concept of a women's art museum (to begin correcting the inequities of underrepresentation) soon evolved.

Since its opening, the collection has grown to more than 2,000 works by artists including Rosa Bonheur, Frida Kahlo, Helen Frankenthaler, Barbara Hepworth, Georgia O'Keeffe, Camille Claudel, Lila Cabot Perry, Mary Cassatt, Elaine de Kooning, Käthe Kollwitz, and many other lesser known but notable artists from earlier centuries. You will discover here, for instance, that the famed Peale family of 19th-century portrait painters included a very talented sister, Sarah Miriam Peale. The collection is complemented by an ongoing series of changing exhibits.

The museum is housed in a magnificent Renaissance Revival landmark building designed in 1907 as a Masonic temple by noted architect Waddy Wood. Its sweeping marble staircase and splendid interior make it a popular choice for wedding receptions. The charming and sunny Mezzanine Cafe serves light lunches Monday through Saturday—soups, salads, and sandwiches.

☉ Phillips Collection. 1600 21st St. NW (at Q St.). ☎ **202/387-2151.** Admission Sat–Sun $6.50 adults, $3.25 seniors and students, free for children 18 and under; contribution suggested Tues–Fri. Sept–May Tues–Wed and Fri–Sat 10am–5pm, Thurs 10am–8:30pm, Sun noon–5pm; June–Aug, noon–7pm. Free tours Wed and Sat 2pm. Closed Jan 1, July 4, Thanksgiving Day, and Dec 25. Metro: Dupont Circle (Q St. exit).

Conceived as "a museum of modern art and its sources," this intimate establishment, occupying an elegant 1890s Georgian Revival mansion and a more youthful wing, houses the exquisite collection of Duncan and Marjorie Phillips, avid collectors and proselytizers of modernism. Carpeted rooms, with leaded- and stained-glass windows, oak paneling, plush chairs and sofas, and frequently, fireplaces, establish a comfortable, homelike setting for the viewing of their art. Today the collection includes more than 2,500 works. Among the highlights: superb examples of Daumier, Dove, and Bonnard paintings; some splendid small Vuillards; five van Goghs; Renoir's *Luncheon of the Boating Party;* seven Cézannes; and six works by Georgia O'Keeffe. Ingres, Delacroix, Manet, El Greco, Goya, Corot, Constable, Courbet, Giorgione, and Chardin are among the "sources" or forerunners of modernism represented. Modern notables include Rothko, Hopper, Kandinsky, Matisse, Klee, Degas, Rouault, Picasso, and many others. It's a collection no art lover should miss. The museum presents an ongoing series of temporary shows, supplementing works from the Phillips with loans from other museums and private collections.

A full schedule of events includes gallery talks, lectures, and free concerts in the ornate music room. (Concerts take place every Sunday at 5pm, September through May; arrive early. Although the concert is free, admission to the museum on weekends costs $6.50.) On Thursdays, the museum stays open until 8:30pm for **Artful Evenings** with music, gallery talks, and a cash bar; admission is $5.

On the lower level, a charming little restaurant serves light fare.

8 Other Attractions

John F. Kennedy Center for the Performing Arts. New Hampshire Ave. NW (at Rock Creek Pkwy.). ☎ **800/444-1324** or 202/416-8341 for information or tickets. Free admission. Daily 10am–midnight. Free guided tours Mon–Fri 10am–6pm, Sat–Sun between 10am and 2pm. Metro: Foggy Bottom (there's a free shuttle service from the station). Bus: no. 80 from Metro Center.

Opened in 1971, the Kennedy Center is both our national performing arts center and a memorial to John F. Kennedy. Carved into the center's river facade are several Kennedy quotations, including, "the New Frontier for which I campaign in public life can also be a New Frontier for American art." Set on 17 acres overlooking the Potomac, the striking $73-million facility, designed by noted architect Edward Durell Stone, encompasses an opera house, a concert hall, two stage theaters, a theater lab, and a film theater. The best way to see the Kennedy Center, including restricted areas, is to take a free 50-minute guided tour (see above for schedule). You can beat the crowds by writing in advance to a senator or congressperson for tickets for a VIP tour, which are given year-round Monday through Saturday 9:30am and 4:45pm, with a 9:45am tour added April through September (details in chapter 2).

The tour begins in the **Hall of Nations,** which displays the flags of all nations diplomatically recognized by the United States. Throughout the center you'll see gifts from more than 40 nations, including all the marble used in the building (3,700 tons), which Italy donated. First stop is the **Grand Foyer,** scene of many free concerts and programs and the reception area for all three theaters on the main level; the 18 crystal chandeliers are a gift from Sweden. You'll also visit the **Israeli Lounge** (where 40 painted and gilded panels depict scenes from the Old Testament); the **Concert Hall,** home of the National Symphony Orchestra; the **Opera House;** the **African Room** (decorated with beautiful tapestries from African nations); the **Eisenhower Theater;** the **Hall of States,** where flags of the 50 states and four territories are hung in the order they joined the Union; the **Performing**

Arts Library; and the **Terrace Theater,** a Bicentennial gift from Japan. Your guide will point out many notable works of art along the way. If rehearsals are being held, visits to the theaters are omitted.

If you'd like to attend performances during your visit, call the toll-free number above and request the current issue of *Kennedy Center News Magazine,* a free publication that describes all Kennedy Center happenings and prices.

After the tour, walk around the building's terrace for a panoramic view of Washington and plan a meal in one of the Kennedy Center restaurants (see chapter 6). See chapter 10 for specifics on theater, concert, and film offerings. There is limited parking below the Kennedy Center during the day at $3 for the first hour, $6 for 2 hours, $8 for 3 hours or longer; nighttime parking (after 5pm) is a flat $8.

✪ **Union Station.** 50 Massachusetts Ave. NE. ☎ **202/371-9441.** Free admission. Daily 24 hours. Shops Mon–Sat 10am–9pm, Sun 10am–6pm. Garage parking: $4 for 1 hour, $7 for 2 hours, $10 for 2 to 24 hours. You get 2 hours free parking with store or restaurant's stamped validation. Metro: Union Station.

In Washington, D.C., the very train station where you arrive is itself a noteworthy sightseeing attraction. Union Station, built between 1903 and 1907 in the great age of rail travel, was painstakingly restored in the 1980s at a cost of $160 million. The station was designed by noted architect Daniel H. Burnham, who modeled it after the Baths of Diocletian and Arch of Constantine in Rome.

When it opened in 1907, this was the largest train station in the world. The Ionic colonnades outside were fashioned from white granite. The facade contains 100 eagles. In the front of the building, a replica of the Liberty Bell and a monumental statue of Columbus hold sway. Six carved fixtures over the entranceway represent Fire, Electricity, Freedom, Imagination, Agriculture, and Mechanics. You enter the station through graceful 50-foot Constantinian arches, and walk across an expanse of white marble flooring. The **Main Hall** is a massive rectangular room with a 96-foot barrel-vaulted ceiling and a balcony adorned with 36 Augustus Saint-Gaudens sculptures of Roman legionnaires. Off the Main Hall is the **East Hall,** shimmering with scagliola marble walls and columns, a gorgeous hand-stenciled skylight ceiling, and stunning murals of classical scenes inspired by ancient Pompeian art. Today it's the station's plushest shopping venue.

In its heyday, this "temple of transport" witnessed many important events. President Wilson welcomed General Pershing here in 1918 on his return from France. South Pole explorer Rear Admiral Richard Byrd was also feted at Union Station on his homecoming. And Franklin D. Roosevelt's funeral train, bearing his casket, was met here in 1945 by thousands of mourners.

But after the 1960s, with the decline of rail travel, the station fell on hard times. Rain damage caused parts of the roof to cave in, and the entire building— with floors buckling, rats running about, and mushrooms sprouting in damp rooms—was sealed in 1981. That same year, Congress enacted legislation to preserve and faithfully restore this national treasure.

Today, Union Station is once again a vibrant entity patronized by locals and visitors alike. Every square inch of the facility has been cleaned, repaired, and/or replaced according to the original design. About 100 retail and food shops on three levels offer a wide array of merchandise. And you'll be happy to find that most of the restaurants in the Food Court are not fast-food joints—you can choose from an eclectic mix of restaurants. The skylit **Main Concourse,** which extends the entire length of the station, is the primary shopping area as well as a ticketing and baggage facility. And a nine-screen cinema complex and beautiful food court have been installed on the lower level. The remarkable restoration, which involved hundreds of European and American artisans using historical research, bygone craft techniques, and modern technology, is meticulous in every detail.

Stop by the visitor kiosk in the Main Hall. See chapter 6 for information on Union Station restaurants and chapter 9 for information about shops.

✪ Washington National Cathedral. Massachusetts and Wisconsin aves. NW (entrance on Wisconsin Ave.). ☎ **202/537-6207.** Free admission, donations accepted for tours (see information below). Cathedral daily 10am–4:30pm; May 1–Labor Day, the nave level stays open weeknights until 9pm. Gardens open daily until dusk. Worship services vary throughout the year but you can count on a daily Evensong service at 4pm, a noon service Mon–Sat, and an 11am service every Sun; call for other service times. Metro: Tenleytown, then about a 20-minute walk. Bus: Any N bus up Massachusetts Ave. from Dupont Circle or any 30-series bus along Wisconsin Ave. Also: This is a stop on the Old Town Trolley Tour.

Pierre L'Enfant's 1791 plan for the capital city included "a great church for national purposes," but possibly because of early America's fear of mingling church and state, more than a century elapsed before the foundation for Washington National Cathedral was laid. Its actual name is the Cathedral Church of St. Peter and St. Paul. The church is Episcopal, but it has no local congregation and seeks to serve the entire nation as a house of prayer for all people. It has been the setting for every kind of religious observance from Jewish to Serbian Orthodox.

A church of this magnitude—it's the sixth-largest cathedral in the world—took a long time to build. Its principal (but not original) architect, Philip Hubert Frohman, worked on the project from 1921 until his death in 1972. The foundation stone was laid in 1907 using the mallet with which George Washington set the Capitol cornerstone. Construction was interrupted by both world wars and by periods of financial difficulty. The cathedral was completed with the placement of the final stone atop a pinnacle on the west front towers on September 29, 1990, 83 years to the day it was begun.

English Gothic in style (with several distinctly 20th-century innovations, such as a stained-glass window commemorating the flight of *Apollo 11* and containing a piece of moon rock), the cathedral is built in the shape of a cross, complete with flying buttresses and gargoyles. It is, along with the Capitol and the Washington Monument, one of the dominant structures on the Washington skyline. Its 57-acre landscaped grounds have two lovely gardens (the lawn is ideal for picnicking); four schools, including the College of Preachers; an herb garden; a greenhouse; and two gift shops (one in the cathedral basement, the other in the "Herb Cottage).

Over the years the cathedral has seen much history. Services to celebrate the end of World Wars I and II were held here. It was the scene of President Wilson's funeral (he and his wife are buried here), as well as President Eisenhower's. Helen Keller and her companion, Anne Sullivan, were buried in the cathedral at her request. And during the Iranian crisis, a round-the-clock prayer vigil was held in the Holy Spirit Chapel throughout the hostages' captivity. When they were released, the hostages came to a service here, and tears flowed at Colonel Thomas Shaefer's poignant greeting, "Good morning, my fellow Americans. You don't know how long I've been waiting to say those words."

The best way to explore the cathedral and see its abundance of art, architectural carvings, and statuary is to take a 30- to 45-minute guided tour. They leave continually, from the west end of the nave, Monday to Saturday 10–11:30am and 12:45–3:15pm, and Sunday 12:30–2:45pm. A suggested donation of $2 per adult, $1 per child is requested. No tours are given on Thanksgiving, Christmas, Palm Sunday, or Easter, or during services. You can also walk through on your own, using a self-guiding brochure available in several languages. Call about group and special-interest tours, both of which require reservations (☎ **202/537-6207**). Special-interest tours cover topics ranging from the cathedral's architecture to its stained glass, and generally cost $4 per person.

Allow additional time to tour the grounds or "close" and to visit the Observation Gallery where 70 windows provide panoramic views. Tuesday and Wednesday afternoon tours are followed by a high tea in the Observation Gallery—see chapter 6, "Swell Places to Take Afternoon Tea," for further information.

The cathedral hosts numerous events: organ recitals, choir performances, an annual flower mart, calligraphy workshops, jazz, folk, and classical concerts, and the playing of the 53-bell carillon. Check the cathedral's Web site for upcoming events and other information at **www.cathedral.org/cathedral**.

9 Further Afield: Arlington

The land that today comprises Arlington County was originally carved out of Virginia as part of the territory ceded to form the nation's new capital district. In 1847, the land was returned to the state of Virginia, although it was known as Alexandria County until 1920, when the name was changed to avoid confusion with the city of Alexandria.

The county was named to honor Arlington House (inside Arlington National Cemetery, see entry earlier in this chapter), built by George Washington Parke Custis, whose daughter married Robert E. Lee. The Lees lived in Arlington House on and off until the onset of the Civil War in 1861. After the first Battle of Bull Run, at Manassas, several Union soldiers were buried here; the beginnings of Arlington National Cemetery date from that time. The Arlington Memorial Bridge leads directly from the Lincoln Memorial to the Robert E. Lee Memorial at Arlington House and symbolizes the joining of forces behind the two figures of Lincoln, representing the North, and Lee, representing the South, into one Union, following the Civil War.

Arlington has long been a residential community, with most people commuting into Washington to work and play. In recent years, though, the suburb has come into its own, booming with business, restaurants, and nightlife, giving residents reasons to stay put and tourists more of an inducement to visit (see the box, "Arlington Row," in chapter 10). Here are a couple of sites worth seeing:

The Newseum & Freedom Park. 1101 Wilson Blvd. (at N. Kent St.). ☎ **888-NEWSEUM** or 703/284-3544. Newseum Wed–Sun 10am–5pm. Freedom Park daily dawn–dusk. Limited parking is available in the building. Metro: Rosslyn.

Kids love this place because they can ham it up as a pretend newscaster, view themselves broadcasting up on the screen, and then talk mom and dad into plunking down $7 so they can take home the videotaped performance.

The Washington area's newest museum opened on April 18, 1997, and is the world's first museum dedicated exclusively to news. The Newseum's 72,000 square feet of space occupy an existing office building, reconfigured into exhibit halls and a 220-seat theater topped by an immense dome. Using state-of-the-art multimedia presentations and interactive exhibits, the museum explores the history of news dissemination and the influence of the First Amendment, granting Americans the freedom of speech and of the press. Highlights include a geodesic globe constructed of stainless steel plates and bearing the names of every existing American daily newspaper and many from around the world; a two-story-high, block-long Video Newswall displaying, via satellite and fiberoptics, more up-to-the-minute news

Pentagon Touring Tips

Tourists under 16 must be accompanied by an adult. Those 16 and older must bring a current photo ID that includes a signature and expiration date (driver's license, passport, college ID, international student ID, and so on) to be admitted. You'll have to go through a metal detector and have your bags X-rayed before the tour.

feeds than any other site in the world; a theater featuring a signature presentation about news; a news forum/TV studio where visitors can view broadcast productions in progress and discuss news events and issues; and a walk-through history of news gathering from the ancient preprint oral traditions to the latest electronic developments. In the news history gallery, look for intriguing artifacts, such as a 1455 Gutenberg Bible and a pen that belonged to Charles Dickens. The museum hosts a series of three photography exhibits during the year. The News Byte Cafe offers snack fare; the gift shop sells T-shirts, hats, and other souvenir items.

Adjoining the museum, **Freedom Park,** which opened in the summer of 1996 and sits atop a never-used elevated highway, celebrates the spirit of freedom and the struggle to preserve it. Here, too, are many intriguing exhibits, among them segments of the Berlin Wall; stones from the Warsaw Ghetto; a bronze casting of a South African ballot box; a headless statue of Lenin (one of many that were pushed over and beheaded when the Soviet Union collapsed in 1991); and a bronze casting of the Birmingham, Alabama, jail-cell door that enclosed Martin Luther King, Jr. The glass-and-steel Freedom Forum Journalists Memorial (honoring more than 900 journalists killed while on assignment) rises above the Potomac, offering views of the Washington Monument, the Lincoln and Jefferson Memorials, and the National Cathedral.

The Pentagon. Off I-395. ☎ **703/695-1776.** Free admission. Guided tours Mon–Fri 9:30am–3:30pm, every 30 minutes. Closed federal holidays and weekends. Metro: Pentagon.

The immense five-sided headquarters of the American military establishment was built during the early years of World War II. It's the world's largest office building, housing approximately 24,000 employees. For their convenience, it contains a complete indoor shopping mall, including two banks, a post office, an Amtrak ticket office, a beauty salon, a dry cleaner, and more. It's a self-contained world. There are many mind-boggling statistics to underscore the vastness of the Pentagon—for example, the building contains enough phone cable to gird the globe three times!

You can take a free 75-minute tour of certain corridors, covering the distance of a mile. Departure is from the registration booth in the Concourse area at the Pentagon Metro entrance. During the tourist season, try to arrive by 9am, when the booth opens. Groups of 10 or more must make reservations.

The tour begins with an explanation of the Department of Defense hierarchy and a short introductory film about the development of the Pentagon. Then a military guide takes you around. You'll visit:

> **The Air Force Art Collection,** which commemorates historic events involving the U.S. Air Force, including cartoons drawn by Walt Disney when he was an ambulance driver during World War I.
> **The Air Force Executive Corridor,** where, as you might have guessed, air force executives have their offices.
> **The POW Alcove,** hung with artists' conceptions of life in POW camps such as the "Hanoi Hilton."

The Marine Corps Corridor, with a small display, because the marines are actually headquartered in the Navy Annex a quarter of a mile away. Did you know that marines are called "leathernecks" because they used to wear leather collars to protect their necks from fatal sword blows?

The Navy Executive Corridor, lined with portraits of former secretaries and undersecretaries of the navy. Glass cases display models of ships and submarines in the navy's current fleet, and the solid oak doors in this corridor are modeled after old ship captain's doors.

The Army Executive Corridor, or Marshall Corridor, named for General George C. Marshall, the first military man to receive a Nobel Peace Prize (for the Marshall Plan that helped Europe recover after World War II). Displayed here are army command and divisional flags and 172 army campaign streamers dating from 1775 through the Gulf War.

The Time-Life Art Collection Corridor. During World War II Time-Life hired civilian artists to paint battle scenes at the front line. Most affecting is *Two-Thousand Yard Stare*, showing a soldier suffering from battle fatigue because of lack of food, sleep, and water.

The MacArthur Corridor honors General Douglas MacArthur. His career spanned 52 years, during which he served in three wars under nine presidents.

The Hall of Heroes is where Medal of Honor recipients (3,409 to date) are commemorated. The medal is given out only during wartime and usually posthumously.

The Military Women's Corridor documents the role of women throughout U.S. armed services history.

The Navaho Code Talkers Corridor tells the story of the code language developed for military communications after the Japanese bombed Pearl Harbor during World War II. The U.S. military recruited the help of 400 Navahos, all marines, to create an indecipherable means of communication from the Navaho language.

The Flag Corridor displays state and territorial flags, from the first Union Jack to the 50-star flag of today. This is where the tour concludes.

Note: The best way to get to the Pentagon is via Metro's blue or yellow lines. If you must drive, call for directions.

10 Parks & Gardens

Like most cities, Washington intersperses manicured pockets of green between office buildings and traffic-laden streets. Unlike most cities, it's also extensively endowed with vast natural areas all centrally located within the district: thousands of parkland acres; two rivers; the mouth of an 185-mile-long, tree-lined canalside trail; an untamed wilderness area; and a few thousand cherry trees. And there's much more just a stone's throw away.

GARDENS

Enid A. Haupt Garden. 10th St. and Independence Ave. SW. ☎ **202/357-2700.** Free admission. Late May–Aug daily 7am–8pm; Sept–mid-May; daily 7am–5:45pm. Closed Dec 25. Metro: Smithsonian.

Named for its donor, a noted supporter of horticultural projects, this stunning garden presents elaborate flower beds and borders; plant-filled turn-of-the-century urns; 1870s cast-iron furnishings; and lush baskets hung from reproduction

Alert

The U.S. Botanic Garden is closed for renovations and is not expected to reopen until the year 2000 or later.

19th-century lampposts. Although on ground level, the garden is really a 4-acre rooftop garden above the subterranean Sackler and African Art Museums. A magnolia-lined parterre, framed by four floral swags, centers on a floral bed patterned after the rose window in the Commons of the Castle; it is composed of 30,000 green and yellow Alternanthera, supplemented by seasonal displays of spring pansies, begonias, or cabbage and kale. An "Island Garden" near the Sackler Gallery, entered via a 9-foot moongate, has benches backed by English boxwoods under the shade of weeping cherry trees; half-round pieces of granite in its still pool are meant to suggest ripples. A "Fountain Garden" outside the African Art Museum provides granite seating walls shaded by hawthorn trees, with tiny water channels fed by fountains and a waterfall or "chadar" inspired by the gardens of Shalimar. Three small terraces, shaded by black sour-gum trees, are located near the Arts & Industries Building. And five majestic linden trees shade a seating area around the Downing Urn, a memorial to American landscapist Andrew Jackson Downing. Additional features include wisteria-covered dome-shaped trellises, clusters of trees (Zumi crabapples, ginkgoes, and American hollies), a weeping European beech, and rose gardens. Elaborate cast-iron carriage gates made according to a 19th-century design by James Renwick, flanked by four red sandstone pillars, have been installed at the Independence Avenue entrance to the garden.

✪ **United States Botanic Garden.** 100 Maryland Ave. at 1st St. SW (at the east end of the Mall). ☎ **202/225-8333.** Free admission. Daily 9am–5pm. Metro: Federal Center SW.

Well, you're out of luck. The Botanic Garden is currently undergoing a major renovation and won't reopen until about 2001. Keep up with its progress by checking the Web site at **www.nationalgarden.org.** You *can* visit the garden annex across the street, **Bartholdi Park.** The park is about the size of a city block, with a stunning cast-iron classical fountain created by Frédéric Auguste Bartholdi, designer of the Statue of Liberty. Charming flower gardens bloom amid tall ornamental grasses here, benches are sheltered by vine-covered bowers, and a touch and fragrance garden contains such herbs as pineapple-scented sage.

United States National Arboretum. 3501 New York Ave. NE. ☎ **202/245-2726.** www.ars-grin.gov/ars/Beltsville/na. Free admission. Daily 8am–5pm; bonsai collection 10am–3:30pm. 40-minute, open-air, tram tour Apr–Oct, weekends 11:30am, 1, 2, 3, and 4pm; $3 per adult, $2 members and seniors, $2 children 4–16. Closed Dec 25. Metro: Stadium Armory, then take bus no. B2 to Bladensburg Rd. and R St. NE (or hop in a taxi; it's only a few dollars). Free parking.

A research and educational center focusing on a vast variety of landscape plants, the U.S. National Arboretum is a must-see for the horticulturally inclined. Its 9½ miles of paved roads meander through 444 hilly acres of azaleas (the most extensive plantings in the nation); magnolias; hollies; dwarf conifers; and boxwoods. One highlight is the National Bonsai and Penjing Museum, which includes a Bicentennial gift from Japan of 53 beautiful miniature trees, some of them more than 3 centuries old. Each one is an exquisite work of art. The exhibit was augmented by a gift of 35 Chinese Penjing trees in 1986, and again in 1990 by the American Bonsai Collection of 56 North American plants; in 1993, a conservatory for tropical bonsai was erected. This area also includes a Japanese Garden and a garden of plants of

American origin. The Herbarium contains 600,000 dried plants for reference purposes. The Herb Garden, another highlight, includes a historic rose garden (150 old-fashioned fragrant varieties), a contemporary interpretation of a 16th-century English-style "knot" garden, and 10 specialty gardens: a dye garden, a medicinal garden, and a culinary garden among them. Along **Fern Valley Trail** is the **Franklin Tree,** a species now extinct in the wild, discovered in 1765 by a botanist friend of Benjamin Franklin. And a magnificent sight is the arboretum's acropolis, 22 of the original U.S. Capitol columns designed by Benjamin Latrobe in a setting created by the noted English landscape artist Russell Page. The **American Friendship Garden** is a collection of ornamental grasses, reminiscent of prairie landscapes, and perennials, with brick walkways, terraces, and a statue of Demeter, the Greek goddess of agriculture. Its colorful spring bulb plants comprise a wide variety of narcissi and irises enhanced by small flowering and fruiting trees and interesting shrubs. Carefully placed teak benches provide a place for quiet contemplation. This garden also features an extensive collection of perennials and bulb plants. And the **Asian Collections** in a landscaped valley include rare plants from China and Korea.

Magnolias and early bulbs bloom in late March or early April; azaleas, daffodils, and flowering cherry trees in mid-April; rhododendrons and peonies in May; daylilies and crape myrtles in summer. In autumn, the arboretum is ablaze in reds and oranges as the leaves change color.

On the open-air tram tour, a guide narrates the tour, telling you about the history and highlights of the arboretum. You purchase tickets at the ticket kiosk (located in the parking lot next to the administration building) for the day of the tour only. In addition, the arboretum offers lectures and workshops (including bonsai classes), and a comprehensive guidebook is available in the gift shop.

PARKS
POTOMAC PARK

West and East Potomac Parks, their 720 riverside acres divided by the Tidal Basin, are most famous for their spring display of cherry blossoms and all the hoopla that goes with it. In all, there are 3,363 cherry trees planted along the Tidal Basin, with another 337 blooming in other pockets of the city. The cherry trees lie along the portion of the Tidal Basin that runs alongside the FDR Memorial. If you're driving, you want to get on Independence Avenue and follow the signs posted near the Lincoln Memorial that show you where to turn to find parking and the FDR Memorial. If you're walking, you'll want to cross Independence Avenue where it intersects with W. Basin Drive (there's a stoplight and crosswalk), and follow the path to the Tidal Basin, where you'll find the trees. There is no convenient Metro stop near here.

West Potomac Park has 1,682 trees bordering the Tidal Basin, some of them Akebonos with delicate pink blossoms, but most Yoshinos with white cloudlike flower clusters. The blossoming of the cherry trees is the focal point of a week-long celebration, including the lighting of the 300-year-old Japanese Stone Lantern near Kutz Bridge, presented to the city by the governor of Tokyo in 1954. The trees bloom for a little less than 2 weeks beginning somewhere between March 20 and April 17; April 5 is the average date. Planning your trip around the blooming of the cherry blossoms is an iffy proposition, and I wouldn't advise it. One thing many people don't realize is that all it takes is one good rain and those cherry blossoms are gone. And the cherry blossoms are not illuminated at night, and therefore, not truly visible, so if you think you're going to beat the crush of tourists touring the Tidal Basin during the day by going at night, you'll be out of luck. The National Park

Service should consider backlighting the trees at night: not only would it be a breathtaking sight, but it would help with the yearly stampede along the Tidal Basin. See the calendar of events in chapter 2 for further details on cherry blossom events.

East Potomac Park cherry trees number 1,681, and 11 varieties. The park also has picnic grounds, tennis courts, three golf courses, a large swimming pool, and biking and hiking paths by the water, all of which are described in "Outdoor Activities," below.

West Potomac Park encompasses Constitution Gardens; the Vietnam, Korean, Lincoln, Jefferson, and FDR Memorials; a small island where ducks live; and the Reflecting Pool.

ROCK CREEK PARK

Created in 1890, Rock Creek Park was purchased by Congress for its "pleasant valleys and ravines, primeval forests and open fields, its running waters, its rocks clothed with rich ferns and mosses, its repose and tranquillity, its light and shade, its ever-varying shrubbery, its beautiful and extensive views." A 1,750-acre valley within the District of Columbia, extending 12 miles from the Potomac River to the Maryland border (another 2,700 acres), it's one of the biggest and finest city parks in the nation. Parts of it are still wild; it's not unusual to see a deer scurrying through the woods in more remote sections.

The park's offerings include the **Carter Barron Amphitheater** (see chapter 10); playgrounds; an extensive system of beautiful wooded hiking trails; and sports facilities, for which there are detailed listings in "Outdoor Activities," below. See also our entry in "More Museums," above, on the formal gardens at Dumbarton Oaks, which border Rock Creek Park in upper Georgetown, that include an Orangery; a 1000-bush Rose Garden; wisteria-covered arbors; herbaceous borders; groves of cherry trees; and magnolias.

For full information on the wide range of park programs and activities, visit the Rock Creek Nature Center, 5200 Glover Rd. NW (☎ **202/426-6829**), Wednesday to Sunday 9am to 5pm; or Park Headquarters, 6545 Williamsburg Rd. NW (☎ **202/282-1063**), weekdays 7:45am to 4:15pm. To get to the Nature Center by public transportation, take the Metro to Friendship Heights and transfer to bus no. E2 or E3 to Military Road and Oregon Avenue/Glover Road.

The Nature Center itself is the scene of numerous activities, including weekend planetarium shows for kids (minimum age 4) and adults; nature films; crafts demonstrations; live animal demonstrations; guided nature walks; plus a daily mix of lectures, films, and other events. A calendar is available on request. Self-guided nature trails begin here. All activities are free, but for planetarium shows you need to pick up tickets a half hour in advance. There are also nature exhibits on the premises. The Nature Center is closed on federal holidays.

At Tilden Street and Beach Drive, you can see a water-powered 19th-century gristmill grinding corn and wheat into flour (☎ **202/426-6908**). It's called **Pierce Mill** (a man named Isaac Pierce built it), and it's open to visitors Wednesday to Sunday 9am to 5pm. Pierce's old carriage house is today the **Art Barn** (☎ **202/ 244-2482**), where works of local artists are exhibited; it's open Thursday to Sunday 11am to 4:30pm (closed federal holidays and one month in summer, either July or August).

Call ☎ **202/673-7646** or 202/673-7647 for details, locations, and group reservations at any of the park's 30 picnic areas, some with fireplaces. A brochure available at Park Headquarters or the Nature Center also provides details on picnic locations.

Poetry readings and workshops are held during the summer at **Miller's Cabin,** the one-time residence of High Sierra poet Joaquin Miller, Beach Drive north of Military Road. Call ☎ **202/426-6829** for information.

There's convenient free parking throughout the park.

THEODORE ROOSEVELT ISLAND

A serene, 88-acre wilderness preserve, Theodore Roosevelt Island is a memorial to our 26th president, in recognition of his contributions to conservation. An outdoor enthusiast and expert field naturalist, Roosevelt once threw away a prepared speech and roared, "I hate a man who would skin the land!" During his administration, 150 million acres of forest land were reserved, and 5 national parks, 51 bird refuges, and 4 game refuges were created.

Theodore Roosevelt Island was inhabited by Native American tribes for centuries before the arrival of English explorers in the 1600s. Over the years, it passed through many owners before becoming what it is today, an island preserve of swamp, marsh, and upland forest that's a haven for rabbits, chipmunks, great owls, fox, muskrat, turtles, and groundhogs. It's a complex ecosystem in which cattails, arrow arum, and pickerelweed growing in the marshes create a hospitable habitat for abundant bird life. And willow, ash, and maple trees rooted on the mudflats create the swamp environment favored by raccoons in search of crayfish. You can observe these flora and fauna in their natural environs on 2½ miles of foot trails.

In the northern center of the island, overlooking an oval terrace encircled by a water-filled moat, stands a 17-foot bronze statue of Roosevelt. From the terrace rise four 21-foot granite tablets inscribed with these tenets of his philosophy: "There are no words that can tell the hidden spirit of the wilderness, that can reveal its mystery, its melancholy, and its charm" and "The Nation behaves well if it treats the natural resources as assets which it must turn over to the next generation increased and not impaired in value."

To get to the island, take the George Washington Memorial Parkway exit north from the Theodore Roosevelt Bridge. The parking area is accessible only from the northbound lane; from there, a pedestrian bridge connects the island with the Virginia shore. You can also rent a canoe at Thompson's Boat Center (see "Outdoor Activities," below) and paddle over, or walk across the pedestrian bridge at Rosslyn Circle, 2 blocks from the Rosslyn Metro station. Picnicking is permitted on the grounds near the memorial.

For further information, contact the District Ranger, Theodore Roosevelt Island, George Washington Memorial Parkway, ℅ Turkey Run Park, McLean, VA 22101 (☎ **703/285-2598;** fax 703/285-2398).

ACTIVITIES ON THE C&O CANAL

One of the great joys of living in Washington is the **C&O Canal** and its unspoiled 184½-mile towpath. One leaves urban cares and stresses behind while hiking, strolling, jogging, cycling, or boating in this lush, natural setting of ancient oaks and red maples, giant sycamores, willows, and wildflowers. But the canal wasn't always just a leisure spot for city people. It was built in the 1800s, when water routes were considered vital to transportation. Even before it was completed, the B&O Railroad, which was constructed at about the same time and along the same route, had begun to render it obsolete. Today, perhaps, it serves an even more important purpose as a cherished urban refuge.

Headquarters for canal activities is the Office of the Superintendent, C&OCanal National Historical Park, P.O. Box 4, Sharpsburg, MD 21782 (☎ **301/739-4200**).

Another good source of information is the National Park Service office at **Great Falls Tavern Visitor Center,** 11710 MacArthur Blvd., Potomac, MD 20854 (☎ 301/299-3613). At this 1831 tavern, you can see museum exhibits and a film about the canal; there's also a bookstore on the premises. And April to November, Wednesday to Sunday, the **Georgetown Information Center,** 1057 Thomas Jefferson St. NW (☎ 202/653-5190), can also provide maps and information. Call ahead for hours at all of the above.

Hiking any section of the flat dirt towpath or its more rugged side paths is a pleasure. There are picnic tables, some with fire grills, about every 5 miles beginning at **Fletcher's Boat House** (about 3.2 miles out of Georgetown) on the way to Cumberland. Enter the towpath in Georgetown below M Street via Thomas Jefferson Street. If you hike 14 miles, you'll reach **Great Falls,** a point where the Potomac becomes a stunning waterfall plunging 76 feet. Or drive to Great Falls Park on the Virginia side of the Potomac.

Stop at Fletcher's Boat House, described below in "Outdoor Activities," to rent bikes or boats or purchase bait and tackle (or a license) for fishing. A snack bar and picnic area are on the premises.

Much less strenuous than hiking is a mule-drawn 19th-century canal boat trip led by Park Service rangers in period dress. They regale passengers with canal legend and lore and sing period songs. These boats depart Wednesday through Sunday from mid-April to early November; departure times and tickets are available at the Georgetown Information Center (☎ 202/653-5190) or the Great Falls Tavern (☎ 301/299-3613). The Georgetown barge ride lasts 45 minutes and the Great Falls barge ride lasts 1 hour, which accounts for the difference in price at each location: in Georgetown, you pay $5.50 per adult, $4.50 per senior over 61, and $3.50 per child ages 3–14; at Great Falls, you pay $7.50 per adult, $6 per senior, and $4.50 per child.

Call any of the above information numbers for details on riding, rock climbing, fishing, bird-watching, concerts, ranger-guided tours, ice skating, camping, and other canal activities (or consult "Outdoor Activities," below).

11 Especially for Kids

Who better would know what kids might enjoy in Washington than other kids? So, I asked my own children, Caitlin (11) and Lucy (6); my nieces, Sarah (9) and Annie (7), and my nephew, Nick (3), what sites in Washington they would recommend to friends and cousins visiting from out of town. Here are some of their suggestions:

Caitlin: "The Washington National Cathedral is interesting because you can have a tour of the inside and outside and maybe, if you're lucky, you can tour the room (I think it's the Choir Room), where, in medieval times, only the priest was allowed. On Saturdays, you can do arts and crafts in the basement and make bookmarks using Medieval characters, and clay gargoyles, and brass rubbings. (This is a hands-on activity offered by the Cathedral's Medieval Workshop, for kids 5 and older, costing $3 per participant; call ☎ 202/537-2934 for exact days and times, which are extended during the summer.) I also like the Hope Diamond (in the Museum of Natural History); the last time I saw it, the line went all the way around the floor of the museum, but it was worth it, the diamond was really intriguing. And I like the National Postal Museum, because you can use special machines there to print cool postcards (you should bring the addresses of your friends), and you can walk through the fake forest along a path that was supposed to be just like the one people would follow to deliver mail a long time ago, before there were roads."

Sarah: "The FDR Memorial, because there are a lot of statues of people waiting in line to get bread and you can stand in line between the statues and have your Mom or Dad take a picture of you."

Annie: "The Air and Space Museum, because there's a spaceship and you can get inside it and look around."

Lucy: "Ford's Theatre, because downstairs in the museum you can see Lincoln's blood on the pillow where he put his head."

Nick: "The Zoo, I like to watch the buffaloes bump their butts into each other."

For more ideas, consult the Friday "Weekend" section of the *Washington Post,* which lists numerous activities (mostly free) for kids: special museum events, children's theater, storytelling programs, puppet shows, video-game competitions, and so forth. Call the Kennedy Center, the Lisner, and National Theatre to find out about children's shows; see chapter 10 for details. Also read the write-up of Discovery Theater, within the Smithsonian's Arts & Industries Building, earlier in this chapter.

I've checked out hotels built with families in mind in chapter 5's "Family-Friendly Hotels"; that hotel pool may rescue your sanity for an hour or two. Public swimming pools are another option—see the swimming listing, and other suggestions for outdoor activities, below. The "Organized Tours" section might be your saving grace when you've either run out of steam or need a jump start to your day.

FAVORITE CHILDREN'S ATTRACTIONS

Check for special children's events at museum information desks when you enter. As noted within the listings for individual museums, some children's programs are also great fun for adults. I recommend the programs at the Corcoran Gallery of Art, the Folger Shakespeare Library, and the Sackler Gallery in particular. (The gift shops in most of these museums have wonderful toys and children's books.) Call ahead to find out which programs are running. Here's a rundown of the biggest kid-pleasers in town (for details, see the full entries earlier in this chapter):

National Air & Space Museum. Spectacular IMAX films (don't miss), planetarium shows, missiles, rockets, and a walk-through orbital workshop.

National Museum of Natural History. A Discovery Room just for youngsters, an insect zoo, shrunken heads, and dinosaurs.

National Museum of American History. The Foucault pendulum, locomotives, Archie Bunker's chair, and an old-fashioned ice-cream parlor.

Federal Bureau of Investigation. Gangster memorabilia, crime-solving methods, espionage devices, and a sharp-shooting demonstration.

Bureau of Engraving and Printing. Kids enjoy looking at immense piles of money as much as you do.

National Zoological Park. Kids always love a zoo, and this is an especially good one.

Ford's Theatre and Lincoln Museum and the House Where Lincoln Died. Booth's gun and diary, the clothes Lincoln was wearing the night he was assassinated, and other such grisly artifacts. Kids adore the whole business.

National Geographic Society's Explorers Hall. A moon rock, the egg of an extinct "elephant bird" (if hatched, it would weigh 1,000 pounds), numerous interactive videos. The magazine comes alive.

Washington Monument. Easy to get them up there, hard to get them down. If only they could use the steps, they'd be in heaven.

Lincoln Memorial. Kids know a lot about Lincoln and enjoy visiting his memorial. A special treat is visiting it after dark (the same goes for the Washington Monument and Jefferson Memorial).

Newseum. Kids can ham it up as an ace news reporter, then take home the videotaped performance to show to their friends.

12 Organized Tours

BY FOOT A TOUR de force, **Guided Tours of Washington** (☎ 703/525-2948) is historian and raconteur Jeanne Fogel's 15-year-old company. She offers a variety of walking and bus tours around the city, revealing little-known anecdotes and facts about neighborhoods, historic figures, and the most visited sites. Fogel's tours are custom-designed, for groups, not individuals. Call for rates.

TourDC, Walking Tours of Georgetown (☎ 301/588-8999; www.tourdc.com) conducts 90-minute ($12) and 2-hour ($15) walking tours of Georgetown, telling about the neighborhood's history up to the present and taking you past the homes of notable residents.

Weekend Walks in Georgetown (☎ 301/294-9514) offers 2-hour walks through the streets of Georgetown, guided by author/historian Anthony S. Pitch. Rates are $9 per person, seniors and students $6.

D.C. Heritage Tours (☎ 202/639-0908), co-sponsored by the D.C. Heritage Tourism Coalition and the Discovery Store, leave twice daily from the front of the Discovery Channel Store in the MCI Center, in downtown Washington. A costumed guide tells tales about 19th-century Washington as she takes you in and out of historic sites and through Chinatown, showing you a side of Washington you won't find out about otherwise. Tours last 90 minutes and cost $7.50 per adult, $5 per child under 6 and per senior 55 and older. Before the tour starts, you might want to see the 15-minute film *Destination DC,* shown on the top floor of the Discovery store; the charge is $2.50 per adult, $1.50 per child under 6 and seniors.

BY BUS **The Gray Line** (☎ 202/289-1995) offers a variety of tours, among them: "Grand Homes and Gardens" (co-sponsored by the D.C. Chamber of Commerce and the D.C. Heritage Tourism Coalition, each tour lasts 4 hours and costs $30 per person), featuring a choice of 3 neighborhoods—Georgetown, Lafayette Park, or Dupont Circle; "Washington After Dark" (3 hours; $25 per adult, $12 per child), focusing on night-lit national monuments and federal buildings; the "Washington, D.C., All-Day Combination Tour" ($42 per adult, $21 per child), which includes major Washington sights plus Arlington National Cemetery, Mount Vernon, and Alexandria; and the full-day "Interiors of Public Buildings" ($36 per adult, $18 per child), which covers Ford's Theatre, the Jefferson Memorial, the Museum of American History, the Capitol, the Supreme Court, the National Air & Space Museum, and the National Archives. There are also trips as far afield as Colonial Williamsburg ($64 per adult, $54 per child), Gettysburg ($50 per adult, $30 per child), and Charlottesville ($64 per adult, $64 per child). Tours depart from Gray Line's Union Station terminal, with pickups at most major hotels. Headsets and tour tapes in certain foreign languages are available for certain afternoon tours, at $30 per adult, $15 per child.

All About Town, 519 6th St. NW (☎ 202/393-3696; fax 202/393-2006), offers a similar range of tours at rates running from $22 to $66 per adult. Pickup is offered at 102 hotels in the Washington area.

Consider, too, Tourmobile and Old Town Trolley tours (see "Getting Around" in chapter 4 for details).

BY BOAT Since Washington is a river city, why not see it by boat? Potomac cruises allow sweeping vistas of the monuments and memorials, Georgetown, the Kennedy Center, and other Washington sights. Read the information carefully, since not all boat cruises offer guided tours.

Some of the following boats leave from the Washington waterfront and some from Old Town Alexandria:

Spirit of Washington Cruises, Pier 4 at 6th and Water Streets SW (☎ **202/ 554-8000;** Metro: Waterfront), offers a variety of trips daily from early March through October, including evening dinner, lunch and brunch, and moonlight dance cruises, as well as a half-day excursion to Mount Vernon and back. Lunch and dinner cruises include a 40-minute, high-energy musical revue. Prices range from $23.50 for a sightseeing (no meals) excursion to Mount Vernon, which takes 5½ hours in all, including a 2-hour tour break, to $65.30 for a Friday or Saturday dinner cruise, drinks not included. Call to make reservations in advance.

The *Spirit of Washington* is a luxury harbor climate-controlled cruise ship with, carpeted decks and huge panoramic windows designed for sightseeing. There are three well-stocked bars on board. Mount Vernon cruises are aboard an equally luxurious sister ship, the *Potomac Spirit.* You board both ships at the Washington waterfront, pier 4, at 6th and Water Streets SW.

Potomac Party Cruises (☎ **703/683-6076**) has been operating for about 20 years. Its boat, *The Dandy,* is a climate-controlled, all-weather, glassed-in, floating restaurant that operates year-round. Lunch, evening dinner/dance, and special charter cruises are available daily. You board *The Dandy* in Old Town Alexandria, the Prince Street pier, between Duke and King Streets (Metro: Waterfront). Trips range from $26 for a 2½-hour weekday lunch cruise to $63 for a 3-hour Saturday dinner cruise, drinks not included.

Odyssey III (☎ **800/946-7245**) is Washington's newest boat and was designed specifically to glide under the bridges that cross the Potomac. The boat looks like a glass bullet, with its snub-nosed port and streamlined, 240-foot-long glass body. The wraparound see-through walls and ceiling allow for great views. Like *The Dandy,* the *Odyssey* operates all year. You board the *Odyssey* at the Gangplank Marina, on Washington's waterfront, at 6th and Water Streets SW (Metro: Waterfront). Cruises available include lunch, Sunday brunch, and dinner excursions, with live entertainment provided during each cruise. It costs $40 for a 2-hour weekday lunch cruise and $104 ($79 if you purchase tickets more than 3 days in advance) for a 3-hour Saturday dinner cruise, drinks excluded.

The Potomac Riverboat Company (☎ **703/548-9000**) offers 3 sightseeing tours April through October, aboard: the *Matthew Hayes,* on a 90-minute tour past Washington monuments and memorials; the *Admiral Tilp,* on a 40-minute tour of Old Town Alexandria's waterfront; and the *Miss Christin,* which cruises to Mount Vernon, where you hop off and reboard after you've toured the estate. You board the boats at the pier behind the Torpedo Factory in Old Town Alexandria, at the foot of King Street (Metro: Waterfront). *Matthew Hayes* tickets are $14 for adults, $7 for children ages 2 to 12; *Admiral Tilp* tickets are $7 for adults, $5 for children ages 2 to 12; and *Miss Christin* tickets are $22 for adults, $18 for children, and include admission to Mount Vernon. A concession stand selling light refreshments and beverages is open during the cruises.

The **Capitol River Cruise's** *Nightingale II* (☎ **800/405-5511** or 301/ 460-7447) is a historic 65-foot steel riverboat that can accommodate up to 90 people. The *Nightingale II*'s narrated jaunts depart Georgetown's Washington Harbour every hour on the hour, from noon until 8pm weekdays and 9pm weekends,

April through October. The 50-minute narrated tour travels past the monuments and memorials as you head to National Airport and back. A snack bar on board sells light refreshments, beer, wine, and sodas; you're welcome to bring your own picnic aboard. The price is $10 per adult, $5 per child ages 3 to 12. To get here, take the Metro to Foggy Bottom and then walk into Georgetown, following Pennsylvania Avenue, which becomes M Street. Turn left on 31st Street NW, which dead-ends at the Washington Harbour complex.

A Boat on Wheels   A company called **DC Ducks** (☎ **202/966-3825**) features unique land and water tours of Washington aboard the red, white, and blue *DUKW,* an amphibious army vehicle (boat with wheels) from World War II that accommodates 30 passengers. Ninety-minute guided tours aboard the open-air canopied craft include a land portion taking in major sights—the Capitol, Lincoln Memorial, Washington Monument, the White House, and Smithsonian museums—and a 30-minute Potomac cruise. Tickets can be purchased inside Union Station at the information desk; you board the vehicle just outside the main entrance to Union Station. There are departures daily during tour season (April to November); hours vary, but departures usually follow an 11am, 1pm, and 3pm schedule. Tickets cost $24 for adults, $12 for children 5 to 12, children under 5 free.

BIKE TOURS   Bike the Sites, Inc. (☎ **202/966-8662**), offers a more active way to see Washington. The company has designed several different biking tours of the city, including an Early Bird Fun Ride, which is a 1-hour, moderately paced ride and costs $25 per person, and the Capital Sites Ride (the most popular), which takes 3 hours, covers many sites along a 10-mile stretch, and costs $35 per person. Bike the Sites provides you with a 21-speed Trek Hybrid bicycle fitted to your size, bike helmet, handlebar bag, water bottle, light snack, and two guides to lead the ride. Guides impart historical and anecdotal information as you go. The company will customize bike rides to suit your tour specifications.

13 Outdoor Activities

BICYCLING   Both **Fletcher's Boat House** and **Thompson's Boat Center** (see "Boating," below) rent bikes, as does **Big Wheel Bikes,** 1034 33rd St. NW, right near the C&O Canal just below M Street (☎ **202/337-0254**). The rate is $5 per hour, with a 3-hour minimum, or $25 for the day. Shop opens at 10am daily, closing times vary. There's another Big Wheel shop on Capitol Hill at 315 7th St. SE (☎ **202/543-1600**); call for hours. Photo ID and a major credit card are required to rent bicycles.

On Fridays, the *Washington Post* "Weekend" section lists cycling trips. Rock Creek Park has an 11-mile paved bike route from the Lincoln Memorial through the park into Maryland. On weekends and holidays, a large part of it is closed to vehicular traffic. The C&O Canal and the Potomac Parks, described earlier in "Parks & Gardens," also have extended bike paths. A new 7-mile path, **the Capital Crescent Trail,** takes you from Georgetown to the suburb of Bethesda, Maryland, following a former railroad track that parallels the Potomac River part of the way and passes by old trestle bridges and pleasant residential neighborhoods.

BOATING   Thompson's Boat Center, 2900 Virginia Ave. at Rock Creek Parkway NW (☎ **202/333-4861** or 202/333-9543; Metro: Foggy Bottom with a 10-minute walk), rents canoes, kayaks, rowing shells (recreational and racing), and bikes. They also offer sculling and sweep-rowing lessons. Photo ID and a credit card are required for rentals. They're open for boat rentals usually from early May to the end of September, daily 8am to 6pm. Bike rentals range from $4 for the most basic to $22 for the fanciest.

Late March to mid-September, you can rent paddleboats on the north end of the Tidal Basin off Independence Avenue (☎ 202/479-2426). You have the choice of renting a four-seater for $14 an hour or a two-seater for $7 an hour. Hours are 10am to about an hour before sunset daily.

Fletcher's Boat House, Reservoir and Canal Roads (☎ 202/244-0461), is right on the C&O Canal, about a 3.2-mile wonderfully scenic walk from Georgetown. The same family has owned it since 1850! Open March to mid-November, daily from about sunrise to dusk, Fletcher's rents canoes, rowboats, and bikes (bikes: $8 for 2 hours, or $12 for the day; boats: $8 for 2 hours, or $16 for the day; you aren't allowed to leave the area of the canal), and sells fishing licenses, bait, and tackle. Identification is required (a driver's license or major credit card). A snack bar and rest rooms here are welcome facilities. There are also picnic tables (with barbecue grills) overlooking the Potomac. You don't have to walk to Fletcher's; it's accessible by car (west on M Street to Canal Road) and has plenty of free parking.

CAMPING   There are numerous camping areas on the C&O Canal starting at **Swain's Lock,** 16 miles from Georgetown. Use of campsites is on a first-come, first-served basis.

FISHING   The Potomac River around Washington holds an abundant variety of fish, some 40 species, all perfectly safe to eat. Good fishing is possible from late February to November, but mid-March to June (spawning season) is peak. Perch and catfish are the most common catch, but during bass season a haul of 20 to 40 is not unusual. The Washington Channel offers good bass and carp fishing year-round.

To make sure you stay the within legal limit of local restrictions, pick up a free regulations book on fishing, available at **Fletcher's Boat House** (☎ 202/244-0461;** details above). You can also obtain the required fishing license here. Cost for nonresidents is $7.50 a year, $3 for a 14-day permit. Residents pay $5. Bring your own fishing equipment.

GOLF   There are dozens of public courses within easy driving distance of the D.C. area, but within the district itself **East Potomac Park** and **Rock Creek Park** have the only public courses. Fees run from $9 weekdays for 9 holes to $19 weekends for 18 holes. The 18-hole Rock Creek Golf Course and clubhouse, at 16th and Rittenhouse Streets NW (☎ 202/882-7332), are open to the public daily year-round from dawn to dusk. You will find a snack bar on the premises, and you can rent clubs and carts.

East Potomac Park has one 18-hole, par-72 layout, and two 9-hole courses. For details, call ☎ 202/554-7660.

HIKING   Check the *Washington Post* Friday "Weekend" section for listings of hiking clubs; almost all are open to the public for a small fee. Be sure to inquire about the difficulty of any hike you plan to join and the speed with which the group proceeds; some hikes are fast-paced, allowing no time to smell the flowers.

There are numerous hiking paths. The C&O Canal offers 184½ miles; Theodore Roosevelt Island has more than 88 wilderness acres to explore, including a 2½-mile nature trail (short but rugged); and in Rock Creek Park there are 20 miles of hiking trails for which maps are available at the Visitor Information Center or Park Headquarters.

HORSEBACK RIDING   There are stables at the **Rock Creek Park Horse Center,** near the Nature Center on Glover Road NW (☎ 202/362-0117).

One-hour guided trail rides are offered Tuesday through Thursday at 3pm, weekends at noon, 1:30pm, and 3pm; they cost $21. Call for reservations or information on riding instruction.

ICE SKATING   If you have your own skates, you can skate on the C&O Canal (call ☎ 301/299-3613 for information on ice conditions). If you need to rent skates, head to one of these 3 locations: the National Gallery Sculpture Garden Ice Rink, on the Mall at 7th Street and Constitution Avenue NW (call the National Gallery's main number, ☎ 202/737-4215, for information; at this writing, the sculpture garden was under reconstruction); the Pershing Park outdoor rink, at 14th Street and Pennsylvania Avenue NW (☎ 202/737-6938); and a huge hockey-size indoor facility, the Fort Dupont Ice Arena, at 3779 Ely Place SE, at Minnesota Avenue in Fort Dupont Park (☎ 202/584-5007). The Sculpture Garden rink is open from late October to mid-March; the Pershing Park rink from about Thanksgiving to February, weather permitting; Fort Dupont, from Labor Day to the end of April. Call for hours and admission prices.

JOGGING   A parcourse jogging path, a gift from Perrier, opened in Rock Creek Park in 1978. Its 1½-mile oval route, beginning near the intersection of Calvert Street NW and Rock Creek Parkway (directly behind the Omni Shoreham Hotel), includes 18 calisthenics stations with instructions on prescribed exercises. There's another Perrier parcourse, with only four stations, at 16th and Kennedy Streets NW. Other popular jogging areas are the C&O Canal and the Mall.

SWIMMING   There are 44 swimming pools in the district run by the D.C. Department of Recreation Aquatic Program (☎ 202/576-6436). They include the **Capitol East Natatorium,** an indoor/outdoor pool with sundeck and adjoining baby pool at 635 North Carolina Ave. SE (☎ 202/724-4495 or 202/724-4496); the outdoor pool in East Potomac Park (☎ 202/863-1309); a large outdoor pool at 25th and N Streets NW (☎ 202/727-3285); and the Georgetown outdoor pool at 34th Street and Volta Place NW (☎ 202/282-2366). Indoor pools are open year-round; outdoor pools, from mid-June to Labor Day. Thirty-nine of the district pools are free; the remaining five charge about $3 per adult, $1 per child. Call for hours and details on other locations.

TENNIS   The D.C. Department of Recreation and Parks, 3149 16th St. NW, Washington, D.C. 20010 (☎ 202/673-7660 or 202/673-7665), maintains 57 outdoor tennis courts throughout the district (25 of them lighted for night play). Court use is on a first-come, first-served basis. Call or write for a list of locations. Most courts are open year-round, weather permitting. At **Rock Creek,** there are 15 soft-surface (clay) and 10 hard-surface tennis courts at 16th and Kennedy Streets NW (☎ 202/722-5949). From April to mid-November you must make a reservation in person at Guest Services on the premises to use them. Six additional clay courts are located off Park Road, just east of Pierce Mill. **East Potomac Park** has 24 tennis courts, including five indoors and three lighted for night play (☎ 202/554-5962). Fees vary with court surface and time of play; call for details.

14 Spectator Sports

Sports venues in Washington, D.C., are new, state-of-the-art, and some of the nicest around. And you pay for it. A Washington Redskins ticket for a game at Jack Kent Cooke Stadium sells at the highest average price ($52.92) in the National Football League; a Wizards ticket for a game at the MCI Center sells at the second highest average price ($51.63) in the National Basketball Association; a Baltimore Orioles ticket for a game at Camden Yards sells for the fourth highest average price ($15.66) in Major League Baseball; and a Washington Capitals ticket for a game at the MCI Center sells for the fifth highest average price ($50.36) in the National Hockey League. But if you're a sports fan, it may be worth it.

The **MCI Center** is especially noteworthy. Even if you don't have tickets to a game, you may want to stop in to visit the Sports Gallery, the Discovery Channel Retail Store, or one of the restaurants, one of which, Velocity Grill, has a glass wall through which you can watch the Wizards practice on the court below.

TICKETS   For tickets to most events, call ☎ 800/551-SEAT or 202/432-SEAT.

BASEBALL   Lovely 48,000-seat Camden Yards, 333 W. Camden St. (between Howard and Conway Streets), Baltimore (☎ 410/685-9800), is home to the American League's Baltimore Orioles. Unlike recent ultramodern sports stadiums and ugly domes, Camden Yards is an old-fashioned ballpark, unafraid to incorporate features of its urban environment, such as the old B&O Railroad yards. A renovated brick warehouse serves as a striking visual backdrop beyond the right-field fence.

It was here on September 6, 1995, that Cal Ripken broke Lou Gehrig's legendary consecutive-game record; he took a lap around the field and was acclaimed with a 22-minute standing ovation and a citywide celebration.

Tickets (which range from $9 to $35) were once impossible to get; now it's possible but still tough, so call ☎ 800/551-SEAT or 410/481-SEAT well in advance of your visit if you want to catch a game. There are usually scalpers outside the stadium before a game; use your judgment if you try this option. And there's a D.C. ticket office as well, at 914 17th St. NW (☎ 202/296-2473). From Union Station in Washington, take a MARC train to Baltimore, where you are let off right at the ballpark. If you're driving, take I-95 north to Exit 53.

BASKETBALL   The Washington Wizards (née Bullets) and the Georgetown Hoyas play home games at the newly opened MCI Center (☎ 202/628-3200), at 7th and F Streets NW, adjacent to the Gallery Place Metro station in downtown Washington. Tickets cost $19 to $65 for the Wizards and $5 to $16 for the Hoyas.

FOOTBALL   The Washington Redskins played their last home game at RFK Stadium in 1997 and now play at the new Jack Kent Cooke Stadium, 1600 Raljohn Rd., Raljohn, MD 20785 (☎ 301/276-6050; Metro: Addison Road, with bus shuttle to stadium). Tickets for Redskins games have been sold out since Lyndon Johnson was in the White House, so forget about getting your hands on one, unless you're willing to shell out $250 for a club-level seat.

The Baltimore Ravens (formerly the Cleveland Browns, until Art Modell moved the team and broke the city's heart) started off the 1998–1999 season in their new home, the Ravens Stadium, right next to Camden Yards. Tickets cost $17 to $75; for more information, call ☎ **410/261-7283.**

HOCKEY   Home ice for the NHL's Washington Capitals is now the MCI Center (☎ **202/628-3200**), at 7th and F Streets NW, adjacent to the Gallery Place Metro station. Tickets cost $19 to $50.

SOCCER   D.C. United, the champions of Major League Soccer in 1996, play at RFK Stadium (☎ **202/547-9077;** Metro: Stadium-Armory). Tickets to their games range from $12 to $32. The Washington Warthogs indoor soccer team plays its games at the US Airways Arena (☎ **301/350-3400**) in Landover, Maryland. Tickets cost $12.50 to $15.50.

8

In & Out of Washington's Historic Houses: Three Walking Tours

One of the best ways to get to know a city is to wander its neighborhoods, popping into historic homes along the way to learn about the long-ago lives of individual Washingtonians, some famous, others not so. These less tourist-traveled attractions offer a respite from the crowds as they reveal an intriguing, more personal perspective on the past. If you'd like to sightsee away from the madding throngs for a while, try one of the following walking tours.

WALKING TOUR 1
Dupont Circle's Historic Homes

Start: 1307 New Hampshire Ave. NW (Dupont Circle Metro station).
Finish: 2320 S St. NW (Dupont Circle Metro station).
Time: Approximately 4 to 5 hours, including tours and breaks.
Best Times: If you want to see all the houses, you should start mid-morning, Wednesday through Saturday.
Worst Times: Before 10am, in late afternoon, and Sunday through Tuesday, when the houses are closed or getting ready to close.

The neighborhood you traverse in this tour gives you a good look at cosmopolitan Washington. At its center is Massachusetts Avenue, the main thoroughfare known as "Embassy Row" because of the number of embassies located along the avenue and on side streets. Many of the embassies are in magnificent mansions built in the early part of the 20th century for the city's wealthy, so it is a treat to stroll here.

From the Dupont Circle Metro station, 19th Street exit, cross 19th Street, continue around the circle to New Hampshire Avenue, and turn left. Follow New Hampshire Avenue to its juncture with 20th Street. Here is the:

1. **Heurich House Museum,** 1307 New Hampshire Ave. NW (☎ **202/785-2068;** www.hswdc.org). This four-story, brown-stone and brick, turreted Victorian castle was built as a residence in 1894 for wealthy German businessman and brewer Christian Heurich and his family. (Heurich's grandson, Gary, revived the business in 1986; you may notice his Foggy Bottom Ale delivery trucks around Washington). Old Heurich was a character, as you'll learn by touring three floors of the mansion. He was more

than cautious: He constructed the house of poured concrete, making it the city's first fireproof dwelling. And though Heurich installed 17 grand fireplaces throughout, he permitted no one to use them; to this day, the fireplaces remain virginal. The proud brewer incorporated his favorite drinking mottoes into the murals painted on the walls of his basement Bierstube (tavern room): "He who has never been drunk is not a brave man" and "There is room in the smallest chamber for the biggest hangover." As you tour, be on the lookout for Heurich's ghost, who has been spotted here "wearing a blue seersucker-like jacket and looking like Colonel Sanders."

Whether or not you spy any ghosts, your jaw may drop at the sight of Heurich's heavy-handed decorating, reflective of Victorian times and the man's indomitable personality. Elaborate embellishments adorn every conceivable space throughout the 31 principal rooms. Allegorical paintings cover the ceilings; decorative brass grilles hide the radiators; intricately carved wood panels encase the fireplaces; gilding gelds the bathroom tiles. The foyer recalls a medieval castle, with its standing suit of armor, mosaic floor, and silvered plaster medallions on the stucco walls. A Victorian garden (open to picnickers) and brick patio lie off the back of the house. The mansion serves as headquarters for the Historical Society of Washington, D.C., whose offices and library are on the second and third floors.

Tours, Hours & Admission: Tours are walk-in, self-guided, Wednesday through Saturday 10am to 4pm. Admission is $3 for adults, $1.50 for seniors and students, free for children under 6. Docents also lead guided tours that highlight varied angles, from technology of the time, to women's history viewed through domestic life, to servants' stories. Call in advance for a schedule and reservations for the guided tours, which cost $5. The gift shop stocks Victorian and turn-of-the-century items, as well as jewelry and decorative arts crafted by local artisans. Closed federal holidays.

TAKE A BREAK   Is it too soon for lunch? Cross New Hampshire Avenue at the corner to reach 20th Street, then cross 20th Street. Walk up 20th Street to P Street NW and turn left. Walk 1 block down P Street, cross 21st Street, and enter the BeDuCi at the corner of P and 21st Streets. **BeDuCi,** 2100 P St. NW (☎ **202/223-3824**), serves Mediterranean cuisine (a range of French, Spanish, Moroccan, and Italian dishes) in a sunporch-fronted dining room that opens to the outdoors in warm weather. See chapter 6 for a full listing.

Back outside, return to the corner of 21st and P Streets, cross P Street, and walk up 21st Street to Massachusetts Avenue NW. Turn left at the Westin Fairfax and proceed to the "house" next door.

2. Anderson House, 2118 Massachusetts Ave. NW (☎ **202/785-2040**). It took 3 years, from 1902 to 1905, to build this palatial beaux arts mansion, which was the winter residence of Larz Anderson and his heiress wife, Isabel. Isabel's $17 million inheritance from her grandfather, shipping magnate William Fletcher Weld, helped pay for Anderson House. Anderson was a career diplomat who served as ambassador to Japan in 1912 and 1913. In 1937, following her husband's death, Isabel gave the house and much of its original art and furnishings to the Society of the Cincinnati, to which Larz had belonged. Anderson was descended from an original member of this society, which was founded in 1783 by Continental officers who had served in the American Revolution. (George Washington was its president-general from 1783 until 1799.) A $6.1 million renovation was completed to preserve, not alter, the magnificent castle.

Walking Tour 1—Dupont Circle's Historic Homes

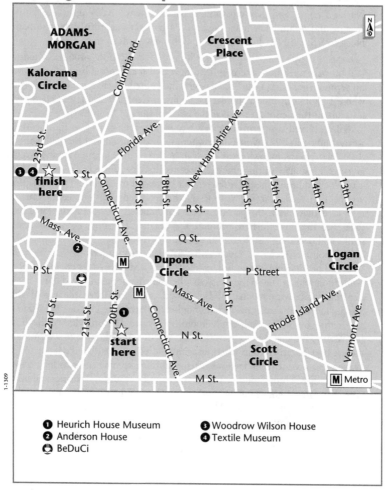

1 Heurich House Museum
2 Anderson House
◐ BeDuCi

3 Woodrow Wilson House
4 Textile Museum

The mansion's 50 rooms stagger the imagination, and include an immense ball-room with a 30-foot-high coffered ceiling and ornate, Louis XV–style French and English parlors embellished in 23-karat gold leaf. Anderson belongings are on display throughout, including Belgian and Flemish tapestries, 17th-century wood choir stalls from Naples, and Asian and European paintings and antiquities. A solarium (with gilt-accented door frames and ceilings) leads through French doors to a lovely courtyard-garden. Open by appointment is the Society of the Cincinnati Library, which houses more than 40,000 works focused on the American Revolution and the "art of war" in the 18th century.

Tours, Hours & Admission: Tours are walk-in, self-guided, Tuesday through Saturday 1 to 4pm. Admission is free. Closed on national holidays. Call about free concert series.

From Anderson House, turn left on Massachusetts Avenue NW, away from Dupont Circle, cross Q Street, proceed down Massachusetts Avenue, cross

Florida Avenue, and then cross Massachusetts Avenue. Walk up Massachusetts Avenue and around Sheridan Circle to 24th Street and turn right. Go half a block to S Street NW, turn right, and walk a few yards to the:

3. **Woodrow Wilson House,** 2340 S St. NW (☎ **202/387-4062**). Woodrow Wilson wasn't just our 28th president, he was also a besotted bean who married his second wife, Edith Galt, after a whirlwind courtship. He was a prolific writer, whose 19 books include a popular biography of George Washington. Here you'll learn about the personal as well as the political sides of Wilson's life.

Wilson served two terms in the White House, then retired to this Georgian Revival home in 1921 with Edith, whom he had courted and married while in the White House, following the death of his first wife. During 45-minute tours given continuously during the day, docents describe Wilson's career and character: He had been a mediocre lawyer, but successful president of Princeton University, then governor of New Jersey, before becoming president. You are reminded that this is the president best remembered for his international outlook, and that his efforts to promote the League of Nations contributed to a stroke and declining health until his death in 1924.

The house is preserved much as it was when the Wilsons lived here in the 1920s. The drawing room is furnished with wedding presents, including a Gobelin tapestry given to the couple by the French ambassador; and it was at the drawing room window that Wilson stood to acknowledge the crowd that had gathered in the street below to honor him on Armistice Day in 1923. Among the items you see in the family room/library are Wilson's desk chair from the White House and the screen that the Wilsons pulled down to watch silent movies by Charlie Chaplin (their favorite) and other stars. Unlike today, when Wilson was president, no laws restricted him from keeping the gifts he received while in office. Throughout the house, you'll notice beautiful tapestries and other gifts that foreign governments bestowed on him. When you reach the dining room, the docent tells you that Wilson insisted that guests at dinner "wear black tie and refrain from discussing religion and politics." Edith died in 1961, bequeathing the house and its belongings to the National Trust for Historic Preservation. The Woodrow Wilson House is the only presidential museum in the capital.

Tours, Hours & Admission: The house is open Tuesday through Sunday 10am to 4pm. Admission is $5 for adults, $4 for seniors, $2.50 for students, free for children age 7 and under. Gift shop. Closed on federal holidays. Call about special events and exhibits.

Now turn right from the entrance and go right next door to:

4. **The Textile Museum,** 2320 S St. NW (☎ **202/667-0441**). The Textile Museum occupies two buildings, the first designed by John Russell Pope, architect of the Jefferson Memorial and the West Wing of the National Gallery, and the adjoining structure designed by Waddy B. Wood, architect for the Woodrow Wilson House.

A man named George Hewitt Myers founded The Textile Museum in 1925, in what was then his home (one of several). Myers was a wealthy man, the founder of Merganthaler Linotype and of the investment firm Y.E. Booker & Co., which is still in operation in Baltimore. His interest in textiles begun in 1896, when Myers purchased an Oriental rug for his Yale dormitory room. By 1925, his collection included 275 rugs and 60 related textiles. When he died in 1957, Myers's collection encompassed not only Oriental carpets, but also textiles from Africa, Asia, and Latin America.

Today, the Textile Museum holds more than 15,500 textiles and carpets, dating as far back as 3,000 B.C. They include Turkish rugs and Peruvian tunics, Suzani embroideries from central Asia, and tapestries from Egypt. Not all are on display, of course. The museum rotates exhibits from its permanent collection in high-ceilinged rooms that are dimly lighted to preserve the fabrics. One of the exhibit areas holds a computer loaded with design software that visitors, especially kids, are invited to use. Friendly interns assist.

Tours, Hours & Admission: Introductory tours take place September through May, Wednesday, Saturday, and Sunday at 2pm. Or you can call 2 weeks in advance to reserve a spot on a docent-led tour. You may also walk in and tour the place on your own: The museum is open year-round Monday through Saturday 10am to 5pm, Sunday 1 to 5pm. Closed on federal holidays and Christmas Eve. Donation of $5 suggested. Call about special lectures and workshops. Poke around the garden and intriguing gift shop.

To get back to the Metro, return to Massachusetts Avenue, turn left, and follow the avenue back around Sheridan Circle, keeping to the odd-numbered side of the street until it meets 20th Street, where you'll find the entrance to the Dupont Circle Metro station.

WALKING TOUR 2
Historic Homes Near the White House

Start: 748 Jackson Place NW (corner of H Street NW on Lafayette Square; Farragut West Metro station).

Finish: 2017 I St. NW (Foggy Bottom Metro station).

Time: Approximately 2½ hours.

Best Times: If you want to see all the houses, you should start mid-morning, Tuesday through Sunday.

Worst Times: Before 10am or in late afternoon, or Monday, when the houses are closed or getting ready to close.

This walking tour centers on another main thoroughfare, Pennsylvania Avenue, best known as the street on which the president lives. You'll walk by the White House, but not go in. (See chapter 7 for information on touring the White House.) Each of the houses on this tour lies in close proximity to the White House, so it makes sense that their individual histories intertwine with particular presidencies.

From the Farragut West Metro station, use the 17th Street exit, cross I Street and walk down 17th Street, cross H Street and then turn left, and continue on H until you reach the gift shop entrance at 748 Jackson Place NW, where you purchase your ticket and begin your tour.

1. **Decatur House,** 748 Jackson Place NW, on Lafayette Square (☎ **202/ 842-0920**). Noted architect Benjamin Latrobe (the Capitol, the White House) designed this Federal-style brick town house in 1817 for Commodore Stephen Decatur, famous War of 1812 naval hero. Decatur and his wife, Susan, established themselves as gracious hosts in the 14 short months they lived here. Two days after hosting a ball for President James Monroe's daughter, Marie, in March 1820, Decatur was killed in a "gentleman's duel" by his former mentor, James Barron, who blamed Decatur for his 5-year suspension from the Navy following a court-martial in which Decatur had played an active role. Susan moved to Georgetown.

Other distinguished occupants have been Henry Clay (while secretary of state), Martin Van Buren, and George M. Dallas (vice president from 1845 to 1849). Since 1956, the National Trust for Historic Preservation has owned and maintained Decatur House, converting the house into a museum and bookstore.

Thirty-minute tours given every hour and half-hour inform you about the house's history, architecture, and interior design. (It's a good idea to call ahead to confirm that the house is not closed for a special group tour, which sometimes take place.) Ground-floor rooms reflect Federal-period decorating and lifestyles. For example, a room on the first floor appears as it might have in Decatur's day, as an office, with naval war scenes on the wall, books from the period on the shelves, and maps showing Decatur's investments around the city; the desk and chair you see belonged to Decatur. The décor upstairs reflects the life of the last occupant, Marie Oge Beale (Mrs. Truxton Beale), during the year of 1944, telling her story as a world traveler, early preservationist, well-known hostess, and writer. Mr. Beale came from a prominent California family, which may explain the California state seal inlaid in the north drawing room's parquet floor.

Tours, Hours & Admission: Decatur House is open for guided tours only, Tuesday through Friday 10am to 3pm, weekends noon to 4pm. Admission is $4 for adults, $2.50 for students and senior citizens. Closed Thanksgiving, Christmas, and New Year's. Annual special events include a Mother's Day Open House in May and a 19th-Century Christmas for 3 weeks in December.

Your tour puts you back on H Street, where you want to turn right, walk to the corner, and turn right again. You are walking past Decatur House now, facing the White House. Your next stop will be the Octagon, but on your way, you pass:

2. **Lafayette Square,** a small public park, known best today as a gathering spot for protestors and as a favorite resting place for homeless people. Originally an open-air market and military encampment, the square takes its name from the day in 1824 when Lafayette visited Washington and crowds swarmed the park for a sight of him. The statue at the center of the park is of General Andrew Jackson—his was America's first equestrian statue when erected in 1853. Elsewhere in the square are memorials to those from other countries who helped the colonists fight in the War for Independence, the Marquis de Lafayette, Steuben (the Prussian drillmaster of Valley Forge), and Kosciuszko (Polish soldier and statesman) among them.

When you reach the corner, you've arrived at:

3. **Pennsylvania Avenue,** the 2-block section that's been closed to traffic since 1995 in an effort to thwart terrorists and crazies from getting near the president. The closing of the street has been controversial, but one good result (aside from ensuring the safety of the president, that is) is that the street has turned into a festive promenade area, especially in warm weather, and a place where in-line skaters and bicyclists whiz around and Frisbee games erupt impromptu. Hovering over Pennsylvania Avenue is:

4. **The White House,** which we cover fully in chapter 7. Now turn right down Pennsylvania Avenue and pass:

5. **The Renwick Gallery** of the National Museum of American Art, where it meets 17th Street NW. See chapter 7 for details about this museum, which specializes in American crafts. Turn left on 17th Street, where you walk right by the:

6. **Old Executive Office Building** (as opposed to the New Executive Office Building, located behind the Renwick Gallery). Known as the "OEB" by insiders who work in or with the Executive Office of the President, this huge, ornately

Walking Tour 2—Historic Homes Near the White House

●1 Decatur House
●2 Lafayette Square
●3 Pennnsylvania Ave.
●4 The White House
●5 Renwick Gallery
●6 Old Executive Office Building
●7 Octagon
◉ Seasons
●8 Arts Club of Washington

styled building originally was called the State, War and Navy Building. It was constructed between 1872 and 1888, and on completion, it was the largest office building in the world. During the Iran-Contra scandal of the Reagan presidency, the OEB became famous as the site of document shredding by Colonel Oliver North and his secretary, Fawn Hall.

Cross 17th Street, walk a couple of blocks to New York Avenue, and turn right. Follow New York Avenue to 18th Street and you have found:

7. The Octagon, 1799 New York Ave. NW (☎ **202/638-3221;** www. amerarchfoundation.com). One of the oldest houses in Washington, the Octagon is also one of the most interesting. The 1801 building served as a temporary president's home for James and Dolley Madison after the British burned the White House in 1814. President Madison sat at the circular table in the upstairs circular room and signed the Treaty of Ghent, ending the War of 1812. The Octagon, which has only six sides (the Tayloe children who lived there preferred to call it the Octagon), was designed by Dr. William Thornton, first architect of the U.S. Capitol (and Tudor Place, see below), and completed in 1801. Built for the wealthy Tayloe family, it is an exquisite example of Federal-period architecture, with unusual features: round rooms, an oval shaped staircase that curves gracefully up three floors, hidden doors, and triangular chambers.

Tours, Hours & Admission: Guided tours last about 30 to 45 minutes, during which you learn about the house, the Tayloes, their slaves, and life in the

1800s. The museum hosts changing exhibits, usually on an architectural theme, in two upstairs rooms and has a permanent exhibit in the English basement, where you learn about the "downstairs" side of life in the 1800s—these were the servants' quarters and work rooms. The American Architectural Foundation administers the Octagon, which is open Tuesday through Sunday 10am to 4pm. Admission is $3 for adults, $1.50 for students and senior citizens.

From the Octagon, head up 18th Street to Pennsylvania Avenue and turn left. Cross Pennsylvania Avenue at 20th Street, proceed 1 block to I Street, and turn left again. In the middle of the block is the:

8. Arts Club of Washington, 2017 I St. NW (☎ 202/331-7282). You will have to ring the buzzer here for entry, and then you'll be on your own to wander. Chances are, too, that a luncheon or some other event will be in full swing in the first-floor rooms. The Arts Club, founded in 1916 to promote the arts in greater Washington, occupies this town house duplex and allows members and others to rent its facilities for special events.

The site is historic because this is where James Monroe lived for the first 6 months of his presidency, while the White House was being rebuilt after being torched by the British in the War of 1812. Monroe's inaugural ball was held here. The rear wing of the structure dates from 1802, the front portion from 1805.

The building is a little bit funky now, as you'll see if you explore a bit: Flights of stairs take you into little alcoves and hidden wings. Art by local artists hangs on the walls throughout the adjoining buildings.

Tours, Hours & Admission: The Arts Club is free and open to the public Tuesday through Friday 10am to 5pm, Saturday 10am to 2pm, and Sunday 1 to 5pm. Call in advance if you'd like a guided tour of the club.

⬤ **WINDING DOWN** Kinkead's, 2000 Pennsylvania Ave. NW (☎ 202/296-7700). There are plenty of sandwich shops in this part of town, but if you want to eat at one of Washington's best restaurants, try Kinkead's. Its attractive, multileveled dining room serves wondrous seafood dishes. Because the restaurant is so popular, consider playing it safe and reserving in advance. See chapter 6 for details.

From Kinkead's, turn left outside the restaurant and walk to the end of the block to reach 21st Street. Turn left and walk the few steps to I Street. Cross 21st Street and follow I Street to the Foggy Bottom Metro station and 23rd and I Streets NW.

WALKING TOUR 3
Georgetown's Historic Homes

Start: 3051 M St. NW (Foggy Bottom Metro station).
Finish: 1703 32nd St. NW (Dupont Circle Metro station).
Time: Approximately 5 hours, including tours and breaks.
Best Times: If you want to see all the houses, you should start first thing in the morning, Wednesday through Saturday, because two of the houses close in midafternoon.
Worst Times: In August, when Dumbarton House is closed, and in late afternoon, when two of the houses are closed.

The Georgetown area famous for its shops, restaurants, and bars is not the Georgetown you'll see on this walking tour. Instead, the circuit will take you along quiet streets lined with charming houses and stately trees that remind you of the town's age and history. The town of George, comprising 60 acres and named for the king of England, was officially established in 1751. It assumed new importance in 1790, when George Washington specified a nearby site on the Potomac River for America's new capital city.

From the Foggy Bottom Metro station, walk up 23rd Street NW to Washington Circle, and go left around the circle to Pennsylvania Avenue. Continue on Pennsylvania Avenue until you reach M Street NW.

TAKE A BREAK   Seasons, Four Seasons Hotel, 2800 Pennsylvania Ave. NW (☎ **202/342-0810**). Before you start walking, give yourself something to walk off. Breakfast here is sumptuous but pricey: $7.75 for blueberry pancakes, $11.50 for continental breakfast, and so on. For a quicker, cheaper fix, stop at the Starbucks at 3122 M St. NW.

Once you are satiated, head to the:

1. Old Stone House, 3051 M St. NW (☎ **202/426-6851**). Located on one of the busiest streets in Washington, the unobtrusive Old Stone House offers a quiet look back at pre-Revolutionary times, when its first owner, a carpenter, used the ground floor as a workshop. The house dates from 1765, making it the only surviving pre-Revolutionary building in the city. Acquired by the National Park Service in 1926, the Old Stone House today shows its four small rooms furnished as they would have been in the late 18th century, during the period when Georgetown was a significant tobacco and shipping port. Park rangers provide information and sometimes demonstrate cooking on an open fireplace, spinning, and making pomander balls. Beyond the house is a pretty, terraced lawn and 18th-century–style English flower garden, a spot long frequented by Georgetown shop and office workers seeking a respite.

Tours, Hours & Admission: The Old Stone House is open to the public Wednesday to Sunday 9am to 5pm. Admission is free. Closed federal holidays.

From the Old Stone House, head to Dumbarton House. First, though, you may want to take a short detour to the **Georgetown Post Office,** around the corner on 31st Street. Recently renovated to the tune of $2.1 million, the 140-year-old building was designed with Italian Renaissance palaces in mind. Step inside to purchase postage stamps for all those postcards you're intending to send, and you'll have the chance to admire the grand space, with its high ceiling, gilded capitals, and cast-iron columns. When you're through, walk back down to M Street, follow it to 28th Street, and turn left. Follow 28th Street to Q Street and turn right, where you'll have no trouble finding:

2. Dumbarton House, 2715 Q St. NW (☎ **202/337-2288**). This stately mansion lies behind a long brick wall and dominates the block. Begun in 1799 and completed in 1805, the house is exemplary of Federal-period architecture, meaning its rooms are exactly symmetrical, below and above stairs, and are centered by a large hall. The house is filled with Federal-period furnishings, like the dining room's late–18th-century sideboard, over which hangs a painting by Charles Willson Peale.

On guided, 45-minute tours, you learn a bit of the history of the house. For example, one of its first owners was Joseph Nourse, first Register of the U.S. Treasury, who lived here with his family from 1805 to 1813. Recent research has confirmed that Dolley Madison stopped here for a cup of tea during her escape from the burning White House in 1812, before crossing by ferry into Virginia.

Tours, Hours & Admission: Dumbarton House serves as headquarters for the Colonial Dames of America, who restored the house. It is open for guided tours only, Tuesday through Saturday starting at 10:15am, with the last tour at 12:15pm. A $3 donation is requested; students are free. Dumbarton House is closed in August, Thanksgiving holiday weekend, and December 25 through January 1.

Turn right when you exit the house and follow Q Street as far as 31st Street. This is a quiet and pleasant stroll, along wide, brick-laid sidewalks, past old town houses with turrets and other examples of Georgetown's fine architecture. For some reason, many of these streets bear no street signs. Fortunately, 31st Street is not only marked, it also tells you to turn right on 31st Street to reach Tudor Place. So, turn right and walk to the grand gates at mid-block and press the buzzer to gain entry.

3. Tudor Place, 1644 31st St. NW (☎ **202/965-0400;** http://tudorplace.org). Occupying an entire city block, Tudor Place is a 5.5-acre estate of sloping green lawn and exquisite gardens. At its summit is the magnificent, Palladian-style manor house designed by Dr. William Thornton, the first architect of the U.S. Capitol. Martha Custis Peter, Martha Washington's granddaughter, purchased Tudor Place in 1805 with an $8,000 legacy left her by her step-grandfather, George Washington. Martha Custis Peter was married to Georgetown mayor Thomas Peter; their descendants lived here until 1984.

The house has an exceptional architecture—note the clever pull-up windows to the domed portico overlooking the south lawn, a feature found in another Thornton creation, the Octagon. Many of the furnishings were inherited or were purchased at auction from Mount Vernon. On your tour, you'll have the chance to scan a loving letter written by George Washington to Martha on June 18, 1775, upon receiving command of the Revolutionary Army: ". . . I should enjoy more real happiness and felicity in 1 month with you, at home, than I have the most distant prospect of reaping abroad . . . ."

Henry Clay, Daniel Webster, and John Calhoun visited Tudor Place. The Marquis de Lafayette attended a reception held here in his honor in 1824. Robert E. Lee was a close friend of the family, who were Confederate sympathizers.

Tours, Hours & Admission: If you arrive between the normal tour times of Tuesday through Friday at 10am, 11:30am, 1pm, and 2:30pm, and Saturday on the hour, 10am to 3pm, take the opportunity to visit the delightful 5-acre Federal-period garden, which includes centuries-old boxwoods; a lily pond; a bowling green; pear trees; ivy-covered arbors; and intimate seating alcoves. You tour the Tudor Place mansion by guide only, in 45-minute sessions. Tudor Place offers several tours on specific subjects, for instance, the "19th-Century Mistresses of Tudor Place," tour. Donations of $6 per adult, $5 for seniors, $3 for students are requested. The gardens are open Monday through Saturday 10am to 4pm for self-guided tours; a $2 per person donation is requested. You receive a map to guide you through the gardens. Tudor Place is closed for major holidays.

From Tudor Place, turn left on 31st Street, away from the direction you came, and follow 31st Street to R Street and turn left again. Walk along R Street for about 2 blocks, and you reach Wisconsin Avenue. Cross Wisconsin Avenue and walk the few steps to:

Walking Tour 3—Georgetown's Historic Homes

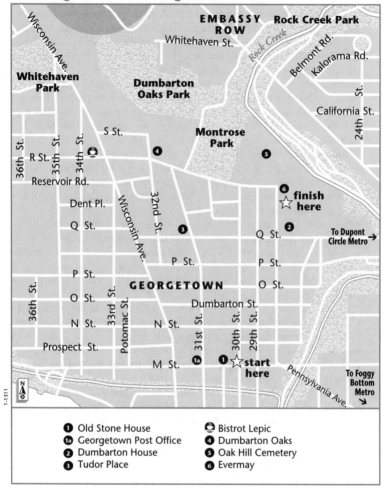

Whitehaven St. EMBASSY ROW · Rock Creek Park

Whitehaven Park · Dumbarton Oaks Park · Belmont Rd. · Kalorama Rd. · California St. · 24th St.

Wisconsin Ave. · Whitehaven St. · Rock Creek

S St. · Montrose Park ❺

36th St. · 35th St. · 34th St. · R St. · Reservoir Rd. · Dent Pl. · Q St. · P St. · O St. · N St. · Prospect St.

Wisconsin Ave. · 32nd St. · ❹ · ❻ ☆ finish here

❸ · Q St. · ❷ · To Dupont Circle Metro →

P St. · P St. · O St.

GEORGETOWN · Dumbarton St.

33rd St. · Potomac St. · N St. · 31st St. · 30th St. · 29th St.

M St. ❶ₐ · ❶ ☆ start here · Pennsylvania Ave. · To Foggy Bottom Metro →

N

1-1311

❶ Old Stone House
❶ₐ Georgetown Post Office
❷ Dumbarton House
❸ Tudor Place

☺ Bistrot Lepic
❹ Dumbarton Oaks
❺ Oak Hill Cemetery
❻ Evermay

☺ **TAKE A BREAK   Bistrot Lepic,** 1736 Wisconsin Ave. NW (☎ 202/
333-0111). Very French, Bistrot Lepic is a small place with a large following.
Because of the restaurant's petite size and great popularity, it's best to reserve a
table in advance if you want to sample its traditional (onion tart) and nouvelle
(grape leaves stuffed with crab) cuisine. See chapter 6 for details.

Now retrace your steps, crossing Wisconsin Avenue again to return to R
Street. Turn right and walk a block to 32nd Street, turning left. Go to the
imposing double doors and enter at:

4. **Dumbarton Oaks,** 1703 32nd St. NW (☎ **202/339-6401;** www.
doaks.org). The oldest part of this grand mansion dates from 1800. Since then,
the house has undergone considerable change, most notably at the hands of a
couple named Robert and Mildred Bliss.

The wealthy Blisses retired here in 1933, ending Robert's 33-year career in the Foreign Service. Over the years, the Blisses amassed collections of Byzantine and pre-Columbian art and books relating to those studies, as well as to landscape architecture. Their move into Dumbarton Oaks began a remodeling of the mansion to accommodate the collections and the library, which now occupy the entire building. When the Blisses relocated in 1940, they conveyed the house, gardens, and Byzantine art collection to Harvard University, Robert's alma mater. In 1963, the house/museum completed two new wings, one to house the pre-Columbian works, the other to hold Mrs. Bliss's gardening books.

You may guide yourself through the exhibit rooms to view these unique artworks, from Byzantine illuminated manuscripts, jewelry, and mosaic icons to pre-Columbian Olmec jade figures (the Olmec is the earliest known civilization in Mexico) and Mayan pottery. Pre-Columbian works are displayed chronologically in an octet of glass pavilions.

In 1944, Dumbarton Oaks hosted two international conferences, which cemented the principles later incorporated into the United Nations charter. The conferences took place in the Music Room, which you should visit to admire the immense, 16th-century stone chimneypiece, 18th-century parquet floor, and antique French, Italian, and Spanish furniture, as well as the El Greco painting, *The Visitation.*

Today, Dumbarton Oaks is a research center for studies in Byzantine and pre-Columbian art and history and in landscape architecture. Most Washingtonians know Dumbarton Oaks for its magnificent 10-acre terraced garden, which includes an orangery; wisteria-covered arbors; groves of cherry trees; magnolias; and herbaceous borders. You can't picnic here, though; for that, you must go down the block to Montrose Park.

Hours & Admission: Dumbarton Oaks' collections are open Tuesday through Sunday 2 to 5pm ($1 donation suggested). The gardens (entrance on R Street) are open November to March, daily 2 to 5pm for no charge; April to October, daily 2 to 6pm for a charge of $4 per adult, $3 per senior citizen and children under 12. Both gardens and collections are closed on national holidays and Dec. 24; the gardens may also close during inclement weather.

You can wind down your tour by walking away from Wisconsin Avenue on R Street, passing Montrose Park and:

5. **Oak Hill Cemetery,** the 25-acre Victorian landscaped burial place founded in 1850 and whose graves include those of William Wilson Corcoran (of the Corcoran Gallery of Art), Edwin Stanton (Lincoln's secretary of war), and Dean Acheson (secretary of state under Truman). If you want to stroll, purchase a map of the graves at the gatehouse, 3001 R St. NW, itself a beautiful brick and sandstone Italianate structure built in 1850. The cemetery is open weekdays 10am to 4pm.

As you leave, note the beautiful house across the street at 2920 R St.: It's the home of *Washington Post* publisher Katherine Graham.

Follow the brick sidewalk and iron fence as it curves down 28th Street to:

6. **Evermay,** 1623 28th St. NW, which you can't visit, since it's a private residence, but which you can ogle from the gate. You also can't see much of it, because the brick ramparts and foliage hide it so well, but what's on view is impressive. As the plaque on the estate wall tells you, Evermay was built in 1792–94 by Scotsman Samuel Davidson, with the proceeds Davidson made from the sale of lands he

owned around the city, including part of the present-day White House and Lafayette Square property.

Note: From here, believe it or not, you are only about a 15- or 20-minute walk from the Dupont Circle part of town—and the Metro. Walk down to Q Street NW, turn left, and follow Q Street across the Dumbarton Bridge to Massachusetts Avenue NW. Walk along Massachusetts Avenue to 20th Street NW and turn left. Continue another block, and you're at the Dupont Circle Metro station.

9

Shopping the District

Here's a fact that may astound you, even if you are an avid shopper: The Potomac Mills Outlet, which lies 30 miles south of the capital on I-395, attracts more visitors annually than any other site in the Washington area. Twice as many more people make the trek here (and it is a traffic-laden trek) than tour the National Air & Space Museum. If Potomac Mills intrigues you, flip to its entry, listed in this chapter among "Malls." If you want to know more about Washington shopping in general, read on.

1 The Shopping Scene

SHOPPING AREAS

ADAMS-MORGAN This is a lively part of town that spills over with the sounds, sights, and smells of different cultures. Defined by 18th Street and Columbia Road NW, Adams-Morgan is a neighborhood of ethnic eateries interspersed with the odd secondhand bookshop and eclectic collectibles store. Although Adams-Morgan has more nightclubs and bistros than actual stores, it's still a fun area for walking and shopping. Parking is possible during the day, but impossible at night, simple as that. Closest Metro: Dupont Circle; exit at Q Street NW and walk up Connecticut Avenue NW to Columbia Road NW.

CONNECTICUT AVENUE/DUPONT CIRCLE Connecticut Avenue NW, which runs from the mini-Wall Street that is K Street north to S Street, is a main thoroughfare, where you'll find traditional clothing at Brooks Brothers, Talbots, and Burberry's; casual duds at the Gap and Liz Claiborne; discount items at Filene's Basement and Hit or Miss; and haute couture at Rizik's. The closer you get to Dupont Circle, the fewer business-types you see. People are younger, mellower, and sport more pierced body parts. This pedestrian-friendly section of the avenue is studded with coffee bars and neighborhood restaurants, as well as art galleries, book and record shops, vintage clothing stores, and gay and lesbian boutiques. Metro: Farragut North, at one end, Dupont Circle at the other.

DOWNTOWN Between 12th and 14th Streets NW lies an interesting stretch of Pennsylvania Avenue. On the White House side, within the Willard Inter-Continental Hotel's courtyard, are three tony shops: Chanel, Harriet Kassman, and Jackie Chalkley.

Down 1 block are the Shops at National Place, a four-level mall whose stores include Curious Kids, Casual Corner, and the newly opened Filene's Basement. This is where beloved, family-owned department stores like Garfinckel's, Raleigh's, and Woodward & Lothrop used to be located. Now, Hecht's, at 12th and G Streets, is the sole carrier of the department store flag downtown. Metro: Metro Center.

GEORGETOWN   Georgetown used to be more fun, when Hare Krishnas hung out on its corners and the streets were less, well, tourist-ridden. These days, Georgetown is a great place to shop, but you may come away with a headache from its crowded streets, sidewalks, and shops. Weekends, especially, bring out all kinds of yahoos, who are mainly there to drink. Visit Georgetown on a weekday morning, if you can. The heart of the shopping district is at the intersection of Wisconsin Avenue and M Street NW, where shops fan out broadly. Weeknights are another good time to visit, for dinner and strolling afterwards. On afternoons, early evenings, and weekends, traffic is heavy, and parking can be tough. Consider taking a bus or taxi—the closest Metro stop is at Foggy Bottom, a good 20- to 30-minute walk away. If you drive, you'll find parking lots expensive and tickets even more so, so be careful where you plant your car.

OLD TOWN ALEXANDRIA   Old Town is becomingly increasingly like Georgetown, warts (heavy traffic, crowded sidewalks, difficult parking) and all. It's still a nice place to visit, though; the drive alone is worth the trip. From Memorial Bridge, near the Lincoln Memorial, follow the George Washington Parkway alongside the Potomac River (the same route that takes you to National Airport) about 14 miles, where the parkway becomes Washington Street. Look for a parking spot on King Street (dream on) or a side street, and then walk. Shops run the length of King Street, from the waterfront up to Washington Street, and from Washington Street west to the Masonic Temple. You can also take the Metro to King Street. See chapter 11, for more information.

UPPER WISCONSIN AVENUE NORTHWEST   In a residential section of town known as Friendship Heights on the D.C. side and Chevy Chase on the Maryland side is a quarter-mile shopping district that extends from Saks Fifth Avenue at one end to Roche Bobois at the other. In between lie the Lord & Taylor, Nieman-Marcus, and Hecht Company department stores; a bevy of top shops, such as Tiffany's and Gianni Versace; two malls, the Mazza Gallerie and its younger, more chi-chi sister, the Chevy Chase Pavilion, whose offerings range from Country Road Australia to Hold Everything; and several stand-alone staples, such as Banana Republic. (A third mall, adjoining the Chevy Chase Pavilion, is due for completion in late 1998.) The street is too wide and traffic always too snarled to make this a place to stroll. Most people head for particular stores and then leave. Drive here if you want; the malls offer 2 hours of free parking. Metro: The strip is right on the red line of the subway, with the "Friendship Heights" exits leading directly into each of the malls and into Hecht's.

2 Shopping A to Z

ANTIQUES

While you won't find many bargains in Washington area antique stores, you will see beautiful and rare decorative furniture, silver, jewelry, art, and fabrics, from Amish quilts to Chinese silks. Antique shops dot the greater Washington landscape, but the richest concentrations are in Old Town Alexandria; Capitol Hill; Georgetown; Adams-Morgan; and Kensington, Maryland.

Anne Pelot Antiques. 1007 King St., Alexandria. ☎ **703/549-7429.** Metro: King St., with a short walk.

A little less expensive than some of its neighbors, this shop specializes in American furniture from the late 18th and early 19th centuries, both Empire and Federal, as well as English ceramics and glass and decorative objects from the 18th and 19th centuries. The pleasant owner is happy to find "the special item" you're desperately seeking.

Antique Row. Howard and Connecticut aves., Kensington, Maryland.

If you're in search of a real deal or true bonanza, then certainly a trip few miles north of the city to 40-odd antique and collectibles shops is worth your while. The stores are in a row along Howard Avenue and offer every sort of item in a mix of styles, periods, and prices.

✪ **Antiques-on-the-Hill.** 701 North Carolina Ave. SE. ☎ **202/543-1819.** Metro: Eastern Market.

A Capitol Hill institution since the 1960s, this place sells silver, furniture, glassware, jewelry, porcelain, and lamps.

✪ **The Brass Knob Architectural Antiques.** 2311 18th St. NW. ☎ **202/332-3370.** Metro: Dupont Circle.

When early homes and office buildings are demolished in the name of progress, these savvy salvage merchants spirit away saleable treasures, from chandeliers to wrought-iron fencing. Cross the street to its other location: The Brass Knob's Back Doors, 2329 Champlain St. NW (☎ **202/265-0587**).

Cherishables. 1608 20th St. NW. ☎ **202/785-4087.** www.washingtonpost.com/yp/cherishables. Metro: Dupont Circle.

An adorable shop specializing in 18th- and 19th-century American furniture, folk art, quilts, and decorative accessories. The furniture is displayed in roomlike settings. The store stocks a world-renowned line of Christmas ornaments designed each year around a new theme: the garden, architecture, and breeds of dogs are some from years past.

GKS Bush. 2828 Pennsylvania Ave. NW. ☎ **202/965-0653.** Metro: Foggy Bottom.

This place has been in business for 15 years selling antique American paintings, furniture, and decorative accessories.

Millenium. 1528 U St. NW. ☎ **202/483-1218.** Metro: U St.–Cardozo.

The TV generation, who consider anything made between the 1930s and the 1970s collectible, come here to shop for antiques. The shop works with 18 dealers and stock changes weekly. Funky wares run from Bakelite, to Heywood-Wakefield blond-wood beauties, to used drinking glasses.

Old Print Gallery. 1220 31st St. NW. ☎ **202/965-1818.** www.oldprintgallery.com. Metro: Foggy Bottom, with a 20-minute walk.

This gallery carries original American and European prints from the 18th and 19th centuries, including British political cartoons, maps, and historical documents. The store is one of the largest antique print and map shops in the United States.

Susquehanna Antiques. 3216 O St. NW. ☎ **202/333-1511.** Metro: Foggy Bottom, with a 25-minute walk.

American, English, and European furniture and paintings are the specialties at this store.

ART GALLERIES

Art galleries abound in Washington, but they are especially prolific in the Dupont Circle and Georgetown neighborhoods and along 7th Street, downtown. For a complete listing of local galleries, get your hands on a copy of *Galleries,* a monthly guide to major galleries and their shows; the guide is available free at many hotel concierge desks and at each of the galleries listed in the publication. Here's a selection of top places.

DUPONT CIRCLE

For all galleries listed below, the closest Metro stop is Dupont Circle.

✪ **Addison/Ripley Gallery, Ltd.** 9 Hillyer Court NW. ☎ **202/328-2332.**

This gallery displays contemporary paintings, sculpture, and drawings by Americans, some but not all by locals. Edith Kuhnle, Richard Hunt, and Wols Kahn are a few of the artists represented here. There is a second location at 1670 Wisconsin Ave. NW (☎ **202/333-3335**).

Affrica. 2010 R St. NW. ☎ **202/745-7272.**

African masks, figures, and artifacts.

Anton Gallery. 2108 R St. NW. ☎ **202/328-0828.**

Expect to find contemporary American paintings, with maybe a little sculpture or photography. Nearly all of the artists who show their work here live locally but hail from around the world, from Japan to Chile, New Zealand to California.

Fondo del Sol Visual Arts and Media Center. 2112 R St. NW. ☎ **202/483-2777.**

This lively gallery in a picturesque town house showcases the art and cultures of Latin American, Native American, Caribbean, and African-American artists.

H. H. Leonards' Mansion on O Street. 2020 O St. NW. ☎ **202/659-8787.**

This is not an art gallery in the usual sense. H. H. Leonards' consists of three Victorian five-story town houses joined together, decorated throughout with more than 5,000 antiques and artworks, in styles ranging from art deco to avant garde. Everything's for sale, even the beds on which owner H. and son Z. sleep. This is the Leonards' home, a special events spot, and a luxurious B&B to boot. (Christie Brinkley, Alec Baldwin, and Kim Bassinger are among her clients.) H. tells you to help yourself to champagne or coffee in the English kitchen and then wander around on your own, which you could do for hours. Parking is such a problem that neighbors are trying to shut her down.

Kathleen Ewing Gallery. 1609 Connecticut Ave. NW. ☎ **202/328-0955.**

This gallery covers everything from 19th century to contemporary photography.

Very Special Arts Gallery. 1300 Connecticut Ave. NW. ☎ **202/628-0800.**

This one-of-a-kind gallery represents about 800 American artists with disabilities who have created astounding works that include folk art, paintings, and sculptures.

GEORGETOWN

If you're not driving, take a cab, a "30" series bus, or the Metro. If you Metro it, hop off at the Foggy Bottom station, walk up to Washington Circle, turn left and follow Pennsylvania Avenue, which becomes M Street, into Georgetown. See the Walking Tour at the end of this chapter for a number of recommendations. Here's one other:

Govinda Gallery. 1227 34th St. NW. ☎ **202/333-1180.**

You read about this one in the newspaper because it often shows pictures of celebrity musicians taken by well-known photographers.

SEVENTH STREET ARTS CORRIDOR

A renaissance is taking place on 7th Street, which lies at the heart of downtown Washington, in the general vicinity of the MCI Center. These galleries were here before (in the case of the Michelson Gallery, try 40 years before) there was even talk of an MCI Center. And where once these galleries languished among office buildings, their neighbors now are trendy restaurants and bars.

406 Group. 406 7th St. NW (between D and E sts.). Metro: Archives–Navy Memorial.

Several first-rate art galleries, some interlopers from Dupont Circle, occupy this historic building, with its 13-foot-high ceilings and spacious rooms. They include **David Adamson Gallery** (☎ 202/628-0257), which is probably the largest gallery space in D.C., with two levels showing the works of contemporary artists, including locals Kevin MacDonald and rising star Renee Stout, and prints and drawings by David Hockney; and the very expensive **Baumgartner Galleries** (☎ 202/347-2211), displaying national and international artists. Although this gallery gets a lot of good press, other galleries have works every bit as impressive, or more so. Try **Touchstone Gallery** (☎ 202/347-2787), which is a self-run co-op of 15 artists who take turns exhibiting their work.

Mickelson Gallery. 707-709 G St. NW. ☎ **202/628-1734.** Metro: Gallery Place/MCI Center.

Around the corner from the 7th Street gang, this is one of the oldest D.C. galleries, approaching 40 years, with a framing business going back 87 years. The gallery shows mostly 20th-century American and European printmakers, painters, and sculptors, and has one of the largest collections of M.C. Escher's works for sale in the United States (you must make an appointment to view them), as well as a large selection of works by George Bellows.

✪ **Zenith Gallery.** 413 7th St. NW. ☎ **202/783-2963**. www.zenithgallery.com. Metro: Archives–Navy Memorial or Gallery Place.

Across the street from the 406 Group, this 19-year-old gallery shows diverse works of contemporary artists, most American, about half of whom are local. You can get a good deal in this gallery, paying anywhere from $50 to $50,000 for a piece. Among other things you'll find here are annual humor shows, annual neon exhibits, realism, abstract expressionism, and landscapes.

BEAUTY

With a few exceptions, the best salons are in Georgetown and cater to both men and women.

Bogart. 1063 Wisconsin Ave. NW. ☎ **202/333-6550.** Metro: Foggy Bottom, with a 20-minute walk, or take one of the 30-series buses (30, 32, 34, 36, 38B) from downtown into Georgetown.

Favored by certain local TV news anchors, this salon specializes in "corrective color." Facials cost $60; haircuts average $50 for women, $35 for men.

Elizabeth Arden. 5225 Wisconsin Ave. NW. ☎ **202/362-9890.** Metro: Friendship Heights.

This place does it all. Facials cost $65; haircuts average $65 for women, $35 for men.

Interiano Salon. 1025 31st St. NW. ☎ **202/333-3455.** Metro: Foggy Bottom with a 15-minute walk.

Gloria (Interiano) has been cutting my husband's hair for 20 years now and mine about half that time. Other patrons are often Washington insiders whose names, if not faces, you will recognize. Gloria, herself, is pretty down to earth, and so are her rates: $35 for men, $60 for women.

IPSA for Hair. 1629 Wisconsin Ave. NW. ☎ **202/338-4100.** Metro: Foggy Bottom, with a 30-minute walk, or take one of the 30-series buses (30, 32, 34, 36, 38B) from downtown into Georgetown.

This salon won the most votes for favorite hair styling salon in a local count, but it only does hair. Haircuts average $60 for women, $35 for men.

✪ **Okyo.** 2903 M St. NW. ☎ **202/342-2675.** Metro: Foggy Bottom, with a 10-minute walk, or take one of the 30-series buses (30, 32, 34, 36, 38B) from downtown into Georgetown.

Owner Bernard Portelli colored Catherine Deneuve's hair in France, and he's so booked that he isn't taking any new clients. They only do hair here, at surprisingly reasonable rates: cuts start at $50 for women, $30 for men.

Saks Fifth Avenue. 5555 Wisconsin Ave., Chevy Chase, MD. ☎ **301/657-9000.** Metro: Friendship Heights, Red.

Saks caters to an older clientele. Facials cost $55; haircuts average $45 for women and men, without a blowdry.

3303 Inc. 3303 M St. NW. ☎ **202/965-4000.** Metro: Foggy Bottom, with a 20-minute walk, or take one of the 30-series buses (30, 32, 34, 36, 38B) from downtown into Georgetown.

This is a good place to run to if you're embroiled in a scandal—at least that's what Monica Lewinsky thinks. Facials start at $42; haircuts start at $45 for women, $30 for men. You have to know what you want, but these stylists can do it.

Ury & Associates. 3109 M St. NW. ☎ **202/342-0944.** Metro: Foggy Bottom, with a 20-minute walk, or take one of the 30-series buses (30, 32, 34, 36, 38B) from downtown into Georgetown.

Lots of models come here, where they get rapt attention from Ury. Non-model types come here, too, for expert styling by other hairdressers. Facials cost $60; haircuts start at $60 for women, $40 for men.

BOOKS

Washingtonians are readers, so bookstores pop up throughout the city. An increasingly competitive market means that stores besides Crown Books offer discounts. Here are favorite bookstores in general, used, and special-interest categories.

GENERAL

Barnes & Noble.

The only Barnes & Noble located in the district is the Georgetown Branch. (See Walking Tour below.)

Other area locations of this discount bookstore and cafe include: 4801 Bethesda Ave. (☎ **301/986-1761**); 12089 Rockville Pike (☎ **301/881-0237**); 3651 Jefferson Davis Highway (☎ **703/299-9124**); 1851 Fountain Dr. (☎ **703/437-9490**); and 6260 Seven Corners Center (☎ **703/536-0774**).

B. Dalton. Union Station. ☎ **202/289-1750.** Metro: Union Station.

Your well-rounded bookstore, heavy on the best-sellers. They sell magazines, too.

Borders Books & Music. 1800 L St. NW. ☎ *202/466-4999.* Metro: Farragut North.

With its overwhelming array of books, records, videos, and magazines, this out post of the rapidly expanding chain has taken over the town. Most hardcovers are 10% off; *New York Times* and *Washington Post* hardcover best-sellers are 30% off. People hang out here, hovering over the magazines or sipping espresso in the cafe as they read their books. The store often hosts performances by local musicians.

A new Borders Books & Music store opened in early fall of 1998, on Wisconsin Ave. NW, in Friendship Heights (upper northwest DC). Other Borders stores in the area include those in North Bethesda, Md., at White Flint Mall, 11301 Rockville Pike (☎ 301/816-1067); Arlington, Va., 1201 Hayes St. (☎ 703/418-0166); Baileys Crossroads, 5871 Crossroads Center Way (☎ 703/998-0404); Vienna, Va., 8311 Leesburg Pike (☎ 703/556-7766).

Bridge Street Books. 2814 Pennsylvania Ave. NW. ☎ *202/965-5200.* Metro: Foggy Bottom.

A small, serious shop with a good selection of current fiction, literary criticism, and publications you won't find elsewhere. Best-sellers and discounted books are not its raison d'être.

Chapters Literary Bookshop. 1512 K St. NW. ☎ *202/347-5495.* Metro: McPherson Square or Farragut North.

Chapters is strong in new and backlisted fiction and is always hosting author readings. The store does not offer discounts. Tea is always available, and on Friday afternoons they break out the free sherry and cookies.

Crown Books. 2020 K St. NW. ☎ *202/659-2030.* Metro: Foggy Bottom.

Crown offers the best discounts: 10% off all paperbacks, 15% off all hardcovers, 40% off hardcover best-sellers, and 25% off *New York Times* paperback best-sellers.

SuperCrown Books. 11 Dupont Circle. ☎ *202/319-1374.* Metro: Dupont Circle.

Same discounts as the main Crown bookstore, but a wider selection.

Kramerbooks & Afterwords Café. 1517 Connecticut Ave. NW. ☎ *202/387-1400.* Metro: Dupont Circle.

The first bookstore/cafe in the Dupont Circle area, this place has launched countless romances. It's jammed and often noisy, stages live music Wednesday through Saturday evenings, and is open all night on weekends. Paperback fiction takes up most of its inventory, but the store carries a little of everything.

✪ **Olsson's Books and Records.** See entry in Georgetown walking tour, p. 254.

✪ **Politics and Prose Bookstore.** 5015 Connecticut Ave. NW. ☎ *202/364-1919.* Metro: the closest is Van Ness–UDC, but you'll have to walk about a half-mile from there.

This is a two-story shop in a residential part of town. A devoted neighborhood clientele helped move this shop, book by book, across the street to larger quarters in 1990 (it's expanded again since then). It has vast offerings in literary fiction and nonfiction alike, with the largest psychology section in the city (possibly on the East Coast), and an excellent children's department. A warm, knowledgeable staff will help you find what you need. Downstairs is a cozy coffeehouse frequented by booklovers of all description: professorial types to moms treating themselves to a cappuccino. Staff-recommended books are discounted 20%; otherwise there are no discounts.

Trover Shop. 227 Pennsylvania Ave. SE. ☎ **202/543-8006.** Metro: Capitol South.

The only general bookstore on Capitol Hill, Trover's strengths are its political selections and its magazines. The store discounts 20% on *Washington Post* hardcover fiction and nonfiction best-sellers, computer books, and cookbooks.

Waldenbooks. Georgetown Park Mall. ☎ **202/333-8033.** Metro: Foggy Bottom, with a 20-minute walk.

Another chain, general-selection bookstore.

OLD & USED BOOKS

Booked Up. 1204 31st St. NW. ☎ **202/965-3244.** Metro: Foggy Bottom, with a 20-minute walk, or take one of the 30-series buses (30, 32, 34, 36, 38B) from downtown into Georgetown.

An antiquarian bookstore in Georgetown, where you can stumble upon some true collectors' items. Specialties include travel and literature.

Idle Time Books. 2410 18th St. NW. ☎ **202/232-4774.** Metro: Woodley Park–Zoo or Dupont Circle.

A dusty, two-story treasure trove of used books in Adams-Morgan; strong on politics.

Second Story Books. 2000 P St. NW. ☎ **202/659-8884.** Metro: Dupont Circle.

If it's old, out of print, custom-bound, or a small-press publication, this is where to find it. The store also specializes in used CDs and vinyl and has an interesting collection of antique French and American advertising posters.

SPECIAL-INTEREST BOOKS

American History Museum Bookstore. National Museum of American History gift shop, Constitution Ave. between 12th and 14th sts. NW. ☎ **202/357-1784.** Metro: Federal Triangle or Smithsonian.

You'll find a wonderful selection of books on American history and culture here, including some for children.

American Institute of Architects Bookstore. 1735 New York Ave. NW. ☎ **202/626-7475.** Metro: Farragut West.

This store carries books and gifts related to architecture.

Back Stage. 2101 P St. NW. ☎ **202/775-1488.** Metro: Dupont Circle.

This is the headquarters for Washington's theatrical community, which buys its books, scripts, trade publications, and sheet music here.

Franz Bader Bookstore. 1911 I St. NW. ☎ **202/337-5440.** Metro: Farragut West.

This store stocks books on art, art history, architecture, and photography, as well as exhibition catalogs.

Cheshire Cat Children's Bookstore. 5512 Connecticut Ave. NW. ☎ **202/244-3956.** On the L2 bus line.

The owners are extremely knowledgeable about children's literature, from the classics to the current market. They are also big promoters of local talent and host frequent author visits. The store's way out on Connecticut Avenue.

Lambda Rising. 1625 Connecticut Ave. NW. ☎ **202/462-6969.** Metro: Dupont Circle.

It was a big deal when this gay and lesbian bookstore opened with a plate-glass window revealing its interior to passersby. Now it's an unofficial headquarters for the gay/lesbian/bisexual community, carrying every gay/lesbian and bisexual book in print, plus videos, music, and gifts.

MysteryBooks. 1715 Connecticut Ave. NW. ☎ **800/955-2279** or 202/483-1600. Metro: Dupont Circle.

The name of the store should give you a clue. Here's where to find out whodunit. It has more paperbacks than hardcovers.

Travel Books & Language Center. 4437 Wisconsin Ave. NW. ☎ **800/220-2665** or 202/237-1322. Metro: Tenleytown.

Its move in November 1997 to new digs tripled the space of this 14-year-old travel bookstore, which has the best-in-the-area assortment of guidebooks and maps covering the entire world, as well as language dictionaries and learning tapes, travel diaries, memoirs, and novels famous for their evocation of particular places.

Yes! Bookshop. See entry in Georgetown walking tour, p. 252.

CAMERAS & PHOTOGRAPHIC EQUIPMENT

Photography is a big business in this image-conscious tourist town. A wide range of services and supplies, from inexpensive point-and-shoot cameras to deluxe German and Japanese equipment, is available at competitive prices. Some shops offer repair services and have multilingual staff.

Congressional Photo. 209 Pennsylvania Ave. SE. ☎ **202/543-3206.** Metro: Capitol South.

This is the professional's choice for custom finishing. Full camera-repair service and budget processing are available.

✪ **Penn Camera Exchange.** 915 E St. NW. ☎ **800/347-5770** or 202/347-5777. Metro: Gallery Place or Metro Center.

Across the street from the FBI Building, Penn Camera does a brisk trade with professionals and amateurs alike. The store offers big discounts on major brand-name equipment, such as Olympus and Canon. Penn has been owned and operated by the Zweig family since 1953; its staff is quite knowledgeable, its inventory wide-ranging. Their specialty is quality equipment and processing—not cheap, but worth it. Also at 1015 18th St. NW (☎ **202/785-7366**).

Ritz Camera Centers. 1740 Pennsylvania Ave. NW. ☎ **202/466-3470.** Metro: Farragut West.

This place sells camera equipment and develops film with 1-hour processing for the average photographer. Call for other locations—there are many throughout the area.

CRAFTS

American Hand Plus. See entry in Georgetown walking tour, p. 251.

Appalachian Spring. See entry in Georgetown walking tour, p. 255.

Corso De-Fiori. 801 Pennsylvania Ave. NW, entrance at 8th and D St. ☎ **202/628-1929.** www.corso.com. Metro: Navy Memorial–Archives.

This Sydney, Australia-based store sells its own line of furniture, made of forged iron or wood in a Spanish colonial style, as well as upholstered pieces. Also on sale are beautiful hand-painted ceramics imported from Deruta, Italy, a village dating from the 15th century and known for its handcrafted ceramics; and Haddonstone limestone English garden accessories.

Indian Craft Shop. Department of the Interior, 1849 C St. NW, Room 1023. ☎ **202/ 208-4056.** Weekday hours only. Metro: Farragut West or Foggy Bottom.

The Indian Craft Shop has represented authentic Native American artisans since 1938, selling their handwoven rugs and handcrafted baskets, jewelry, figurines, paintings, pottery, and other items. You need a photo ID to enter the building.

✪ **The Phoenix.** 1514 Wisconsin Ave. NW. ☎ **202/338-4404.** Metro: Foggy Bottom, with a 30-minute walk, or take one of the 30-series buses (30, 32, 34, 36, 38B) from downtown into Georgetown.

Around since 1955, the Phoenix still sells those embroidered Mexican peasant blouses popular in hippie days; Mexican folk and fine art; handcrafted, sterling silver jewelry from Mexico and all over the world; clothing in natural fibers from Mexican and American designers like Eileen Fisher and Flax; collector-quality masks; and decorative doodads in tin, brass, copper, and wood.

✪ **Torpedo Factory Art Center.** 105 North Union St. ☎ **703/838-4565.** Metro: King St., then take the DASH bus (AT2 or AT5) eastbound to the waterfront.

This three-story, converted munitions factory houses more than 83 working studios and the works of about 160 artists, who tend to their crafts before your very eyes, pausing to explain their techniques or to sell their pieces, if you so desire. Artworks include paintings, sculpture, ceramics, glasswork, and textiles.

CRYSTAL/SILVER/CHINA

Neiman-Marcus (see "Department Stores," below) and **Tiffany's** (see "Jewelry," below) sell many of these items, so you may want to visit them. First, though, consider visiting two Georgetown landmarks, **Little Caledonia** and **Martin's.** For more information, see the Georgetown walking tour, below.

DEPARTMENT STORES

Bloomingdale's. White Flint Mall, North Bethesda, MD. ☎ **301/984-4600.** Metro: White Flint.

This outpost of the famous New York–based chain features trendsetting fashions for men, women, and children, as well as shoes; accessories; household goods; furnishings; and cosmetics. Don't look for the same variety and selection found in New York, however, since the Washington versions seem restrained by comparison.

Hecht's. Metro Center, 1201 G St. NW. ☎ **202/628-6661.** Metro: Metro Center.

Everything from mattresses to electronics, children's underwear to luggage, can be bought in this mid-priced emporium.

Lord & Taylor. 5255 Western Ave. NW. ☎ **202/362-9600.** Metro: Friendship Heights.

This is another lesser version of a New York chain, although lately the store has vastly improved its selections. The staff, too, seems more professional and helpful than in the past. Its women's clothing and accessories departments are probably its strong suit; go elsewhere for gadgets and gifts.

Macy's. Fashion Center at Pentagon City, 1000 S. Hayes St., Arlington, VA. ☎ **703/ 418-4488.** Metro: Pentagon City.

A household name for many East Coasters, this Macy's (although nowhere near the size of its Manhattan counterpart) hopes to fulfill the same role for Washington customers. Expect mid- to upscale merchandise and prices.

Neiman-Marcus. Mazza Gallerie, 5300 Wisconsin Ave. NW. ☎ **202/966-9700.** Metro: Friendship Heights.

The legendary Texas institution's catalogs and "his-and-hers" Christmas gifts are exercises in conspicuous consumption. Look for remarkably good bargains at their "Last Call" half-yearly sales; otherwise, this store is pretty pricey. It sells no furniture or home furnishings, except for exquisite china and crystal.

✪ **Nordstrom.** Fashion Center at Pentagon City, 1400 S. Hayes St., Arlington, VA. ☎ **703/ 415-1121.** Metro: Pentagon City.

This Seattle-based retailer's reputation for exceptional service is well deserved—a call to the main information number confirms this. In keeping with the store's beginnings as a shoe store, this location has three entire departments devoted to women's shoes (designer, dressy, and just plain fun); if you can't find your size or color, they'll order it.

Saks Fifth Avenue. 5555 Wisconsin Ave., Chevy Chase, MD. ☎ **301/657-9000.** Metro: Friendship Heights.

If you can make it past the cosmetics counters without getting spritzed by the makeup-masked young women aiming perfume bottles at you, you've accomplished something special. On other levels, you'll find designer and tailored clothing for men and women, and some for children.

FARMERS' & FLEA MARKETS

Alexandria Farmers' Market. 301 King St., at Market Sq. in front of the city hall, in Alexandria. ☎ **703/370-8723**. Sat 5:30–10am. Metro: King St., then take the DASH bus (AT2 or AT5) eastbound to Market Square.

The oldest continually operating farmers' market in the country (since 1752), this market offers the usual assortment of locally grown fruits and vegetables, along with delectable baked goods, cut flowers, and plants.

D.C. Open Air Farmers' Market. Oklahoma Ave. and Benning Rd. NE (at RFK Stadium parking lot no. 6), ☎ **202/678-2800.** Year-round, Thurs and Sat 7am–5pm; June–Sept., Tues 7am–5pm. Metro: Stadium/Armory.

This market features fresh vegetables, seafood, hams, and arts and crafts.

✪ **Eastern Market.** 225 7th St. SE (between North Carolina Ave. and C St.). ☎ **202/ 546-2698.** Metro: Eastern Market.

This is the one everyone knows about, even if they've never been here. Located on Capitol Hill, Eastern Market is an inside/outside bazaar of stalls, where greengrocers, butchers, bakers, farmers, artists, crafts people, florists and other merchants vend their wares daily (except Monday), but especially on weekends. Saturday morning is the best time to go. On Sundays, the food stalls become a flea market.

✪ **Georgetown Flea Market.** In a parking lot bordering Wisconsin Ave. NW (between S and T sts.). ☎ **202/223-0289.** Open Mar–Dec, Sun 9am–5pm. Metro: Foggy Bottom, with a 30- to 40-minute walk, or take one of the 30-series buses (30, 32, 34, 36, 38B) from downtown into Georgetown.

Grab a coffee at Starbucks across the lane and get ready to barter. The Georgetown Flea Market is an institution frequented by all types of Washingtonians looking for a good deal—they often get it—on antiques, painted furniture, vintage clothing, and decorative garden urns. Nearly 100 vendors sell their wares here.

Montgomery County Farm Woman's Cooperative Market. 7155 Wisconsin Ave., in Bethesda. ☎ **301/652-2291**. Sat 7am–3:30pm. Metro: Bethesda.

Vendors set up inside every Saturday to sell preserves; homegrown vegetables; cut flowers; slabs of bacon and sausages; and mouthwatering pies, cookies, and breads.

An abbreviated version operates on Wednesdays. Outside, on Saturdays and Wednesdays, are flea-market vendors selling rugs, tablecloths, furniture, sunglasses, everything.

GOOD FOOD TO GO

Demanding jobs and hectic schedules leave Washingtonians less and less time to prepare their own meals. Or so they say. At any rate, a number of fine-food shops and bakeries are happy to come to the rescue. Even the busiest bureaucrat can find the time to pop into one of these gourmet shops for a moveable feast.

The Bread Line. 1751 Pennsylvania Ave. NW. ☎ **202/822-8900.**

Owner Mark Furstenberg is credited with revolutionizing bread baking in Washington (he started the Marvelous Market chain [see below], although he has since bowed out). At the Bread Line, he concentrates on selling freshly baked loaves of wheat bread, flat breads, baguettes, and others kinds; sandwiches made from these breads, like the roast pork bun or the muffaletta; tasty soups; and desserts such as bread puddings, pear tarts, and delicious cookies. Seating is available.

Dean & Deluca. 3276 M St. NW. ☎ **202/342-2500.** Metro: Foggy Bottom.

This famed New York store has set down roots in Washington, in a historic Georgetown building that was once an open-air market. Although it is now closed in, the building still feels airy because of the scale of the room, its high ceiling, and the presence of windows on all sides. You'll pay top prices, but maybe it's worth it, for the charcuterie, fresh fish, produce, cheeses, prepared sandwiches and cold pasta salads, and the hot-ticket desserts, like crème brûlée and tiramisu. Also on sale are housewares; on site is an espresso bar/cafe. In addition, the chain has two other cafe locations, where you can sit and eat, or take out: 1299 Pennsylvania Ave. NW (☎ **202/628-8155**) and 19th and I Streets NW (☎ **202/296-4327**).

Firehook Bakery. 1909 Q St. NW. ☎ **202/588-9296.**

This bakery is known for sourdough baguettes, apple-walnut bread, fresh fruit tarts, and, at its Farragut Square store, 912 17th St. NW (☎ **202/429-2253**), sandwiches like the smoked chicken on sesame-semolina bread.

Lawson's Gourmet. 1350 Connecticut Ave. NW. ☎ **202/775-0400.** Metro: Dupont Circle.

At this Lawson's, with outside tables and chairs clustered at the entrance to the Dupont Circle Metro station, you're at a real Washington crossroads, watching the comings and goings of sharply dressed lawyers, bohemian artistes, and panhandlers. You can buy elaborate sandwiches made to order and, very nice desserts, wines, breads, and salads. Other locations include 1350 I St. (☎ **202/789-0800**), 1776 I St. (☎ **202/296-3200**), and Metro Center, 601 G St. NW (☎ **202/393-5500**).

Marvelous Market. 1511 Connecticut Ave. NW. ☎ **202/332-3690.** Metro: Dupont Circle.

First there were the breads: sourdough, baguettes, olive, rosemary, croissants, and scones. Now, there are things to spread on the bread, like smoked salmon mousse and tapenade; pastries to die for, from gingerbread to flourless chocolate cake; and prepared foods, such as soups, empanadas, and pasta salads. The breakfast spread on Sunday mornings is sinful, and individual items, like the croissants, are tastier and less expensive here than at other bakeries. This location is grand, with 18th-century chandeliers, an antique cedar bar, and a small number of tables. Another store is at 5035 Connecticut Ave. NW (☎ **202/686-4040**).

Reeves Bakery. 1305 G St. NW. ☎ **202/628-6350.** Metro: Metro Center.

Razed to the ground in 1988 to make way for yet another office building, this dieter's nightmare took more than 3 years to find a new home 2 blocks away. Meanwhile, fans pined for the famous strawberry pie, the pineapple dream cake, the blueberry doughnuts, and chicken-salad sandwiches at the counter. The offerings here are 1950s-style, tasty but not elegant. See chapter 6 for further information.

Sutton Place Gourmet. 3201 New Mexico Ave. NW. ☎ **202/363-5800.**

Sutton Place opened in 1980 as the first full-scale, one-stop fancy food store in the Washington area, and residents took to it immediately. Now there are six. Shoppers can be obnoxious—everyone who comes here is "somebody," or thinks he is. It's an expensive store, but reliable: You'll always find the best meats; raspberries when no one else has them; a zillion types of cheeses; and ingredients for recipes in *Gourmet* magazine.

Uptown Bakers. 3313 Connecticut Ave. NW. ☎ **202/362-6262.** Metro: Cleveland Park.

If you're visiting the zoo and need a sweets fix, walk down the street to this bakery for a muffin, sweet tart, or a delicious "Vicki" bun, a cinnamon roll named for the long-gone worker who invented it. Coffee, sandwiches, and a wide range of breads are also available.

JEWELRY

Beadazzled. 1507 Connecticut Ave. NW. ☎ **202/265-BEAD.** Metro: Dupont Circle.

The friendly staff helps you assemble your own affordable jewelry from an eye-boggling array of beads and artifacts.

Charles Schwartz & Son. Willard Hotel, 1401 Pennsylvania Ave. NW. ☎ **202/737-4757.** Metro: Metro Center.

In business since 1888, Charles Schwartz specializes in diamonds, sapphires, rubies, and emeralds. The store is also one of the few distributors of Baccarat jewelry and repairs watches and jewelry. There's another branch at the Mazza Gallerie (☎ **202/363-5432**), Metro: Friendship Heights.

✪ **Galt & Brothers.** 607 15th St. NW. ☎ **202/347-1034.** Metro: Metro Center.

In existence since 1802, Galt's is the capital's oldest business and America's oldest jewelry store. The shop sells and repairs high-quality jewelry, diamonds, and all manner of colored gems. Gifts of crystal, silver, and china are also sold.

✪ **Tiffany and Company.** 5500 Wisconsin Ave., Chevy Chase, MD. ☎ **301/657-8777.** Metro: Friendship Heights.

Tiffany's is known for exquisite diamonds and other jewelry that can cost hundreds of thousands of dollars, but what you may not know is that the store carries less expensive items, as well—for example, $35 candlesticks. And if you've ever seen the movie *Breakfast at Tiffany's,* you know Tiffany's will engrave, too. Other items include tabletop gifts and fancy glitz: china; crystal; flatware; and bridal-registry service.

✪ **Tiny Jewel Box.** 1147 Connecticut Ave. NW. ☎ **202/393-2747.** Metro: Farragut North.

The first place Washingtonians go for estate and antique jewelry.

MALLS

Chevy Chase Pavilion. 5345 Wisconsin Ave. NW. ☎ **202/686-5335.** Metro: Friendship Heights.

This is a manageably sized mall, with about 50 stores and restaurants, anchored by an Embassy Suites Hotel. The inside is unusually pretty, with three levels winding around a skylit atrium. Giant palm trees, arrangements of fresh flowers, and seasonal events, such as a ballet performance by a visiting Russian troop at Christmastime, add panache. Stores include the Limited; a 2-level Pottery Barn; a Bath and Body shop; and a Joan and David shoe store. A small food court, the Cheesecake Factory, and the California Pizza Kitchen are among the eating options.

Fashion Center at Pentagon City. 1400 S. Hayes St., Arlington, VA. ☎ **703/415-2400.** Metro: Pentagon City.

Nordstrom's and Macy's are the biggest attractions in this block-long, five-story, elegant shoppers' paradise that also houses a Ritz-Carlton Hotel (the site where Ken Starr nabbed Monica Lewinsky); office suites; multiplex theaters; and a sprawling food court. Villeroy and Boch, Crate & Barrel, and Eddie Bauer are among the nearly 167 shops.

Mazza Gallerie. 5100 Wisconsin Ave. NW. ☎ **202/966-6114.** Metro: Friendship Heights.

Undergoing a renovation scheduled for completion in 1999, the mall is looking down at its heels right now, despite the presence of Neiman-Marcus. And the fact that McDonald's is the mall's main restaurant doesn't help. With sprucing up, the Mazza should return as an attractive shopping center, with its skylit atrium and stores like Ann Taylor and Benetton's. The mall has theaters on the lower level, and there is access to Chevy Chase Pavilion, the subway, and to the Hecht's department store via the Metro tunnel.

The Pavilion at the Old Post Office. 1100 Pennsylvania Ave. NW. ☎ **202/289-4224.** Metro: Federal Triangle.

This is a tourist trap with souvenir shops and a food court. Noontime concerts are a draw, as is the view of the city from the building's clock tower, 315 feet up.

Potomac Mills. 30 miles south on I-95. Accessible by car, or by shuttle bus leaving from designated places throughout the area, including Dupont Circle and Metro Center. Call ☎ **800/VA-MILLS** or **703/490-5948** for information about Potomac Mills; call ☎ **703/551-1050** for information about the shuttle bus service.

When you are stuck in the traffic that always clogs this section of I-95, you may wonder if a trip to Potomac Mills is worth it. Believe it or not, this place attracts more visitors than any other in the Washington area, and twice as many as the next top draw, the Smithsonian's National Air & Space Museum. It's the largest indoor outlet mall around, with more than 225 shops, including New York's Barney's, DKNY; Nordstrom's, IKEA, Samsonite, and Jones New York.

The Shops at Georgetown Park. 3222 M St. NW. ☎ **202/342-8180.** Metro: Foggy Bottom, then a 20-minute walk.

This is a deluxe mall, where you'll see beautiful people shopping for beautiful things, and paying stunning prices at stores with European names: Nicolo (men's clothes) and Arpelli's (leather goods). The diplomatic set and well-heeled foreign travelers favor these stores, so you're bound to hear a number of languages, especially French and Italian. For more information, see the description in Georgetown walking tour, below. Wander here, then set off for the streets of Georgetown for more shopping.

The Shops at National Place. 1331 Pennsylvania Ave. NW. ☎ **202/662-1250.** Metro: Metro Center.

You enter through the J. W. Marriott Hotel or at F Street, between 13th and 14th Streets. National Place has more than 75 specialty shops and eateries, including Arpelli Leather, Casual Corner, the Russian Store, the newly opened Filene's Basement discount department store, an international food court; and the National Cafe restaurant.

Tyson's Corner Center. 9160 Chain Bridge Rd., McLean, VA. ☎ **703/893-9400.** Tyson's Corner II, The Galleria, 2001 International Dr., McLean, VA. ☎ **703/827-7700.** Metro: West Falls Church, take shuttle.

Facing each other across Chain Bridge Road, these two gigantic malls could lead to shopper's overload. Tyson's Corner Center, the first and less expensive, has Nordstrom's, Bloomingdale's, and JCPenney, and specialty stores, such as Abercrombie & Fitch and Crabtree & Evelyn. The Galleria has Macy's, Saks Fifth Avenue, and more than 100 upscale boutiques.

✪ **Union Station.** 50 Massachusetts Ave. NE. ☎ **202/371-9441.** Metro: Union Station.

After the National Air & Space Museum, this is the next most popular stop in Washington. The architecture is magnificent. The mall's more than 120 shops include the Nature Company, Brookstone, and Appalachian Spring; among the places to eat are America, B. Smith, and an international food court. There's also a nine-screen movie theater complex.

White Flint Mall. 11301 Rockville Pike, Kensington, MD. ☎ **301/468-5777.** Metro: White Flint, then take the free "White Flint" shuttle, which runs every 12 to 15 minutes.

Another Bloomingdale's and another long trip in the car or on the Metro, but once you're there, you can shop, take in a movie, or dine cheaply or well. Notable stores include Lord & Taylor's, a huge Borders Books & Music, Ann Taylor, and Coach.

MEN'S CLOTHES & SHOES

Banana Republic. Wisconsin and M sts. ☎ **202/333-2554.** Metro: Foggy Bottom, with a 20-minute walk.

Everything bears a Banana Republic label, and clothes run from casual to dressy: wool gabardine and wool crepe pants; khakis; shorts; vests; and jackets. Expect mid to high prices. Women's clothes are also available Another location is at F and 13th Streets NW (☎ **202/638-2724**).

Beau Monde. International Sq., 1814 K St. NW. ☎ **202/466-7070.** Metro: Farragut West.

This boutique sells all Italian-made clothes. Some double-breasted traditional suits are available, but the styles are mostly avant-garde.

Britches of Georgetown. See entry in Georgetown walking tour, p. 254.

Brooks Brothers. 1840 L St. NW. ☎ **202/659-4650.** Metro: Farragut West or Farragut North.

This is where to go for the K Street/Capitol Hill pinstriped power look. Brooks Bros. sells the fine line of Peal's English shoes. This store made the news as the place where Monica Lewinsky bought a tie for President Clinton. The store has other locations at Potomac Mills (see "Malls," above) and at 5500 Wisconsin Ave., in Chevy Chase, MD.

Burberry's. 1155 Connecticut Ave. NW. ☎ **202/463-3000.** Metro: Farragut North.

Here you'll find those plaid-lined trench coats, of course, along with well-tailored but conservative English clothing for men and women.

Gianfranco Ferre. 5301 Wisconsin Ave. NW. ☎ **202/244-6633.** Metro: Friendship Heights.

Shop here for the sleek and sexy European look. This store also features interesting suits and some casual wear.

Giotto. Georgetown Park. ☎ **202/338-6223.** Metro: Foggy Bottom, with a 20-minute walk.

You'll find Italian designer sports and dress wear here.

MISCELLANEOUS

Al's Magic Shop. 1012 Vermont Ave. NW. ☎ **202/789-2800.** Metro: McPherson Square.

This first-rate novelty shop is presided over by prestidigitator and local character Al Cohen, who is only too happy to demonstrate his latest magic trick or practical joke.

Animation Sensations. See entry in Georgetown walking tour, p. 251.

Chocolate Moose. 1800 M St. NW. ☎ **202/463-0992.** Metro: Farragut North.

Here's where to go when you need a surprising and unexpected gift—they stock wacky cards; a range of useful, funny, and lovely presents; candy; eccentric clothing; and jewelry.

Discovery Channel Store: Destination D.C. 601 F St. NW. ☎ **202/639-0908.** Metro: Gallery Place/MCI Center.

This flagship store for the Discovery Channel is purposely designed to resemble a museum as much as a store, with interactive displays, like the virtual dinosaur "dig," that invite participation. The idea is, once you've become involved, you'll want to buy. And there's plenty to buy. The store arranges merchandise according to theme for each of its four levels: Paleo World (fossils, jewelry, gems, minerals); Ocean Planet (ceramics, clothing, games); Wild World Cultures (books, home decorating, music, gardening); Sky Science (science kits, telescopes, and globes). Make sure you make it to the top floor to see the 15-minute film, *Destination D.C.*

Ginza, "Things Japanese". 1721 Connecticut Ave. NW. ☎ **202/331-7991.** Metro: Dupont Circle.

Everything Japanese is here, from incense and kimonos, to futons and Zen rock gardens.

Map Store. 1636 I St. NW. ☎ **202/628-2608.** Metro: Farragut West.

Going somewhere? Or just daydreaming about leaving? This fascinating boutique is always packed with map and globe enthusiasts. It's a good spot for D.C. souvenirs.

MUSEUM SHOPS

The gift stores in the Smithsonian's 14 Washington museums are terrific places to shop, with wares related to the focus of the individual museums. The largest Smithsonian store is in the National Museum of American History. The mart in the Smithsonian's Arts & Industries Building is nearly as extensive, since it sells all of the items offered in the museum catalogs. Smithsonian's museum shop buyers travel the world for unusual items, many of which are made exclusively for the shops.

The Smithsonian doesn't corner the market on museum merchandise, however. Here's a sample of smaller museum gift shops and some of the unique gifts that make them worth a stop. (See chapter 7 for museum locations and hours.)

The National Gallery of Art gift shop. (on the north side of the Mall, on Constitution Avenue NW, between 3rd and 7th streets) is not so small, actually. Its wares include printed reproductions, stationery, and jewelry, and designs are all based on works in the gallery's permanent collections, as well as those from special exhibitions. The shop also has one of the largest selections of books on art history and architecture in the country and a generous offering of children's products (books, art kits, games, and so on).

The gift shop at the **Textile Museum** (2320 S St. NW; Metro: Dupont Circle, Q St. exit, then walk a couple of blocks up Massachusetts Avenue until you see S. Street.) offers an extensive selection of books on carpets and textiles, as well as Indian silk scarves, kilim pillows, Tibetan prayer rugs, and other out-of-the-ordinary items.

Washington National Cathedral's main shop (Massachusetts and Wisconsin avenues NW; entrance on Wisconsin Avenue), in the crypt of the Gothic cathedral, sells books, stained glass, and tapes. The Herb Cottage, located across the lane from the Cathedral is a delightful oasis, selling dried herbs and garden gifts. The Greenhouse shop, located elsewhere on the grounds, is one of the best and certainly most charming places in town to buy flowering plants and live herbs.

POLITICAL MEMORABILIA

Capitol Coin and Stamp Co. Inc. 1701 L St. NW. ☎ **202/296-0400.** Metro: Farragut North.

A museum of political memorabilia—pins, posters, banners—and all of it is for sale. This is also a fine resource for the endangered species of coin and stamp collectors.

✪ **Political Americana.** Union Station. ☎ **202/547-1685.** Metro: Union Station.

This is another great place to pick up souvenirs from a visit to D.C. The store sells political novelty items; books; bumper stickers; old campaign buttons; and historical memorabilia. A second location is at 685 15th St. NW (☎ **202/547-1817**).

RECORDS, TAPES & CDS

Borders Books & Music. 1800 L St. NW. ☎ **202/466-4999.** Metro: Farragut North.

Besides being a fabulous bookstore, Borders offers the best prices in town for CDs and tapes and a wide range of music.

HMV. 1229 Wisconsin Ave. NW. ☎ **202/333-9292.** Metro: Foggy Bottom, with a 20-minute walk.

This London-based record and tape store is fun to visit, with its cunning clientele, party atmosphere, and headphones at the ready for easy listening. But you can get a better deal almost anywhere else.

Melody Record Shop. 1623 Connecticut Ave. NW. ☎ **202/232-4002.** Metro: Dupont Circle, Q St. exit.

CDs, cassettes, and tapes are discounted 10% to 20% here, new releases 20% to 30%. Melody offers a wide variety of rock, classical, jazz, pop, show, folk music, and international selections. This is also a good place to shop for discounted portable electronic equipment, blank tapes, and cassettes. The knowledgeable staff is a plus.

Olsson's Books & Records. See entry in Georgetown walking tour, p. 254.

Tower Records. 2000 Pennsylvania Ave. NW. ☎ **202/331-2400.** Metro: Foggy Bottom.

When you need a record at midnight on Christmas Eve, you go to Tower. The large, funky store, across the street from George Washington University, has a wide choice of records, cassettes, and compact discs in every category—but the prices are high.

12" Dance Records. 2010 P St. NW, 2nd floor. ☎ **202/659-2010.** Metro: Dupont Circle.

Disco lives. If you ever moved to it on a dance floor, Wresch Dawidjian and his staff of DJs have got it, or they can get it. There's always a DJ mixing it up live in the store, and they pump the beats out into the street.

WINE & SPIRITS

The following liquor stores are among the best in the city for choice and value.

Calvert Woodley Liquors. 4339 Connecticut Ave. NW. ☎ **202/966-4400.** Metro: Van Ness–UDC.

This is a large store with a friendly staff, nice selections, and good cheeses (about 300 to choose from) and other foods to accompany your drinks.

✪ **Central Liquor.** 917 F St. NW. ☎ **202/737-2800.** Metro: Metro Center or Gallery Place.

This store's great volume allows it to offer the best prices in town on wines and liquor.

Eagle Wine & Liquor. 3345 M St. NW. ☎ **202/333-5500.**

Georgetown residents come to this longtime establishment (here for 50 years) for its discounts and for assistance from a well-informed staff.

MacArthur Liquor. 4877 MacArthur Blvd. NW. ☎ **202/338-1433.**

It's always busy, because the staff is so knowledgeable and enthusiastic, and because the shop has such an extensive and reasonably priced selection of excellent wines, both imported and domestic.

WOMEN'S CLOTHES & SHOES

If Washington women don't dress well, it isn't for lack of stores. The following boutiques range in styles from baggy grunge to the crisply tailored, from Laura Ashley to black leather.

Ann Taylor. Union Station. ☎ **202/371-8010.** Metro: Union Station.

Specializes in American-style, chic clothing, Joan and David and other footwear, and accessories. Other locations include 1720 K St. NW (☎ **202/466-3544**), 600 13th St. NW (☎ **202/737-0325**), and Georgetown Park, 3222 M St. NW (☎ **202/338-5290**).

Betsy Fisher. 1224 Connecticut Ave. NW. ☎ **202/785-1975.** Metro: Dupont Circle.

A walk past the store is all it takes to know that this shop is a tad different. Its window front and racks show off whimsically feminine fashions, including hats, of new American Designers.

Chanel Boutique. 1455 Pennsylvania Ave. NW, in the courtyard of the Willard Inter-Continental Hotel. ☎ **202/638-5055.** Metro: Metro Center.

A modest selection of Chanel signature designs, accessories, and jewelry, at immodest prices.

✪ **Commander Salamander.** 1420 Wisconsin Ave. NW. ☎ **202/337-2265.** Metro: Foggy Bottom, with a 20-minute walk.

Too cool. Commander Salamander has a little bit of everything, including designer items, some of which are quite affordable: Dolce and Gabanna dresses; Jean Paul Gaultier and Oldham creations; $1 ties; and handmade jackets with Axl jewelry sewn on, for more than $1000. Loud music, young crowd, funky and sweet.

Hit or Miss. The Shops at National Place. ☎ **202/347-0280.** Metro: Metro Center.

Here you'll find a mixture of professional and casual clothes for women at bargain prices. Other locations include 1140 Connecticut Ave. NW (☎ **202/223-8231**), 1701 K St. NW (☎ **202/833-8344**), and 900 19th St. (☎ **202/785-2226**).

Pirjo. 1044 Wisconsin Ave. NW. ☎ **202/337-1390.** Metro: Foggy Bottom, with a 20-minute walk.

Come here for funky, baggy, and pretty creations of designers including the Finnish Marimekko and others: Bettina, Flax, VIP. Styles range from casual to dressy; Pirjo sells elegant jewelry to boot.

Rizik's. 1100 Connecticut Ave. NW. ☎ **202/223-4050.** Metro: Farragut North.

This is downtown high fashion, closer to art than clothing. Designs are by Caroline Herrara, Armani, Oscar de la Renta, and their ilk.

Saks-Jandel. 5510 Wisconsin Ave., Chevy Chase, MD. ☎ **301/652-2250.** Metro: Friendship Heights.

This store displays elegant afternoon and evening wear by major European and American designers: Giorgio Armani, Hervé Leger, Vera Wang, Louis Féraud, Christian Dior, Sonia Rykiel, Yves Saint-Laurent Rive Gauche, Isaac Mizrahi (this was the site of the designer's promo for his movie, *Unzipped*), John Galliano, and many others. Saks-Jandel has an international clientele.

Secondhand Rose. See entry in Georgetown walking tour, p. 255.

Talbots. 1227 Connecticut Ave. NW. ☎ **202/887-6973.** Metro: Farragut North.

Talbots sells career and casual clothes with a decidedly conservative bent, and accessories to go with them. Another branch is at Georgetown Park, 3222 M St. NW (☎ **202/338-3510**).

Toast & Strawberries. 1608 Connecticut Ave. NW. ☎ **202/234-2424.** Metro: Dupont Circle.

You'll see clothes from around the world and from local designers, too. Many in the collection are one of a kind, some are casual and some ethnic, but all are fun to wear. The shop also sells some accessories.

Victoria's Secret. Union Station. ☎ **202/682-0686.** Metro: Metro Center.

Washington women really like the chain's feminine, sexy array of lingerie, so you'll find you're never too far from one of the shops. Other locations at Connecticut and L sreets NW (☎ **202/293-7530** and Georgetown Park (☎ **202/965-5457**).

WALKING TOUR
Georgetown Shopping

Start: M and 29th Streets NW.

Directions: To get to Georgetown by public transportation, you can either ride the Metro to Foggy Bottom and walk for 10 or 15 minutes, or take one of the 30-series buses (30, 32, 34, 36, 38B), all of which travel from downtown into Georgetown. Call Metro (☎ **202/637-7000**) for exact information.

Finish: Wisconsin Avenue and Q Street NW.

Time: Allow 1 to 3 hours, depending on how much time you spend browsing or actually shopping.

Best Times: During store hours—most stores open at 10am daily; antique, art, and crafts stores keep more conventional hours, usually closing at 5pm or 6pm; book and record stores and some of the more offbeat clothing stores stay open later, until 7pm at least, and as late as midnight for some on weekends.

In Georgetown, you can combine shopping and browsing (there are hundreds of stores) with a meal at a good restaurant, crowd-watching over cappuccino at a cafe, and even a little sightseeing. The hub is at Wisconsin Avenue and M Street, and most of the stores are on those two arteries. In addition to shops, you'll encounter street vendors hawking T-shirts and handmade jewelry.

If you drive into Georgetown, check out the side streets off Wisconsin Avenue above M Street for spots. The Shops at Georgetown Park (see below) offers validated parking with purchases of $10 or more.

ALONG PENNSYLVANIA AVENUE, WHICH QUICKLY TURNS INTO M STREET NW For the first part of this shopping tour, stroll along M Street, with a few diversions, from 29th to 33rd Streets. Start at the:

1. **Animation Sensations,** 2820 Pennsylvania Ave. NW (☎ **202/337-5024**). It's fun to peruse this collection of original animation cels and drawings, comic book/strip art, vintage movie posters, movie star autographs, Disney/Warner Brothers/Hanna-Barbera character figurines, and movie memorabilia. Open Monday to Saturday 10am to 6pm, Sunday noon to 5pm.

   As you continue along the block, Pennsylvania Avenue becomes M Street. Dip left on 29th Street to:

2. **Spectrum Gallery,** 1132 29th St. NW (just below M St.) (☎ **202/333-0954**), a cooperative venture since 1968, in which 30 professional Washington-area artists, including painters, potters, sculptors, photographers, collagists, and print-makers, share in shaping gallery policy, maintenance, and operation. The art is reasonably priced. Open Tuesday to Saturday noon to 6pm, Sunday noon to 5pm, and by appointment.

   Walk around the corner onto M Street to:

3. **Grafix,** 2904 M St. NW (☎ **202/342-0610**), which carries a noteworthy collection of vintage posters (mostly French), 16th- to 20th-century maps, 19th-century prints, vintage magazines from the turn of the century through the 1930s, and other collectibles. Open Tuesday, Wednesday, and Friday 11am to 6pm; Thursday 11am to 9pm; and Saturday 11am to 5pm. Next door is:

4. ✪ **American Hand Plus,** 2906 M St. NW (☎ **202/965-3273**), which features exquisite contemporary handcrafted American ceramics and jewelry, plus international objets d'art. Open Monday to Saturday 11am to 6pm, Sunday 1 to 5pm. A little farther down the street you'll stumble upon:

5. **Georgetown Antiques Center,** 2918 M St. NW, which houses the Cherub Antiques Gallery (☎ **202/337-2224**) and its collection of art nouveau and art deco, art glass (signed Tiffany, Steuben, Lalique, and Gallé), Liberty arts and crafts, and Louis Icart etchings. Sharing the premises is **Michael Getz Antiques** (☎ **202/338-3811**), which sells American, English, and continental silver; porcelain lamps; and many fireplace accessories. Open Monday to Saturday 11am to 6pm, Sunday noon to 5pm; closed Sunday July and August.

⬤ **TAKE A BREAK** At Washington Harbour (30th St., a block south of M St.) is a riverside development with an esplanade leading to a fountain and a group of restaurants with indoor windowed and outdoor umbrella-table seating overlooking the Potomac. The best of these is **Sequoia,** which features American fare (details in chapter 6).

Backtrack to M Street and turn left, walking until you see:

6. **Barnes & Noble,** 3040 M St. NW (☎ 202/965-9880), a wonderful three-story shop that discounts all hardcovers 10%, *New York Times* hardcover best-sellers 30%, and *New York Times* paperback best-sellers 20%. It has sizable software, travel-book, and children's sections. A cafe on the second level hosts concerts. Open daily 9am to 11pm.

7. **Eddie Bauer** (☎ 202/342-2121), which shares the same address, is a handsome two-level emporium specializing in outdoorsy sportswear for men and women. Come here for fly-fishing equipment (and books about fishing), backpacks, English Barbour jackets, hunter's caps, Stetson hats, luggage, flashlights, binoculars, hiking boots, Swiss Army knives, and other accoutrements of the adventurous lifestyle. Open Monday through Saturday 10am to 9pm, Sunday noon to 6pm.

Turn left on 31st Street NW and continue past the canal; on your left is the:

8. **Yes! Bookshop,** 1035 31st St. NW (☎ 800/YES-1516 or 202/338-7874 for a free catalog). The shelves of this unique store are stocked with a wealth of literature (both books and books on tape) on personal growth and personal. The store also sells books on health, natural medicine, men's and women's studies, mythology, creative writing, Jungian psychology, how to save the planet, ancient history, and Native American traditions. Cassettes and CDs include non-Western music, instrumental music, New Age music, and instruction in everything from quitting smoking to astral projection and hypnosis. Also available is a large number of instructional videocassettes. Open Monday to Saturday 10am to 7pm, Sunday noon to 6pm.

Cross 31st Street to South Street, which takes you over to Wisconsin Avenue, which you cross. Walk 1 block up to Grace Street and turn left:

⬤ **TAKE A BREAK** Stop for croissants and cappuccino, a Camembert sandwich on a baguette, or afternoon tea with sumptuous desserts at Patisserie Café Didier, 3206 Grace St. NW.

Now continue along Wisconsin Avenue, crossing the canal and walking until you reach:

9. ✪ **The Shops at Georgetown Park,** 3222 M St. NW, at Wisconsin Ave. (☎ 202/298-5577). This four-story complex of about 100 shops belongs, architecturally, to two worlds: outside, quietly Federal, in keeping with the character of the neighborhood; inside, flamboyantly Victorian, with a huge skylight, fountains, and ornate chandeliers. You could spend hours here exploring branches of the nation's most exclusive specialty stores. Represented are **Ann Taylor, Caché, J. Crew,** and **Polo/Ralph Lauren** (for men and women). Men will find GQ-caliber Italian designer sportswear at **Giotto** and Italian-designer evening wear at **Nicolo.** Also featured are many gift/lifestyle boutiques, such as **Circuit City Express, Sharper Image, Crabtree & Evelyn,** and the fascinating **Gallery of History** (framed historical documents). If you have kids, take them to **F.A.O. Schwarz** and **Learningsmith** (billing itself as "the general store for the curious

Walking Tour—Georgetown Shopping

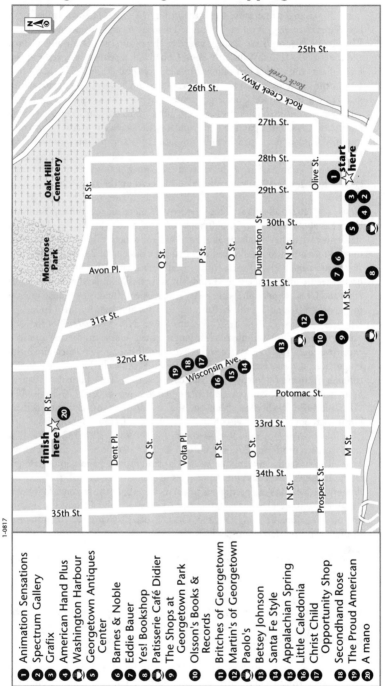

1. Animation Sensations
2. Spectrum Gallery
3. Grafix
4. American Hand Plus
5. Washington Harbour
6. Georgetown Antiques Center
7. Barnes & Noble
8. Eddie Bauer
9. Yes! Bookshop
10. Patisserie Café Didier
11. The Shops at Georgetown Park
12. Olsson's Books & Records
13. Britches of Georgetown
14. Martin's of Georgetown
15. Paolo's
16. Betsey Johnson
17. Santa Fe Style
18. Appalachian Spring
19. Little Caledonia
20. Christ Child Opportunity Shop
21. Secondhand Rose
22. The Proud American
23. A mano

1-0817

mind," it has many interactive facilities for children). An Old Town Trolley ticket booth (see chapter 4) is on the premises. There are several restaurants, including **Clyde's** (see chapter 6 for details), gourmet emporium/cafe **Dean and Deluca,** and the parklike **Canal Walk Café Food Court** with a painted sky overhead, and many plants and garden furnishings. An archaeological exhibit of artifacts found during the complex's excavation can be viewed on Level 2. Georgetown Park maintains a full-service Concierge Center offering gift wrapping, worldwide shipping, postal/fax/photocopy services, gift certificates, and even sightseeing information. Validated parking in the underground garage is available with minimum $10 purchase. Open Monday to Saturday 10am to 9pm, Sunday noon to 6pm.

Exit onto M Street, turn right, cross at the corner of Wisconsin Avenue, then cross Wisconsin Avenue to the other side and head up the avenue to:

10. ✪ **Olsson's Books and Records,** 1239 Wisconsin Ave. NW, between M and N sts. (☎ **202/338-9544**). This 21-year-old, independent, quality bookstore chain has about 60,000 to 70,000 books on its shelves. Members of the helpful staff know what they're talking about and will order books the store doesn't have in stock. Competition has forced them to offer discounts: 25% off *Washington Post* best-sellers, 20% off certain hardcover books, and 10% off certain paperbacks that are promoted as "good reads" by store staff. Similar discounts exist for tapes and CDs. Regular prices are pretty good. Open Monday to Thursday 10am to 11pm, Friday and Saturday 10am to midnight, Sunday 11am to 11pm.

11. **Britches of Georgetown,** 1247 Wisconsin Ave. NW (☎ **202/338-3330**), is much patronized by well-dressed Washington men. It sells moderately priced to expensive dress apparel, both designer wear and from its own label. You'll find Hugo Boss, Donna Karan, and St. Andrews, Southwick. Hours are Monday through Wednesday, Friday, and Saturday 10am to 7pm; Thursday 10am to 8pm; and Sunday noon to 6pm. Another location is at 1776 K St. NW (☎ **202/347-8994**). Also check out the casual/sportswear division, Britches Great Outdoors, at 1225 Wisconsin Ave. NW (☎ **202/333-3666**).

12. **Martin's of Georgetown,** 1304 Wisconsin Ave. NW (☎ **202/338-6144**). This shop has been proffering exquisite wares since 1929. Come in and feast your eyes on Martin's selection of Lalique vases, Christofle silver, hand-painted Herend china, Limoges boxes, and other fine lines of china, silver, crystal, flatware, and dinnerware. Martin's is a prestigious bridal registry (both the Nixon and Johnson daughters registered here). You'll find stuffed animals, baby gifts, picture frames, and other quality gift items here, too. Open Tuesday to Saturday 10am to 6pm; Georgetown Inn, next door, validates parking.

☕ **TAKE A BREAK** **Martin's Tavern,** 1264 Wisconsin Ave. NW ☎ 202/333-7370.

13. **Betsey Johnson,** 1319 Wisconsin Ave. NW (☎ **202/338-4090**). New York's flamboyant flower-child designer has a Georgetown shop. She personally decorated the bubble-gum-pink walls. Her sexy, offbeat play-dress-up styles are great party and club clothes for the young and the still-skinny young at heart. Open weekdays 11am to 7pm, Saturday 11am to 8pm, Sunday noon to 6pm.

14. **Santa Fe Style,** 1413 Wisconsin Ave. NW (☎ **202/333-3747**). Here you'll find high-quality southwestern merchandise, mostly handmade items from New Mexico and Arizona. The inventory includes silver jewelry, picture frames, oxidized-iron animal decorations, barbed-wire art, furniture, pottery, colorful painted sculptures made from barn-roof tin, birdhouses, southwestern cookbooks, and more. Open Monday to Saturday 10am to 6pm, Sunday noon to 5pm.

15. Appalachian Spring, 1415 Wisconsin Ave. NW, at P St. (☎ **202/337-5780**), brings country crafts to citified Georgetown. They sell pottery, jewelry, newly made pieced and appliqué quilts, stuffed dolls and animals, candles, rag rugs, hand-blown glassware, an incredible collection of kaleidoscopes, glorious weavings, and wooden kitchenware. Everything in the store is made by hand in the United States. There's another branch in Union Station (☎ **202/682-0505**). Open Monday to Saturday 10am to 8pm, Sunday noon to 6pm.

16. ✪ Little Caledonia, 1419 Wisconsin Ave. NW (☎ **202/333-4700**), is a delightful warren of tiny rooms filled with indoor and outdoor furnishings (18th- and 19th-century mahogany reproductions are featured), ceramic figures, exquisite upholstery and drapery fabrics, candles, tablecloths, wallpapers, lamps, and much, much more. It's been here for 60 years. Open Monday to Saturday 10am to 6pm, and Thanksgiving to Christmas Sunday noon to 5pm.

17. Christ Child Opportunity Shop, 1427 Wisconsin Ave. NW (☎ **202/333-6635**). Proceeds from merchandise bought here go to children's charities. Among the first-floor items (all donations), I saw a wicker trunk for $5 and the usual thrift-shop jumble of jewelry, clothes, shoes, hats, and odds and ends. Upstairs, higher quality merchandise is left on consignment, it's more expensive, but if you know antiques, you might find bargains in jewelry, silver, china, quilts, and other items. Open Tuesday to Saturday 10am to 3:45pm, closed in August.

18. Secondhand Rose, 1516 Wisconsin Ave. NW, between P St. and Volta Place (☎ **202/337-3378**). This upscale second-floor consignment shop specializes in designer merchandise. Creations by Chanel, Armani, Donna Karan, Calvin Klein, Yves Saint-Laurent, Ungaro, Ralph Lauren, and others are sold at about a third of the original price. Recent offerings included a gorgeous Scaasi black velvet and yellow satin ball gown for $400 (it was $1,200 new) and Yves Saint-Laurent pumps in perfect condition for $45. Everything is in style, in season, and in excellent condition. Secondhand Rose is also a great place to shop for gorgeous furs, designer shoes and bags, and costume jewelry. Open weekdays 11am to 6pm, Saturday 10am to 6pm.

19. Gore-Dean/The Proud American, 1529 Wisconsin Ave. NW (☎ **202/625-1776**), is somewhat of a misnomer. Although its offerings include some American pieces, the store specializes in 18th- and 19th-century European furnishings, decorative accessories, paintings, prints, and porcelains. Open Monday to Saturday 10am to 6pm, Sunday noon to 5pm.

20. ✪ A mano, 1677 Wisconsin Ave. NW (☎ **202/298-7200**), sells unique handmade imported French and Italian ceramics that owner Adam Mahr brings back from his frequent forages to Europe. Open Monday to Saturday 10am to 6pm, Sunday noon to 5pm.

10

Washington, D.C., After Dark

Two kinds of tickets in Washington are nearly impossible to obtain without a subscription: tickets to Redskins games (forget about it) and tickets to the Washington Opera (if you act now, it may not be too late). Fortunately, that still leaves you a cornucopia of entertainment options, from attending a Shakespeare play to laughing it up at the Improv Comedy Club. The venues for every type of theater, dance, and musical entertainment are here, with new ones opening everyday.

Of course, not all forms of nightlife require tickets. If your idea of relaxation involves a visit to a bar or a nightclub, you will find plenty of options. For a civilized bar experience, see chapter 5, "Behind Hotel Bars: The Willard's Round Robin Bartender Tells All." The bars and clubs listed within this chapter are recommended for livelier adventures.

Even if you're on a limited budget, you'll find lots to do at night in Washington. For one thing, many of the museums and other attractions you visit during the day often stage free or inexpensive cultural performances in the evening. Secondly, if you are here in late spring through early fall, you'll want to know about all the free outdoor entertainment taking place throughout the city—flip to "Free Shows" at the end of this chapter for more information. Finally, you should know about the **Kennedy Center's "Performing Arts for Everyone" program.** Launched in the spring of 1997, the successful program offers free concerts by mostly local performers each evening at 6pm in its Grand Foyer. The Kennedy Center is also one of several Washington theaters that operates a "pay what you can" program, whose tickets are good on certain days for selected performances on the center's stages. Read on for details.

In addition to the listings below, check the Friday "Weekend" section of the *Washington Post,* which will inform you about children's theater; sports events; flower shows; and all else. The *City Paper,* available free at restaurants, bookstores, and other places around town, is another good source.

TICKETS

TICKETplace, Washington's only discount, day-of-show, ticket outlet, has one location: in the Old Post Office Pavilion, 1100 Pennsylvania Ave. NW (Metro: Federal Triangle). Call ☎ **202/ TICKETS** for information. TICKETplace is a service of the

Cultural Alliance of Greater Washington. On the day of performance only (except Sunday and Monday, see below), you can buy half-price tickets (with cash, select debit cards, or traveler's checks) to performances at most major Washington area theaters and concert halls, not only for dramatic productions, but for opera, ballet, and other events as well. TICKETplace is open Tuesday to Saturday from 11am to 6pm; half-price tickets for Sunday and Monday shows are sold on Saturday. Although you purchase the ticket for half price, you will have to pay a service charge, 10% of the full face value of the ticket.

Full-price tickets for most performances in town can be bought through **Ticketmaster** (☎ **202/432-SEAT**) at Hecht's Department Store, 12th and G Streets NW, and at George Washington University's Lisner Auditorium, 1730 21st St. NW (at H Street; Metro: Foggy Bottom). You can purchase tickets to Washington theatrical, musical, and other events from home by calling ☎ **800/551-SEAT.** Another similar ticket outlet is **Protix** (☎ **800/955-5566** or 703/ 218-6500).

1 Theater

Theatrical productions in Washington, D.C., are first-rate and varied. Almost anything on Broadway has either been previewed here or will eventually come here. Washington, D.C., also has several nationally acclaimed repertory companies and a theater specializing in Shakespearean productions. Additional theater offerings, including those at the Kennedy Center, are listed under "Other Performing Arts" later in this chapter.

Arena Stage. 1101 6th St. SW at Maine Ave. SW. ☎ **202/488-3300.** Tickets $26–$45; discounts available for students, people with disabilities, groups, and senior citizens. A limited number of half-price tickets, called HOTTIX, are available 90 minutes before most performances (call for details). $5 reserved parking on-site and in satellite lots, as well as street parking. Metro: Waterfront.

Founded by the brilliant Zelda Fichandler, the Arena Stage, now in its fifth decade, is home to one of the oldest acting ensembles in the nation. Several works nurtured here have moved to Broadway, and many graduates have gone on to commercial stardom, among them Ned Beatty, James Earl Jones, Robert Prosky, Jane Alexander, and George Grizzard.

Arena presents eight productions annually on two stages: the **Fichandler** (a theater-in-the-round) and the smaller, fan-shaped **Kreeger.** In addition, the Arena houses the **Old Vat,** a space used for new play readings and special productions.

The 1997–1998 September-to-June season included productions of Chekhov's *Uncle Vanya; Lovers and Executioners* by Montfleury, adapted by John Strand; *Black No More,* by Syl Jones; and Moss Hart and George Kaufman's *You Can't Take it with You.* The 1998–1999 lineup promises Williams's *Cat on a Hot Tin Roof; Expecting Isabel,* by Lisa Loomer; *Thunder Knocking on the Door,* a musical by Keith Glover; *The Faraway Nearby,* by John Murrell; Clare Booth Luce's *The Women;* the Marx Brothers' *Animal Crackers;* the 1998 Pulitzer Prize winning play, *How I Learned to Drive,* by Paula Vogel; and *Oak and Ivy,* about African-American poet Paul Dunbar, by Kathleen McGee-Anderson.

Should you have any questions, call the number above. Arena Stage staff and volunteers are remarkable for their courtesy and helpfulness. The theater has always championed new plays and playwrights and is committed to producing the works of playwrights from diverse cultures. Molly D. Smith is the Arena Stage's new artistic director.

Ford's Theatre. 511 10th St. NW (between E and F sts.). ☎ **202/347-4833,** TDD 202/ 347-5599 for listings, 800/955-5566 or 703/218-6500 to charge tickets. Tickets $27–$40; discounts available for families, also for senior citizens at matinee performances and any time on the "day of" for evening shows; both seniors and students with ID can get "rush" tickets an hour before performances if tickets are available. Metro: Metro Center or Gallery Place.

This is the theater where, on the evening of April 14, 1865, actor John Wilkes Booth shot President Abraham Lincoln. The assassination marked the end of what had been John T. Ford's very popular theater; it remained closed for more than a century. In 1968, Ford's reopened, completely restored to its 1865 appearance, based on photographs; sketches; newspaper articles and samples of wallpaper and curtain material from museum collections. The presidential box is decorated and furnished as it was on that fateful night, including the original crimson damask sofa and framed engraving of George Washington.

Ford's season is more or less year-round (it's closed for a while in the summer). Several of its productions have gone on to Broadway and off-Broadway. Recent shows have included *Paper Moon, Twilight in Los Angeles* with Anna Deavere Smith, and *Kudzu,* a Southern musical.

A big event here is the nationally televised "A Festival at Ford's," which is a celebrity-studded bash usually held in the fall and attended by the president and first lady. A Washington tradition is the holiday performance of Dickens' *A Christmas Carol.*

National Theatre. 1321 Pennsylvania Ave. NW. ☎ **202/628-6161** or 800/447-7400 to charge tickets by phone. Tickets $30–$75; discounts available for students, seniors, military personnel, and people with disabilities. Metro: Metro Center.

The luxurious, Federal-style National Theatre is the oldest continuously operating theater in Washington (since 1835) and the third-oldest in the nation. It's exciting just to see this stage where Sarah Bernhardt, John Barrymore, Helen Hayes, and so many other notables have performed. The National is the closest thing Washington has to a Broadway-style playhouse. Managed by New York's Shubert Organization, it presents star-studded hits, often pre- or post-Broadway, most of the year. The 1998 season included productions of *Rent* and *Ragtime.* The National seats 1,672.

The National also offers free public-service programs: Saturday-morning children's theater, free summer films, and Monday-night showcases of local groups and performers. Call ☎ **202/783-3372** for details.

Shakespeare Theatre. 450 7th St. NW (between D and E sts.). ☎ **202/393-2700.** Tickets $14–$56, $10 for standing-room tickets sold 1 hour before sold-out performances; discounts available for students, groups, and senior citizens. Metro: Archives–Navy Memorial or Gallery Place.

This internationally renowned classical ensemble company, which for 2 decades performed at the Folger Shakespeare Library, moved to larger quarters at the above address in 1992. Under the artistic direction of Michael Kahn, it offers 3 Shakespearean productions plus two other modern classics each September-to-June season. The 1997–1998 season included *The Tempest, Othello* (starring 1997 William Shakespeare Award winner Patrick Stewart in an otherwise all African-American cast), *The Merry Wives of Windsor,* Ibsen's *Peer Gynt,* and Tennessee Williams's *Sweet Bird of Youth* (starring Elizabeth Ashley). Playing in the 1998–1999 season are *Edward II* (by Christopher Marlowe), *Twelfth Night, King John,* Euripides's *The Trojan Women,* and *The Merchant of Venice,* which will star Hal Holbrook. Other well-known actors, such as Jean Stapleton, Tom Hulce, Kelly McGillis, and Richard Thomas, have joined the company for specific productions. This is top-level theater. The company also offers one admission-free, 2-week run of a Shakespeare production at the Carter Barron Amphitheatre in Rock Creek Park (see listing for Carter Barron below, under "Outdoor Pavilions and Stadiums").

Source Theatre Company. 1835 14th St. NW (between S and T sts.). ☎ **202/462-1073** for information or 301/738-7073 to charge tickets. Tickets $20–$25, OFF HOURS shows $15, Washington Theatre Festival shows $8–$15.

Washington's major producer of new plays, the Source also mounts works of established playwrights—for example, Anton Chekhov's *The Cherry Orchard,* Arthur Miller's *A View from the Bridge,* and A. R. Gurney's *A Cheever Evening.* It presents top local artists in a year-round schedule of dramatic and comedy plays, both at the above address and, during the summer, at various spaces around town. The theater is also used for an OFF HOURS series of productions geared to a contemporary urban audience. Annual events here include the **Washington Theatre Festival** each July, a 4-week showcase of about 50 new plays. The Source, which produces many African-American works, welcomes original scripts from unknowns.

Studio Theatre. 1333 P St. NW. ☎ **202/332-3300.** Tickets $17.50–$34.50, Secondstage shows $15. Discounts available for groups of 15 or more, students, and senior citizens. Metro: Dupont Circle or McPherson Square or U St.–Cardozo.

Under artistic director Joy Zinoman, the Studio has consistently produced interesting contemporary plays, nurtured Washington acting talent, and garnered numerous Helen Hayes Awards for outstanding achievement. Many plays come here from off-Broadway. Past seasons have included Sebastian Barry's *The Steward of Christendom,* David Mamet's *The Cryptogram,* John Osborne's *Look Back in Anger,* and Terrence McNally's *Love! Valour! Compassion!* The Studio also houses **Secondstage,** a 50-seat space on the third floor where emerging artists, directors, and actors can showcase their work. The season runs year-round. A $4.5-million renovation completed in 1997 remodeled the main theater and added a wonderful new one, **the Milton.** Street parking is easy to find, and there's a pay lot at P Street between 14th and 15th Streets.

Woolly Mammoth Theatre Company. 1401 Church St. NW (between P and Q sts.) ☎ **202/393-3939.** For tickets, call Protix ☎ **800/955-5566** or 703/218-6500. Tickets $15–$28. A range of ticket discounts is available, including reduced prices for seniors and students and pay-what-you-can nights; inquire at the box office. Free parking across the street. Metro: Dupont Circle, about 5 blocks away. You might prefer to take a cab from there, since the neighborhood is often deserted at night; on request, theater staff will call a cab for you after the show.

Established in 1980, the Woolly Mammoth offers as many as six productions each year-long season, specializing, according to a publicist, in "new, offbeat, and quirky plays." "I'm not interested in theater where people sit back and say, 'That was nice. I enjoyed that,'" says artistic director Howard Shalwitz. "I only look for plays that directly challenge the audience in some important way." The 1998–1999 lineup includes *The Last Orbit of Billy Mars,* by Robert Alexander, and Friedrich Durrenmatt's comedy *The Marriage of Mr. Mississippi.* This company has garnered 14 Helen Hayes Awards, among other accolades, and is consistently reviewed by the *New York Times.*

2 Other Performing Arts

The following listings are a potpourri of places offering a mixed bag of theater; opera; classical music; headliners; jazz; rock; dance; and comedy. Here you'll find some of the top entertainment choices in the district.

MULTICULTURAL FACILITIES

DAR Constitution Hall. 18th and D sts. NW. ☎ **202/628-4780,** 800/551-SEAT or 202/ 432-SEAT to charge tickets. Tickets $15–$50. Metro: Farragut West.

Housed within a beautiful, turn-of-the-century, beaux arts–style building is this fine, 3,746-seat auditorium. Its excellent acoustics make it a prime venue for hearing the eclectic music that plays here—the Boston Symphony; John Hiatt; Count Basie Orchestra; Los Angeles Philharmonic; Lee Greenwood; Diana Ross; Ray Charles; Buddy Guy; The Temptations; Trisha Yearwood; Roy Clark; Kathleen Battle; and Marilyn Horne.

The Folger Shakespeare Library. 201 E. Capitol St. SE. ☎ **202/544-7077.** Students and seniors receive discounts with proof of ID. Call for information about ticket prices, which can range from $5 to $40, depending upon the event. Metro: Capitol South.

The Folger Shakespeare Library is open year-round for exhibits in and tours of its Tudor-style great rooms (see chapter 7 for details). Its theatrical programs and special events generally coincide with the academic year, from October through May. Among the offerings are the **Folger Consort,** a music ensemble that performs medieval, Renaissance, and baroque music; troubadour songs; madrigals; and court ensembles. Between October and May, the group gives 30 concerts over the course of 7 weekends.

The Folger presents theatrical and musical performances, lectures, readings, and other events in its Elizabethan Theatre, which is styled after the innyard theatre from Shakespeare's time.

In addition, an evening lecture series called **"Places in the Mind"** features writers, artists, actors, and performers (such as playwright Wendy Wasserstein and writer Roger Angell) speaking on cities around the globe. On selected evenings, poets—such as Jorie Graham, Seamus Heany, Gwendolyn Brooks, Michael Ondaatje, and John Ashbery—read from their works. Another exciting program is the **Friday-night PEN/Faulkner series of fiction readings** by noted authors Joyce Carol Oates, Ann Beattie, Susan Power, Albert Murray, Joan Didion, and Richard Ford. And the Folger offers Saturday programs for children ranging from medieval treasure hunts to preparing an Elizabethan feast.

John F. Kennedy Center for the Performing Arts. At the southern end of New Hampshire Ave. NW and Rock Creek Pkwy. ☎ **800/444-1324** or 202/467-4600. kennedy-center.org. 50% discounts are offered (for most attractions) to students; seniors 65 and over; people with permanent disabilities; and enlisted military personnel with a valid ID. Garage parking $8. Metro: Foggy Bottom (it's a fairly short walk, but a free shuttle between the station and the Kennedy Center departs every 15 minutes from 7pm to midnight). Bus: 80 from Metro Center.

Our national performing arts center, the hub of Washington's cultural and entertainment scene, is actually made up of six different theaters. You can find out what is scheduled during your stay (and charge tickets) before leaving home by calling the above toll-free number. Half-price tickets are available for full-time students, senior citizens, enlisted military personnel, people with disabilities, and persons with fixed, low income (call ☎ **202/416-8340** for details).

The Kennedy Center's free concert series, known as **"Millennium Stage,"** features daily performances by area musicians, staged each evening at 6pm in the center's Grand Foyer. The Friday "Weekend" section of the *Washington Post* lists the free performances scheduled for the coming week. Also call about "pay what you can" performances, scheduled throughout the year on certain days, for certain shows.

The 27-year-old center is in the process of a $50-million overhaul scheduled to continue until the year 2007. The Concert Hall was the first to be renovated; after 10 months of work, the hall reopened in October 1997 with improvements that include wheelchair accessibility for 4% of the seats and enhanced acoustics.

Opera House   This plush red-and-gilt, 2,300-seat theater is designed for ballet, modern dance, and musical comedy, as well as opera, and it's also the setting for occasional gala events such as the Kennedy Center Honors, which you've probably seen on TV (Neil Simon, B. B. King, Lauren Bacall, and Bob Dylan have been honorees). Other offerings have included performances by the Joffrey Ballet, the Bolshoi Ballet, the Kirov Ballet, the Royal Ballet, and the American Ballet Theatre. The Washington Opera (**www/dc-opera.org**) stages many of its performances here and in the Eisenhower Theater. Tickets often sell out before the season begins. In 1999, the Washington Opera, under the artistic direction of Placido Domingo, brings, among others, Mozart's *The Abduction from the Seraglio,* a comedy, and *The Crucible,* based on Arthur Miller's play, to the Eisenhower. *Boris Godunov* by Mussorgsky and Wagner's *Tristan and Isolde* are scheduled to appear in the Opera. The Opera House has also staged such musicals as *The King and I* (starring Hayley Mills), *Phantom of the Opera,* and *Footloose;* in July 1999, the musical *Titanic* will play here.

Eisenhower Theater   A wide range of dramatic productions can be seen here. Some recent examples: *Master Class* starring Zoë Caldwell as the legendary diva Maria Callas, and Neil Simon's *Proposals.* The Eisenhower is also the setting for smaller productions of the Washington Opera from December to February; solo performances by the likes of Harry Belafonte; dance presentations by the Paul Taylor Dance Company; and others. Tickets for most theatrical productions are in the $25 to $70 range. Prices for opera seats tend to soar higher.

Concert Hall   This is the home of the National Symphony Orchestra, which presents concerts from September to June. Tickets are available by subscription and for individual performances. Guest artists have included Itzhak Perlman, Vladimir Ashkenazy, Zubin Mehta, Pinchas Zukerman, André Previn, Jean-Pierre Rampal, and Isaac Stern. Headliner entertainers such as Ray Charles, Patti LuPone, Bill Cosby, and Harry Belafonte also have appeared here. Among the 1999 performances planned are a premiere on March 11 of *Symphony No. 2* by John Corigliano, based on texts by Dylan Thomas; a percussion festival in April; the annual Mozart festival in June; vocalist Bobby McFerrin conducting the NSO in a production of Gershwin's *Porgy and Bess;* and Placido Domingo's NSO debut as conductor, leading works by Haydn, Falla, and Tchaikovsky (December 3–5).

Terrace Theater   Small chamber works, choral recitals, musicals, comedy revues, cabarets, and theatrical and modern-dance performances are among the varied provinces of the 500-seat Terrace Theater, a bicentennial gift from Japan. It's been the setting for solo performances by violinist Eugene Fodor, pianists Santiago Rodriguez and Peter Serkin, soprano Dawn Upshaw, and jazz singer Barbara Cook. Performance artists Laurie Anderson and Michael Moschen have performed here, and jazz evenings have included tributes to Count Basie, Louis Armstrong, and Duke Ellington. More recently, a production of Athol Fugard's *The Captain's Tiger* took the stage of the Terrace. Every spring the Terrace (along with the Theater Lab) hosts productions of six finalists in the American College Theatre Festival competition.

Theater Lab and More   By day, the Theater Lab is Washington's premier stage for children's theater. Evenings it becomes a cabaret, now in a long run of *Shear*

Madness, a comedy whodunit (tickets are $25 to $29). Elsewhere at the center, there are family concerts by the National Symphony Orchestra several times each year, not to mention clowns, jugglers, dance troupes, improvisational theater, storytellers, and films. Many events are scheduled around the Christmas and Easter holidays.

Parking   Limited underground parking at the Kennedy Center is $8 for the entire evening after 5pm; if that lot is full, go to the Columbia Plaza Garage, at 2400 Virginia Ave. NW, which runs a free shuttle back to the facility.

Lincoln Theater. 1215 U St. NW. ☎ **202/328-6000.** Tickets range in price from $10 to $25 and are available at the theater box office and through Ticketmaster outlets or by calling 800/551-SEAT or 202/432-SEAT to charge tickets. Metro: U St.–Cardozo.

In the heart of happening U Street, the Lincoln was once a movie theater, vaudeville house, and nightclub featuring black stars like Louis Armstrong and Cab Calloway. The theater closed in the 1970s and reopened in 1994 after a renovation returned the theater to its former elegance. Today the theater books jazz, R&B, gospel, and comedy acts, and events like the D.C. Film Festival.

Lisner Auditorium. On the campus of George Washington University, 21st and H sts. NW. ☎ **202/994-1500.** www.gwu.edu/~Lisner. Tickets average $15–$50 depending upon event. Tickets are available through Protix (703/218-6500) or Ticketmaster (800/551-SEAT or 202/432-SEAT). Discounts may be available for students and others, depending upon promoter. Metro: Foggy Bottom.

One of my favorite places to hear good music, the Lisner is small (only 1,500 seats), so you always feel close to the stage. Bookings sometimes include musical groups like Los Lobos and Siouxsie and the Banshees, comedians like "Weird Al" Yankovic, and children's entertainers like Raffi, but most of the theater's lineup centers on cultural shows, everything from a Pakistani rock group to the Washington Revels' annual romp at Christmas.

Warner Theatre. 1299 Pennsylvania Ave. NW (entrance on 13th St., between E and F sts.). ☎ **800/551-SEAT,** 202/783-4000, or 202/432-SEAT to charge tickets. www. warnertheatre.com. Play tickets $20–$60. Metro: Metro Center. Parking is available in the Warner Building PMI lot on 12th St. NW, for $6.

Opened in 1924 as the Earle Theatre (a movie/vaudeville palace) and restored to its original appearance in 1992 at a cost of $10 million, this stunning neoclassical-style theater features a gold-leafed grand lobby and auditorium. Everything is plush and magnificent, from the glittering crystal chandeliers to the gold-tasseled, swagged-velvet draperies. It's worth coming by just to see the theater's ornately detailed interior. The 2,000-seat auditorium offers year-round entertainment, alternating dance performances (from Baryshnikov to the Washington Ballet's Christmas performance of *The Nutcracker*) and Broadway/off-Broadway shows (the fabulous *Stomp* and *Jelly's Last Jam*) with headliner entertainment (Sheryl Crow, k. d. lang, Natalie Merchant, Chris Isaak, Wynton Marsalis). Call ahead for a schedule of events taking place during your visit.

ARENAS

Ticket prices for arena performances vary widely, reflecting the very different types of events typically held in these large spaces—from trade fairs to popular sports events to sold-out rock-and-roll concerts. So it's best to call for ticket price information.

Baltimore Arena. 201 W. Baltimore St., Baltimore, MD. ☎ **410/347-2020,** 800/551-SEAT or 410/481-SEAT for tickets. To get here by car, take I-95 north to I-395 (stay in the left lane) to the Inner Harbor exit and follow Howard St. to the arena. You can also take a MARC train from Union Station.

This 13,500-seat arena, a few blocks from Baltimore's Inner Harbor and around the corner from Camden Yards, is home to several local sports teams. When the teams are not playing, the arena hosts big-name concerts and family entertainment shows. The Beatles appeared here back in the 1960s. More recently, they've presented *Sesame Street Live,* Ringling Brothers and Barnum and Bailey Circus, *Disney on Ice.* Headliners have included New Edition, Alan Jackson, Reba McEntire, Brooks & Dunn, Paul Simon, Liza Minnelli, Luther Vandross, and Vince Gill.

MCI Center. 601 F St. NW, where it meets 7th St. ☎ **202/628-3200.** To charge tickets by phone, call 800/551-SEAT or 202/432-SEAT. Very limited parking on-site; surface lots and garages in neighborhood; but your best bet is the Metro. The Gallery Place stop lies just beneath the building.

Set on 5 acres in a prime downtown location, the MCI Center is the new home for the Washington Wizards (formerly the Bullets) and the Georgetown Hoyas basketball teams and the Washington Capitals hockey team, with seats for 20,600 fans to watch the games. This is also the site for the world championship figure skating competition and the Franklin National Bank Classic competition for college basketball. See chapter 7 for more information about sports events.

The center is open 365 days a year, not just as a sports facility, but as a location for music concerts and business conferences. Among the 1998 concerts were ones by Billy Joel, Yanni, and Janet Jackson. Within the three-story complex are a 25,000 square-foot Discovery Channel, Destination D.C. retail store, a National Sports Gallery (an interactive sports museum), and three restaurants.

The Patriot Center. George Mason University, 4400 University Dr., Fairfax, VA. ☎ **703/ 993-3000,** 800/551-SEAT or 202/432-SEAT to charge tickets. The facility has 4,000 free parking spaces. To get here by car, take the I-495 to Braddock Rd. W, and continue about 6 miles to University Dr.

This 10,000-seat facility hosts major headliners. Performers here have included Randy Travis, David Copperfield, Gloria Estefan, Tom Petty, Natalie Cole, Sting, Counting Crows, and Kenny Rogers. There are family events such as *Sesame Street Live* here, too.

US Airways Arena. 1 Harry S Truman Dr., Exit 15A or 17A off the Capital Beltway in Landover, MD. ☎ **800/551-SEAT** or 301/350-3400.

This 19,000-seat arena hosts a variety of concerts and headliner entertainment, including Pavarotti, AC/DC, Rod Stewart, Neil Diamond, and Garth Brooks, the Washington Warthogs indoor soccer games, Washington International Horse Show, and monster trucks events.

OUTDOOR PAVILIONS & STADIUMS

When summer comes to Washington, much of the entertainment moves outdoors. As city theaters go dark or cut back on performance schedules in July and August to catch their breath and gear up for a new season, a handful of Washington area amphitheaters pick up the slack.

Carter Barron Amphitheater. 4850 Colorado Ave. NW, at 16th St. ☎ **202/260-6836.** Take Metro to Silver Spring, transfer to bus no. S2 or S4, with "Federal Triangle" destination sign, and let the driver know you wish to hop off at the 16th St. bus stop nearest the Carter Barron; the amphitheater is a 5-minute walk from that stop.

Way out on 16th Street (near the Maryland border) is this 4,250-seat amphitheater in Rock Creek Park. Summer performances include a range of gospel, blues, and classical entertainment, though each year is different; my husband still talks about the Bruce Springsteen concert he saw here years ago. You can always count on

Shakespeare: **The Shakespeare Theatre Free for All** takes place at the Carter Barron usually for 2 weeks in June, Tuesday through Sunday evenings. The free tickets are available the day of performance only, on a first-come, first-served basis (call ☎ **202/628-5770** for details).

Merriweather Post Pavilion. 10475 Little Patuxent Pkwy. (just off Rte. 29 in Columbia, MD). ☎ **410/730-2424** for information; 800/955-5566, 410/481-6500, or 703/218-6500 to charge tickets. Tickets $17–$50 pavilion, $15–$23 lawn.

During the summer there's celebrity entertainment almost nightly at the Merriweather Post Pavilion, about 40 minutes by car from downtown Washington. There's reserved seating in the open-air pavilion (overhead protection provided in case of rain) and general-admission seating on the lawn (no refunds for rain) to see such performers as James Taylor, Tina Turner, Van Halen, the Beach Boys, Liza Minnelli, Sting, Julio Iglesias, Joan Rivers, Hootie and the Blowfish, Jimmy Buffett, Elton John, Al Jarreau, and Barry Manilow. If you choose the lawn seating, bring blankets and picnic fare (beverages must be bought on the premises).

Nissan Pavilion at Stone Ridge. 7800 Cellar Door Dr. (off Wellington Rd. in Bristow, VA). ☎ **800/455-8999** or 703/754-6400 for concert information; 800/551-SEAT or 202/432-SEAT to charge tickets. Tickets $25–$55 pavilion, $9.50–$29. To get here by car, take I-66 west to Exit 43B, turn left on Route 29, continue half a mile, and turn left onto Wellington Rd.; the Nissan Pavilion is about a mile down on your right.

With a capacity of 22,500 seats (10,000 under the roof, the remainder on the lawn), this immense state-of-the-art entertainment facility just 25 minutes from the Beltway features major acts varying from classical to country. Since its opening in the summer of 1995, featured performers have included Yanni, Dave Matthews Band, Rush, Melissa Etheridge, Phish, Reba McEntire, The Cranberries, James Taylor, Van Halen, Jimmy Buffett, David Bowie, Nine Inch Nails, Hanson, R.E.M., and Spice Girls. The action is enhanced by giant video screens inside the pavilion and on the lawn.

Robert F. Kennedy Memorial Stadium/D.C. Armory. 2400 E. Capitol St. SE. ☎ **202/547-9077**, 800/551-SEAT or 202/432-SEAT to charge tickets. Metro: Stadium-Armory.

Until 1998, RFK was the home stadium for the Washington Redskins football team, who now play at the new Jack Kent Cooke facility in Raljohn, Maryland. The stadium continues as a spring, summer, fall event facility, packing crowds of 55,000-plus into its seats to hear concerts by the Rolling Stones, the Eagles, and other big name groups, and to watch D.C. United Major League soccer and college football.

The D.C. Armory, right next door, is a year-round venue for the Ringling Brothers Barnum and Bailey Circus, antique shows, and other events that require space for as many as 10,000 people.

Wolf Trap Farm Park for the Performing Arts. 1551 Trap Rd., Vienna, VA. ☎ **703/255-1868**, or Protix (703/218-6500) to charge tickets. www.wolf-trap.org. Filene Center seats $18–$70, lawn $7–$20; Barns tickets average $14–$20. By car, take I-495 (the Beltway) to Exit 12W (Dulles Toll Road); follow the signs and exit (after paying a 50¢ toll) at the Wolf Trap ramp. Stay on the local exit road (you'll see a sign) until you come to Wolf Trap. The park is also accessible from Exit 67 off I-66 west. There's plenty of parking. In summer only, you can get to Wolf Trap by taking the Metro to the West Falls Church stop, to and from which the Wolf Trap Shuttle ($3.50 round-trip) runs every 20 minutes. The shuttle runs start 2 hours before performance time and (on the return trip) either 20 minutes after the performance ends or 11pm (whichever comes first).

The country's only national park devoted to the performing arts, Wolf Trap, just 30 minutes by car from downtown D.C., offers a star-studded Summer Festival Season from late May to mid-September. The 1998 season featured performances by the National Symphony Orchestra (it's their summer home), adopted daughter Mary Chapin Carpenter, Grover Washington, Jr., Ray Charles, Peter, Paul, and Mary, the San Francisco Ballet, Pilobolus, and Riverdance.

Performances take place in the 7,000-seat Filene Center, about half of which is under the open sky. You can also buy cheaper lawn seats on the hill, which is sometimes the nicest way to go. If you do, arrive early (the lawn opens 90 minutes before the performance), and bring a blanket and a picnic dinner; it's a tradition.

Wolf Trap also hosts a number of very popular festivals. The park features a daylong **Irish Music Festival** in May; two major festivals in June, the **Louisiana Swamp Romp Cajun Festival** and a weekend of jazz and blues; and the **International Children's Festival** each September.

From late fall until May, the 350-seat **Barns of Wolf Trap,** just up the road at 1635 Trap Rd., features jazz, pop, country, folk, bluegrass, and chamber musicians. The Barns are the summer home of the Wolf Trap Opera Company, which is the only entertainment booked here May through September. Call ☎ **703/938-2404.**

3 The Club & Music Scene

You don't have to go to an enormous auditorium or a fancy concert hall to enjoy live entertainment in the capital. If you're looking for a tuneful night on the town, Washington offers smoky jazz clubs, lively bars, warehouse ballrooms, places where you sit back and listen, places where you can get up and dance, even a roadhouse or two. If you're looking for comic relief, Washington can take care of you there, too (the pickings are few but good).

A lot of nightlife sites fall into more than one category: for example, the **Black Cat** is a bar and a dance club, offering food and sometimes poetry readings; **Coco Loco** is a hot Brazilian restaurant and an even hotter nightclub on weekend nights. So I've listed each nightspot according to the type of music it features, and included the details in its description.

The best nightlife districts are **Adams-Morgan;** the area around **U and 14th Streets NW,** a newly developing district yet still a relatively dangerous part of town; the **7th Street NW corridor** near Chinatown and the MCI Center; and **Georgetown.** If you don't mind venturing into the suburbs, you should know about Arlington's hot spots—see the box called "Arlington Row." As a rule, while city-clubbing—even in Georgetown—stick to the major thoroughfares and steer clear of deserted side streets. The best source of information about what's doing at bars and clubs is *City Paper,* which is available free at bookstores, movie theaters, drugstores, and other locations.

COMEDY

In addition to the places listed below, be sure to catch **Gross National Product,** a political satire troupe that appears at Chief Ike's Mambo Room every Saturday night. (See Chief Ike's listing, below.) Big-name comedians also perform around town at such places as Constitution Hall.

Chelsea's. 1055 Thomas Jefferson St. NW (in the Foundry Building on the C&O Canal). ☎ **202/298-8222.** $50 for dinner and show, $33.50 for show only. Fri and Sat nights. Metro: Foggy Bottom, with a 10-minute walk. Complimentary parking in building garage.

This nightclub in the Foundry Building on the C&O Canal is home base for the Capitol Steps comedy satire troupe, whose claim to fame is poking fun at Washington institutions through song. You may have heard of them via their many

Washington, D.C. Clubs & Bars

Asylum **33**
The Ballroom **2**
The Bar **25**
The Bayou **44**
The Big Hunt **14**
Black Hat **22**
Blues Alley **42**
Brickskeller **15**
Café Milano **39**
Champions **40**
Chelsea's **45**
Chief Ike's Mambo Room **34**
The Circle **16**
City Blues **36**
Club Heaven and Hell **28**
Coco Loco **7**
Columbia Station **27**
The Dubliner **5**
Fado **8**
Fox and Hounds **17**
Habana Village **30**
The Improv **12**
J.R.'s **18**

Kala Kala **31**
Latin Jazz Alley **29**
Lucky Bar **13**
Madam's Organ **32**
Metro Café **21**
Mr. Smith's **43**
Nathans **41**
New Vegas Lounge **20**
9:30 Club **23**
One Step Down **46**
Ozio **11**
Polly Esther's **9**
Post Pub **10**
The Rock **6**
State of the Union **24**
The Tombs **38**
Townhouse Tavern **19**
Tracks **1**
Tune Inn **4**
Tunnicliff's Tavern **3**
Twins Lounge **35**
Twist and Shout **37**
Utopia **26**

albums and appearances on national TV shows. And they certainly know their material: The Steps are ex-Congressional staffers, well acquainted with the crazy workings of government. Their shows are at 5:30pm Saturday, 6pm Friday. See Chelsea's listing under "International Sounds," this chapter, for information about Latino and Arabic music and dancing nights here.

The Improv. 1140 Connecticut Ave. NW (between L and M sts.). ☎ **202/296-7008.** www. dcimprov.com. Cover: $12 Sun–Thurs, $15 Fri–Sat, plus a 2-drink minimum (waived if you dine). Open every night but Monday. Metro: Farragut North. Parking garage next door $4.

The Improv features top performers on the national comedy club circuit as well as comic plays and one-person shows. *Saturday Night Live* performers (David Spade, Chris Rock, Adam Sandler) have all played here, as have comedy bigs Ellen DeGeneres, Jerry Seinfeld, David Alan Grier, Robin Williams, Rosie O'Donnell, and Brian Regan. Shows are about 1½ hours long and include three comics (an emcee, feature act, and headliner). Show times are 8:30pm from Sunday to Thursday, 8:30 and 10:30pm on Friday and Saturday. The best way to snag a good seat is to have dinner here (make reservations), which allows you to enter the club as early as 7pm. Dinner entrées ($7.95 to $13.95) include prime rib, sandwiches, and pasta and seafood selections. Drinks average $3.25. You must be 18 to get in.

POP/ROCK

The Ballroom. 1015 Half St. SE (at K St.). ☎ **202/554-1500.** www.cellardoor.com. Cover: Fri–Sat $9–12; Sun–Thurs $8–$30, depending on the performer. Open most weekend nights, and often weeknights, depending upon performance schedule. Metro: Navy Yard.

Occupying a vast converted boiler-company warehouse consisting of a cavernous space, a bigger cavernous space, and a half dozen bars, this place is generally a Gen-X mecca (although some performers attract an older crowd). It's also D.C.'s largest club, accommodating upward of 1,500 people a night. Friday night Buzz Parties here feature six DJs playing techno, house, and jungle music from 10pm to 6am (except for once-a-month raves, when the action continues until about 9am). Saturday nights are similar, although the music is a mix of alternative/industrial, progressive, and techno. The rest of the week is given over to live concerts, mostly featuring nationally known acts (such as 311, David Bowie, Tool, The Artist-previously-known-as-Prince), and, occasionally, local groups. You can buy tickets in advance via Ticketmaster (☎ **202/432-SEAT**). The Ballroom is all ages for concerts; for dancing you must be 18 to get in. The game room and state-of-the-art lighting/laser/sound systems are a plus.

The Bayou. 3135 K St. NW (under the Whitehurst Fwy., near Wisconsin Ave.). ☎ **202/ 333-2897.** www.cellardoor.com. Cover: $5–$25. Open most weekend nights, and often weeknights, depending upon performance schedule. Metro: Foggy Bottom, with 25-minute walk.

This lively nightclub, located on the Georgetown waterfront, features a mixed bag of live musical entertainment, mostly progressive, reggae, and alternative sounds. Performers are up-and-coming national groups, with occasional big names (Hootie and the Blowfish, Dave Matthews, John Popper with Blues Traveler) who like to pop in for old times' sake. On Wednesday nights the Bayou hosts the disco band Boogie Fever, from New York City, and discounts $2 off the $5 cover if you're dressed in disco attire.

The Bayou is a funky, cavelike club, with exposed brick-and-stone walls and seating on two levels. Sandwiches and pizza are available during the show. Most shows are for people 18 and older, but call or check the local listings to be sure. You

Dancing in D.C.

"Where can we go to dance? It's the question asked most frequently by my readers," says Eric Brace, who reports on the city's nightlife for the *Washington Post*. (See his column, "Nightwatch," which appears every Friday in the *Post*'s Weekend section.) Sadly, says Brace, "I just have to tell them, there's really not much."

Dance places do exist in D.C., and if you like to dance, the following suggestions will help you figure out where to go and what to expect. For clubs not already listed within this chapter, I provide an address and phone number; otherwise, refer to full entries within the main text to find out this and other information.

To begin with, let me tell you that one clear deficiency is the absence of a dinner-dance club. There used to be a couple, the best of which was the River Club, a romantic sort of place with good food and a dance floor for swaying to big-band and swing tunes. If that's the kind of thing you have in mind, you might want to try either **Marley's Lounge at the Henley Park Hotel,** 926 Massachusetts Ave. NW (☎ **202/414-0500**), for live jazz standards Friday and Saturday nights, or the **Melrose Bar, at the Park Hyatt Hotel,** 1201 24th St. NW (☎ **202/955-3899**), for live jazz on Saturday nights.

Latin jazz continues to be popular in Washington, and one of the funnest places to go to salsa and rhumba and all that jazz is Adams-Morgan's **Habana Village** (1834 Columbia Rd. NW; see p. 274). Habana Village, which happens to be Eric Brace's current favorite spot, is open Wednesday through Saturday evenings for both lessons and dancing. Other choices include Latin Jazz Alley, also in Adams-Morgan, the downtown **Coco Loco** (see p. 273), and Georgetown's **Chelsea** (see p. 273).

Adams-Morgan, in general, is a convenient neighborhood to travel if you're in a dancing mood. Stop in at **Chief Ike's** and **Club Heaven and Hell** for disco-driven dance music, or at **Madam's Organ,** if live jazz, blues, or R&B turn you on (on Thursday nights, though, a DJ spins funk and rock). (See listings below for more information.) And speaking of blues, two other locations outside Adams-Morgan offer live performances: the **New Vegas Lounge** (see p. 272), which really isn't a dance club, but turns into one, if the music is good.

Dance venues where live bands play contemporary music include the **Ballroom,** the **Bayou, Black Cat, Metro Café, State of the Union,** and, in Arlington, **IOTA** (see "Arlington Row," later in this chapter). Alas, the live rock-dance scene is another category woefully underrepresented in Washington.

If you're into dancing while a DJ spins the music, you're in luck, since this is the most prevalent dance option. All but the Metro, from the paragraph above, stage DJ music on certain nights. In addition, you might consider **Club Heaven and Hell** or **Chief Ike's** (as previously mentioned), for choices ranging from alternative to hip-hop; or **Polly Esther's** for '80s retro dance music and disco. **Nathan's,** the **Spy Club** (805 15th St. NW, ☎ **202/289-1779**), **Club Zei** (1412 I St. NW, ☎ **202/842-2445**), and **Sesto Senso** (1214 18th St. NW, ☎ **202/785-9525**) play a combination of international, Euro, and Top 40 rock.

can buy tickets in advance from Ticketmaster (☎ **202/432-SEAT**). There's convenient parking at the corner of Wisconsin and K Streets.

Black Cat. 1831 14th St. NW (between S and T sts.). ☎ **202/667-7960.** Cover: $5–$10 for concerts; no cover in the Red Room. Bar open Sun–Thurs until 2am, Fri–Sat until 3am. Concerts held 4 or 5 nights a week, begining around 8:30pm (call for details). Metro: U St.–Cardozo.

This comfortable, low-key, everyone-in-black-clothes bar has a large, funky, red-walled living-roomy lounge with booths and tables, a red-leather sofa, pinball machines, a pool table, and a jukebox stocked with a really eclectic collection. College crowds gather here on weekends, but you can count on seeing a 20- to 30-something bunch here most nights, including members of various bands who like to stop in for a drink. There's live music in the adjoining room, essentially a large dance floor (it accommodates about 400 people) with stages at both ends. Entertainment is primarily alternative rock (mostly locals, but some bigger names such as Blur, Morphine, Foo Fighters, and The Cramps), with a little jazz, swing, folk, and occasional poetry readings thrown in. Light fare, such as kebab dinners, is available, and the bar has microbrew beers on tap.

Chief Ike's Mambo Room. 1725 Columbia Rd. NW. ☎ **202/332-2211.** www.tlac.net/users/chiefike. Cover: $3 Sat–Sun. Open from 4pm–2am or 3am nightly. Metro: Woodley Park–Zoo, with a 20-minute walk.

In early 1998, Chief Ike's served as a location shot for a scene in Will Smith's movie *Enemy of the State.* Its more usual role is as a place where professional musicians jam on Tuesday nights; local DJ legend Stella Neptune spins dance tunes once or twice a week; and the Gross National Product, a political satire troupe, performs Saturday nights. People come here to dance, drink, flirt, and yes, to eat. Chief Ike's, unlike other clubs, sets a great store by its regional American grub. Happy hour lasts weeknights from 4 to 8pm. The crowd is (for the most part) young, with lots of politicos and local artists stopping in. Downstairs is where you'll find the dancing, upstairs is good for kibitzing and pool-playing.

Club Heaven and Hell. 2327 18th St. NW. ☎ **202/667-HELL** (club phone), or 703/522-4227 (for bookings and information). Cover in Heaven: $3 Tues, $3 Wed, $5 Thurs, $5 Fri and Sat; no cover in Hell. Hell open daily, Heaven is closed Sun–Mon. Metro: Dupont Circle (Q St. exit) or Woodley Park–Zoo, with a 20- to 30-minute walk.

This schizophrenic club is in Adams-Morgan. Heaven (upstairs, of course) is a psychedelic version of paradise with black walls and strobe lights, Buddhas, Egyptian art, and paintings based on Michelangelo's *David* and *God Creating Adam.* The balcony allows an escape from the dense mob of dancers and very loud music. Weather permitting Thursday through Saturday, you can go up on the rooftop patio, one of the larger ones, in Adams-Morgan at least. The crowd is interracial, clean-cut, casual, and 25 to 35 (picture the cast of *Friends*). The music (till 2am Tuesday to Thursday, 3am Friday and Saturday) is alternative, Gothic, and industrial on Tuesday; progressive, alternative, and techno on Wednesday; '80s retro (Prince, Madonna, Michael Jackson), DC's Original Dance Party, or played by DJs Jim'n'Jon on Thursday; hip-hop, progressive, or alternative on Friday; and house sounds on Saturday. The ground floor is occupied by a dark, minimalist Italian restaurant called the Green Island Café, which serves pastas and veal dishes and features live traditional/mellow jazz on Friday and Saturday nights. Go down a flight of stairs to the smoke-filled, low-ceilinged cellar, with bar and pool table and a mural of hellfire and backlit eerie masks: this is Hell. The crowd is not especially satanic; it's basically the same as upstairs.

Metro Café. 1522 14th St. NW. ☎ **202/518-7900,** for advance tickets, call ☎ 202/884-0060. Cover: $5 until 12:30am. Shows usually start daily at 9pm. Free parking across the street. Metro: Dupont Circle, about 5 blocks away.

The space at the Metro fits about 100 people in a room that holds a big stage, an L-shaped bar, red velvet curtains, and high ceilings. Acts range from hip-hop to good local rock bands, to national acts like Holly Cole. The club, a newcomer, seems to be attracting all ages, everyone in black. Like several other nightclubs (State of the Union for one; see below), the Metro is also into drama and presenting short plays on various nights.

9:30 Club. 815 V St. NW. ☎ **202/393-0930.** Tickets $5–$40, depending on the performer. Open days of performance only. Metro: U St.–Cardozo.

Housed in yet another converted warehouse, this major live-music venue hosts frequent record-company parties and features a wide range of top performers. In 1998, the concert trade publication *Pollstar* named the 9:30 the nightclub of the year. You might catch Sheryl Crow, the Wallflowers, Smashing Pumpkins, Shawn Colvin, or even Tony Bennett. It's only open when there's a show on (call ahead), and, obviously, the crowd varies with the performer. The sound system is state of the art. There are four bars, two on the main dance-floor level, one in the upstairs VIP room (anyone is welcome here unless the room is being used for a private party), and another in the distressed-looking cellar. The 9:30 Club is a standup place, literally; there are no seats. Tickets to most shows are available through Protix (☎ **800/955-5566** or 703/218-6500).

Polly Esther's. 605 12th St. NW. ☎ **202/737-1970.** Cover: $6 Fri nights, $8 Sat nights. Open Thurs–Sun. Metro: Metro Center.

Seventies decor and music reign here, with artifacts from that decade hanging on the walls (a John Travolta memorial, anything to do with the Brady Bunch) and disco dance music (think YMCA, Abba, the BeeGees) blaring from the sound system. Downstairs is more Culture-Clubish, where you dance to '80s tunes.

State of the Union. 1357 U St. NW. ☎ **202/588-8810.** Cover: generally $5–$7. Open through 2am Sun–Thurs, 3am Fri–Sat. Metro: U St.–Cardozo.

DJ and live music highlight reggae, hip-hop, and acid jazz sounds in this nightclub that plays on a Soviet Union theme: hammer and sickle sconces, a bust of Lenin over the bar, and a big painting of Rasputin on a back wall. The hip crowd is diverse, "different every half hour," says a bartender, ranging from mid-20s to about 35, interracial, and international. The music, both live and DJ-provided, is avant-garde. On Friday and Saturday nights, live bands play from 9 to 11pm, followed by renowned D.C. DJs playing rare grooves, funk, soul, hip-hop, and house; Wednesday there's live reggae; Monday from 10pm to 2am is live jazz night; and other nights there's live entertainment, generally, straight, funk, and acid jazz. You might also happen upon a poetry reading. The music is pretty loud. Weather permitting, the back room has an open-air screen (actually more like a cave wall). There's an interesting selection of beers and more than 30 flavored vodkas.

JAZZ/BLUES

Blues Alley. 1073 Wisconsin Ave. NW (in an alley below M St.). ☎ **202/337-4141.** Cover: $13–$40, plus $7 food or drink minimum, plus $1.75 surcharge. Open nightly. Metro: Foggy Bottom, with a 20-minute walk.

Blues Alley, in Georgetown, has been Washington's top jazz club since 1965, featuring such artists as Nancy Wilson, McCoy Tyner, Sonny Rollins, Flora Purim,

Herbie Mann, Wynton Marsalis, Charlie Byrd, Ramsey Lewis, Rachelle Ferrell, and Maynard Ferguson. There are usually two shows nightly, at 8 and 10pm; some performers also do midnight shows on weekends. Reservations are essential (call after noon), and because seating is on a first-come, first-served basis, it's best to arrive no later than 7pm and have dinner. Entrées on the steak and creole-seafood menu (for example, jambalaya, chicken creole, and crab cakes) are in the $14 to $22 range; snacks and sandwiches are $5.25 to $9, and drinks are $5.35 to $9. The decor is of the classic jazz club genre: exposed-brick walls, beamed ceiling, and small candlelit tables. Sometimes well-known visiting musicians get up and jam with performers.

City Blues. 2651 Connecticut Ave. NW. ☎ **202/232-2300.** Cover: $5 Thurs–Sat. Open Nightly. Metro: Woodley Park–Zoo.

This is a neighborhood club that offers live entertainment 7 nights a week, mostly blues and some jazz, performed mainly by locals but with big names sitting in from time to time. Look for groups like the Mary Ann Redmond Band, and names like Timothy Ford, who plays piano with the Marianna Previti Band. The 6-year-old club is a cozy den of three interconnected rooms on one floor of a converted town house. Seating is at tables and at the bar. The full menu features American cuisine, with a few pastas and Cajun dishes. The crowd ranges in age from 21 to 65 and includes lots of repeat customers.

Columbia Station. 2325 18th St. NW. ☎ **202/462-6040.** No cover, but a $6 minimum. Breakfast served Fri–Sat 1am–5am. Open weeknights until 1:30am. Metro: Dupont Circle Q St. exit) or Woodley Park–Zoo, with a 20- to 30-minute walk.

Another fairly intimate club in Adams-Morgan, this one showcases live blues and jazz nightly. The performers are pretty good, which is amazing, considering there's no cover. Columbia Station is also a bar/restaurant, and the kitchen is usually open until midnight and serves Cajun-style cuisine.

Madam's Organ. 2461 18th St. NW. ☎ **202/667-5370.** Cover: never more than $5–$8. Open Sun–Thurs 5am–2am, Fri–Sat 5pm–3am. Metro: Dupont Circle (Q St. exit) or Woodley Park–Zoo, with a 20- to 30-minute walk.

This beloved Adams-Morgan hangout fulfills owner Bill Duggan's definition of a good bar: where there's great sound and people sweating. The great sounds are provided courtesy of jazz guitarist Peter Beck on Mondays, bluesman Ben Andrews on Tuesdays, bluegrass open mike on Wednesday, and live R&B, including the likes of Bobby Parker, on Friday and Saturday provides the great sounds. You provide the sweat. DJ and local "character" Stella Neptune spins funk and dance tunes on Thursday nights. The club features a wide-open bar decorated eclectically with a 150-year-old gilded mirror, stuffed fish and animal heads, and paintings of nudes. The second-floor bar is called Big Daddy's Love Lounge & Pick-Up Joint, which tells you everything you need to know. Other points to note: You can play darts, and redheads pay half-price for drinks.

New Vegas Lounge. 1415 P St. NW. ☎ **202/483-3971.** Cover: $7–$10. Open Sat–Sun, Tues–Sat. Sun–Thurs 8pm–2am, Fri–Sat 8pm–3am. Metro: Dupont Circle.

When the Vegas Lounge is good, it's very good. When it's bad, it's laughable. This dark, one-room joint is crowded with tables at which sit a mix of Washingtonians, black and white, college kids and their elders. If you're lucky, you might find a blues band out of Chicago playing Otis Redding's "Try a Little Tenderness," making the room swoon, and eventually putting everyone on their feet dancing. On the other hand, on an open-mike night, you're likely to hear a neighborhood group who has no business appearing in public. Thursdays are college nights.

One Step Down. 2517 Pennsylvania Ave. NW. ☎ **202/955-7141.** Cover: $5 Mon–Thurs, typically $12.50 or $13.50 Sat–Sun; 2-drink minimum every night. Open Mon–Thurs 5:30pm–1am, Sat–Sun until 2am. Live music 6 nights a week. Metro: Foggy Bottom.

This quintessential, hole-in-the-wall jazz club is the constant on this stretch of Pennsylvania Avenue just outside of Georgetown. After 36 years, One Step Down has seen its neighbors change names and owners too many times to count. The One Step showcases the talents of names you often recognize, and some you don't: sax player Paul Bollenbeck, the Steve Wilson Quartet, Ronnie Wells, and Ron Elliston. Blues night is the last Thursday of every month (cover $5). Every Saturday and Sunday, from 3:30 to 7:30pm, the club stages a free jam session. The people who come to the One Step tend to be jazz enthusiasts who stay quiet during the sets.

Twins Lounge. 5516 Colorado Ave. NW. ☎ **202/882-2523.** No cover, but a $7 minimum weeknights; variable cover weekends, plus a $10 minimum. Open Sun–Thurs 6pm–2am, Fri–Sat 6pm–3am. Take a taxi or drive.

Four blocks from the Carter Barron Amphitheater (see p. 265) on the outskirts of town is this intimate jazz club, which offers live music every night. On weeknights you'll hear local artists (open mike on Wednesday nights); on weekends, expect out-of-town acts, such as Bobby Watson, Gil Scott Heron, and James William. Sunday night is a weekly jam session attended by musicians from all over town. The menu features Italian, Ethiopian, and Caribbean dishes. Twins attracts a mixed crowd—"75% white, ages 25 to 90," according to the staff.

Utopia. 1418 U St. NW. ☎ **202/483-7669.** No cover. Sun–Thurs until 2am, Fri and Sat until 3am. Metro: U St.–Cardozo.

Unlike many music bars that offer snack fare, the arty New York/Soho–style Utopia is serious about its restaurant operation. A moderately priced international menu features lamb couscous; blackened shrimp with creole cream sauce; pastas; and filet mignon béarnaise. There's also an interesting wine list and a large selection of beers and single-malt Scotches. The setting is cozy and candlelit, with walls used for a changing art gallery show (the bold, colorful paintings in the front room are by Moroccan owner Jamal Sahri). The eclectic crowd here varies with the music, ranging from early 20s to about 35, for the most part, including South Americans and Europeans. On Wednesday nights, live blues and jazz groups perform; Thursday, there's live Brazilian jazz; Friday, there's jukebox only (everything from Algerian Ray to the Gypsy Kings); and on Sunday, bluesy jazz singer Pam Bricker takes the stage. There's no real dance floor, but people find odd spaces to move to the tunes.

INTERNATIONAL SOUNDS

Chelsea's. 1055 Thomas Jefferson St. NW (in the Foundry Building on the C&O Canal). ☎ **202/298-8222.** Cover: $10. Open Wed–Mon. Complimentary parking in the building garage. Metro: Foggy Bottom, with a 10-minute walk.

Wednesday and Sunday, 10pm to 2am, are Arabic nights, here, featuring an Arabic band and a belly dancer. Thursday through Saturday nights are devoted to Latino music, with a DJ playing disco Latino tunes Thursdays 10:30pm to 2am, and bands playing live music 10:30pm to 4am on Friday and Saturday nights.

Coco Loco. 810 7th St. NW (between H and I sts.). ☎ **202/289-2626.** Cover: $5–$10. Open every night but Sunday. Metro: Gallery Place.

This is one of D.C.'s liveliest clubs, heralded by marquee lights. On Friday and Saturday nights, you can come for a late tapas or mixed-grill dinner (see chapter 6 for details) and stay for international music and dancing, with occasional live bands.

On Saturday night, the entertainment includes a sexy 11pm floor show featuring Brazilian exhibition dancers who begin performing in feathered and sequined Rio Rita costumes and strip down to a bare minimum. Laser lights and other special effects enhance the show, which ends with a conga line and a limbo contest. There's dancing until 3am on Friday and Saturday; occasionally there's dancing on Thursday nights, too, which lasts until 2am. Coco Loco draws an attractive upscale international crowd of all ages, including many impressively talented dancers. It's great fun.

Habana Village. 1834 Columbia Rd. NW. ☎ **202/462-6310.** Cover $5 only on Friday and Saturday nights after 10pm, and only for men. Open Wed–Sat 6:30pm–2am. Metro: Dupont Circle, with a 15-minute walk, or Woodley Park–Zoo, with a 20-minute walk.

The 2-story nightclub holds a bar/restaurant on the first floor, a dance floor and bar on the second level. Salsa and merengue lessons are given every Wednesday and Thursday evening, from 7 to 9:30pm, tango lessons every Friday and Saturday evening, same time; each lesson is $10. When dance lessons are not taking place, a DJ plays danceable Latin jazz tunes.

Kala Kala. 2439 18th St. NW. ☎ **202/232-5433.** After midnight –Sat, a $5 cover charge, for men only, includes 1 drink. Open Mon–Thurs until 2am, Fri–Sat until 3am.

The owner of this Adams-Morgan African club originally hails from Madagascar. It's a claustrophobic narrow space with a variety of African sculptures displayed on the wall. The clientele is about half African/Caribbean and half young neighborhood residents. You can order an African beer or a spicy shish kebab. A DJ plays African reggae, zouk (French Caribbean), soca (from Trinidad), salsa, and the occasional Top 40 tune.

Latin Jazz Alley. 1721 Columbia Rd. NW, on the 2nd floor of the El Migueleno Cafe. ☎ **202/328-6190.** $5 for salsa instruction; $5 for beginner, $8 for intermediate mambo lesson; or 2-drink minimum. Open Wed–Thurs 6pm–midnight, Fri–Sat 6pm–3am. Metro: Dupont Circle (Q St. exit) or Woodley Park–Zoo, with a 20- to 30-minute walk.

Another place to get in on Washington's Latin scene, this one is in Adams-Morgan. At the Alley, you can learn to dance: salsa for beginners on Wednesday, Friday, and Saturday nights at 7:30pm; and mambo, rumba, and cha-cha on Thursday nights at 7:30pm. Friday, and Saturday nights, from about 10pm to 2am, a DJ plays Latin jazz; there's no cover but there is a 2-drink minimum. Dinner is served until midnight (the food comes from El Migueleno, the Salvadorean/Mexican restaurant on the first floor.)

GAY CLUBS

Dupont Circle is the gay hub of Washington, D.C., with at least 10 gay bars within easy walking distance of one another. At either of the two Dupont Circle locales listed below, you'll find natives happy to tell you about (or take you to) the others.

The Circle Bar & Tavern. 1629 Connecticut Ave. NW (between Q and R sts.). ☎ **202/462-5575.** No cover. Sun–Thurs until 2am, Fri–Sat until 3am. Metro: Dupont Circle.

This impressively slick-looking three-story club is the largest gay bar in the Dupont Circle area. It attracts a racially mixed gay and lesbian crowd (about 80% male), mostly in the 25 to 35 age range. The Underground level, which has a dance floor, is the setting for many weekend events: lesbian rugby team parties; Log Cabin Club parties (they're a gay Republican group); gay rodeos; and gay proms. Candice Gingrich (Newt's half sister) has held receptions here. The main floor, with black-painted brick walls hung with artwork from a local gallery, has two bars, a great jukebox stocked with a variety of music, and two pool tables. The upstairs Terrace, which centers on a big rectangular bar, is adorned with fabulous floral displays. Up here, monitors show music videos; there are also pinball and video games; and, when the weather is fine, the big open-air terrace beckons.

J.R.'s. 1519 17th St. NW (between P and Q sts.). ☎ **202/328-0090.** No cover. Sun–Thurs until 2am, Fri–Sat until 3am. Metro: Dupont Circle.

More intimate than the above, this casual all-male Dupont Circle club draws a crowd that is friendly, upscale, and very attractive. The interior—not that you'll be able to see much of it, because J.R.'s is always sardine-packed wall to wall—has a 20-foot-high, pressed-tin ceiling and exposed-brick walls hung with neon beer signs. The big screen over the bar area is used to air music videos, showbiz sing-alongs on Mondays, and *South Park* viewings on Wednesdays. Thursday is an all-you-can-drink-for-$5 night, from 5:30 to 8pm; at midnight you get free shots. The balcony, with a pool table, is a little more laid-back. No food is served.

Tracks. 1111 1st St. SE. ☎ **202/488-3320.** Cover: $5–$10. Metro: Navy Yard.

This vast, high-energy club (a converted auto dealership, with 21,000 square feet inside and a 10,000-square-foot patio) is a favorite place to dance in D.C. Its chic-rather-than-funky interior houses a main dance floor centered under a mirrored ball and another with a zigzag display of video monitors, both offering great sound and light systems. DJs provide the music, and the crowd is appealingly unhinged. Thursday nights, there's progressive house and techno in the main room, progressive industrial video in another, and the crowd is predominantly straight (there's an open bar from 9 to 10pm, and pitchers of beer are $4 all night; some nights there are rave parties). Friday also draws a straight crowd for progressive and house music. Saturday is a gay night (mostly men but some women and a sprinkling of straights); the music is high-energy house in the main room, deep underground and club house in the video room. Gay country-and-western tea dances are featured Sunday afternoons through 9:30pm followed by house music, and the crowd is mostly gay and African-American. The last Tuesday of every month is lesbian night. On warm nights, much of the action centers on the fountained outdoor deck, which has a volleyball court! Other pluses: a pool table, video games, and a snack bar. Liquor service is available through 2am Thursday and Friday, till 3am Saturday and Sunday; the club often stays open until 6am.

4 The Bar Scene

Washington has a thriving and varied bar scene. If you're in the mood for a sophisticated setting, seek out a bar in one of the nicer hotels, like the Jefferson, the Willard, the Westin Fairfax, or the Carlton (see chapter 5 for more information and suggestions). If you want a convivial atmosphere and decent grub, try bars that are known for food as well as a good time. Refer to chapter 6 for details about these in particular: Capital City Brewing Company, Clyde's of Georgetown, Martin's Tavern, Music City Roadhouse, Old Ebbitt Grill, Old Glory Barbecue, and Sequoia.

But if you're looking for the more typical, drink-and-mingle, drink-and-converse, or drink-and-get-rowdy place, try these:

Asylum. 2471 18th St. NW. ☎ **202/319-9353.** No cover. Sun–Wed 8pm–2am, Thurs 5pm–2am, Fri 5pm–3am, Sat 7pm–3am. Metro: Dupont Circle, with a 15-minute walk, or Woodley Park–Zoo, with a 20-minute walk, that takes you across the Calvert St. Bridge.

This below-street joint has room for about 100 people; plays rock CDs; and has a pool table, a bar, tables for sitting and drinking, and an atmosphere made fun by the youngish patrons.

The Bar. 1416 U St. NW. ☎ **202/588-7311.** No cover. Wed–Thurs 7:30–2am, Fri–Sat 7:30–3am. Metro: U St.–Cardozo.

The Bar is a mellow place to get comfortable and listen to good music. It's cozy, with candles, sofas, and brick walls topped with a mural of dancers, diners, card players; platters of food; and bottles of wine. Musicians, usually jazz, set up in the front window. The bartender is amiable and the food not bad.

The Big Hunt. 1345 Connecticut Ave. NW (between N St. and Dupont Circle). ☎ **202/785-2333.** No cover. Sun–Thurs until 2am, Fri–Sat until 3am. Metro: Dupont Circle.

This casual and comfy Dupont Circle hangout for the 20- to 30-something crowd—billing itself as a "happy hunting ground for humans"—has a kind of *Raiders of the Lost Ark*/explorer/jungle theme. A downstairs room (the floor where music is the loudest) is adorned with exotic travel posters and animal skins; another area has leopard skin–patterned booths under canvas tenting. Amusing murals grace the balcony level, which adjoins a room with pool tables. The candlelit basement is the spot for quiet conversation. Typical bar food is available on the menu; more to the point is a beer list with close to 30 varieties on tap, most of them microbrews. New since 1998 is the outdoor patio off the back pool room.

Brickskeller. 1523 22nd St. NW. ☎ **202/293-1885.** No cover. Wed–Thurs 7:30–2am, Fri 11:30am–3am, Sat 6:30pm–3am, Sun 6:30pm–2am. Metro: Dupont Circle or Foggy Bottom.

If you like beer and you like a choice, head for Brickskeller, which has been around for nearly 40 years and offers about 1,000 beers from the world over. If you can't make up your mind, ask one of the waiters, who tend to be knowledgeable about the brews. The tavern draws students, college professors, embassy types, and people from the neighborhood. Brickskeller is a series of interconnecting rooms filled with gingham tablecloth–covered tables; upstairs rooms are open only on weekend nights. The food is generally OK; more than OK are the burgers, which include the excellent Brickburger, topped with bacon, salami, onion, and cheese; and the Ale burger, made with beer.

Café Milano. 3251 Prospect St. NW. ☎ **202/333-6183.** No cover. noon–1am daily. Metro: Foggy Bottom, with a 25-minute walk.

Located just off Wisconsin Avenue in lower Georgetown, Café Milano has gained a reputation for attracting beautiful people. You might see a few glamorous faces, and then again, you might see a bunch of people on the prowl for glamorous faces. It's often crowded, especially Thursday through Saturday nights. The food is good; in fact, Café Milano could rightfully be included in the restaurant section (the owner also runs the well-received Villa Franco; see chapter 6). Salads and pastas are excellent.

Champions. 1206 Wisconsin Ave. NW (just north of M St.). ☎ **202/965-4005.** No cover. Sun–Thurs 6pm–2am, Fri–Sat 6pm–3am. Metro: Foggy Bottom, with a 20-minute walk.

Smells like beer. This is a sports bar, where both sports fans and athletes—Redskins players among them—like to hang out. Champions lies at the end of an alley off Wisconsin Avenue—be careful at night. The two-story bar is a clutter of sports paraphernalia, with TV monitors airing nonstop sporting events. Conversation has two themes: sports and pickup lines. Champions is often packed and doesn't take reservations; in the evening, you can expect to wait for a table, so arrive early.

Cheap Eats: Happy Hours to Write Home About

Even the unfanciest of bars puts out some free nibblies to complement your drink, peanuts or pretzels at the very least. And then there are those bars that go all out: certain fine restaurants and hotels around town that set out gourmet food during happy hour, either at no cost or for an astonishingly low price. Sometimes the establishments offer specially priced drinks, and often entertainment, during specified hours on weekdays. Here are a few that even many Washingtonians don't know about:

- **Gabriel,** 2121 P St. NW, in the Radisson Barceló Hotel (☎ **202/956-6690**). This may be the best value in town. On Wednesday, Thursday, and Friday evenings, from 5:30 to 8pm for a mere $7.50, you are entitled to a superb, all-you-can-eat buffet, with a choice of about seven scrumptious tapas, quesadillas made to order, and reduced drink prices including microbrew drafts for $2.50. A more extensive lunch buffet (weekdays 11:30am to 2pm, $9.50), also with a quesadilla station, offers a similar array of tapas plus marvelous salads, cheeses, and entrées such as paella and cassoulet.
- **McCormick & Schmick's,** 1652 K St. NW, at corner of 17th St. NW (☎ **202/861-2233**). In the bar area, Monday through Friday 3:30pm to 6:30pm, Monday through Thursday 10:30pm to midnight, and Friday and Saturday 10pm to midnight, for only $1.95 each you can your pick among a giant burger, fried calamari, quesdadillas, fish tacos, and more. Friendly bartenders make you feel at home as they concoct mixed drinks with juice they squeeze right at the bar (the drinks, alas, are not discounted).
- **The Potomac Lounge,** in the Watergate Hotel, 2650 Virginia Ave. NW (☎ **202/965-2300**). Oh, dear. This posh hotel prefers to refer to its Tuesday, Wednesday, and Thursday evening specials as "taste sensations," rather than as "happy-hour buffets." Call them what you will, just be sure to dress tastefully when you sit yourself down in the hotel lounge to enjoy unlimited caviar on Tuesday, sushi on Wednesday, or salmon (prepared in a variety of styles, including smoked, herbed, and cured) on Thursday. The buffets, which cost $5 per person, are presented from 5:30 to 8pm, are offered from the fall through spring, and include music played by a pianist. Drinks are not discounted; expect to pay upwards of $6 for each.
- **Town and Country Lounge,** in the Renaissance Mayflower Hotel, 1127 Connecticut Ave. NW (☎ **202/347-3000**). This clubby, mahogany-paneled pub is the setting weeknights, from 5:30 to 7:30pm, for complimentary cocktail-hour hors d'oeuvres that change from night to night: slices of roast beef served with toast, or chicken/beef fajitas, or pastas, and so on. Here, you also have the pleasure of watching the personable bartender, Sambonn Lek, at work, whether mixing drinks or performing magic tricks. Drinks are regular price.
- **Pullman Lounge,** in the Hotel Sofitel, 1914 Connecticut Ave. NW (☎ **202/797-2000**). Weeknights, from 6 to 7pm, this lounge offers complimentary hot hors d'oeuvres, mostly French whimsies, like canapés, mini croque monsieurs, and the like. It's a buffet, so go ahead and help yourself. Beer is $1.50, mixed drinks and wine $3 each. Stay on past happy hour to hear pianist Peter Robinson and his jazz trio play between 8 and 11pm. There's no cover for the entertainment, and the hotel offers free parking.

The Dubliner. In the Phoenix Park Hotel, at 520 N. Capitol St. NW, with its own entrance on Massachusetts Ave. NW. ☎ **202/737-3773.** No cover. Sun–Thurs 11am–1am, Fri–Sat 11am–2:30am. Metro: Union Station.

This is your old Irish pub, the port you can blow into in any storm, personal or weather-related. It's got the dark wood paneling and tables, the etched-and-stained glass windows, Irish-accented staff from time to time, and, most importantly, the Auld Dubliner Amber Ale. You'll probably want to stick to drink here, but should you look at a menu, choose a burger, grilled chicken sandwich, or the roast duck salad. The Dubliner is frequented by Capitol Hill staffers and journalists who cover the Hill. Irish musical groups play nightly.

Fadó. 808 7th St. NW. ☎ **202/789-0066.** No cover. Open daily until 2am. Metro: Gallery Place/Chinatown.

Another Irish pub, this one opened in the spring of 1998, in Chinatown of all places. It's gotten a lot of attention from the start, partly because it was designed and built by the Irish Pub Company of Dublin, who shipped everything—the stone for the floors, the etched glass, and the milled wood—from Ireland. The pub has separate areas, including an old Irish "bookstore" alcove and a country cottage–style bar. Authentic Irish food, like the potato pancake, is served to accompany your Guinness. Fadó, Gaelic for "long ago," doesn't take reservations, which means that hungry patrons tend to hover over your table, waiting for you to finish.

Fox and Hounds. 1533 17th St. NW (between Q and Church sts.). ☎ **202/232-6307.** No cover. Mon–Thurs 11:30am–1:30am, Fri 11:30am–2:30am, Sat 9am–2:30am, Sun 9am–1:30am. Metro: Dupont Circle.

Although it's in the heart of the Dupont Circle gay district, Fox and Hounds is a basically straight and very friendly neighborhood bar that offers pretty good singles action. It's under the same ownership as the Trio restaurant and offers its identical extensive menu (see details in chapter 6). Genial owner George Mallios describes it as "Cheers for the 20-something set." In the beery-smelling interior, the walls are hung with fox-hunting prints and posters from the Disney movie *The Fox and the Hound.* The jukebox blares the latest hits, and sporting events are aired, to enthusiastic commentary, on a TV over the bar. Spring through fall, the large patio fronting 17th Street is packed nightly. Customers like the wide variety of coffee-liqueur drinks, premium wines by the glass, imported beers, and microbrews.

Lucky Bar. 1221 Connecticut Ave. NW. ☎ **202/331-3733.** No cover. Mon–Thurs 3pm–2am, Fri–Sat noon–3am. Metro: Dupont Circle or Farragut North.

You used to be able to dance here, when the place was known as Planet Fred. As the name has changed, so has the focus: to sitting back and relaxing. DJ or jukebox music plays, but never so loud that you can't carry on a conversation. The bar has a front room overlooking Connecticut Avenue, and a back room decorated with good-luck signs; couches; hanging TVs; booths; and a pool table.

Mr. Smith's of Georgetown. 3104 M St. NW. ☎ **202/333-3104.** No cover. Sun–Thurs 11:30am–1:30am, Fri–Sat 11:30am–2:30am. Metro: Foggy Bottom, with a 15-minute walk.

Mr. Smith's bills itself as the Friendliest Saloon in Town, but the truth is that it's so popular among regulars, you're in danger of being ignored if the staff doesn't recognize you. The bar, which opened about 30 years ago, has a front room with original brick walls, wooden seats, and a long bar, at which you can count on finding pairs of newfound friends telling obscene jokes, loudly. At the end of this room is a large piano around which customers congregate each night to accompany the pianist.

(Have a daiquiri—Mr. Smith's is known for them.) The garden room, an interior light-filled room that adjoins an outdoor garden area, lies beyond.

Nathans. 3150 M St. NW. ☎ **202/338-2600.** No cover. Mon–Thurs 2pm–2am, Fri 2pm–3am, Sat 2pm–3am, Sun 11am–2am. Metro: Foggy Bottom, with a 20-minute walk.

Nathans is on the corner of M Street and Wisconsin Avenue, in the heart of Georgetown. If you pop in here in mid-afternoon, it's a quiet place to grab a beer or glass of wine and watch the action out on the street. (I know someone who uses Nathans as an in-town office for his suburban Virginia–based business.) Visit at night, though, and it's the more typical bar scene, crowded with locals, out-of-towners, students, and a sprinkling of couples in from the suburbs. That's the front room. The back room at Nathans is a civilized, candlelit restaurant serving classic American fare prepared by Markey Marks's brother, Paul Wahlberg, who's getting good reviews. Thursday through Saturday, once dinner is over, this room turns into a dance hall, playing DJ music and attracting the 20-somethings Thursday and Friday nights, 20- to 40-somethings on Saturday nights.

Ozio, Martini and Cigar Lounge. 1835 K St. NW. ☎ **202/822-6000.** Cover: $20 Fri–Sat after 10:30pm. Open Mon–Wed until 2am, Fri–Sat until 3am. Closed Sun. Happy hour weekdays 4–7pm. Metro: Farragut West, Farragut North.

Winston Churchill's rule of life reigns here: "Smoking cigars and drinking of alcohol before, after, and if need be, during all meals, and intervals between them." Ozio has a whimsical/upscale art-deco interior, with distressed walls and columns, Persian rugs strewn on concrete floors, and comfortable seating in plush armchairs, sofas, and banquettes. The lighting is nightclubby, and the music mellow (light jazz, blues, Sinatra, Tony Bennett). People dance wherever they can find a space. Ozio is the kind of place where limos are parked out front, and the suit-and-tie crowd is comprised of senators, hotshot professionals, and local sports figures. Exotic-looking cigar men (the stogie equivalents of sommeliers) come by during the evening with humidors. Vodka and gin martinis are a favorite drink as are single-malt Scotches (choose from a list of 20). The menu ranges from tapas and pastas to filet mignon.

Post Pub. 1422 L St. NW. ☎ **202/628-2111.** No cover. Mon–Fri 11am–midnight, Sat 11am–8pm. Metro: McPherson Square.

This joint fits into the "comfortable shoe" category. Situated between Vermont and 15th Streets, across from the offices of the *Washington Post,* the pub gets busy at lunch, grows quiet in the afternoon, and picks up again in the evening, but the place is never empty. Post Pub has two rooms, which are furnished with old-fashioned black banquettes, faux wood paneling, mirrored beer insignias, juke-boxes, cigarette machines, and a long bar with tall stools. There are different happy hour specials every night, like the 5 to 9pm Thursday "Anything Absolute," which offers drinks made with Absolut vodka for $2.50 each. The food is homey and inexpensive (under $10)—onion rings, sandwiches, chicken parmigiana, and the like.

The Rock. 717 6th St. NW. ☎ **202/842-7625.** No cover. Mon–Thurs 3pm–2am, Fri–Sat noon–3am, Sun noon–2am. Metro: Gallery Place.

The Rock is the district's newest sports bar, situating itself in probably the best location a sports establishment could have: across the street from the MCI Center. The 3-floor bar fills a former warehouse, its decor a montage of preexisting exposed pipes and concrete floors, and TV screens, pool tables, and sports memorabilia. The most popular spot is the third floor, where the pool tables and a cigar lounge are located. In good weather, folks head to the rooftop bar.

Arlington Row

As unlikely as it seems, one of the hottest spots in Washington's nightlife corner, suddenly, is a stretch of suburban street in Arlington, Virginia. I'm talking about a section of Wilson Boulevard in the Clarendon neighborhood, roughly between Highland and Danville Streets. For many years, people referred to this area as "Little Vietnam," because of the many Vietnamese cafes and grocery stores that flourished here. Now some are calling it "the new Adams-Morgan," because, in addition to the still-strong Vietnamese presence, six or seven pretty darn good nightclubs have popped up. The clubs join other recent additions to the area: town houses, condominiums, a fancy (and huge) Fresh Fields gourmet emporium, and several well-reviewed restaurants.

Let's get one thing straight: this isn't Adams-Morgan. Adams-Morgan is urban, ethnic, and on the edge. Black clothes, body piercings, colorful hair, tatoos, and bad attitudes are de rigueur. Arlington Row is a lot tamer, attracting, so far anyway, a mostly white crowd of all ages, dressed, usually, for comfort. Certainly, the clubs in Arlington Row are more accessible: Metro stops are nearby, parking is easier, streets are safer, and clubs front right on the street with picture windows drawing passersby in, and letting you see out. Adams-Morgan clubs, by contrast, lie a bit inconveniently off the Metro line, in a crowded part of town where parking is impossible, and tend to be stacked within a town house, where space is tight, making entry exclusive.

But there's one key reason why I'm recommending this area: the music. It's live, it's good (most of the time), and it's here nightly in most of these clubs, in greater supply than in Adams-Morgan, believe it or not. So take the Metro to the **Clarendon stop** and walk down Wilson, or drive up Wilson from Key Bridge, turn left on Edgewood Road, and park in the vast (and free) lot where the street dead-ends. Then walk to these spots and check 'em out. Food is served at each site.

Galaxy Hut, 2711 Wilson Blvd. (☎ **703/525-8646**). No cover. Although it's small, Galaxy Hut is a comfortable bar on weeknights, with far-out art on the walls and a patio in the alley. There's live music on the weekends, of the "new music" variety (original rock and roll).

IOTA, 2832 Wilson Blvd. (☎ **703/522-8340**). Cover: If there's a cover it runs about $4, but can be as high as $10 when the band is really good.

The Tombs. 1226 36th St. NW. ☎ **202/337-6668.** Cover sometimes on Tuesday nights, never more than $5. Open Mon–Fri 11:30am–1:30am, Sat 11am–1:30am, Sun 10:30am–1:30am. Metro: Foggy Bottom, with a 40-to-45-minute walk.

Housed in a converted 19th-century Federal-style home, the Tombs, which opened in 1962, is a favorite hangout for students and faculty of nearby Georgetown University. (Bill Clinton came here during his college years.) GU types tend to congregate at the central bar and surrounding tables, while local residents tend to head for "the Sweeps," the room that lies down a few steps and has red-leather banquettes.

Directly below the upscale 1789 restaurant (see chapter 6 for details), the Tombs benefits from menu supervision from 1789 chef Riz Lacoste. The menu offers burgers, sandwiches, and salads, as well as more serious fare.

Townhouse Tavern. 1637 R St. NW. ☎ **202/234-5747.** No cover. Sun–Thurs 8am–2am, Fri–Sat 8am–3am. Metro: Dupont Circle, with a short walk.

Here, up-and-coming local bands take the stage nightly in a setting with minimal decor (cement floor, exposed brick walls and wood-beamed ceiling). There's a patio in back.

Whitlow's on Wilson, 2854 Wilson Blvd. (☎ **703/276-9693**). Cover: $3 Fri–Sat after 10pm.

Spread throughout 3 rooms, Whitlow's is the biggest of the bunch in the area. The first room showcases music, usually blues, with anything from surfer music to rock and roll thrown in. The place has the appearance of a diner, from Formica table-booths to soda fountain, and serves retro diner food. The two other rooms hold coin-operated pool tables, English dartboards, and air-hockey games.

Clarendon Grill, 1101 N. Highland St. (☎ **703/524-7455**). Cover: $2–$5. This one wins for best decor, which sports a construction motiff: murals of construction workers, building materials displayed under glass-covered bar, and so on. The music is a mix of modern rock, jazz, and reggae and is live Tuesday through Saturday.

Now, get in your car, hop the Metro, or get out your rambling shoes to visit two other places, at opposite ends, each about 1 mile in either direction from this stretch of Wilson:

Rhodeside Grill, 1835 Wilson Blvd. (☎ **703/243-0145**). Cover: averages $3. Tues–Sat, starting at 9:30pm.

Heading toward the district on Wilson you reach Rhodeside Grill (3 blocks from the Courthouse Metro stop). A well-liked restaurant serving American cuisine occupies the first floor, while downstairs you'll find the rec room–like bar, which features excellent live bands playing roots rock, jazz funk, Latin percussion, country rock, blues —you name it.

Bistro Bistro, 4301 N. Fairfax Dr. (☎ **703/522-1800**). No cover.

Heading the opposite direction from the Clarendon neighborhood, up Wilson, deeper into Arlington, you reach Bistro Bistro (just off the boulevard or within a short walk from the Ballston Metro stop). Here again, the food (more American cuisine) gets kudos. In addition to a jazz brunch on Sundays, the restaurant/bar features jazz, jump blues, Texas swing, or rock groups every Saturday night

Anytime you go by this place, people are going in and out. It appears to be a home away from home for much of the neighborhood. You can sit outside at a sidewalk table or move indoors, either to the basement bar, with a fantastic CD jukebox, pool table, and pinball machines; or to the upstairs bar with its TV turned to a sports event. Owners and bartenders R.T. Smith and Doug Edgerton are known to many from their stints at Fox and Hounds, nearby (see listing above). Bar food at the tavern is a cut above: black-bean soup, cajun popcorn, and lamb chops. The Townhouse occupies the same building that for decades belonged to the Spanish restaurant El Bodegon (upstairs) and the Mexican restaurant La Fonda (downstairs), which I, for one, miss.

The Tune Inn. 33½ Pennsylvania Ave. SE. ☎ **202/543-2725.** No cover. Sun–Thurs 8am–2am, Fri–Sat 8am–3am. Metro: Capitol South.

Capitol Hill has a number of bars that qualify as "institutions," but the Tune Inn is probably the most popular. Capitol Hill staffers and their bosses, apparently at ease in dive surroundings, have been coming here since it opened in 1955. Or maybe it's the cheap beer and greasy burgers that draw them. Anyway, stop in.

Tunnicliff's Tavern. 222 7th St. SE. ☎ **202/546-3663.** www.tunnicliffs.com. No cover. noon–2am daily. Metro: Eastern Market.

Directly across from Eastern Market is another Capitol Hill institution, named for the original, circa-1796 Tunnicliff's Tavern. (This Tunnicliff's opened in 1988.) An outdoor cafe fronts the tavern, which includes a great bar and a partly set-apart dining room. You're likely to see Hill people here; the last time I was there, Louisiana Senator John Breaux and his wife stopped by. Proprietress Lynne Breaux, though not related to the senator, hails from New Orleans and cultivates a Mardi Gras atmosphere that includes live music (no cover) on Saturday nights. The menu features some standard New Orleans items, like po'boys, gumbo, and fried oysters, as well as nachos and other bar fare. Breaux likes to make everyone feel welcome, including families, and has toys and coloring books at the ready.

XandO. 1350 Connecticut Ave. NW. ☎ **202/296-9341.** No cover. Mon–Thurs 6:30am–1am, Fri 6:30am–2am, Sat 7am–2am, Sun 7am–1am. Metro: Dupont Circle, 19th St. exit.

Popular from the start, XandO (pronounced "zando") is a welcoming place in the morning for a coffee drink, and even more inviting for a cocktail as the day progresses. Men, you'll see a lot of cute girls hanging here, drawn perhaps, by the s'mores, which you make yourselves, and other delicious desserts. (XandO also serves sandwiches and soups.) The music is loud, the decor a cross between bar and living room.

5 More Entertainment

CINEMA

With the advent of VCRs, classic film theaters have almost become extinct. Other than the **Mary Pickford Theater** in the Madison Building of the Library of Congress (see chapter 7), there is only one choice in this category (and at this writing, the program was entering into a period of transition; to the best of my knowledge, the following is still true):

AFI (American Film Institute) Theater. At the Kennedy Center, New Hampshire Ave. NW and Rock Creek Pkwy. ☎ **202/828-4090** (information) or 202/785-4601 (box office). $6.50; $5.50 for members (AFI Theater memberships are $20 a year), senior citizens, and students under 18 with ID. Underground parking at the Kennedy Center, subject to availability, is $8 for the entire evening after 5pm. Metro: Foggy Bottom.

This marvelous facility shows classic films, works of independent filmmakers, and foreign films, and presents themed festivals and the like in a 224-seat theater designed to offer the highest standard of projection, picture, and sound quality. There's something showing almost every Wednesday to Sunday evening and weekend afternoon. The AFI also sponsors audience-participation discussions with major directors, film stars, and screenwriters; for example, Linda Yellin, Sigourney Weaver, Milos Foreman, Gore Vidal, Nora Ephron, Faye Wray, and Jonathan Demme.

FREE SHOWS

In D.C., some of the best things at night are free—or very cheap. See chapter 7 for information about free entertainment offered year-round by individual museums and historic sites; see information earlier in this chapter about the free performances staged by the **Kennedy Center,** the **Shakespeare Theatre,** and the **Carter Barron Amphitheater.**

The city comes especially alive in summer when numerous outdoor concerts take place all around town. Choose a night, any night, and you will find a military band playing at one of three locations in Washington, D.C.: the **U.S. Capitol,** the **Sylvan Theater** on the grounds of the Washington Monument, or the **Navy Memorial Plaza.** These bands perform jazz, show tunes, blues, music for strings—you name it. The concerts begin at 8pm and continue every night June through Labor Day. For details about military events, call the individual branches: the U.S. Army Band, "Pershing's Own" (☎ **703/696-3399**); the U.S. Navy Band (☎ **202/433-2525** for a 24-hour recording or 202/433-6090); the U.S. Marine Band, "The President's Own" (☎ **202/433-4011** for a 24-hour recording or 202/433-5809); and the U.S. Air Force Band, "America's International Musical Ambassadors" (☎ **202/767-5658** for a 24-hour recording or 202/767-4310).

On the southeast side of town, you'll find renowned Washington blues and jazz artists doing their thing at the **Fort Dupont Summer Theatre,** Minnesota Ave. SE at Randle Circle, in Fort Dupont Park (☎ **202/426-7723** or 202/619-7222), every Friday and Saturday at 8:30pm from sometime in July to the end of August. Bring a blanket and a picnic dinner; arrive early to get a good spot on the lawn. Fort Dupont features both talented local performers and nationally known acts, such as Marion Meadows, Miles Jaye, the Sensational Nightingales, Pieces of a Dream, and Roy Ayers. No tickets are required, and admission is free.

Concerts at the Capitol, an American Festival, is sponsored jointly by the National Park Service and Congress. It's a series of free summer concerts by the National Symphony Orchestra that takes place at 8pm on the west side of the Capitol on Memorial Day, July 4, and Labor Day. Seating is on the lawn, so bring a picnic. Major guest stars in past years have included Ossie Davis (a narrator and host), Leontyne Price, Johnny Cash, Rita Moreno, Mary Chapin Carpenter, and Mstislav Rostropovich. The music ranges from light classical, to country, to show tunes of the Gershwin/Rodgers and Hammerstein genre. For further information, call ☎ **202/619-7222.**

Two only-in-Washington, not-to-be-missed outdoor events are the **Smithsonian's Festival of American Folklife,** which offers a potpourri of musical and cultural performances and takes place for 5 to 10 days always including July 4; and the **National Independence Day Celebration** on the Mall. For more information on these events, see the "Calendar of Events" for June and July in chapter 2.

Finally, the Washington National Cathedral and its grounds are a magnificent setting for the cathedral's annual **Summer Festival** series of musical events, which include on Saturdays at 12:30pm a weekly carillon recital ("best heard from the Bishop's Garden," according to a staff member). Call ☎ **202/537-6200** for details.

11

Side Trips from Washington, D.C.

If you have the time and inclination, head by Metro, car, bike, or boat to visit George Washington's home, Mount Vernon, stopping on the way to tour the town he hung out in, Alexandria. There's plenty to see at each of these sites. But don't expect to find them less crowded than Washington attractions; their suburban locations and proximity to the downtown make them popular spots for local tourists and out-of-towners alike.

1 Mount Vernon

No visit to Washington would be complete without a trip to Mount Vernon, the estate of George Washington. Only 16 miles south of the capital, this southern plantation dates from a 1674 land grant to a certain Washington—the president's great-grandfather.

ESSENTIALS

GETTING THERE If you're going **by car,** take any of the bridges over the Potomac into Virginia to the George Washington Memorial Parkway (Rte. 1) going south; the parkway ends at Mount Vernon. **Tourmobile buses** (☎ 202/554-5100) depart daily, April through October only, from Arlington National Cemetery and the Washington Monument. The round-trip fare is $22 for adults, $11 for children 3 to 11 (free for children under 3) and includes the admission fee to Mount Vernon (for details on the Tourmobile, see p. 62 in "Getting Around" in chapter 4).

Gray Line bus tours go to Mount Vernon, as do several boat cruises. **Boat tours** to Mount Vernon include the Spirit Cruises line's *Potomac Spirit,* which leave from the Washington waterfront; and the Potomac Riverboat Cruise's *Miss Christin,* a two-level vessel, which departs from the pier adjacent to the Torpedo Factory, at the bottom of King Street in Old Town Alexandria. See the section on "Organized Tours," in chapter 7 for further information about boat and bus excursions to Mount Vernon.

If you're in the mood for exercise in a pleasant setting, **rent a bike** (see "Outdoor Activities" in chapter 7 for rental locations) and hop on the pathway that runs along the Potomac. In Washington, this is the Rock Creek Park Trail; once you cross Memorial Bridge into Virginia, the name changes to the Mount Vernon Trail, which,

Side Trips from Washington, D.C.

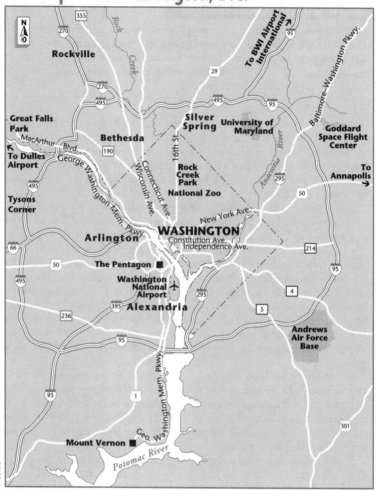

1-0818C

as it sounds, is a straight shot to Mount Vernon. The section from Memorial Bridge to Mount Vernon is about 19 miles in all.

TOURING THE ESTATE

Mount Vernon. ☎ **703/780-2000.** www.mountvernon.org. Admission $8 adults, $7.50 senior citizens, $4 children 6–11, children under 6 free. Apr–Aug, daily 8am–5pm; Mar, Sept, and Oct, daily 9am–5pm; Nov–Feb, daily 9am–4pm. Allow at least 2 hours to see everything A map is provided at the entrance. To get here by car, take any of the bridges over the Potomac into Virginia to the George Washington Memorial Parkway South, which ends at Mount Vernon. Tourmobile also stops here. The *Spirit of Mount Vernon* (☎ **202/554-8000**) plies the Potomac to Mount Vernon from the District.

Mount Vernon was purchased for $200,000 in 1858 by the Mount Vernon Ladies' Association from John Augustine Washington, great-grandnephew of the first

Special Activities at Mount Vernon

There's an ongoing schedule of events at Mount Vernon, especially in summer. For adults, these might include tours focusing on 18th-century gardens, slave life, colonial crafts, or archaeology; for children there are hands-on history programs and treasure hunts. Call ☎ **703/780-2000** to find out if anything is on during your visit.

---

president. Without the group's purchase, the estate might have crumbled and disappeared, for neither the federal government nor the Commonwealth of Virginia had wanted to buy the property when it was earlier offered for sale. The restoration is an unmarred beauty; many of the furnishings are original pieces acquired by Washington, and the rooms have been repainted in the original colors favored by George and Martha.

Mount Vernon's mansion and grounds are stunning. Some 500 of the original 8,000 acres (divided into five farms) owned by Washington are still intact. Washington delighted in riding horseback around his property, directing planting and other activities; the Bowling Green entrance is still graced by some of the trees he planted (unfortunately, the cherry trees he cut down are long gone). The American Revolution and his years as president took Washington away from his beloved estate most of the time. He finally retired to Mount Vernon in 1797, just 2 years before his death, to "view the solitary walk and tread the paths of private life with heartfelt satisfaction." He is buried on the estate. Martha was buried next to him in May 1802. Public memorial services are held at the estate every year on the third Monday in February, the date commemorating Washington's birthday; admission is free that day.

Mount Vernon has been one of the nation's most-visited shrines since the mid-19th century. Today more than a million people tour the property annually. There's no formal tour, but attendants stationed throughout the house and grounds provide brief orientations and answer questions. The best time to visit is off-season; during the heavy tourist months, avoid weekends and holidays if possible, and year-round, arrive early to beat the crowds.

The house itself is an outstanding prototype of colonial architecture, an example of the aristocratic lifestyle in the 18th century, and of course, the home of our first president. There are a number of family portraits, and the rooms are appointed as if they were in day-to-day use.

After leaving the house, you can tour the outbuildings: the kitchen, slave quarters, storeroom, smokehouse, overseer's quarters, coachhouse, and stables. A 4-acre exhibit area called "George Washington, Pioneer Farmer" includes a replica of Washington's 16-sided barn and fields of crops that he grew (corn, wheat, oats, and so forth). Docents in period costumes demonstrate 18th-century farming methods. A museum on the property exhibits Washington memorabilia, and details of the restoration are explained in the museum's annex; there's also a gift shop on the premises. You'll want to walk around the grounds (most pleasant in nice weather), and see the wharf, the slave burial ground, the greenhouse, the tomb containing George and Martha Washington's sarcophagi (24 other family members are also interred here), the lawns, and the gardens.

WHERE TO DINE

At the entrance to Mount Vernon you'll find a snack bar serving light fare, and there are picnic tables outside. If a picnic is what you have in mind, drive a mile north on the parkway to Riverside Park, where you can lunch at tables overlooking the Potomac.

Mount Vernon Inn. Near the entrance to Mount Vernon. ☎ **703/780-0011.** Reservations recommended at dinner. Lunch $4.50–$8.50, dinner $12–$24, prix-fixe dinner $14. AE, DISC, MC, V. Mon–Sat 11am–3:30pm and 5–9pm, Sun 11am–3:30pm. AMERICAN.

Lunch or dinner at the inn is an intrinsic part of the Mount Vernon experience. It's a quaintly charming, colonial-style restaurant, complete with period furnishings and three working fireplaces. The staff sports 18th-century costume. Be sure to begin your meal with an order of homemade peanut and chestnut soup. Lunch entrees range from colonial turkey pye (a sort of Early American quiche served in a crock with garden vegetables and a puffed pastry top) to 20th-century-style burger and fries. There's a full bar, and premium wines are offered by the glass. At dinner, tablecloths and candlelight make this a plusher choice. Fortunately, a prix-fixe dinner means that it is also affordable. The meal includes soup (perhaps broccoli cheddar) or salad, an entree such as Maryland crab cakes or roast venison with peppercorn sauce, homemade breads, and dessert (like Bavarian parfait or English trifle).

2 Alexandria

Founded by a group of Scottish tobacco merchants, the seaport town of Alexandria came into being in 1749 when a 60-acre tract of land was auctioned off in half-acre lots. Colonists came from miles around, in ramshackle wagons and stately carriages, in sloops, brigantines, and lesser craft, to bid on land that would be "commodious for trade and navigation and tend greatly to the ease and advantage of the frontier inhabitants. . . ." The auction took place in Market Square (still intact today), and the surveyor's assistant was a capable lad of 17 named George Washington.

Today, the original 60 acres of lots in George Washington's hometown (also Robert E. Lee's) are the heart of Old Town, a multimillion-dollar urban-renewal historic district. Many Alexandria streets still bear their original colonial names (King, Queen, Prince, Princess, Royal—you get the drift), while others like Jefferson, Franklin, Lee, Patrick, and Henry are obviously post-Revolutionary.

In this "mother lode of Americana," the past is being restored in an ongoing archaeological and historical research program. The present can be seen in the abundance of shops, boutiques, art galleries, and restaurants capitalizing on tourism, but it's easy to imagine yourself in colonial times by smelling the fragrant tobacco; listening to the rumbling of horse-drawn vehicles over cobblestone; envisioning the oxcarts piled with crates of chickens, country-cured ham, and casks of cheese and butter; and picturing the bustling waterfront where fishermen brought in the daily catch and foreign vessels unloaded exotic cargo.

ESSENTIALS

GETTING THERE   If you're traveling **by car,** take the Arlington Memorial or the 14th Street Bridge to the George Washington Memorial Parkway south, which becomes Washington Street in Old Town Alexandria. Washington Street intersects with King Street, Alexandria's main thoroughfare. Turn left from Washington Street onto one of the streets before or after King Street (southbound left turns are not permitted from Washington onto King Street), and you'll be heading toward the waterfront and the heart of Old Town. Turn right onto King Street and you'll find an avenue of shops and restaurants. You can obtain a free parking permit from the Alexandria Convention and Visitors Association (see below), or park at meters or in garages.

The easiest way to make the trip may be the **Metro's yellow line** to the King Street station. From there, you can catch a blue-and-gold DASH bus (AT2 or AT5 eastbound) to the Visitors Association, or you can walk, although it's about a mile from the station into the center of Old Town. The town is compact, so you won't need a car once you arrive.

VISITOR INFORMATION The **Alexandria Convention and Visitors Association,** located at Ramsay House, 221 King St., at Fairfax St. (☎ 800/388-9119 or 703/838-4200; fax 703/838-4683), is open daily from 9am to 5pm (closed January 1, Thanksgiving, and December 25). Here you can obtain a map/self-guided walking tour and brochures about the area; learn about special events that might be scheduled during your visit and get tickets for them; and receive answers to any questions you might have about accommodations, restaurants, sights, or shopping. The association supplies materials in five languages.

If you come by car, get a free 1-day parking permit here for complimentary parking at any 2-hour meter for up to 24 hours. It can be renewed for a second day.

ORGANIZED TOURS It's easy to see Alexandria on your own by putting yourself in the hands of colonially attired guides at the various attractions, but you might consider taking a comprehensive walking tour. The three tour companies listed below rotate the role of guiding you on the daily walking tour offered at 11am and leaving from Ramsay House Visitor Center, for $5 per person (no price breaks for kids). Tours offered individually by these companies are as follows:

Doorways to Old Virginia (☎ 703/548-0100). Doorways operates 1-hour ghost tours on weekend evenings spring through October (weather permitting), departing from 221 King St. at 7:30pm and again at 9pm Friday and Saturday, at 7:30pm only on Sunday; the cost is $5 for adults, $3 for children ages 7 to 17, free for children 6 and younger.

Alexandria Tours (☎ 703/329-1122). This company offers daily 1-hour **Overview Tours** at noon for $5 per person (ages 6 and under free) and 1-hour **Ghosts, Legends, and Folklore Tours** beginning at Market Square, nightly at 8pm, for $5 per person. Reservations are required.

The Old Town Experience (☎ 703/836-0694). On this guided tour of Alexandria's historic district, you learn about Alexandria's hospitality symbols, merchant houses, flounder houses, busybodies, and more. The tour takes in the Gadsby's Tavern Museum, Carlyle House, and the Stabler-Leadbeater Apothecary Shop. Call ahead; their $5 tours are by appointment only.

CITY LAYOUT Old Town is very small. It's helpful to know, when looking for addresses, that Alexandria is laid out in a grid. At the center is the intersection of Washington Street and King Street. Streets that run parallel to Washington Street, running north and south, are identified according to which side of King Street they lie, so Alfred Street, for example, is N. Alfred Street on the side of King Street closest to the city of Washington; once it crosses King Street, it becomes S. Alfred Street Understand? Take a look at the map and these instructions should become clear.

SPECIAL EVENTS

The events listed below are only the major events. If you're planning to participate in any of them, book your accommodations far ahead and contact the Visitors Association for details and advance tickets. Whenever you come, you're sure to run into

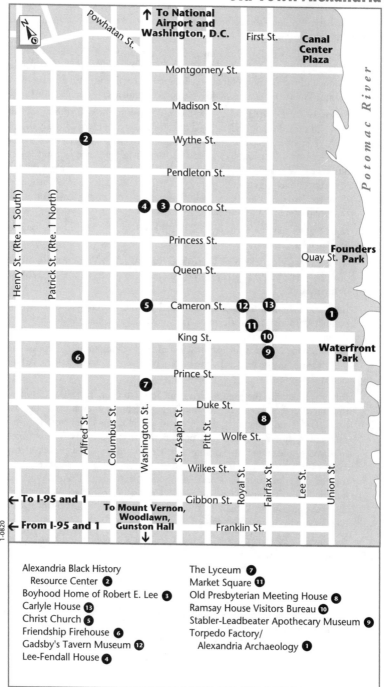

Old Town Alexandria

Alexandria Black History
  Resource Center **2**
Boyhood Home of Robert E. Lee **3**
Carlyle House **13**
Christ Church **5**
Friendship Firehouse **6**
Gadsby's Tavern Museum **12**
Lee-Fendall House **4**

The Lyceum **7**
Market Square **11**
Old Presbyterian Meeting House **8**
Ramsay House Visitors Bureau **10**
Stabler-Leadbeater Apothecary Museum **9**
Torpedo Factory/
  Alexandria Archaeology **1**

some activity or other—a jazz festival, tea garden or tavern gambol, quilt exhibit, wine tasting, or organ recital.

January The birthdays of Robert E. Lee and his father, Revolutionary War Colonel "Light Horse Harry" Lee, are celebrated together at the Lee-Fendall House and the Boyhood Home of Robert E. Lee on the third Sunday of the month. The party features period music, refreshments, and house tours.

February Alexandria celebrates **George Washington's Birthday,** on the weekend preceding the federal legal holiday, usually the third Monday in February. Festivities typically include a colonial-costume or black-tie banquet followed by a ball at Gadsby's Tavern, a 10-kilometer race, special tours, a Revolutionary War–style encampment at Fort Ward Park (complete with uniformed troops engaging in skirmishes), the nation's largest George Washington Birthday Parade (50,000 to 75,000 people attend each year), and 18th-century comic opera performances.

March On the first Saturday in March, King Street is the site of a popular **St. Patrick's Day Parade.**

April Alexandria celebrates **Historic Garden Week** in Virginia with tours of privately owned local (usually historic) homes and gardens the third Saturday of the month.

June The **Red Cross Waterfront Festival,** the second weekend in June, honors Alexandria's historic importance as a seaport and the vitality of its Potomac shoreline today with a display of historic tall ships, ship tours, boat rides and races, nautical art exhibits, waterfront walking tours, fireworks, children's games, an arts and crafts show, food booths, and entertainment. Admission is charged.

July Gather with the clans for **Virginia Scottish Games,** a 2-day Celtic festival the fourth weekend of the month that celebrates Alexandria's Highland heritage. Activities include athletic events (such as the caber toss, in which competitors heave a 140-pound pole in the air), musicians (playing reels, strathspeys, and laments), fiddling and harp competitions, a parade of clan societies in tartans, a Celtic crafts fair, storytelling, Highland dance performances and competitions, booths selling Scottish foods and wares, dog trials featuring Scottish breeds, and a Scottish Country Dance Party. Admission is charged; you can get a small discount on tickets purchased in advance at the Ramsay House Visitors Center.

September Chili enthusiasts can sample "bowls of red" at the **Hard Times Chili Cookoff** in Waterfront Park. Contestants from almost every U.S. state and territory compete, and for an admission charge of a few dollars, you can taste all their creations. Proceeds go to charity. Fiddling contests, jalapeño-eating contests, and country music are part of the fun.

October Explore the ghosts and graveyards of Alexandria on a **Halloween Walking Tour** with a lantern-carrying guide in 18th-century costume. The tour focuses on eerie Alexandria legend, myth, and folklore. See "Organized Tours," above, for phone numbers and costs.

November The **Historic Alexandria Antiques Show,** on the third weekend of the month, features several dozen dealers from many states displaying an array of high-quality antiques in room settings, including jewelry, silver, rare books, rugs, paintings, folk art, furniture, pottery, and decorative objects.

Admission charged; proceeds help restore historic sites. Pricier activities include a gala opening party (about $75 admission) and a champagne brunch with a featured speaker (about $40).

There's a **Christmas Tree Lighting** in Market Square the Friday after Thanksgiving; the ceremony, which includes choir singing, puppet shows, dance performances, and an appearance by Santa and his elves, begins at 7pm. The night the tree is lighted, thousands of tiny lights adorning King Street trees are also illuminated.

December   Holiday festivities continue with the **Annual Scottish Christmas Walk** on the first Saturday in December. Activities include kilted bagpipers, Highland dancers, a parade of Scottish clans (with horses and dogs), caroling, fashion shows, storytelling, booths (selling crafts, antiques, food, hot mulled punch, heather, fresh wreaths, and holly), and children's games. Admission is charged for some events.

The **Old Town Christmas Candlelight Tour,** the second week in December, visits seasonally decorated historic Alexandria homes and an 18th-century tavern. There are colonial dancing, string quartets, madrigal and opera singers, and refreshments. Purchase tickets at the Ramsay House Visitors Center.

There are so many holiday season activities, the Visitors Association issues a special brochure about them each year. Pick one up to learn about decorations, workshops, walking tours, tree lightings, concerts, bazaars, bake sales, crafts fairs, and much more.

WHAT TO SEE & DO

In addition to the annual events mentioned above, there's much to see and do.

Admissions Tip: Available at Ramsay House (see "Visitor Information," above) is a money-saving block ticket for admission to five historic Alexandria properties: Gadsby's Tavern, the Boyhood Home of Robert E. Lee, the Carlyle House, Stabler-Leadbeater Apothecary Shop, and the Lee-Fendall House. The ticket, which can also be purchased at any of the buildings, costs $12 for adults, $5 for children ages 11 to 17; children under 11 enter free. You can also purchase block tickets for the Lee Houses alone ($6 adults, $3 children) or for the three "Market Square" sites: Gadsby's Tavern, the Apothecary Shop, and Carlyle House ($3 adults, $2 children), but I would recommend that you visit all five.

Alexandria Black History Resource Center. 638 N. Alfred St. (at Wythe St.). ☎ **703/ 838-4356.** Free admission (donations accepted). Tues–Sat 10am–4pm.

In a 1940s building that originally housed the black community's first public library, the center exhibits historical objects, photographs, documents, and memorabilia relating to African-American Alexandrians from the 18th century forward. In addition to the permanent collection, the museum presents twice-yearly rotating exhibits and other activities. If you're interested in further studies, check out the center's Watson Reading Room.

✪ **Boyhood Home of Robert E. Lee.** 607 Oronoco St. (between St. Asaph and Washington sts.). ☎ **703/548-8454.** Admission $4 adults, $2 children 11–17, free for children under 11; or buy the block ticket. Tours given Mon–Sat 10am–3:30pm, Sun 1–3:30pm. Closed Easter, Thanksgiving, and Dec 15–Jan 31 (except for the Sun closest to Jan 19, Robert E. Lee's birthday).

Revolutionary War cavalry hero Henry "Light Horse Harry" Lee brought his wife, Ann Hill Carter, and five children to this early Federal-style mansion in 1812, when

Robert, destined to become a Confederate military leader, was just 5 years old. A tour of the house, built in 1795, provides a glimpse into the gracious lifestyle of Alexandria's gentry. George Washington was an occasional guest of two earlier occupants, John Potts (the builder of the house) and Colonel William Fitzhugh. In 1804, the Fitzhughs' daughter, Mary Lee, married Martha Washington's grandson, George Washington Parke Custis, in the drawing room. And the Custises' daughter, Mary Ann Randolph, married Robert E. Lee.

General Lafayette honored Ann Hill Carter Lee with a visit to the house in October 1824 in tribute to her husband, "Light Horse Harry" Lee, who had died in 1818. Lafayette had been a comrade-in-arms with Lee during the American Revolution. The drawing room today is called the Lafayette Room to commemorate that visit.

On the tour, you'll see the nursery, with its little canopied bed and toy box; Mrs. Lee's room; the Lafayette Room, furnished in period antiques, with the tea table set up for use; the morning room, where *The Iliad* translated into Latin reposes on a gaming table (both "Light Horse Harry" and Robert were classical scholars); and the winter kitchen. The furnishings are of the Lee period but did not belong to the family. The house was occupied by 17 different owners after the Lees left. It was made into a museum in 1967.

✪ **Carlyle House.** 121 N. Fairfax St. (at Cameron St.). ☎ **703/549-2997.** Admission $4 adults, $2 children 11–17, free for children under 11; or buy a block ticket. Tues–Sat 10am–4:30pm, Sun noon–4:30pm. Tours are given every half-hour on the hour and half hour.

Not only is Carlyle House regarded as one of Virginia's most architecturally impressive 18th-century houses, it also figured prominently in American history. In 1753, Scottish merchant John Carlyle completed the mansion for his bride, Sara Fairfax of Belvoir, a daughter of one of Virginia's most prominent families. It was designed in the style of a Scottish/English manor house and lavishly furnished. Carlyle, a successful merchant, had the means to import the best furnishings and appointments available abroad for his new Alexandria home.

When it was built, Carlyle House was a waterfront property with its own wharf. A social and political center, the house was visited by numerous great men of the time, including George Washington. But its most important moment in history occurred in April 1755 when Major General Edward Braddock, commander-in-chief of his majesty's forces in North America, met with five colonial governors here and asked them to tax colonists to finance a campaign against the French and Indians. Colonial legislatures refused to comply, one of the first instances of serious friction between America and Britain. Nevertheless, Braddock made Carlyle House his headquarters during the campaign, and Carlyle was less than impressed with him. He called the general "a man of weak understanding . . . very indolent . . . a slave to his passions, women and wine . . . as great an Epicure as could be in his eating, tho a brave man." Possibly these were the reasons his unfinanced campaign met with disaster. Braddock received, as Carlyle described it, "a most remarkable drubbing."

A tour of Carlyle House takes about 40 minutes. Two of the original rooms, the large parlor and the adjacent study, have survived intact; the former, where

Planning Note

Many Alexandria attractions are closed on Monday.

Braddock met the governors, still retains its original fine woodwork, paneling, and pediments. The house is furnished in period pieces, but only a few of Carlyle's possessions remain. In an upstairs room an architecture exhibit depicts 18th-century construction methods with hand-hewn beams and hand-wrought nails.

Christ Church. 118 N. Washington St. (at Cameron St.). ☎ **703/549-1450.** Suggested donation $2 per person. Mon–Fri 9am–4pm, Sun 2–4:30pm. Tours given on a walk-in basis. Closed all federal holidays.

This sturdy, redbrick, Georgian-style church would be an important national landmark even if its two most distinguished members had not been Washington and Lee. It has been in continuous use since 1773.

There have, of course, been many changes since Washington's day. The bell tower, church bell, galleries, and organ were added by the early 1800s. The "wineglass" pulpit arrived in 1891. But much of what was changed later has since been restored to its earlier state. The pristine white interior with wood moldings and gold trim is colonially correct, although modern heating has obviated the need for charcoal braziers and hot bricks. For the most part, the original structure remains, including the hand-blown glass in the windows that the first worshipers gazed through when their minds wandered from the service. The town has grown up around the building that was first called the "Church in the Woods" because of its rural setting.

Christ Church has had its historic moments. Washington and other early church members fomented revolution in the churchyard, and Robert E. Lee met here with Richmond representatives to discuss assuming a command of Virginia's military forces at the beginning of the Civil War. You can sit in the pew where George and Martha sat with her two Custis grandchildren, or in the Robert E. Lee family pew.

It's a tradition for U.S. presidents to attend a service here on a Sunday close to Washington's birthday and sit in his pew. One of the most memorable of these visits took place shortly after Pearl Harbor, when Franklin Delano Roosevelt attended services with Winston Churchill on the World Day of Prayer, January 1, 1942.

Of course, you're invited to attend a service. There's no admission, but donations are appreciated. A guide gives brief lectures to visitors. The old Parish Hall today houses a gift shop and an exhibit on the history of the church. Walk out to the weathered graveyard after you see the church. It was Alexandria's first and only burial ground until 1805; its oldest marked grave is that of Isaac Pearce, who died in 1771. The remains of 34 Confederate soldiers are also interred here.

Fort Ward Museum & Historic Site. 4301 W. Braddock Rd. (between Rte. 7–Leesburg Turnpike–and Seminary Rd.). ☎ **703/838-4848.** Free admission. Park, daily 9am–sunset; museum, Tues–Sat 9am–5pm, Sun noon–5pm. Call for information regarding special holiday closings. From Old Town, follow King St. west, turn right on Kenwood Ave., then left on West Braddock Rd.; continue for ¾ mile to the entrance on the right.

A short drive from Old Town is a 45-acre museum, historic site, and park that take you on a leap backward in Alexandria history to the Civil War. The action here centers, as it did in the early 1860s, on an actual Union fort that Lincoln ordered erected. It was part of a system of Civil War forts called the "Defenses of Washington." About 90% of the fort's earthwork walls are preserved, and the Northwest Bastion has been restored with six mounted guns (originally there were 36). A model of 19th-century military engineering, the fort was never attacked by Confederate forces. Self-guided tours begin at the Fort Ward ceremonial gate.

Visitors can explore the fort and replicas of the ceremonial entrance gate and an officer's hut. A museum of Civil War artifacts on the premises offers changing exhibits that focus on subjects such as Union arms and equipment, medical care of the wounded, and local war history.

There are picnic areas with barbecue grills in the park surrounding the fort. Concerts are presented on selected evenings June to mid-August in the outdoor amphitheater. A living-history program takes place in mid-August (call for details).

Friendship Firehouse. 107 S. Alfred St. (between King and Prince sts.). ☎ **703/838-3891** or 703/838-4994. Free admission. Fri–Sat 10am–4pm, Sun 1–4pm.

Alexandria's first fire-fighting organization, the Friendship Fire Company was established in 1774. In the early days, the company met in taverns and kept its fire-fighting equipment in a member's barn. Its present Italianate-style brick building dates from 1855; it was erected after an earlier building was, ironically, destroyed by fire. Local tradition holds that George Washington was involved with the firehouse as a founding member, active firefighter, and purchaser of its first fire engine, although extensive research does not confirm these stories. Fire engines and fire-fighting paraphernalia are on display.

✪ **Gadsby's Tavern Museum.** 134 N. Royal St. (at Cameron St.). ☎ **703/838-4242.** Admission $4 adults, $2 children 11–17, free for children under 11; or buy the block ticket. Tours given Apr–Sept, Tues–Sat 10am–5pm, Sun 1–5pm; Oct–Mar, Tues–Sat 11am–4pm, Sun 1–4pm. Closed all federal holidays except Veterans Day. Tours depart 15 minutes before and after the hour.

Alexandria was at the crossroads of 18th-century America, and its social center was Gadsby's Tavern, which consisted of two buildings (one Georgian, one Federal) dating from circa 1770 and 1792, respectively. Innkeeper John Gadsby combined them to create "a gentleman's tavern," which he operated from 1796 to 1808; it was considered one of the finest in the country. George Washington was a frequent dinner guest; he and Martha danced in the second-floor ballroom, and it was here that Washington celebrated his last birthday. The tavern also saw Thomas Jefferson, James Madison, and the Marquis de Lafayette. It was the scene of lavish parties, theatrical performances, small circuses, government meetings, and concerts. Itinerant merchants used the tavern to display their wares, and traveling doctors and dentists treated a hapless clientele (these were rudimentary professions in the 18th century) on the premises.

The rooms have been restored to their 18th-century appearance with the help of modern excavations and colonial inventories. On the 30-minute tour, you'll get a good look at the Tap Room, a small dining room; the Assembly Room, the ballroom; typical bedrooms; and the underground icehouse, which was filled each winter from the icy river. Inquire about a special "living history" tour called Gadsby's Time Travels, which is given four or five times a year. Cap off the experience with a meal at the restored colonial-style restaurant that occupies three tavern rooms (see "Where to Dine," below).

✪ **Lee-Fendall House Museum.** 614 Oronoco St. (at Washington St.). ☎ **703/548-1789.** Admission $4 adults, $2 children 11–17, free for children under 11; or buy the block ticket. Tues–Sat 10am–3:45pm, Sun 1–3:45pm. Tours given on the hour, 10am–3pm. Closed Jan 1, Thanksgiving, and Dec 24–25.

This handsome Greek Revival–style house is a veritable museum of Lee family furniture, heirlooms, and documents. "Light Horse Harry" Lee never actually lived here, although he was a frequent visitor, as was his good friend George Washington. Lee did own the original lot, but sold it to Philip Richard Fendall (himself a Lee on his mother's side), who built the house in 1785. Fendall married three Lee wives, including Harry's first mother-in-law and, later, Harry's sister.

Thirty-seven Lees occupied the house over a period of 118 years (1785 to 1903), and it was from this house that Harry wrote Alexandria's farewell address to Washington, delivered when he passed through town on his way to assume the presidency. (Harry also wrote and delivered, but not at this house, the famous funeral oration to Washington that contained the words: "First in war, first in peace, and first in the hearts of his countrymen.") During the Civil War, the house was seized and used as a Union hospital.

Thirty-minute guided tours interpret the 1850s era of the home and provide insight into Victorian family life. You'll also see the colonial garden with its magnolia and chestnut trees, roses, and boxwood-lined paths. Much of the interior woodwork and glass is original.

The Lyceum. 201 S. Washington St. (off Prince St.). ☎ **703/838-4994.** Free admission. Mon–Sat 10am–5pm, Sun 1–5pm. Closed Jan 1, Thanksgiving, and Dec 25.

This Greek Revival building houses a museum that depicts Alexandria's history from the 17th through the 20th century. It features changing exhibits and an ongoing series of lectures, concerts, and educational programs.

Information is also available here about Virginia state attractions, especially Alexandria attractions. You can obtain maps and brochures, and a knowledgeable staff will be happy to answer your questions.

But even without its many attractions, the brick and stucco Lyceum merits a visit. Built in 1839, it was designed in the Doric-temple style to serve as a lecture, meeting, and concert hall. It was an important center of Alexandria's cultural life until the Civil War, when Union forces appropriated it for use as a hospital. After the war it became a private residence, and still later it was subdivided for office space. In 1969, however, the city council's use of eminent domain alone prevented the Lyceum from being demolished in favor of a parking lot.

Old Presbyterian Meeting House. 321 S. Fairfax St. (between Duke and Wolfe sts.). ☎ **703/549-6670.** Free admission. Mon–Fri 9am–3pm. Sun services at 8:30am and 11am, with a 10am service added mid-June to mid-Sept.

Presbyterian congregations have worshipped in Virginia since the Reverend Alexander Whittaker converted Pocahontas in Jamestown in 1614. This brick church was built by Scottish pioneers in 1775. Although it wasn't George Washington's church, the Meeting House bell tolled continuously for 4 days after his death in December 1799, and memorial services were preached from the pulpit here by Presbyterian, Episcopal, and Methodist ministers. According to the Alexandria paper of the day, "The walking being bad to the Episcopal church the funeral sermon of George Washington will be preached at the Presbyterian Meeting House." Two months later, on Washington's birthday, Alexandria citizens marched from Market Square to the church to pay their respects.

Many famous Alexandrians are buried in the church graveyard, including John and Sara Carlyle, Dr. James Craik (the surgeon who treated—some say killed—Washington, dressed Lafayette's wounds at Brandywine, and ministered to the dying Braddock at Monongahela), and William Hunter, Jr., founder of the St. Andrew's Society of Scottish descendants, to whom bagpipers pay homage on the first Saturday of December. It is also the site of a Tomb of an Unknown Revolutionary War Soldier, and the tomb of the minister between 1789 and 1820, Dr. James Muir, who lies beneath the sanctuary in his gown and bands.

The original Meeting House was gutted by a lightning fire in 1835, but parishioners restored it in the style of the day a few years later. The present bell, said to be recast from the metal of the old one, was hung in a newly constructed belfry in

1843, and a new organ was installed in 1849. The Meeting House closed its doors in 1889, and for 60 years it was virtually abandoned. But in 1949 it was reborn as a living Presbyterian U.S.A. church, and today the Old Meeting House looks much as it did following its first restoration. The original parsonage, or manse, is still intact. There's no guided tour, but there is a recorded narrative in the graveyard.

Stabler-Leadbeater Apothecary Museum. 105 S. Fairfax St. (near King St.). ☎ **703/ 836-3713.** Admission $3 adults, $2 children 11–17, children under 11 free; or buy a block ticket. Mon–Sat 10am–4pm, Sun 1–5pm. Closed Wed during the winter, Jan 1, Thanksgiving, Dec 25. Tours Sun 1–5pm.

When its doors closed in 1933, this landmark drugstore was the second oldest in continuous operation in America. Run for five generations by the same Quaker family (beginning in 1792), its famous early patrons included Robert E. Lee (he purchased the paint for Arlington House here), George Mason, Henry Clay, John C. Calhoun, and George Washington. Gothic Revival decorative elements and Victorian-style doors were added in the 1840s.

Today the apothecary looks much as it did in colonial times, its shelves lined with original hand-blown gold-leaf-labeled bottles (actually the most valuable collection of antique medicinal bottles in the country), old scales stamped with the royal crown, patent medicines, and equipment for bloodletting. The clock on the rear wall, the porcelain-handled mahogany drawers, and two mortars and pestles all date from about 1790. Among the shop's documentary records is this 1802 order from Mount Vernon: "Mrs. Washington desires Mr. Stabler to send by the bearer a quart bottle of his best Castor Oil and the bill for it."

There are tours Sundays from 1 to 5pm; other times a 10-minute recording will guide you around the displays. The adjoining gift shop uses its proceeds to maintain the apothecary.

✪ **Torpedo Factory.** 105 N. Union St. (between King and Cameron sts., on the waterfront). ☎ **703/838-4565.** Free admission. Daily 10am–5pm; archaeology exhibit area Tues–Fri 10am–3pm, Sat 10am–5pm, Sun 1–5pm. Closed Easter, July 4, Thanksgiving, Dec 25, Jan 1.

This block-long, three-story building, once a torpedo shell-case factory, now accommodates some 160 professional artists and craftspeople who create and sell their own works on the premises. Here you can see artists at work in their studios— potters, painters, printmakers, photographers, sculptors, jewelers, as well as those who make stained-glass windows and fiber art.

On permanent display here are exhibits on Alexandria history provided by **Alexandria Archaeology** (☎ 703/838-4399), which is headquartered here and engages in extensive city research. The special exhibit area and lab are open to the public during the hours listed above with a volunteer or staff member on hand to answer questions. An ongoing exhibit, "Archaeologists at Work," highlights current excavation finds and methodology.

SHOPPING

Old Town has hundreds of charming boutiques, antique stores, and gift shops selling everything from souvenir T-shirts to 18th-century reproductions. Some of the most interesting are at the sites (for example, Museum Shop at the Lyceum), but most are clustered on King and Cameron streets and their connecting cross streets. Plan to spend a fair amount of time browsing in between visits to historic sites. A guide to antique stores is available at the Visitors Association. Also see chapter 9, which includes some Alexandria shops.

WHERE TO DINE

There are so many fine restaurants in Alexandria that Washingtonians often drive over just to dine here and stroll the cobblestone streets.

EXPENSIVE

Landini Brothers. 115 King St. (between Lee and Union sts.). ☎ **703/836-8404.** Reservations recommended. Lunch $10–$13, dinner $17–$35. AE, CB, DC, DISC, MC, V. Mon–Sat 11:30am–11pm, Sun 4–10pm. NORTHERN ITALIAN.

The classic, delicate cuisine of Tuscany is featured at this rustic, almost grotto-like restaurant with stone walls, a flagstone floor, and rough-hewn beams overhead. It's especially charming by candlelight. There's additional seating in a lovely dining room upstairs. Everything is homemade: the pasta, the desserts, and the crusty Italian bread. At lunch you might choose a cold seafood salad or spinach- and ricotta-stuffed agnolotti in buttery Parmesan cheese sauce. At dinner, try the prosciutto and melon or the shrimp sautéed in garlic with tangy lemon sauce. Many proceed to an order of prime aged beef tenderloin medallions sautéed with garlic, mushrooms, and rosemary in a Barolo wine sauce. Others opt for linguine with scallops, shrimp, clams, mussels, and squid in a garlic/parsley/red-pepper and white-wine sauce. Dessert choices include tiramisu and custard-filled fruit tarts.

✪ **Le Refuge.** 127 N. Washington St. (1 block from King St.). ☎ **703/548-4661.** Reservations recommended. Lunch $9–$14, dinner $15–$21, pretheater $16.95. AE, DC, DISC, MC, V. Mon–Sat 11:30am–2:30pm and 5:30–10pm. FRENCH.

This is a cramped, but still appealing, space. Le Refuge is dark and busy and inexorably French. The food is mostly old-fashioned: onion soup, bouillabaisse, rack of lamb, and chicken in mustard cream sauce. Perfectly prepared vegetables surround all entrées: potatoes lyonnaise, coins of zucchini, and bright bunches of broccoli florets. Desserts, like everything here, are homemade and include fruit tarts, crème brûle, and profiteroles.

MODERATE

Bilbo Baggins. 208 Queen St. (at Lee St.). ☎ **703/683-0300.** Reservations recommended. Lunch/brunch $7.50–$12, dinner $15–$18. AE, DC, DISC, MC, V. Mon–Fri 11:30am–2:30pm and 5:30–10:30pm, Sat 11:30am–5:30pm and 5:30–10:30pm, Sun 11am–2:30pm and 4:30–9:30pm. AMERICAN/CONTINENTAL.

Named, in case you didn't know, for a character *in The Hobbit,* Bilbo Baggins is a charming two-story restaurant offering scrumptious fresh and homemade fare. Plants flourish in the sunlight throughout the rustic downstairs area and among the stained-glass windows and murals of scenes from *The Hobbit* upstairs. Candlelit at night, it becomes an even cozier setting. The restaurant adjoins a skylit wine bar with windows overlooking Queen Street.

Offered here are many pasta dishes, such as tortellini stuffed with crabmeat, fresh salmon, and dill, in an apple-ginger chardonnay cream sauce. Other entrees range from grilled salmon and scallops in lemon-dill vinaigrette to chicken breast stuffed with feta cheese, accompanied by potato croquettes or seasonal vegetables. An extensive wine list is available (32 boutique wines are offered by the glass), as are all bar drinks, 10 microbrewery draft beers, and out-of-this-world homemade desserts such as the Lord of the Rings—seven layers of raspberry-filled white and chocolate cake topped with chocolate ganache.

East Wind. 809 King St. (between Columbus and Alfred sts.). ☎ **703/836-1515.** Reservations recommended. Lunch $6–$8, dinner $8–$14, prix-fixe lunch $7. AE, CB, DC, DISC, MC, V. Mon–Thurs 11:30am–2:30pm and 5:30–10pm, Fri 11:30am–2:30pm and 5:30–10:30pm, Sat 5:30–10:30pm, Sun 5:30–9:30pm. VIETNAMESE.

The decor of this Vietnamese restaurant is very appealing: The works of Vietnamese artist Minh Nguyen adorn the sienna stucco and knotty pine–paneled walls, accompanied by flowers on each pink-clothed table and a large floral display up front. The owner personally visits the market each morning to select the freshest fish.

An East Wind meal might begin with an appetizer of *cha gio* (delicate Vietnamese egg rolls) or a salad of shredded chicken and vegetables mixed with fish sauce. A favorite entree is *bo dun:* beef tenderloin strips marinated in wine, honey, and spices, rolled in fresh onions, and broiled on bamboo skewers. Also excellent are the grilled lemon chicken or charcoal-broiled shrimp and scallops served on rice vermicelli. Vegetarians will find many appealing selections on East Wind's menu. There's refreshing ginger ice cream for dessert. A good bargain is the prix-fixe lunch, which includes soup, an entrée, and coffee or tea.

Gadsby's Tavern. 138 N. Royal St. (at Cameron St.). ☎ **703/548-1288.** Reservations recommended. Lunch/brunch $7–$10, dinner $15–$23. Half-price portions available on some items for children 12 and under. CB, DC, DISC, MC, V. Mon–Sat 11:30am–3pm and 5:30–10pm, Sun 11am–3pm and 5:30–10pm. COLONIAL AMERICAN.

In the spirit of history, pass through the portals where Washington reviewed his troops for the last time, and dine at the famous Gadsby's Tavern. The setting evokes the 18th century, with period music, wood-plank floors, hurricane-lamp wall sconces, and a rendition of a Hogarth painting over the fireplace (one of several).

Servers are dressed in authentic colonial attire. George Washington dined and danced here often. A strolling violinist entertains Sunday and Monday nights and at Sunday brunch. Tuesday through Saturday night, an "18th-century gentleman" regales guests with song and tells the news of the day (200 years ago). In clement weather, it is possible to dine in a flagstone courtyard edged with flower beds.

All the fare is homemade, including the sweet Sally Lunn bread baked on the premises daily. You might start your meal with soup from the stockpot served with homemade sourdough crackers. Then try an entree, perhaps baked ham and cheese pye (a sort of Early American quiche), or hot roast turkey with giblet gravy and bread and sage stuffing on Sally Lunn bread, or George Washington's favorite: slow roasted crisp duckling served with fruit dressing an Madeira sauce. For dessert, try the English trifle or creamy buttermilk-custard pye with a hint of lemon. Colonial "coolers" are also available: scuppernong, Wench's Punch, and such. The Sunday brunch menu adds such items as thick slices of toast dipped in a batter of rum and spices, with sausage, hash browns, and hot cinnamon syrup. And a "desserts and libations" menu highlights such favorites as Scottish apple gingerbread and bourbon apple pye, along with a wide selection of beverages.

INEXPENSIVE

The Deli on the Strand. 211 The Strand #5 (entrance on S. Union St. between Duke and Prince sts.). ☎ **703/548-7222.** Sandwiches $2.75–$7. AE, MC, V. Daily 8am–8pm. DELI.

Who could refuse a sunlit picnic in Fort Ward Park (described under "What to See and Do," above), in the Old Town at Founders Park, bordering the Potomac at the foot of Queen Street, or in the Market Square? The park doesn't have picnic tables, but there are benches and plenty of grass to sit on. Buy the fixings at the Deli on the Strand. The divine aroma of baking bread wafts through the air, and you can get reasonably priced cold-cut sandwiches on it, as well as muffins, brownies, and (on the weekend) bagels. Also available are homemade seafood or pasta salads, cheeses, beer, wine, and champagne. There are a few picnic tables outside under an awning.

⚫ **Hard Times Café.** 1404 King St. (near S. West St.). ☎ **703/683-5340.** No reservations. Main courses $4–$7. AE, MC, V. Sun–Thurs 11am–10pm, Fri–Sat 11am–11pm. AMERICAN/ SOUTHWESTERN.

Will Rogers once said he "always judged a town by the quality of its chili." He would have loved Alexandria, where the fabulous Hard Times Café serves up top-secret-recipe homemade chilies and fresh-from-the-oven cornbread. It's a laid-back hangout where waiters and waitresses wear jeans and T-shirts; country music is always playing on the 100-CD jukebox; and the Texas decor features Lone Star flags, a longhorn steer hide overhead, and historic photos of the Old West on the walls. The chili comes in three varieties: Texas, Cincinnati (cooked with sweeter spices, including cinnamon), and vegetarian. I favor the Texas style: coarse-ground chuck simmered for 6 hours with special spices in beef sauce. If chili isn't your thing, order grilled chicken breast, a burger, or salad. Side orders of steak fries cooked with the skins, cheddar-filled jalapeños, and deep-fried onion rings are ample for two. Wash it all down with one of the menu's 30 beers, including a Hard Times label and many selections from western microbreweries. The Hard Times has garnered many a chili cook-off award, and CHILI-U.S.A., a resolution before Congress "to make chili the official food of this great nation," was conceived by Oklahoma lobbyists over a "bowl of red" here. There's additional seating upstairs; the Colorado flag overhead was brought in by a senator from that state.

La Madeleine. 500 King St. (at S. Pitt St.). ☎ **703/739-2854.** No reservations. Lunch $2.99–$6, dinner $6.99–$10.49. AE, DISC, MC, V. Sun–Thurs 7am–10pm, Fri–Sat 7am–11pm. FRENCH CAFE.

This is part of a self-service chain, charming nonetheless. Its French-country interior has a beamed ceiling, bare oak floors, a wood-burning stove, and maple hutches displaying crockery and pewter mugs. The walls are hung with copper pots and antique farm implements.

Come in the morning for fresh-baked croissants, Danish, scones, muffins, and brioches, or a heartier bacon-and-eggs breakfast. Throughout the day, there are delicious salads (such as roasted vegetables and rigatoni), sandwiches (including a traditional croque monsieur), and hot dishes ranging from quiche and pizza to rotisserie chicken with a Caesar salad. After 5pm, additional choices include pastas and specials such as beef bourguignonne and salmon in dill cream sauce, both served with a crispy potato galette and sautéed broccoli. There are about two dozen fabulous fresh-baked French desserts, including yummy fruit tarts and a chocolate, vanilla, and praline triple-layer cheesecake with graham-cracker crust.

⚫ **South Austin Grill.** 801 King St. (at S. Columbus St.). ☎ **703/684-8969.** Reservations not accepted. Lunch, Sat–Sun brunch, and dinner $8–$15. AE, DC, DISC, MC, V. Mon–Thurs 11:30am–11pm, Fri 11:30am–midnight, Sat 11am–midnight, Sun 11am–10pm. TEX-MEX.

One of five Austin Grills in the area, this one is larger than the original outpost in Glover Park. The two dining floors are cheerfully decorated, with roomy booths painted in bright primary hues and walls hung with Austin music club posters and other Texas memorabilia. A corner location permits lots of sunlight to stream in. Otherwise, menu, music, and ambience are the same as at the Glover Park location (see p. 152 in chapter 6 for that information).

Appendix: Useful Toll-Free Numbers & Web Sites

AIRLINES

Air Canada
☎800/776-3000
www.aircanada.ca

Alaska Airlines
☎800/426-0333
www.alaskaair.com

America West Airlines
☎800/235-9292
www.americawest.com

American Airlines
☎800/433-7300
www.americanair.com

British Airways
☎800/247-9297
☎0345/222-111 in Britain
www.british-airways.com

Canadian Airlines International
☎800/426-7000
www.cdnair.ca

Continental Airlines
☎800/525-0280
www.flycontinental.com

Delta Air Lines
☎800/221-1212
www.delta-air.com

Kiwi International Air Lines
☎800/538-5494
www.jetkiwi.com

Midway Airlines
☎800/446-4392

Northwest Airlines
☎800/225-2525
www.nwa.com

Southwest Airlines
☎800/435-9792
www.iflyswa.com

Tower Air
☎800/34-TOWER
  (800/348-6937) outside
  New York (☎718/553-8500
  in New York)
www.towerair.com

Trans World Airlines (TWA)
☎800/221-2000
www.twa.com

United Airlines
☎800/241-6522
www.ual.com

US Airways
☎800/428-4322
www.usairways.com

Virgin Atlantic Airways
☎800/862-8621 in
  Continental U.S.
☎0293/747-747 in Britain
www.fly.virgin.com

CAR RENTAL AGENCIES

Advantage
☎800/777-5500
www.arac.com

Alamo
☎800/327-9633
www.goalamo.com

Auto Europe
☎ 800/223-5555
www.autoeurope.com

Avis
☎800/331-1212 in the Continental U.S.
☎800/TRY-AVIS in Canada
www.avis.com

Budget
☎800/527-0700
www.budgetrentacar.com

Dollar
☎800/800-4000
www.dollarcar.com

Enterprise
☎800/325-8007
www.pickenterprise.com

Hertz
☎800/654-3131
www.hertz.com

Kemwel Holiday Auto
☎800/678-0678
www.kemwel.com

National
☎800/CAR-RENT
www.nationalcar.com

Payless
☎800/PAYLESS
www.paylesscar.com

Rent-A-Wreck
☎800/535-1391
rent-a-wreck.com

Thrifty
☎800/367-2277
www.thrifty.com

Value
☎800/327-2501
www.go-value.com

MAJOR HOTEL & MOTEL CHAINS

Best Western International
☎800/528-1234
www.bestwestern.com

Clarion Hotels
☎800/CLARION
www.hotelchoice.com/
   cgi-bin/res/webres?clarion.html

Comfort Inns
☎800/228-5150
www.hotelchoice.com/
   cgi-bin/res/webres?comfort.html

Courtyard by Marriott
☎800/321-2211
www.courtyard.com

Days Inn
☎800/325-2525
www.daysinn.com

Doubletree Hotels
☎800/222-TREE
www.doubletreehotels.com

Econo Lodges
☎800/55-ECONO
www.hotelchoice.com/
   cgi-bin/res/webres?econo.html

Fairfield Inn by Marriott
☎800/228-2800
www.fairfieldinn.com

Hampton Inn
☎800/HAMPTON
www.hampton-inn.com

Hilton Hotels
☎800/HILTONS
www.hilton.com

Holiday Inn
☎800/HOLIDAY
www.holiday-inn.com

Howard Johnson
☎800/654-2000
www.hojo.com/hojo.html

Hyatt Hotels & Resorts
☎800/228-9000
www.hyatt.com

ITT Sheraton
☎800/325-3535
www.sheraton.com

La Quinta Motor Inns
☎800/531-5900
www.laquinta.com

Marriott Hotels
☎ 800/228-9290
www.marriott.com

Motel 6
☎ 800/4-MOTEL6 (800/466-8536)

Quality Inns
☎ 800/228-5151
www.hotelchoice.com/
   cgi-bin/res/webres?quality.html

Radisson Hotels International
☎ 800/333-3333
www.radisson.com

Ramada Inns
☎ 800/2-RAMADA
www.ramada.com

Red Carpet Inns
☎ 800/251-1962

Red Lion Hotels & Inns
☎ 800/547-8010
www.travelweb.com

Red Roof Inns
☎ 800/843-7663
www.redroof.com

Residence Inn by Marriott
☎ 800/331-3131
www.residenceinn.com

Rodeway Inns
☎ 800/228-2000
www.hotelchoice.com/
   cgi-bin/res/webres?rodeway.html

Super 8 Motels
☎ 800/800-8000
www.super8motels.com

Travelodge
☎ 800/255-3050

Vagabond Inns
☎ 800/522-1555
www.vagabondinns.com

Wyndham Hotels and Resorts
☎ 800/822-4200 in Continental U.S.
   and Canada
www.wyndham.com

Index

See also separate Accommodations and Restaurants indexes, below.
Page numbers in italics refer to maps.

304 Index

WHEREVER YOU TRAVEL, *H*ELP IS NEVER FAR AWAY.

From planning your trip to providing travel assistance along the way, American Express® Travel Service Offices are always there to help you do more.

Washington, D.C.

American Express Travel Service
1150 Connecticut Avenue N.W.
202/457-1300

American Express Travel Service
Mazza Gallerie, 5300 Wisconsin Avenue N.W.
202/362-4000

do more AMERICAN EXPRESS
Travel

http://www.americanexpress.com/travel

**American Express Travel Service Offices
are located throughout the United States.
For the office nearest you, call 1-800-AXP-3429.**